Glyndon G. Van Deusen is Research Professor of History Emeritus at the University of Rochester, where he has taught history for more than three decades, and has served both as chairman of the History Department and Associate Dean for Graduate Students. Professor Van Deusen is the author of biographies of Henry Clay and Horace Greeley and of Seward's political mentor, Thurlow Weed; and he also wrote *The Jacksonian Era, 1828-1848* for the New American Nation series. He has earned degrees at the University of Rochester, Amherst College, and Columbia University, and was the winner of the Albert J. Beveridge Prize of the American Historical Association in 1950. In 1951-52 he was Fulbright Lecturer in American History in New Zealand.

The present biography of Seward is largely based on the Seward Papers, a collection of some 150,000 items which Professor Van Deusen helped acquire for the University of Rochester. These include thousands of family letters which have not heretofore been available for any study of Seward.

WILLIAM HENRY SEWARD

BY GLYNDON G. VAN DEUSEN

William Henry Seward
(New York, 1967)

Sieyes: His Life and His Nationalism (New York, 1932)

The Life of Henry Clay (Boston, 1937)

Thurlow-Weed: Wizard of the Lobby (Boston, 1947)

Horace Greeley: Nineteenth-Century Crusader
(Philadelphia, 1953)

The Jacksonian Era: 1828–1848 (New York, 1959)

The United States of America: A History,
with Dexter Perkins (New York, 1962)

The American Democracy: Its Rise to Power,
with Dexter Perkins (New York, 1964)

EDITOR

Foreign Policy and the American Spirit,
with Richard C. Wade (Ithaca, 1957)

Readings in American History,
with Herbert Bass (New York, 1963)

William H. Seward. A Brady photograph, *c.* 1863.
University of Rochester Library.

William Henry Seward

GLYNDON G. VAN DEUSEN

New York OXFORD UNIVERSITY PRESS 1967

Copyright © 1967 by Oxford University Press, Inc.
Library of Congress Catalogue Card Number: 67-28131
Printed in the United States of America

To Ruth

Contents

Introduction

This biography concludes a project in American political history that began many years ago, one that has centered chiefly in studies of national leaders in the middle nineteenth century. This particular volume is the product of years of research, and has monopolized my time since 1962.

I have written this book with three aims in view. One is to portray as accurately as possible the career and personality of an extraordinary man. Another is to show Seward's place in the times in which he lived. My third purpose is to stimulate the interest of the general reader in a fascinating period of American history.

Some years ago H. R. Trevor Roper, in his inaugural lecture as professor of modern history at Oxford University, said that those subjects we group together as the humanities are meant primarily for the benefit of laymen. If such subjects "once lose touch with the lay mind, they are rightly condemned to perish." I heartily subscribe to this statement. While I hope that this book will be useful to professional historians and to students, I am even more anxious that laymen find in it both pleasure and profit. As for myself, during many months of work my interest in William Henry Seward never flagged. And my feeling of having come to know him—to understand why he thought and acted as he did—has been an unfailing source of strength and excitement.

It would be presumptuous of me to claim sole credit for whatever is good in this biography. It owes much to John R. Russell, Director of Libraries at The University of Rochester, who helped me to obtain the Seward Papers for the University; and who provided me with that indispensable adjunct of a scholar's life, a study. It owes a great deal to Mrs. Margaret Butterfield Andrews and Miss Catherine Davidson Hayes, who preside over the Special Collections in Rhees Library. They organized and indexed the Seward Papers. Experts in deciphering Seward's handwriting, and always ready to help in solving innumerable problems, they have earned my gratitude in countless ways. Mrs. Margaret K. Toth is another expert to whose help I have had recourse in deciphering Seward's scrawl, and I have only praise for the entire staff of Rhees Library, so co-operative have they been in this project.

Every conscientious biographer is aware that, despite his best efforts, he is responsible for errors of commission and omission. That many of my mistakes and oversights have been corrected is the result of labor generously bestowed by four eminent historians. David M. Ellis of Hamilton College, Don E. Fehrenbacher of Stanford University, Richard W. Leopold of Northwestern University, and Eric L. McKitrick of Columbia University have read large sections of the manuscript. For their comments, critical and otherwise, I am deeply grateful. And I shall never forget the skillful editing and encouragement given by Sheldon Meyer of the Oxford University Press.

Many others have contributed to this book. I am deeply grateful for the patient co-operation of university and library archivists all over the United States who took time out of their busy lives to furnish pertinent materials from their manuscript collections. Mrs. William H. Seward III told me of valuable papers stored away in the attic of Seward House, and has heartened me by her interest in the progress of the manuscript. Others of whose aid I am appreciative are Professors Charles Adler, Martin B. Duberman, Frank Gatell, Harold M. Hyman, William H. Gilman and Howard S. Merritt. Dr. William M. Franklin of the State Department furnished valuable assistance, as did Lyman H. Butterfield, editor-in-chief of the Adams Papers, and Messrs. Mark Eckoff and A. H. Leisinger, Jr., of the National Archives. Mr. I. N. Zemskov, Chief of the Historical and Political Division of the Ministry of Foreign Affairs in

Moscow, aided me in obtaining a microfilm of portions of the Stoeckl-Gortchakov correspondence in the archives of the USSR that would not otherwise have been available. I appreciate the courtesies extended by M. Chamson, Le Directeur Général des Archives de France, the trustees of the Broadlands Archives in England, and Joseph W. Scott, Librarian of University College, London. Mr. George Patterson Crandall of Westfield, New York, gave valuable assistance. The generous financial aid furnished by The University of Rochester was important to my research.

Finally, I owe more than I can say to my wife, Ruth Litteer Van Deusen, an authority on the history of the Seward family. As my research assistant, she took notes on important source materials. She typed the entire manuscript. She and I have spent many hours discussing problems of authorship. Out of these discussions have come ideas that have been woven into the Seward story. In a very real sense, it is our book.

Rochester, New York G. G. V. D.
April 1967

WILLIAM HENRY SEWARD

∼§ I §∽

Portrait of an Ambitious Young Man

Orange County, New York, is a land of broad, fertile valleys and rolling hills. At the beginning of the nineteenth century it was farming country, with here and there a little huddle of houses. In Florida, one of these hamlets, a modest, gambrel-roofed structure sheltered Samuel Sweezy Seward and Mary Jennings Seward and their children. There on May 16, 1801, was born their son William Henry.

Harry Seward, as he preferred to be called in his youth, came of forebears who had immigrated in the reign of Queen Anne and were of English and possibly Welsh stock, with some Irish blood on the Jennings side.[1] His mother was a kindly, warm-hearted woman, much loved by her children and by the townsfolk round about. She had humor and a patient understanding, qualities that were needful in a household dominated by her husband.

Samuel Seward was a restless, ambitious, driving man, always on the lookout for new ventures. A Jeffersonian Republican in politics, he served at various times as postmaster and county judge. He was also a doctor, merchant, and land speculator. Much of what he touched turned into gold, and before his death in 1849 he had amassed a fortune of over $300,000.

Samuel loved his children but ruled them harshly, being quick to punish verbally or with the rod. For him duty rather than love ruled the household. Harry, his brothers Benjamin Jennings, Edwin Polydore, and George Washington, and his sister Louisa Cornelia, chafed and at times rebelled against the tyranny of their father.

Harry's frail health and active mind set him apart from the other children of the family. Samuel decided that this son should go to college, and in preparation Harry received the best schooling the neighborhood could furnish. His father urged him to study hard, that he might one day become a great lawyer. Tradition and his own recollections give fleeting pictures of a generous, affectionate little boy, quick to learn, popular in the neighborhood, and adored by the two or three slaves in the Seward household.

Harry later recalled the kitchen of the Seward home—

> . . . the kitchen in the chimney corner of which I spent my winter evenings [he wrote to a friend in 1864] had two doors opposite each other, through which the horse passed when he drew in the back log. Secondly, there was a setoff in the chimney just above the jamb in which the witches used to rendezvous when going out before their mischievous errands. Third, there was a slave bunk for the people who were the lawful proprietors of the kitchen, and who kindly yielded its hospitalities to good white children who would teach the black ones how to read. That old New York kitchen is still standing. So long as our country was at peace I visited it once a year, and I mean to do so when we have peace again, which I hope will be soon. But the specialties I have mentioned are gone. For the fireplace there is a patent cooking stove. The witches, I learn, have long ago abandoned their hiding place, and the black people have homes and kitchens of their own.[2]

When Harry was fifteen years old he was admitted to Union College at Schenectady, New York. His record there reveals certain aspects of his mind and character. Letters to an Orange County friend show his lively interest in such pranks as burning a college outhouse, and filling the lock of a recitation room with brick dust and chips so as to thwart the will of an unpopular teacher. He loved to play cards, a pastime to which he was devoted all his life. Summoned to chapel from a game one day, he and his companions hastily concealed the evidence of play in his hat, only to have the cards fall in a shower to the chapel floor when he removed it.

Anxious to be popular with the student body, Harry stopped

going to his Latin teacher for guidance when classmates derided him for doing so, and he gained goodwill by prompting other students who stumbled in recitation. "The confidence which he has in himself and the ease of his manners renders him quite pleasing," a friend of the family wrote to Samuel after seeing Harry on the college campus.

If Harry could be charming, he could also be stubborn. When he refused to recite after being called upon out of turn by one of his teachers, he received a two weeks' suspension that ended only when President Eliphalet Nott apologized for the teacher and Harry apologized to the president. The rebel then went back to his classes, but his troubles in college were not over.

Samuel provided Harry with quite a skimpy allowance, one that soon melted away before the needs of college living and the pleas of improvident young borrowers. When Harry felt classmates were smiling at his country clothes he promptly visited the Schenectady tailor shops—and went into debt. The tailors billed his father, and Samuel refused to pay. Harry thereupon flew into revolt and on New Year's Day, 1819, left college with a classmate who was bound for a teaching post in Georgia.

The two young men traveled by ship and stage to Atlanta. There Harry's friend found employment, and he himself went on to Putnam County in the northwestern part of the state, where he took the post that originally had been offered to his companion. The trustees of the school, which was happily entitled Union Academy and which was scheduled to open on April 19, advertised in the local paper that Mr. William H. Seward, "late from Union College, New York," came highly recommended as of good moral character, industry, and literary requirements. "He will teach," they informed the public, "the Latin and Greek languages, theoretical and practical Mathematics, Logic, Rhetoric, Natural and Moral Philosophy, Chemistry, Geography, English grammar, and such other branches as are usually taught in Northern Colleges." There would also be instruction in reading, writing, and spelling.[3] Harry's contribution in these various branches of knowledge could not have been great, for his term of office lasted only eight weeks.

Seward's departure from Union College created a furor in the family home at Florida. Harry's father, who had gone to New York in a vain endeavor to stop his wayward son, urged him to return and sent him $100 traveling money—which the youth promptly spent. Samuel then stormed and threatened, Harry's mother implored him to come back, and his sister, Cornelia, to whom he was deeply attached, added her entreaties. Moved by mother and sister, and recognizing that he had acted somewhat rashly, Harry gave in, and in June 1819 returned to a joyful mother and an irate father.

Years later, Harry's Georgia sojourn had repercussions. In the 1850s there was thunder from the South about his supposed mulatto offspring. In 1866 a former slave of Major Alexander (in whose house he had lived in Georgia) wrote to him for aid and said that her mother Milly and the Major had always said that Seward was her father. This is evidence of a most dubious character. Seward himself often recalled his hospitable treatment by people in Georgia, and said his trip had strengthened an aversion to the institution of slavery that was already deeply formed.[4]

During the summer of 1819 Harry read law in John Duer's nearby Goshen office and collected debts for his father. In the fall he went back to Union, this time to stay until he graduated in July 1820.

Seward was a junior Phi Beta Kappa at Union and a member of the Adelphic debating society. His self-confidence grew apace, and in the middle of his senior year he confided to a friend that he was intellectually inferior to none of his fellows—that if he were not chosen a speaker at the commencement, he would not return in the spring to "listen to some whom he considered beneath even his notice." He did speak at graduation and received highest honors, but this did not mean a high level of intellectual achievement. Eliphalet Nott had used lotteries successfully in relieving the college's financial problems, but had done little as yet to improve instruction, which relied chiefly on recitation from memory. Harry left college without mastering, or even becoming proficient in, any subject or field. Writing to a friend some years later, he complained that he had been "hurried mechanically through the miserable rudiments of an American collegiate education." [5]

After graduation Harry read law in Goshen for over a year and then in the fall of 1821 continued his legal training in John Anthon's

New York office. There he met a young man with whom he formed a Damon and Pythias friendship.

David Berdan was one of Harry's fellow students, a brilliant youngster, poor, gentle, and generous, who studied law under parental compulsion, though his real interest was in languages and literature. He and Harry were both religious skeptics, and they also had common interests in books, the theater, and the opposite sex. Together they roamed the New York streets, and dissipated to the extent permitted by their finances. Afterward they carried on a voluminous correspondence in which they poured out their souls to each other until Berdan died of consumption in 1827. Seward once told his wife that he could never love anyone as deeply as he had loved David Berdan.[6]

Harry completed preparation for his legal examination in the Goshen office of Ogden Hoffman, and was admitted to the bar in October 1822. He was now ready to begin practice and began looking for a suitable location. Two junior partnerships were available in the bustling village of Auburn, New York. Seward went up there to look the ground over, and be looked over in turn, arriving on Christmas Day 1822. He had the offer of both places, took the one that did not require him to purchase a law library, and early in the new year became a partner of Judge Elijah Miller.

Harry Seward was now nearly twenty-two years old, slight of build, and about five feet six inches in height. He had wavy red hair (a family characteristic), a red beard, so heavy that he sometimes shaved twice a day, blue eyes, and a thin, light-complexioned face with a jutting, aquiline nose. His chin was firm and his voice slightly husky. He had no interest in music and was awkward on the dance floor, but he liked pomp and circumstance and loved sociability. Ardent and impetuous in temperament, agreeable by nature, he could when necessity arose be coldly calculating, and he was intensely ambitious.

Harry wrote freely to Berdan about all the girls who interested him. Berdan replied that Harry was continually in his thoughts, "but the gods forbid that I should draw you from your present situation, even in imagination. You have too many fair damsels at your disposal to be tempted to occupy half a couch 2 feet in width with a person of your own sex." One of them would be sure to find himself on the floor in the morning. He still could not entirely understand Harry's motives in attaching himself to every girl he met. What of this shoemaker that he had kissed on a public street? And David was amazed at his friend's exchanging vows of faithfulness with another girl on a hill summit at Goshen.

Harry did not confine his pursuit of women to the Goshen and Florida region. There was Mary Ann Kellogg of Skaneateles, a pretty, flirtatious miss with a wealthy father. Harry had met her while still a law student, and by the fall of 1822 was on the verge of declaring himself, if indeed he did not propose. So deeply was he involved that some years later Berdan destroyed all Seward's letters so that the latter could feel easy about what he had written concerning Mary Ann.[7]

There was also Frances Adeline Miller, daughter of his law partner and classmate of Cornelia Seward at Mrs. Willard's seminary in Troy. Harry had met Fan, as he sometimes called her, in 1821 when she was visiting Cornelia in Florida. She was there again the following spring, and he told Berdan that he found her charming. Still the choice between Frances and Mary Ann was not easy, and it was only in the summer of 1823 that he made up his mind. Carefully he explained the reasons for his decision to his father.

There were for him, Harry wrote, three bases for marriage— mutual love, a wife with "a strong mind together with a proper respect for me," and financial security. From a practical point of view a connection with the rich Mr. Kellogg might be advantageous, but that gentleman had seven children, might have more, and his property had been obtained by extortion and oppression. To be in his power might be disastrous. Also, Mary Ann blew hot and cold in her love for Harry, and this wounded his self-respect. On the other hand, Miss Miller's dowry could not be much inferior to that of Miss Kellogg, and Judge Miller had only two children and was honest and magnanimous. Also, Frances had a strong mind, was not a dissembler, and loved and respected him.

When Harry wrote to his father, he had been engaged to Frances for nearly a month. Now he was about to ask the Judge for her hand, and so took her to visit her cousin in Ludlowville, some thirty miles south of Auburn, that she might be absent during the interview. After this conference Harry wrote briefly but jubilantly that the Judge had "adopted" him "as a son." There is no record of Samuel's reply to this news, but David Berdan could not help wondering what Miss Kellogg would have to say when she heard it, and whether or not father Samuel would pay Harry's debts before his marriage.[8]

Shortly after the engagement was announced, Seward's father and mother came to Auburn for a visit, and both families went on an excursion to Niagara Falls. In Rochester a wheel came off their coach, and the party found itself mired in a muddy street. Among those who came to their assistance was a tall, broad-shouldered, dark-complexioned individual with kindly eyes, the editor of a local newspaper. His name was Thurlow Weed, and so began a fateful friendship.

Harry and Fan were married in St. Peter's Episcopal church in Auburn on October 20, 1824. Harry wanted Berdan for his best man, but the latter, pleading poverty, declined. It was, nevertheless, a gala affair with several hundred guests at the ceremony and a small reception afterward at the home of the bride. Then the happy couple, together with seven relatives and friends, piled into a great barouche and drove to Rust's Hotel at Onondaga Hill on the out-skirts of Syracuse, where they all spent the night. The next day they were back in Auburn.[9]

Young Harry Seward was now a member of the Miller house-hold. At its head was the fifty-two-year-old judge—lawyer and land speculator, a man of prodigious memory and an independent spirit. His religious beliefs shifted from Quakerism to Episcopalianism and finally to Universalism. Six feet in height and 200 pounds in weight, genial in a patriarchal manner, he had a passion for regularity at meals and for being entertained in the evening. These comforts he looked to his daughters to provide, his wife having died in 1810 of consumption.

The elder daughter was Lazette Maria—elegant and vivacious, her head a mass of dark chestnut curls. Intelligent and attractive to men, she was also willful and was soon to marry against her father's wishes Alvah Worden, president of the Auburn Manufacturing Company. If both girls left the parental home on South Street it would leave there only the Judge's seventy-four-year-old mother,

Paulina Titus Miller, and his stately maiden sister Clarinda. To guard against this possibility, the Judge stipulated that when Frances and Henry married they should live with him.

The bride was nineteen years old and just over five feet six inches in height, slightly taller than her husband. Frances Adeline had black eyes, hair that was glossy black, a long aristocratic nose and neck, and a fine figure—one of the dresses she wore thirty-five years later still measured only twenty-five inches at the waist. She was beautiful, "almost very beautiful" Chester Harding thought her in 1843 when he painted her portrait, and she was intelligent, read avidly, and possessed a keen, though sometimes bitter sense of humor. She also had high standards of morality, a conventional sense of decorum, and an equally conventional Christian faith. More critical of women than of men, modest but strong-minded, she shrank from the social intercourse that Henry loved but was hurt when she felt herself slighted by society. Her dream of conjugal bliss was a quiet life in Auburn with a few close friends, children to be loved and cherished, and a devoted husband by her side.[10]

Henry, as Frances called her husband, was anything but the quiet type. Warm and outgoing, immensely energetic and boundlessly ambitious, he must have come into the quiet town and the ordered Miller household with something of the effect of a bombshell. It was impossible to disregard him. Skeptic though he was, he rented a pew in the Episcopal church when he first arrived in Auburn. He also proceeded to enroll in the militia, attend political rallies, and even manage dancing assemblies. It was inevitable that he should have a part in the tumultuous reception accorded the Marquis de Lafayette when the Revolutionary hero visited the town in 1825. A leader in the town's social activities, he also plunged vigorously into the work of his profession.

Politics beckoned to every young lawyer in those days. Party politics had become largely personal factionalism, with individuals frequently shifting allegiance, and Henry was no exception to the rule. As a stripling he had felt a lasting sense of outrage at the carping attitude taken by the Federalist party toward the War of 1812. In 1816, among New York candidates, outright Jeffersonian Republican Daniel Tompkins had been his choice for President, rather than DeWitt Clinton. The latter had a Republican background but sometimes consorted with Federalists. Four years later Henry told a friend that the most consummate treason on Tompkins's part "would not wipe away one stain from the character of Clinton," and pronounced the Clinton-proposed Erie Canal an idle dream that, if completed, would be the financial ruin of the state. At the beginning of the 1820s, he was a Bucktail and as such a supporter of the Albany Regency which was then being built up by Martin Van Buren, the "Red Fox of Kinderhook." Then came a change, and in the election of 1824 Henry supported John Quincy Adams for President and Clinton for governor on a People's party ticket in direct opposition to the Regency.

Why Henry changed his politics must remain a matter of conjecture. He himself in 1824 declared the Regency had become corrupt and that its leaders had "sunk into cunning and chicanery." Van Buren was, indeed, a wily politician whose ways were sometimes devious. In the early 1820s, before he saw the way to political success, he opposed universal suffrage and the election of officials. His faction fought successfully against a law that would have given to the people the privilege of choosing presidential electors, and by 1824 his opponents were calling the Regency a "cabal" and a "Royal Cabinet" that sought to deprive the people of their just rights. These things may have disgusted Henry, who had a strain of idealism in his makeup, but it is likely that more practical reasons also influenced his decision. He lived in a community that yearned for progress and development, and to those ends strongly favored educational advance and internal improvements, both of which were articles of faith with John Quincy Adams. Henry's father-in-law and senior partner, a man of pronounced and dogmatic opinions, was a National Republican, as such being defeated for Congress in 1826, and Henry's father was an ardent Adams man. Finally, Cayuga County during the middle 1820s was not decisively committed to Regency candidates, and a united opposition marching under the banner of freedom from the increasingly autocratic rule of Van Buren and his associates could reasonably hope for success at the polls. It is probable that practical as well as idealistic considerations sent Henry into the National Republican and Clintonian ranks.

Andrew Jackson was Henry's second choice for President in

1824, chiefly because of Old Hickory's military exploits, but Henry remained a National Republican, though on occasion complaining of Adams's "pedantry." Early in 1828 he went to Albany seeking appointment as surrogate of Cayuga County. Clinton favored Jackson, and the Clintonian leaders at the capitol urged Henry to come out in support of the hero of New Orleans. He "wavered," as he later described it, and this helped him get the desired nomination from the governor. Then the Jackson men in the senate rejected his appointment, Clinton died, and Henry was left free of any obligation to support Jackson in 1828. There was perhaps some wavering still, for in 1841 he told Christopher Morgan that, had it not been for the firmness of Francis Granger, "I might not have been at so early a period as I was an opponent of Andrew Jackson." [11]

During the remainder of 1828 Seward was active in National Republicanism, and in September of that year a convention of the party's young men at Utica elected him chairman of the meeting. At the same time he was co-operating with a new political movement that rapidly took form in western New York.

William Morgan of Batavia, New York, a recreant member of the Masonic order, published in 1826 his *Illustrations of Masonry*, describing the first three degrees of that secret society. His erstwhile brethren, wild with anger, had him arrested on a charge of theft. He was then abducted from a Canandaigua jail and hustled off to the Niagara frontier, never to be seen or heard from again.

When it became apparent that Masons were obstructing the ensuing investigation, excitement rose among the citizenry in western New York. Masonry was an elite organization, numbering in its ranks many prominent and wealthy individuals, and the word spread that New York State was in the grip of selfish aristocrats who swore secret oaths and pursued objectives that were hostile to the welfare of the common man. Out of the furor arose an Antimasonic movement that emphasized its devotion to the great principles of freedom and social equality. Its strength lay among the farmers and the little people of the towns.

Antimasonic political activity began in 1827, and that fall western New York sent fifteen sworn foes of Masonry to the state assembly. A state-wide Antimasonic party appeared in 1828, one of its leaders being Seward's former rescuer, Thurlow Weed. Already a wily politician, Weed carried water on both shoulders, supporting Adams for President and also doing his best to foster the rise of political Antimasonry.[12]

Seward's political course now ran parallel to that of Weed. He was active in National Republican meetings, but when Antimasonry invaded Cayuga County in the winter of 1827–28, capturing hundreds of National Republicans, Seward helped in the drafting of Antimasonic addresses and speeches. The Cayuga Antimasons agreed to form a coalition ticket with the National Republicans, but without Seward's knowledge nominated him for Congress. He hoped that the National Republicans would accept him, but when he was hissed in their county convention he withdrew from the race. Each party then nominated its own candidate, and the Regency won easily against a split opposition.

The election of 1828 demonstrated the demoralization of the National Republicans in New York State. Antimasonry, however, increased in vigor. It offered formidable battle to the Regency, and Seward now threw himself wholeheartedly into the Antimasonic movement. In February 1829 he attended an Antimasonic state convention in Albany, and in January 1830 at a Cayuga County convention he drew up an address denouncing Masonry as a "secret government" that made its own laws and enforced them, even to the death sentence. Political Antimasonry, he declared, was the only practical way of dealing with this menace to liberty. He boasted of the rapid growth of his party throughout the East, and of its opposition to Federalists and Federalism. It was, he asserted, the party of the common man. Shortly thereafter he was made a delegate to a national Antimasonic convention in Philadelphia which was to meet in the fall of 1830. He also raised $400 in the Auburn area to help start Weed's Albany *Evening Journal*, a considerable feat since only $1200 was obtained in all of western New York.[13]

By 1830 the Antimasonic party had not only a hard core of fanatics on the subject of Masonry but also included ardent devotees of freedom and equality in the abstract and a mélange of quondam National Republicans and professional office-seekers. Welcome as all these were, more adherents were needed if the party was to prosper, and Weed had already begun broadening the specific bases of the Antimasonic political creed to include a protective tariff, internal improvements, abolition of imprisonment for debt, repeal of the militia system, and even temperance. That the party was something more than an attack upon a secret society became evident when its state convention met at Utica in August, 1830.

The convention had to nominate a state ticket, and Francis Granger, a young Canandaigua lawyer and rising politician, was the obvious candidate for governor. As for lieutenant-governor, Weed had thoroughly canvassed the situation in New York City, and had come to the conclusion that Samuel Stevens, not an Antimason but the favorite of a New York Working Men's party which contained bankers and businessmen as well as laborers, must be the man. Seward had the task of persuading the convention that Stevens should be nominated. It was a hard assignment, for Stevens was an affront to fanatical Antimasons, but Seward carried the day. Moreover, he was prominent in securing the passage of resolutions that, in addition to assailing Masonry, attacked the Regency for extravagance, partiality to banks, lack of interest in a protective tariff, and failure to provide the canals and other internal improvements needed by a long-suffering public.

Antimasonry had by this time spread into New England, Pennsylvania, and other neighboring states, and was challenging Jacksonian Democracy on a national scale. In the Antimasonic Philadelphia convention of 1830, "a gathering of defeated and desperate politicians," according to the Regency's Albany *Argus,* the New York delegation far outnumbered those from any other state. It issued a call for a national nominating convention to be held in Baltimore the following year. Seward drew up and presented the report of its committee on resolutions and, as chairman of another committee, gave a glowing account of the progress of Antimasonry in the United States. Granger was president of the convention, but the red-headed young man from Auburn had also played a prominent role.[14]

Seward was now a leading Antimason, and Thurlow Weed's eye was upon him. Weed pushed him as a candidate for the state senate; while he was in Philadelphia Seward received the party's nomination in the seventh district. In the ensuing election the Regency's Enos

Throop defeated Granger for the governorship by over 8000 votes, but the seventh district sent Seward to the state senate with a 2000 majority. Cayuga, he told Weed exultantly, was safe from now on. For the next four years he would spend a considerable part of his time in Albany.

2

A Budding Politician

Albany was a growing town in 1830, its population of 24,000 having increased 92 per cent during the past ten years. It boasted a variety of manufacturing establishments, several banks, a state library and, when the river was open, a bustling waterfront. The Dutch had settled it originally; Dutch names and accents were still common; and Dutch high-gabled houses with stoops in front were much in evidence. There were slums down by the Hudson, and affluence further up State Street hill. There were a number of taverns and coffee houses, but Cruttenden's Eagle Tavern at 453 South Market Street, Bement's Hotel at 82 State Street, and Congress Hall on Capitol Park at the corner of Washington Street provided the best accommodations for travelers and legislators.

Henry Seward, senator, went by stagecoach from Auburn to Albany, a two and one-half days' journey. Following Weed's advice, he lodged at the Eagle, and on January 4 in a state of some nervousness took the oath of office. He thought his post would have great importance, but within a few days it began to appear dull and commonplace. He found, however, that he had some interesting colleagues.

Seward was one of seven Antimasons in the senate, whose leaders were the very able William H. Maynard of Utica, the jovial and well-to-do Trumbull Cary of Batavia, and Albert Haller Tracy of Buffalo. In the assembly John C. Spencer of Canandaigua stood out as the leading Antimason in that body "always forward and assuming," as Seward discovered, but a very able and conscientious member of the party. Millard Fillmore of Buffalo, only a year older than Seward, also represented the Antimasons, together with the handsome, affable, and just-defeated candidate for governor, Francis Granger. Soon Henry and those with whom he associated himself most closely were calling one another "Uncle" and their wives "Aunty" as symbols of the Antimasonic tie that bound them together.

Albert Tracy and his wife Harriet fascinated Henry. Harriet was both beautiful and sympathetic. She and Henry discovered a mutual interest in gardening, and before long he regarded her as a confidante. Her thirty-seven-year-old husband bore a striking resemblance to Thomas Jefferson, in manner and physical appearance, a fact of which he was fully conscious. He had been six years in Congress, where John Quincy Adams had held him to be extremely able and "a man of pure morals." Tracy's health was poor and his temperament mercurial, but he was a man of culture and refinement, warm and affectionate by nature, eloquent, and a brilliant conversationalist. Decided in his opinions, he tried to exert a dominating influence on those around him. Henry looked up to him, and the two men quickly developed a very strong attachment.[1]

Thurlow Weed ranked as the most influential Antimasonic leader in the state. Six feet one inch in height and powerfully built, with big hands and feet, a strongly marked, darkly ruddy face, warm-hearted, generous, vital, endlessly devising political maneuvers, Weed counselled his political associates in both public and private affairs. He and Seward both had a sense of humor, a capacity for affection, and a fondness for current literature and for the theater. Both were ambitious for political power, the one as a manager, the other as a leader. Weed, self-educated and strongly masculine, could and did on occasion knock a man down in a fist fight, and always drove hard toward his goal. Seward had had more opportunity for cultural development, and his personal qualities, especially his sense of refinement and his sense of humor, had a delicacy lacking in his friend.

Weed would come to Seward's room and, with Frances present or absent, the two men would sit down before the coal-grate fire, puff cigar smoke into one another's faces, and talk endlessly. "How deeply are all the associations and recollections of your room impressed upon my heart!" wrote Weed after Seward's last year in the senate. It was not long before Seward found Weed even more interesting and likeable than Tracy.[2]

Seward had four busy and eventful years in the senate. At first he felt a painful sense of inadequacy, a feeling that he had in more or less degree until late in life when entering upon any new sphere of activity. His knees knocked together and his mouth went dry at the thought of making a speech. But Tracy and Weed encouraged him, party spirit was moderate in the senate, and by the end of the first session he was taking an active part in the proceedings. He spoke in favor of the law abolishing imprisonment for debt that the Antimasons pushed through the legislature. He demanded reform of the state's unwieldy militia system, urged the direct election of mayors, and wrote the party's *Address* at the end of the session which lauded their achievements and blasted the Jacksonians. All through the session he deliberately avoided personal hostility in debate, and his relations with political opponents were amicable.[3]

During the summer and fall of 1831 Henry caught up on his legal work, but he also delivered a patriotic and Antimasonic Fourth of July oration at Syracuse and corresponded with Weed and Tracy about presidential possibilities. Weed favored Richard Rush as the Antimasonic candidate, though he also thought of John C. Calhoun as a possibility, but Tracy was strong for John McLean of Ohio. Seward had little interest in Rush and none in Calhoun. "The cold, clear, intelligent North is the field for the growth of Anti Masonry," he told Weed, and in September he made an expedition to Boston in an effort to persuade the New England Antimasons that, even though McLean was not a member of the party, he should be the Antimasonic nominee.

Seward went to Boston by way of New York, visiting art galleries and historic sites en route. He conferred with Antimasonic leaders in Massachusetts, made a speech in Boston that delighted the brethren there, and called on John Quincy Adams at Quincy. The former President spoke coolly of McLean and Calhoun, but was favorable to Rush. Adams also evinced support for Antimasonry and said that, if it were deemed essential, he would take the nomination. He expressed himself in measured, deliberate phrases. Seward, so used to eliciting warmth from others, found none in the ex-President.

Seward's journey proved otherwise politically fruitless. Massachusetts and Rhode Island still wanted Adams, while the New Yorkers felt that his administration had been so unpopular that he would not be a good candidate. McLean ended their hopes in his direction by refusing to run.[4]

Meanwhile, back in Auburn, Judge Miller became restive. His son-in-law was politicking so much of the time that their law business suffered. Seward calmed his father-in-law's fears and, a few days after his return from Boston, took both the judge and his own father with him to Baltimore, where all three were delegates to the Antimasonic national convention. There he joined in the search for a candidate and helped persuade Thaddeus Stevens of Pennsylvania, who wanted to draft McLean, that the nominee must be William Wirt. This former Mason bore no hatred towards "the knights of the cable-tow," as the Antimasons injuriously designated their opponents. But he was a distinguished man and was accepted gladly by most of the delegates.

The New York State Antimasons were badly beaten in the 1831 elections, but Seward refused to be disheartened. Clay and the National Republicans were a thorn in the flesh, he told Weed, but Jackson would defeat Clay in 1832 and then the Antimasonic party would have its day. He went back to the senate ready to carry on the political battle with all the energy at his command.[5]

In the senate session of 1832, Seward urged penal reform, especially a separate prison for women, denounced monopolies, and at least on one occasion voted in favor of the individual liability of stockholders for the debts of a corporation. A score of railroad charters came before the senate, and Seward voted for all save two. Most of them were visionary projects, he informed his father, but they were part of the spirit of the times. He wanted railroads, like canals, to be owned and operated by the state.

Seward's outstanding effort in the senate that year was his speech on the recharter of the Bank of the United States. The Bank performed many valuable services. It helped to keep the state banks honest by calling on them periodically to redeem their notes, and itself furnished the nation with a sound currency. Both merchants and farmers found useful its powers of exchange. Nevertheless the Bank was not subject to anything like effective regulation, and its president, Nicholas Biddle, conferred its favors practically at will on influential people. Moreover it had come into disfavor with Old Hickory, who believed that it had been against him in the election of 1828. Jackson regarded it as a "Monster" and a "hydra of corruption." The Bank's recharter impended, the leader of the national Democracy was determined that it should not be renewed, and the Democratic majority in the New York legislature (which wished to free the state banks it had chartered from the "Monster's" surveillance) proposed a resolution supporting the President.

Beginning on January 31, Seward spoke for parts of two days. Varying solid argument with irony and sarcasm, he praised the services and trustworthiness of the Bank as compared with the state banks, and contrasted its approval by the Presidents and Secretaries of the Treasury before Jackson with the opposition of State Senator Edmonds, who had brought in the resolution against recharter. Let the Bank live, said Seward, with such restraints upon its power as might be deemed necessary. With clarity and vision he urged the necessity of a sound, well-regulated paper currency for the development of the nation's resources.[6]

John C. Spencer advised Seward tartly to stop paying attention to the Bank and give a little time to Antimasonry, but his other associates gave the speech the praise it deserved. It would do great things for him, said Weed, not merely for its merit in defending the Bank but also as a demonstration of his principles. This comment pleased the young senator immensely, for he had been very nervous about the effect of his efforts.

At the close of the session Seward again drew up the *Address* of the Antimasonic members of the legislature to the people of the state, a document which castigated the Regency for its laxity in performance, extravagance, and indifference to progress and reform. The *Address* emphasized economic matters; only at the close did it deliver a blast against Masonry.

Henry came home that spring to a county that had just defeated him for supervisor, his friends having put him up in his absence. Any possible qualms on his part because of this humiliation were, however, soothed by a military honor. He had refused a promotion and had resigned his post as a colonel of artillery in the 33rd. militia regiment, but he now found himself elected brigadier general, in large part through the support of his political opponents.

Brigadier General Seward appeared frequently in the Court of Common Pleas and the Circuit Court that summer, but he also kept his eye on the political scene. The center of interest for him and for other politicians, was Jackson's veto of the bill rechartering the Bank of the United States. Seward deplored the veto, deeming its arguments faulty, but recognized that it had a prodigious popular effect as a rallying ground for Jacksonism in New York State. "We have not half the spirit we had in 1828," he told Weed.[7]

The New York Antimasons and National Republicans joined hands that fall in what the Democrats described as a "Siamese twin" party, both nominating Granger for governor and selecting a combined electoral ticket that would go for Clay or Wirt, whichever had the best chance of defeating Jackson. Seward helped Weed perfect the working arrangement with Clay's followers, but he also signed a circular which specifically stated that the split ticket was wholly and unequivocally for Wirt. Clay's refusal to come out against Masonry disgruntled Seward, who found it difficult to maintain enthusiasm for the uphill fight Clay was making against Jackson.

The election of 1832 was indeed a Democratic triumph. The leaders of the Democracy, Jackson and Van Buren, stood for certain principles. They believed in maintaining the Union, in economical administration, and in keeping at a minimum the activities of the national government. They professed sympathy for the desire of westerners for cheap land, and Jackson catered to land-hungry easterners in his determination to remove the Indian tribes of the South to areas west of the Mississippi. Their best issue, however, was the bill rechartering the Bank of the United States, which Clay and Webster had pushed through Congress and Jackson had vetoed. The veto message was a ringing blast against recharter as prostituting the government to the wealthy; it promised that the Democratic party would stand always for the best interests of the people. Under these circumstances the opposition's arguments about the Regency spoilsmen and Jackson's use of the veto to enhance executive power had little effect. The Regency candidate for governor, William Learned Marcy, beat Granger by a 10,000 majority, and Jackson carried the state in even more impressive fashion. "What a Waterloo rout we have suffered!" moaned Tracy, "Horse, foot and dragoons all gone." Conspiring with the National Republicans, he asserted, had left the Antimasons no ground of principle to stand on.

Seward, too, was disheartened, but if he felt there was any loss of principle he took pains not to show it. After consultation with Weed and other Antimasonic leaders, he wrote a manifesto for the Albany *Evening Journal* which admitted that the Democratic victory had been an expression of the popular will, but pledged a continuance of the struggle against Jacksonism. It contained no clarion call for the preservation of the Antimasonic party. As an Antimasonic manifesto, it was pitched at least a couple of octaves too low.

Seward's record on matters of state interest in the 1833 legislative session was much like that of the two preceding years with the exception of a vote against the Chenango Canal, which was to run from Binghamton through the Chenango Valley and connect with the Erie Canal at Utica. On the national scene, when collision between the federal government and South Carolina threatened, he voted for resolutions upholding Jackson and denouncing nullification or secession by a single state. At the same time, however, he offered two resolutions supporting strict construction of the Constitution. These slaps at "King Andrew" received the support of his Antimasonic colleagues, but the senate promptly voted them down.[8]

The following summer brought a change of scene for the young senator. Samuel Seward wanted to go abroad and asked Henry to go with him, offering to pay his expenses. Judge Miller opposed the trip on the ground that the law firm's business would suffer; Tracy wrote that stability and concentration of purpose were more important than any European jaunt; but Henry was determined to go. He loved travel; he could plead filial duty, for his father was sure that his own health would benefit by the journey, and there can be no doubt that Seward saw in it political advantages. He had an understanding with Weed that letters descriptive of his journey would be published in the *Evening Journal*. This salutary procedure, as the canny editor remarked, would keep unbroken the chain between Seward and his constituents.

The two travelers sailed on the *Europe* on June 1 and were gone for five months, two spent in ocean travel, the rest in the British Isles and on the Continent. Henry engaged in a whirlwind of activity that ranged from improving his French by conversations with a pair of pretty Belgian girls to visiting Lafayette at LaGrange. Guide books helped him inspect innumerable museums and cathedrals. While in Switzerland he climbed almost to the top of Mont Blanc, and he walked half the distance on the journey from Geneva to Paris, often rising in the early morning so that he might start out ahead of the stagecoach. He appreciated the scenery and picked mountain flowers which were carefully preserved for Frances. It was all very exciting for the young traveler, and Samuel, with some reason, complained that he was being neglected.

Seward kept a journal which he wrote at night in the form of letters to various people. Some seventy of these missives, revised for publication, appeared in the *Evening Journal* during 1834 and 1835, Weed solemnly assuring his readers that they had been written without the slightest expectation of their ever appearing in print. They bore testimony in their original form to the young traveler's good qualities—his insatiable curiosity and love of nature, his interest in people and pride in America, and a shrewdness of observation, such as his disappointment that no clear view of St. Paul's cathedral could be obtained from any street leading to that magnificent edifice. Jabez D. Hammond, historian, Democratic politician, and himself widely traveled in Europe, praised them for their descriptive powers and their freedom from both dullness and romantic imaginings.

These letters disclosed on the other hand some of their author's limitations. Henry was shocked by the nude statues in the Tuileries gardens, and he had no real taste or appreciation for painting. An hour that he spent in the Louvre, he later told his wife, had been sufficient instruction in that art so that ever afterward he had been able to distinguish a good work from a bad one, and one school from another.[9]

Henry returned to an accumulation of legal work that kept him busy until the 1834 legislative session. There once again he took an active part in the debate. The Regency had controlled the granting of state bank charters for so long that it had great economic power. This was an issue made to order for the opposition, and Seward took a much more critical attitude toward the chartering of such institutions than had been the case in previous years. He also made two major speeches, neither very statesmanlike. In one he denounced Jackson's removal of deposits from the Bank of the United States as an act of usurpation, which was, to say the least, an exaggeration. In the other, Seward attacked a Regency bill establishing a $6 million credit for the state banks that were being hurt by Biddle's policy of contracting credits.

Contraction, at first a legitimate defense against attack, had been transformed by the Bank into an attempt to force recharter of the institution, but Seward ignored this aspect of the situation. He pictured the Bank as both powerless and defenseless, and called the loan a corruption fund more dangerous than that paid to Benedict Arnold.

The *Address* of the minority members of the legislature, which Seward again drew up at the close of the session, was similar in tenor to his major speeches. The Bank was right, Jackson was wrong. The $6 million loan meant that the state was going deeper and deeper into debt. Direct taxation loomed ahead. The Democratic party had become a menace to the nation's most cherished institutions. The time had come, said Seward, to decide whether the government should continue as a republic, "or whether it should be converted into a monarchy, with the form only of popular power." [10]

At such times Seward did not rise above the level of political partisanship, but on balance his record in the senate was good. To be sure, he had voted rather indiscriminately for railroad and banking charters, save when he felt that the latter were too closely aligned with Regency interests, but he had also urged improvement of the militia system, abolition of imprisonment for debt, and prison reform. He had generally supported internal improvement measures and bills to improve education, both male and female, and his speech on the recharter of the Bank of the United States had been masterly.

A shrewd political observer in 1834 might have noticed that in two instances Seward had taken a stand that could well be detrimental to his political future. In 1833 he had voted against the Chenango Canal and in 1834 against an appropriation for surveying the New York and Erie Railroad, both apparently because of popular opposition to these projects in Cayuga County and the central part of the state.[11] But even though his popularity was not marked in the southern tier of counties, he was in close rapport with Thurlow Weed, and was generally regarded as a coming man.

Even while Seward was flaying the Democratic party for high crimes and misdemeanors, the National Republican and Antimasonic state organizations were in process of dissolution. Both Weed and himself were busy preparing the ground for a new political structure, and during the winter of 1833–34 the state Whig party came into being. It was a strange sort of amalgam. States' righters and nationalists, Masons and Antimasons, pro- and anti-Clay men, pro- and anti-Bank men, merchants and manufacturers, farmers and laborers, rallied under the Whig banner. This uneasy combination held together chiefly because of dislike of Jackson, distrust of Van Buren, and animosity directed toward a Regency which had made enemies during its years of power by its distribution of bank and railroad charters and the patronage.

Most of the Antimasons became Whigs, and for years the heavy majorities they rolled up in western New York played a large part in Whig victories. They were following leaders who felt, Seward declared, that the one indispensable principle was opposition to "the Kinderhook politician." Most of them accepted the situation with good grace, but the zealots were bitter at desertion of the war against "the old handmaid," Masonry, and they accused Seward of betrayal.[12]

Politicians of the Seward stripe act from a mixture of motives. They have a real desire to serve the people, to make the country a better place than they found it. They are aggressive by nature, and at the same time seek to bolster self-esteem by political activity. Gamblers by instinct, they are fascinated by the element of chance in a political contest. They covet power and, if convinced that a given political course rides the wave of the future they will be loyal to it, even though its triumph may be of dubious social value. But they are reluctant to commit themselves to a cause the success of which is doubtful, and once convinced that it has outlived its usefulness they abandon it without reluctance.

To say that Seward joined Antimasonry simply out of lust for office would be to brand him a cynic, and that he was not. Charges that the movement was anything but sincere, or that he had become an Antimason as a politician on the make, roused in him a fury of indignation. His letters and speeches show beyond the shadow of a doubt that he believed, as did the rank and file Antimasons, that "the cause" was based on the great principle of democratic freedom. Weed, also, felt that they had a high purpose in view. "Will we ever again," he wrote to Seward in 1835, "have our better and higher sympathies so warmly excited and so nobly directed. I fear not." [13] But by 1834 most of the Masonic lodges in New York State had been closed, and both men were astute enough to realize that opposition to a secret society was altogether too narrow a base for a successful political structure.

Seward's term in the senate was now over. His father-in-law wanted him to quit politics for a few years and make some money; Weed and a number of other friends wanted him to stand for re-election; Henry had his own ideas, and at first they differed from those of everyone else, even though they were directly related to the state campaign of 1834.

It was clear to all that the Whigs would battle against great odds in 1834. Their party was new and untried, and jealousies between Antimasons and National Republicans rent its ranks. The Democracy, on the other hand, had a veteran organization, command of the patronage, and a host of friends among state banks that provided both money and influence. Furthermore, Marcy had been a reasonably good governor and was now up for re-election. The Whigs desperately needed a first-class candidate for the governorship.

Weed and Tracy wanted Jesse Buel, the unassuming farmer-editor of Albany County, to head the ticket. Many in the western counties wanted Granger to run again, despite his being a two-time loser. Luther Bradish, from the agricultural north, had support there and in the central part of the state. John A. Collier, Binghamton lawyer, was the candidate of the southern tier, and Gulian Verplanck, a quondam Democrat who had broken with Jackson on the Bank, was popular in New York City. The only mention of Seward was for lieutenant-governor, a post in which at first he professed great interest. Then the contest over the gubernatorial nomination began to work in his favor.

Buel's star faded. The Antimasons distrusted him, and it was hard to discover whether he was a Whig or a Democrat, Granger did not want the nomination, Verplanck was anathema to the former National Republicans, and Bradish, landed proprietor and world traveler, had little appeal for the common man. The candidates were canceling out and, almost in despair, men such as Granger and John C. Spencer began to mention Seward's name. The latter's eagerness was unmistakable, and reluctantly, for he had the votes against the Chenango Canal and the Erie Railroad in mind, Weed began laying the groundwork for Seward's nomination.

The Whig state convention met at Utica in September. Granger was the favorite candidate of the delegates, but he positively declined to be considered. Weed pledged himself that Seward really favored both the Chenango Canal and the Erie Railroad, and the delegates finally nominated the man from Auburn by acclamation, with Silas M. Stilwell, New York lawyer and friend of the workingman, as his running mate. An enthusiastic young men's convention met shortly thereafter in Syracuse and ratified the ticket, half of the group then moving on to Auburn where they paid their respects to the candidate with much cheering and a salute of fifty guns.

All of this moved Henry deeply. The tumult and the shouting appealed to him greatly, and he was especially touched by Weed's efforts on his behalf. William Henry Seward already felt a sense of "infinite obligations" to Weed.

The Democrats renominated William L. Marcy for governor, and the campaign was the usual slam bang affair of the period. The Whigs charged that "ruffled shirt party," the Regency, with extravagance and corruption. They lived in marble palaces, rode in coaches, drank wine imported from Madeira, and had mortgaged the state to sustain their banks. Elect Seward, the voters were told, and he would reform the state government.

The Democrats affected to regard Seward as a diminutive stripling, and spread the report that he was only twenty-two years old. They made great play on the Chenango Canal and Erie Railroad votes, so much so that Seward wrote a letter, widely distributed, to prove that he was a great friend of the road and of internal improvements in general. Seward was the Bank candidate, Edwin Croswell of the Albany *Argus* declared, and also was supported by apostate Antimasons. So alarming was this latter charge that Weed took $3500 provided by wealthy New York and Albany Whigs into the western part of the state, where it was used for hiring speakers and buying votes.[14]

Weed warned Seward against optimism, and the result of the campaign justified the warning. Marcy carried the state by some 11,000 majority, and seven of the eight senatorial districts returned Democratic senators. Seward had run well in the western part of the state, but in the east and in New York City the Democrats had rolled up heavy majorities.

Seward's spirits sank under the defeat, but he quickly rallied. He wrote to Whig leaders in various parts of the state asking if they were disposed to keep up the Whig organization, to which they all replied in the affirmative. "I have got quite over being beat," he told his friend Trumbull Cary a week after the election, "and I don't mean to preach or keep school either—Don't let it vex you. We have had glory enough already." In a more serious vein, he urged Weed not to let the victors see his dejection, for they could yet serve and might possibly live to save the country.[15] Though a defeated candidate, he was now a leading figure in the New York State Whig party.

ᥩ3᥎

Family and Fortune

Seward's rise to political leadership in the state was only one aspect of his public career. Side by side with it went his law practice, which flourished from the start. Judge Miller guaranteed him a first-year income of $500, but he earned at least that amount. An early case, in which he obtained the acquittal of a petty thief by proving factual errors in the indictment, gave him a reputation for shrewdness. Applications for his services mounted; the trustees of Auburn village appointed him their attorney in 1825; he drew up deeds and indentures, settled estates for creditors as far away as New York, and handled legal aspects of land sales. Judge Miller gradually withdrew from the business and in 1831, when Seward went to the state senate, he took as his law partner Nelson Beardsley who, three years before, had come into the office as a law student. The firm continued to prosper, the senior partner handling its Albany affairs when the legislature was in session, and arguing cases in various courts during the remaining eight months of the year. Pressure of legal work mounted after the campaign of 1834, and in 1835 Seward told his father that he was "little better than a galley slave."

The young lawyer was successful in a profession for which he had no love. He disliked its technicalities and uncertainties, and its drudgery repelled him. The practice of law, he told Weed, was a barren and frustrating experience, one in which, after lengthy litigation, the lawyer was all too apt to find that either he, or the court and jury, were entirely wrong. He could not, however, think of any better line of work, and he did appreciate the money that he earned.

By 1826 Seward was anticipating a yearly income of $5000. This was a trifle exuberant, though he probably approached that figure by 1830. After he became a senator and formed the partnership with Beardsley, his share of the profits was some $2000 a year. This doubled in 1835.

In addition to income from legal fees, he profited from railroad stock and from real estate operations during the flush times of the early 1830s. In 1834, overextended speculations made him fearful of bankruptcy, but in 1836 he estimated that he was worth $50,000 in Auburn real estate, owed $10,000, and had "twenty dollars" in cash. He was not yet financially secure, he told Weed, but he hoped to be independent of the law by 1840.[1]

A flourishing law practice, a growing estate, and political honors were satisfactions, but they were not enough to make Seward a contented man. Auburn cramped him, and repeatedly he thought of moving—to New York, or Albany, or Chicago. Achieving much, he continually aspired to more, but he felt the pull of so many forces that he could not achieve any clear conception of the meaning of his existence. "I am an enigma, even to myself," he told one of his friends. Always outward looking, he throve on friendships, most of them superficial rather than intimate. Aggressive by nature, he was restless and threw himself with vigor into the occupation of the moment. This made for storm and stress in private as well as in public affairs.

Problems early beset Seward's married life. Frances had a miscarriage in January 1825 and for weeks thereafter Henry was concerned about her health. Not long thereafter he himself fell victim to what was apparently a serious but short-lived depression. The affairs of his father's family caused him constant anxiety. His sister, whom he deeply loved, married a man of whom her father bitterly disapproved; his brothers, shiftless and wayward, drained his resources. He had to supply his mother with pin money, if she were to have any at all, and the parsimonious Samuel kept putting pressure on him to come back to Orange County. These troubles made life strenuous, and Frances's problems added to its difficulties.

Through visits Frances established an amicable relationship with her in-laws, but she shared Henry's concern over their troubles. Nor did she find married life easy. Henry's frequent absences were hard to bear, especially when her father fell ill, for then he was gruff and forbidding. One winter the judge put up his bed in the sitting room and drove nails in the wall to hang his clothes on, declaring that he would sleep there all summer, while Frances looked on in horrified helplessness.

Frances could cope with such difficulties in her own home, but life in Albany, when she was there in the winter months with Henry, brought strain that she found hard to endure. Her health was poor; she disliked most of the people that she met; the rounds of calls and the other social obligations of a senator's wife were repugnant to her; and Henry was everlastingly at the capitol, or engaged in long political discussions with Weed and Tracy at home. During two of the senate sessions Frances remained in Auburn. In 1832 and 1834 she went to Albany, staying at Congress Hall and at Bement's. In December 1833 Henry went early to attend the Court of Errors, and then wrote that he would come for her. She was not ready, but he arrived in Auburn at four o'clock one morning, having traveled two nights by stagecoach. "As usual," she wrote to her sister, "Henry made all smooth and convinced me that it would be the easiest thing in the world to get ready to go." Frances had an ingrown life, dominated by increasing anxiety over the way in which she and her husband were growing apart. And as she worried, her health worsened, with nervous headaches, dyspepsia, eye trouble that deprived her of the solace of reading, and the "hypos" and "vapours" that sent her to her room until she could reappear with her "bright face." Their children were her chief consolation.

Henry had feared that children would make him miserable, but these fears proved unfounded. Their first child, Augustus Henry, was born October 1, 1826, and a second son, Frederick William, came four years later. Their father, busy with law and politics, saw little of them at first, but as they grew he became more interested and would write them affectionate letters when he was away from home.

Henry's relations with his father-in-law were good, even though the judge was not the easiest man in the world to live with and was

not, Henry thought, as generous as he might be in their early financial arrangements. During the latter 1820s, the young lawyer earnestly considered moving to Goshen or to New York. In 1830 on
plea of his pregnant wife's health and comfort, they did move into a
house they both loved, opposite the Miller residence. Then Henry
went to the senate. Frances, averse to staying alone, moved back
across the street, and in the spring of 1831 they sold the new house.

Henry and Frances were in love, and they meant to keep their
affection alive. They wrote to each other every day when apart, the
letters being sent once a week. Frances read the Albany *Evening
Journal*'s political news and her husband's speeches and became,
Seward told Weed, quite a politician. She glowed with him in his
triumphs, comforted him in his moods of despondency, and
achieved a real liking for Weed and Tracy. Henry was proud of her
and of their two boys, but little by little the paths of husband and
wife diverged.

The truth was that politics and law pre-empted practically all of
Henry's time and most of his thoughts. He did enjoy domestic life,
he told Frances in 1831, but he had to admit that for the past four
years there had been scarcely any time for such enjoyment. And religion, to which she turned for comfort, left him indifferent. This
was another source of worry for his wife.

Henry's neglect of his family increased as the years went on. Cornelia, with sisterly frankness, told him that Frances scarcely knew
she had a husband, and that the little boys could not realize that he
was more to them than Grandfather Miller. Frances, divided between loyalty to her husband and regret over the course he was taking, reproached him for coldness and indifference, but to no avail. In
1833 he went abroad for five months. On his return and much to
Frances's disappointment, he stopped in Albany to see Weed before
coming home. He was in Auburn nine days, and then was off again
to Albany. Next came the political activities of the 1834 legislative
session and after that the gubernatorial campaign. Politics had become the absorbing interest of his life.

Rivalry between Weed and Tracy for Henry's loyalty further
complicated the Seward family situation. Tracy affected to regard
Seward as a hot-headed impulsive young man who needed guidance.
He and Henry had quickly developed what they described as

"womanish" feelings of fondness for each other, and at first Henry
took the older man for his mentor in politics. At the same time he was
also impressed by Weed's kindliness and devotion and his great political knowledge. Weed was "a real wizard," Henry told Frances.
The "wizard" gave Henry presents. Henry lent him money and
raised $700 to help him pay off a court judgment. By 1834 Henry
was relying on Weed's rather than on Tracy's political advice.

When Henry was abroad his letters came intermittently, and
Frances took comfort in correspondence with Tracy. "I love him
very much," she artlessly confessed to her sister. She determined to
learn French, and the following winter in Albany Tracy was often
at Bement's, reading in French with Frances and playing with the
little boys. He told Henry and Frances repeatedly that he loved
them both. Tracy was charming, and Frances was glad of his
company.

The reasons for what followed were probably, on Tracy's part,
a compound of pique, because Henry was turning to Weed for
political counsel, and of genuine concern over Henry's neglect of his
wife. It is impossible to tell whether he made improper advances to
Frances, or whether her half-estrangement from her husband led her
to misinterpret the affection of their mutual friend. Whatever the
cause, Tracy's attitude toward Frances overstepped the bounds of
prudence. From then on Henry held him at arm's length, and
Tracy, pleading illness, refused to campaign for Seward that fall.

Shortly after the election of 1834 Seward went to Albany to
attend the Court of Errors. His first letters to his wife were filled
with the usual chitchat about calls, the theater, and politics. Then at
seven o'clock one morning he poured out a torrent of fears and a
confession of error.

For two days and nights, Henry wrote, he had been awakening
"from a long and feverish and almost fatal dream." He knew now
that he loved her, a fact that she had "so often and with such bitter
tears doubted." Ever since their marriage his ambition had driven
them apart. He had been cruel and selfish, regarding her as incidental to his career, and as the spoiled child of romance. He
had looked with pity upon her interest in religion and her efforts to
win him to religious faith. He had denied her the love that was her
due, "and when the wretched T. took advantage of my madness and

offered sympathy and feelings and love such as I had sworn, and your expelled heart was half won by his falsehoods, still I did not know and see that I was the criminal."

He did not know, Henry told his wife, what had produced this "convulsion of thought and passion." He did not know that he could become a Christian, though he felt that he might become one through reason and reflection. He did know that when he left home he was still the slave of ambition, but now he wanted only her understanding love.

Frances replied that Henry reproached himself too severely. He had always been good and kind, and he could become a Christian with the aid of God's grace. She had come to believe that he could not love her as deeply as she loved him, but she had also reproached herself for expecting a return of her "too intense affections." She had sorrowed over losing her influence with him, but another's love was not the answer. At last winter's crisis, she had said "that I could never love another better than yourself unless God utterly deserted me." God had helped her, and if Henry could only subordinate ambition to love and Christian faith, she believed they might be happier "than in the earliest and brightest days of our marriage."

Husband and wife recognized that they had passed through an emotional crisis. It had been compounded for Frances by worry and neglect. The crisis, on Henry's part, had been brought on by depression over political defeat, recognition of his failings as a husband, and fear that his political ambition had wrecked their marriage.

Tracy believed, or affected to believe, that his own course had been beyond criticism. He protested that he had always been devoted to Seward's happiness and honor, deplored the change in their friendship, and suggested that Henry was incapable of reciprocating his affection. Henry replied that Tracy's action the previous winter, while not dishonorable in intent, might well have destroyed the peace and happiness of his home. He had forgiven, even though he could not forget, Tracy's weakness, and could still sign himself "your friend."

Henry's plea for his wife's forgiveness and promise of reform cleared the matrimonial air, but did not bring about any fundamental change in his way of life. So far as Tracy was concerned, both men appealed to Weed, who wanted no part of the quarrel, and relations between the two principals never came back to the old intimate footing. There was a patching up of differences, however, and six months later Seward was calling Tracy one of his "beloved friends," and the latter was protesting "I love you all." There had been fault on both sides in the affair. Tracy justly remarked that Seward was altogether too prone "to despise the *juste milieu,* and to rush with distempered eagerness to the extreme," a comment that he might also have applied to himself.[2]

Frances's health was very poor in the winter of 1834–35.

Family silhouette, *c.* 1833. (Left to right) Paulina Titus Miller (mother of Judge Miller), Judge Miller, Clarinda Miller (sister of Judge Miller), William Henry Seward, Augustus Seward, Frederick Seward, Frances Adeline Seward. *Seward House, Auburn, New York.*

Dyspepsia, a troublesome cough, and general debility assailed her; she would not see company and kept most of the time to her room. Henry's practice kept him at the office all day and far into the night, and she would have been lonesome indeed if seventeen-year-old Harriet Weed had not come for a long visit. Timid, affectionate, and anxious to please, Harriet spent much of her time reading to the invalid.

Henry sought advice from various doctors in regard to his wife's condition. Their counsel, some improvement in Frances's health as spring came on, and his own belief that travel would cure anything, led them to plan a trip that began on May 23, 1835, and extended over the summer. It was made in a light carriage drawn by a pair of horses, with William Johnson, their Negro servant, as driver. Five-year-old Frederick went with them. Traveling from eighteen to twenty miles a day, their route led them through Pennsylvania and as far as Natural Bridge, Virginia, with stops at Charlottesville, Washington, Philadelphia, and the seashore on the return journey.

Both the travelers loved natural scenery. They found the Virginia plantation seats imposing and the Old Dominion inns better than those of the North, and Henry pronounced the University of Virginia superior to any northern college with which he was acquainted. But the most vivid impression they retained from the trip was of the blighting effects of slavery. Virginia was suffering from soil exhaustion, times were hard there, and many Negroes were being sold south. The travelers saw numbers of fugitive slaves in southern Pennsylvania and, after they crossed the state line, the worn-out farms, the wretched roads, and the tragedy and horrors of slavery made a deep impression on their minds. Their driver could not be out after sundown without a pass. They talked with a Negro woman whose husband and six children had been sold away from her, and saw a coffle of ten naked boys between six and twelve years of age driven to a horse trough to drink and then to a shed for an uneasy night's rest. These youngsters were destined for the cotton and sugar cane plantations of the Deep South. Years later when Seward became a champion of the anti-slavery movement, the memory of these Virginia scenes must have been indelibly printed on his mind.

Sully painted their portraits in Philadelphia, and Frances consulted the famous Dr. Philip Physick, whose advice to her was to avoid taking cold. In Washington the high point was an interview with the President. They could not help being impressed when the old general, dressed in black, rose and shook hands with them and Frederick. Seward noticed that Jackson surrounded himself with busts, pictures, and other evidences of the devotion of his followers, and that he was extremely dogmatic on all subjects. But he had to admit that the President's remarks were "perspicuous and intelligent," and that, to sum it all up, he was "polite, firm, chivalrous, vain, passionate and petulant." Politics had been skirted in the conversation.[3]

Frances's journal of the trip, especially for the first two months, listed a notable series of afflictions—headaches, toothaches, chest pains, insomnia, and just plain "sick"—but when they reached home on September 3 her health had definitely improved. Two months later she was pregnant with their third child, and during the winter the usual train of illnesses afflicted her. In the spring, to her bitter disappointment, Henry became committed to a business deal that kept him much of the time at Westfield in Chautauqua County. Once more, Harriet Weed came to the rescue, arriving in Auburn early in the summer and staying until after the birth of a girl, Cornelia, who arrived on August 25.

For a few short months after Cornelia's birth, Frances was happier than she had been in years. Henry's affairs in Westfield were going well, and he came home as often as possible. Cornelia was entrancing, a redhead, all smiles and baby talk, and she grew at the rate of a pound a week. Then early in January she contracted smallpox through the carelessness of the family doctor. Seward rushed home to find her blinded and disfigured. She died on January 14, and within a few days both her father and Gus came down with mild forms of the same dread disease.

Seward returned to Westfield as soon as he was well again. He wanted to take his remaining family with him, but this was impossible because of Judge Miller. Within a month Frances was imploring her husband to come back, for Fred was desperately ill with pneumonia, but then came word of his improvement and his father remained in Chautauqua County.

The sorrows of this winter affected Seward deeply, bringing home to him, as had the crisis of 1834, the importance of his family. He decided to join the church. On March 26, he received baptism and communion in St. Peter's Episcopal Church in Westfield. As he stood by the baptismal font, he told his wife, his thoughts were of her and the boys and Cornelia. That same day he wrote to Weed—

> I may as well be explicit with you—I profess not to have experienced any miraculous change of heart or to have in any way gone through that ordeal of despair so commonly supposed to be the entrance and the only entrance upon Christian life. I have always been sensible that I was an offender, and a grievous one against the duty I owed to God and my fellow

men. I have endeavoured now to repent and resolve with God's grace to live more in the fear of and under the influence of love and gratitude to God, and to that end to study his revelation. I do not anticipate that it will make any considerable change in my habits of life, but I humbly trust that it will gradually elevate and refine my motives of action.[4]

It may be as well to add here that no particular change is observable in his manner or mode of life as a result of the step which he had taken.

Land speculation brought Seward to Westfield. Years before, the Holland Land Company, a group of Dutch businessmen, had purchased millions of acres of wild lands in the United States, including much of the area in New York State that lies west of the present city of Batavia. The Company's golden dreams did not materialize, and by 1835 it was disposing of its holdings. In the spring of that year, Trumbull Cary and George W. Lay of Batavia and Abraham M. Schermerhorn (a Rochester banker) purchased for $919,175.59 all the Company's holdings in Chautauqua County, comprising some 365,000 acres. The new owners paid the Company an advance of $50,000. One-fourth of the purchase price was to be handed over by January 1, 1836, the rest by the end of 1837.

The Holland Land Company had been lenient, if not generous, with the settlers, and they were disturbed by this sale to native landlords. Grumblings changed to wrath and violence when it became apparent that the latter were determined to collect compound interest on old debts, and were raising the price of land to those asking renewal of contracts. Early in 1836, encouraged by rumors that the Holland Company had no title and that they could avoid all further payments, the settlers sacked the Mayville, Chautauqua County, land office. William Peacock, the land agent, fled in terror of his life, and land receipts dwindled. The new owners, distraught at this turn of affairs, began looking for an agent who had no connection with their rigorous policies and who might calm the settlers' wrath. They asked Seward to take the position.[5]

Discontented with the law and convinced that he would benefit financially by the move, Seward wrote to Weed, who, though at first staggered, finally admitted that it might be a wise venture. All arrangements were made by the end of June. Seward received an annual salary of $5000, plus expenses, and a two-ninths share in the project, assuming in return entire management of the business for a period of up to five years. He withdrew from the law firm in Auburn, with the privilege of re-entry, one John Porter taking his place.

Seward now went to Batavia, where the Company's main land office was located. There he found a state of wild excitement, with the settlers in that area holding meetings almost daily and the office fortified and guarded by armed men. He ordered transcripts of the records, the originals of which had been destroyed in the rioting, and then went on to Chautauqua County. There he moved the land office from Mayville, the center of the disturbance, to the little village of Westfield, and announced his terms to the settlers.

He went to Westfield determined to deal justly, and his terms were moderate. If a settler paid one-fourth of the debt he owed the associates, and gave bond and mortgage payable in five annual installments, he received a deed to his property. Five hundred delinquent mortgagors were threatened with foreclosure unless they paid the back interest, and of these all save a few complied with the demand. Seward eventually extended debt payments over a ten-year period to all who desired it and gave evidence of good faith. Out of the mortgages in default, he later estimated, there were less than fifty foreclosures.

The results of fair dealing were soon manifest. Excitement abated, payments were promptly made, and a generally mellow spirit came to prevail in the county. By January 1, 1837, some 80,000 acres of land had been conveyed to the settlers and a large part of the associates' debt to the Holland Land Company had been paid.

When business was good the land office was thronged from morning till night. Then the tide of settlers would ebb, and Seward would have time to drive about the countryside. In the long winter evenings he read Dickens and Scott, Tacitus and Bacon, and was particularly impressed by the depth and brilliance of Bacon's reasoning. All this was a pleasant change from what he was wont to refer to as the constant slavery of the legal profession.

Not all the affairs of the associates ran as smoothly as did the dealings with the settlers, for jealousy and suspicion were rife among Seward's partners. Jared L. Rathbone, an Albany merchant who had come into the venture when Seward entered it, and who was grasping in money matters, complained that Seward was selling land at too low a price, was being too lenient with the settlers, and was too much involved in politics. Cary told Seward that Schermerhorn would cheat his own wife and children, if it were to his advantage, and Lay, too, was suspicious of "Schem." On one thing, however, all Seward's associates were agreed. They looked to him to wind up the speculation with the utmost profit in the shortest possible space of time.[6]

Over and above discord in the partnership loomed the problem of paying off the entire debt to the Holland Land Company during 1837. Seward tried unsuccessfully to interest a Boston financier, Israel Munson, in financing the undertaking. In November 1836 he went to Philadelphia and concluded an arrangement with the Holland Company's agent that eased the pressure for payments. Panic descended upon the country, however, money became tight, and by February 1837 Seward had to plead for more time with J. J. VanderKemp, the Holland Company's agent. VanderKemp agreed not to force payments that would have thrown the Chautauqua lands back into the Company's possession. Then the depression increased in intensity, all attempts at borrowing money failed, trouble was brewing in the state assembly over the Holland Land Company's title, and Seward's associates were enveloped in a mood of darkest gloom.

Despite the increasing difficulty of the situation, Seward did not despair. In May 1837 he made a refinancing arrangement with the American Life Insurance and Trust Company of Baltimore, only to have it vetoed by the Holland Land Company and the Bank of the United States. Four months later, he again went to Philadelphia, and this time concluded what looked like a real triumph in financial diplomacy.

The arrangement now made involved the Holland Land Company, the American Life and Trust, and Biddle's Bank. American Life and Trust would issue, against the security of the Chautauqua lands and mortgages, trust certificates to the amount of $650,000, payable in twenty years and bearing interest at 5 per cent. These were to be turned over to the Bank of the United States, with authorization to sell enough of them at once so that the Chautauqua associates could pay off the $50,000 that they had borrowed in 1836 to make their advance payment to the Holland Land Company, and in addition a $10,000 draft discounted by the Bank. The remaining trust certificates would be marketed by the Bank, terms to be later decided. The money realized from marketing the certificates would be used to discharge the obligations of the Chautauqua associates to the Holland Land Company and to the American Life and Trust Company. "The long agony is finally over," Seward wrote to Weed,[7] but this did not prove to be the case.

Seward, and John Duer and Morris Robinson of the American Life were appointed to act as trustees for the Chautauqua property, and they carried on the negotiations with Biddle over marketing the trust certificates. Arrangements were completed in the late spring of 1838, and that fall the Holland Company received some $550,000 and in return deeded its Chautauqua lands to Duer, Robinson, and Seward.

But now another difficulty arose. Rathbone felt that the Bank charged too much for marketing the certificates, and he again complained about Seward's leniency with the settlers. The Albany merchant wanted to get out of the venture, and in the summer of 1838 by agreement of all the trustees, a new arrangement of the Chautauqua lands was made. In a division of the remaining property Seward purchased Rathbone's share. Henry now owned four-ninths of the speculation and owed $32,000, most of it to Rathbone, over and above his share of the debt to the American Trust Company. To hedge against this heavy involvement he began negotiating an exchange of part of his Chautauqua holdings for Auburn real estate.[8]

The Chautauqua land purchase had appeared to offer great possibilities of profit, and Seward had embarked on the project with his accustomed energy and enthusiasm. His reports to the Holland Land Company, to the American Life and Trust Company, and to Biddle on the background of the purchase, and on relations with the settlers, were clear and detailed, and evidently inspired confidence. The financial arrangements that he made with the settlers and at the East constituted real achievements. Unfortunately, he was now so

heavily in debt and real estate speculation that his financial future
was most uncertain. This, however, did not weigh him down, for he
was of a sanguine temperament and believed that the depression and
the accompanying collapse of land values would be of short duration.

⤸ 4 ⤹

The Road to the Governor's Mansion

Seward's retirement from the senate and his defeat in the contest for governor in 1834 in no way dimmed his enthusiasm for politics. "Keep me informed upon political matters," he wrote to Weed, "and take care that I do not so far get absorbed in professional occupation that you will cease to care for me as a politician." There was little danger this would happen. He still hoped to be governor, and Weed declared that they would start rebuilding their political cob-houses as soon as Frances's health was restored. They kept up a steady correspondence, and there were visits back and forth. Weed's appearance in Auburn was as welcome to the Seward children as to their father, for he usually came laden with presents.

Both men realized that political conditions forbade any immediate rebuilding of cob-houses, and the bleak outlook fostered a bitter jealousy of the Jacksonians. Weed was sick at heart over political prospects within and without the state. Virginia and Michigan were gone, he moaned, there was little hope in Pennsylvania, and in New York the Democrats were planning a $5–8 million canal enlarge-ment that would help enslave the people of the state for ten yea[r] more. When trouble with France over American debt claims m[ade] the headlines, the Albany boss wrote to Patterson that he wa[nted] French war; the country required a bleeding to purify the[ ] atmosphere.

Seward showed no interest in bloodletting as a politi[c]

though he did believe that the national administration should be upheld in any controversy between the United States and a foreign government. But loyalty to the government and admiration for Old Hickory were two different matters. When Jackson narrowly escaped assassination in 1835, Seward remarked that, while it was a subject of great satisfaction that the attempt failed, it was not to be regretted. It would now go down in history "that the chief who violated the Constitution, proscribed public virtue and patriotism and introduced high handed corruption into public affairs and debauchery into private circles was the first President who received insult to his person and was an object of assassination." This might impress posterity with the justice and patriotism of those "who refused to be among the betrayers of their country."

In contrast Seward found it refreshing to contemplate the grandeur of Webster. Black Dan, however, was "too great, too wise, too pure" to be a good candidate for the presidency. In addition, Seward noted, Webster had begun his political career as an Old Federalist.

It would be impossible, Seward declared, to defeat Van Buren in 1836. The people believed that he symbolized the principle of the Democracy—the poor against the rich—and since 1834 the Whig party had become far too conservative, thanks to the nativists, the anti-Catholics, and conservative editors like William Leete Stone and James Watson Webb. Whiggery would never be successful "except in some tremendous popular convulsion, when suffering shall make men feel and *because* they feel think! . . . until there is some great modification of the elements of parties all is hopeless." But even though the political future looked dark, he was not one to remain gloomy for long. He exhorted Weed to cheer up, and offered to raise $1200 so that the latter could go to France and Italy. As for the rest of the Whigs, they ought to adopt the hickory pole for heroes, especially those of the War of 1812, and shout hurrah for Harrison. That would leave nothing but the slippery elm for n Buren.

ere was, indeed, considerable cause for the pessimism of the aders. They could not match the appeal of the Democrats to n-born and Catholic voters; bank and patronage power y in the hands of their opponents; Van Buren was d Jackson had become a charismatic leader.

But the Whig cause was far from hopeless. The Whigs possessed Weed's political astuteness and his capacity for enlisting the confidence and support of monied men; they had a vision of economic progress that the Democrats, prone to equate equality with liberty, could not match; most important of all, they were destined to have the good fortune to be out of power when the Panic of 1837 swept across the land.

There were no signs of panic in 1835, however, and Seward felt that economic prospects were far brighter than those of politics. He advised Weed not to sell if stocks went down. The nation's resources were so great and its productivity increased so much every year that a long depression was impossible. When the depression did come two years later, he urged the passage of a law that would provide general rules for establishing and regulating banks, thus ending the practice of chartering each institution by a special act of the legislature. This, he felt, would also increase credit facilities, foster the development of the great resources of the state, and put an end to hard times.

The remedy for the depression proposed by Seward became the New York Free Banking Act of 1838, a Whig measure. Scarcely a sufficient curb for the depression, it was nevertheless an extremely important piece of legislation. It ended the iniquitous practice of lobbying bank charters through the legislature, provided strict rules of practice and means of regulation for the state banks, and was a significant factor in democratizing the banking that had flourished under the Regency. Two of Seward's close friends, George W. Patterson and Samuel Ruggles, had a hand in framing and passing the bill.[1]

Seward had an abiding faith in the economic future of the state and nation, but he and Weed kept an eye on a small but growing demand for social reform. Northern anti-slavery societies were multiplying and the leaders of both parties were weighing the political significance in the state of this phenomenon, as well as the South's growing reaction to the movement. In response to southern demands a Democratic Congress gagged abolitionist petitions, and Postmaster-General Kendall restricted their circulation through the mails. Weed believed that these moves would tranquilize the South, which he feared meant to leave the Union, but Seward disagreed. The attempts to dampen the anti-slavery fire would fail, he declared, and the South would be more excited than ever. Moreover, such restrictions tended to create "a permanent Geographical line between the parties," and this would be most unfortunate. The southerners might rant and rave in Congress but, save for South Carolina, the masses of the southern people were as unionist as those of the North. If ever the Union fell to pieces, it would be divided by a parallel of longitude, not latitude.

Seward felt that the madness of the southern defenders of slavery was far worse than the madness of the extreme opponents of slavery, the abolitionists, who were right in principle. But it was not the time for the New York State Whigs to maintain that principle, for to do so would identify the Whig party with what was still a small minority. The best course was to preach moderation to both abolitionists and the South.[2]

Seward did not confine himself to speculations on political affairs. During his journey into Virginia with Frances he conferred with politicians in Harrisburg, Washington, and other places. He kept a hand in Cayuga County politics, helped Granger secure the Antimasonic nomination for Vice President in 1836, and in that same year campaigned for Jesse Buel (the Whig candidate for governor) and for William Henry Harrison. The latter, Seward felt after the presidential election was over, should be "a candidate by continuation," and in December he persuaded the Auburn *Journal* to come out again for Old Tippecanoe. Henry firmly rejected entreaties that he run for either the state assembly or the senate, but in 1837 he made nine election speeches in Cayuga County, blaming the depression on the Democrats. He was still very much the politician, and indications multiplied that he would be a candidate for the Whig gubernatorial nomination in 1838.

Encouraged by definite improvement in his wife's health, Seward began clearing the path that led toward Albany. In the spring of 1837 he persuaded his brother, Benjamin Jennings (B. J. Seward, as he was usually known), who had been organizing Sunday schools in Missouri for the General Sunday School Union and speculating in western lands, to come to Westfield to take over the administration of the land office. To calm the fears of his associates at this move, Henry described his brother as possessing great industry and skill in business. "Blue Jay," as the Westfieldians soon learned to call him, scarcely lived up to these encomiums, but he did free Henry to return to politics.

Seward kept before the public by speaking on education and internal improvements, the major speeches published as pamphlets. Better education, he told the voters, would enable Americans to take advantage of the opportunities spread before them, and to act intelligently in elevating and controlling their leaders. There was much need for improvement of the curricula in both common schools and colleges, and women should have equal educational opportunities with men. Improvement of the mind should be a lifetime process, the individual learning ever more about himself and Nature and the Universe. When Americans were really educated vice and crime would disappear, truth would triumph, and tolerance would become a rule of conduct.

Education fostered American culture; internal improvements, in Seward's way of thinking, were of equal importance in the realm of material things. He regarded the American potential for industrial, commercial, and agricultural expansion as practically limitless, if only means of transportation were provided. New York City of 1837, he told a railroad convention, was merely the nucleus of the great urban center that in years to come would maintain the balance between the commerce of the Old World and the New; just as the United States itself was destined to be the great exemplar of republican democracy opposed to the corrupting and enslaving systems of Europe. Within a few years all the internal improvements now projected for New York State would be inadequate to meet its needs, and then more must be provided. There was no instance in history of a state or nation being impoverished because it constructed means of transportation.

These speeches, if a trifle exuberant in tone, helped to identify Seward as a man of vision, an ardent proponent of a better life for persons of every degree. Weed approved the glowing predictions but, being a thoroughly down-to-earth politician, added a practical warning against selling out any of the Chautauqua settlers. This, he cautioned, could be very dangerous. Seward agreed as to procedure, advised his brother to suspend all harsh measures, and was confident that his policy in this regard left nothing to fear.[3]

The Panic of 1837 had violent political repercussions. The Whigs

swept New York State that year, electing a host of sheriffs and
county clerks, and 101 out of 128 members of the assembly. Seward
and Weed were jubilant, sensing victory in 1838, and Seward's
friends in the western part of the state toasted him as the next
governor. But the auspicious outlook produced other Whig candidates for the nomination. Granger wanted it badly; so did the kindly
but "prim, precise and corsetish" Luther Bradish, and Jesse Buel was
anxious to run again. All professed a willingness to withdraw from
the race, if party harmony demanded it, but none became convinced
that such action was necessary.

Seward made two more speeches early in 1838. One denounced
the 1835 state law prohibiting bills less than five dollars in value (a
monument to the Democracy's hard money policy) and demanded a
currency and credit adequate to the nation's needs. In the other he
argued that social equality was essential to national prosperity.
Social equality could best be achieved, not by setting class against
class, but by internal improvements, education, and laws preventing
the growth of "future monopoly and undue accumulation." Internal
improvements were particularly important because they counter-
acted sectionalism. He also pleaded for an increase of cultural
interest. Material aims were now dominant, but at some future time
America, too, should have an Augustan age.

Social idealism of the conservative variety was all very well, but
Seward's main activities in 1838 were on a much more practical
plane. The ever observant Weed had discovered a penniless New
York editor with a gift for the use of the English language who
could render valuable service to him and his ally. This individual
was Horace Greeley, and Weed engaged him to edit a campaign
weekly, *The Jeffersonian*. Seward rounded up 300 subscribers for
this paper and so began a partnership that was destined to become
famous. Seward also used his influence in the senate to ensure the
passage of a bill granting aid to the staggering Erie Railroad, and
gave a toast to Henry Clay at a New York dinner that seemed to
identify him as the Kentuckian's supporter. He wrote frequently to
Weed about his organization efforts among the Cayuga County
Whigs, and about his hopes and fears, and urged the Dictator (as the
Whigs now called Weed) to come out for him in the *Evening
Journal*. In August he visited Chautauqua, sounding out localities en

route and even trying to see Tracy in Buffalo. He traveled about so much that Weed had to warn him to lie low. This he grudgingly did, complaining that it was "not the most agreeable life—idle, and useless, and excited." By September he had persuaded himself that his nomination was essential to a Whig victory.[4]

It was Weed who laid the groundwork for Seward's nomination. He moved cautiously, professing perfect willingness to let the convention decide but dropping a hint here, a suggestion there, among influential Whigs, always to Seward's benefit, and using lieutenants such as Frederick Whittlesey in Rochester and E. P. Pellet in Norwich to organize Seward strength for the convention. Carefully he kept on good terms with Fillmore, who wanted Granger, the while he dangled support for the vice presidential nomination in 1840 before Granger's eyes. He told George W. Patterson of Livingston County, a formidable Granger supporter, that if Bradish were nominated for governor, Patterson should have second place on the ticket while if Seward or Granger were nominated the second place should go to Bradish—and immediately rumors, apparently inspired in Albany, reached the western counties that Patterson was ditching Granger for Bradish. Despite these efforts, however, very considerable strength developed for both of Seward's chief rivals, and it became evident that the battle would be fought out in the convention.

The Whig convention met in Utica on September 12. Seward's strength came mainly from the Mohawk and Hudson River counties and from New York City, where the friends of Clay rallied to him. The west supported Granger, and a Granger-Bradish deal provided that if one fell out of the running his delegates would go to the other. But Weed was there, armed with all his persuasive powers and with figures to show that in 1834 Seward had run ahead of all the Whig members of Congress elected in New York State, and ahead of all the Whig candidates for state senator. Such arguments, the preliminary spadework, and the contributions Seward had made to the party's welfare, paid off, and he was nominated on the fourth ballot. The next day it was made unanimous, second place going to Bradish.[5]

There was some bitterness among the supporters of Granger and Bradish, but the latter was on the ticket, the former received the

Whig nomination for Congress in the Canandaigua district, and Fillmore poured oil on troubled waters in the western part of the state. All turned upon the Democrats, charging them with land speculation and fomenting the depression. In the same vein the Whigs blasted the Independent Treasury, a proposal of Van Buren's administration by which the Democrats hoped to divorce the national government entirely from banking. They also made much of the Regency's small bill law, claiming with considerable justice that its prohibition of bank notes less than five dollars was responsible for the scarcity of currency that plagued the state.

Both parties bought votes. Seward refused to contribute money for illegal purposes, but he profited by the lack of squeamishness in others. Richard M. Blatchford, New York lawyer and ardent Whig, was fund-raiser extraordinary for the campaign. He got only $200 from "old Astor," but by the end of October had $10,000 in cash and the promise of $7000 more if the Whigs carried the election. Weed distributed the cash in the proper places, and James G. King, Samuel P. Lyman, and Samuel Ruggles, all prominently connected with the Erie Railroad, toured the southern counties with good effect.

The Regency tried hard to re-elect Marcy. The Whigs were just Old Federalists in disguise, said the *Argus*, and Seward himself came of Federalist lineage. He was a blow-hot, blow-cold advocate of internal improvements, for he had voted against both the Chenango Canal and the Erie Railroad. He was also a lackey of Biddle's Bank and the agent of wealthy speculators in Chautauqua County lands. The Democrats concentrated their fire on the southern tier, especially Chautauqua County, where they hoped to diminish an almost certain Whig majority, but it was uphill work.

Greeley wanted Seward to campaign vigorously, but Weed cautioned him to keep out of the limelight. He did go out to Chautauqua, where he published a letter explaining his connection with the Holland Land Company and appealing for votes on the ground of his generous policy as land agent. Otherwise he remained in Auburn, where a stream of visitors rang his doorbell. Anxious for victory, he still professed indifference as to the result of the contest. A baby destined to be William Henry, Jr., was three months on the way, Frances was unwell, and Seward told Weed on the eve of the election that "the conviction that her happiness is best promoted by our defeat contributes greatly to the contentment with which I regard it." [6]

One reason for Seward's pessimism about the outcome of the election was the attitude of the opponents of slavery, for there were 369 anti-slavery groups in the state. The New York State Antislavery Society held its annual meeting at Utica in September, and adopted resolutions binding members to withhold votes from men who would not endorse the cause they had at heart. They asked the candidates for governor and lieutenant governor if they were in favor of jury trial for fugitive slaves in New York State, Negro suffrage, and repeal of the law authorizing the holding of slaves in the state for a nine-month period. Marcy's reply to these questions was unsatisfactory. Bradish, without consulting anybody, answered all in the affirmative. Seward, after anxious consultations with Weed, replied with a considerable amount of circumlocution that he favored any state law providing jury trial that did not conflict with the Constitution of the United States; that he would not favor repealing the nine months' law; and that he opposed granting suffrage to Negroes. The executive committee of the Society then published a resolution asking voters to cast their ballots for Bradish, but not for either Seward or Marcy.

Weed had first advised Seward not to answer these questions, for many New Yorkers disliked the anti-slaveryites, but Bradish's action had forced Seward's reply. The *Argus* falsely reported that he had said "no" in all three cases, and it looked as though the abolition vote might bring defeat. Such fears were groundless. Seward carried the state over Marcy by some 10,000 votes, and only fifty-four voters scratched his name from the Whig ballot. All the furor had demonstrated was that Seward had handled the situation not as an idealist but as a practical politician, and that the anti-slavery leadership had as yet little weight at the polls.

The Seward vote had been heavy in the western part of the state, Chautauqua County alone giving him a 2000 majority. He had also run well in the river counties and in New York City. The depression was undoubtedly the principal cause of his victory, but there were contributing factors such as the small bill law, the support of Senator Nathaniel P. Tallmadge and his Conservative Democrats, and the fears many bankers entertained of the left-wing (Loco Foco) Democracy which hated banks in general. The Whigs also profited from a rebellion that had broken out against the Canadian government. An American ship, the *Caroline*, which carried supplies to the insurgents, had been seized and burned by Canadian militia. A Canadian steamer, the *Sir Robert Peel*, was burned in revenge, and American "Patriots" threatened to invade Canada. There was much sympathy in the frontier counties for the Canadian rebels, and Marcy's efforts to keep the peace lost him a considerable number of votes.[7]

Seward was in the office of the Auburn *Journal* when the returns from the western counties came in. They assured his election, and he exclaimed, "God bless Thurlow Weed! I owe this result to him." His moods, however, alternated with startling rapidity. On November 11 he wrote to Weed that he shuddered at his own temerity in seeking this "fearful post." Frances had taken to her bed, insisting that she would not go to Albany, and he didn't know how to keep house alone. Weed must come at once to Auburn. The next day, buoyed up by a salute of one hundred guns that his fellow townsmen had fired in honor of "glorious Chautauqua," he told his brother Benjamin that Frances was improving in health and that everything looked rosy.

Congratulations poured in from all over the state, and life grew brighter day by day. Weed came to Auburn and helped persuade Frances that after a couple of months she would be able to come to Albany. Henry bought himself a "genteel" black suit and dress overcoat and a covered sleigh that cost $265, ordered supplies of wine, whiskey, and champagne, and borrowed $5000, which he spent on furnishings for his Albany home.

There was a problem as to where he would live in Albany. Marcy occupied a house owned by Edwin Croswell, one of a solid row of structures across the park from the capitol. Weed had poured scorn on this domicile, calling it Croswell's "three-walled house." Seward despised Croswell and his house, and all save Greeley and a few Whigs with quarters on the hill thought it advisable for him to have a new residence. Weed busied himself in finding a more suitable abode, and Seward finally took the Kane Mansion, a stately, yellow brick edifice set in a wooded, four-acre lot on the corner of Broad and Westerlo streets, not far from the river. The furnishings and the rent for a year cost him twice as much as his $4000 salary, the roof leaked persistently, the governor's study was cold and damp, but the house was grand and spacious, and Seward loved it.[8]

Seward chose his new home amid a welter of activities and decisions. Callers and letters requesting appointments flooded into Auburn. New York editors William Leete Stone and James Watson Webb were jealous of one another and importunate in their demands. No one had a stronger claim to reward than Richard M. Blatchford, who had worked hard in the campaign and was acting as Seward's legal agent in regard to the Chautauqua lands and other financial affairs. Blatchford asked that his eighteen-year-old son Samuel be given the post of private secretary, and with some reluctance Seward granted his request. Other pleas were acknowledged, and the task of dealing with most of these importunate petitioners was handed over to Weed.

Seward and Weed worked as a team in organizing the state government. Seward spent much of his time preparing his message to the legislature, however, and many of the most important decisions were made by Weed, who was cartooned as "The Drummer Boy," and was now known to friend and foe alike as "The Dictator." Six weeks before the legislature convened, Weed told Patterson that he would be the speaker of the assembly. Weed shouldered the delicate task of persuading the Whigs to re-elect Conservative Democrat Nathaniel P. Tallmadge to the United States Senate. He also took upon himself the major responsibility for selecting state officers, such as secretary of state and comptroller, Seward taking the position that it was his duty not to make a cabinet but to receive one. Save for Fillmore, who refused the comptrollership, the ones chosen by the Dictator accepted and were approved by the legislature.[9]

The Drummer Boy did not beat to quarters without grumbling among the lieutenants of the Whig army. Granger was critical of some appointments, Fillmore sulked, as did John Collier of Binghamton, and Tracy was openly rebellious, but Weed and Seward were now in control of the party, and their word was law.

Seward put a great deal of thought and effort into his message to the legislature, a document which, Patterson warned him, would be read by everybody. It took form out of his own ideas and solicited and unsolicited advice. Friends urged him to give the Erie Railroad an encouraging word. He asked Samuel P. Ruggles for his opinions on internal improvements and received a seventeen-page letter in reply urging him to cover the state with state-owned railroads. The heads of colleges and academies sent information about their respective institutions, prison wardens did likewise, and Comptroller Azariah Flagg, on request, furnished detailed information about the state's finances. It was "a Herculean task," as Henry told Weed, to transmute this mountain of material into a state paper, and he approached it with trepidation; but he was determined to have it drafted before he went to Albany. It was finished in a burst of composition and read to Judge Miller and Frances before he left for Albany, on December 21, together with twelve-year-old Augustus. After Weed subjected the document to meticulous criticism, it was then put in final form and turned over to Sam Blatchford, who made a fair copy.[10] Meanwhile Henry settled himself in his new house. All was ready for the inauguration.

ᦉ 5 ᦊ

Governor Seward
Philosophy and Practice

Young Augustus Seward thought inauguration day was wonderful, and he wrote all about it to his Aunt Lazette and his Cousin Frances.

> My dear Aunt & Cousin
>
> I recieved your letter on the 5 of Jan and as you were goig home I do not think my New Years letter will reach you so I will write one to Canindaigua. New Years we had 5 tables set with turkeys ham beef corn beef alamode beef new years cakes crackers chees champaign wine. We had eight barrels of New Years cakes 1 barrel of crackers 4 heads of chees 8 baskets of bottles of champaign 1 barrel of wine all of the meat was trimed off with fringed paper of all coulers, white, red, blue, straw couler, pink
>
> I was up to the capitol and saw Pa sworn in his office. And I went into the Assembly and saw some of the officers ellected and heard the Message read but while the Message was being read Pa come home and let about 2 or 3 thousand people in the house and they crowded in so fast that they upset one of the tables. When I come back from the Capitol I tried to get in I went up on the stoop and could not get in now I could not get off of the stoop again any way except to jump off of the side of

the stoop so I jumped off of the side and went around the
house two or three times trying to get in the house but after a
while I got in the kitchen window and upstairs where Mrs
Dewitt was a back way then after a while, I got out of the setting room window and went down to Mr. Weeds and staid
about an half hour then I come up home and got in the kitchen
window with about a dozen boys at my heals as quick as I got
in, another boy got half way in then we shut the window
down on him then he began to squel to get out we kept him
there about a minute then we let him out this is all I shall write
I guess this time. . . .

Your Nephew & cousin
Augustus H. Seward

Augustus's mother, back in Auburn, did not think so highly of
the inaugural festivities. There had been some disorder in the Kane
Mansion, with glassware smashed, carpets muddied, and food strewn
about. The "canaille," she commented acidly, had been feasted and
made tipsy—the house had been "torn to pieces." During the next
three years she dreaded these New Year revels, and when each was
over it was apt to be assessed as better or worse than that first
tumultuous affair.

Seward had more catholic social tastes than his wife, and he was
not distressed by the Kane Mansion celebration. There was still
more feasting and noisy gaiety there before Frances arrived in
February, so much so that it brought a stern rebuke from Samuel
Sweezy about living at the rate of $20,000 a year on a $4000 salary
and about the dignity befitting a governor who in public invoked
the blessing of the Almighty and in private besought his mother's
prayers. Both men could agree, however, that there was more to be
said for Henry's new position as commander in chief of the state
militia. In that capacity he gratified his love for display by appearing
at military reviews in a blue-gray uniform with epaulettes, a buff
sash, and a gilt sword, finery which cost him $224.50.[1]

Dinner parties and military parades were all well enough, but a
governor out to make a name for himself had to think chiefly of
more serious matters. Young, by nature impulsive, fertile in ideas
for the public welfare, and fully aware of the delights of power,

Seward determined to take a major role in shaping the course of events. His first message to the legislature was a lengthy document which began with somewhat premature thanks to God for restoration of the country's prosperity, and thereafter consisted mainly of proposals for progress and reform. He outlined the economic advantages that would result from speedy completion of the Erie Canal enlargement, and the building of three railroad lines—northern, central, and southern—constructed by the state if private enterprise was not equal to the task. He warned the legislature against extravagance, but he also declared that the canal revenue alone would warrant the state's spending $4 million annually for the next ten years on internal improvements. This sum, the governor asserted, was far more than the amount required to complete a transportation system that would tap the nation's wealth and provide funds for essential educational and charitable enterprises.

Wealth and education, Seward declared, were reciprocal influences that, working together, would make secure republican institutions, enable Americans to reach a higher degree of social perfection than had ever before been attained, and generate in them a spirit that would renovate the world. He proposed the establishment of a board of education, improvement of the curricula in the schools and colleges and, for immigrants, "schools in which their children shall enjoy advantages of education equal to our own, with free toleration of their peculiar creeds and instructions." Citing the high rate of crime among Negroes in the state, he urged better educational provisions for the colored population.

A spate of other requests rounded out the governor's message—prison reform, reduction in the costs of litigation, repeal of the law prohibiting small bills, improvement of the General Banking Act of 1838, provision against illegal voting, and an appropriation for gathering historical documents relating to the history of New York Colony. It was a comprehensive document.

Reaction to the message varied from Weed's "earnest, energetic, —clear and strong" to Croswell's "a curious piece of patchwork— the effusion rather of the sophomore than of the statesman." Seward had done nothing for internal improvements while a senator, complained the *Argus*. Now he wanted to do everything, and it went on to note that spending $4 million a year for ten years could mean a

$40 million debt. Another sour noted came from the Whig nativist press in New York City, which barely tolerated the message because of its friendly references to foreigners.

Nor was the legislature, with an assembly composed of largely new and mediocre talent, and a senate controlled by the Democrats, ready to implement Seward's proposals in any major fashion. The legislators did continue the enlargement of the Erie Canal and the prosecution of a number of other public works. They repealed the small bills law, passed a few minor acts designed to improve the common schools and, after some prodding, appropriated $4000 for collecting documents relative to the colonial history of the state. But they did nothing about establishing a state board of education, or about providing educational facilities for the children of foreigners or Negroes. Neither did any grand program of internal improvements take shape. Endlessly busy with local appropriations and continual log-rolling, the legislature dragged its slow length along until the time came for the spring adjournment.[2]

If the legislature was a burden to a man of vision, Seward found appointments even more grievous and hard to bear. The clamor for office began as soon as the election was over and by January was prodigious. "I begin to sicken at the evidences of human infirmity with which you are to be surrounded," wrote Weed, and events bore out this melancholy comment.

The executive patronage consisted chiefly of judicial offices, and such posts as inspectors of agricultural products and commissioners of loans. In making selections among the candidates Seward had the benefit of Weed's counsel, and of the so-called "Wall Street Clique"—Richard M. Blatchford, Simeon Draper, Jr., James Bowen, and Moses H. Grinnell—New Yorkers prominent in law and business, a jovial quartet who poked fun at one another, housed the governor when he came to the metropolis, and made him presents of cigars and champagne. Their advice was helpful, but the burden fell on Seward's shoulders. It was bad enough in 1839, when he made 611 nominations for office, many of them rejected by the Democratic senate, but in 1840 the Whigs had both houses of the legislature, and in five months he had 10,000 requests for 1500 offices. Six days in the week, from eight in the morning until midnight, the applicants laid personal siege to the governor's office.

Begging letters rained upon him from persons of high and low degree. He talked with some fifty individuals every day and appointed, on an average, a hundred a week. He would not go through it again, he told a friend, for the next emission of Treasury notes.

The New York City appointments gave the worst trouble. There nativists, conservatives, Clay supporters, inveterate beggars for office like James Watson Webb, and disgruntled Irishmen raised a continuing and discordant clamor until the selections were made; and then those appointed were apt to squabble among themselves. Auburn was scarcely better, for it had Whig factions at war with one another. Five candidates for surrogate of Cayuga County appeared in 1840, and Seward declared that the choice gave him more pain than all his other official duties. When he finally made his decision, the wife of one of the disappointed candidates, meeting Frances Seward on the street, froze her with a glance "as cold as a Lapland winter."

The general nature of the requests for place shows that a real Whig weakness in New York State was in the county organizations, where ambitious individuals engaged in a rivalry for position that all too often resulted in clique-controlled county conventions and resultant bitterness and feuds. In defense against such local machinations, and because he wanted to make good appointments, Seward established a set of rules for his own use.

The governor sought the greatest possible amount of information about applicants, and would not be a party to resignations made so that a specified individual might take the vacated post. Where there were several candidates for one position, each with his ardent supporters, he tried to find still another qualified man. He strove never to interfere with appointments made by the legislature or by the federal government. He prided himself on making no selection because of personal interest, favor, or prejudice, and he never inquired where a man's presidential preferences lay.

There was one question, however, that Seward always asked about a candidate for office—"Is he a Whig?" The reason for this he expressed succinctly in a letter to James Brooks of the New York *Express:* "It certainly was not and is not my intention to confer appointments upon those who are engaged in destroying the politi-

cal ascendancy from which my power to make appointments has
proceeded——." ³

It would be foolish to suppose that Seward never made exceptions
to the rules that he laid down for his own guidance, or that there
were never errors of judgment in the selections finally made from
the hordes of aspiring candidates. Such errors did occur, and there
were sometimes egregious mistakes, as when he conferred an appointment on a man long since dead. But the evidence indicates that
Seward did as well with the appointing power as a governor could
reasonably be expected to do under the spoils system.

The outcries of disappointed office-seekers were not the only
troubles that afflicted the governor. The cabinet, he declared, was
"excellent, harmonious, prudent and efficient," but this was altogether too rosy a picture. Seward found Attorney General Hall
hard to work with; Bates Cooke, the comptroller, had never wanted
that office and remained in it only until he was replaced by John A.
Collier, between whom and the governor there was mutual dislike.
Secretary of State John C. Spencer was able, efficient, and difficult.
He became Secretary of War in Tyler's Cabinet in 1841, much to
the governor's relief. There was more truth than fancy in the
drummer boy cartoon that showed an uneven and recalcitrant line
of state officers following behind Weed and the governor.

Another source of difficulty for the state administration was the
alliance of Seward and Weed with United States Senator Nathaniel
P. Tallmadge and his Conservative Democrats. The Conservatives,
who favored banks and paper money and had no love for Van
Buren, had helped elect Seward in 1838, and Tallmadge's re-election
to the United States Senate was a logical quid pro quo. Nevertheless
it was resented by no less than five prominent New York Whigs, all
of whom wanted his place. When Fillmore, one of the aspirants, was
also refused nomination as vice chancellor of the state he was outraged and declared that he was being treated as though he were an
enemy of Weed and Seward.

Such were some of the problems that confronted a governor eager
to have a good, progressive administration. When to them were
added perpetual houndings for great and small favors, the attacks of
Whig conservatives, the apostasy of Tracy (who went over to the
Democrats in 1840), Greeley's complaint that he was not being sup-

ported in founding the New York *Tribune* ("I could have begged patronage and done better. Now it seems to be all begged away, while I was getting down to the begging point"), and the continual need to be on guard against the attacks of the Regency, it is clear that the head of the New York State Whig party had his moments of bitterness and frustration.[4]

While Seward and Weed wrestled with state problems, they kept an eye on the national scene, for the choice of a Whig presidential nominee was in the offing. Webster, Harrison, Clay, and Winfield Scott were all anxious to lead the fight against the Democrats, and in the ensuing melee the New York Whig leaders took an eminently practical view of the situation. As Seward wrote to a New York Congressman, "it is not a question of who [sic] we would prefer, but whom can we elect?" They felt sure that Clay could not carry New York, and they decided to foster a Scott boom. This may have been at first simply a stop Clay move, but it developed into a bona fide effort to get the nomination for Scott.

Clay came north in the summer of 1839 on a fence-mending expedition. He reached Auburn late in July, staying overnight at Seward's house, where he met local politicians of various degrees. It was rather like *Hamlet* with Hamlet left out, however, for Seward was not there. He avoided a formal conference with the Kentuckian, though the two men did meet by chance at Port Kent on Lake Champlain and Seward rode on Clay's boat as far as Burlington. He told the Kentuckian that the abolitionists did not want him for President, but Clay replied that many of that ilk were devoted to him; that Granger and Tracy were for him; and that demonstrations everywhere convinced him that he was well thought of by the people. Each man used his best efforts to charm the other. After Clay returned to Kentucky he wrote to Seward that the latter might, if he wished, contradict the report that Clay was about to withdraw from the presidential contest—a suggestion that, it is needless to say, fell on deaf ears.

The Scott boom grew apace in New York State. The six-foot-five hero of the War of 1812 had gained fame as a pacifier of the frontier and of the Indians, and was also a prominent advocate of temperance reform, a movement rapidly gaining popularity. Weed and Seward did their best to rally New York sentiment for Scott, and Weed took a sizable group of Scott delegates with him to Harrisburg; but there Pennsylvania, Ohio, and Indiana carried the day for Harrison. Scott, disappointed but appreciative, took pains to assure Clay's friends that Seward and Weed had really wanted Clay, but the Kentuckian and his New York City supporters knew very well that the New York State leaders had been instrumental in his defeat.[5]

Seward and Weed had failed at Harrisburg, but Whig efforts resulted in capturing the New York State senate that fall. Weed poured money into the third district, which included Albany, and stationed bullies at the polls. The result, to the horror of the Regency which had controlled the senate since 1818, was the election of three additional Whigs and a consequent Whig majority in the upper house.

Seward kept aloof from these sordid efforts. He did, however, travel through the state during the year making speeches on internal improvements, education, and equal rights for the Irish; and at the close of the campaign he opened the Kane Mansion to a motley array of Whig stalwarts bent on celebration. They "came here," Frances wrote to her sister, "to drink champain [sic] and cover the carpet with mud tobacco spittle and lamp oil (from their torches). O the beauties of democracy—." [6]

No sooner was the election of 1839 over than Seward found himself confronted by an explosion of social discontent that became known as "the Helderberg War." The tenants on the Van Rensselaer manor, an area of some 700,000 acres in Rensselaer and Albany counties that included the mountainous region of the Helderbergs, were in revolt against the payment of perpetual rent and obligations to the patroon. Tin horns sounded from the hills, and irate farmers offered such violence to the sheriff when he tried to serve ejection writs that he asked the governor for help.

Seward's sympathies were with the tenants, victims of a social system that had long outlived its usefulness. He also knew that there were similar leases of semi-feudal character in some ten counties and that the tenants constituted a formidable body of voters. He had to move carefully, however, for law and order were on the side of patroon Stephen Van Rensselaer IV, who had inherited the west manor in Albany County. After consulting with Weed and others, Seward told the sheriff to take as a posse the armed military companies of Albany, which included ex-governor Marcy and "Prince John" Van Buren, son of the President. This force also found it expedient to beat a humiliating retreat before the enraged farmers. The governor, after an all-night session with members of his cabinet, then called out some of the state militia and issued a proclamation summoning the rioters to obey the law, while at the same time promising to bring their grievances before the legislature. These measures ended open resistance for the time being, and the sheriff served his papers. In his next message to the legislature Seward took a firm stand against manorial tenures, but it was not until the 1850s that the tenants obtained a satisfactory adjustment of their grievances.

Seward's attitude toward anti-rentism was that of his party's liberal wing. Horace Greeley and the New York *Tribune* championed the cause of the tenants, as did Ira Harris, later United States Senator, and John Young, who in 1846 became governor of the state. On the other hand, Whig conservatives berated Seward for the support he gave the embattled farmers. Anti-rentism was one of the issues that weakened and eventually destroyed the Whig party in New York State.[7]

Seward's handling of the Helderberg War was only one illustration of his desire to be both humane and politically realistic. This intention also underlay his efforts at prison reform, which were not only undertaken as a means of exposing Democratic faults but also because Seward genuinely desired to improve prison conditions. These ends he sought to attain by turning out incompetent or brutal officials at Auburn and Sing Sing and by fostering educational, religious, and manual training, the last especially in the development of silk manufacture. Under his regime prisoners received greatly improved treatment. They were no longer half-starved in the name of economy, the lash was restricted at Sing Sing and abolished at Auburn, and the new prison superintendents undertook programs to rehabilitate the inmates.

Unfortunately these changes did not last. Silk manufacturing did not prosper, and prison labor that turned out products competing with those produced by free labor aroused the ire of the working class. When the Democrats came back into power food economies were restored, the lash returned, and the prisons again run as places of punishment rather than as places of reform. It is noteworthy that when one of the leading Democratic prison officials, John W. Edmonds, finally became convinced of the need for reform, Seward came to his aid in organizing citizens' committees for improving conditions among the prisoners.[8]

Interest in reform and an instinct for political advantage also prompted Seward to fall in line with the mushrooming movement for the prohibition of intoxicating liquors. The Six Reformed Drunkards of Baltimore and their cohorts in the Washington Temperance Society were making converts by the thousands. A reform undertaken in the name of morality, temperance also made plain economic common sense, for drunkenness had proved economically wasteful, and the politicians began to take notice. Early in 1842 (just about the time that a young Illinois lawyer named Abraham Lincoln delivered an address on temperance before the Springfield Washingtonian Society) the governor signed the pledge of abstinence, asserting that his action would have the more influence while he was still in office. He even made a temperance speech at Warwick, New York, and a thirteen-year-old who signed the pledge later remembered how Seward put his hand on his head and said, "My little fellow, if you hold fast to that you will be a good man when you grow up." Whiggism was thus put on record as being in sympathy with the Washingtonian movement, and alcoholic beverages promptly disappeared from the Kane Mansion table.

Her husband's interest in moral reform delighted Frances, who declared that he had taken this step without consulting anyone in advance. She could not help wondering, however, about the effect of wineless dinners on legislators, who "were not remarkable for their vivacity when under the influence of that article."

The governor also devoted considerable thought to the Indian and Negro problems. He believed that the Indians had rights that should be respected. The red man nevertheless could not be an integral part of white civilization, and his removal from lands desired by the whites would be for the benefit of society. In consequence, while not opposing removal, Seward exerted his influence to prevent abuse of the continent's original inhabitants. The Senecas, in particular, had some reason to be grateful for his efforts to shield them from exploitation, even though he did not keep them from being cooped up on reservations.[9]

The governor's attitude toward slavery was, like his stand on the Indian question, a combination of the practical and the humane. On the one hand, he regarded human bondage as a great moral and political evil, a violation of inalienable rights, and a detriment to the prosperity and happiness of any people among whom it existed. As early as 1825 he had declared that the North would never give up the aim of gradually emancipating the slave by federal legislation, and with this attitude his wife had the deepest sympathy. Profoundly religious and with high moral standards, she regarded slavery as the antithesis of morality and Christianity, and the Seward household reflected this point of view. Henry and Frances habitually employed Negro servants and brought up their children without color prejudice—no mean feat in Auburn, where such prejudice was pervasive. They also sympathized with Negroes who attempted to escape from slavery, and there is some evidence that in the 1850s their Auburn estate served as a station on the underground railroad.[10]

But Seward was a politician, and he could not afford to view the slavery question from a purely moral standpoint. He had to consider the ballot box and how far the populace would go, or could be made to go, in supporting an anti-slavery attitude. It was therefore important that, when he took office as governor, the slavery question was becoming more and more of a major political issue in the state. Reports poured in to him about the growing power of the anti-slavery movement in the central and western counties, and late in 1839 he felt that the time had come to present his views on slavery to the public.

Three colored seamen, citizens of New York, made an unsuccessful attempt to help a slave escape from Virginia, and that state demanded their surrender. This Seward refused, declaring that they were accused of a crime not recognized as such in New York, and that all men, regardless of their race or condition, had a right to freedom. Virginia regarded slaves as property, but Seward asserted that human beings could not be so considered and that therefore the would-be "stealers" had committed no crime.

The controversy over the seamen dragged on and on, with the New York legislature coming to the governor's support by providing jury trial for fugitive slaves, to which Virginia replied by inspection of ships under New York registry. Virginia also asked the cooperation of other southern states, and Seward found himself involved in similar controversies with Georgia and South Carolina. Georgia in particular sought to confound the New York governor by asking the return of fugitive John Greenman, who in fleeing the state had sought to take with him certain blankets, shawls and, with intent to seduce her, a Negro woman named Kezia. In this case, also, Seward refused to surrender the Negro.

Seward told his close friend, Christopher Morgan, that he knew he was right in this slavery controversy. John Quincy Adams and Jabez D. Hammond praised the stand he took, and abolitionists like Lewis Tappan were delighted by his action. But a chorus of condemnation swelled up from the South, and the conservative northern press either denounced him as a rattlepated boy, or accused him (incorrectly) of having John C. Spencer write the letters in the Virginia correspondence. Conservative and moderate Whig politicians, too, were critical, and Hammond could say, truthfully, that they had left the governor "almost alone, exposed to the fire of the enemy."

Seward's reaction to the *Creole* affair of 1842 showed the gulf that separated him, so far as the slavery question was concerned, even from moderate Whig leadership. Slaves on this American ship overpowered master and crew and took the vessel into port at Nassau, where the British authorities freed the Negroes. Secretary of State Webster vigorously protested this action, declaring that the *Creole's* captain should have been allowed to take the slaves ("mutineers and murderers," Webster called them) back to the United States. Seward termed this protest "a miserable and unmanly effusion" that extinguished the last hope of favor in the North for President John Tyler and his Secretary of State.[11]

The position that Seward took in the fugitive slave cases was bold, even daring. The federal constitution states expressly that a person charged with crime who flees from one state to another shall on demand be delivered up to the state from which he fled, and it was not until 1842, in *Prigg v. The Commonwealth of Pennsylvania*, that the Supreme Court ruled that the enforcement of fugitive slave laws rested not with the states but with Congress. Seward went beyond the position taken by the Supreme Court, for he held that a human being could not "by the force of any human constitution or laws be converted into chattel or a thing in which another being like himself can have property—." This was virtually the "higher law" position that he was to take nine years later in the United States Senate.

The controversy over slavery brought Seward into national prominence during the early 1840s. Negroes thanked him for his efforts on behalf of their race, and the abolitionists tried to make him their candidate for high office. They urged him to run for Congress in 1842; Gerrit Smith assured him that James G. Birney, the Liberty party candidate for President in 1844, would withdraw if Seward would take the nomination; and a rising anti-slavery spokesman in Ohio named Salmon P. Chase avowed that Seward would be the right presidential candidate for the Liberty party in 1848. To these suggestions and proposals Seward turned a deaf ear, but he obviously was becoming more and more identified in the popular mind as a leader in the anti-slavery movement.[12]

While Seward battled with the southern governors over slavery, he became involved in another controversy that generated much bitterness. This arose out of his effort to promote education for the children of foreigners. No attention had been paid to his suggestion in 1839 that something be done for them. He therefore returned to the attack in his 1840 message to the legislature, recommending "the establishment of schools in which they may be instructed by teachers speaking the same language as themselves and professing the same faith." This was substantially what he had already asked, but New York City Catholics renewed a previous demand on their part for public funds with which to support parochial schools, whereupon a veritable explosion ensued.

The governor had a number of reasons for insisting on the importance of schooling the children of foreigners. He saw education and internal improvements as twin keys to American progress. He had declared publicly that prejudices retarding educational advance in any direction must be banished and that he favored "free schools accessible to the children of the most humble." Furthermore, the efforts of such progressive leaders in educational thought as Henry Barnard and Horace Mann were finding a popular response that indicated the temper of the times. Seward corresponded with both Mann and Barnard, and found in John C. Spencer an earnest partner in his effort to improve the state school system.

The governor was particularly concerned about the thousands of immigrant youngsters who roamed the streets of New York without any schooling whatever. This was due in part to the rapid increase in German immigration (many of these children spoke only German), and in part to the attitude of the Public School Society, a semi-public, semi-private agency that controlled the city's public school funds and imbued the schools with a distinctly Protestant bias.

Seward determined to remedy this waste of human potential, and he also saw it as an opportunity for gaining political advantage. His reputation as a sympathetic supporter of Catholic immigrants had just been enhanced when he ordered that a priest be permitted to administer confession without witnesses to a condemned prisoner—a humane step that both he and Weed felt would have a most favorable effect on the Irish vote. There can be no doubt that he saw the school question in a similar light.[13]

Though his motives in dealing with the school question were, on the whole, creditable, Seward acted without sufficient investigation of the circumstances involved. After the storm over his proposal had burst, he told the Reverend Samuel Luckey (a prominent New York Methodist clergyman) that when he sent his messages of 1839 and 1840, he "had never heard of the New York Public School Society its foundation its powers or its funds nor of the disputes which had existed concerning the apportionment of the public school monies." [14] But act he had, and now the fat was in the fire.

Attacks upon Seward's proposal came from various quarters. The Democratic press assailed it as a nefarious attempt to unite church and state and to seduce Catholics into voting the Whig ticket. The conservative Whig press denounced it, and there rose a chorus from nativists and Protestants accusing the governor of seeking support for Catholic schools, of being in league with the Pope, and of wishing to have Protestant children instructed by Catholic priests.

What Seward had in mind, so he later told a friend, was "to let the Catholics support schools of their own and receive their own share of the public monies." While the controversy raged, he answered critics that his objective was not to educate children in foreign languages or in particular creeds or faiths—but simply to see that all children should have opportunity for instruction. Surely this was worthwhile. Why should any American hate foreigners, he asked. "It is to hate such as their forefathers were." The foreign-born were entitled "by the Constitution and the laws, and by the higher laws of God Himself" to the rights, privileges, and political power possessed by other citizens.

Seward, Weed, and their New York friends, aided by John Power, Vicar General of the New York diocese, made energetic efforts in 1840 to capitalize politically on the governor's friendship for foreigners. At Power's request Richard M. Blatchford sent him some 2400 copies of speeches Seward had made to the St. Patrick's Society of Albany. These were for distribution in the churches of New York, but Power's prediction that 2000 Irishmen would go over from the Democrats to the Whigs was only a dream, and the Democrats raised an outcry about prostituting the churches to political purposes.

Bishop John Hughes came back from Ireland in July 1840 and assumed leadership of the drive for support of Catholic schools from the public funds. An abler man than Power, he took pains to avoid association with public political maneuverings, though privately he sought a state job for his brother-in-law, a gesture that brought a quick and favorable response from Weed. Frances thought the bishop assumed the garb of humility altogether too easily, but Weed and Seward were both drawn to him, and his picture hung under that of Washington in the governor's mansion.[15]

The bishop and the governor now formed a private alliance. It was a league between a Catholic churchman and a Protestant political leader, in which each respected the other's point of view and valued the assistance that the other could give. The prelate lavishly praised the governor's high ideals and noble efforts in education and his general rectitude and sincerity. Hughes hoped and believed that Seward would rise to still greater heights in the political world, but regretted that he could not come out publicly in his support, since his own parishioners were politically divided and he would be called a Whig.

Bishop Hughes did, however, help to promote the passage of an education bill that the governor regarded as a vindication of his policy. This measure, drawn up by John C. Spencer, prohibited state support to religious schools in New York City, and put the city's school system under the supervision of elected school commissioners. In other words, it extended the public school system used in other parts of the state to the metropolis.

Assured that Spencer's bill would pass the senate in 1841, Seward sought to placate rabid Protestant opinion in New York by nominating Hiram Ketchum, a violent opponent of the bill, for a circuit judgeship. Ketchum responded by raising such a storm in the senate that the Spencer measure went down to defeat. Hughes complained of Ketchum's conduct, and Seward withdrew the latter's nomination, much to the disgust of Protestant bigots in New York City.

The main features of Spencer's bill became law in 1842. This broke the monopoly that the Public School Society had theretofore exercised and that had so irritated the Catholics; but both the bishop and the governor lamented that the measure had to be enacted by a Democratic legislature. Even so, Hughes declared that the new education law gave Catholics equality of rights in the schools, and that they owed this victory to Seward's constancy and firmness.

This unstinted praise was not entirely merited. John C. Spencer and others had made notable contributions to the final solution of the school problem. Seward's ambiguous original proposal had stirred up needless controversy; and there can be no question that, in subsequent maneuvering, he sought political as well as cultural benefits. He could, however, maintain with truth that the net result had improved the educational situation in New York City and had made it easier to bring the children of the foreign-born into the broad stream of American culture. Years later Jabez D. Hammond told Seward his action in the school question was one of "the best and most meritorious acts of your life." [16]

Seward's association with Bishop Hughes continued for many years. The governor and Weed regarded their friend as a tower of political strength, a belief that the prelate turned to account by seeking reciprocal favors, such as a $10,000 loan and a jaunt through Europe at government expense. Hughes was a helpful influence in state politics, and later, during the Civil War, he was an influential supporter of the Union. In 1862 Seward asked the Vatican to make his friend, then archbishop of New York, a cardinal. Pius IX did not see fit to grant this request, which would have made Archbishop Hughes the first American cardinal.

What may be said about the governor's efforts on behalf of social reform? They were usually made with some attention to political advantage, a consideration seldom absent from his thoughts. They hardly resulted in any great or spectacular achievements. But Seward did gain a reputation for being in harmony with the reform zeal that characterized that age. There is also no question that Seward genuinely believed in liberty as man's inalienable birthright, and that he felt that freedom and education in conjunction would make for equality of opportunity among men.

Seward was neither a radical nor a dyed-in-the-wool conservative. He brushed aside as relatively unimportant the power of great wealth, declaring that the laws and institutions of the United States made it well-nigh impossible for estates to become so large that they would menace the interests of the general public.[17] But he was equally indifferent to the argument that government ownership of internal improvements imperilled freedom. He was convinced that both private enterprise and state direction and ownership must be used in achieving the American promised land. A shrewd politician, he approached reform more with an eye to the practical than the theoretical.

◄§ 6 §►

The Fortunes of Political War

While battling southern governors over slavery and Democrats and nativists over his school proposal, Seward found himself confronted by still another thorny issue: a registry law for New York City voters.

Whigs and nativists had long been clamoring for protection against illegal voting by foreigners, and on March 30, 1840, the Whig legislature passed a registry law for New York City. Under its terms the governor was to appoint three commissioners of election who would divide the city into districts of approximately 500 voters each. It also made provision for election inspectors, the registration of voters, challenging votes of doubtful propriety, and punishment for false registration and illegal voting. The New York City Whig press loudly praised the bill; the New York *Evening Post* and the Albany *Argus* poured out anathemas upon it as a costly and unwarranted restriction upon "the free and unbiased expression of the popular will."

Seward had told Weed in 1835 that such a law would alienate the whole Irish nation and provide the Democrats with proof of Whig imbecility. Both he and Weed disliked the measure that now lay upon the governor's desk, and some of his most influential New York City friends urged a veto. They pointed out that the bill made an invidious distinction between the city and the rest of the state, and that it would identify the Whigs as a Federalist, Alien-and-

Sedition-Law party. Veto and let the better classes go, urged James Bowen. The common people would rally to the governor and the party would be purged of those "who had better be against us." Conversely, such influential Whigs as Frank Granger and Philip Hone warned that a veto would hopelessly alienate thousands of good Whig voters, while it would have no influence on the foreign vote. The excitement in the city was intense, with most of Seward's friends there believing that he would refuse to sign the bill.[1]

Seward prepared a veto message. This declared that the bill's provisions for registration of voters could throw an election into chaos and would make voting difficult for the poor and the laboring class. He criticized its unilateral application to New York City and its doubtful constitutionality. The message contained such a ringing affirmation of his belief in universal suffrage that Frances declared it converted her into a democrat.

Seward's friends in New York were rallying to support the veto, but meanwhile other influences were at work. The governor received a petition for the bill with 20,000 signatures. The Whig senators urged him to sign, and Weed, convinced that a veto would break up the party, exerted all his influence. Reluctantly Seward gave in, simply notifying the senate that the measure needed amendments.

Weed described this course of events to Granger, but Seward gave his friend, Congressman Christopher Morgan, a very different account. The law, he said, was folly, for it gave the Democrats a good issue for the 1840 campaign, but he had never had any intention of vetoing it. His hesitation and delay were designed to make clear his own dislike of the bill. Time would sicken the supporters of the measure and vindicate him.

Seward had written hastily, without consulting Weed, in an effort to convince the New York congressional delegation that he had played the part of a skillful politician. His letter to Morgan, clearly disingenuous (for if he had never intended to veto why did he prepare a veto message?), stands in sharp contrast to a comment he made to a friend less than a year later—"Quite the opposite of concealment is the error of my character as a public man." [2]

There was no doubt of Seward's renomination in 1840, especially after a fence-mending trip to New York City that enabled him to exert all his charm on lukewarm and hostile Whigs. The thirteen-man delegation to the Whig state convention from that troublesome metropolis was, as James Bowen put it, "a miserable batch but all ardent Seward men." A few troublemakers of course did appear when the state convention assembled at Utica, but the proceedings, as Christopher Morgan reported, were "all that could be desired." Seward again received the Whig nomination, and he believed firmly that his course of action during the preceding two years had energized and liberalized his party.

The Democrats nominated William C. Bouck, a popular canal commissioner who had been a familiar figure jogging up and down along the Erie on his white horse until the Whigs removed him from his post. Bouck, like Seward, strongly advocated enlargement of the canal.

The confident Whigs blamed the Democrats for the depression, made great play of Van Buren's supposedly extravagant and luxurious tastes, and glorified the log cabin—symbol of Whig identification with the common man. Bouck, they declared, was a man of extravagant notions who wanted the Erie Canal enlarged beyond anything reasonable. They vigorously repelled all Regency assaults upon the governor, who took little part in the campaign, though he did write a letter for publication that paid tribute to the log cabin as "peculiarly American" and a "cradle of patriotism and valor."

Van Buren went into the presidential campaign of 1840 a beaten man. The Democrats had no reason to hope that they could re-elect a President who was identified with hard times, and who was confronted in Whig candidate William Henry Harrison by a military hero and a campaign of ballyhoo that rolled on as irresistibly as one of the huge victory balls that Whig zealots propelled for miles along the highways. The New York State Regency therefore centered its fire upon Seward.

The governor, said Croswell ironically, had asserted in his 1839 message that the American people were destined to reach ever higher standards of social perfection. Who could doubt it, when they saw the array of living raccoons, horned owls, masked foxes, and stuffed dogskins that paraded around the country, or heard the cogent reasoning about log cabins, hard cider, and gingerbread?

Seward was a false prophet, and an advocate of a $40 million debt that would mean either perpetual borrowing or grinding taxation. He had called out the militia against peaceful citizens at a cost of $3000 a day. He had prostrated the state's credit and was the agent and the servant of the Holland land speculators. In sober truth he was identified with the old Hartford Convention, Blue Light Federalists, the enemies of the people. In a last desperate effort at the close of the campaign the Democrats charged that in 1838 one James B. Glentworth had been hired by the New York City Whigs to import thousands of fraudulent voters from Philadelphia, and that for bringing in these "pipe layers" he had been rewarded with the post of tobacco inspector. The Whigs were now repeating that performance. REPUBLICANS OF THE EMPIRE STATE, shrilled the *Argus*, WE ARE ABOUT TO BE OVERRUN WITH FRAUDULENT VOTERS. The rumor spread that Seward had been arrested for his part in these nefarious proceedings.[3]

It is doubtful that the uproar over Glentworth had much to do with the result of the election, but the Democratic charge of extravagance hurt, for the Whig legislature had spent steadily on the Erie Canal enlargement and other internal improvements, and the aggregate state debt had increased over 50 per cent since 1838. It is equally certain that Seward's attitude toward the registry law and his New York City school proposal cost him a considerable number of Whig votes. There was disaffection, too, among the lawyers on account of legal reforms that had lowered their fees, there were a number of bitter and revengeful office-seekers, and it is likely that some of Henry Clay's ardent followers defected.

Harrison received 234 electoral votes to 60 for Van Buren, and carried New York State by 13,000 votes. But Seward's 1838 majority of 10,000 was cut in half. If western New York had not remained sturdily loyal to the governor, he might well have gone down to defeat. It was a bitter pill for a man who, in February, had been supremely confident of a 20,000 majority.[4]

With the election over, Seward busied himself in preparing his message to the legislature and catching up on a heavy correspondence. He kept late hours, smoked too much, took little exercise, and was half sick with a recurrent malady—always described as "a rush of blood to the head." He was also despondent over the election. For three months, he told Weed, he had had to bear the burden of not only his own mistakes but also those of all other Whigs. He was willing to admit being either wounded or killed, as the interests of the party might require. If only the former, he urged Weed to come to his support. There had been mistakes of judgment on his part, he told other friends, but in one respect at least his course had been right—in regard to the proscription of foreigners by conservative Whigs. Said the still embattled governor—

> This right hand drops off before I do one act with the Whig or any other party in opposition to any portion of my fellow citizens on the ground of difference of their nativity or of their religion. No pretense of policy, no sense of injury, shall induce me to join, aid, or abet such miserable efforts.[5]

One of Seward's first acts in 1841 was to remove Glentworth as tobacco inspector, a post that, according to Horace Greeley, brought to its recipient an income of from $20,000 to $30,000 a year. In answer to the Democratic campaign charges, the Whigs stoutly averred that Glentworth had been sent to Philadelphia in 1838 to prevent New York's Democrats from importing illegal voters. When they discovered that he was bringing Whig "pipe layers" from Philadelphia to New York, he was rebuked and ordered to desist. He had been an untrustworthy fellow, they sadly observed.

The truth was, however, that he had been given his lucrative position as inspector at the urgent demand of the leading New York City Whigs, who with one voice had then testified to his indispensable and exceedingly valuable services in the 1838 election. Such services he had undoubtedly rendered by providing bullies and fraudulent voters at the polls. But it was now in the open that he was something of a rogue, and he was thrown to the wolves.[6] This sticky business over, the governor turned to a controversy that had already begun boiling up over relations with Canada.

From the start of the Canadian rebellion in 1837 Seward had determined that no action of his should increase tensions along the border. The *Caroline* affair, he told Weed, was a horrible business. During the 1838 election he took toward Canadian affairs a noncommittal attitude that the Democrats strove to represent as opposition to the insurgents and their American sympathizers. As governor, his messages of 1839 and 1840 made no mention of the excitement along the frontier. He supported President Van Buren's efforts to maintain order, but that was all. In November 1840, however, an incident occurred which he could not ignore, and which involved him in a controversy with the government at Washington.

On November 12, 1840, one Alexander McLeod, a Canadian deputy sheriff whose efforts to prevent gun-running had made him unpopular with the Patriots, was arrested at Lewiston, New York, and indicted by a grand jury at Lockport on charges of murder and arson that were based on his alleged participation in the attack on the *Caroline*. Habeas corpus proceedings were instituted, and McLeod was ordered freed on $5000 bail, but enraged Patriots surrounded the jail at Lockport, beat drums, repeatedly fired a small cannon, and prevented his release. The New York Supreme Court directed a change of venue from excited Lockport to Utica, where it was obvious that McLeod would have to stand trial.

The aroused Lord Palmerston, British Minister of Foreign Affairs, made vigorous representations to the federal government, demanding McLeod's release on the ground that he could not be held responsible for acts committed under orders from the authorities in Canada. Washington replied that it could do nothing, since McLeod was being tried by and under the laws of New York State. Palmerston responded that, if New York hanged McLeod for murder, Britain would fight.

Daniel Webster became Secretary of State in the midst of this crisis. An Anglophile, Webster saw maintenance of good relations with Great Britain as basic American policy. He accepted the British contention that McLeod could not be held responsible for what happened during the *Caroline* affray, and wanted the prosecution dropped; but he found himself confronted in the spring of 1841 by a governor determined to uphold all the prerogatives of the sovereign State of New York. Seward told John J. Crittenden, a special emissary from the government at Washington, that he was convinced that McLeod had an alibi and would be acquitted; that if convicted he would be pardoned; but that there must be a trial.

McLeod's day in court did not come until October, and during the intervening months Seward carried on with Webster and President Tyler a spirited controversy over procedure, a discussion that was all the more acrid because Seward was quarreling with Tyler's home state over slavery, and the governor and the Secretary of State had long been cool to one another. Some years before, John Quincy Adams had told Seward that he doubted Webster's integrity, a remark that Seward promptly retailed to Gerrit Smith and that probably found its way to Webster's ears. Furthermore it was an open secret that Weed and Seward regarded Webster as so closely identified with Biddle's bank and so lacking in personal popularity that he could not be considered as a presidential candidate.

Seward complained that he was not informed regarding negotiations with Great Britain over the affair, and that Washington kept trying to interfere in the proceedings of the New York State courts. He protested having a federal district attorney act as McLeod's counsel, but was snubbed or, as he averred, "answered by ribaldry" from the White House. Webster was petulantly nervous over the possibility of war with Great Britain and vastly irritated by Seward's conduct—"savage as a meat axe," wrote Richard M. Blatchford from Washington after a conference with the Secretary of State. It took the combined efforts of Blatchford, Bowen, and Weed at the nation's capital to soothe the Secretary of State's ruffled feelings. Then came McLeod's trial and prompt acquittal, and the controversy ended, but there had been a rupture between Seward and the Tyler administration for all the world to see. The irate governor felt, and continued to feel, that the President and all his Cabinet had done him grievous wrong.[7]

Seward's attitude toward the delicate border situation had been correct, for he had steadily co-operated with the federal government in seeing that the proper steps were taken to preserve order and prevent the Patriots from making forays into Canada. In regard to McLeod he had been perhaps ultra sensitive in upholding state prerogative—so much so that one correspondent felt there was not much ground left to stand on in opposing nullification, if any state followed the example set by South Carolina in 1832—but this was partly the result of pique over the conduct of Webster and Tyler, and partly because the Democrats were eager to make political capital out of any apparent magnanimity toward the prisoner. Certainly New York State courts had jurisdiction, and Seward had no choice but to uphold that jurisdiction.

McLeod's acquittal had a good effect upon Anglo-American relations, which were in a strained condition because of boundary disputes and other matters. The Secretary of State shortly concluded
the Webster-Ashburton treaty of 1842, which settled many of the
points at issue between the two countries. Seward warmly approved
the treaty. It contained a provision for the mutual surrender of
criminals that he had urged on the authorities at Washington and
Ottawa. More important to him was the general improvement of relations between the United States and Canada, for he was convinced
that Canada would eventually become independent of Great Britain,
and that if it did not become part of the American Union, at least
some portion of it might well unite with New York State.[8]

Canadian affairs did not provide the only occasion for close contact between Albany and Washington during Seward's second term
as governor. He claimed, when it was convenient to do so, that he
had made it a general rule not to interfere with the distribution of
federal patronage in the state, but this did not prevent him from
attempting to procure James Watson Webb's appointment as postmaster of New York, or from energetic interference on behalf of
that staunch anti-Clay and pro-Scott man, Edward Curtis, for collector of the New York port. Despite President Harrison's death
after only a month in office and Tyler's emergence as leader of the
Whig party, Seward hoped for a federal legislative program that
would provide for internal improvements and a better national currency. He tendered the new President his high respect, his "humble
approval" of the inaugural address, and his "confiding support of
your administration," but the quarrel between Clay and Tyler over
reinstituting a national bank made the New York governor very
uneasy. More than this, he knew that Clay was a protective tariff,
internal improvements Whig, while Tyler was a states' rights Democrat turned Whig on account of his hostility to Andrew Jackson.
His predilections were southern, and the South wanted slavery
maintained and disliked internal improvements. Seward wrote of his
fears to John A. King. In Van Buren's time, he said, they had had a
northern man with a southern Cabinet, and now they had a southern
man with a northern Cabinet. If the sins of the former administration were not rectified by the latter, it would be apparent that the
South was determined to control the whole government—a state of
affairs that he could not believe would ever come again.

Clay had demanded and obtained from Harrison an extra session of Congress and, after Tyler became President, husbanded through Congress two bank bills which Tyler vetoed. The man in the White House was determined to be the leader of the Whig party, a role that Clay felt was his by right of past performance. Webster, who had his own aspirations, sided with the President and remained in the Cabinet after its other members resigned in protest over the vetoes. The ensuing bitterness among the leaders threatened to disrupt the Whig party.

In this melee Seward and Weed played a cautious role, deploring the Washington imbroglio because it weakened Whiggery and rendered most unlikely a program of constructive legislation. Seward laid the trouble at Clay's door, declaring that the Kentuckian should never have insisted upon an extra session of Congress. Years later, Seward and Lincoln agreed that Clay, like Webster, had been a selfish man whose personal ambition had damaged the Whig party.

Weed went down to Washington in order to exert a soothing influence and keep on good terms with both sides in the quarrel. One reason that he and Seward backed Spencer for Secretary of War in the fall of 1841 was the short-lived hope that putting a man in Tyler's Cabinet who had a following among Clay's supporters might help heal the Whig factionalism in New York State and elsewhere caused by the Clay-Tyler controversy. But, like most of the Whigs, they became convinced that the President was not to be trusted and they looked to the future with foreboding.[9]

Despite Seward's best efforts to be a popular governor, the decline of Whig fortunes in the state matched their decline in Washington. His 1841 inaugural address was determinedly optimistic; 1840 had been a year "of health, plenty and peace," he declared, and he deplored the Democracy's shift to a "stop and tax" attitude. He denied the charge of extravagance. Faced by the mounting costs of canal construction, he had insisted that the state's debt should be kept within such bounds that the interest on its obligations would not exceed the net revenue from canal tolls, and that further increase in that revenue should be devoted to extinguishing the public debt. This was all very well as to purpose, but what the voters could plainly see was that the state debt had been steadily increasing, that the state was having difficulty in borrowing money, and that the securities of the commonwealth were selling as low as eighty cents on the dollar. In an effort to bolster the state's credit, Seward and Samuel B. Ruggles developed a plan whereby the federal government would buy the right to use state canals and railroads, thus helping New York and other states to pay their debts; but this scheme, as visionary as any cloud-capped towers, left not a wrack behind.[10]

The disappointing showing he had made in the 1840 election, the growing influence on the voters of Democratic charges of extravagance, and the drumfire of criticism from conservative Whig quarters led Seward to decide during the spring of 1841 not to seek a third term. To run again would be hazardous, he told Christopher Morgan, and defeat after two terms as governor would be disgraceful and ruinous. Furthermore, his principles, he felt, were "too liberal, too philanthropic if it be not vain to say so for my party," and to seek a third nomination would divide the state convention.

That retirement was the part of wisdom became even more evident when, in the fall of 1841, the Whigs lost both houses of the legislature, and the triumphant Democrats serenaded the governor's mansion with a "dead march." Party leaders were disposed to blame the catastrophe on the quarrel between Tyler and the Congressional Whigs, but Seward felt that the inveterate apathy of Whig voters and an anti-Catholic bigotry, as archaic in his opinion as the Salem witchcraft delusion, were contributing factors. Now, instead of the progress for which he had fought, there would be a period of Democratic inaction. Melancholy as this prospect made him, however, he would have nothing to do with a suggestion that he convene the senate early and so make appointments before the Democrats took control of that body. Such procedure, he felt, would be contrary to the spirit of the state's laws and constitution.

A considerable portion of Seward's message to the 1842 legislature was devoted to urging continuation of the state's internal improvements program. Once more he told the legislators of his conviction that the public debt should not rise above an amount the interest on which could be paid out of the current surplus revenue from the canals, but he was sure that this still left room for generous state participation in the building of railroads and additional water-

ways. The Erie enlargement was vital, especially in view of the possible rivalry for western commerce of a St. Lawrence seaway; of
equal importance was the construction of railroads by the state, for
waiting on private capitalists often delayed needed works, since
capitalists thought in terms of their own profits rather than what
was good for the economy as a whole. Such improvements should be
regarded as parts of the general system of interior communications
designed to promote the general welfare, rather than as "mere investments for gain," and to bring them to a halt would have an evil
effect upon the state's prosperity. It would put a blight upon commercial expansion, depreciate property values, and bring suffering to
thousands of laborers by aggravating the unemployment problem.

When the legislature met in special session for the purpose of
Congressional redistricting, Seward repeated his arguments for continuing to enlarge the Erie and for constructing more railroads and
canals. Always optimistic about the state's economic potential, he
was not afraid of deficit financing when it meant building for the
future, and he welcomed work relief as a means of ameliorating the
economic condition of the masses.

Democrats were unimpressed by Seward's argument for the continuation of internal improvements. Azariah Flagg, the state comptroller, pointed out that in four years the state debt had increased
over $16 million. It had now passed, he asserted, the point of safety,
and in April the legislature suspended the development of public
works and passed a tax bill levying a dollar per thousand upon the
assessed valuation of all taxable property in the state. The zeal for
retrenchment was so great that at least $425,000 was paid to con-
tractors as a result of the suspension of contracts.

A generally brightening economic situation accompanied these
conservative measures, which Seward reluctantly accepted. The
market value of the state's obligations increased, the 7 and 6 per
cent bonds reaching par before the end of 1842. The Democrats
claimed all the credit for this, while the disgruntled Whigs could
only sneer that, now the state's bonds had proven sound, the Democracy could resume internal improvements and get credit for
them also.

"Stop and tax," as events were to prove, was a political gambit
that paid off for the Democrats, but the long-range course of events

justified Whig faith in internal improvements. Between 1839 and 1851 the revenue received from the state's canal tolls increased from $1,617,369.41 to $3,329,304.60. This revenue might easily have reached $5 million a year had the Whig enlargement program been completed. Not until the middle 1850s could a Whig legislature speed up canal construction by means of a bond issue anticipating canal revenue.[11]

Internal improvements were not the only source of friction between Governor Seward and his Democratic opponents. Once again, as in 1839, the senate rejected a number of his appointments. The Democracy passed some bills, including one designed to take the state printing away from Weed, which the governor vetoed. The legislature also criticized his handling of the Virginia controversy, and sought to embarrass him in other ways. Seward accepted without protest a repeal of the registry law, but he chafed under the hostility of the legislative branch. The Locos had done everything unwise and unfortunate that a party could do, he told Christopher Morgan, but even so the Whig party remained in the doldrums and he had little hope for its immediate future.

Seward's difficulties that spring were not made easier by a conversation he had with Congressman Joseph L. White of Indiana on a steamboat trip down the Hudson. Seward commented upon Tyler's policies and criticized Spencer's reasons for accepting the post of Secretary of War. White transmitted Seward's comments to Spencer. It took a five-page letter compounded of apology, denials, and self-justification to assuage the resentment of the Secretary of War, who still felt that time alone could restore his confidence in Seward.

Seward's effort to appease Spencer clearly indicated his anxiety over the political future, and the state election of 1842 justified his obvious pessimism. The Democrats again ran Bouck for governor, while the Whigs nominated Luther Bradish, for whom Seward had little respect. After Bouck had won by some 20,000 votes, Seward Whigs gleefully told how Bradish had refused to go home to vote because he needed time to prepare his message to the legislature; how he had the message well along by election time; and how he had measured the rooms in the house he proposed to occupy as governor, in order to see where and how his own furniture could be used.[12]

The closing months of Seward's administration brought on a flurry of demands for pardons. He believed, as did Dorothea Lynde Dix, that the restraining influence of justice was destroyed by a liberal exercise of executive clemency and, where Marcy had released an average of over 100 prisoners a year, Seward pardoned an average of under seventy. He weighed the applications for pardon carefully and made it a general rule to issue none before half of the sentence had been served, granting clemency chiefly where there were doubts as to the justice of the conviction, where punishment had been unduly severe, or where the culprit was youthful or insane. He made penitence an indispensable condition of release. He showed courage in refusing to pardon the convicted murderer John C. Colt, despite great pressure from influential quarters. Colt cheated the hangman by committing suicide in his cell on the day of execution. On the other hand, Seward did pardon a convicted bully who thereupon became very useful to the Albany Whigs on election day. He also pardoned James Watson Webb, who was in the Tombs for flagrantly violating the state's anti-duelling law, although here clemency was expressly conditioned on there being no further violation of the law—a rebuke which Webb did not relish, but which his wife thoroughly approved.[13]

Despite his difficulties with the legislature and the problems inevitably connected with the pardoning power, Seward could feel that his last year in the governor's chair had not been wholly barren. Toward the Dorr Rebellion in Rhode Island that year he preserved a correct attitude—taking steps to see that the Dorrites did not obtain arms in New York State, but also manifesting his sympathy with their demand for extension of the suffrage. Deeply interested in the historical background of the state, he had selected John R. Brodhead to obtain transcripts from the Dutch, English, and French archives relative to the colonial history of New York, had constantly encouraged Brodhead's labors, and now looked forward with satisfaction to the completion of his work. Seward took an equal interest in the geological survey of the state begun under Governor Marcy. He met the famous geologist Sir Charles Lyell in 1841, probably when Sir Charles received an honorary degree at Union College, and doubtless found it a stimulating experience. On the completion of the state survey he wrote in haste a lengthy and none too accurate introduction to the published results, and saw to it that collections of New York minerals were placed in the colleges and universities of the state.

Seward had other reasons for feeling that his gubernatorial career had been constructive. His interest in education had not produced drastic changes, but he had helped improve the educational situation in New York City, and a quarter of a century later Henry Barnard wrote of how Seward's warm appreciation had strengthened his own faith in the work he did as secretary of the board of education in Connecticut. Seward could tell himself with justice that he had helped stigmatize slavery as a vicious institution, and had demonstrated the vital importance of internal improvements to the prosperity of the state. Though still inclined to be provincial in outlook, a condition of mind that he himself recognized,[14] he had grown accustomed to thinking in terms of the welfare of a great and growing community, and had had the valuable experience of state leadership. Power and responsibility had matured him.

Honors, too, had come his way. He had been elected a corresponding member of the recently established National Institution for the Promotion of Science, had been tendered numerous testimonial dinners, and already artists were competing for the honor of painting his portrait that would hang in the Governor's Room of the New York City Hall. It was evident that retirement by no means meant oblivion.

The governor viewed his approaching return to private life with mingled feelings of relief and regret. He was too conservative, he told his friends, to be a member of an unprincipled and opportunistic Democracy, too democratic to share the errors and follies of the prevailing majority of Whigs. The Whig party was, by its very nature, unable to correct its inherent weaknesses. He wanted to see a reorganization of parties, though he recognized that the time was not yet ripe for this. To John Quincy Adams, who hoped that Seward was not retiring from public service, the latter replied that he had charted his course to free himself from jealousies that hindered his usefulness, and that if his services were needed in the future he would be ready. Consciously or unconsciously, he projected an image of himself as a man of wisdom and high principle, unappreciated but still ready to serve his country when duty called.

The time was drawing near when he must leave Albany. He moved from the Kane Mansion to the Eagle, where he had lived on the eve of becoming governor. Bouck had the keys and the state seal, but for himself there were recollections of times past and of the loyalty of friends, most of all of Weed, memories that made "tears like such as woman sheds flow whenever I am alone. How delightful is such solitude. I am a mystery to myself. What am I? What is there belongs to me that has entitled me or secured to me without a claim, such friendship and affection." [15]

Seward attended Bouck's inauguration on Monday, January 2, and publicly wished him well, a precedent-breaking gesture of good will that left the audience open-mouthed. During the rest of the week, he made a multitude of calls, and received hundreds of well-wishers at the Eagle. On his last day in town he was a guest at two dinners and the principal figure at a farewell supper party, where gloom disappeared under the influence of whiskey, oysters, and champagne. Seward and Weed joined in this dissipation.

Saturday morning, January 7, Seward left Albany for the twelve-hour train ride to Auburn. He reached his destination ahead of schedule and made his way "solitary and alone through the dark streets wet with plashy snow and ice" to come upon his family unawares. The next morning three-year-old Willie awakened his father to show him a set of toy carpenter's tools, a present from Weed. Willie said that, now all the family including the white and black children and the servants were in Auburn, nobody lived at Albany but Mr. Weed and Harriet Weed.[16]

~§ 7 §~

New Horizons

Seward on his return to Auburn was faced with a financial problem. Still under heavy bond to the American Life Insurance and Trust Company, he had lived beyond his income in Albany, and at one time in 1841, faced by mounting debts and insistent creditors, he had become deeply despondent and thought seriously of resignation and bankruptcy.

Thurlow Weed and Richard M. Blatchford had saved the governor from financial ruin. Weed was indefatigable in smoothing creditor relationships, giving good advice, and lending money. Blatchford, a wealthy New York lawyer and specialist in banking operations, virtually took over the handling of Seward's financial affairs. An ardent Whig, Blatchford was enthusiastic over Seward's political leadership, and grateful for the appointment of his son, young Sam Blatchford, as the governor's private secretary. "Your kindness to me—your confiding and generous bearing towards me is indelibly impressed on my heart and won it long ago," the father wrote in 1841. "I shall always love you, and you may rest assured it will give me the greatest pleasure to serve you." He gave Seward notice when notes had to be renewed, handled his arrangements with the American Life Insurance and Trust Company and with the Bank of the United States of Pennsylvania and, like Weed, lent money to the governor. Seward's gratitude, and his respect for his friend's financial astuteness, were such that he would gladly have made the New Yorker either comptroller or secretary of state, but Blatchford was not interested in holding office.

Blatchford and Weed kept Seward's head above the financial waves that threatened to engulf him but when, back in Auburn, he took stock of his situation, he found himself sadly in arrears. He owed Jared Rathbone some $30,000, Blatchford $13,000, Weed over $11,000, lesser but still considerable amounts to Trumbull Cary and Judge Miller, and all of these debts were steadily mounting because no interest was being paid. Over and above all this was his heavy holding in Chautauqua lands, a speculation that had so far not paid off. His obligation there had lessened as some of the lands were sold, but such fragmentary records as remain make it apparent that his bond to the American Life was at least $150,000. His total obligations amounted to over $200,000, a load that he was determined to lighten.[1]

Seward also had to adjust himself to the life of a private citizen. He had not been home a week before he was complaining that the days in Auburn were very long—"he would prefer to be in a hustle," Frances wrote to her sister. All sorts of projects filled his head. He would establish his law office in his home, improve the house and grounds, spend part of his time writing a commentary on American government, politics, and law, publish his state papers and, of course, make money in his law practice.

To the first of these plans Frances had decided objection. When Henry was at home all the time, the whole house was his office and there was a constant stream of muddy-booted, spitting and smoking visitors. This ended the home law office idea. Henry hung up his shingle in the Exchange Building, and shortly Frances was complaining that she never saw him, except at meals. He did establish a study at the house, but he wrote nothing there save letters. No publication appeared. Life was complicated enough as it was.

Clients thronged into the law office. Henry took a couple of partners (nearly all the lawyers in town coveted that association), and soon there gathered about him a number of young law students. Cases multiplied, and before the winter was over he began paying interest on his debts and enjoying "a sense of pecuniary independence and ease." Reducing the principal of his indebtedness did not for the moment bother him very much, and he could indulge an

always generous spirit, giving free legal advice to the impecunious
and paying the fare back to New York of a poor Irish girl stranded
in Westfield. By the fall of the year his legal business was sending
him across the state, and he was not more than half of his time in
Auburn.

When not in his office, Seward spent hours in the garden. Some
ten years before, he and other Auburn citizens had each agreed to
plant at least three shade trees along their own streets, and their
efforts had done much to improve the town. Now he had another
burst of gardening activity, planting pinks and other flowers in his
yard, digging out dead trees, and bringing from the woods over 100
elms, acacias, firs, and shrubs to beautify the grounds around the
house.[2] There was also the time-consuming business of having his
portrait painted for the New York City Common Council.

The Council wanted his portrait for the Governor's Room in City
Hall, and Seward asked Blatchford, Ruggles, and other friends to
form a committee to choose the artist. The consequence of this
apparently simple request was a lengthy and formidable contention,
the committee differing violently among themselves as to what
artist should be chosen, and the Common Council waxing wroth
because it was not consulted. At one stage it looked as though five
portraits would be painted by five different artists. Henry was
summoned to New York, made a weary round of the studios, and
even inspected portraits in various private houses, but was unable or
too shrewd to state a preference. The committee finally decided that
he should sit for both Chester Harding and Henry Inman. These
two artists came to the Seward home, fortunately at different times,
and Henry found that he could play whist and talk politics with
Harding and that Inman shared his love of nature. The latter was a
friend of Ruggles, the former a friend of Weed, and Henry was
diplomacy personified in his judgment of their work. Frances clearly
thought Inman's portrait the better of the two, a judgment that has
been borne out by posterity. The one to hang in City Hall was
determined, at Inman's suggestion, by the toss of a coin. His portrait
won the toss, and the committee purchased that by Harding as a
present for Seward's children.[3]

Between the visits of the two artists came that of another eminent
man. John Quincy Adams, defender of free speech, opponent of

slavery, and now approaching the end of a distinguished career, had been on a family excursion to Canada and Niagara Falls. The return trip, much to his surprise, had become a triumphal journey through New York State. Accompanied by his daughter-in-law, Abigail Brooks Adams and her father, Peter Chardin Brooks (who was paying for the trip), Adams arrived in Auburn toward the close of a blistering July day. The Brooks father and daughter stopped at the hotel, but a torchlight procession escorted the great man to the Seward home. There some fifty chosen souls followed him into the parlor, the rest of the multitude milling around in the garden.

This visit took Frances completely by surprise, although it was characteristic of Henry to extend hospitality without consulting his wife beforehand. She hurriedly slipped into a fresh dress and met the elder statesman, but scarcely heard Henry's welcoming remarks or Adams's reply because of Aunt Clara's anguished exclamations at the window—"There goes a rose bush"—"they have broken one of the oleanders"—"the gates are down"—"the fence is falling."

Adams was hardly a lively guest. Exhausted by his journey, the heat, and the attentions lavished upon him, he took a glass of wine and promptly retired to his room. Henry routed him out at five o'clock the next morning for a visit to Auburn prison.

Meanwhile, word had been sent to the hotel that Frances would call for the Brookses and bring them up to the house for an eight o'clock breakfast, but Mr. Brooks met her at the hotel door with word that Abigail declined to come. The two ladies met later in the day, and Frances, who could appreciate what Abigail had been enduring on the trip, found her "spirited and decidedly clever." Adams's speech that morning, Frances thought, was a miserable effort, and she put him down as no orator.[4]

The house was always full of visitors, Henry's relatives among them. Uncle John Seward, a sickly old man of eighty, appeared one summer for an indefinite stay. In the spring of 1843 Henry's father and mother came to Auburn. "*They purpose remaining here all summer*—a pleasing prospect," Frances informed Lazette. Remain they did, most of the time very feeble and confined to their room. They had brought their maid with them and, with a little encouragement, would have stayed for the rest of their lives. It would not have been a long visit for Mary Seward. She died December 11,

1844, but Samuel lingered on, increasingly difficult and demanding, for almost five years.

"It is not for ourselves, chiefly, that we live or labor, but for those whom Providence has committed to our care and who are destined to survive us," Seward once declared in the Supreme Court of the United States. Despite his other manifold interests and activities, he took a deep interest in his children's welfare. They were growing up, and he would often take one of them with him on his travels. When they did not go he would write to them, usually some piece of moral instruction, but with flashes of humor and interesting descriptions. "I am glad that you saw the Siamese twins. They are very nice young men, as I am informed. Would you like to see them when they are hunting? I wonder whether they both fire at once?" Again he wrote of a splendid sunset that he saw when coming from Mount Vernon.

> The sun like a chariot seemed begirt with golden clouds. The swallows impatient for the twilight had come out from their retreats and alighted on the telegraph wires. They crowded together as closely as they could sit on the wires and they covered it for a long distance, as far as from our house to the farthest garden wall. The wires trembled under their feet, and so they were all gently in motion looking towards that glorious setting sun.

There was also a delightful bit of nonsense, addressed to

> Master William H. Seward
>   in the Nursery
>   close by the stove
>   between the stove and the cradle
> North Room

> Mr. Seward accepts with much pleasure Master Willie's polite invitation for this evening; but as the weather is inclement hopes that the giver of the Party will send a sleigh and horses for his guests—with plenty of buffalo skins.

Frederick, naturally studious, entered Union in 1845, where he did well and quite suddenly emerged from little boy into young gentleman, annoyed by his father's insistence that he board with the Eliphalet Notts. Clarence, orphaned son of Benjamin Jennings and now a ward of the Auburn Sewards, a gay lad of extravagant tastes, was put through Geneva College at their expense. William Henry, Junior, the Seward's third son, had great trouble with his eyes during his childhood, and his schooling was intermittent, but he was merry, loved games and animals, and was by nature adventurous and an organizer. In 1848 he led the neighborhood boys in political parades, and when the California fever hit Auburn in the fall of that year Frances wrote to Lazette that nine-year-old Willie said "that he would like to go—of all things." The eldest son, Augustus, moved more or less by accident into a military career. He was a sturdy lad, and General Winfield Scott, at dinner one day with the family, declared that he should without question go to West Point. Augustus and his father thought this was excellent advice, and he was duly enrolled at the Point. There he had great difficulty in adjusting to the rigid disciplinary requirements of cadet life, but he became a second lieutenant during the Mexican War, and saw a limited amount of service in Mexico.

The Seward's last child, Frances Adeline, was born December 9, 1844. Chubby, sprightly, and affectionate, she promptly became "Fanny" to the household. Henry at once took out a life insurance policy to provide for her maintenance in case of need. He was devoted to her, saying that she reminded him of his mother. When she reached the game-playing age and he had any time to spare out of his busy life, he would join Fanny and her friends in riotous games of blind man's buff and puss-in-the-corner.

As their children grew up around them, Henry and Frances moved into middle age. He began to wear glasses when he read and worked, and by 1849 Frances was "rinsing" the gray out of her hair and wearing very troublesome false teeth. Both led busy lives that moved along different paths, she preoccupied with the children and household cares, he with law and politics.

As in any family, there were differences between husband and wife. Frances could not understand Henry's lack of respect for homeopathy. She could see no reason at all for his playing squire to Mrs. Maury (an eccentric Englishwoman of enormous vitality, eleven children, an invalid husband, and exuberant admiration for the governor) who, with one of her brood, was entertained for two days at the Seward home.

But it was Augustus's army career that produced really serious conflict in the family. Frances had been horrified by the idea of his becoming a soldier. She fought against his going to West Point and tried to prevail upon him to leave before graduation. When the Mexican War broke out, her state of mind was such that Henry feared she would become insane. After the war ended, she urged her husband to use his influence to get their son out of the army. Her pleas to Augustus and Henry were of no avail and, having no decided inclination elsewhere, Augustus remained wedded to a military career. Frances felt that a major share of the responsibility for this rested on his father's shoulders.

Frances also felt that Henry was away from home altogether too much. She did urge him for the sake of his health to go on a trip to the Great Lakes ("to the Far West," as Henry said) with Colonel James Bowen in the summer of 1845, although she scarcely relished the prospect of entertaining Mrs. Bowen while the two men were away. But she could not see why he took on legal work that required his journeying all over the country east of the Mississippi, and she tried to use Fanny in an effort to curtail these legal expeditions. She would write to Henry, "Fanny says I must tell her father she wants him to come home," or "Fanny says she shall have a father one of these days," but she might as well have kept her thoughts to herself.[5]

Gradually but inexorably the lives of Henry and Frances were drifting apart. But a strong bond of sympathy and affection still existed between them, and in the middle of the 1840s they were drawn together by a legal battle that became famous throughout the land.

Two Negroes, Henry Wyatt and William Freeman, each accused of murder, were brought to trial in Auburn in 1846, and for a variety of reasons Seward became interested in the two men. It seemed likely that both culprits had lost their reason, and while governor his sympathetic interest in insane prisoners had been so marked that in 1843 Dorothea Lynde Dix had come to Auburn for his advice on steps that might be taken to improve the lot of the demented. His sympathy for Negroes was even better known.

Seward did not believe that the black man in America was the equal of the white, or that he was capable of assimilation as were the Irish and German immigrants. But he did believe that the Negro was a man, and as such deserved and should have all the privileges of the whites. This was true in regard to equal opportunities in education and the equal protection of the laws. As for the franchise, he declared in 1846 that he would "give the ballot to every man, learned or unlearned, bond or free." It was his hope that the Negro, given his rights and given time, would gradually become an harmonious element in American society, and he meant to do what he could to bring that day nearer by giving the two murderers an adequate defense.

There were also more practical reasons, public and private, for Seward's decision to help Wyatt and Freeman. He believed that he could so conduct their defense as to further his own legal reputation and thereby enhance his private fortunes, and he was convinced that the trials would be politically useful.

For Seward and Weed were now fully convinced that it was politically necessary to champion the Negro. Southern control of the Democratic party, nationally speaking, indicated its commitment to pro-slavery, low tariff, and anti-internal improvement policies. The anti-slavery Liberty party, growing in strength, threatened to weaken the Whig party in the North, ensuring Democratic triumph in New York and other states and in the nation itself. The obvious answer for the Whigs was to attack slavery and uphold the cause of Negro rights. By so doing Whiggery might well absorb the anti-slaveryites and, if it successfully championed Negro suffrage, it would have the benefit of Negro votes. The Seward-Weed Whigs were now wooing the anti-slavery groups and arguing for Negro suffrage in the state. Seward believed that defending the accused men would provide valuable publicity for the Whig cause.[6]

Wyatt was first tried in February 1846, Seward defending him on the ground that he was insane. The jury disagreed, and a second trial was scheduled for June. In the interim Freeman was arrested, and a court of oyer and terminer was convened in special session to try both men before Judge Bowen Whiting.

William Freeman, born in Auburn in 1824, was partly Indian with possibly a tincture of French blood. His brother and sister were insane and his father died of brain disease. William grew up a happy-go-lucky and irresponsible member of a small Negro community whose children were not permitted to go to school with the whites. In 1840 he was falsely convicted of horse-stealing and sentenced to Auburn prison for five years. Miserable in confinement, chafing under the wrong done him and the hardships of prison labor, he became sullen and refractory. The guards then brutalized him—flogging him repeatedly and on one occasion striking his head with a board so hard that he was deafened and his skull permanently injured. Evidences of derangement ensued, and after his discharge from prison in September 1845 he wandered about mumbling that he was going to have his pay.

There is evidence that Freeman thought that John Van Nest, a popular farmer living some three and one-half miles south of Auburn, had sworn him into prison. At any rate, he determined to get his "pay" from the Van Nests. On the evening of March 12, 1846, armed with two knives, he went to the Van Nest home and butchered four of its inmates. He was captured the next day and jailed amid great popular excitement. There were threats of burning and lynching, and the pastor of the Van Nests' church called for Freeman's blood. People knew that Wyatt was still unpunished and feared that some smart lawyer would get both men off by an insanity plea.

When it became known that Seward would defend Freeman as well as Wyatt, there were threats of violence against him. Judge Whiting, too, was anything but unprejudiced in his attitude toward the prisoners. "I am crushed," Seward wrote to Weed a few weeks later, "between the nether millstones of judicial tyranny and popular anger. But there will be a consoling reflection by and by that I was not guilty of hanging the poor wretches whom the State Prison tormentors drive to madness."

The second Wyatt trial ended in conviction, and the judge sentenced Wyatt to hang. Freeman was arraigned on June 1, 1846, and Seward offered a plea of insanity. The judge ordered a preliminary trial to determine whether the prisoner was now sane. The jury, under pressure from Whiting, brought in a verdict that Freeman could tell right from wrong, which the judge declared was equivalent to pronouncing the prisoner sane, and on July 10 Freeman

went on trial for his life before a jury that could scarcely be called
unprejudiced. Seward, and Attorney General John Van Buren for
the prosecution, each called a parade of doctors who presented conflicting testimony as to Freeman's sanity at the time of the murders,
the judge having ruled that no testimony would be allowed as to the
prisoner's present mental state, since it had been determined that he
was now sane. This made things very difficult for the defense, since
Freeman on the witness stand showed evidence of great mental
confusion, if not imbecility.

When the time came for summation, Seward told the jury that he
was shocked at the spectacle "of trying a maniac as a malefactor."
He asked them not to be influenced by the color of the prisoner's
skin or the form of his features "—he is still your brother, and
mine—Hold him to be a man." Skillfully Seward reviewed Freeman's history, showing how he had changed from a moderately
intelligent boy to a stupid individual who laughed for no cause and
could not answer rationally the simplest questions. He quoted the
bitter plaint of another Negro, John Dupuy—"They have made
William Freeman what he is, a brute beast; they don't make
anything else of any of our people but brute beasts; but when we
violate their laws, then they want to punish us as if we were men."
Years later Charles Francis Adams, reading over this summation,
though that it had a boldness, breadth, and strength that rose "to the
uppermost region of eloquence."

All argument was unavailing. On July 23 the jury returned a
verdict of guilty, and the following day Judge Whiting sentenced
Freeman to die. Seward promptly appealed on the ground of the
Court's prejudice against the defendant. The Supreme Court reviewed the case, declared that the judge had made serious mistakes
in his rulings in both trials, reversed the judgment, and ordered a
new trial.

Freeman was kept in jail, for the circuit court judge declared that
he was incapable of standing a new trial. Seward visited him as he
lay deaf, with putrid discharges from his ears, indifferent now to the
world about him. He remained in his cell until August 21, 1847,
when he died of consumption. A post mortem showed clearly that
his brain "presented the appearance of a chronic disease." [7]

Seward had calculated on spending from two to three weeks on the Wyatt and Freeman trials. When they were over nearly three months had elapsed, and he emerged "exhausted in mind and body, covered with public reproach, stunned with duns & protests." They were also a disappointment politically, for they did not bring Negro suffrage to the State of New York. From his personal point of view, however, it was not time spent in vain. The publicity given to the trials spread his fame far and wide, and his *Argument in Defense of William Freeman*, prepared from Sam Blatchford's notes, went into four editions that same year. Clients flocked to his office, and his business grew by leaps and bounds. And the trial had forged a new bond between husband and wife. When the other members of his household had urged him not to go on with the Freeman defense and Judge Miller had tormented him with advice to "abandon the nigger," Frances had stood loyally by her husband, giving him aid and encouragement.

During Freeman's preliminary trial Seward, engaged in an appeal to the sympathies of the jury, voiced the hope that the stone on his grave would bear the epitaph, "He was Faithful." That he was faithful to this tragic human being was a tribute to his wife as well as to himself.[8]

The Wyatt and Freeman trials, though remunerative in the long run, temporarily interrupted Seward's attempt to increase his income. There were other and more serious interruptions. Political campaigns found him on the hustings, sometimes for months at a time. His health was none too rugged. He took cold easily, once more had occasional 'rushes of blood to the head,' which were probably migraine headaches. In 1844–45 he had four attacks of erysipelas that laid him low for short periods of time. Moreover, in December 1844, he had a serious accident. Returning from Florida after his mother's death, he rode as usual on the driver's seat of the stagecoach so that he could smoke and view the scenery. The axle of the coach broke and Seward fell on hard frozen ground, dislocating his right shoulder and spraining his hip. He was in bed for days and then hobbled for months on crutches or with a cane, his obstinate determination to use both arm and leg retarding his recovery. It was not until February that he was able to put in a full day's work.[9]

Seward still thought occasionally of leaving the law, perhaps for teaching, but his financial situation precluded any such move. Then, too, his proficiency in the courtroom made him a man of note. Quick to seek out weak spots in the presentation of an opponent's case, able in the use of precedents, fertile in the discovery of evidence and in handling a case in such a way as to blunt the force of the argument on the other side, he was an opponent to be feared, and more people sought his services.

Forensic ability began to pay Seward large dividends in 1845. James G. Wilson, owner of the patents on a planing machine, heard Seward win a case in an Albany court and offered him a retainer. Seward accepted hesitantly, for he knew nothing of patent law, but a new legal vista now opened before him. The planing machine was so valuable that there were numerous infringements on the patent involved. In January 1846 he won an important suit for Wilson in the Supreme Court of the United States, and then prosecuted a number of similar litigations that took him to various cities in the South and Middle West. By 1849 these suits had brought thousands of dollars in fees, and the golden tide continued to flow.[10]

As Seward's law practice increased, he found still other means of improving his economic affairs. He made an arrangement with the American Life Insurance and Trust Company that left him a trustee of the Chautauqua land operation, but relieved him from financial pressure in that direction. Further relief came in 1845 as a result of the death of his importunate creditor Jared Rathbone. After protracted negotiations Seward obtained an agreement that settled his $31,000 debt to the Rathbone heirs for $10,000.[11]

At various times Seward still toyed with the idea of moving to Chicago or of transferring his law office to Albany as a means of bettering his fortunes, but such ideas were abandoned toward the close of the decade. This was due to his flourishing practice and, so far as Chicago was concerned, to two other considerations. One was that Samuel Seward's ill health made it apparent that responsibility would soon devolve upon Henry for settling his father's estate. A second reason was political. Moving to the West would mean abandoning a power base that had been built up during two decades, and separating himself from Thurlow Weed.

~8~

Political Maneuvers

Despite his cares and tribulations in the 1840s, Seward never abandoned the idea of resuming his political career. "It is seldom that persons who enjoy intervals of public life are happy in their periods of seclusion," he wrote to his friend Alvah Hunt soon after leaving Albany, and Hunt had a vivid picture of him in his Auburn office, "long nine in mouth, legs cocked up, *Evening Journal* in hand— reading the debates, stopping from time to time and giving one of his real out and out horse laughs."

Politics drew Seward as surely as a magnet draws iron. Weed and Lewis Benedict, an Albany businessman and politician, went on a political journey in April 1843. They reached Auburn at midnight and sent word to Seward of their arrival. He rose from his bed, came down to the hotel for a two-hour conference, and in the morning accompanied them to Rochester. He wrote to Weed every week while Weed was abroad that summer to bring his friend up to date on political affairs. When called on to make a public speech he seldom missed an opportunity to tell Irishmen how right they were in agitating for Irish home rule. And he utilized on occasion a gift that he had for making extemporaneous remarks at public gatherings. At the State Fair in Rochester that year, when Webster as the principal speaker "pleaded sickness," Seward took his place and spoke with such happy effect that at dinner that night Webster pledged him the lasting support of the great New England Confederacy, and then proceeded to get thoroughly drunk.[1]

Anti-slavery supporters three times in 1844 suggested that Seward run for President on the Liberty ticket. Politely but firmly, Seward rejected these proposals. He was on the Clay bandwagon and, as far as he was concerned, he told his friends, Fillmore might have second place on the national ticket. It was a spot Fillmore would have liked, but instead Fillmore bowed to Weed's demand that he run for governor, another in the list of grievances he harbored against Weed and Seward.

The appearance of the Liberty party indicated the extent to which the older political organizations in New York and to varying degrees throughout the nation were disintegrating during the 1840s. The Whig triumph in the 1840 national election showed that the Democrats could not hope to keep on winning elections by posing as the champions of liberty and equality. The national Democracy began looking for new issues, and as it did so factionalism within the party over economic issues and over slavery increased in virulence. The Whigs, united temporarily in the hullabaloo campaign of 1840, soon reverted to disputes over banks, tariffs, internal improvements, and nativism. And in the Whig party the slavery question also arose.

Nowhere was this breakup of the major political organizations more clearly defined than in New York State. There the Democrats split into two factions, Hunkers and Barnburners. The former were pro-South in their attitude toward slavery, catered to the New York state banks, and favored canal enlargement. They looked to William Learned Marcy for leadership. The Barnburners, led eventually by Martin Van Buren and Silas Wright, were economy-minded in state policies and viewed banking with a skeptical eye, while on the national scene they opposed the extension of slavery into the territories of the Union. The two groups also quarreled bitterly over the spoils of office, and as the decade wore on the separation increased.

The New York Whigs, like their rivals, were torn by dissensions, and Seward, who gained comfort from the feuds in the Democratic party, knew that the Whigs were in an equally perilous condition. He and Weed led the Whig progressive element, which was friendly to the foreigner and the Negro and anxious to foster a rapid development of the state's transportation system. But they faced vigorous and formidable opposition. Disappointed office-seekers such as Fillmore of Buffalo and John Collier of Binghamton vented their spite on Weed and his friend. Wealthy Whigs criticized Seward and Greeley for championing the tenants against the Hudson Valley landlords. Embittered Clay supporters accused Seward of double dealing in 1839 that deprived Clay of his great chance for the White House. New York City nativists, strong enough to sweep the city's election in 1844, were ardent in their dislike of foreigners and Catholics. They railed at Weed's leadership, looked askance at Seward's attitude toward the school question and the registry bill, and viewed with deep suspicion his friendship with Bishop Hughes.

Weed, conscious of the bitterness of this opposition and fearful that Fillmore might after all decline the gubernatorial nomination, threatened in the spring of 1844 to retire from the *Journal*. This brought an anguished appeal from Auburn. Such a move, Seward declared, would leave him defenseless against those jealous members of the Whig party who would only be satisfied when he was "without the possibility of restoration, without a defender, without an organ." To Seward's relief, Weed remained at his post.[2]

Clay and Van Buren seemed the logical presidential candidates in 1844, and the former did receive the Whig nomination from a united and enthusiastic national convention which assembled early in May at Baltimore. But the Democratic party forsook Van Buren. Previous to the conventions both Clay and Van Buren had come out against the annexation of Texas, which the Tyler administration was pushing through the Senate. The Whigs at Baltimore accepted Clay's Texas stand without difficulty, but the southern Democrats would have none of Van Buren and deadlocked the Democratic convention. Out of the ensuing struggle came the first dark horse presidential candidate in American history, James K. Polk of Tennessee, an ardent expansionist. The Liberty party chose an ex-slaveholder, James G. Birney, as its standard bearer.

The campaign had the usual amount of name-calling and mud-slinging but, from an over-all national point of view, the great issue was Texas. It began to appear that the country, especially the South, agreed with Polk about annexing Texas. As this trend became obvious, Clay began to explain, much to the disgust of the anti-slavery

Whigs, that he would like to see Texas annexed if it could be done in an honorable and peaceful fashion.

Seward paid little attention to Fillmore's race in New York, publicly or privately, and Clay's backing and filling on Texas made him gloomy, but he did campaign vigorously for the national ticket. He wrote at Clay's request a strong letter to Bishop Hughes urging his active support, but if the prelate responded it was to little effect. Seward also made a number of speeches. In some of these he sought to counter the effect on the foreign vote of the Philadelphia anti-Catholic riots that had taken place in the spring, with nativist mobs destroying Irish homes and Catholic churches; but most of his attention centered upon Texas and slavery. The Democratic party, he told his audiences, was the slavery party. The acquisition of Texas meant war with Mexico, the addition to the Union of from one to five new slave states, and new demands by the Slaveholding Power, demands to which the democratic free labor states could not yield and "which will be made the ground for secession, nullification and disunion."

The contest was close, and New York was decisive. Polk took the state by some 5000 votes over Clay, but the Liberty party candidate, Birney, polled 15,000 ballots, most of them cast by Whig defectors who hated slavery. It was antislavery Whigs who sent Clay down to defeat. In the struggle for control of the state government, Fillmore lost to Democrat Silas Wright by 10,000 votes.

While the loss of anti-slavery votes in the state proved in itself decisive, the Whig disaster also resulted from nativism. Fillmore, who had tried to curry favor with the foreign-born by helping establish a German language newspaper in Buffalo, told Weed that practically the whole foreign vote in Erie County had gone Democratic, cutting the expected Whig majorities there by almost 1000 votes. Greeley and Weed, both shrewd analysts of election returns, were convinced that the Whig flirtation with nativism had been sufficient to give the state to Polk and Wright.

Seward, too, held that nativism had been a major cause of Whig defeat in New York, and he told Clay that this had been the case. To others he protested bitterly that the Whig candidates had been soft on slavery. He also felt that, so far as Clay and Fillmore were concerned, he had been supporting men who would almost prefer defeat to sharing with him any of the honors of victory. It had not been a happy experience.[3]

Seward was now convinced that slavery had become the great political question of his time.

> The reckless folly of the Administration in regard to Texas [he wrote to his friend Edward A. Stansbury] and the unprincipled adoption of it by our opponents have loosed our tongue stays. Slavery is now henceforth and forever among the elements of political action in the Republic. Let Mr. Clay treat it as he may, and be the result of this canvass what it may, the ground the public mind has traveled cannot be retraced.

> What then? The work of manumission begun in the Revolutionary age as a natural work, prosecuted until it reached Mason and Dixon's line and suspended there long ago by force of political combinations, is to be resumed, to be arrested no more. How is it to be prosecuted? I think by firm decisive urgent advocacy in the North, tempered nevertheless by moderation, in making it collateral and if need be subordinate to other questions of Administration raised by the two great parties, and above all tempered by conciliation. Let the world have assurance that we neither risk nor sympathize with convulsive, revolutionary or sanguinary measures. That our desires are benevolent and that emancipation will be beneficent to the Master as well as to the Slave. For in truth humanity teaches and obliges us to feel sympathy for our white brethren before or at least equally with compassion to the Black. Caution and Compensation should be always proclaimed, and they will ultimately commend our great enterprise to the wise and good men of the South of whom there are enough to join us when the character of our designs shall be truly understood. . . . If the sentiments I have expressed meet your views I shall be most happy.

This Stansbury letter outlined a plan of action to which Seward remained faithful in principle down through the secession crisis of 1861 and beyond.

In 1845 in a letter to Salmon P. Chase that he asked the latter to burn, Seward again outlined his views on the connection between slavery and politics, and on his own relationship to the Whig party. He loved the party, he declared, but not it or any part of it when it was lukewarm on slavery. He never used the term "Democratic party," which was a misnomer to him for what was, actually, the slavery party. There could only be two parties, one for slavery, the other more or less against slavery. "Whether more or less at one time or another depends on the advancement of the public mind and the intentness with which it can be fixed on the question of slavery." The name of the anti-slavery party did not matter too much but, unlike Chase, he did not think that the Liberty party could displace the Whig party and give "a new name to the same mass." He would remain with the Whig party, to which he owed so much, where he had influence that he would lose if he changed his political allegiance, and which in New York State had steadily supported every position he had ever taken in regard to slavery.[4]

There was small comfort for Seward in Polk's administration, or in the state government headed by Silas Wright, though he continued to watch with pleasure the growing feud in the state Democracy between the Hunkers and the Barnburners. Vigorously disclaiming any intention of returning to public life, when in Washington on legal business he dined with the Marcys and squired Mrs. Marcy to a ball given by Secretary of State Buchanan. On this same visit to the capital he consulted with the leading congressional Whigs on what attitude they should take toward an increase of American possessions in the Far West.

The Manifest Destiny of the United States to expand westward was very much in the air at this time, and the leaders of a national Democracy in search of new issues readily accepted its slogans. To these men it seemed only logical that a rapidly growing population needed for self-protection more land, and also natural frontiers. Together with the obvious duty of carrying the dogmas of freedom to unenlightened peoples, this made necessary an expansion of American territory. President Polk, foremost in the van, dedicated himself to the outright acquisition of land jointly owned with Great Britain in the Far Northwest, and to obtaining California from Mexico.

The dispute with Great Britain over possession of the Oregon Territory was at its height when Seward reached Washington, and he urged his party friends to show that they were not afraid to stand up for American rights. He approved going along with the administration in giving notice to the government in London that joint occupation of Oregon must end, not because he yearned to beard the British lion but because he felt that such a stand would be popular with the voters. Some Whig extremists demanded possession of the whole Northwest coast as far as Alaska, trumpeting the slogan "fifty-four forty or fight." Seward felt that this was going too far, but he thought it wise to give a measure of support to these fire-eaters on the ground that it would strengthen the ties between eastern Whigs and those of the Old Northwest.

The Oregon crisis faded with acceptance by both nations of the forty-ninth parallel as a boundary in the Far Northwest, but the quarrel with Mexico over Texas deepened into war. Seward was never a warmonger, and this conflict had the additional odium of being brought on by a Democratic administration. It was a "bastard war," he said, but he cautioned Whigs to pursue a circumspect policy. Best, he felt, to vote army supplies, the while they kept a watchful eye on the democratic agitation for the acquisition of California and even Mexico. Who could tell where it all might end? He had a vision of Spanish America under the domination of the United States, and of American economic interests reaching ever outward until there was an eventual collision with imperial Britain. "We shall begin to need more room in India and China," he told Weed. "The battle between Britain and America is to be fought if not *in at least for* Asia! We are not ready for it. It will come off when we have grown strong and England begun to decline."

He gave public expression of this expansionist mood in a letter to his Chautauqua constituents. In it he charged slavery with preventing a stronger stand for all of Oregon up to 56° 40', and then went on to declare that, while he did not want war, he recognized that the American people had an irresistible passion for expansion. They would not rest until there was no European colony on the continent and they were confronting Oriental civilizations on the shores of the Pacific. Since this was the case, America must prepare for its destiny by setting its own house in order. Moves in this direction should be made by providing freedom for the foreign-born and by giving the suffrage to free Negroes as the first step in a peaceful but inexorable march toward the abolition of slavery.[5]

This pronunciamento drew menacing growls from Whig conservatives and alarmed Thurlow Weed. He told the ex-governor that his radicalism on slavery and expansion, together with efforts by the Fillmore faction to reheat for its own advantage the old quarrel with Webster over McLeod, threatened his political future. Seward leaped to the conclusion that Weed thought all was over for them both, and wrote defending his course—"I cannot, I will not change, to win the highest honor of the Republic. And you know I scorn any humbler one." He felt deep sorrow, however, that his course had damaged his friend's fortunes and would do all that he could to repair them. Weed had only to tell him that he might "relinquish all thought of the castles you have conjured up for me," and he would never again write or speak on public affairs "without first knowing that it shall not injure you."

Weed felt that Seward's letter, in effect, put their relationship on a cash basis, and he was deeply hurt. Seward vehemently protested that he was thinking only of his friend's welfare, protested his devotion, and apologized for misapprehending Weed's admonitions. It was months, however, before Weed's ruffled plumage was smoothed.[6]

Where Seward's political fortunes could be rebuilt was not easily determined. Weed and Seward considered and discarded another term as governor. As Seward remarked, if he were elected to that post, "it would be thought by many that claims for much more were cancelled." He was not yet well enough known to be a serious competitor for the Whig presidential nomination in 1848, but the Vice Presidency or the United States Senate might well be within reach. To attain either of these goals it was necessary to keep his public image bright.

Seward continued speaking at meetings which urged repeal of the Act of Union between England and Ireland. Daniel O'Connell, the great champion of Ireland's independence, died in 1847, and Seward delivered a panegyric, praising "the Liberator" in the warmest terms. When in Washington that same year, he called on John Quincy Adams, finding him depressed in spirits but "affectionate to me beyond my former most pleasant experience." Adams died February 23, 1848, and two days later Seward delivered a eulogy before the court of chancery in Albany. Humanity, he said, had "lost her most eloquent, persevering, and indomitable advocate—I have lost a patron, a guide, a counsellor, and a friend—one whom I loved scarcely less than the dearest relations, and venerated above all that was mortal among men." Shortly thereafter he gave Old Man Eloquent a more extended tribute before the Albany legislature. He also undertook a biography of Adams, a task largely taken over by a ghost writer, the Reverend John M. Austin of Auburn, which was published in 1849 with Seward's name on the title page.

Seward gained public attention when he collaborated with Salmon P. Chase in arguing the Van Zandt fugitive slave case before the Supreme Court. They lost the case, but Chase told Lewis Tappan that Seward's conduct had been "noble and generous. I regard him as one of the very first public men in our country."

Nevertheless, Seward was rebuffed when he offered his services in a Washington slave case the following year. Horace Mann and others felt that he was a publicity-seeker who would contribute little to the defense, and made excuses to keep him from active participation.[7]

The 1848 presidential campaign began early, and Seward had little use for the candidates who came into view. He did not want Clay, was dubious about Scott, who had flirted with the nativists, and was scarcely more enthusiastic about Weed's choice, slaveholder General Zachary Taylor, the hero of the battle of Buena Vista. Seward himself was being mentioned as a possible candidate, and he drew up a statement of the principles that would govern him, if chosen to lead the nation. He favored restricting the power of the Chief Executive, reposing the utmost confidence in Congress, avoiding war whenever possible, and obtaining from Mexico such parts of its territory as would be commercially advantageous to the United States.

Seward's name was mentioned more frequently for the vice presidential nomination, but there is scant evidence that he wanted to run and none whatever that he wanted second place on a Taylor ticket. He was a statesman who had the wisdom and the patience to bide his time, said the *Evening Journal*, and this well summed up his point of view. Just before the Philadelphia convention that nominated Taylor, he remarked that the Democrats had a strong candidate in Lewis Cass and that for himself, "I see no danger to come from leaving me where I am." His only fear was that Fillmore might get second place and so encourage "factious counsels that would weaken the influence which of course we believe we ought to possess for the safety of the Whig party of the state and of the Union. But even this consideration does not incline me to consent to be second to a nomination that will emasculate the virtue of our party." He would, however, trust to Weed's discretion in the matter, and Weed would be at Philadelphia. It is possible that both men had hopes of a deadlocked convention with Seward emerging as a presidential, dark horse candidate.

As Weed and Seward had expected, the Whig national convention preferred Taylor to Henry Clay. Taylor was nominated on the fourth ballot and at once John Collier moved that Fillmore be given second place on the ticket as a peace offering, so he declared, to disappointed presidential aspirants Clay and Webster. Weed hesitated. His own preference had been Abbott Lawrence, millionaire New England textile manufacturer, but cotton on both ends of the ticket would not do. Fillmore, restless and ambitious, had had a good record in Congress and was now the New York comptroller, a post to which he had been elected by a large majority. Weed and Seward mistrusted him, for there had been indications of his alliance with their outright enemies in the party. Seth Hawley of Buffalo, one of the Seward-Weed stalwarts, believed Fillmore was slippery, but Philo C. Fuller of Livingston County, an astute man and friend of both Weed and Fillmore, thought the latter was honest and incapable of Machiavellian tactics. To Weed's complaints of Fillmore's machinations Fuller had replied that Fillmore might well have been led into foolish ways by others, but also that "there may be some spunk under your own jacket." This comment was fresh in Weed's mind, and he must also have realized that thwarting Collier at this juncture would precipitate a bitter quarrel in the New York Whig party. He threw his support to Fillmore, the influential Truman Smith of Connecticut added his backing, and Fillmore was nominated for Vice President on the second ballot.[8]

Fillmore's nomination demonstrated that the supposed Weed-Seward-Greeley partnership had its flaws. Weed accepted the nomination with misgivings; Greeley, already disposed to fly off on tangents such as Fourierism and to doubt Weed's political acumen, was enthusiastic; Seward was alarmed. What would this mean to the

Wilmot Proviso, which squarely opposed the admission of slavery to the territories acquired from Mexico and which they both supported, Seward asked Weed. What would it do to their influence in the national government, and what would be the fate of their friends in New York State if the Whig national ticket were elected? Time would soon show how correct were these forebodings.

The Democratic national convention, riven by contending factions, nominated Lewis Cass of Michigan for President. Neither the Democrats nor the Whigs took any stand on the paramount issue of the day—whether or not slavery should be given an opportunity to expand into the territories gained by the Mexican War. A new third party also appeared. Disgruntled anti-slavery Whigs and Democrats, such men as Henry Wilson, the "Natick cobbler," and Gideon Welles, a Connecticut newspaper man, met with Liberty party leaders in a convention at Buffalo on August 9, 1848, and formed the Free-Soil party, with Martin Van Buren as its presidential candidate and Charles Francis Adams of Massachusetts as his running mate. The Free-Soil platform promised to "fight ever" for "free soil, free speech, free labor and free men."

Deeply disturbed by the Whig party's course, Seward at first threatened to stay out of the campaign, since "what would be effectual when said I should be unwilling and ashamed to read." This was not for long. Soon he was making fresh contacts with Colonel J. P. Taylor, the nominee's brother, whom he had met some time before. He also drew up a memorandum which he hoped Taylor would use in reply to the notification of his nomination.

Before the summer ended, the reluctant campaigner was speaking at one Whig rally after another in New York and Massachusetts, Pennsylvania and Ohio. He was never at home, and Frances grew more and more discontented. When Henry strove to placate her with presents she wrote sharply, "Do not on any account get me a velvet dress. I have one which is nearly useless. Neither do I want a hat though I am much obliged." Even such words as these had little effect, for her husband was caught up in the fever of the campaign.

Seward frankly avowed in his speeches that he would have preferred candidates who would stand boldly for slave emancipation. Whigs opposed the extension of slavery into any free territory, he declared before a huge Tremont Temple audience in Boston, with

Abraham Lincoln sitting with him on the platform, and his emphasis on the slavery question impressed Lincoln. Our first duty as American citizens, Seward told an audience in Ohio, was to preserve the Union as a voluntary organization, for "a Union upheld by force would be despotism." At the same time, they must see to it that the onward march of American democracy was not impeded. This meant educational advance, economic development, but most of all the establishment of equality for all men—a principle basic to the democratic system. Slavery warred against both justice and humanity, and was the great antagonist of liberty. In words that were to haunt him in later years, he declared that slavery "can and must be abolished, and you and I can and must do it." When he spoke, as he frequently did, of the Free-Soil party and its candidate, Martin Van Buren, he asserted that a vote for Van Buren could not help the antislavery movement. The hopes of that movement lay in no third party, and certainly not in a Democracy which was more and more aligning itself with the slaveholding interest. The Whig party was the rightful, logical home for opponents of slavery.[9]

The election of 1848 brought about a rather dubious Whig triumph, for the outcome showed no decisive voter preference for either of the major parties. It demonstrated above all a significant increase in free soil sentiment, especially in the east-north-central states where it drew heavily from the Whig voters. In New York State the Free-Soil party split the Democracy, bearing witness to the feud between Hunkers and Barnburners and to Van Buren's influence more than to the growth of anti-slavery sentiment. This split gave Hamilton Fish an easy triumph in the governor's race and the Whigs a majority in the legislature. It also paved the way, so Weed and Seward hoped, for Seward's election to the United States Senate.

A number of aspirants appeared for the Senate seat that was to become vacant on March 3, 1849, but Seward's outstanding rival was John Collier of Binghamton, the candidate of Fillmore and his friends. For months before the legislature met, Weed was busy marshaling support among the legislators before they reached Albany, enlisting the aid of New Yorkers in Congress and of loyal henchmen throughout the state, brandishing a letter from Colonel Taylor saying that he would be delighted with Seward's election and could see no reason why President-elect Taylor would object. The opposition, however, was determined not to have Weed's protégé. Collier's supporters declared that Seward was an anti-slavery radical and would be ineffectual in the Senate. Furthermore, he would never support the Taylor administration. The Collier forces published excerpts from a supposed Seward letter to Seth M. Hawley of Buffalo which said that Collier must be "headed" for the good of the party—a letter that both Seward and Hawley pronounced a forgery. All of these efforts proved vain, for when the legislature met it became apparent that Collier could not be elected.

With Collier out of the running, his Whig supporters turned to other expedients. They made a bargain with the Democrats to send Governor Fish to the Senate, and then urged him to be a "compromise" candidate. Rebuffed in that quarter, they put great pressure on Washington Hunt to play the same role, only to find that Hunt had promised Weed that he would be comptroller in the Fish administration. The fight was carried to the bitter end, but Weed had his way. On February 6, Seward was elected by a vote of 121 to 32. Fillmore, who was present, said that he would like to exchange places with the victor. It had been a galling struggle, Frances told her sister. John Collier had "acted so like the father of evil" that for once in her life she was glad that Henry was elected.[10]

Seward had been in Washington and New York while the conflict raged. Toward its close Weed wrote that he had been attempting to satisfy inquiries as to Seward's position on public questions. Fillmore had twice expressed a desire to be certain that Seward would support the administration, to which, said Weed, "I replied that I knew a Whig Administration would ever have your support." He suggested that Seward write a letter to Webb or to Fish that could be published after the election was over, pledging loyalty to Taylor and to the Constitution.

In response to Weed's advice, Seward wrote to Webb declaring his allegiance to the national administration and asserting that he would attack slavery only within the limits defined by the Constitution. He added that his so-called radicalism was really only his ability to see into the future weeks, months, and years earlier than others who were "less hopeful of human progress and less confiding in human virtue" than himself. Webb could be sure that he would never seek the fulfillment of his hopes by any course endangering the Union.

Weed took one look at this letter and wrote immediately to Seward, warning him to keep it out of the press. It would cheapen and tarnish his triumph, especially the paragraph about Seward's prophetic powers, which "looks as if it might have been written under the Astor House table." Seward rewrote the letter, softening its language somewhat and leaving out all reference to his second sight, but even so it was never published.

One problem remained to be settled before the Senator-elect took his seat—who should have charge of distributing the federal patronage in the state? Seward and Fillmore, on their way to Washington for the inaugural ceremonies, stopped off in Albany and at dinner with Weed an arrangement was made. The Vice President and the Senator would consult from time to time and agree upon New York State appointments.[11] It was a deceptively simple plan utterly impossible of implementation, considering the struggle for power in which the two men had been engaged.

❧ 9 ❧
"A Higher Law"

Seward's election to the Senate brought rejoicing to anti-slaveryites and liberals in general. "Probably no man ever yet appeared for the first time in Congress so widely known and so warmly appreciated as William H. Seward," wrote Greeley in the *Tribune*, adding that "the lofty anticipations which the prospect of his election has excited will not be disappointed." Seward had made the masses his friends, wrote Eliphalet Nott, and had come to his high office as a defender of the rights of the Irish, the Negroes, the Catholics, and the poor. He must stand by these principles, for even if he could not bring the Whig party to accept them, "some party will be brought there and it will become the predominent [sic] party." Others were not so laudatory. The Democrats looked askance at this firebrand from New York; Whig conservatives were alarmed; and southerners felt that his election was an ominous and aggressive act. The Washington correspondent of the Baltimore *Sun* declared that New York had sent a fanatical anti-slavery man to the Senate, a radical who would run after every popular humbug and would sorely embarrass the Taylor administration.

The new Senator was sworn in at a short special session that began the day after Taylor's inauguration. He spoke several times during the ensuing weeks, but always gently and moderately in a deliberate effort to overcome the prejudice against him. Even Webster forgot his wrath over McLeod and unbent to Seward's charm,

especially after the latter, though privately complaining about Webster's nepotism, helped make Fletcher Webster district attorney for
Massachusetts. A short-lived intimacy sprang up between the two
Senators. Seward was confident that by the end of the session he
would have the good wishes of all the Whigs and no unkindness
from the opposite side of the aisle.[1]

Seward also sought the favor of the President and his Cabinet. At
first Taylor, gentle and guileless, had been inclined to leave all
patronage appointments to Fillmore, as one who understood these
things far better than himself, but was soon disabused of any such
notion. Seward's friends told Taylor how wrong this would be,
even while the energetic Senator from New York exploited his
acquaintance with the old hero's brother, Colonel J. P. Taylor.
Busily cultivating mutual acquaintances and exerting all his charm,
by inauguration day Seward had several conferences with the
President-elect, and was on confidential terms with the new Secretary of State, John M. Clayton. In the weeks that followed, he
became Clayton's means of communication with the Senate and lent
support to Taylor's plan for having California and possibly New
Mexico organize as states and apply for admission to the Union.
Toward the close of March, Seward attended a full Cabinet meeting, the President presiding, which approved and ordered printed
the New Yorker's vindication of Taylor's policy. Obviously, the
New York anti-slavery champion sat at the right hand of the
slaveholding President from Louisiana.

Popularity in the Senate and access to the inner counsels of the
administration opened the way to control of the patronage in New
York State. A struggle over those spoils was inevitable, in part because Seward and Weed distrusted Fillmore and his linkage with
New York conservatives who abhorred progressivism in such matters as slavery and coddling the foreigner, and even more because
each side had importunate allies who were clamoring for office.
Weed kept up a drumfire of instructions from Albany concerning
the claims of hundreds who, in Seward's words, "have reckoned on
our favor;" Fillmore was equally beset by Collier, John Young, and
his own law partner Nathan Kelsey Hall, men who hated Weed and
wished to destroy his power in the party. Before Taylor had been
three days in office Fillmore was claiming that a compromise had

been arranged at Albany which provided that Seward should become Senator and John Collier be made naval officer at New York. This Weed categorically denied, and Seward promptly obtained Philip Hone's nomination for the post. Henry wrote to Frances on March 10 that Fillmore would agree only on appointments for his own followers, and that he, himself, had about decided to terminate their working arrangement.

Differences between the two men multiplied. Young and Hall came down to help Fillmore; John L. Schoolcraft, wealthy, handsome Albany merchant and Whig Congressman, supported Seward strongly; and tempers flared as the battle waxed hot. Fillmore supporters accused Seward of trickery in securing the nomination of P. V. Kellogg as United States marshal in northern New York. Hall declared that Weed cheated Fillmore; Weed asserted that Fillmore had fooled him altogether too long.[2]

As the contest between the Senator and the Vice President became grim, the Cabinet wavered and became uncertain. Seward then asked for and received a letter signed by Weed, Governor Fish, and other leaders in the state government saying that Seward's wishes were those of the New York State Whig party and the state administration. This worked wonders. Henry wrote to Frances that, though the administration still needed "the wisdom to profit by my mind," he had become its chief agent in the Senate, and he told Weed that Fillmore, shepherding a job applicant around the government departments, reminded him of Falstaff's soliloquy—"I am a sow that hath overlaid all her litter but one."

Meanwhile the fight had spilled over into county after county of the state. Even an agreement between Fillmore and Seward to keep out of their respective bailiwicks proved useless, and in Erie County, which was more vulnerable to outside aggression than Cayuga, Seward men scarcely distinguished for either energy or talent won the offices of postmaster and collector of the port of Buffalo.[3] All did not turn to the Seward-Weed advantage, however, for the appointments had yet to be confirmed by the Senate. In New York City, by what appeared to be a sad mischance, Secretary of the Treasury Meredith appointed enemies of Weed and Seward to the important posts of sub-treasurer and collector of the port.

Seward left Washington at the end of the special session in a mood of elation that was not altogether warranted, and plunged into a mass of work. Legal cases, patent and otherwise, sent him to Charleston, South Carolina, and when he returned kept him busy in the New York State courts. A combination of dysentery and erysipelas laid him low for a week during the summer and brought a warning from Weed about his killing labors, but the admonition had no effect, and Frances saw him at home only at brief intervals.

A new complication arose in the midst of all this legal work. Samuel Sweezy Seward died in August 1849 and Henry, as co-executor with his kinsman George Grier of a $300,000 estate, found its settlement a heavy burden. By the terms of the will, the shares left to his brothers, nephews, and nieces were in trust, and they virtually became Henry's wards. Samuel had willed between $75,000 and $100,000 in securities and real estate to Henry and Frances, but he had also set aside $20,000 for the Samuel Sweezy Seward Institute, an educational venture which had opened its doors in 1847, and of which Henry now became president. He faithfully carried out the provisions of the will, though often with considerable difficulty. It was 1871 before the estate was finally settled.

Samuel had been a hard man, not one to be deeply mourned, but Henry ordered the customary stationery with deep black borders. After four months had gone by, Weed wrote to him—"Pray dispense as soon as may be with black-edged letter paper. People say things to me which you can only hear through me." [4]

Settling his father's estate was not the only family worry for Seward. Augustus, now twenty-three and with no future save an army career, was a constant anxiety for his mother, and Henry also worried about his future. Frederick, though he had done well at Union, had no enthusiasm for the law. Willie's eyes did not permit him to read much, and the active ten-year-old's thoughts centered chiefly on his pony. Fanny's health was uncertain, and Frances had only misgivings about life in Washington. She wanted to remain in Auburn, and only Henry's insistence upon her coming with him— Webster had convinced him that an establishment at the capital was essential—won her reluctant consent.

Problems rising out of the terms of his father's will kept Seward from attending a railroad convention that was held in St. Louis early in October, but in a letter to that body he avowed himself an enthusiastic supporter of a transcontinental railroad. This should be built at once, and by the national government. Doubts about the constitutional power of Congress must be removed, or it would "be left for the States yet to be organized, and even yet to be peopled, to construct link by link the chain which the federal power ought to forge at a single blow."

The invitation to attend the railroad convention was only one evidence of Seward's growing national reputation. His correspondence was enormous, often running over fifty letters a day. He had paid fellow townsman B. F. Hall to publish a transcript of the Freeman trial, and Hall was working on a biography with a view to the next presidential campaign. Seward corresponded with Charles Sumner of Massachusetts, who thought he had found a kindred spirit in this New Yorker; with a young newspaper man in Indiana named Schuyler Colfax, who wished to follow in his footsteps; with an even younger Utica lawyer named Roscoe Conkling, who asked, "with high respect and regard," permission to put Seward's name on his card as a business reference.

Seward felt about publicity for himself that there could not be too much, provided it was favorable. Weed was more cautious. The *Daily Atlas* of Cincinnati mentioned Seward as a contender for the Whig nomination in 1852, and Henry forwarded a clipping to his friend. Some months later, when the New York *Evening Post* had intimated the same possibility, Weed wrote, "I have with great misgiving mentioned a few words about you today. The *Evening Post* opened the door. You will have, for a few months, difficulties enough to encounter without being advertised as a candidate." But Weed exploded when Seward told him that two Washington clerks who wanted to get out a 400-page book of his papers and speeches, had asked if they could have a file of the *Evening Journal*. "If it is needful that your enemies should be envenomed and stirred up, let's have a Book," wrote Weed. "It is about as much as you can do to stand up against reproach and obloquy while no great cause for either is found in your conduct; but if, after the manner of Presidential aspirants, you are advertised, in a Book, the whole Pack will be let loose." He might better, Weed added, have his name at the editorial head of the *Journal*. "Of all times this is the worst for a Book." [5] No book appeared.

The Sewards and their children, save for Augustus, came to Washington in November, and Henry plunged into legal work that kept him busy until two days before the opening of Congress. They rented a house on F Street for $400 a year, a red brick, ten-room structure with a pump in the yard and a woodhouse and a small privy at the back. It was a good location, next door to Secretary of War Crawford and in a respectable residential district, close by the shops on Seventh Street and within walking distance of the Capitol. Their furniture, mostly purchased in New York and Philadelphia, was slow in arriving, and for two weeks they and their Negro servants (two of them brought from Auburn) slept on straw-filled bags placed on the floor. John L. Schoolcraft became a member of the household in December, bringing with him barrels and boxes of coffee, tea, and other comestibles. By Christmastime they were engulfed in the social whirl that Henry loved and Frances detested.

While the Seward family settled itself in its new home the capital buzzed with rumors. In the North, public opinion was hardening against any further extension of slavery; in state after state free soil movements were gaining strength. In the South, Mississippi, spurred on by South Carolina, had issued a call for a convention of the slave states to meet in Nashville in June 1850, and southern orators and newspapers were declaring that slavery was more to be prized than the Union.

This sectional division quickly manifested itself in Congress. A protracted struggle over the election of a Speaker for the House unleashed a riot of emotion that extended even to the choice of a doorkeeper. Southerners and anti-slavery northerners shouted insults at one another, and threats of secession were hailed by southern cheers.

> We are in a trying crisis here [Seward wrote to Hamilton Fish]. Every demonstration which passion and design can make to change the purposes of the Free States is resorted to on the one side, self respect, prudence and patriotism counsel moderation on the other side, and yet moderation is liable to produce timidity among ourselves and encourage faction at home. I hope that our friends in the Legislature and in the Press will remain not only firm but bold and active. The future destiny of our country is full of hope if we only remain faithful now.

It was a time not only of tension between North and South but also one of political flux. The old issues between Whigs and Democrats had largely vanished, and talk of political reorientations was much in the air. Seward shared in such speculations. For a number of years he had been impatient with a Whig party which harbored cheek by jowl nativist bigots and advocates of liberty and equality for all men. In 1845 he had told Gerrit Smith that the abolition of slavery should be "the first, the leading, the paramount question of the day," and nothing had occurred since then to change his opinion. He believed in a two-party system, balanced so that each could stand watch over the other, with each compelled to put forward its best men and measures in its quest for victory at the polls. Still thinking of himself as a Whig, he hoped to have a hand in shaping the party so that it would stand for a reasonable degree of protection, internal improvements and educational development at national expense, resistance to nativism, and steady pressure for emancipation. Such a party would have sufficient appeal in the South so that it could with truth call itself national, for he believed that the movement for secession, which he had seen at first hand in South Carolina in the spring of 1849, was an abortion got up by schemers who were using it to wring concessions from the North.[6]

Seward came to Washington in one sense as a Whig politician, tied to his party by very practical considerations. But when he thought in terms of political ideals, he was wont to argue that principles and the power to transform them into legislation were considerations that transcended party shibboleths. The important thing was not whether a man called himself a Whig or a Democrat, but whether the club to which he belonged was right on important issues and had a reasonable prospect of elevating its leaders to office and of achieving its goals. In another and very real sense he came as the evangelist of a movement for human freedom that, he hoped, would carry him into the presidency.

It was in this latter mood that Seward took his place in the Senate which assembled in December 1849, and he immediately drew fire from the southern extremists. A resolution was introduced giving Father Theobald Mathew, an Irish temperance advocate, the privilege of the Senate floor. Southerners objected because in Ireland some years previously he had spoken out against slavery. Seward supported the resolution. He hoped it would be passed unanimously,

not only as homage to a great benefactor of humanity but also as
evidence that they deplored the existence of slavery in the United
States. The resolution passed, 33 to 18, but not before Jefferson
Davis, Henry Foote of Mississippi, and other southern Senators had
denounced the New Yorker for his stand on slavery. It was noteworthy that not one Whig Senator came to his support.

"I am *alone* all *alone* in the Senate, in Congress, and almost in the
United States—I dare to build on the rights of disfranchised men,"
Seward told his friend Judge Conkling. He continued in this course
much to the rage of southern Senators. They declared that he
favored foreigners over Americans when he advocated giving land
from the public domain to Hungarian exiles who had fled from their
native country in the 1848 revolution, and they were bitterly
scornful when he proposed a measure that would authorize jury trial
for fugitive slaves and recognize their right to writs of habeas
corpus.[7] Schoolcraft wrote to Weed that Seward was in great
danger. The confidant of the administration, he had to guard
against the envy of both Whig and Democratic Senators. The free
territory question is soon coming up, said Schoolcraft, and "W. H.
Seward destiny is to be decided within the next six months."

Seward recognized his vulnerability, but he bore the jibes and
taunts of his opponents with composure. When Foote threatened to
currycomb him, metaphorically speaking, if he did not mend his
manners in the Senate, he invited his tormentor to dinner, and Foote
came to feast on stewed terrapin, fried oysters, and roast duck, and
to wax eloquent over the dissolution of the Union. The New
Yorker felt that his crusade was gaining momentum every day at the
national capital. He was also responsible for strong anti-slavery
resolutions that passed the New York State legislature, resolutions
that caused an anguished Fillmoreite to declare that a move was on
to denationalize New York State Whiggery and convert it into an
abolition party.[8]

While Seward was busy establishing his position as a defender of
human freedom, the conflict over slavery and its extension deepened
and became more violent. Passion was aroused daily in congressional
debates, and the press of both sections fed the bitterness of feeling
exhibited by the nation's legislators. Northern anti-slavery zealots
opposed any compromise on slavery for the sake of the Union, and

southern extremists were equally obdurate. By January 1850 there was controversy in and out of Washington over the Wilmot Proviso, the continuation of slavery in the District of Columbia, and the growing problem of how the South would recover its runaway slaves in the face of northern efforts to abet their escape. The country was in a crisis.

At this critical juncture in the nation's history Clay proposed his plan of compromise. His crusade for peace and Union took the form of a series of resolutions. He would admit California as a state (the Californians wished admission as a free state) without reference to slavery; the remaining territories acquired from Mexico should be organized by Congress without restriction or condition as to slavery; a boundary line should be drawn between Texas and New Mexico favorable to the latter's territorial claims, and the United States should pay the public debt owed by Texas at the time that state entered the Union. Clay would also abolish the traffic in slaves brought into the District of Columbia for sale (coupling this with the assertion that it was inexpedient to end slavery in the District without compensation); recommended the passage of a more rigorous fugitive slave law; and proposed a declaration that Congress had no power to interfere with the trade in slaves between slaveholding states.

On February 5 and 6, Clay spoke in defense of his proposals. He began by invoking the aid of Heaven at this critical moment in the nation's history, brought on, he declared, by "the violence and intemperance of party spirit" and the efforts of Whigs and Democrats in their struggle for power to obtain the assistance of "a small party called abolitionists." Then, skillfully and eloquently, he defended each of his resolutions, urged the sections to compromise for the sake of the Union, and closed with a vigorous assertion that there was no such right as secession, and an appeal to his countrymen to pause at the edge of that precipice before they leaped to certain destruction. The Senate then launched into a great two months' debate on the Compromise.

Seward was hostile to Clay's plan from the first, and its approval by Webster roused his indignation, sentiments shared by Frances, who had gone down to the Senate to hear both men speak. Caught up in the great controversy, she was deeply involved. The Kentuckian, she grudgingly admitted, had made doughfaces out of half the Congress by his eloquent appeal, but he had made her indignant by his talk about northern men being moved only by considerations of policy and party spirit. "Now if Henry Clay has lived to be 70 years old and still thinks slavery is opposed only from such motives I can only say he knows much less of human nature than I supposed." As for Webster, she found him less eloquent than Clay because his heart was colder—but what could one expect from a man who had never yet raised his voice in behalf of oppressed people? Henry speaks tomorrow, she told her sister. "I shall not go—the interest I feel is too deep to make it pleasant to be there."

Seward's speech had been weeks in preparation, for he felt sure that it would be his major effort of the session. He and Weed had agreed in advance on its main themes—a sketch of the nation's destiny, the certainty of slavery's destruction, the impossibility of dissolving the Union. Schoolcraft knew what its approach would be; Ewing had seen the notes for the speech and had approved them. News had spread around that the firebrand from New York was to make a major effort, and on the appointed day, March 11, Samuel P. Lyman stood for four hours in a crowded gallery to hear what his friend had to say.[9]

Seward was not, in the popular sense, a great orator. He had no well-calculated gestures, his voice was husky, and he often gave the impression of communing with himself rather than addressing an audience. When he first rose on this momentous day, he hesitated and spoke in such a subdued monotone that the New York *Tribune*'s correspondent feared the speech would be a failure. Benton did not lift his eyes from his book, Webster paid no attention, and Calhoun fidgeted. But all this changed as Seward developed his theme.

He began with a lengthy argument for the admission of California. National interest demanded it, lest she set up for herself, and this, he said, was so important that he would have voted for her entrance even if she had wished to come in as a slave state. Then, declaring that he regarded all legislative compromises as "radically wrong and essentially vicious" because they were surrenders of judgment and conscience, he examined the proposals made by some of the previous speakers in the session. Calhoun had demanded safeguards for the South and its peculiar institution, safeguards that, Seward declared, meant a return to a government as weak and unworkable as it had been under the Articles of Confederation. He clashed with Webster over admitting additional slave states carved out of Texas, and over spending $80,000,000 for removing free Negroes from the South—a move, he said, that would strengthen slavery. One by one he took up and rejected Clay's compromise proposals, and then attacked the very principle of the compromise. It assumed that slavery was a ruling institution in the southern states, but it was in truth transient, while freedom was a permanent institution and fundamental to the very existence of those states. Then, too, the compromise principle regarded the public domain only as a possession to be enjoyed by the citizens of all the old states. The domain did belong to the nation's citizens, but they held no arbitrary authority over it. The Constitution devoted it

> . . . to union, to justice, to defence, to welfare and to liberty.
>
> But there is a higher law than the Constitution, which regulates our authority over the domain, and devotes it to the same noble purposes. The territory is a part—no inconsiderable part—of the common heritage of mankind, bestowed upon them by the Creator of the universe. We are his stewards, and must so discharge our trust as to secure, in the highest attainable degree, their happiness.

Slavery in the territories, Seward declared, would be incompatible with "the security of natural rights, the diffusion of knowledge, and the freedom of industry," for it subverted the principle of democracy and converted the state into either an aristocracy or a despotism.

Webster had argued that slavery would not go into the new territories because it was shut out by God's design. To this Seward answered that all just human laws were re-enactments of the law of God, and that it was sometimes desirable to reaffirm the dictates of the Almighty by the sanctions of civil authority. History showed that slavery could rear its head anywhere.

Seward also assailed the argument that compromise was necessary to preserve the Union. Natural and economic factors made a north-south division impossible. There was no adequate reason for secession, for slavery had solid guarantees in its support from the Demo-cratic party, the North's economic aristocrats, the prejudice of caste and color, and its control over the national government. When it eventually gave way to economic and humane influences, its elimina-tion would be peaceful or violent as it was hastened or hindered in the going. He would hasten it, but only by lawful, constitutional, and peaceful means, including compensation.

He heard much these days, said Seward, of state loyalties. As for himself, he had good reason to be loyal to New York, but he "knew only one country and one sovereign—the United States of America and the American people." He had confidence in the Union, and therefore felt no need for compromise as a means of its salvation. He would vote for the admission of California "directly, without con-ditions, without qualifications, and without compromise." As for the new territories, he could see their countless generations of inhabi-tants yet unborn saying, "the soil you hold in trust for us, give it to us free—free from the calamities and sorrows of human bondage." [10]

Seward's arguments were clear and cogent, and he had rallied a formidable array of authorities—Burke and Montesquieu, Vattel, Bacon, and Machiavelli—to his support. The speech immediately produced violent repercussions all over the country. His first mail brought criticism from both North and South. Then anti-slavery sentiment made itself felt, enthusiastic letters flooded in, and more and more northern newspapers rallied to his support. The South, however, remained hostile, and its press and public men raised a chorus of bitter indignation. The New Yorker was a ranter, an extremist, a man without principle. The Richmond *Enquirer* as-serted that he was a "wretch whom it would be a degradation to name"; Calhoun declared that Seward had defended the North's treachery toward the South; and half a dozen South Carolina clergymen sent him copies of his speech with insulting remarks written on the pages. "I am going to examine the list of names and ascertain what denomination these clergymen belong to," wrote Frances to her sister, "but I am inclined to think it is the Episcopal as they are more opposed to progress of all kinds than most others. Henry had a commendatory letter from Bp. Potter but he is not of the narrowest kind."

The South's dislike erupted among the Senate Whigs. Clay, who had invoked the higher law in defense of the admission of California, now spoke contemptuously of it and of its would-be expositors. Mangum of North Carolina told the President that, if Seward's speech represented administration policy, he would go into opposition, and Taylor, stuttering in his excitement, urged Bullitt of the Washington *Republic* to write a disclaimer. A blistering editorial promptly appeared, accusing Seward of overriding the Constitution and presuming to legislate as the steward of God Almighty.

Bullitt's onslaught brought a vigorous rejoinder from Greeley. Seward had appealed to a higher law not in opposition to but as a reinforcement of the Constitution, a fact that his critics ignored. The doughty *Tribune* editor, always at his best when battling in a moral cause, pointed out that instead of nullifying a constitutional obligation Seward had enforced it by the sanction of divine law. He had, moreover, put into words "the thought of that gathering, swelling, advancing host with whom Democracy is not a fig leaf device, a gainful craft, but a living, pervading, controlling aspiration." Greeley was inclined to favor Clay's compromise proposals, but it was still his opinion that "Seward's speech will live longer, be read with a more hearty admiration, and exert a more potential and pervading influence on the national mind and character than any other speech of the session."

The *Republic*'s attitude indicated a rift between Seward and the administration. Democrats and Fillmore supporters gleefully predicted the end of Seward's influence, but Taylor's irritation with his New York mentor was short-lived. Seward rallied the Cabinet, with which Bullitt was at war, to his support, arguing that he alone among the Whig Senators was in line with the President's plan. Within little more than a week he was again high in Taylor's favor.[11]

Not so short-lived was the effect of the speech on the Seward-Weed relationship. Reading it gave the Albany boss a restless night and left him ridden with anxiety. Able and eloquent though it was, he wrote to Seward, it suggested no remedies for the evils it portrayed and gave no ground for hope that there was a way to salvation. Seward had raised a storm that would divide the Whig party in New York State. Pointedly opposing Webster was also a mistake, for it gave Webster a party in the North. One paragraph in support of Taylor's plan would have meant the support of the administration, but Taylor and his patriotic efforts had been ignored, and now Seward stood alone. Weed was also troubled by the higher law statement, and he took pains in the *Journal* to insist on Seward's loyalty to the President.

Seward was hurt by Weed's criticism. The timing of his difference with Webster was unfortunate, he admitted, but the difference was there and had to be met. Support of the President's plan could not logically fit into the main body of his speech. Had he dragged it into his conclusion, the changes would have been rung on that charge of insincerity that had been so industriously circulated against him by his enemies for a dozen years. "The first element of political character, or rather of public character," Seward told Weed, "is sincerity. I thank God that this element so unjustly lost is retrieved." He could not with consistency or with safety, he declared, have been less bold or less firm.

There were three main reasons for Weed's discomfort. He had been giving Taylor all-out support in the *Journal*, and Seward's speech appeared to weaken that position. Second, Weed feared the effect of the speech on the power of the Weed-Seward machine in New York State, for the anger of southern Senators, joined to the hostility of northern Democrats, imperilled the confirmation of many a hard-won federal appointment in New York. If there were wholesale rejections, the Fillmore conservatives would be riding high in the state. Third, Weed felt that Seward's action indicated disregard for his advice, want of appreciation for his friendship, and an overweening ambition. Seward argued that to have taken any other course would have been "a dereliction of principle equally wrong in itself and ruinous in its consequences." It took years to restore their relationship to the old footing of trust and intimacy—if, indeed, it was ever completely restored.[12]

Seward could put noble aspirations into eloquent words. He could also, in the name of political expediency, do some devious things. Old Eliphalet Nott had seen these two sides of his character and, when Seward entered the Senate, had warned him to adhere to his principles, lest he turn out to be like Samson with his locks shorn. Frances gave him the same warning when she wrote to him in 1850, "My earnest prayer to God is that the high intellectual eminence which you have attained may cast no shadow on your naturally clear moral perceptions." When the New Yorker rose in his seat on March 11 he had been true to his better self and, despite Weed's strictures and forebodings, he took a stubborn pride in what he had done.

As the spring of 1850 wore on, the impact of the speech became more and more apparent. It was in tremendous demand. Within three weeks Seward had franked out 50,000 copies and at least as many more had been distributed by his friends in and out of Congress. The American and Foreign Antislavery Society printed 10,000 copies, thousands more were printed in German for German voters, and Greeley's *Tribune* circulated it through the Middle West in a special edition. Other papers sent it out in supplements that mounted into the tens of thousands.

Enthusiastic letters came in floods. Bishop Hughes thought it likely to overwhelm slavery. "You have revived the age of Burke. All his comprehension, his eternal truth is yours," wrote a Union College professor. Lewis Henry Morgan, Whig lawyer and celebrated ethnologist, praised it as clear and direct. Many spoke of Seward as being destined for the presidency. The *American Whig Review* in its June issue featured his picture and a flattering 14,000-word sketch of his life by Horace Greeley.[13]

But while his friends applauded, his critics belabored him, their attacks centering on the "higher law" portion of his speech. It was customary at that time for men to appeal to a law that was above human law. John Quincy Adams had done so in his controversy with Georgia over the Indians; Chief Justice Marshall and Justice Story had done so in their opinions; William Ellery Channing had declared that the will of God was the "higher law." Seward, too, had repeatedly invoked the sanction of a higher law without subjecting himself to any criticism on that account. But this time it was different, for he was now a national figure speaking in a time of crisis, and he had used the expression in conjunction with an attack on slavery. "The unscrupulous demagogue," as the New Orleans *Picayune* called him, had said that the provision in the Constitution for the return of fugitive slaves was in conflict with the law of God and could not be enforced against the moral convictions of the North. This, taken together with his statement that there was a higher law than the Constitution (a statement ripped out of context by his detractors), was used to depict him as a dangerous radical who was ready to trample the Constitution under foot. It was an unwarrantable description of a moderate who believed that emancipation must come slowly, constitutionally, and with compensation to the slave-owners.[14]

Seward's mood in the midst of all this publicity was mainly one of elation. To be sure, in a moment of humility he told Weed that the latter's apprehensions about the speech had caused him much anxiety; that he was covered with shame and sorrow; that he would gladly withdraw from public life if it would do any good, for he knew that he was "incapable of so mean a thought as of acquiring fame for myself," or even of advancing the cause of humanity "at the cost of confiding political associates." But even so he did not see how he could have done differently. "I know," he declared, "that I have spoken words that will tell when I am dead, and even while I am living, for the benefit and blessing of mankind, and for myself this is consolation enough."[15] Perhaps, despite his protestations to the contrary, an even greater satisfaction lay in the knowledge that this speech had made him the outstanding political leader of the anti-slavery forces of the North.

⊰ 10 ⊱

Aftermath

The Compromise was the principal business of the Senate during the spring and summer of 1850. Clay's proposals went to a select committee of thirteen in April, out of which three bills emerged. The first, or so-called "Omnibus bill," provided for the admission of California as a free state, the organization of Utah and New Mexico territories without mention of slavery, and adjustment of the Texas boundary with compensation to Texas for abandoning her pretension to some one hundred and twenty-five thousand square miles of territory claimed by New Mexico. A second measure provided a rigorous fugitive slave law, and a third prohibited bringing slaves into the District of Columbia either for future transportation or for sale. These bills produced in their turn a flock of amendments; little progress was made; and as the hot summer came on tempers became worn and frayed. Clay, pleading for action, vigorously attacked Taylor's plan for the immediate admission of California as a free state, declaring that the committee proposed to heal five bleeding wounds, whereas the President was concerned with only one, and the breach between the two men became wide as the outlook for the passage even of the Omnibus became dim.

For some two months after his March assault on Clay's proposal, Seward spoke frequently and on relatively non-controversial topics, but his opposition to the Compromise did not waver. He tried vainly to enlist Greeley's support for Taylor's plan, only to be told that he

A Fable—In the Reign of Zackery 1st the Goddess of Liberty Designed a Statue, a Model of a Man which she exhibited before the King, his Ministers, & the People. The Beauty of the Statue Elicited such shouts of Approbation from the People that the King's Ministers fired with Jealousy determined to Destroy it, but after many Ineffectual attempts were obliged to Desist amidst the Laughter of the Court & the People.

had too high an opinion for dexterity in statesmanship. Tired, almost ill, but determined to answer Clay's attack on "the noble old chief," Seward went for a weekend in late June to Auburn, where he read what he had written to Frances. He went back to the capital heartened by her approval; on July 2 he rose to deliver his second major speech of the session.

Now, as he had not done in March, Seward specifically supported Taylor's plan, the while he subjected the Compromise to blistering attack. He wanted each controversial problem to be considered by itself, with the whole settlement based on the great principles forming the basis of American government.

> The abstractions of human rights [he said] are the only permanent foundations of society. It is by referring to them that men determine what is *established* because it is RIGHT, in order to uphold it forever; and what is *right* only because it is *established*, in order that they may lawfully *change* it, in accordance with the increase of knowledge and the progress of reason.

He defended the Wilmot Proviso vigorously as the rule for action regarding the new territories. The interest expressed by southern Senators in the extension of the Missouri Compromise line of 36° 30' to the coast betrayed their hopes of slavery expansion, against which the Proviso would stand as a bulwark, and its opponents no longer had the excuse of a secession threat, for the Nashville convention, where the southern states had met, had come and gone with no one the worse for it. There were not five bleeding wounds; California was the only one, and that one should be healed at once for the country was impatient.

Compromise would not end the slavery problem, declared Seward, for there was a radical and perpetual antagonism between slavery and freedom. Immigration and expansion would go on in obedience to laws higher than the Constitution, he would say, if

---

The Compromise of 1850. Pro-Clay and the Compromise, it satirizes Taylor and his Cabinet. Seward, "little Billey," clings to his protector, the President. *The Library of Congress.*

such laws were acknowledged in Congress, and here he paused to quote Algernon Sydney's dictum that the constitution of countries "ought not to be followed unless they are rightly made; they cannot be rightly made if they are contrary to the universal law of God and nature." So, too, the struggle for freedom would continue. "You may slay the Wilmot Proviso in the Senate Chamber, and bury it beneath the Capitol today. The dead corse, in complete steel, will haunt your legislative halls tomorrow." Compromise only impaired the vigor of the Constitution and was a concession to threats of disunion. It was high time that panic about the Union should cease.

The true policy, said the Senator from New York, was to leave slavery in the states where it existed, but with a federal government devoted to keeping it within bounds and favoring its ultimate extinction. Then, gradually and without sudden change or violence, "ten, or twenty, or even fifty years hence," men might bring about the emancipation of labor, its restoration to its rightful dignity and power. In that happy time the nation, reconciled and in accord, could pursue its rightful aims "in the most sublime and beneficent enterprise the earth has witnessed."

Frances felt, as she read the speech in the *Tribune*, that it was just as good as she had thought it to be when he had read it to her at home. Weed was ecstatic. He told Frances that it was the greatest speech ever heard in the Senate, and that shouts of homage for Seward would resound throughout the land. Hundreds of congratulatory letters poured into Seward's Washington office.[1]

Then, within a week, the attention of the country was centered in another quarter. Zachary Taylor was stricken with acute gastroenteritis. He died on the evening of July 9, and Millard Fillmore became the President of the United States. The Cabinet resigned; Webster became Secretary of State. It was obvious that a new order was at hand, and once again the cob houses that Seward and Weed were building began to crumble.

The enemies of the two men had been trying for months to destroy their control over the New York State Whig party. John Young and Nathan Kelsey Hall led this movement, the Vice President having been kept informed of their tactics, but taking little or no active part in their development. An unsuccessful effort had been made to take control of the 1849 state convention away from Weed, and a rival to the *Evening Journal*, the *Register*, had been established in Albany to support Webster and the Compromise and to oppose Seward.

Men wondered whether this opposition would take on added force with White House sanction, or whether an arrangement could be made that would keep the Whig party in the state from splitting wide apart. A second question, relevant to the first, was what attitude would be taken by Fillmore's administration toward the Compromise. Would Fillmore support it, or would he go along with Weed and Seward in opposing it?

On the news of Taylor's death, Seward telegraphed Weed to come at once to Washington. Instead, and more astutely, the Dictator sent Washington Hunt as an emissary to the White House with a message that Weed would support Fillmore if the latter would follow in Taylor's footsteps. An editorial in the *Evening Journal* conveyed the same information to the public. Some of Fillmore's friends considered this attitude belligerent and peremptory, but during the next few months Albany manifested an earnest desire to establish a rapprochement with the national administration. Seward, half-sick and thoroughly dispirited, went along with this policy, although after advice that he sent Fillmore about the Cabinet was ignored, he had little hope of any agreement.

What made this effort at accommodation fruitless was the fact that the national patronage, which had been to a large extent under the control of Weed and Seward when Taylor was in the White House, was now in the hands of the Fillmore administration. The President, if let alone, might have acted with moderation—his instincts were all for peace—but his friends' drive for place gave him no rest. On July 23 Nathan Kelsey Hall became Postmaster General, and at that moment the post-office appointments slipped out of the Seward-Weed control. Rumor said that Fillmore hated Seward, and the course of events gave credence to the allegation. The Detroit *Tribune* lost its federal patronage, so the anguished editor wailed, because of its "Sewardism"; Hugh Maxwell, confirmed as collector of the port at New York, openly proscribed the friends of the beleaguered Senator; Seward's nominee for collector of the port at Buffalo was withdrawn, and a Fillmore supporter, William Ketchum, was confirmed in that important post; in another bitter blow, Fillmore withdrew the name of Lewis Benedict, close ally of Weed and Seward, for postmaster at Albany.

The national as well as the local scene found Seward and Fillmore at odds. It speedily became apparent that the President favored the Compromise, while Seward continued vehemently to oppose it. On July 26, fighting against the adoption of the Omnibus, he introduced an amendment providing for the immediate admission of New Mexico as a state under a constitution prohibiting slavery. His was the only voice raised for this amendment, and Senator Pratt of Maryland, Fillmore's chief spokesman in the Senate, led the attack upon the New Yorker, declaring that he should be expelled from the Senate. Seward's proposal was in line with Taylor's plan, which was now laid in the dust with the Old Chief himself.[2]

Through the weeks that followed this rebuff, Seward opposed all the Compromise measures save the California bill. The Omnibus collapsed at the end of July, but under the management of Stephen A. Douglas and with the aid of Democrats and Fillmore Whigs the separate bills of the Compromise became law. Seward proposed a measure abolishing slavery in the District of Columbia, but this was roundly defeated. The swing to the Compromise began to resemble a stampede. Frances, who was with Henry in Washington and watched the proceedings in Congress with close attention, wrote to her sister that there were only about seven Whigs in the House who could be counted upon to follow Seward's leadership.[3]

The passage of the Compromise bills put new heart into the movement to wrest control of New York State from Weed and Seward, but Weed's selection of the moderate Washington Hunt for governor blunted the conservative drive. Seward liberals had a majority in the state convention that met on September 26, 1850, and nominated Hunt, but when the convention adopted resolutions praising Seward's course in the Senate and approving the Wilmot Proviso, the conservatives, or nationalists as they styled themselves, bolted. Silver-maned Francis Granger, who had been chairman of the convention, led them out of the hall and gave them the name of the Silver Grays, sometimes known as the Cotton Whigs to distinguish them from the Sewardites, who in derision were dubbed Woolly Heads.

The Silver Grays also nominated Hunt and the rest of the regular state ticket, but they adopted a set of principles that were enthusiastically pro-Compromise, and that omitted commendation of Seward. In the ensuing election, Hunt bested Democrat Horatio Seymour by 262 votes, but the Whigs lost all the other state offices, a result not to be wondered at when extremists like N. K. Hall (conservative) and E. G. Spaulding (liberal) were in favor of throwing the election to the Democrats, each as a means of teaching the opposite wing of the party a lesson. Only great Whig strength in the rural districts gave the Whigs control of the assembly and a shaky majority of two in the senate.

An uneasy truce within the New York State Whig party followed the election of 1850, each side professing an ardent desire for peace, but each profoundly distrusting the other's good intentions. Seward was calm but gloomy, his spirits not improved by Greeley's informing him that he had lost all his personal popularity in the Senate and had very little with the officeholders and anti-reformers out of that body. The Senator had formulated a plan of non-action, and, though he made clear his desire for the repeal of the fugitive slave law, only once in the second session of the Thirty-first Congress did he refer to the slavery question.[4]

Frederick Douglass thought Seward had lost his enthusiasm for freedom, that he and other anti-slavery leaders in Congress had been "shorn of their moral strength," but this was unfair. Seward had been, and continued to be, a financial supporter of Douglass's paper, *The North Star;* he was mulling over plans for modifying the fugitive slave law and for fostering gradual emancipation with consent and compensation; and he wrote a little essay on "The Basis of the American Constitution" in which he argued that this basis was "the absolute and inherent equality of all men." There was, he averred, a supreme law of creation, based on the equality of nations, races, and men; and there was a common humanity, evidenced by the similarities of codes of moral conduct, common elements in languages and religions, and the inexorable march of human civilization toward freedom.

Now, however, the country was in the grip of reaction and Seward thought it best to be quiet for a time on slavery, even though ardent spirits murmured at this "masterly inactivity." He accepted without enthusiasm Weed's determination to force the election of the moderately conservative Hamilton Fish to the Senate, and took a like course with the Albany boss's efforts to play along with Fillmore and the Cotton Whigs in order to keep the New York State Whig party from falling apart. As for himself, he told Weed, "I shall be out of the play, at best behind the scenes, for a long time. The Drama will go on without me." But he was also sure that new slavery aggressions would again awaken the North and that then the fight for freedom would have to be renewed.[5]

Letting slavery alone meant Seward had leisure time to read Swift and Beaumont and Fletcher, as well as to find ways to build up his political image. He told the country that commercial opportunities in the Pacific should be broadened, and that the merchant class was justified in seeking from the federal government indemnification for French spoliations of the 1790s. He argued for the right of immigrants to acquire land and engage in mining on even terms with the native-born—"the only difference that I can see between a citizen by birth and one by adoption is, that the one was made a citizen by his ancestors, and the other by his own voluntary action." He pleaded for two-cent postage. He urged using the public domain for internal improvements and educational development, and in a major speech came out for free land for actual settlers with security against seizure for debt. He also paid $400 to have 40,000 pamphlet copies of these speeches printed for distribution to the public.

The New York merchants greeted his speech on French spoliations with great joy, and report had it that Supreme Court Chief Justice Taney said its argument was conclusive. Seward at once asked permission to inscribe the pamphlet copy to the Chief Justice, an honor that was politely declined.

In June, Seward appeared for the defense in a conspiracy case in Detroit, where the Michigan Central Railroad accused fifty men of destroying the company's property. He needed the promised fee (from $1500 to $2000) and, he told Weed, the case would help him professionally. Besides, he added wryly, "the accused, if they are guilty, are white." The trial dragged on all summer, with Seward more and more convinced that his clients were innocent. When twelve of them were convicted and sentenced to prison terms, he wrote bitterly to Greeley about corruption covered by the judicial ermine, a reaction at least partly justified by subsequent revelations before a grand jury which led to the indictment of a number of the Michigan Central's witnesses as perjurers. His Albany friends thought that the trial would be used to smear him as an irresponsible radical, but he did not share their fears.[6]

The Detroit case was an exhausting business, but Seward had time for only a short rest at home before he left for Goshen and work on the settlement of his father's estate. While he was there, excitement over the fugitive slave law boiled up in Auburn and in nearby Syracuse due to the famous rescue by abolitionists of the fugitive slave Jerry in the latter city. Frances wrote that arrests were expected in Auburn and that two fugitive slaves, one of them "our acquaintance John," had gone to Canada. Eight of the Jerry rescuers were brought before the court in Auburn, and Seward arrived in time to sign their bail bonds. "The reaction in this state against slavery is signal," he wrote to Greeley, "and yet I do not see who is to shape or in what way the course of events. We are at sea without rudder or compass." Deeply dissatisfied with the policies of both of the major parties, Seward went to Washington for the first session of the Thirty-second Congress which opened on December 1, 1851.[7]

Among the Senators who gathered on Capitol Hill was Charles Sumner, newly elected by a Massachusetts Free-Soil–Democratic coalition. This humorless, sensitive, handsome Free-Soiler had occasionally exchanged letters, speeches, and compliments with Seward since 1846, and now formed the habit of dropping in at the Seward home, sometimes appearing at dinner time without the formality of an invitation. Frances found him fearless, sincere, a man of high moral perceptions, one whose bent was definitely in a literary rather than a political direction, and she hoped that he was not, as Henry surmised, headed toward becoming a Democrat. Then, too, what she regarded as Sumner's naïveté interested and amused her. Schoolcraft, who thought Sumner a Democrat already, would have nothing to do with him—leaving the room when he entered it, and refusing to sit at the same table. One day at dinner, after Schoolcraft had been behaving in this way for some time, Sumner proposed that Henry invite Schoolcraft to meet him at the Sewards for a meal, as he wanted to make his acquaintance. "Somehow or other," said

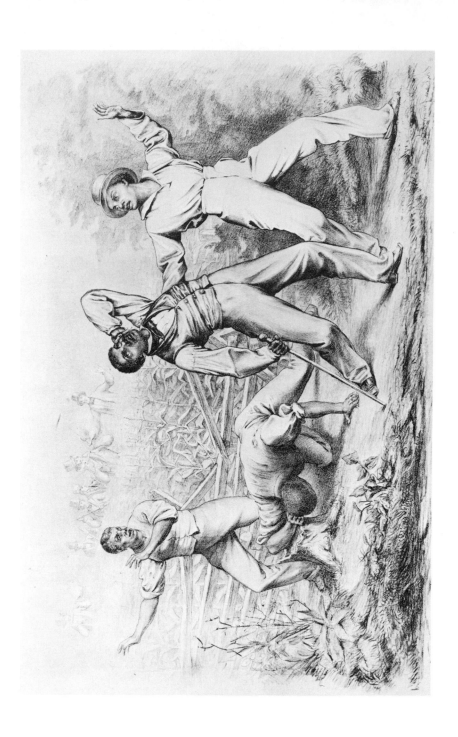

Sumner, "he always leaves the room when I come. I suppose," turning to Henry who was intently regarding his plate, "he thinks I wish to see you alone." Frances said that Schoolcraft was an old acquaintance of whom they were fond, and Henry added that it would be nice for them all to dine together.[8]

In the Senate Seward found himself on the commerce committee, but his first activities that session concerned Lajos Kossuth. The distinguished Hungarian patriot and exile landed in New York early in December, where he was received with great enthusiasm. Russia and Austria together had crushed the Hungarian movement for independence, and Kossuth was seeking help for his native land. After a round of banquets and financial contributions he moved on to Washington, where he was met by government consternation, the stony dislike of southern Congressmen, and the warm approbation of free-soilers and libertarians.

Seward stood among Kossuth's most fervid admirers. The New Yorker extolled his virtues and proposed a welcome to the capital and to the country in the form of a resolution which, after acrimonious debate, passed both houses of Congress. He spent a great deal of time with Kossuth while the latter was in the capital; he actually knew more about the Hungarian's entourage and plans than did either Webster or Fillmore. After Kossuth departed for a tour of the country, Seward offered a resolution of solemn protest against Russia's suppression of Hungary's independence, supporting it in a lengthy speech that put great emphasis on sustaining the cause of human freedom.

Late in May Kossuth and his wife spent a weekend at the Seward home in Auburn, a visit marked by much pomp and ceremony and

---

HOLY BIBLE	DECLARATION OF INDEPENDENCE
Thou shalt not deliver unto the master his servant which has escaped from his master unto thee. He shall dwell with thee. Even among you in that place which he shall choose in one of thy gates where it liketh him best. Thou shalt not oppress him. Deut XXIII 15, 16.	We hold that all men are created equal, that they are endowed by their Creator with certain unalienable rights; that among these are life, liberty, and the pursuit of happiness.

A cartoon of 1850 entitled "Effects of the Fugitive-Slave-Law". Seward was opposed to the law. *The Library of Congress.*

the vociferous support of Willie Seward's boy friends, who called themselves the Young Hungarian Association. When the Kossuths returned to Europe Seward secured free passage for them on the Collins Steamship Line, the subsidization of which the Senator had supported.

Approbation of Kossuth was in accord with Seward's belief that liberty was the rightful heritage of all men. "How strange that people will go mad *for* the freedom of *white* men and *against* the freedom of *black* men," he wrote when the Hungarian was tumultuously received in New York. And on the southern attitude—"You see how timid Slavery is. It dare not tolerate freedom in Europe." [9]

Slavery was a loathsome institution and must be eliminated from the American scene, but the relief with which the Compromise had been greeted convinced Seward that the moral education of the American people must come first. Political movements could proceed only as fast as public opinion was ready to sustain them, and so, as in the preceding year, he let the Compromise alone and turned to promoting the nation's economic development. In a spate of speeches and resolutions he supported government participation in the building of railroads and other internal improvements, government subsidies for American steamship lines, and a survey of the Arctic and Pacific oceans for the benefit of the whaling industry and for the general expansion of American trade in the Far East. He also gave advice to Vermont farmers about developing the agricultural science and education that were so essential if America's wealth and her territory were to expand beyond her present borders. When difficulties with Great Britain over the fisheries arose, and southerners belabored the government for not upholding the national honor, he responded with an extremely able defense of the administration's handling of the dispute. He made a lucid review of the problem, based in part on information furnished by John F. T. Crampton, the British Minister to the United States. His speech in the main had a dispassionate tone, and, though Crampton objected to some of its judgments on British policy, he felt that it stated the questions involved "in a manner more consistent with justice and common sense than has yet been done by any of the speakers on the subject." Webster called it "a great speech." By such activities, by happy eulogies of Clay and Webster (both of whom died in 1852), and by his caution in dealing with the slaveholders, he added to his reputation for statesmanship.[10]

While Seward built up his image as a conservative-liberal, the battle over presidential candidates for 1852 got into full swing. Fillmore would have liked the Whig nomination, and his friends made it appear that he was duty bound to run as the great apostle of Unionism and the savior of the Whig party. Webster, ambitious to the last, was an avowed aspirant, and so was the man characterized by Greeley as that "immeasureably conceited, aristocratic ass, Gen. Scott." [11]

There is some evidence that Seward was at first inclined to let Fillmore have the nomination, and it is clear that he was not enthusiastic about either Webster or Scott. He had never thought of Webster as a suitable presidential candidate. As for Scott, his pomposity was annoying, he had a positive genius for coining fatuous phrases, and his earlier nativist leanings were sure to be exhumed by the Democrats and used where they would have the greatest effect. But he was a military hero, had favored the Compromise without becoming embroiled in controversy over it, and if he could be nominated without platform concessions to the South and then remain silent on slavery during the campaign, he would be acceptable from Seward's point of view.

The Democrats met at Baltimore on June 1, 1852, and after a protracted struggle nominated a dark horse, Franklin K. Pierce of New Hampshire, on a ticket pledging all-out support for the Compromise. The Whigs gathered in the same city on June 16. Many of the delegates had come to the convention by way of Washington, and there Seward had been in the thick of the Scott-men's consultations. In vain, Congressman Meredith P. Gentry blistered both Seward and Scott in the lower house; in vain, Fillmore supporters whispered "Seward" as a word with which to frighten delegates away from Scott. The Scott men carried the day in the convention after fifty-three ballots but, much to Seward's disgust, the platform endorsed the Compromise.[12]

To allay southern suspicions that Scott was Seward's pawn, the latter published a statement that he would not accept any public station or preferment at the hands of the General. This had little effect, and Seward thought seriously of resigning from the Senate. He con-

sulted Frances, who agreed to the move if he obtained the assent of
six friends, including Schoolcraft and Weed; the proposal came to
naught.

During the campaign of 1852 Seward, in common with most of
the northern Whigs in the Senate, sought to avoid stirring up passions over slavery. Accordingly, much to Frances's disgust, he voted
against Sumner's effort in late August to repeal the fugitive slave
law. In part because of continued and vehement attacks upon him
by southern Whigs and Silver Grays, in part because of the
"wretched platform" to which Scott felt in honor committed
(despite Seward's assurance that he was under no obligation to
execute it), the senior Senator from New York played only a
nominal role in the presidential contest. On election day he voted
for Scott "with a protest." [13]

When the election was over the Whigs took account of their
losses. The Democrats had carried every section of the country, had
won all but four states, and their victory in the South had been
overwhelming. Henry J. Raymond put on a brave front in the editorial columns of the New York *Times*, but privately he compared
the result to the flood in the time of Noah, and saw no hope for the
resurrection of the Whig party as such. Charles Francis Adams
dubbed Whiggery a "crazy bark." Charles Sumner, too, felt that the
time had come for a new organization, a party of freedom. Seward,
himself, could not help being downcast, not only because of the
Whig defeat but also because of the "kill Seward" slogan of the
mercantile element in the Whig party, those businessmen who were
all for conciliation of the South. "Well!" he wrote to Weed, "the
play is played out for this time and played out practically for us
perhaps forever." But he was not yet ready to abandon the Whig
ship. Instead he began considering the possibility of a North-West
alliance of Whigs and Free-Soil party members, with a moderate
anti-slavery program, an alliance that would march to victory by
1860 under the Whig banner. This was just like a New York politician, Charles Francis Adams confided to his diary. Seward was
equal to the ordinary demands of his station, but was always thinking of himself. This scheme of preserving the Whig party must be
made as difficult as possible, Adams felt.

The election of 1852 was, indeed, a crucial point in a Whig disintegration that had been going on for years. Southern Whigs were beset by faction and torn between loyalty to the Union and devotion to the South's way of life. Perturbed by Seward's dominance over Taylor, they had rallied to the Compromise of 1850, but remained deeply suspicious of the anti-slavery Northern Whigs. Drifting from their moorings more and more, they had flocked eagerly into the Union parties that had appeared in Georgia, Alabama, and Mississippi, pledged to the Compromise. These parties had been short-lived, and Whig disorientation became more pronounced; whereas the erstwhile southern Democrats could more easily go back to a national organization that had produced no such immensely influential leaders in an anti-slavery direction as William Henry Seward or such a powerful anti-slavery newspaper as Greeley's *Tribune*. Scott's nomination produced still further alienation, and by the end of 1852 the southern wing of the Whig party had ceased to exist as a vital entity.

Northern Whiggery had also been wracked by dissension. Its adherents, East and West, were by no means unanimous in their views of tariff, land, and internal improvement policies. Nativism rent their ranks, and throughout the North the Conscience and Cotton Whigs were vigorously and often bitterly voluble. Nowhere did these elements of dissension seem more plainly apparent than in New York State.

Since 1850 the Whig party in New York had steadily deteriorated as a political organization. Dissension over the fugitive slave law added new fuel to the long disputes involving nativism, anti-rent difficulties, and the never-ending conflict over the spoils of office. The efforts of Fillmore's supporters to put him forward as the Whig candidate for President in 1852 produced violent reactions from the liberal Seward-Weed wing of the party, and the President's efforts to use proscription of those loyal to Seward as a means of enforcing party harmony made for further discord. In the fall elections of 1851 the Whigs went down to defeat, with anti-renters deserting to the Democrats, and Fillmore supporters in New York City knifing the ticket that Weed had painfully and carefully put together. Then came the debacle of 1852, when the Democrats carried their entire state ticket and gained a two to one majority in the assembly, the while they elected twice as many Congressmen as did the Whigs.

Similar tales of woe came from other parts of the North. All signs indicated that the party of Clay and Webster, those dead giants, had run its course.

Despite, or perhaps because of, the small part that Seward had taken in the 1852 campaign, Washington gossips spread the word that he had been responsible for Scott's defeat. Shortly after returning to the capital for the opening of Congress that winter, Seward called at the General's house and was not received. The Senator's feelings as he went down the walk may be imagined, but that evening Scott wrote that it had all been a mistake. He had been busy with guests, the light was bad when Seward's card was brought in, and he had not realized who was at the door.[14]

The Whig defeat in the election of 1852 was the harbinger of a political change that would have a profound effect on Seward's career. Changes of a more intimate nature were occurring in his family life. Augustus remained in the army, and his mother's conviction that military life was ruining her eldest child made for much unhappiness in the family. Her desperate pleas even shook her husband's belief that their son must be left to go his own gait. Henry made an effort to find him employment as a civil engineer, but the young lieutenant refused to resign his commission. Henry then used his influence with Scott and others to have Augustus transferred to the Coast Survey.

The other boys presented no unusual problems. Frederick, undecided as to a career after college, looked to his father for guidance. Seward advised the law, and in 1851 Frederick was admitted to the bar, only to turn his back on that profession and join the staff of the Albany *Evening Journal,* where he became junior editor. Twelve-year-old Willie's eye trouble prevented his having any regular education, and his interests continued to be non-academic. He craved excitement, whether it was riding his pony, organizing a boys' club, or planning an exploring expedition. He much preferred Auburn to Washington and remained at home under the wing of a relative when his parents went to Washington in the fall of 1851.

A couple of months later Sam Blatchford wrote that Willie was falling on evil courses. He was eating oysters and drinking beer at Bemis's tavern, spending his money on the theater, and riding about town in a loud and unseemly manner. His parents promptly haled him off to Washington, where they soon satisfied themselves that all was well. It was Willie's misfortune, Frances wrote to her sister, to do the things other boys did in so open a manner that it was bound to attract attention. There was nothing to worry about in his behavior.

Frances had the main responsibility for guiding the childrens' day-by-day development, Henry's control over them being of necessity intermittent, but relatives on both sides of the family took up much of his time. He acted as guardian for no less than ten nephews and nieces under the terms of his father's will, and gave generous financial assistance to sister-in-law Lazette and her daughter Frances. He also bore the expense of bringing up and educating his nephew Clarence Seward, a burden that had been his ever since Benjamin Jennings's death in 1840.

Clarence in 1852 had a wife and baby and was just starting on a promising legal career in Auburn. The question of where he and his wife were to live inevitably arose, and Frances said that it was not to be in the old homestead. Henry invited them anyway, but Clarence had bought a house before he knew what his uncle had in mind. "Men are strange," wrote Frances to her sister. "Clarence writes that he would have accepted the offer had he not made the purchase previous to receiving his uncle's letter. *It would have been pleasant.*"

Family responsibilities and Seward's own propensity for free spending meant heavy financial outlays. "Great leaks," to use his own expression, absorbed his means, but somehow the necessary funds always came to hand. His law practice gave him all the work he could handle outside of his senatorial duties, and in the early 1850s two other sources of revenue appeared. Judge Miller succumbed to gout and old age in November 1851, and his will provided that the Auburn homestead and two-thirds of the residual estate should go to Frances, the other third to her sister. These latter bequests consisted of property in land on the outskirts of Auburn. Seward bought additional property and began dividing the whole into village lots. These were either disposed of outright or houses were constructed, house and lot being sold at around $700. By May 1854 he had a booming real estate operation, which became increasingly profitable with the years. Seward's Chautauqua affairs also reached a settlement that left him with clear title to some 3000 acres of land and between $55,000 and $60,000 in mortgages and contracts, from all of which he derived a comfortable income. By the middle 1850s his finances had improved so much that he no longer had to devote all his time outside the Senate to arduous legal work. This was fortunate, for he would soon be caught up in a savage political storm.[15]

᪥ II ᪥

Twilight of the Whigs

During the year that followed the election of 1852, Seward's speeches in the Senate, save for a spirited defense of protection for iron manufacturers, were concerned primarily with foreign affairs. Manifest Destiny was still an article of faith, especially in the slave-holding states. The acquisition of California and the settlement of the Oregon boundary had made the United States a Pacific power. Schemes of expansion abounded, whether of trade with the Orient, extension of American territory in Mexico and Central America, or the acquisition of Cuba, and they produced spirited debates.

Seward was anxious to promote American commercial activity in the Pacific region. An ardent exponent of a transcontinental railroad, he saw its iron bands as not only uniting the American East and West but also as affording a means of providing national communication with the Orient. But he viewed with suspicion and dislike any projects for expansion that would involve an increase of slave territory. He admitted that the safety of the southern states required a "watchful jealousy" of the pressure of European Powers in Central America and the exercise by the United States of "a paramount influence in the affairs of the nations situated in this hemisphere," but he was not at all interested in clearing the way for expansion southward of slavery.

The consequences of this attitude speedily became obvious. Others might become excited about Britain's sinister designs in

Honduras and demand American intervention in that part of the hemisphere, but Seward took a very temperate view of British policy in Central America. He was equally cool to the idea about a right of transit across the Isthmus of Tehuantepec, for he thought that such a move involved the danger of a speedy acquisition of all Mexico by the American government. As for Cuba, he felt that island, like Mexico, must eventually become a part of the United States, but he saw no urgent need for its annexation and did not see how he could vote for its acquisition until its slaves became free. His fear of slavery expansion also led him to oppose the Gadsden Treaty of 1853, by which the United States acquired the lowest pass over the southern Rocky Mountains.

In two public addresses that same year Seward let his vision range into the future. A grand prospect lay before the United States, he declared at the dedication of Capital University in Columbus, Ohio. The country was united in spirit, for the strongest public passion in all the states was loyalty to the Union. The nation was also steadily expanding its power and influence. There was no foreign foe of whom to be afraid, and Canada, already half-annexed, would ultimately become a member of the Union if allowed to do so. The urge for freedom that was paramount in this country characterized men everywhere, and if the United States preserved the principles bequeathed to it by the founding fathers, if its material advancement was paralleled by intellectual and moral achievement, its borders would ultimately extend from the tropics to the polar circle, and thus it would take its place among the few great states that have exercised a commanding influence upon world history.

A speech he made in New York before a society devoted to sponsoring a protective tariff took as its theme American progress in the arts and civilization. This must be achieved, Seward declared, through that individual independence which, "when it pervades the whole state is national independence." His fellow countrymen had the least excuse of all peoples for lacking this quality and the greatest need for achieving and maintaining it. They were homogeneous and self-sufficient, geographically and economically, and also sprang from pure and gentle ancestors. Their nation was new and vigorous, with constitutions and laws that established political equality and that, by preventing monopolies of land and great accumulations of wealth, also operated to produce social equality. A vigorous, vital people, they were never satisfied with the present and were continually changing old laws, customs, and constitutions.

But the American people were not perfect. Too much racial and political intolerance existed among them, too much dependence upon foreign goods and foreign cultures. They should develop their own virtues and opportunities, and in so doing take "the first place in the great family of nations." Then, addressing himself specifically to the members of the society before which he spoke, he attacked free trade and made an appeal for building an ever greater and diversified economy under the shelter of a protective tariff.[1]

In these speeches, Seward gave slavery only passing mention, for he was still being cautious about emphasizing the issue. He told Frances that for her to become an active and open abolitionist would do the cause more harm than good. His own actions as a politician, so he wrote to Theodore Parker, must be tempered by the winds of public opinion. Nevertheless, he continued to make clear in a variety of ways his hostility to slavery. "I did not fail to note the concluding words. Good!" wrote Charles Sumner in praising a Niagara Falls speech which Seward concluded with an appeal for the maintenance of justice and the extension of liberty. The New York Senator also kept his anti-slavery position before the public when he avowed his readiness to serve in defense of the Jerry rescuers, who were threatened with prosecution by the federal government.

The second volume of Julia Griffith's *Autographs for Freedom* had as its first number a short piece by W. H. Seward entitled "Be Up and Doing." All lovers of freedom and the rights of man, he said, should see to it that the following principles were taught in the homes, schools, and churches of the land. Caste prejudice must be overcome; the fugitive slave should be received and defended "as you would your household gods"; congressional action could ameliorate slavery. If this course was followed with moderation and benevolence, he declared, the southern states would ultimately be brought to renounce slavery. Even Frederick Douglass began to see Seward as one of the true friends of the oppressed, and evidence to this effect mounted in the months ahead.

While Seward sought to show that he was an honest and principled opponent of slavery, he and Weed worked hard and effectively to strengthen their hold on the Whig party in New York State. The Whig state convention of 1853 was a tribute to Weed's management and to the anti-slavery feeling of the Whig rank and file. Only one Silver Gray, Ogden Hoffman, gained a place on the ticket. After it was over, the New York *Herald* observed bitterly that the Whig abolitionist party was in the ascendant, with Seward as its master spirit. He had great skill and talent, the *Herald* admitted, and was headed for the Presidency in 1856.[2] The state election, a Weed-Seward triumph, gave weight to this prediction, but now came a development in Congress that was to have momentous consequences for parties, politicians, and the nation itself.

Early in January 1854, Stephen A. Douglas, chairman of the committee on territories in the Senate, reported a bill providing for organization of the territories of Kansas and Nebraska, a huge portion of the Louisiana Purchase. Seward wrote at once to Frances that the measure in its earliest form (which left clouded the status slavery would have in those territories) went as far as the Democrats dared to go toward repealing the Missouri Compromise of 1820, which had settled that all lands above the 36°30′ line should be forever free. Seward promised grimly that he would do his duty in the matter.

There is evidence that Seward did more than his duty during the hectic weeks that followed Douglas's first proposal. Talk of destroying the Missouri Compromise was at once in the air, and on January 8 Seward wrote to Weed that he hoped to get Clayton to lead the opposition to any such move. Then another thought occurred to him, or so he later declared. Would it not be politically advantageous to make the Democracy go the whole distance and commit itself to repeal of the Compromise of 1820? It was evident that anti-slavery Senators wished to make the Douglas bill as objectionable as possible by way of amendment, and Seward, as he subsequently told both Charles Francis Adams and Montgomery Blair, went to Whig Senators Dixon of Kentucky and Jones of Tennessee and suggested that it would be a good party stroke to propose outright repeal of the Compromise. One of them, presumably Dixon, who was pro-slavery as well as Whig, exclaimed, according to Seward, "By God, that's a good thought. I'll do it." Shortly thereafter Dixon gave notice in the Senate of his intent to offer such an amendment;

southern Democrats as well as Whigs took it up; and Douglas, under pressure, finally consented to incorporate the repeal in his bill, though commenting wryly that it would "raise a hell of a storm." [3]

The Kansas-Nebraska bill, in its final form, not only repealed the Missouri Compromise, but also took away from Congress and gave to the people of those territories the right to decide all local questions pertaining to slavery. It was a fateful measure, rousing a storm of indignation in the North that increased when, on January 24, Chase, Giddings, and others issued an "Appeal of the Independent Democrats in Congress to the People of the United States," a highly emotional arraignment coupled with allusions to a "monstrous plot" aimed at extending slavery throughout all the trans-Mississippi West. The South rallied with equal warmth to the support of the bill, and contenders on both sides gathered their forces for a four months' long debate in Congress.

When the Appeal was first published, Seward was listed as one of the signers. The mistake was a natural one, for he had already swung into vigorous opposition. He urged Weed to foster public meetings and legislative resolutions opposing the measure, and tried to foment division in the South by urging southern Whigs to oppose repeal of the Missouri Compromise; he wrote to a protest meeting of northern merchants that the surrender of the New Mexico vantage ground in 1850 had furnished the basis for the proposed extension of slavery to Kansas and Nebraska, and that the North might well have to fight for freedom in the whole Far Northwest; and he began working strenuously on a speech that would put him among the leaders in opposition to the measure.

On January 30, Douglas opened debate on the bill, while Chase, Sumner, and Seward marshaled the meager forces of the anti-Nebraska men in the Senate. Seward spoke for three hours on the afternoon of February 17. It was private bill day and few had expected a major effort, but when word got around that Seward had taken the floor the galleries soon filled up. Chase, Sumner, Judah P. Benjamin of Louisiana, John Bell of Tennessee, and other Senators listened attentively; Douglas and his supporters bustled about or ostentatiously left the chamber. The speaker's voice was low, his physical appearance unimpressive, but some happy spell, he told his wife, seemed to come over him, and he spoke with more ease and freedom than ever before.

Carefully he sketched the history of American slavery—its first footholds, the efforts of the forefathers to prevent its spread, the attempt to find a *modus vivendi* with it through the compromises of 1820 and 1850. Now a bill had come "bowing, stooping and wriggling into the Senate" that violated both those agreements. It was a measure of transcendent importance, for the extension of slavery into Kansas and Nebraska would endanger communication of the free states with the Far West, would ominously increase the power of the slave states in the federal government, and might well endanger the Union itself. The slavocracy was already pushing toward Central America and Cuba. What territories would be safe from its insatiable desire for power?

The bill, said Seward, illustrated the eternal conflict "between conservatism and progress, between truth and error, between right and wrong." He demonstrated with powerful logic that the Compromise of 1850 had not superseded that of 1820; that compromise in any form had proved to be only a temporary palliative in this struggle. The Wilmot Proviso had continued to stalk the halls of Congress, and now the South itself had broken the compromises it had gained. The supporters of the bill claimed they wanted peace as well as victory. The latter they might have, but not the former, for the anti-slavery forces of the North would continue the struggle for freedom, their numbers and their strength were on the increase, and they had supporting them "a higher Power" that would bring the still distant but inevitable triumph "of the equal and universal liberty of all men." [4]

Seward was on doubtful ground in depicting the danger of slavery expanding into the Far Northwest, though many northerners shared this fear. He was at his best in arguing that the Compromise of 1820 had validity, despite the threat now centered upon it, and in demonstrating the futility of the hope that any compromise could check the conflict between slavery and freedom.

Anti-Nebraska men of various shades of opinion—the smug and power-hungry abolitionist Sumner, the timid compromiser Edward Everett, the cautiously conservative Hamilton Fish, and Weed, the canny politician—united in praising Seward's speech. William

Herndon wrote from Springfield that Seward's popularity in Illinois was growing fast, and that "Mr. Lincoln my partner and your friend . . . thinks your speech most excellent." Other letters poured in, amounting to what Frances called "a torrent of applause." But Douglas, Toombs, and the fire-eaters of the South abused him as a perverter of facts, a man guilty of "pertinacious misrepresentations." Seward, said A. P. Butler of South Carolina, was a man who pretended to be in direct communication with divinity but was "like the condor that soars in the frozen regions of ethereal purity, yet lives on garbage and putrefaction."

Despite the efforts of its opponents, the Kansas-Nebraska bill ground on through the legislative mill. Overwhelming southern support, the energetic leadership of Douglas, and the backing of President Pierce more than offset the efforts of its opponents. The first triumph of its advocates came on March 4 after an all-night session of the Senate. Douglas, rough, dynamic, quick to spot weaknesses in his opponents' logic, his "God damns" and "by Gods" audible in the galleries, dominated the proceedings. "Ah, you can't crawl behind that free nigger dodge," he told Seward, who had offered an explanation at one point in the debate, and it may have been at this time that Seward made the remark later credited to him—"Douglas, no man who spells Negro with two gs will ever be elected President of the United States."

The vote was 37 to 14 for the passage of the bill. Then the weary Senators trooped down the Capitol steps, while southern sympathizers jubilantly fired cannon from the adjoining terrace. "They celebrate a present victory," said Chase to Sumner, "but the echoes they awake will never rest till slavery itself shall die." [5]

Seward felt much as Chase did about the situation. He told Theodore Parker that the tide was changing, the spirit of freedom was awake, and those opposed to slavery would thenceforth speak with more boldness and with greater effect. Parker and himself were not far apart, he added, even though their temperaments and perhaps their hopes were somewhat different. Anxiously he watched the struggle in the House, where the rising tide of opposition to the bill got in its work and the northern Whigs and half the northern Democrats stood firm against passage. The House was about equally divided, pro and con, and when the two sides held caucuses they

were attended without distinction of party. It was common talk on
Capitol Hill that, if the Missouri line went, past lines of party
division would follow.[6]

The bill passed the House on May 22 by a vote of 113 to 100 and,
as amended, came back to the Senate, where its final passage was
certain. Seward was one of the speakers in the last hours of the
struggle. Freedom, he said, was suffering a severe but not a final
blow. He was "quite sure" that slavery could at most get no more
than Kansas, since Nebraska's soil and climate were unfavorable to
southern crops. Even Kansas was doubtful, for free soil settlers would
throng into the territory, "and God give victory to the side which is
stronger in numbers as it is in right." The fundamental antagonism
between slavery and freedom must end in a separation of the slave
and free states, or in victory for one side or the other. Yet it could
not end in separation, for the ties that bound the Union together
could not be broken by any voluntary secession, either of the North
or of the South. The day of compromises was past, and from now
on the great questions at issue between the two social orders would
be decided on their merits and not by "bargains of equivocal
prudence, if not of doubtful morality." Hopefully he pointed to the
increasing northern majority in the House, and to the growing split
in the Democratic party over slavery.

Seward acknowledged that he had borrowed some of the ideas in
this speech from Theodore Parker, but its optimism must have been
surprising to Parker, for it certainly was to others. The Boston
Unitarian divine was beginning to think that civil war was inevitable, and Edward Everett told Seward that he himself was in
despair at the way in which southern extremists were playing into
the hands of those of the North. Even Henry Raymond, who had
been encouraged by Seward's speech—"I had no idea such a rain-
bow could be hung out on such a cloud"—was forced to add that he
was not as loyal to the Union as Seward, and that freedom was a
loftier ambition than empire.[7]

On May 25 the Kansas-Nebraska Act passed the Senate, 35 to 13.
President Pierce signed it and it became the law of the land.

As Congress closed its sessions in June 1854 Seward wrote an
"Address to the People of the United States" for the members of
Congress, irrespective of party, opposed to the Kansas-Nebraska

bill. This manifesto gave an account of the rise of slavery and of the way in which the North had repeatedly submitted to the extension of slave territory. Both parties in 1852 had deprecated any renewal of the slavery agitation, but now the Pierce administration was responsible for the Kansas-Nebraska Act and the turmoil that was sweeping the land. There was evidence that the administration and the representatives of the slave states were planning the annexation of Cuba, half a dozen states in northern Mexico, Santo Domingo, and an alliance with Brazil and the extension of slavery in the valley of the Amazon. The public would have to judge whether slavery, having made these additions to the United States, would then demand unconditional submission by the free states or, failing that, would attempt to withdraw the slave states from the Union and then organize a separate empire. "We appeal to no sectional spirit," said the Address. "We appeal equally to the North and to the South. . . . It is no time for exaggeration or for passion." The signers pledged themselves to do all in their power to restore the Missouri Compromise, and to take such measures for the recovery of the ground lost by freedom and for the prevention of further aggressions by slavery as an aroused people might demand.

The Address made charges difficult to substantiate, but its tone was temperate. Frances thought it lukewarm, but her husband hoped that its dignity and moderation would win support in both sections and strengthen the cause of freedom. At the same time, he urged Theodore Parker to continue his attacks upon slavery. "Just so fast as you can awaken the public conscience," he told Parker, "just so fast shall I be willing to cooperate in the reforms it shall demand," and added that he would do what he could to help in the awakening by resisting in Congress the further designs of the Slave Power.[8]

The Kansas-Nebraska Act came in the midst of signs that a major political reorganization was at hand. The virtual collapse of the Whig party of the South in 1852 had been one evidence of this impending change; another was the growing conflict over slavery, splitting party lines in the North; a third was the appearance in the early 1850s of a host of minor parties and factions—Temperance, People's, Fusion, Conscience and Cotton Whigs, Hard and Soft Democrats, a spectacle bound to obfuscate the voting population.

One perspicacious observer remarked that he would not be surprised to see a spectrum of political and social opinions grouped together, with Gerrit Smith, Martin Van Buren's son "Prince" John, Frederick Douglass, and Seward marching hand in hand. He was nearer right than he knew.

In the midst of this political confusion came the rapid rise of the American, or Know-Nothing party. Chronic American fears of Catholics and foreigners were given marked impetus as churchmen renewed their demands for public support of parochial schools, while hundreds of thousands of German and Irish immigrants entered the job market. President Pierce, it was widely held, had been elected by the votes of foreigners, and as the Whigs saw their party collapse they went over to the Know-Nothings by the thousands. North and South, the members of this new political movement differed over slavery extension, the tariff, internal improvements and land policy, but they organized nevertheless as a national party. The Know-Nothings were also a vast secret society, with passwords and degrees, grips, signs, and a solemn initiation. If one brother wished to inquire of another the object of a particular mass meeting, he would say "Have you seen Sam?" and would then receive the desired information. This rigmarole fascinated thousands of American citizens.[9]

The Know-Nothing movement's meteoric rise was paralleled by another and far more enduring political development. The Kansas-Nebraska Act produced a political explosion in the North, for millions of voters believed that it presaged a movement of slavery into vast areas beyond the Mississippi. Many had moral convictions about slavery, others hoped for free land, tariff protection, internal improvements, or financial reforms, all of which were opposed by the South. As if by magic, hundreds of committees formed, city and state conventions were held, Free-Soil Leagues and anti-Nebraska clubs sprouted up, and state political parties committed to the defense of freedom appeared. Out of this spontaneous movement emerged the Republican party, taking its name from the party formed by that critic of slavery, Thomas Jefferson.

Seward viewed these political developments with deep concern, for his future was at stake. His correspondents began urging him to cut loose from the Whig organization. Greeley wanted him to do so;

"Oh! I do long for *Union* among men who think substantially alike," wrote Charles Sumner; and Henry Wilson told Seward that, if Seward would abandon the idea of preserving the national Whig party, there was no man in the country whom he would do more to aid in becoming President.

But Seward still hesitated. Prominent though he was in the anti-slavery crusade, and no stranger to shifts in political allegiance, he still held back because of a variety of considerations. The success of the new movement could not be predicted with any degree of certainty. If successful, it would likely gather to itself other reforming groups, and would necessitate co-operation not only with anti-slaveryites but also with temperance folk, who regarded him with suspicion, and anti-Nebraska Know-Nothings, who held him in abhorrence. Then, too, as he confessed to Charles Sumner, he had a prejudice against Democrats, especially New York Democrats. Finally, there was the problem of timing, an important element in any politician's plan of action.

Gloomy after the election of 1852, Seward had for once thought seriously of retiring from public life. This was his "fixed purpose," he told Alvah Hunt the following May, and their mutual friends had so understood it ever since Pierce's inauguration. But that fall the New York Whigs won majorities in both houses of the state legislature and, as always when party prospects were looking up, his political hopes revived. He would, in all probability, be up for re-election in 1855. The New York State Whig party, though by no means a stable quantity, was more attractive as a base of operations than this burgeoning Republicanism, a movement that the New York merchant class viewed with anxiety and that might prove to be evanescent. Seward's political instincts urged caution and, though he was "plagued to death with letters asking about disbanding and reorganizing," he remained uncommitted to the new course. Weed did the same. For a season, at least, both men wanted to keep the New York State Whig party intact.[10]

While Seward considered the collapse of the party and its implications, he busied himself in many other ways. He denounced Pierce for vetoing a bill granting 10,000,000 acres of the public domain to the states for relief of the indigent insane, a measure sponsored by Dorothea Lynde Dix. He urged passage of a homestead law, defended the rights of immigrants, and attacked Know-Nothingism. That summer he told the Yale Phi Beta Kappa that America's democratic principles were among the chief reasons for the nation's already being a World Power with a glorious future. And all the while he was anxiously watching the New York State political situation.

Some influential Whigs wanted Seward to run for governor in 1854, but he was reluctant to do so, and Weed was certain that the Maine-Law question would be fatal to him. The temperance people were active, and Seward had long ago forgotten the abstinence pledge that he took in 1842. Furthermore, the political situation in the state looked extremely uncertain.

For in New York State, as well as in the nation at large, the Whig party was well-nigh a shattered lamp. In August 1854 a Saratoga gathering of Old Whigs, Old Democrats, abolitionists, and free-soilers heralded the birth of a Republican party. Fillmore men were moving into the Know-Nothing organization, though many Silver Grays and Know-Nothings, too, were still active in the decimated Whig ranks. Prohibitionists had become noisy and powerful. Weed-Seward henchmen, dubbed Choctaws, infiltrated the Know-Nothing units in various localities, but Weed was uncertain of his power to control events. He went to the Whig state convention fearful that a Silver Gray-Know-Nothing combination might get second, or even first, place on the ticket. In the end, Myron H. Clark, a Whig dry and supposedly a Know-Nothing, was the nominee for governor, with Henry J. Raymond, editor of the New York *Times*, as his running mate.

The Know-Nothing standard bearer was Daniel Ullman, an erstwhile Whig whose alleged birth in India of German-Jewish parentage resulted in his New York followers being dubbed the "Hindoos." The only bright spot in the picture, from the Weed-Seward point of view, was that the Democrats, Hard and Soft, nominated separate tickets, and that the Saratoga convention reassembled in Auburn and endorsed the Whig slate. In the outcome, Clark won a narrow victory, and the legislature went heavily Whig in both branches. But many Whigs were Know-Nothings in disguise, and the situation at the state capital was confused and uncertain.[11]

Seward had a busy law practice during the fall of 1854 and took no active part in the campaign, though he doubtless gave advice about candidates. Ullman drew a heavy vote on election day, and Seward in disgust foresaw another year or two of nativist hysteria. "Sam" was a troublesome problem, and so, it now developed, was Horace Greeley.

The partnership of Weed, Seward, and Greeley had been in existence some fourteen years and it had not been an altogether smooth relationship. The squeaky-voiced editor had a tendency to go off on tangents, such as Fourieristic social experiments, and he had only contempt for political expediency; but his moral earnestness and his marvelous pen were great assets to the senior partners. By 1854, however, Greeley was in a querulous frame of mind. He did not like the way that Weed was running the party, for he wanted to plunge forthwith into Republicanism; he was bitterly critical of that "Little Villain," Raymond, who had set up a rival newspaper that was eating into the *Tribune*'s circulation, and who, Greeley felt, was being unduly favored by Seward and Weed; he had also developed an itch for office which Weed showed no disposition to gratify.

The crisis came with the election of 1854. Greeley, himself a dry, wanted either first or second place on the ticket, but the convention ended with that temperance reformer and "bogus Know-Nothing" Clark for governor with, of all people, Raymond as his running mate. Greeley had had enough.

The *Tribune* went down the line for Clark, but its editor was in a bitter frame of mind. Toward the close of the campaign he wrote a grumbling letter to Seward in which he said that he wanted to know about plans for the future. If there were none, he would try to form a plan of some sort for himself. On November 11, after the narrow Whig victory, he wrote again to Seward and withdrew from the triumvirate. The letter showed plainly his jealousy and his sense of neglect. It also indicated his appreciation of Seward's legal services and his intention to help in the campaign for re-election to the Senate. "I trust I shall never be found in opposition to you," he said at the close.

Seward was disturbed by Greeley's outburst, which was, he wrote to Weed, "full of sharp pricking thorns." Greeley was difficult, but he had a basic "nobleness of disposition," and it was a shame to see him so unhappy. Could not something be done for him? Perhaps he could be put on the Board of Regents.

Seward had an interview with the disgruntled editor that emphasized the depth of the latter's unhappiness, but a second letter struck a more resigned note. To all appearances the storm had blown over, and Seward thought that the partnership was still in operation. Some years later, Henry B. Stanton, visiting in Auburn, asked the Senator if it would not have been better to let Greeley have an office. Seward puffed out a blue cloud of cigar smoke, the while gazing intently at his visitor, and then replied, "I don't know but it would." [12]

The state election decided, all political elements made ready for the battle over Seward's re-election. Both Silver Grays and Know-Nothings vowed to defeat him, and Weed knew that it would be a battle. There was a momentary falling out between Weed and Seward. Some cautionary words by Weed, about becoming a perennial candidate for a White House which he might never occupy, ruffled Seward, who declared that he would at once decline being a candidate—and then took back his words. His temperamental friend once again in line, Weed concentrated on preparations for the fight.

The contest involved chiefly the Sewardites on the one hand and the Know-Nothings and Silver Grays on the other, for the Democrats were a feeble element in both houses of the legislature. Always resourceful when the odds were against him, Weed worked with his customary energy and skill. To keep anti-Nebraska spirit at fever pitch, the Albany *Evening Journal* published excerpts from the Richmond *Whig* blasting Seward as a menace to the nation. Under the spell of Weed's seductive influence, so many Know-Nothings voted for Seward in the Whig legislature caucuses that the Know-Nothing Councils sent thugs to Albany in a vain effort to keep their errant legislators in line. Weed also took full advantage of the opposition's inability to agree upon a single candidate. On February 6, the balloting showed Seward the victor by clear majorities in both houses. The legislature then met in joint session, Lieutenant-Governor Raymond declared the result, and a great roar of applause shook the rafters of the capitol.

Jabez D. Hammond, when convinced of the certainty of Seward's triumph, declared that he was the choice of 99 per cent of the state electorate and 95 per cent of the Democrats. This was a touch exuberant, but there can be no doubt that the result met with popular approval.[13]

The victor's Albany partisans fired 300 cannon, or at least cannon shots, and held a joyous Hindoo funeral ceremony. Seward's home town, not to be outdone, celebrated with 700 cannon shots. Congratulations flooded in, Democrats vying with Whigs in their approval. Abram S. Hewitt and Peter Cooper wrote from New York that they were pleased with the victory of a man of principle —and an advocate of protection for iron manufacturers. Theodore Parker sent his congratulations, and the wish that Seward's next six years might be as honorable and productive as the last, "nay, even more so, for the experience gives you additional power, moral as well as intellectual." Seward was now the most powerful man in the Senate, said Parker, and they would all look to him for great things. Most of the letters of congratulation, whether from within or without the state, showed deep hostility to slavery and a conviction that its expansion must be checked.

Seward was elated by his re-election. He had left all the labor to Weed, and now he wrote to Albany, expressing his gratitude and his amazement at his friend's sagacity and skill in the face of what was practically an oath-bound majority bent on defeating their "hopes for the benefit of our state, our country and mankind." He knew that he would need all of Weed's wisdom in the years that lay ahead.

Seward's happiness was not unalloyed, however. Frances, nerve-wracked and despondent, had been too ill that winter to go to Washington. She had followed the course of the contest and had heard the roar of the cannon celebrating victory, but her heart was heavy. Washington had become almost unbearable to her, and congratulations from Blatchford—"I wish my wife had such a husband"—were like seed sown on stony ground. She could not bring herself to write until a letter from Henry—"either you do not speak or else the words have frozen on the way"—brought what seemed to him eloquent and wise comment on the election.[14] Seward had set his eyes on the White House, and for Frances the future held little promise of joy.

⊰ 12 ⊱

A Frustrated Republican

Seward was in high spirits after his triumphant re-election, and he played a prominent role in the Senate during the closing weeks of the Thirty-third Congress. Free homestead and protective tariff bills, generous pensions for veterans, subsidization for the Collins steamship line and for a transcontinental railroad—these projects had Seward's support. His most notable effort, however, was an assault upon the fugitive slave law.

A bill came before the Senate for the protection of officers and other persons representing the United States. It proposed to transfer suits involving those who sought to apprehend fugitive slaves from state to federal courts, and the anti-slavery Senators became engaged in acrimonious debate with the supporters of the measure.

Seward spoke on February 23. He used the occasion to refute Douglas's sneer that he owed his re-election to the Know-Nothings by a lengthy and grandiloquent denial of connection with that or any other secret organization, but the burden of his speech concerned the measure in question. The bill, he said, was one more concession to the Slave Power, and those who opposed it were, as usual, being showered with denunciations, calumnies, and epithets. There was no necessity for such an act of federal aggrandizement at the expense of the states. All this furor was due to the fugitive slave law, which suspended the writ of habeas corpus, denied the right of trial by jury, and was unfair to the fugitive. Neither it nor any harsher law could be enforced. Once more, as so often in times past, he urged compensated emancipation upon the South.[1]

This speech fairly represented Seward's attitude toward a law that was becoming more than ever unenforceable in the North after the passage of the Kansas-Nebraska Act and the appearance of the Republican movement. That movement was well advanced by the summer of 1855, and Republican mass meetings in a number of states invited him to join in their deliberations. Still cautious and reluctant, he declined such participation, and it was Weed who saw at length that "the necessity for getting into line with other states is imperative." Weed did successful spade work in New York City, though Hamilton Fish was recalcitrant and at the other end of the state Washington Hunt refused to go along. Late in September 1855, Whig and Republican conventions met on the same day in Syracuse; the Whigs moved over into the hall occupied by the Republicans, and together they named a state Republican ticket.

Seward had kept in touch with these preliminaries. He told an Orange County delegate, perplexed as to which convention he should attend, that it made no difference; they would go in by two doors and come out by one. But his heart was heavy, for he had cherished the dream of maintaining the national Whig party on a moderate anti-slavery platform, and he had no illusions about the difficulties that lay ahead. The revolution had been inaugurated, he said, but it would proceed slowly, unevenly, and with difficulty. They were only at the beginning of the end for slavery. Political reformations in a democracy should allow the people time to appreciate their worth, and the sponsors of such movements must calculate on many disturbances and caprices.

The new party having been formed, Seward spoke in its behalf that fall at both Albany and Buffalo. They were engaged, he said, in a struggle for freedom, equality, and justice against a privileged class of slaveholders. The power of this class was everywhere, and Republicans ought to contend with it on a national level and should never forget that they should always be faithful to the Constitution, the Union, and the rights of man. They must rescue Kansas and see to it that hereafter only free states were admitted to the Union. There need be no fear of secession. Patriotic and economic ties, as well as fear of a servile war, a slave rebellion, bound the South fast to the Union.

Fanatical abolitionists criticized Seward for refusing to support any interference with slavery in the slave states, except by constitutional methods, but the speech pleased Charles Sumner so much that he read part of it aloud to the Longfellows, who joined him in approbation. Kentucky abolitionist Cassius Clay also was jubilant. He wrote, "You'll soon be as much a 'Fanatic' as myself! Good." [2]

Much to Seward's disgust, the Know-Nothings showed great strength in New York State that fall. They polled more votes than any of the other three parties and elected thirty-nine members of the state assembly. But he refused to be disheartened. It was enough, he said, to have kept Republicanism from pollution by this fanaticism. Like a balloon filled with gas, Know-Nothingism was bound to come down, and quickly.

Seward challenged the spirit of both Know-Nothingism and slavery in a speech that December at Plymouth before the Pilgrim society. It was a tribute to reform and reformers. The Pilgrims, he declared, had come from a Europe that, though teeming with change and progress, showed signs of slipping into reaction. They believed themselves to be God's chosen emissaries on earth, and they appealed to the law of God and Nature as their highest authority. Firm and unwavering, scorners of compromise, they sought to establish a better life for themselves and for all mankind. From their teachings and their example there derived in America the inviolability of the right of conscience, the right of all men to political equality, the absolute separation of church and state, and the great principle of republican government. The Puritans were reformers who wrought in toil and suffering, and their efforts had borne fruits they scarcely dreamed of. We should take courage from their example and recognize that progress in society and government, though slow, is not only possible but certain, and that the primary objective of American patriots is the preservation of that freedom which is the soul of the republic.

This tribute to the Pilgrim Fathers reflected fully Seward's higher aspirations, and the New Englanders greeted it with approval. As Theodore Parker and Wendell Phillips listened to it, wrote the former, they felt "that you were erecting a tower of strength for humanity." Even the crusty Charles Francis Adams, savagely critical of Seward two years before, wrote that, in these degenerate days, it was a consolation to pick up a diamond from the dross that littered the streets.[3]

After the Plymouth oration, Seward returned to Washington, where he was on the commerce, Pacific railroad, and pensions committees of the Thirty-fourth Congress. There, early in the session, he introduced a bill for a Pacific railroad, and a little later earned the gratitude of writers for his aid in the passage of a Dramatic Authors' Copyright Act. His first major speech of the session discussed the Central American question.

As Americans pushed into the Far West and gold poured out of California, the American people became keenly aware of the need for contact with that region. One possible route of travel lay across Central America, and there Britain had a protectorate over the Mosquito Indians on the east coast of Nicaragua, and claimed Belize, or British Honduras, as a crown colony. Any indication that Britain planned to extend these holdings was bound to create tensions in the American capital.

In 1850, the two nations signed the Clayton-Bulwer Treaty, a mutual agreement never to establish or maintain exclusive control over the Nicaragua canal route, never to build fortifications near it, and never to colonize or exert dominion over Nicaragua, the Mosquito Coast, or any part of Central America. The United States claimed that this meant Great Britain would surrender the holdings she already had in Central America. At the same time, President Pierce, much under the influence of southern expansionists, looked the other way while William Walker, a southern adventurer and filibuster, made himself dictator of Nicaragua. The British Foreign Office, on its part, viewed Walker's exploits as evidence of American aggressive designs in the Isthmus area. Britain also stoutly maintained that the Clayton-Bulwer Treaty applied only to the acquisition of new territories and protectorates, not to the existing situation.

When reports reached the United States during the winter of 1855–56 that Her Majesty's government was expanding its controls in Central America, Senators became much alarmed. They invoked the Monroe Doctrine and threatened the use of force against Great

Britain if she did not fulfill the obligations of the treaty. The diplomatic corps in Washington feared that an Anglo-American war was imminent.

Seward took part in the debate over the Central American situation for two reasons. He shared the general concern over Britain's intentions. He also wished to delay as much as possible the impending debate over the chaotic situation in Kansas, for the House was still trying to elect a Speaker, and the Republicans there were in a disorganized state. He realized that relations with Great Britain were in a parlous state, but he would try, he told Weed, to walk on eggs without breaking them. He took the floor on January 31.

He began with the assertion that it was necessary to review the American position for,

> If it is right, we cannot recede without dishonor, never to be incurred. If it is wrong, we cannot recede too soon. If we shall not recede, we may involve our country in no common war— an evil to be avoided if possible, consistently with duty. I shall therefore take care not to say, consciously, anything that might tend to inflame our own country, or to exasperate Great Britain.

As he always did when speaking on foreign affairs, Seward went into a careful survey of the historical background of the dispute. He praised the Clayton-Bulwer Treaty which, he declared must be maintained at all costs. Britain was violating that agreement, and American alarm was justified. He deplored the possibility of war with a "fraternal state" and potential champion of freedom, especially one that was fighting in the Crimea against Russian despotism, but we could not yield our determination that the British government cease the expansion of its power in Central America. Neither could we propose arbitration without weakening our case. We must adhere to our position, casting the responsibility for peace or war upon our adversary. He proposed giving notice to Great Britain that the United States would "interfere to prevent her exercise of dominion in South America, if it shall not be discontinued within one year. . . ." Having given this notice, he would then "go to the very verge of accommodation."

If war came, Seward declared, it would be fought in Canada,

which could not refuse annexation if tendered "on just terms." But he predicted that without war on our part Great Britain would "wisely withdraw and disappear from this hemisphere" within twenty-five, or perhaps fifty years. Britain was the center of a European, as we were of an American, system. She had had her day in the Western hemisphere while, "almost in spite of ourselves," we were "steadily extending and increasing our control over these continents." War might hasten but might also delay the period of our undisputed control over the Western world. In preparation for that happy day he urged beginning what was already too long delayed, the building of transcontinental railroads. These were necessities, "for a nation that strikes for continental supremacy must at once render itself self-sustaining and independent."

Senator John M. Clayton, co-author of the Clayton-Bulwer Treaty, wrote that Seward's speech was "an admirable exposure of British chicanery & did you infinite honor." His other correspondents generally applauded the position he had taken, although a Quaker neighbor in central New York thought a word of caution only fitting—"William the must not alow thy Passions to rise to High in Regard to that Clayton & Bulwer affair. But the knows more about thyn own business than I do." The speech was also well received across the water, where the London *Times*, though warning that Britain's defense of her rights would not be affected by defiant speeches or hostile resolutions, declared that it could not complain of the tone in which Seward had discussed the question.[4]

The furor over Central American affairs (which resulted in years of diplomatic negotiation before a satisfactory adjustment was achieved) did not prevent the Senate from turning its attention to Kansas, where a state of disorder prevailed that was almost anarchy. The rapidly growing population of that territory in large measure opposed slavery. Missourians, however, determined not to have another free state as a neighbor, interfered in the territorial elections. In 1855, some 5000 crossed the border into Kansas and elected a pro-slavery legislature which set itself up at Shawnee Mission, just across the Missouri line, and then passed laws punishing any anti-slavery activity with Draconian severity. The free settlers thereupon set up a government of their own at Topeka and drew up a constitution prohibiting slavery in Kansas after July 4, 1857. This was approved by a free-soil vote, practically none of the pro-slavery settlers voting, and the Topeka "government" submitted it to Congress. Kansas now had two rival governments.

President Pierce took the pro-slavery side in the Kansas dispute. He sent a special message to Congress, January 24, 1856, declaring that it was not his duty to preserve the purity of elections in the territory and denouncing the Topeka government as revolutionary and treasonable in tendency. He recommended delay in framing a state constitution until the populace was large enough to constitute a state, and asked for a special appropriation to defray expenses in maintaining order in Kansas.

Seward had letters from Kansas asserting that a large majority of the settlers were opposed to slavery and describing the outrages of the Missourians. He knew that Republican newspapers were fanning popular excitement over what Greeley called the "Border Ruffians," and he saw at first hand how Know-Nothing influence in Congress was trying to water down opposition to Pierce's Kansas policy. The logic of the situation suggested vigorous resistance to slavery extension on the ground of principle, and the use of the Topeka constitution as an issue on which to rally the Republican party in the 1856 election.

Such was the basis of his policy during this hectic session. The House of Representatives with its northern majority was the best hope of the anti-slavery forces, and Seward and other like-minded Senators sought to guard that body against any infringement of its prerogatives by the Senate. They even tried, vainly, to prevent the finance committee of the Senate reporting appropriation bills, on the ground that all measures concerning revenue should properly originate in the lower house of the legislature. And, though a little band, they flung themselves headlong into the battle over Kansas.

In March, Douglas sponsored a bill providing for the admission of Kansas as a state when her population should reach 93,420 and she could send a representative with full powers to Congress. Seward countered with a proposal to admit Kansas at once under the Topeka constitution. Both bills smacked of politics, and both had weaknesses. The Douglas bill gave the governor and the Shawnee Mission legislature control of the territory for what might be a considerable time, and also control of the arrangements for the convention that would draw up the state's constitution. The Seward proposal would give Kansas a constitution made by a legislature that had no legal sanction and that in no sense represented the pro-slavery minority of the population. Furthermore, neither bill had the slightest chance of passage. The Douglas proposal was utterly unacceptable to the House, where the Republicans outnumbered the Democrats and, with Know-Nothing aid, had chosen Nathaniel P. Banks as Speaker. Seward's bill had as little chance in the Senate, where it was anathema to the Democrats.

The New Yorker threw himself with a will into the struggle that at once developed over the two measures. His major speech, on April 9, was a formidable effort in a dubious cause. Stoutly he defended the proceedings of the Topeka legislature as regular and devoid of partisanship, and his denunciation of Pierce for exercising a "foreign tyranny" over the people of Kansas was dramatically effective. As he held up before his colleagues the arraignment of George III in the Declaration of Independence, and in his grave, husky voice read off the list of grievances with variations adapted to the Kansas crisis, the Senate sat in hushed silence, and some in the chamber wept from sheer excitement. He was on stronger ground when he depicted the territory as revolutionized by armed invaders, rather than by the free-soil majority, and when he defended abolitionism as "a slow but irrepressible uprising of principles of natural justice and humanity." The anti-slavery movement, though still in its first century, compared as a force to Christianity in its early stages, while slavery was a waning institution that could only be upheld by bayonets. He adjured the country to abandon "the miserable delusion that we can safely extend empire when we shall become reckless of the obligations of Eternal Justice, and faithless to the interests of universal freedom."

Thousands of copies of this speech sped out across the country in pamphlet form, and it was reprinted in newspapers all over the North. Congratulations flooded into Washington, more than one correspondent expressing the hope that it would carry Seward into the White House. Governor Salmon P. Chase of Ohio wrote in praise of its "splendid argument," adding that "your place hereafter, I trust, will be higher and more conspicuous still." [5]

The running debate over Kansas, acrimonious enough from the

start, was now aggravated by an act of violence. On May 19 and 20, Sumner made a speech in the Senate that became famous for the title that it afterwards bore, "The Crime Against Kansas." It was a vitriolic attack on slavery, Pierce, the Missourians, and on some of the Senator's own colleagues. Vituperation was common in the Senate of that day, but Sumner outdid all the rest. At its close he singled out for special denunciation the state of South Carolina and its Andrew Pickens Butler, called by his admirers the Nestor of the Senate.

Sumner made reference to South Carolina's "shameful imbecility from slavery," and declared that were the state's whole history blotted out there would be small loss to civilization. Kansas would be "a ministering angel to the Republic, when South Carolina, in the cloak of darkness which she hugs, lies howling." He then paid his respects to Butler who, though popular among his colleagues and proud of being a southern gentleman, was no mean hand at scarifying his opponents. Sumner denounced Butler's "loose expectoration" of speech, declaring him incapable of accuracy—"He cannot ope his mouth, but out there flies a blunder."

On May 22, Representative Preston Brooks, Butler's cousin and neighbor in South Carolina, incensed by the insults to his state and to his kinsman, entered an almost deserted Senate chamber and walked up to where Sumner sat at his desk. Brooks struck Sumner over the head with a light but strong gutta percha cane. Sumner, well over six feet in height and long-legged, had difficulty in getting his legs out from under his desk. The blows continued until he wrenched the desk loose from its fastenings and fell, stunned and bleeding, in the aisle. Word of this flashed out over the country, and a great clamor arose, northern opponents of slavery denouncing the assault as a cowardly outrage while southern extremists applauded it as well-merited chastisement.

Before Sumner addressed the Senate he had read his speech to Seward, who advised him to tone it down, omitting personal attacks, but the Massachusetts Senator paid no heed. It had been in many respects outrageous, but Brooks's response had grossly affronted the dignity of the Senate, and now Sumner's colleagues had to determine their proper course of action. On the evening after the attack, the little handful of Republican Senators met at Seward's house and agreed that Henry Wilson, the other Senator from Massachusetts, should raise the point that Brooks had violated the rules and decorum of the Senate.

On May 23, Wilson rose in the Senate chamber, described the assault, and called upon the senior members to take such action as would vindicate the honor and dignity of the Senate. No one stirred. Then Seward offered a resolution that a committee of five Senators be appointed to inquire into the assault and report a statement of the facts and their opinion thereon. The majority promptly amended this resolution so that the committee would be elected, rather than appointed and, needless to say, none but Sumner's political opponents were chosen to serve. A whitewash would obviously follow, and this became clear when the committee reported that the only thing the Senate might do was make complaint to the House about Brooks's action.

In the running debate on this affair during the succeeding weeks, Senator Brown of Mississippi argued that Sumner was personally answerable for his attacks upon South Carolina and Senator Butler and that, since the assault took place when the Senate was not in session, there had been no affront to that body. Suppose, said Brown, that *he* got up in the Senate and said that Seward could not open his mouth without uttering a falsehood. Would not the Senator from New York think it rather mean if Brown did not give him satisfaction for the insult? To this Seward replied that he did not know anything that could be said about the Senator from New York that had not been said about him on the floor of the Senate. He had never called a Senator to order for these remarks. His position had been, and would be that

> A moral, sensible and well-bred man
> Will not affront me and no other can.

Seward deplored the assault upon Sumner, but he was critical of the latter for having provoked it. Frances, on the contrary, felt only bitter indignation. Asked if she thought Brooks would be hanged if Sumner died, she replied that he ought to be hanged now, but that if Sumner did die his assailant's life would not be in danger. Only slaves were punished in Washington for rebelling against their masters, and for them hanging was regarded as too mild a penalty.

The events of that winter, she said, were graven on her soul, "and the certainty that we are all becoming slaves ourselves is not calculated to make the grievance more tolerable." [6]

Alarmed by the rising tide of Republicanism, and the effective use that that party was making of the Kansas turmoil and the caning of Sumner, the Democratic leadership made a final effort to take Kansas out of the presidential campaign. On June 23 Senator Toombs introduced a new version of the Douglas bill, one designed to meet Republican objections. It provided for five commissioners, appointed by the President, to supervise a fair census of residents and registration of voters in the territory, with a constitutional convention to be held in November. Every effort was made by way of amendment to meet Republican objections.

Had settlement of the Kansas troubles been the paramount consideration with both parties, a satisfactory bill could have been constructed, but deep suspicion of Pierce and of Democratic motives, together with the Republicans' awareness of the attractiveness of the Kansas turmoil as a campaign issue, prevented any agreement. Seward deemed the Douglas-Toombs offer "an ingenious dodge," and on July 2, as the bill moved toward passage in the Senate, he charged that the real intent of its proponents was to make Kansas a slave state. It was a compromise, and the day of compromises was past.

Kentucky Senator John J. Crittenden, on whom Clay's mantle had fallen, defended the bill as honest, and criticized Seward for not accepting it when doing so would ensure peace in the distracted territory. Toombs flayed the New York Senator as a conscienceless ranter who traduced and abused those who stood in his way to power. Those who qualify themselves for treason, said Toombs, get Seward's plaudits. Those who stand up for the country get Seward's condemnation—"an honor to be coveted."

Boldly, Seward answered these attacks. He was touched, he declared, by Crittenden's appeal for peace, but he could not compromise principle. By no act of his should slavery be established or extended, or any human being "ever hereafter be made or held a slave." The Douglas-Toombs measure did not go far enough, for the people of a territory where slavery did not legally exist should not be given a choice between slavery and freedom; they needed the guardian care, the counsel, of Congress in establishing the institutions under which they would live. Stubbornly he defended his bill. All Kansans had been invited to participate in voting on the adoption of the Topeka constitution. Many had been alarmed by the Missouri foray; but even so, 1731 had voted for the Topeka document with only 46 opposed. Slavery was disappearing throughout the world, and it was wretched sophistry to charge him with exercising tyranny over the territories because he would deny them "the ruinous privilege of choosing an evil and a curse which no matured State, already exempt from it, will adopt, and which all such states afflicted with it relieve themselves from as speedily as possible!" He would be contented with nothing less than the admission of Kansas under the Topeka constitution.

Seward's argument in this speech was partly motivated by political considerations, but it also made clear his intent to control slavery by means of the ever-growing northern representation in Congress. He looked to Congress to check slavery expansion and, hemming in the peculiar institution by unfriendly legislation, put it in the way of ultimate extinction.

The debate on the Douglas-Toombs bill, replete with charge and countercharge, continued throughout the night. Then the measure passed by a vote of 33 to 12, and the weary Senate adjourned, four hours after sunrise. The measure failed in the House.

The fight over Kansas now took on another aspect. The House inserted in an army appropriation bill a clause forbidding the President to employ the army in enforcing laws passed by the Shawnee Mission legislature. Seward defended the House proposal in a speech that met the approval of former Territorial Governor Reeder, and the controversy continued without the two houses coming to an agreement. Both adjourned *sine die* on August 18, and it was only after Congress had been called back in special session that the House gave in to the Senate on the army bill. The main problem confronting Congress remained unsolved; Kansas was still a territory; and the Republicans had their issue for the campaign.[7]

The excitement over Kansas, the passion roused by the caning of Sumner, the sweeping and continued popularity in the North of Harriet Beecher Stowe's *Uncle Tom's Cabin*, with its vivid portrayal of the evils of slavery, made it obvious that the anti-slavery movement had developed tremendous vote appeal. It was equally apparent that the Republican party, still a congeries of local movements, badly needed a wider organization for combat with the American and Democratic parties on anything like equal terms. This was all the more true since the Know-Nothings, or Native Americans, though still strong, were split on the slavery issue, and the northern wing of the party might be won over to Republicanism.

During the Christmas holidays in 1855, Salmon P. Chase, Francis P. Blair, Sr., Nathaniel Banks, Preston King, and others began preparations for calling a convention to meet at Pittsburgh on Washington's birthday, 1856, and there formally launch the national Republican party. King, acting as an emissary of this group, told Seward that the plan was for a national ticket that was half Republican, half Know-Nothing, and that they wanted him in on the movement. He refused to participate, saying that he was emphatically against any combination with Know-Nothings or Know-Nothing candidates. King said that Weed had told him that Seward did not think of being a candidate, and Seward said that this was true. He told Weed of these developments and was chided for being so precipitate in his refusal to consult, but he remained adamant. Getting mixed up with the Hindoos, he said, was profanation of a good cause. "I mean to keep my record clear," he declared.

Despite his protestation that he was not a candidate, Seward hoped for the Republican nomination. His ambition for the Presidency was never more keen than it was in the early 1850s. He had printed at his own expense hundreds of thousands of copies of his speeches, and Congressional associates, working late into the night, helped him frank and bundle them for distribution throughout the country. In 1853 he published a three-volume edition of his *Works*. Weed disapproved; Greeley doubted the wisdom of publishing before death what a man had said in the course of thirty years; but Seward plunged doggedly ahead, and his editor, George E. Baker, scoured the country for subscribers and other purchasers. In 1855 Baker brought out a one-volume *Life and Works* that was essentially a campaign biography, which sold for one dollar. In January of that same year, the Albany *Evening Journal*, of which Frederick Seward was an associate editor, declared that Henry was the political heir of John Quincy Adams—this with little more basis than a letter from Adams to Seward urging him to uphold the cause of universal freedom.

Seward also had a lengthy list (on which Walt Whitman, for one, asked to be enrolled) of individuals to whom he sent all kinds of government documents—a bid for popularity akin to a modern Senator's report to his constituents and particularly useful in a day when such materials were one of the main sources of information about the doings of the government. These publicity arrangements, together with the great public interest excited by his speeches, helped to enhance his reputation as the outstanding anti-slavery leader in the political arena and would, he hoped, serve as stepping stones to the White House.[8]

By 1856, however, there was a rapidly growing boom for another candidate. John Charles Frémont, a dashing, handsome adventurer, had focused attention upon himself by his explorations in the Far West, his "California Battalion" in the Mexican War, and his elopement with Jessie Benton, daughter of "Old Bullion" Benton, long-time Senator from Missouri. Banks, Henry Wilson, Blair, and a number of newspapers began raising Frémont's standard. Hamilton Fish told Weed that Seward was neither sufficiently national nor sufficiently conservative to be a good candidate, and suggested Frémont on an anti-Nebraska platform. The tide for Frémont was strong and moving toward the full.

Weed played a cautious role as nomination time drew near. He kept telling Seward about the all-importance of the popular will; how essential it was that members of Congress should not take the nomination away from the "People." But he kept watching the Know-Nothings. When northern supporters began leaving that party after it nominated Fillmore for President on a platform that ignored the slavery issue, Weed became convinced that the Republican candidate must be one who would attract rather than repel Know-Nothing votes. He was confirmed in this opinion by Greeley and by John L. Schoolcraft, both of whom felt that nativist prejudice against Seward was too strong and that he should not be thought of for the nomination.

Weed, like Seward, had a long record of opposition to nativism, but he could always co-operate with those who might be useful to him either in his pursuit of money or political victory. His quest for

the former had already taken him into Wall Street, and was probably one reason why he was watching over Democrat Erastus
Corning's interests in the New York legislature while the president
of the New York Central was traveling abroad. As for victory at the
polls, if northern Know-Nothings could be brought into the Republican fold, Weed could lay aside his principles for the sake of a political triumph. He was working closely with Banks and Wilson, both
of whom had risen to prominence by way of Know-Nothing support, and they went along with him in fostering the Frémont
boom.[9]

Seward was in a difficult position. Some of his friends, Webb for
one, insisted that he keep his name before the public, and reports
that scores of delegates from Pennsylvania, New York, Michigan,
and other states in the Old Northwest were eager to vote for him in
the convention whetted his appetite for the nomination. He felt that
Frémont would be a sop to voters who were not ardently anti-
slavery, and that to choose him would weaken the movement for the
immediate admission of Kansas as a free state, but Seward had to
recognize that Republican leadership in Congress leaned strongly to
the Californian. So did the New York *Times* and *Tribune*, papers
which, Seward said bitterly, were demoralizing "the party so far as
to make it willing to reject me." Embarrassed, frustrated, he once
more began to talk about retirement from public life.

The Democratic national convention met at Cincinnati early in
June and nominated James Buchanan for the Presidency. "Old
Obliquity," as his enemies called him, just back from service as
Minister to England, had had no part in the Kansas troubles, or in
the Brooks-Sumner episode. He was a strong candidate, and Weed
felt that his nomination made that of Seward impossible.

Immediately after Buchanan's nomination, Weed asked Seward to
sign a letter that would show his hearty acceptance of the candidate
chosen at the Republican convention. Seward refused to do so, for
he did not wish to make any statement that might be used to
prejudice his chances for the nomination.

The *Tribune*'s Washington correspondent, James S. Pike, reported from Philadelphia, where the Republican national convention was to convene on June 17, that he had surveyed the ground
and felt that Frémont's nomination was inevitable. The New York

delegation, however, though committed to Frémont, found Seward sentiment much stronger than it had expected. Vermont, Rhode Island, Michigan, the Southwest, kept asking why New York had dropped its favorite son. Weed, embarrassed by this clamor, requested James Watson Webb, an ardent Seward man, to get in touch with the Senator and ask him what should be done. At ten o'clock on the evening of June 16, Webb wrote a frantic letter to Seward, telling him that the nomination was within his grasp and begging him to respond by telegraph and "say go ahead." If Seward would not run, said Webb, he could name the candidate, and added in a postscript—"I am pressed to death in writing this. For God sake *speak* & say aye, or if this may not be say *who*."

There were scores of delegates at Philadelphia to whom Seward was unquestionably the greatest man in the party. When Henry Wilson, speaking on June 18, merely suggested the possibility of nominating "the foremost statesman of America, William H. Seward," the convention rose *en masse*, cheering as it had not done at the mention of any other candidate. Had he said "go ahead" in response to Webb's appeal, it is probable that he would have received the nomination. Instead, and in what bitterness of spirit no man can fully know, he bowed to the opinions of his closest advisers. He wrote to his wife of June 17 that he had peremptorily declined to have his name go before the delegates on the ground that that body was not prepared to accept all his principles and policy, but the records of the convention show that his name was withdrawn by his friends before this message reached Philadelphia, if, indeed, it was ever sent. One delegate cast a ballot for him. The convention nominated Frémont, with William L. Dayton of New Jersey, supposedly acceptable to the Know-Nothings, as his running mate. The platform was strongly anti-Nebraska and anti-slavery.[10]

Seward had allowed himself to be guided by Weed and Schoolcraft. They had decided that it was not the time for him to run, partly because of fear that Know-Nothings would not vote for him, partly because they felt sure that Buchanan would win against the candidate of a party that had been nationally organized for only a few short months, partly because their sights were set on 1860. Seward accepted their decision, but he could not help feeling that he had been thrust to one side, thrown by like a squeezed orange, to use

Edward Everett's expression. "Forbidden to doubt" that the nomination was for the best, he hoped that it would not disappoint its
"inventors." Deriving what solace he could from a satisfactory platform, he took up again in Congress his fight for the Topeka constitution.

Frances sympathized with her husband in his hour of disappointment, and in doing so passed judgment on Weed. "His abandonment," she wrote, "seems to have been a matter of very cool
calculation. Worldly wisdom certainly does impel a person to 'swim
with the tide'—and if they can judge unerringly which way the tide
runs, may bring them to port. A magnanimous friendship might
suggest a more elevated course and even reconcile one to struggling
against the current if necessary but magnanimous friendships are
rare—incompatible I think with an absorbing desire for power." [11]

Congress, what with the special session, did not adjourn that election year until the end of August, and before it was over Seward
was weary as well as dispirited. Washington heat, a mountainous
correspondence with uncertain secretarial help, and the bitterness of
disappointed hopes all afflicted him. The political future seemed
dark, and he found it difficult to reconcile himself to being passed
over at Philadelphia. "Frémont, who was preferred over me because
I was not a bigoted Protestant is nearly convicted of being a
Catholic," he wrote to Frances as this false Democratic charge swept
over the land. Plans for coming home by way of a sea voyage to
Halifax collapsed because of the special session, and this disappointment added to his malaise. He reached Auburn in early September,
weary, short of temper, and more than half resolved to go to Europe
and bask in the sun on the shores of the Mediterranean. His desire to
keep out of the campaign was obvious.

Seward's friends were prompt to protest what looked altogether
too much like poor sportsmanship. They pointed out that the worst
possible construction would be put on his going abroad; that he
owed it to himself and the party to do at least a minimum of
campaigning. Weed wrote impatiently that Hale and Wilson were
asking why Seward kept out of the fight. "The answer is obvious,"
said Weed tartly, "but is [it] not best to ask ourselves whether it will
do, in a time like this, to stand back."

Under this prodding, Seward reluctantly abandoned his plan to go to Europe. He agreed to speak in Detroit and half a dozen places in New York State, but turned down urgent requests for speeches in Illinois and other states in the Old Northwest, states where he was to need support badly four years later.[12]

The election in which Seward became thus tardily involved was a three-cornered affair, for the Know-Nothings, rallying their dwindling forces, had nominated Millard Fillmore for President on a moderately nativist platform that straddled on the slavery issue. The Whig remnants also endorsed Fillmore, but they were bitter-enders, and the Know-Nothings were hopelessly divided, North and South, over slavery. The main contest, therefore, was between the Republicans and the Democrats. The former asserted that all the territories must be free soil, and denounced the atrocities in Kansas and the greed of the Slave Power. The Democrats declared that Frémont was a Catholic, and illegitimate to boot, and that the Republicans were fanatical extremists whose triumph would make inevitable the secession of the South. In the North at least it was a wild, free-swinging campaign.

The slaveholding class bore the brunt of Seward's attack in his campaign speeches. It was, he said, perverting the government and endangering the Union. Its power must be curtailed, for between the slave and free labor systems there was "an ancient and eternal conflict." Compromise between them was impossible, and he raised the specter of a triumphant South reopening the African slave trade and of Negro slave displacing free white labor in the fields and cities of western New York. Voting Republican, Seward declared, would halt this menace. Know-Nothingism and its candidate Fillmore evaded the slavery question and rejected the principle of political equality so basic in the republic, while the Democracy and Buchanan were in the hands of the slaveholders. Only the Republican party and its leader upheld the cause of freedom.[13]

Seward believed that Frémont would be beaten, and the result bore out his prediction. The national election of 1856 was a Democratic victory—the last for a generation. "Old Obliquity" received 45.3 per cent of the popular vote, and with it the Presidency. Fillmore, candidate of the dying Know-Nothing and Whig parties, carried only Maryland, but Frémont, plagued though he was by Democratic canards and threats of secession, swept New England

and New York, carried state after state in the Old Northwest, and garnered 33.1 per cent of the ballots cast. The character of his support stamped the party as sectional, for the Republican vote south of the Mason and Dixon line was practically nil, but it was nevertheless an impressive showing of strength. As one of Seward's embattled correspondents wrote, they could at least say with the old Duke of Argyle,

> If 'twas na weel bobbit,
> we'll bobbit again.

Seward met calmly the threats of secession that were commonplace in the South. Captain Abner Doubleday at Fort Monroe wrote to him that, if Frémont were elected, Governor Wise of Virginia and others planned to seize that fortress and talked of taking over the navy yard at Portsmouth and Harper's Ferry. Intelligent Virginians would prevent such action, Doubleday thought, and Seward shared that opinion. He could say in a campaign speech that the slaveholders were endangering the Union, but to him southern secession was now, as it had always been, an impossibility.

What interested Seward more than the danger of secession was a move for the prompt renomination of Frémont for 1860. The New York *Herald* urged this step, one that Webb doused with cold water by a rejoinder in the *Courier and Enquirer*. He wrote to Seward, "You will, of course, read; and I hope, approve." There can be no doubt that Seward approved. His closest friends and he himself were already looking forward to his running in the next presidential election.[14]

There was good reason for Seward to anticipate being the nominee in 1860. He was one of the party's outstanding leaders, and Frémont had run on what was essentially a Seward platform. The latter's friends, especially his powerful New York friends, would then be united behind him, instead of holding him back, and Frémont, though the titular party head, was not really presidential timber. Know-Nothingism, Seward's *bête noire* in 1856, was obviously on a decline, and within four years might well drop out of sight. All this was most encouraging, but there was another side to the shield.

The Republican party had begun in 1854 as a revolt against

slavery and the Slave Power, and Seward was the outstanding opponent of both in the political sphere. He had, however, as Greeley phrased it, adhered in that early time to "the vacated shell of Whiggery" instead of striding to the forefront of the Republican movement. Two years later, when anti-slavery sentiment dominated the Republican national convention and the presidential nomination might well have been his for the asking, his friends held him back, and he accepted their dictum that his name should be withdrawn from consideration. Others, and one in particular, did not shun the fight for office in 1856. On the informal ballot for the vice-presidential nomination Abraham Lincoln ranked second to William L. Dayton with 110 votes, but in the race for the higher post Seward had stood to one side.[15]

There is a Biblical saying that "No man, having put his hand to the plough, and looking back, is fit for the kingdom of God." Seward did not exactly look back from the cause of which he was the pre-eminent champion, but in the hour of decision he faltered, and in the years that lay ahead there was cast across his path the long shadow of another champion of human rights. Neither he nor Weed could know it, but once again the cob houses that they laboriously constructed were beginning to crumble.

ᴥᴥ 13 ᴥᴥ

Seedtime

The third session of the Thirty-fourth Congress opened in December 1856 with a flurry of partisan bickering. Pierce's message flayed Republicanism as a sectional movement that could only accomplish its mission through civil and servile war. In the thrust and counterthrust that followed, Mason of Virginia declared that a Republican victory would have torn the Union to fragments, while Brown of Mississippi quoted Seward's assertion in 1848 that slavery could and would be abolished. Seward replied that 1860 would be the time for a conclusive and good-tempered vindication of Pierce, or of Republicanism.

Little business of a significant character appeared in this lame duck session, for Congress was marking time until Buchanan took office and the new administration laid down its lines of policy. Aside from his customary defense of a protective tariff, Seward's most noteworthy effort was his vigorous promotion of a transatlantic cable to run between Newfoundland and Ireland. He urged a government subsidy for this project, the brain child of Cyrus W. Field, not only because it was economically feasible but also because it would be a means of promoting good relations with Great Britain. The bill was well-nigh buried under floods of oratory, pro and con. It passed eventually, although the cable itself did not become a permanent success until the middle of the next decade.

Buchanan took the presidential oath on March 4, 1857, and two days later Chief Justice Taney handed down one of the most fateful decisions in American history. Dred Scott, a Missouri slave, had sued for his freedom on the ground that his master's having at one time taken him into free territory made him a free man. His suit was based on the supposition that Negroes were citizens of the states in which they resided and, as such, could sue in the federal courts.

Taney held that Negroes of slave ancestry could not be citizens and that therefore Scott's suit must be thrown out. The old Chief Justice and the Court majority then went on to declare that the Missouri Compromise was unconstitutional because it was, in effect, a deprivation of property without due process of law. In other words, a slaveholder had the right to take his slaves into any territory of the Union. Buchanan had learned from one of the judges what the decision would be, and in his inaugural had remarked that all good citizens would, of course, submit to it.

The Dred Scott case had long been pending, and in 1856 Lewis Tappan had solicited Seward's participation. Certain expressions in Tappan's letter, however, had ruffled Seward's feelings, and he had had no part in Scott's defense. Nor did he now join in the general Republican outcry against Taney and the decision. As events a year later were to prove, he was only saving his fire.[1]

While Greeley and Weed thundered against the Dred Scott decision in the *Tribune* and the *Evening Journal,* Seward was revolving in his mind projects for a trip abroad. He and Senator Thomas Jefferson Rusk of Texas half planned a nine months' tour around the world, and there was some talk about his going to Europe with Weed and Blatchford. What finally developed was an excursion and fishing jaunt into Canada that took him as far as the coast of Labrador.

At its start the Canadian trip included Preston King, Mr. and Mrs. Francis P. Blair, Sr., and Frederick and his wife Anna. After visiting the Falls, Toronto, and the Thousand Islands, the party separated at Montreal, with Seward and Frederick and Anna going on to Quebec, where they hired a fifty-five foot fishing schooner, *Emerence.* Leaving Quebec on August 1, they reached Labrador after eleven days of fishing, sightseeing, and innumerable games of whist. Then they came back to Quebec. The journey had its rough moments and was undoubtedly enjoyed more by the Senator than by the young people. At its end the steward made off with the *Emerence* cooking utensils, leaving Seward to foot the bill; but that incorrigible traveler felt that the voyage had benefited his health if not his pocketbook. It also enabled him, the following winter, to lecture Senator Hale of New Hampshire on the fine points of cod and mackerel fishing.[2]

While Seward explored the reaches of the St. Lawrence, the situation in Kansas went from bad to worse. Buchanan had appointed Robert J. Walker of Mississippi governor of the territory, with the clear understanding that the Kansans should have a fair opportunity to make known their desires regarding slavery. An election to a constitutional convention held in June 1857, however, was based on a census that had been rigged before Walker arrived on the scene, and was boycotted by the free-soilers. As a result, a pro-slavery convention at Lecompton drew up an extraordinary document, which barred free Negroes from Kansas, safeguarded property rights in the some two hundred slaves already there until at least 1864, and also contained a special clause guaranteeing slavery in the state. The whole was submitted to the voters, but in such a way that they could only vote for or against the special clause—not for or against the constitution itself. Once again the free-soil majority refused to vote. Only a rigged constitution, anything but representative of the popular will, was ready for submission to Washington.

Events moved swiftly. Walker, knowing Kansas sentiment, came East to protest against what had happened in the territory, but Buchanan, under heavy southern pressure, abandoned the governor. When Congress opened in December 1857, the President defended the admission of Kansas under the Lecompton constitution. Douglas, determined not to accept such a caricature of popular sovereignty, moved into open revolt, and the Democratic party began to split apart.

Hale and other Republicans were eager to assail Buchanan for his stand on Lecompton, but Seward took a different line. He had a fairly accurate picture of the Kansas situation from correspondents there and from Walker himself, and was as strongly opposed as any to Lecompton. Nevertheless he urged delay until Douglas and his supporters had acted, for he wanted the Democratic quarrel to develop unhindered by Republican interference. It was a typical piece of dexterous Seward political maneuvering.

Not so dexterous was his move in January 1858 in regard to the troubled situation in Utah. There Brigham Young was defying the laws of the United States, and Buchanan prepared to send a military force under Albert Sydney Johnston against him. In connection with this move, a bill providing for a maximum army increase of 7000 men came before the Senate. The troops were professedly for use in Utah, but Republican Senators declared that the increase was actually for the purpose of suppressing the anti-slavery men in Kansas.

Seward thought that for the Republicans to lay themselves open to the charge of abandoning the army in Utah would be bad tactics. As he later explained to John Hay in reference to this same army bill, "the fundamental principle of politics is to be always on the side of your country in a war." Much to the surprise of his friends, he supported the measure, making his argument on the ground that the additional troops were needed to deal with the Utah situation.

Hale, in a bitter speech, declared that Seward was defeating the Republican effort to ride herd on Buchanan, and the New Yorker, stung by this charge, replied in an irritable outburst. Party regularity meant nothing to him, he said. Ten years from now no one would be able to tell from his record whether he had belonged to one party or the other. "I know nothing, I care nothing, I never did, I never shall, for party." He voted only for the nation's good. Hale wanted the battle over Kansas fought by skirmishes. "Sir, I regard this battle as already fought. It is over," he declared. There were now sixteen free to fifteen slave states, and before the year was out the count would be nineteen to fifteen. Kansas was free, and the administration could do nothing about it.

This speech produced astonishment and dismay among Republicans. The New York *Tribune* and *Evening Post* were critical; Hale compared Seward's stand to the fall from grace of Daniel Webster; a number of agitated correspondents berated him for boasting and for betraying the party. Smarting under these attacks, Seward wrote a long letter to be used by Blatchford in New York as a defense and explanation of his stand.

The Republican party was like a common scold, declared Seward. It saw only wickedness in the Democracy, a wickedness for which it held the South exclusively to blame. This kept Republicanism weak in the South, and also kept Know-Nothings and Silver Grays in the

North arrayed against it, for they feared that this Republican attitude would consolidate the northern opposition to the Democracy at their expense. His own rule was to concentrate on only one issue—the slavery question—agreeing with the Democrats, where possible, in other matters. This was helpful, he found, in commercial circles, in the South, and among the Silver Grays. The letter continued with a puff for the services of the *Tribune* in the fight against slavery, and a bid for Greeley's support. As for himself, Seward averred, he was not conscious of being ambitious as other men were, and he was being subjected to unmerited criticism. He had given up all aspirations for office and would on no account accept another term in the Senate.

Blatchford sent Greeley a copy of this contrived effusion, which had little effect on the cantankerous editor. Weed also read it with mixed emotions. He deplored aiding the administration, he told Seward, but the very bad thing about the army speech was its injudicious comments about caring nothing for party, and the assertion that the battle was already won. Not fifty men in the North would know what was meant by that last remark, or comprehend the sense in which it was true. "If Blatchford keeps letters," continued Weed, "he can show a dozen from Webster complaining, as you do, of the injustice and ingratitude of his friends; and finally he inquired, 'where shall I go?' " [3]

Weed's criticism touched Seward on a sensitive nerve, and there ensued another of their periodic fallings out. Seward admitted that his remarks about independence of party and the battle being won had been mistakes, but he maintained that his vote on the army bill had been right. All he had from Weed, he said, was harsh and unjust criticism. The altercation then harked back to Weed's course in 1856, with Seward declaring that Weed thought him weak and vain and selfish, the victim of disappointed ambition, while Weed defended his course at the Philadelphia convention and accused Seward of being morbid about the past. As usual in these quarrels, Seward declared that he would retire from public life. He was, however, careful to leave an out—Weed must let him know when he could go to the rest he desired.

Seward's morbidity, as Weed termed it, was in part due to his disappointment of 1856, but there was another factor as well. Weed's financial operations had brought charges of corruption, and

Seward knew this, for Lewis Benedict and Samuel Wilkeson told him of the gang of thieves who hung about the Dictator, destroying his power and influence. Moreover, Greeley was feuding openly with Weed. These things, coupled with Seward's known closeness to Weed, were detrimental to the former's political hopes. There can be little doubt that Seward was troubled about his relationship with the Albany boss. Nevertheless, he knew that Weed was indispensable as security for his own power base in New York State, and by the spring of 1859 their differences, if not forgotten, had been at least thrust into the background.[4]

Seward's defense of his stand on the army bill, while in part labored, did illustrate his main policy at this time. He was trying to carry water on both shoulders; to remain the great protagonist of the anti-slavery cause, and at the same time to make it clear that he was a man who could be trusted by both sides in the deepening sectional conflict—a safe man.

There were many evidences of this policy. During 1857 and at the beginning of 1858 he made gestures of friendship toward northern conservatives and toward the South. He indicated that it might be well to leave to popular sovereignty the question of slavery in the territories. He cultivated the friendship of Virginians. Proposals for spending federal money in the South found favor in his eyes, whether for building a naval depot in Georgia, or for giving Virginia and Maryland some $200,000 from federal funds on the ground that they had advanced this amount for erecting public buildings in the District of Columbia. He would, he declared, be glad to help make Andrew Jackson's home, the Hermitage, a national shrine. Seward persuaded his wife not to lend her support to a project for a Negro school in the nation's capital, a proposal that was bound to draw southern fire, and repeatedly he used his good offices to smooth over quarrels in which southern Senators became involved. For much the same reason Seward regarded Senator Rusk's suicide in the summer of 1857 as little short of a national tragedy. "The event is a public misfortune," he wrote to Fish, "to me a personal disaster. I know of no Southern Senator capable of balancing himself against the passion which makes them all violent and fanatical—now that he is gone. With his cooperation I could do something for the North and for the whole country." [5]

While Seward cultivated good feeling in the South, he kept close watch of northern public opinion. He supported homestead bills, a transcontinental railroad and, of course, protection for the nation's industries. In regard to the tariff, he was especially tender of the Pennsylvania iron interest and of "The Great Winnebago Chief," Simon Cameron, who assured him that he had high hopes of putting Pennsylvania in the Seward column in 1860. Delaware's Senator Bayard remarked that Seward's vigorous support of river and harbor improvements, especially for the West, had about it a presidential odor.

In his effort to present a widely pleasing portrayal of himself as a public man, the New Yorker did not forget the anti-slavery element. He took pains to lavish praise on Governor Salmon P. Chase of Ohio, and even on Joshua Giddings, a fervent hater of slavery who regarded Seward as a politician on the make. When radical abolitionists held a meeting in Worcester, Massachusetts, for the purpose of urging disunion, Seward, in common with Henry Wilson, Theodore Parker, and others, wrote a letter denouncing such action, but unlike them he kept the letter in his files, probably fearing that its publication would hurt him with the anti-slavery element in the Republican party.

Seward felt these efforts at conciliation were paying off. Early in 1858 he told Edwin D. Morgan, chairman of the Republican National Committee, that prejudices and passions against him had died away, and that he did not know that he had "an enemy in the society political or otherwise in which I move." The expiration of his present term would bring him "to the climacteric. . . . My ambition is satisfied. . . . My work is entirely done. . . . I shall go into retirement without a wish unsatisfied."

The era of good feeling that Seward described to Morgan came to an abrupt end early in March 1858. Perhaps Seward felt that his policy of general conciliation had gone too far, especially since the report spread that he had left the Republican party and had given up the anti-slavery cause.[6] He may also have felt that the time was ripe for leaping into the quarrel between Douglas and Buchanan. Whatever the cause, he rose in a crowded Senate on March 3, 1858, to make a slashing attack upon slavery, the administration, and the Lecompton constitution.

The country faced, he said, the same old struggle between "two

antagonistical systems," slave labor and free labor, the one aristocratic, the other democratic in character. The outcome of this conflict was certain. The northern economic and social order must, by
its very nature, expand, and in so doing new free states would come
into being. No such need existed for slavery expansion. Indeed, he
believed, "to some extent," in the isothermal theory—that there
were colder regions where slavery, if planted, would die out—and
he was sure that 36°30′ was too far north for this isothermal line to
be drawn (a suggestion that there need be no fear of slavery flourishing in New Mexico Territory). Kansas must and would be free,
and the slaveholding region must continue to diminish. Inexorably,
but with moderation, free labor would restrict the area controlled
by the slaveholders. The effort of expansion to make new slave
states "will only fail to be a great crime because it is impracticable;
and, therefore, will turn out to be a stupendous imbecility."

But despite the rejection of Lecompton by Kansas, continued
Seward, Buchanan was determined to force slavery upon the territory. To that end, he had connived with the Supreme Court which,
to please him, had rendered the Dred Scott decision. Then, as the
galleries hushed, Seward drew a graphic picture of the 1857 inauguration, with the President and Taney whispering together on the
portico of the Capitol about this act of "judicial usurpation," this
"political game." Doubtless, sneered the New Yorker, at the Executive Palace reception on March 5, the President had received the
judges as graciously as Charles I did those who, at his instance,
subverted English liberty. And, having organized "this formidable
judicial battery" at the Capitol, Buchanan was now with assurances
"apologetical and jesuitical" urging Congress to admit Kansas under
the fraudulent Lecompton constitution.

What should be done, Seward asked, in the present situation?
Whether or not the Court receded from the position it had taken, it
must be reorganized in such a way as to bring its political sentiments
and practices "into harmony with the Constitution and the laws of
nature." As for Kansas, Lecompton was an impossibility. There it
would be wise to restore the Missouri Compromise, but the same result could be achieved by going back to the popular sovereignty of
the Kansas-Nebraska bill. In doing this, he would cheerfully co-
operate with Senator Douglas, Senator Broderick of California, and

other like-minded men. The speech closed with another affirmation of slavery's inevitable extinction and of the triumph of freedom.

This speech drew marked reactions from all quarters. It met with George Bancroft's "hearty concurrence." Gerrit Smith praised it as "temperate but firm"; Charles Francis Adams thought it "statesman-like." Chase declared it worthy of the occasion and of its author. Chase would distrust Seward's devotion to the cause of anti-slavery when he distrusted his own, but he did wish there had been no support for the popular sovereignty doctrine. Others responded with more violent emotion. Buchanan, outraged, forbade Seward access to the White House, and Taney, equally indignant, declared subsequently that if Seward had been elected President he would have refused to administer the oath of office.

The South shared Taney's rage and contempt, for it was touched to the quick by Seward's confident description of slavery's twilight. Southern Senators were raising the specter of disunion if Kansas were not admitted under Lecompton, and Senator James H. Hammond of South Carolina, an exemplar of southern courtesy and owner of 400 slaves, answered Seward on the floor of the Senate.

Seward, said Hammond, had spoken as though the South was a conquered province to be ruled by the North. Far from it. The South was an empire of 850,000 square miles, with 1,000,000 men on its muster roles. It was perfectly capable of independence, and it would be a peaceful independence, for all the world needed its cotton. "No sir, you dare not make war on cotton. No power on earth dares make war upon it. Cotton is king."

Every social system, continued Hammond, had to have a mudsill class to perform the drudgeries of life. In the South it was the slaves; in the North it was the manual laborers, the white slaves, who could vote and were far more dangerous than the South's vigorous, docile, happy, contented blacks. How would the North like it, he asked, if the South sent agitators into the North to teach its manual laborers the power of the ballot box, to help them combine, to lead them?— And at this there came a chorus from the Republican side, "Send them along." [7]

As Seward had predicted, Lecompton was doomed. A combination of Republicans, anti-Lecompton Democrats, and six Know-

Nothings defeated it in the House of Representatives. Then the administration, determined to have its way, devised another plan. The so-called English bill coupled submission of the Lecompton constitution to the Kansas voters with what amounted to a threat. If the constitution was accepted, Kansas would receive 5 per cent of the proceeds from the sale of 2,000,000 acres of the public domain. If it were rejected, the state could not enter the Union until a census showed it possessed 90,000 inhabitants. This would mean a delay of about two years in statehood and in the customary grant of public lands.

Seward opposed the English bill as an act of immorality in legislation. He had no confidence that Buchanan would administer fairly the bill's provisions for ratification by the Kansas voters. Douglas, too, opposed it, but the administration brought enormous pressure, including bribery, to bear. The measure became law, but when it was submitted to the voters, the Kansas electorate, assisted by the well-placed efforts of Republicans sent out to see that Kansas voted right, rejected it by a 6 to 1 majority.[8]

The Lecompton struggle saw Seward moving in concert with Stephen A. Douglas. This, together with his announced willingness to accept Douglas's brand of popular sovereignty, filled the air with rumors of a partnership of the two men. The New York *Herald* declared that there was a definite Seward-Douglas alliance looking to Douglas's re-election in 1858, and the New Yorker's elevation to the Presidency two years later. Lincoln himself thought that Seward was one of a group of eastern Republicans such as Greeley and Henry Wilson that favored returning Douglas to the Senate, but this was hardly the case.

Seward was delighted by the split in the Democracy and after it occurred counseled with Douglas on strategy, but he also distrusted Douglas as an ally; like the other anti-Lecompton Democrats he could not be relied upon, Seward thought, in the struggle against slavery. Furthermore, his nomination on the Republican ticket in Illinois was at best a doubtful possibility. A journey to Chicago in the fall of 1857, partly on behalf of his investments in Illinois, enabled Seward to look over the political situation there. In the months that followed, letters from and conversations with Lincoln's law partner Herndon and with his own relative Thomas C. Miller (a Detroit newspaper man who surveyed the ground in Illinois) furnished abundant evidence that Illinois Republicans would never agree to support Douglas. There was no Seward-Douglas alliance. But neither did Seward give Lincoln any support.

During the Illinois contest, Douglas tried to exploit the anti-Negro sentiment in Illinois. He declared that Lincoln's "house-divided" speech was abolitionist doctrine. Douglas charged that Republicans believed in complete equality between Negroes and whites, and he forecast intermarriage in the event of Republican victory. Lincoln countered by asserting that he did not believe in social and political equality for the Negro. There was, he said, a physical difference between the races that forever prohibited their living together as social and political equals.

After the Lincoln-Douglas debates were over and Douglas had gained a narrow victory, Herndon assured Seward that Illinois Republicans had no hard feelings about the course pursued by some easterners. They would fight to the end against the pro-slavery Democracy under Seward, Chase, Banks, or any other leader. Seward replied that he sorrowed over Lincoln's defeat, for he was needed in the Senate. It would have been pleasant, he added, if excitable persons had not become querulous about himself, but that was a customary inconvenience.

Querulous was a mild term for what Illinois Republicans felt toward Seward. Though Herndon absolved him of blame for Lincoln's defeat, many were disposed to hold him equally responsible with Greeley, and the New Yorker lost the high ground he had held in the state as a candidate for 1860.[9]

Seward spent most of the summer of 1858 in Auburn, watching over the development of his real estate projects there. In September he argued a railroad bridge case before the United States Circuit Court in Albany and in New York, winning the right to span the Hudson at Albany. He based his argument on the state's police power, its right to regulate its internal commerce, and the growing transportation needs of the nation. Meanwhile, he received appeals for speeches from several quarters. James Wilson, prominent Indiana Republican, urged him to take part in that state's fall election, for such action might give him the state in 1860. To this request and to all others Seward turned a deaf ear. He was concentrating his attention upon the coming New York State campaign.

The New York situation was crucial. There the Republicans under Weed's leadership nominated Edwin D. Morgan for governor, and the Know-Nothings, incensed by their failure to get second place on the ticket, ran a separate slate. They were out to beat Seward, their long-time enemy, who had opposed the fusion at Syracuse that they desired and whose senatorial record was warmly endorsed by the Republican convention. Defeat of Morgan would be defeat for Seward.

The election turned out to be a four-cornered affair, for in addition to Republican, Democratic, and Know-Nothing slates, Gerrit Smith ran for governor on a People's State Ticket, with a program advocating temperance, anti-slavery, and land reform. Seward was anxious to see a decisive Republican victory, for 1860 was only two years away.

Seward made a number of speeches in the campaign, but the one that excited most attention came on October 25 at Rochester. His main theme there was that the Democratic party was unworthy of the confidence of the American people. He then, as he had done many times before, declared that the United States had two different political systems, one resting on slave, the other on free labor. These systems were incompatible, yet as the country grew they came into closer and closer contact. The result was an "irrepressible conflict," and it meant that, sooner or later, the United States must become an entirely slaveholding or an entirely free labor nation. Slavery could scarcely triumph without violating the Constitution; nor did he expect that freedom would gain the victory otherwise "than through the action of the several states cooperating with the federal government, and all acting in strict conformity with their respective constitutions."

The effort of slavery to expand must be defeated, Seward declared. Therefore the Democratic party must be turned out of office, for it was a tool of the slaveholders and had become a sectional and local party "having practically its seat within the slave states. . . ." The true principles of justice for all men were now upheld by the Republican party. The people were gathering together the forces with which to gain back all that had been surrendered by the Democracy, "and to confound and overthrow, by one decisive blow, the betrayers of the constitution and freedom forever."

This "irrepressible conflict" speech produced torrents of praise and of abuse. Eighty-six-year-old Josiah Quincy took pen in trembling hand to give his hearty approval; the artist, Chester Harding, wrote that it was the most statesmanlike utterance he had read in years. But the South, and northern conservatives, denounced it in unsparing terms. The New York *Herald* declared that it advocated abolition of slavery by the national government, and the Albany *Atlas* asserted that it called for the invasion of South Carolina and Georgia and the forcible emancipation of the slaves on the plantations. Even the New York *Times* felt that it gave the impression that Seward advocated the extirpation of slavery in the South by the federal government. Everywhere the changes were rung on the expression "irrepressible conflict." Sometime later, Seward told Rose Greenhow, a famous southern beauty and Washington hostess, that, if heaven would forgive him for stringing together two high-sounding words, he would never do it again.[10]

There followed a speech in Rome, New York, where Seward declared that the time for decisive action had come. A blow for freedom and humanity would be struck by Congress in 1859 and 1860, and all would be recovered that had been so shamefully lost. The Republican party was now organized in the free states, and during the next two years men like Frank P. Blair, Jr. and Cassius M. Clay would establish it south of the Mason and Dixon line. Even now, a Republican victory in New York would ensure a Republican Congress in Washington.

At this point Seward's argument took what looked like a curious turn. The speech was given to help Roscoe Conkling win election to Congress over his Democratic opponent in the Oneida district. With this in view, and perhaps also with the intent of encouraging anti-slavery sentiment in the South and of quieting the fears of timorous and conservative northerners, he went on to assert that the "war" was no longer with southerners. Indeed, the slaveholders were now "subdued in spirit," divided in their counsels, and had ceased to menace disunion. Forbearance, tolerance, and patriotism might be expected of them, were it not for the Democratic party in the free states. That party's leader, President Buchanan, had procured the Dred Scott decision from the Supreme Court and, by his support of the Lecompton constitution, encouraged the slaveholders to insist upon maintaining slavery in Kansas. The real enemy was the northern Democracy and Buchanan.

It was now plain, declared Seward, why this election was so important. With a Republican Congress, and a Republican President elected in 1860, the Supreme Court would recede from its untenable position, and all that the slave states had gained in violation of the Constitution would be relinquished. Peace and harmony would once more brood over the country, and the great problem of removing slavery from the land would be settled in a constitutional way, without danger to the Union and without injustice to 30,000,000 people living under "the best of Constitutions that human wisdom has ever devised."

Seward told both James Watson Webb and Theodore Parker that this Rome speech, like the one at Rochester, was meant to rally the Republican voters in the rural regions of the state who had been made uneasy by the way in which the urban elements of the party were trying to propitiate Know-Nothingism. Neither he nor his audiences, he declared, thought there was anything new or bold in his statements. Such may have been his intent, and it is true that both speeches were concerned with the great struggle waged between the friends and foes of freedom, a struggle in which one side or the other must triumph. But it was little short of ridiculous for him to assert that the Democratic party was dominated by the slaveholding South and then, four days later, to declare that the real struggle was not with a chastened South but with the Democrats of the free states. The latter statement was false. The conclusion is inescapable that the Rome speech represented mainly an electioneering effort, with truth cast to the winds in an effort to win votes. It is no wonder that Seward omitted it from his published *Works*.

After the campaigns of 1858 were over, Herndon wrote from Springfield that Seward and Lincoln had taken the same position on the slavery issue, both having declared that two such absolute antagonisms as slavery and freedom could not permanently co-exist. This was but partly true. Lincoln in his "house-divided" speech had emphasized containing slavery where it already existed, leaving its ultimate extinction to perhaps a century later. Seward, while careful to point out that only constitutional measures must be used against slavery, had spoken in terms that seemed to promise extreme action. "Irrepressible conflict" and overthrowing slavery by "one decisive blow" had a far more ominous ring than did talk about a house-divided and the nation's inability to endure permanently half-slave and half-free. Furthermore, Lincoln's stand on Negro rights was more conservative than the position taken by Seward, although their thought on the subject ran along much the same line.

When the count was taken in November, Edwin D. Morgan had a majority over his Democratic rival, Amasa J. Parker, of 17,440 votes. Two years before, John A. King had had a 65,000 majority over his Democratic opponent. The American candidate, Lorenzo Burrows, polled 60,000 votes in 1858, and Greeley, who had deplored the "Syracuse folly" of avoiding fusion with the Know-Nothings, declared that the "irrepressible conflict" speech and "Sewardism" in general had cost the party many votes. Seward, putting on a brave face, told Morgan that the election meant they had reached safe ground at last. But for 1860 the omens were not auspicious.[11]

The election over, Seward went to Washington for the second session of the Thirty-fifth Congress. There he found the Democrats thoroughly demoralized by the Buchanan-Douglas split, and northern and southern Senators at odds over the tariff and the Pacific railroad. He spoke that winter for a transcontinental road built by the federal government, with public lands given to settlers instead of to private railroad companies. He also demanded an increase in the tariff, with special reference to the mining and manufacture of iron, and opposed all schemes that seemed to smack of slavery expansion, whether plans for the purchase of Cuba or for adventuring in Central America. Meanwhile, he made arrangements for an extended European journey.

"All our discreet friends unite in sending me out of the country to spend the recess of Congress," he wrote to George W. Patterson. In other words, going abroad meant safety from entanglements at home that might lessen his chances of reaching the White House. Commodore Vanderbilt provided him with the best cabin on the steamship *Ariel* and, having armed himself with letters to a flock of

European dignitaries and a credit of £1000 at Baring Brothers in London, Seward left home for New York at the end of April. There were a few hectic days at the Astor House. Then on May 7, heartened by the music of bands, the firing of cannon, and the cheers of hundreds of supporters—to say nothing of Weed's last-minute assurance that Greeley was now all right politically and was going to California to be useful—the departing statesman bade adieu to the friends who had gathered to wish him well.

He was going abroad, he told them, to renew his health and to study the people and institutions of the Old World so that he might better serve his native land. Then he boarded the *Ariel* and, as it moved down the harbor, he stood on the wheelhouse waving his hat and handkerchief in response to the cheers from the accompanying boats and from two other ocean-going steamers, whose bells and whistles added to the general din.[12]

≈§ 14 §≈

The Higher Destiny

Many of Seward's critics—radical abolitionists, conservative Republicans, and Democrats—declared him to be merely a time-serving, clever, ambitious seeker after power and place. There was an element of truth in this contention. His posturing in the Senate, his use of what Greeley called dexterity in statesmanship, his veering from universal conciliation to bitter condemnation of the southern slaveholders, gave color to his enemies' attacks. But a close examination of his views as mirrored in his senatorial career shows that he possessed certain fundamental convictions which he strove to translate into action; that the man who put on his table service the motto *Esse quam videre*—To be rather than to seem—had a vision of the good society that transcended any desire for power and place. It would be too much to say that he sought political advancement solely for the purpose of serving his country's welfare. It is, nevertheless, true that his conception of what his country was, and what it should become, formed a basis for much of his thought and action during the national period of his career.

Central to Seward's thinking was his concept of the United States as a national entity. While in the early part of his career he occasionally recognized the experimental nature of the Union, his attitude became more and more one of firm belief in the permanence of the nation.

Let him who doubts the stability of the Union [he said to the Phi Beta Kappa Society at Union in 1844] repair for one day to the place where the impatient Niagara gathers within its narrow banks the floods of the Lakes, Erie, Huron, Michigan, Superior, and the Woods—hindering yet accelerating them on their descent to the capacious basin below. Let him there watch the vessels as they heave in sight, burthened with the agricultural and forest productions of the interior States, and bearing them to Atlantic ports; and then number the barques, which, having gathered fabrics and merchandize from all that once was civilized America, and from the earth's broad surface, are conveying them on to be distributed in individual homes throughout the communities which cluster and ripen on the Western Lakes and Rivers. If not yet satisfied, let the doubter then transfer himself to the confluence of the Ohio and the Mississippi, and see the great Father of Waters projecting his broad arms Northward till he almost grasps the great fountains of the St. Lawrence, and Westward till he takes hold of the base of the Mountains. There let the distrustful patriot contemplate the ever-passing, ever-swelling tides of inland trade, and then ask himself, are these fit stations for custom houses and walls and castellated towns and frontier armies? Shall these ever-busy steamers, employed in paternal commerce, give place to armed Ships of War; and these Lakes and Rivers no longer whitened with canvass, be crimsoned henceforth with human blood? No! he will forget that the Union was formed by compact, and is political, and will exclaim, The Union exists, because it is inevitable; and must endure, because it is indispensable.

The Union would be permanent, he told Weed two years later, if only because of these same geographical factors. The great rivers, running north and south, bound it together and "no political convulsion can shake it to pieces. The Union is the handiwork of Nature."

In the 1850s, as the trans-Mississippi West became a vital part of the nation, he put greater emphasis on other unifying factors. Railroads, canals and telegraph lines, the rapid assimilation of immigrants, the people's consciousness of the superiority of American social and political institutions, and the growth of national pride all combined, in Seward's estimation, to make for an inevitable, indispensable, and therefore enduring Union. Addressing the members of the New York legislature when they visited New York City, he emphasized the interrelationship of the city, the state, and the nation, a condition which he pictured as indissoluble and eternal. If he should ever hear a New York man avow himself a disunionist, he would think that the Bloomingdale Asylum at Utica was "the fittest place for his correction."

This American Union was a nation, and as such it had certain qualities and characteristics. The nation, Seward declared, was, in fact, "a human person consisting of many persons." Like human individuals, it had moral and social responsibilities, and like them it could live and grow strong, or languish and die. The American nation would take the former course, for it was "quick and vigorous of thought, free and bold in speech, prompt and resolute in action, and just and generous in purpose." Its sense of nationality must be cherished, and local, sectional, and foreign influences must be watched and repelled, since they made for social derangement and tended to subvert its democratic character.[1]

If the nation was to last and be strong, it obviously had to have the proper kind of government. There must be political and civil equality, for Seward accepted the equalitarian principles of Jefferson and the Declaration of Independence. Therefore the government should properly be, in form, a federal republic, consisting of states bound together under a revered Constitution that provided a balance of power between the executive, the legislative, and the judicial departments.

What of the allocation of power between the states and the central government? While governor, Seward had been zealous in upholding the prerogatives of New York, but in the 1850s he took a more nationalistic viewpoint, one that emphasized the limited sphere of state sovereignty. States could demand the loyalty of their citizens; they could and should exercise normal police powers over strictly intrastate affairs. But they had no absolute jurisdiction over matters affecting other states, such as interstate commerce, and certainly none over foreign relations.

As for the national government, Seward believed that, where interstate relations and foreign affairs were concerned, the power of Washington ruled supreme. Furthermore Washington derived its authority, not from the states but directly from the people, for the nation was constituted of the mass of "citizens throughout all the several states." These millions of voters by exercising the power of election gave motive and energy to the governmental activity at the nation's capital. The cardinal principle of the American government, he said in 1856, the characteristic that rendered it "practically eternal," was that it relied not on force or fraud, or on the corporate consent or action of the states, "but upon the consent and acquiescence of the people in the action of the Government itself. . . ."

Seward did not see this central government as a passive policeman. It had a positive function, the active promotion of national strength and security. To that end, it should make judicious use of the tariff, whether for fostering such industries as iron and textiles, or for combating economic recession. Washington should also subsidize projects, such as the merchant marine and the Atlantic cable, that would bring profit and prestige to America, and he urged generous federal support for all manner of internal improvements, from the dredging of rivers and harbors to the building of a transcontinental railroad. The preamble to the Constitution, he asserted, furnished the authority for such federal action, since it declared that the purpose of the central government was to establish justice, maintain domestic tranquillity, and secure the blessings of liberty to ourselves and our posterity. Under such a construction of the ark of the covenant, there was practically no limit to what the government might do in fostering the national welfare. The one exception was interference with the right of the southern states to maintain slavery within their borders.[2]

Government and people alike, Seward contended, must labor for the nation's welfare, for both its cultural and its material development. There were three great wheels of American prosperity, he told a New York audience in 1853: agriculture first, then manufacturing, and finally commerce. Primarily these wheels were put in motion by individual initiative and private enterprise.

Unlike his friend Theodore Parker, who was deeply concerned about the shortcomings of the merchants, the vicious aspects of

nineteenth-century industrial feudalism, and the need for governmental action on behalf of the common man, Seward saw no need
for a program of social legislation on behalf of the masses. Education, the ballot box, the expansion of economic opportunity, and the
existing forms of government were sufficient, in his opinion, to take
care of such social inequities as existed on the American scene. They
would prevent great land monopolies and accumulations of wealth,
and so afford "incentives to universal activity and emulation."
Furthermore, the West with its resources, and the cheap fares to
that region, relieved Americans from seeking solutions of existing
evils such as those offered by Robert Owen or the Fourierites.[3]

Seward would promote agriculture, first of the great wheels of
national prosperity, primarily through land policy. The public
domain, he contended in 1850, should be used to foster internal
improvements and facilitate settlement, which in turn would increase national wealth and unity. It would also encourage immigration, which would promote prosperity. As early as 1851 Seward
came out for free land granted to settlers in limited amounts with
provision against alienation. Such disposal of the public domain
would populate the frontier, hinder the development of great
manorial estates, and put a curb on land speculation and absentee
ownership. It would also promote the introduction of new states
into the Union, and in general furnish a firm agricultural base for
the development of the American economy. Seward consistently
supported free homestead legislation during the decade before the
Civil War.

Seward advocated other uses for the public domain. He urged
land grants that would be used by the states to establish schools
teaching agricultural science, and hospitals devoted to caring for the
indigent insane. These grants, as well as free homesteads, would
promote the prosperity of the agricultural regions and of the nation
at large. He became convinced, however, that land subsidies to
railroad companies, which he favored in the early part of the decade, should be discontinued. In 1858 he denounced such grants,
for he felt the roads used them for speculative purposes; he urged
instead that this land should be given to actual settlers in holdings
suitable for cultivation. This way it could be used to promote
America's prosperity and power.

Seward's appreciation of the role of the West in American society led him to anticipate in some respects the frontier hypothesis of Frederick Jackson Turner. The New Yorker's conception of the West as a barrier to radicalism in essence was Turner's safety valve theory, and he, like the great historian of a later generation, emphasized the role of the frontier as a seedbed of democracy, a source of freedom. Speaking at St. Paul in the autumn of 1860, Seward extolled the rapidity with which Germans and Irishmen, Frenchmen and Italians, Hollanders and Norwegians became, almost within their own generation and entirely in that of their children, American citizens. And the West represented something more than a melting pot of races.

> Do you not see and feel . . . that when men from Maine, and from Carolina, and from Mississippi, and from New Hampshire, and from England and Ireland, and Scotland, from Germany and from all other portions of the world come up here, the atmosphere becomes the atmosphere not only of health, but of liberty and freedom? Do we not feel when we come up here, that we have not only found the temple and the shrine of freedom, but that we have come into the actual living presence of the goddess of freedom herself? Once in her presence, we see that no less capacious temple could be fit for the worship that is her due. I wish, my fellow citizens, that all my associates in public life could come up here with me, and learn by experience, as I have done, the elevation and serenity of soul which pervades the people of the great northwest. It is the only region of the United States in which I find fraternity and mutual charity full developed.[4]

Industry and internal commerce shared the importance of the land in Seward's vision of America transformed into an affluent and free society. Industry, he declared, deserved special encouragement, for so far the United States had put its main emphasis upon agriculture, sending its raw materials out of the country and relying altogether too much upon Europe for its manufactured goods. America, to be strong, required a balanced economy, and industry was an essential part of that balance. Industrial development would also bring industrial independence and would thereby foster a spirit of national pride. It would create bonds between the sections, for as more and more domestic goods were manufactured there would come into being a truly national market, and the internal trade thus established "would constitute the firmest possible national union."

Seward proposed a variety of means for stimulating industrial production: the improvement of patent laws, bounties for the cod-fishing industry, the subsidization of railroad and telegraphic communication with the Far West and, especially desirable from the point of view of industry, a protective tariff. The latter would enable infant industries to grow and help America achieve an independent national economy and would lessen the effects of economic depressions. Not so extreme a protectionist as Henry C. Carey in the 1850s, Seward believed that American industry would develop and prosper whether or not duties remained at the lowered levels of the 1846 Walker tariff. But he generally raised his voice against any further reductions; he fought against a number of the lowered duties in the tariff of 1857 (though he finally voted for the bill); and he firmly supported Justin Morrill's high protective tariff measure which passed Congress after the secession of the southern states in 1861.

Seward also sought to foster a national economy by promoting internal commerce through the development of transportation and communication. While the canal-building era had largely ended by the 1850s, rivers still needed dredging and harbors improving, and Seward supported a vast number of such bills in Congress. Indeed he hardly ever failed to back such measures when they came to a vote in the Senate, and he was equally enthusiastic about the development of railroads and telegraph lines. They not only facilitated the transport of raw materials and the products of industry, but they greatly helped the cross-fertilization of ideas between the various sections of the country. They were, Seward declared, "vastly more powerful for holding civil communities together than were any mere covenants, though written on parchment or engraved upon iron." Telegraph wires stretching to the Pacific would be valuable, he believed, in breaking up distinctions between East and West, North and South. He demonstrated his faith in this line of reasoning when, in January 1861 he proposed as one of a number of remedies for ending the secession crisis that the nation unite in building two transcontinental railroads, one by a northern the other by a southern route.[5]

Industry, commerce, and agriculture all benefited, Seward believed, from the influx of the foreign-born. The Irish and German immigrants streaming into the country each year by the hundreds of thousands increased the nation's military strength and, more important, provided workers for the mills, factories, and farms. They built railroads, stoked the fires that moved the wheels of industry, and put millions of additional acres into wheat and corn and oats. Experience showed that they were easily assimilated with the native-born population. They should, therefore, be encouraged to come to the United States, rather than hindered by restrictions on their civil liberties or their acquisition of land, or by persecution for their religious beliefs. He steadily and consistently opposed bigotry and intolerance in the treatment of aliens, and ironically this stand on principle rated as one of his most severe political handicaps.

Slavery, like Know-Nothingism, was an obstacle to the realization of Seward's American dream. He did not believe that the United States would become a completely integrated society, for he found miscegenation unnatural and repulsive, and felt that, like the Indians, the "African race" was "incapable of assimilation." Nevertheless, the black man was a human being, and as such was entitled to certain rights. Seward objected to slavery on moral grounds; he believed and argued at great length that it hindered the nation's economic development, but, more fundamental still, was his conviction that the nation's claim as the home of freedom and equality and its right to a position of world leadership, were challenged by the existence of an institution that consigned millions of its citizens to servitude, forbade them opportunity for social and economic progress, and denied the democratic principle by its tolerance of an aristocratic, slaveholding class wielding great power in the national government. He knew how difficult it would be to end slavery in the South, sheltered as it was by the sovereignty of the states. Time and patience, he knew, would be required to work out this problem, but eventually a nation dedicated to the great principle of freedom must itself become entirely free. Repeatedly during the 1850s he presented to the Senate petitions praying for the abolition of the peculiar institution with compensation from the proceeds of land sales.

This was one way, he felt, in which to deal with America's greatest social problem.[6]

Seward also laid great stress upon universal education. This was essential, if we were to have an elevated and intelligent citizenry, capable of shouldering the duties that devolved upon it in a democratic society. Education should be extended as widely as possible, to black and white, male and female. Primary and secondary schools remained its basic constituents, with the apex the university, which should hold "a chief place among the institutions of the American Republic." Universities should teach both science and the arts; they should be conservative, exercising moderation and charity while holding to that which had been proven good and true, but they also should boldly root out superstition and false practices. Most of all, they should be institutions "where opinion is left free, and reason is ever active and vigorous." Himself a voracious reader and avid for knowledge all his life, Seward felt that education was a fundamental means of building that great American society the outlines of which would emerge more and more clearly in succeeding generations.

Belief in the idea of progress, that is to say, faith in the progressive improvement of the condition of mankind, had been current since the time of Francis Bacon. It received a great impetus in the nineteenth century through the spectacular advances made in invention and in the creation of wealth. Seward shared this belief, and he would sometimes prophesy that the human race was making its way toward "an ultimate and glorious destiny." He acknowledged that many obstacles lay in the path toward ultimate felicity, but the race advanced toward this goal, he declared, because this was the Divine purpose. That purpose, he believed, manifested itself in a supreme, universal law—the essential equality of nations, of races, and of men. According to this law, "one nation, race, or individual may not oppress or injure another, because the safety and welfare of each is essential to the common safety and welfare of all." Knowledge and virtue must be disseminated and increased if men were to understand and follow this precept, for political and social democracy must triumph over the outworn principles of monarchy and aristocracy.

Among all the nations, the United States was best suited to promote the progress of civilization. Its multiplying wealth and population, its advantageous geographical position, gave it security and power, and it derived continued inspiration and strength from the great ideals of the Founding Fathers. Their political philosophy was enshrined in the Constitution, and the democratic government established under that instrument would ensure America's position of leadership in the great struggle for human progress.[7]

The United States, then, must "take up the cross of republicanism and bear it before the nations." Then our internal development, material and intellectual, would excite the world's admiration. It would prompt other peoples to abandon outworn systems of social and political organization and pattern their lives after our own. Even more, an expansion of communication with the rest of the world would have far-reaching results.

Seward put great emphasis upon the world-wide effects of the expansion of communication. Railroads, the telegraph, the Atlantic cable, would carry the American message and increase American influence. The iron bands stretching across the continent would make Britain's maritime supremacy crumble and cause the commerce of the world to roll down upon the United States as inevitably as a magnet draws steel. Indeed, the importance of such a development could not be exaggerated. Not only would it be a great co-operative enterprise enabling North and South to meet on a common field as they labored to improve the West "for the common benefit of our posterity and for the welfare and happiness of the human race"; it would also be

> the realization of what all Europe has been striving for for the last four hundred years. . . . It changes the commerce of the world. It transfers it, in my judgment, across the American continent, from across its old and ancient channels by the Red Sea and the Arabian Gulf, and around the Cape of Good Hope. It is the great agency by which this Government is to become the highest and most important and beneficent among the Powers of the earth in promoting and advancing civilization and the progress of the human race.

The national and world progress which Seward envisioned would not only be tied up with the expansion of communication and the development of commerce within the United States, it would also be accompanied by the growth of foreign commerce. He heartily approved the opening of Japan by Commodore Perry, and joined with him in urging the appointment of Townsend Harris as America's first commissioner to the Land of the Rising Sun. He was anxious to foster commercial relations with South America and Turkey. He wanted to see fleets of trading vessels flying the American flag in the Bering Strait and Hudson's Bay, and a steady growth of commerce with Hawaii and with China. He told Weed in 1845 that we would meet Great Britain in Asia in a final contest for world leadership, and eight years later he declared in the Senate that the Pacific area was the center of the great conflict for world power. It would be a contest for commerce, and America should concentrate its efforts upon victory. Seward's belief in the benefits of an American-controlled external trade, together with his lively conception of Britain as the great rival of the United States in the contest for world supremacy, were undoubtedly the motivating factors in his stubborn insistence upon governmental subsidization of ocean-going commerce. The Collins Line, costly and uneconomical though it was, especially offered a direct challenge to the British-subsidized Cunarders.[8]

The expansion of American influence, ideologically and commercially, would have far-reaching consequences, in Seward's estimation. As the United States became the strongest power in the world, and as its influence promoted the spread of democratic institutions, its geographical limits would be steadily enlarged. This would not happen by war but by a process of osmosis, selective in character. He opposed, for the time being, any attempt at expansion in Central America, or Cuba, or any other area where it might be used to perpetuate slavery. He disclaimed belief in a Manifest Destiny that would accept war as an instrument of national policy. While it was as natural for nations to be politically active and seek to expand their borders as it was for birds to fly, such efforts could be either irenic or martial. Peaceful activity, he felt, was safer, cheaper, surer, and it conserved national strength. War was desolating, and history taught that it was "incompatible with the maintenance of our free republican institutions." When his imagination kindled, he foresaw a pacific, gradual expansion of American sovereignty as Canada, Mexico, Central America, Hawaii, and the Caribbean Islands, their institutions moulded after those of the United

States, their trade connection with the great republic becoming more and more important, would ask for admission to the Union. In keeping with his desire to promote such a development, despite objections from friends and supporters, he took a leading part in putting through the Senate the 1855 reciprocity treaty with Canada, and he always looked for similar ways of expanding American influence. "I would not seize in haste, and force the fruit, which ripening in time, will fall of itself into our hands," he told the Senate. "But I know nevertheless, that the stars will come out even if the moon delay its rising. I have shown you then that a continent is to be peopled, and even distant islands to be colonized by us." He envisioned a vast, federal, American empire, democratically organized, itself the culmination of trends that would be years, perhaps centuries, in the making. In time, he declared in 1858, the center of the Union would be nearer the Valley of Mexico than the Valley of the Mississippi.[9]

What are we to think of Seward as a man of intellect? A voracious reader, he had a mind crammed with information gleaned from the literature of Europe and America, and from a host of American contemporaries ranging from Washington Irving to Jean Louis Rodolphe Agassiz. He had a remarkable ability to organize information, and he unquestionably possessed imaginative power, a breadth of view, a knowledge of human nature, and a capacity for logical argument that, combined with fertility of expression, marked him as a man of outstanding intellectual capacity. On the other hand, he had certain qualities and viewpoints that prevented his becoming an intellectual force of the first order. He used, at times, the lawyer's trick of subtle qualification—a means of obscuring his real intentions when he judged such obscurantism to be politically expedient—and his critics seized upon this to cast doubt upon his integrity as a public man. Then, too, the visionary in him sometimes got out of hand, especially when he projected the American future. And his line of reasoning, when affected by political considerations, often became subjective.

Seward could give high priority to political expediency. His boast that he had prompted Senator Dixon to move the repeal of the Missouri Compromise is a good example of this propensity. In his speeches on the Kansas problem, he sought political advantage rather than peace in that strife-ridden territory. The best way to fight the Democrats, he told Samuel Ruggles in 1852, was to make the country believe that the Whigs were the only true repositors of national grandeur and glory.[10]

This man who challenged the views of the South in the fateful decade before the Civil War was a party leader who sought victory at the polls and the power that comes with victory. But he was also a statesman. He argued convincingly for the value and the necessity of the Union, and supported freedom and the democratic ideal. He envisioned a federal government based on universal suffrage and actively employing its energies under a broad construction of the Constitution to build internal improvements, promote the settlement of the West, and foster industry by a protective tariff. As a means to these ends he avowed repeatedly that slavery must be ended, and that the immigrants who were building up northern manpower and developing northern resources must be welcomed with open arms. And he took steps as a leader and legislator to translate these views from ideas into reality. His influence in the North was immense.

To a South dominated by an aristocratic ideal, opposed to tariff protection, to internal improvements at federal expense and to free land, devoted to keeping slaves that it at once valued and feared, profoundly distrustful of expanding the power of the national government and of endowing it with capacity for expenditure on a grand scale, Seward became the outstanding symbol of a northern viewpoint hated and despised. Who, asked Jefferson Davis in February 1861, had been "more industrious, patient and skillful as a sapper and miner against the foundations of the Constitution" than had William Henry Seward? It was so that the South came to picture him in the decade before the Civil War—able, intelligent, sinister, the head and front of those subversive forces that threatened to destroy the southern way of life. No other man of his generation points up as clearly the tragic differences between North and South that set the bugles blowing in 1861.[11]

❧ 15 ❧

The Best Laid Plans

The *Ariel* had a smooth and sunny passage and by May 19, 1859, reached the English Channel; a day later Seward was in London. There he stayed for the major part of the two months he spent in the British Isles, while the aristocracy vied with one another to do honor to the man whom they regarded as the next President of the United States. The Reform Club made him an honorary member for one month, explaining to him that this was the greatest length of time permitted by its constitution, and the Travellers' Club admitted him as a visiting dignitary. In 1833 he had only obtained a glimpse of King William IV by bribing a guard in the chapel at Windsor. Now, garbed in knee breeches, white waistcoat and cravat and a black dress coat, and carrying a three-cornered collapsible hat, he was presented at Court. Queen Victoria, "a sturdy, small, unaffected and kind person," exchanged comments with him on progress in the Anglo-Saxon countries, and Seward told her Majesty of his hope that peace could be preserved "between the two branches of our great family." He met Gladstone and Nassau Senior, attended the opening of Parliament, visited the law courts, and made the usual excursions to Oxford and Cambridge. Palmerston and Russell entertained him. The flood of other invitations was so great that in the confusion he forgot to appear at a dinner given by the royal physician, Sir Henry Holland. Such a crowd of great and titled personages beat a path to his door that, to his amusement, the hotel management bowed and scraped before him with ever-increasing vigor.

Before leaving home, Seward had intended to spend most of his time in France. Now he told Weed that he remained in London so that he might discover the interests of the government and its leaders. Actually, his love of English society and the adulation he received, more than a study of institutions and policies, led him to stay in London as long as he could find any excuse for prolonging his visit. He finally visited historic sites in Scotland and England for two weeks, saw something of the Midlands, and spent several days in Staffordshire at Trentham, the magnificent seat of the Duke and Duchess of Sutherland.[1]

Seward's views on the inner structure of English society and on the national future were scarcely based on profound observation, but they did illustrate his penchant for prophecy and his own social outlook. The class distinctions that he saw everywhere repelled him, and he foresaw a crumbling of the aristocracy into ruins as mournful as the castles of Warwick and Kenilworth. The immense estates of the landed aristocracy, he believed, would fall into the hands of "the active and industrious classes." He seems not to have foreseen the rise of an English laboring class, distinct from the bourgeoisie and with interests and a program of its own. Laborers, while they would be given the vote, would thankfully accept the economic betterment and improved educational opportunities that would be the fruits of democratic progress.

From England Seward went by way of Paris to Rome and Naples; visited northern Egypt and the Holy Land; and then came back through central Europe, Belgium, and Holland to the French capital, the while recording his impressions in voluminous letters home. Rome was "old and dull and black, medieval and inconvenient," but its art and architecture were majestic and surpassed in elegance all the other world capitals. He deplored the Papal government's rabid anti-Semitism, but found Pius IX a "good, old man," gracious and vivacious, who thanked him for his attitude toward Catholics and wished him well in regard to his "higher advancement." The trip to the Middle East was full of hardship, but it convinced him that the Jews would eventually triumph over Moslems and Christians in the Holy Land. In Beirut he obtained three

Seward and daughter Fanny, *c.* 1850. Seward House, Auburn, New York.

Frances Adeline Seward (1805-65).
Portrait by Jocelyn. Seward House, Auburn, New York.

Early portrait of Seward by an unknown artist.
Frick Art Reference Library.

Frances Adeline (Fanny)
Seward (1844-66). Seward
House, Auburn, New York.

Olive Risley Seward,
at about the age of 25.
University of Rochester Library.

Anna Wharton Seward
(1835-1919). Portrait by
Leutze. Seward House,
Auburn, New York.

Frederick W. Seward (1830-1915),
c. 1865. Seward House,
Auburn, New York.

Charlotte Cushman (1819-76).
Seward House, Auburn, New York.

Frances Adeline Seward,
c. 1860. Seward House,
Auburn, New York.

The Seward House in Auburn, New York,
as enlarged by Seward.
Seward House, Auburn, New York.

John Quincy Adams (1767-1848).
Seward regarded Adams as his political mentor.
U.S. Signal Corps photo (Brady Collection) in the National Archives.

Henry J. Raymond (1820-69). Courtesy of *The New York Times*.

Richard Milford Blatchford (1798-1875).
University of Rochester Library.

Horace Greeley, the powerful
editor of the New York *Tribune*.

fine Arabian horses for himself and purchased one for Simon
Cameron. On his return trip he visited Cavour at his country estate,
and had an audience with King Victor Emanuel, dined with King
Leopold I at Brussels, and was received by Napoleon and Eugenie at
Compiègne. He had hoped to meet Tocqueville. Had this been possible history might have had the record of an interesting dialogue,
but the author of *Democracy in America* had died in April.

The traveler saw many things on the Continent he did not like.
The Austro-Sardinian conflict, together with visits to the battlefields
of Solferino and Waterloo, caused him to reflect solemnly on the
tragedy of war and the transient character of earthly glory. The
despotism that reigned in France repelled him. Nevertheless, he felt
that, by and large, the signs of progress pointed to a better European
future. "Standing here as I do," he wrote to Frances from England,
"and looking with American eyes on what I see, the war in Europe
seems to me less a war between states and nations than a civil war; for
the European states, though not politically united, like the American
states, are nevertheless in fact one great commonwealth." Here was
a conception that was to underly the twentieth century struggle of
Europe toward unity.

Seward came home on the *Arago*, landing at New York in zero
weather on December 28 to the accompaniment of a hundred-gun
salute and the greetings of a crowd of well-wishers at the Astor
House. He held conferences with Republican leaders that took a
little more than a day, and on December 30 arrived in Auburn,
where he was greeted by a tumultuous reception. A great crowd
thronged the railroad station, banners and arches were everywhere,
bands played, church bells rang, and the boom of a brass six-
pounder that he had procured years before from the state arsenal at
Albany repeatedly interrupted his speech of acknowledgment for
this enthusiastic welcome. Speech-making over, he got into his sleigh
and, escorted by two military companies, rode from the railroad
station to his home. It was the sort of welcome that he loved.[2]

Speeches and jubilation over Seward's return were well enough,
but they could not conceal the growing state of tension between the
sections. Northern anti-slavery sentiment was on the rise. Helper's
Impending Crisis, with its appeal to the non-slaveholding southern
whites to cast aside the shackles of the "slaveocrats," circulated by

the hundreds of thousands of copies, and in state after state personal liberty laws, backed by the attitude of public officials and by public opinion, made it practically impossible to return fugitive slaves. The radical northern press poured scorn and abuse upon slavery and slaveholders, while northern resentment toward the South was enflamed by tales of plots for expanding slave territory in the Caribbean region, and of deliberate reopening of southern ports to the importation of black chattels.

Tempers also flared in the South. Many southerners felt bitter because of the way in which northern fanatics were defying the Constitution and the laws of the national government; over the way in which northern presses poured out a stream of vilification that might well produce slave uprisings. And then, in October 1859, as though in proof of this diabolical northern intent, had come John Brown's raid at Harper's Ferry.

Brown's effort to raise a slave rebellion was a dismal failure; Virginia tried and hung him for treason and other crimes committed against that state. But the tragic end of this fanatic's life only served to excite the passions of the South. That section raged when the northern press portrayed Old Brown as a martyr and men like Emerson and Thoreau glorified him as a saint. Southern newspapers teemed with denunciations of the abolitionists and also of the "Black Republicans," accused of being partners in Brown's schemes.

Seward was one of the Republican leaders branded as a Harper's Ferry conspirator, but not a scintilla of evidence was ever offered to prove the assertion. He had met Brown but once in his life, so he later averred, and at that time had been impressed by his honesty and truthfulness, but also by an eccentricity so marked as to border on an unsettled state of mind. He followed the news of Brown's trial as best he could while traveling in Europe, writing to his wife that he wondered "at the stoical firmness of the monomaniac" who "rises morally above his prosecutors so much that you almost forget his criminality." However, his views, though spread abroad by his supporters, had little effect, for when he came home he found southerners determined to identify him with the raid. James Chestnut of South Carolina charged in the United States Senate that Seward's reference to free labor "invading" the South had stimulated "much of the violence we have seen in the country." An advertisement in a Richmond paper offered $50,000 for the head of that traitor William H. Seward, and some southern hotheads talked of kidnapping him so that he could be hung without trial.

In Congress southerners showed milder forms of the same antagonism. When Seward resumed his seat the southern Senators were distinctly cool toward him. Representative Elbridge Gerry Spaulding, visiting the upper chamber, noted that Senator Mason, garbed in a suit of Virginia homespun and occupying a seat immediately to Seward's left, acted "like an old ass" in snubbing his neighbor, and that other southern Senators gave a similar exhibition of "plantation manners." Former Governor William Smith of Virginia, now in the House of Representatives, spread on the pages of the *Congressional Globe* the story of a conversation between himself and the New York Senator in which Seward had remarked that he was more than willing to accept free Negro voters from Virginia in exchange for the German and Irish voters in New York State who were such stubborn Democrats. The South was doing everything in its power to make clear its detestation of a man who talked about a higher law and an irrepressible conflict.[3]

The Republican national convention was now little more than four months away and Chicago had been chosen as the place for the Republicans to meet, all members of the national committee save Norman Judd of Illinois (who was Lincoln's campaign manager) regarding it as neutral ground. New York's political leaders were determined to give Seward the nomination at long last. To strengthen Seward support in such states as New Hampshire and Minnesota Weed had furnished funds for their 1859 elections. His lieutenants were everywhere surveying the ground, and a report from Illinois stated confidently that "Long John" Wentworth, a power in Chicago, was "right," and that the state would go for Seward. Weed built up a war chest by soliciting contributions from New York City business men, and by shaking down Republican officeholders in the state. He obtained the promise of large contributions to the campaign fund from the promoters of New York City street railways whose franchises he guided through the state legislature. Under his tutelage the Republican state convention, meeting at Syracuse on April 18, picked a solid Seward delegation for Chicago. He obtained assurances of support from Nathaniel P. Banks, former Know-Nothing and now governor of Massachusetts, rallied Archbishop Hughes to the cause, and moved cautiously but energetically to obtain the support of Pennsylvania. Evading Cameron's request that he come to Philadelphia before the convention, apparently because it was not clear that the Pennsylvania boss could control that state's delegation, he contributed $600 to the Pennsylvania state central committee for use in the Philadelphia municipal election of 1860.[4]

Weed oscillated between confidence and doubt. Just after the New York State election of 1859, when it looked as though the entire Republican slate had been elected, he said jubilantly to Richard M. Blatchford, "Blatch, I consider now that Seward's nomination and election are sure." A few days later, when it developed that the Republican candidate for secretary of state and two others had been defeated, he was not so certain, and there were times as the convention drew near when he spoke in gloomy tones of the fight for the nomination.

Seward did his best to smooth the path to victory. He drew up a disclaimer of any connection with the Harper's Ferry affair, one that could be used wherever necessary. He entertained lavishly at Washington, and exerted his charm, with considerable effect, to win back his old southern friends in the Senate. Such efforts blurred the image of his "radicalism." Moderation was now his watchword, and this became clear on February 13, when he rose in the Senate to deliver a eulogy on David C. Broderick, late Senator from California.

Broderick, elected to the Senate as a Democrat, had turned against Buchanan and the powerful slavery party in California. The state's chief justice, David S. Terry, challenged him to a duel. Broderick fell, mortally wounded, and his last words were supposed to have been, "They have killed me because I was opposed to the extension of slavery and a corrupt administration." Seward had regarded him as a valuable anti-slavery ally and, together with Weed, E. D. Morgan, and Blatchford, had arranged to go on his note for a $16,000 debt Broderick owed in California, so that he would be freed from paying 3 per cent a month interest upon it. It would have been only natural to make the observance of Broderick's death the occasion for a slashing attack on the slavocracy, but Seward did not do so, merely paying tribute to his friend as a man of honor and a frontier statesman who had been untimely slain.[5]

The Broderick eulogy was a straw in the wind. Far more important was a major speech, carefully planned. Seward wrote to Patterson, asking his advice, and sent the manuscript to Weed who approved it, saying it was in a "new vein, unambitious and yet effective." This was to be Seward's great effort for the nomination, and when he learned that Sumner was preparing an oration, he suggested that Charles Francis Adams head him off. Seward wanted the floor all to himself. On February 21 he gave notice that he would introduce a bill for the admission of Kansas and intended to speak on the subject. The news was out, and when he rose in his place on February 29 the floor and galleries of the Senate were packed to suffocation.

Seward began with a memorial from the Kansas legislature asking admission as a free state. Then, speaking slowly and distinctly in his quiet, conversational manner, he proceeded to his main subject. The "labor states," he said, regard the laborer as a free man; the "capital states" regard him as a slave. "What is just," he declared, "to one class of men can never be injurious to any other; and what is unjust to any condition of persons in a State is necessarily injurious in some degree to the whole community." Moderately, without rancor, he then rehearsed the historical development of the contest over slavery, which had now reached a point where the Democratic party, masked "behind the battery of the Supreme Court," had taken upon itself the defense of human bondage in the territories of the Union. The Republican party embodied the popular protest and reaction to a policy so allied with despotism. It sought to save the territories, by constitutional and lawful means, from slavery and polygamy. It also championed other important interests of freedom—an untrammeled speech and press, the rights of the individual safeguarded by the Constitution, and the prosperity of mining, manufacturing, and internal commerce.

Republicanism, Seward declared, was national in its viewpoint, and it would meet threats of disunion "seriously and with a just moderation." He rejected the charge that it was any more sectional in outlook than its opponent. Was it easier for the North to bear the sway of another section of the country than it was for the South? Let each section extend the privilege of free debate to the other, "and I will engage that you will very soon have in the South as many Republicans as we have Democrats in the North"—at which the galleries roared applause and the presiding officer, Benjamin Fitzpatrick of Alabama, threatened to have them cleared.

A better test of the nationalism of parties than "accidental location," continued Seward, was their labor policy. Its opponents charged the Republican party with trying to introduce Negro equality, but what it really sought was the equality of white men as that equality existed in the free states, where the laborer was the political equal of the employer. Furthermore, "we do not seek to force, or even to intrude, our system on you." The southern states were sovereign within their borders on the subject of slavery, and new and future states were a subject for discussion between North and South "with mutual toleration and in a fraternal spirit."

The South's complaints about anti-slavery propaganda should be tempered by regard for the great principle of freedom of speech. Then turning to Vice President Breckinridge's lament over the cleavage between North and South manifested in Congress, Seward declared that, while he could not answer for the South, he could give assurance that there was not one disunionist or disloyalist among the northern members. "We have never been more patient and never loved the representatives of other sections more than now," he said, and this was true also of the districts and states the northerners represented. As for John Brown's raid, that was "an act of sedition and treason," perpetuated by misguided and desperate men who acted under provocation and "earnest though fatally erroneous convictions." The deaths of these offenders, though "pitiable," were "necessary and just."

The Republican party, vindicated against the charge of hostility to the South, would take for its motto "UNION and Liberty. . . ." How could it ever practise tyranny under the checks interposed by the Constitution? If it attempted to do so, it could be thrown out of office. Hasty threats of disunion, Seward concluded, were so unnatural that they would find no hand to execute them. This was a government of the whole people, one in "race, language, liberty, and faith." Their strongest bonds "are the millions of fibers of millions of contented, happy human hearts," whose affections, ambitions, and hopes bound them to a government "the first, the last, and the only such one that has ever existed." This government could not cease to be, even though "a great policy fastened upon the country . . . is to be relaxed and changed." The winds of controversy might blow and the pillars of the government seem to tremble, but "the earth is firm as always before, and the wonderful structure, for whose safety we have feared so anxiously, now more firmly fixed than ever, still stands unmoved, enduring and immovable."

As the New Yorker sat down, Douglas sprang to his feet. Seward's attempt to pin responsibility for the present crisis on the Democratic party was unjust, he said. Seward held Negroes and white men equal by Divine law, and maintained that, where the Constitution recognized slavery, it violated Divine law. He championed Negro equality, but at the same time claimed that Republican doctrine was the equality of white men. If the signers of the Declaration of Independence had understood the matter as Seward did, sneered Douglas, they would have been bound to emancipate their slaves, but not one of them did so. This was a government of white men and should be administered by them only. He derided the terms "labor states" and "capital states" as a dodge to get votes from the working class and, as proof of Seward's radicalism, quoted Seward's statement at Cleveland in 1848 that "slavery must be abolished and you and I must do it."

Jefferson Davis seconded Douglas's assault. It was the North and not the South, he said, that was destroying the Union by its attacks upon slavery. Seward was one of the chief sappers and miners of the foundations of the Constitution. Even today, he had decried states' rights and talked "about the individual masses coercing the sovereign states of the Union." Seward in his zeal depicted the Negro slave as a human being reduced to a mere chattel. This was false. In the South the slave was "still a person, protected by all the laws which punish crime in other persons. . . . the criminal law covers them as perfectly as it covers the white man," taking into consideration that by their nature they "are not fit to govern themselves." [6]

The immediate riposte of Seward's opponents in the Senate stood as the best possible tribute to the effectiveness of his speech. The Republican Executive Congressional Committee alone ordered 250,-000 copies printed, and in all half a million in pamphlet form went out to the country. The New York *Times* put it out in a special supplement, and it was reprinted in the major northern newspapers.

The speech had its critics. Ultra-abolitionists complained because

Seward had said that Brown was justly punished. The South's opinion of Seward as a dangerous character remained unchanged. Henry A. Wise, governor of Virginia, wrote to Edward Everett that the speech had been a miserable failure, and that Seward had been so drunk on the evening after it was delivered that not even his toadies could understand a word he said.

Such cavils were inevitable, but were far outweighed by a flood of praise. The typesetters on the New York *Tribune* applauded the speech as they set it up. James Bowen wrote that it was "without a blunder. . . . The only mistake that can be made is to make *another* speech." Horace Binney Sargent declared that it provided a national platform. Sumner told the Duchess of Argyle that it "is cautious & has insight & elegance. It undertakes to plead the right cause without giving offense, & especially not to furnish expressions, phrases or sentences that might be used against him, & in this he seems to have succeeded." Russell of the London *Times* wrote an editorial on the speech that John Bigelow described as most liberal and encouraging to the Republicans. Seward himself believed that it had been a success, at once an olive branch and a statement of Republican principle that was consistent with loyalty to the Union and patriotism.[7]

Pleased by the reception of his speech, Seward wore an air of confidence in public and among his friends. Charles Francis Adams thought him certain of the nomination, and an ambitious young New York politician named A. Oakey Hall, after talking over the prospects with the Senator, bet $250 that he would be the Republican standard bearer. Nevertheless, the reports that came in to Seward and Weed were of a decidedly mixed character.

Not all the news was bad. The February 29 speech had good effects in various quarters, and the Democratic split at Charleston in April, when the cotton states walked out of the convention, augured a cleavage in the opposition that might well clear the way for Seward's nomination. Prestigious individuals, Charles Sumner and Henry Wilson, for example, were encouraging about his chances as convention time drew near. But such straws in the wind were more than counterbalanced by evidence that came in from state after state and from Congress itself.

Many in the Middle West, so went these reports, were hostile to

Seward's candidacy. Conservative Middle Westerners disliked slavery as a campaign issue and were against him on that ground. The Indiana *State Journal* was anti-Seward, and the Cincinnati *Gazette* charged that he was an exponent of equality between Negroes and whites. In Illinois, Joseph Medill and the Chicago *Tribune* frowned on his nomination, Judd was hostile, and anti-Sewardism was rampant in the central and southern portions of the state. In Wisconsin some doubted his availability. Even Kansas, for which he had been a spokesman in the Senate, was dubious. There the impulsive firebrand Jim Lane claimed to be his special friend and favorite, and for this and other reasons, powerful Charles Robinson declared that Seward had no prestige in the territory. Reports from California told of opposition there. In the East, Know-Nothingism was strong and venomous. It made Pennsylvania a contested ground and created a similar situation in New Jersey, where doubts circulated about whether Seward could carry the state. In New York the Know-Nothings were active in some quarters, and Greeley was continually suggesting in the *Tribune* that Seward would be a weak candidate. Know-Nothingism and the availability argument cooled the ardor of many a New Englander, and others were hesitant because they felt that Seward was too closely linked with corruption in New York State affairs. In the corridors of the Capitol Seward's enemies whispered incessantly that, if nominated, he would surely be beaten. Some Congressmen praised his speech of February 29, but at the same time kept arguing that he was not really available; that conservatives would not support him; that he was in advance of his age. Even Charles Francis Adams, stout anti-slavery man that he was, believed that if Seward were nominated the convention might do well to dispense with a declaration of principles. Seward's nomination, he thought, would have enough significance so that Republican views need not be stressed in a platform.[8] And as if such difficulties were not enough, there was a host of potential candidates—Bates, Chase, Banks, Cameron, Frémont, Lincoln, and others —all with their zealous supporters.

Despite his public protestations of confidence, Seward sensed the strength of this conservative movement against him. "I am half a mind to go back to Westfield," he wrote to Patterson, who had just been elected a supervisor in Chautauqua County, "where it seems they don't think it an objection to a man that he is identified with their own party"; and he told his wife a few days later that Republicanism was seeking to disavow its basic principle of uncompromising antagonism between slavery and freedom.

It was undoubtedly with such opposition in mind that he wrote to Weed about Henry Winter Davis as a running mate. Davis was a Maryland Know-Nothing who had gone Republican that winter in the protracted struggle over the House speakership. Seward understood that Davis would be glad to be on the ticket, and he could bring a large block of votes with him. What did Weed think?

Weed wrote at once to Congressman Elbridge Gerry Spaulding, who knew Davis well. Spaulding decried putting on the ticket a man with such pronounced nativist principles, and there the matter ended. Nevertheless, both Weed and Seward were deeply concerned and, as convention time drew near, felt that much reliance would have to be placed "on the tone of the times and the temper of the delegates to overrule aspirations, jealousies, and animosities." [9]

The Republican convention was to meet at Chicago on May 16 in the Wigwam, a building specially erected for the occasion. Some of Seward's supporters felt that this date was a happy omen, for it was his birthday. As he left Washington for Auburn on May 11, his manner indicated certainty that all was well. He had in preparation a farewell speech to the Senate, for his resignation would follow hard upon his receiving the Republican nomination.

While Seward shook the dust of Washington off his feet, Weed made his last-minute preparations for Chicago. He and the New York delegation, a large and motley crew, arrived there on May 12. Men like Governor King, Blatchford, Moses H. Grinnell, Schoolcraft, and William M. Evarts lent dignity to the group, but others were politicians of a rougher sort. This gentry, heartened by the music of the famous Dodsworth's band, drank everybody's whiskey, slapped backs, boasted that New York had oceans of cash to spend on the campaign, and made vociferous complaint about that "damned old ass" Horace Greeley when they were not rending the air with shouts for "Old Irrepressible."

Weed wanted a running mate for Seward from a southern state. His thoughts had turned to Edward Bates of Missouri, an Old Whig who was being pushed by the Blairs and Greeley, and who was so conservative that Joseph Medill once described him as a fossil of the Silurian era. When the New York Dictator reached Chicago, however, and sized up the ground, he moved with caution. Michigan, Wisconsin, Minnesota, and northern Illinois were strong for Seward, but the size and vehemence of the opposition was impressive. Indiana Republicans declared that, if he were nominated, their state ticket would go down to defeat. Greeley, on the back of whose coat some joker had pinned a Seward badge, told everyone that Seward could not carry Pennsylvania, New Jersey, Indiana, or Illinois, all important states. Many former Democrats were either hostile or lukewarm. The Connecticut delegation and its chairman, Gideon Welles, went about among the other New Englanders arguing against Seward. "Old Blair and his pups," Spaulding noted, were bitter in opposition, and Blair went around showing delegates a letter from William Cullen Bryant of the New York *Evening Post* which said that Seward's nomination would be a blunder. Followers of Chase, Cameron, and McLean downgraded the New Yorker.

Meanwhile, the Illinois delegation pushed Lincoln vigorously, and was lavish with promises of Cabinet and other posts. The New York *Tribune*'s correspondent believed that all the Northwest would cheerfully accept Lincoln, and Weed sought to counter the drive by making it known that Seward would be glad to have Lincoln for Vice President.[10]

The New York leaders worked hard and remained confident, for they believed that the opposition would be unable to agree upon a candidate. Schoolcraft, with a heart too weak to stand the strain, labored for his friend until he became fatally ill. Weed visited one delegation after another, exerting all his persuasive powers. He promised lavish financial support for Andrew G. Curtin and Henry S. Lane, the gubernatorial candidates in Pennsylvania and Indiana, if they would swing their states to Seward; he helped to ward off the two-thirds rule in the choice of candidates. On the evening of May 16, even Greeley conceded that Seward had a fifty-fifty chance of victory, and twenty-four hours later the doughty editor telegraphed the *Tribune* that it looked as though Seward would be nominated. That evening the New York delegation had a champagne supper at the Richmond House to celebrate their triumph on the morrow.

While Weed strained every nerve at Chicago, Seward remained in

Auburn waiting anxiously for the outcome. On the 17th, telegrams came from Governor Morgan and from Spaulding, assuring him that there was no doubt of his nomination, and the next morning there was a message from Preston King, Evarts, and Blatchford—"All right. Everything indicates your nomination today sure." Seward's friends thereupon moved a cannon, probably the brass six-pounder, to a street close by the Seward home. The plan was that when the good news came, the gun would be placed in the little park adjoining the Seward grounds and fired in celebration.

The convention assembled at ten o'clock that morning, some communications were read, and the credentials of certain delegates from Maryland were considered at length. Then came the nomination of candidates, and finally the balloting, a lengthy procedure.

It was a fine spring day in Auburn, and that afternoon Seward sat with a neighbor, the Reverend John M. Austin, under the shade of one of his own trees close by the park fence. Another friend, Dr. Theodore Dimon, had assumed the role of messenger boy, bringing the news from the telegraph office as fast as it arrived. Early that morning, or the night before, Weed had telegraphed that Seward would be nominated on the third ballot.

The first ballot showed Seward ahead with 173½ votes. Lincoln was next with 102, and the rest were scattered, the largest block being cast for favorite sons. Then came the second ballot, showing Seward with 184½, while Lincoln had shot up to 181. It was clear that something serious was happening in Chicago. Seward could not know the details, but New Hampshire, which had promised the night before to go for Seward on the next day, had given Lincoln 7 of its 10 votes on the first ballot and had now given Lincoln 9 and Seward 1; Vermont had switched its 10 votes from favorite son Jacob Collamer to Lincoln; Pennsylvania, abandoning Cameron, had now given Lincoln 48 of its 54 votes; and Connecticut, Rhode Island, Ohio and one or two other states had begun shifting to Lincoln. In a last desperate effort to stave off defeat Weed promised a rally of Seward men to Bates if the third ballot produced no nomination, but it was in vain. Already the roll of the states was being called, and in one state after another the favorite son vote was switching to the railsplitter from Illinois.

When the third ballot ended, Seward had 180 and Lincoln 231½ votes. Nomination required 233. In a hall that became tense and still, D. K. Carrter, chairman of the Ohio delegation, rose and announced a shift of four votes from Chase to Lincoln. Then amid a mighty roar of applause other shifts came, and William M. Evarts rose on behalf of the downcast New York delegation to move that they make the choice unanimous.

The convention had made its decision. Horace Greeley beamed in triumph. Thurlow Weed buried his face in his hands, and the tears ran down his cheeks.

While these dramatic events took place in Chicago, Seward and Austin sat waiting for news of the third roll call. Finally, and the time must have seemed long to both men, they saw Dr. Dimon coming up the street with a telegram in his hand. It was from Governor Morgan and it read—"Lincoln nominated third ballot."

As Dimon remembered it, there was no change in Seward's easy, lounging attitude, or the interested look on his face, as he read those four words. He said, "Well, Mr. Lincoln will be elected and has some of the qualities to make a good President." There followed a little "quiet conversation," and then Dimon and other friends had a hasty consultation and hauled the cannon away. A couple of hours later, in another part of the town and with the powder provided for Seward's triumph, it barked out a salute to Abraham Lincoln.[11]

Why had Seward gone down to defeat at Chicago? For one thing, Weed, the master bargainer, had been outbargained. David Davis and Lincoln's other campaign managers went to the convention with an admonition from Lincoln to buy no support in his name, and then made promises of Cabinet posts and other positions that their candidate later made good. The noisy shouts of thousands of Lincoln rooters from Indiana and Illinois, both inside and outside the convention, undoubtedly had a psychological effect upon the delegates. Some, perhaps only a few, were influenced by the stories of unsavory doings at Albany and the fear that corruption might reign at Washington if Seward were elected.

But in the main, success or failure for Seward in the Wigwam hinged on availability. As he himself had said on an earlier occasion, the fundamental question was, whom could the party elect? Here nativism was one powerful consideration. Tens of thousands of nativists had trooped into the ranks of Republicanism as Know-

Nothingism collapsed, and Seward had been one of their long-standing and outspoken enemies. The Greeley argument that he would lose four of the states in which nativism was still strong undoubtedly carried weight.

And just as important as nativism was Seward's supposed radicalism on slavery. Plainly the delegates, opposed though they were to its extension, committed though they were to its eventual extinction, were anxious to enhance the party's chances in the border slave states, and to ensure victory in Illinois and Indiana where there was strong pro-slavery sentiment. How could this be done with Seward as a candidate? To be sure he had stated that the extinction of slavery would be a slow process, perhaps taking half a century to accomplish, but he had also said that northerners must free the slaves, and he had become identified in the popular mind as a believer in a "higher law" than the Constitution, and in the existence of an "irrepressible conflict" between North and South. Willy-nilly he had created for himself an image of extremism that made the delegates turn against him.

The politicians who, by 1860, had built up a smoothly running political machine that garnered votes from high- and low-tariff men, abolitionists and Negro-haters, advocates of temperance and lovers of Demon Rum, saw in Lincoln an availability that Seward lacked. Lincoln was a symbol of the common man, a railsplitter who had been born in a log cabin. A friend of labor, he had publicly approved the right to strike. He had taken pains to curry favor with the Illinois Germans, but he had not committed himself on nativism as Seward had done. He had lagged behind Seward in open opposition to slavery, and when he did come out had taken no position that could be regarded as extreme. Had he not been for putting a southern man in second place on the ticket? Had he not repudiated both Hinton Helper and John Brown? Had he not made clear his belief that he opposed social and political equality for the Negro? Even his "House Divided" speech had stressed moderation and time as indispensable in the elimination of the Negro's bondage.

The delegates at Chicago had no vision of Seward in the White House disappointing the ultras on both sides and trying, perhaps more effectively than Lincoln tried, to avert the final breach between the sections. They were practical politicians, and they did the best they knew. They chose a canny politician who had assumed no vulnerable positions and had made no major mistakes, and in so doing they happened to nominate a great man. And Seward was left alone in Auburn to watch and weigh and consider his next move.[12]

❧ 16 ❧

Into the Breach Once More

Seward's loyal following took his defeat hard. Weed, in a state of
gloom that bordered on complete despair, wrote that he had little
inclination to think or speak or write, and still less to go where he
could be seen or questioned. Young Henry Adams declared that,
while the Italians had stood by their heroes, Garibaldi and Cavour,
the Americans had rejected their Garibaldi in 1856 and now in 1860
had "done still better; we have deserted our Cavour." Poughkeepsie
Republicans fired a salute in honor of the nomination but, mourned
one of their number, "the swearing is awful. Oh, its rough, its very
rough." Something like a mantle of sadness enveloped Auburn.

Auburn's leading citizen had mixed reactions. He took the blow as
a champion should—smiling as he told Frances in three words,
"Abraham Lincoln nominated"; writing to Weed of his "un-
bounded gratitude for this last as for the whole life of efforts in my
behalf"; promptly announcing his support of the ticket and urging
all his friends and followers to do likewise. But it was impossible to
keep other thoughts from crowding into his brain. He could not
face, for the moment, appearing at public ratifications; he could not
help dwelling on the bitter humiliation of going back to Washington, "a leader deposed by his own party in the hour of organization
for decisive battle." It was, he felt, the lukewarm Republicans, the
Laodiceans, those who blew neither hot nor cold in the struggle
against slavery, who had been responsible for his defeat. They had

turned him down and, though he put on a brave front before his family and the world, underneath his proud spirit was mortified. He was on the Mount, he wrote to his friend, Benjamin D. Silliman, with Jordan at his feet, Canaan on the other side, and the Republican hosts crossing the river. "It is best that I be content to rest and wait, even if I am not appointed to die on the bank. Who would be content to see me lead? Who would be satisfied with my lead? How could it be that I should not become the head of a faction or reduce the Administration to that condition if I should remain in office. . . ." It was only some months later, when the shock had worn off and hope of a sort had revived, that he could say half ruefully, half whimsically, how fortunate it was that he did not keep a diary, for if he had there would be a record of all his cursing and swearing on the day after the news came.[1]

Mingled with Seward's dejection there was also bitterness. Nothing else can account for the blunder he made about Greeley. Weed had written that the *Tribune*'s editor had acted both malignantly and unscrupulously at Chicago, and just as this letter arrived Raymond and Webb appeared at Auburn on their way back from the convention. They brought news of the desperate illness of Seward's close friend Schoolcraft, who had gone to Chicago a sick man and, as a result of his efforts there, was now near death. This did nothing to relieve Seward's feelings, which were further harried by their account of Greeley's doings at the Wigwam. Seward then said it was right that they should know the cause of Greeley's enmity; that he had a letter from Greeley which showed that he was a disappointed office-seeker. At their request he read them the famous missive of 1854 with its complaints about political errors and lack of recognition for service rendered. Seward told them, so they later declared, that no reference should be made to it. Such an injunction would have been in keeping with his character, but if it was laid down, he did it lightly, for Raymond paid it no attention. He and the *Tribune*'s editor had been long at odds, and now he wrote out a blistering editorial for the *Times*, dating it at Auburn.

Seward, said Raymond, regarded his public life as closed. He would serve out his term in the Senate and then retire to Auburn, where he was deeply loved. Greeley had given credit to the Blairs and certain governors for the result at the Wigwam, but Greeley himself had been the major cause of Seward's defeat. Greeley had special qualifications as well as a special love for the task. Supposedly a friend, he had been preparing the event for half a year by his doubts and innuendos in the *Tribune,* and he had worked ceaselessly to that end at the convention. Six years ago, he had privately broken the alliance of Weed, Seward, and Greeley and had menaced Seward with hostility—all because the latter had never helped him get office. Let us, snarled Raymond, give this disappointed office-seeker the full credit that his modesty does not claim, at least until the post-election rewards are distributed.

Raymond's attack filled Greeley with fury, all the more because there was in it an element of truth. As he himself admitted, during the past six years his relations with the Senator "had always been frank and kindly." He had breakfasted and dined at Seward's home, and mutual friends had understood him to say that he was a Seward supporter. Furthermore he had complained in the famous letter that he was passed by in patronage distribution. Now he began calling for that document, declaring that Seward withheld it so that his devotees could pervert it to their purposes. As a result the *Tribune,* the *Times* and the *Evening Journal* all published the fateful letter with extensive comment, and from then on any chance of a rapprochement between Seward and Greeley vanished. The latter apparently made a tentative bid for reconciliation the following February through their mutual friend, Samuel Wilkeson, but it came to nothing. Wilkeson did not mention any possibility of reconciliation with Weed, for by that time Weed and Greeley were carrying on unrelenting war.

While the feud with Greeley gathered force, Seward went back to the Senate, where Mason, Davis, and other Democrats extended their sympathy, showing, as he told Frances, "that their past prejudices had been buried in the victory they had achieved over me." He found Washington dispiriting, the more so because the congressional Republicans seemed to be completely disorganized, and he took little part in the closing days of the session.[2]

Just before Seward left for Auburn, two prominent members of the House, Charles Francis Adams and Israel Washburn, called at his Washington home. The *Tribune* was industriously circulating reports of his resignation from the Senate, and there were other

rumors of his retirement from public life. The two men urged him
to remain an active Republican leader, for they were alarmed lest,
with Lincoln at the helm, the party might lose direction. Seward
listened to them and, much to their relief, appeared to be receptive.

Seward was the more disposed to listen to Adams and Washburn
because he had received a flood of letters, many of them distrustful of
Lincoln and all urging him to remain an active guide of the party's
course. Badly hurt though he was, he was still ambitious. He was
certain that, with the Democrats hopelessly split, a Republican
victory lay ahead, and while he did not wish to rush into the canvass
so impetuously that it would look as if he feared he was being forgotten, he did want to be in the thick of the fray. After all, a politician in whom hope died hard would have to spike the rumor that
New York Sewardites were willing to have Stephen A. Douglas,
candidate of the northern Democracy, carry the state. More com-
pelling still, he had a natural desire to keep the incoming administration from falling into the hands of his enemies. On July 10 he accepted an invitation to speak in Minnesota. Then came a deluge of
requests, one from Springfield, seconded by Lincoln, to speak there
on August 8. This was turned down, on the ground of a previous
commitment in New England, but a western itinerary soon took
shape.[3]

Early in August, Seward had a rendezvous at William M. Evarts's
home in Windsor, Vermont, with Weed and some New Yorkers
who could be expected to furnish financial sinews for the campaign.
Then came a barnstorming trip through New England, during the
course of which he made seven or eight speeches urging support of
the Republican ticket. He ignored Sumner in Boston, much to that
worthy's disgruntlement, but Charles Francis Adams was a different
matter. They occupied the same platform and, after a speech in
which he paid full tribute to John Quincy Adams, Seward asked
Charles Francis if he intended taking him out to Quincy. Adams had
had no such idea, but he rose to the occasion, and Seward spent the
next day at the Adams ancestral mansion.

During the course of this impromptu visit, Seward pressed Adams
to join him on his projected western tour, not only because he
personally wanted him along but also because of Adams's political
influence. Urged by Charles Francis, Jr., who was invited to come

along too, Adams reluctantly consented. He cautiously recorded in his diary that, from the tenor of Seward's conversation, it looked as though the New Yorker expected to wield considerable influence in the Lincoln administration. Adams was not the only one saying this. The New York *Herald* was declaring openly that the Senator from New York had dreams of being the real President of the United States.

The western tour started early in September with a swing through Michigan and into Wisconsin and Minnesota, then down into Iowa and Kansas, back through Illinois and home by way of Cleveland. Seward loved to have an entourage about him on such a trip, and the one he now assembled certainly had the merit of diversity. It included his fifteen-year-old daughter Fanny and her friend Ellen Perry, the two Adamses and George E. Baker (editor of Seward's *Works*), George W. Patterson, and General James Nye, a coarse, back-slapping politician with a fund of off-color stories, whose pretty seventeen-year-old daughter completed the feminine contingent. Others who were asked to go along begged off, and not all of those who went lasted out the journey.

Seward's speeches on this western tour paid tribute to the role of the foreign-born in developing America's resources and, in that same connection, emphasized the importance of free labor. He repeatedly extolled the virtues of the West in the development of American democracy. At St. Paul he told his listeners that the ultimate center of American power would be near the head of navigation of the Mississippi, for Canada and Alaska eventually would be part of the American Union. He paid little specific attention to the economic planks in the Republican platform—protection, internal improvements, a homestead act, a railroad to the Pacific—probably assuming that other speakers would cover those familiar themes. But he had a great deal to say about slavery.

With plentiful references to the higher law and the irrepressible conflict, he portrayed the peculiar institution not only as morally bad but also as stultifying democracy and crippling industry, agriculture, and commerce. Repeatedly he stressed the futility of compromises with slavery, but he emphasized with equal earnestness the theme of moderation and peace. The nation needed quiet, he told his audiences, and there would be quiet after the fourth of March, for the next administration would rely on justice and moral suasion in dealing with the South. He scoffed at the idea of secession. "Who's afraid?" he asked on one occasion. As for the Negro, while he was incapable of assimilation, he lived in a land of liberty, and therefore must have freedom of thought, speech, and religion, and also the right to vote.[4]

This foray into the West took some four weeks. During it Seward made at least ten major speeches, and any number of shorter ones at whistle stops. Everywhere there were companies of Republican marchers, Wide Awakes and Little Wide Awakes, who roared out the campaign song "Ain't You Glad You Joined the Republicans?" Everywhere there were parades with bands and fife and drum corps, the booming of cannon, and at night bonfires, torchlight processions and fireworks. The noise, the endless crowds of politicians and well-wishers, the night travel demanded by the schedule of the trip, made it an exciting and exhausting experience.

On the way back from Kansas the train on which Seward rode made a twenty-minute stop on October 1 in Springfield, and Lincoln came aboard. Young Charles Francis Adams noted the awkward manner of the Republican nominee, noticed, too, that Seward seemed constrained in manner. Lincoln suggested a point that he would like Seward to make in his speech at Chicago on October 3, and Seward said that he would do so. Seward wrote later that he had followed the suggestion but the newspapers had reported it rather briefly. But he had made the same point "freely and strongly," he wrote, in an earlier speech at Dubuque which was reported in the New York *Times*. Lincoln replied that he was satisfied with what Seward had said at Chicago and would "look up the speech made at Dubuque and published in the N. Y. *Times*." If this was all a bit of swordplay, the honors were about even. Seward's letter could be interpreted as suggesting that he had previously covered the ground that Lincoln wanted covered at Chicago, and Lincoln's reply could be taken to indicate that he had not bothered to read Seward's Dubuque speech.[5]

Seward consumed a considerable amount of brandy and other alcoholic beverages, and smoked incessantly during the trip. Young Adams, who had also acquired the cigar habit, jotted down in his diary an account of an early morning resort to the baggage car which served as a smoker, with Seward (wrapped in a remarkable gold-embroidered cashmere cloak that he had acquired in Syria) saying that they had made themselves 'independent on this tobacco question.' On route from Chicago to Cleveland they crawled, fully dressed, into berths that were merely shelves on the side of the car. The train stopped at Toledo in the middle of the night, and the candidate of the Northern Democracy rushed into the car, a bottle of whiskey clutched in one hand. He urged Seward to come out and "speak to the boys," but Seward refused on plea of being sleepy. Douglas left, taking a drink as he did so, and Seward remarked that he was of no mind to make an exhibit of himself for the sake of the Douglas's political capital.

As the train rolled along from Rochester to Auburn, Seward told young Adams the names of the lakes and bridges, and at local stations he would alight and exchange greetings with all and sundry, for he seemed to know everyone. At the Auburn station a friendly crowd fussed over him until they put him, greatly pleased, into a coach that took him to his house. It was a politician's homecoming.

Exhausting as this western campaign trip must have been, Seward's Auburn stay was short. By the middle of October he was in Albany for a dinner at Governor Morgan's with "Lord Renfrew," the Prince of Wales who was traveling in America incognito and whose tour Seward had done much to arrange. Then came an arduous speaking tour through the state. The pace took its toll, and in late October, while in the Fredonia area, he had attacks of fever and ague. Patterson warned him against further engagements, but Seward would not listen.

There was good reason for him to be anxious about the New York State situation. Three candidates opposed Lincoln—Douglas, John C. Breckinridge for the Southern Democracy, and John Bell of Tennessee for the Constitutional Union party. Desperate efforts at fusion were being made between these three as the campaign drew toward its close, and nowhere were they more significant than in New York. If the Douglas-Bell-Breckinridge electoral ticket there concocted could carry that state, Lincoln would not have a majority in the electoral college, and the election would go into the House of Representatives, where in all probability he would be defeated. The chief hope of the fusionists was New York City, where they counted on the great bulk of the powerful merchant class to support their ticket.

On October 25 Weed wrote to Seward urging him to make a soothing speech at New York, one showing that the Republican party was all for peace, union, and prosperity. Exhausted though he was, Seward consented and on November 2, four days before the election, spoke to an enormous crowd at Palace Garden. The election of Lincoln and the Republican ticket, he said, would mean the peaceful limitation of slavery to the areas where it then existed, and this in turn would mean freedom for the nation's economic development. There would be no acts of aggression against the slave states, and he discounted the threats of secession. He closed with an affirmation of faith in the American people's sense of justice and humanity and in their loyalty to the Union.

Seward's reception at Palace Garden had been enthusiastic to the point of tumult. The crowd was so great that benches were smashed in the crush, and there were overflow meetings. Evarts's attempt to address the multitude before the main speaker appeared on the platform was greeted by cries of "Seward," and adjurations to "Cut it short." Seward's speech was interrupted repeatedly by cheers and applause, and at its conclusion there was a deafening ovation. Then "Old Abe's Choir" rendered "Ain't We Glad Abe's Going to the White House," and a glee club sang

> In '64 with peace secured
> We will have our William Seward.

Judging by the reception of this speech, Seward played no inconsiderable part in holding the fusion ticket's New York City majority to 30,000, which was wiped out by the enormous Republican vote upstate.[6]

The election of 1860 demonstrated that southern domination of the national government, evident for three generations and so marked during the 1850s, had ended. It also presaged the breakup of the Union. It was almost as though two parties in two different countries were competing for the prize, so weak were Lincoln and Douglas in the South, and Breckinridge and Bell in the North.

When the balloting was over, and it became clear that the Railsplitter from Illinois was to be in the White House, shock, amazement, and indignation swept over the people of the slaveholding states. In the Upper South the mood varied from anger to something like resignation, but there a desire for peace predominated. The border slave states drew back from any rash action that might precipitate a sanguinary struggle. There was even a feeling that perhaps Lincoln was not so bad after all. The Democracy would still control the Senate, the Supreme Court was a bulwark against extremism, and this minority President could do little harm save by the negative power of veto.

But in the Deep South, extremists bestirred themselves to violence and carried all before them. They ignored the fundamentally conservative approach of the Republican leadership to the slavery question, the gradualism preached by Lincoln and Seward, the weakness of Lincoln's position as a minority President. To men like Rhett of South Carolina, Toombs of Georgia, and Yancey of Alabama, the all-important fact was that a party hostile to slavery and championing economic policies which threatened the southern way of life—a party that slowly, perhaps, but inexorably would force the South to abandon a slavery-dominated economic and social order—had elected a President of the United States. To these men and to the masses that followed them it was the handwriting on the wall, an awful admonition that the destruction of things they cherished was near at hand. Sparked by the inflammatory speeches of such leaders, an explosion of rage and resentment swept through South Carolina, Georgia, Alabama, Mississippi, and Florida, states where belief in the dogma of states' rights and the self-sufficiency of the South was particularly strong.

It was South Carolina that set the course toward disaster. There violence became the talk of the day. The old palmetto flag of the American Revolution, and a states' rights emblem, white with a red star, blossomed out over Charleston; the legislature called for an election of delegates to a convention that would determine whether or not the state would leave the Union. Georgia, Alabama, Mississippi, and Florida followed the example thus set, and by the end of November the Deep South, save for Louisiana, was on the way to secession.

Meanwhile in the North, even though the thunder of the drums became plainer every day, very few were conscious of imminent danger to the Union. When Congress met on December 3, neither Republicans nor Democrats had what could be called a policy for dealing with the growing crisis.[7]

What would be Seward's attitude in this crucial time? All his life he had preached the importance, the necessity, of national existence and had emphasized the strength of the ties that made the states united, ties so strong that he knew the masses would be for liberty and union when it came to a question of whether the nation was to endure slave or free. The first duty of Americans, he had said at Cleveland in 1848, was to preserve the Union's integrity, for without it there would be chaos. But in that same speech he had asserted that it must be a voluntary Union; that one upheld by force "must be despotism." [8] And all his public life he had opposed the idea of compromise. Where would he stand now, what policy would he adopt, when the cords that bound the nation together were fraying, one by one?

⋙ 17 ⋘

To Save the Union

During the campaign Seward had not foreseen the crisis that was now fast approaching. He had planned to remain in Auburn until after the Christmas holidays, but by the middle of November the signs of conflict were too ominous to be ignored. Five days after the election, Adams wrote to him of southern threats and fury, and of the necessity for his taking command of the incoming administration; and Seward replied, though rather enigmatically, that he too was anxious about the course of events. On November 18 he wrote to Weed that the "southern disturbances" made him feel that he should be in Washington for the opening of Congress, though as for himself, he was "without schemes or plans, hopes, or desires or fears."

Seward reached Washington on November 30. The blindness of Republican members to the danger threatening the Union was all too evident, but cases he argued in the Supreme Court kept him busy for several days. Weed presented another problem. Frightened by the dour look of things, he had sent up a trial balloon on November 24 in the *Journal*, suggesting a strengthening of the fugitive slave law and restoration of the Missouri Compromise line of 36° 30′. Six days later, while emphasizing that he had spoken and was speaking only for himself, the Albany editor proposed a constitutional convention with delegates appointed by the states. This clearly indicated the adoption of constitutional amendments to safeguard slavery.

Busily revolving in his mind ideas for saving the Union "without sacrifice of principle," Seward found Weed's action well-intentioned but impulsive and embarrassing, and he made this clear to Weed. He, himself, felt compromise was not the answer; and that any constitutional amendment satisfactory to the South could not pass Congress. He believed that South Carolina and the Deep South would go out of the Union, but that then passion would be succeeded by perplexity about whether to conciliate the Union or fight it. The best policy, he felt sure, was one of moderation, kindness, and reticence, in order to reconcile southerners to the incoming administration. He did his best to scotch rumors, emanating from the *Tribune* office, that Weed's views on compromise really were Seward's; he prevailed on a Republican Senatorial caucus to keep the excitable John P. Hale from making a speech, and to drop the idea of a Force Bill. When they asked him what he proposed to do, he told them that they would know when he knew himself.[1]

Such was the position Seward took during the first two weeks of December. Then, suddenly, he left the capital for Albany. Lincoln had offered him the post of Secretary of State.

Ever since the Chicago convention there had been rumors about Seward's subsequent role in the party. There was talk of his remaining in the Senate, of being Minister to England, of the State Department, and of retirement. After the election, many of his friends were convinced that he would be Secretary of State. It seemed a logical choice, not only on account of his position as a party leader but also because, since 1857, he had been a member of the Senate Committee on Foreign Relations. Cameron wrote that the offer was certain and its acceptance essential, both for Seward's future and for the success of the administration. Adams declared that his opinion and that of everyone he had spoken to in Boston was that the post would be offered and that Seward must accept in order to give the country confidence in Lincoln's administration.

Such arguments were hard for a man of Seward's temperament to combat, but he preserved a waiting attitude and was careful not to indicate any open interest in the post. Old Democrats such as Chase could scarcely be expected to be enthusiastic over him as premier, reports from Maryland indicated that the Blairs were intriguing against him, and the future seemed at best uncertain. New York had done well in the election, he told Patterson. The retreat from Chicago had so far been conducted safely, but it was not yet ended. "I shall await the development of events and act as wisely as I can." [2]

As for Lincoln, some thought that he was lukewarm toward Seward, and was reluctant to take him into the Cabinet. The weight of evidence, however, indicates that he wanted Seward to head the State Department; that he was sincere when he assured the New Yorker on December 8, in a warm letter accompanying his formal offer, that the rumors of his lack of interest were false, and that Seward's position, integrity, learning, and great experience "all combine to render it an appointment preeminently fit to be made."

Now Lincoln's invitation had come, and Seward was excited. He told Preston King about it, intimating that, in view of the present state of the country, which people ascribed mainly to him, he could not refuse the offer. Lincoln's letter had requested his co-operation in handling patronage matters "with justice to all," and in reply Seward promised his "hearty concurrence." As for the State Department, he asked for a few days so that he might consult with his friends. Then he posted off to Albany and Weed. The two men agreed that the latter, who had received an invitation to come to Springfield, should go, find out how the land lay, and, among other suggestions, propose Charles Francis Adams for the Treasury. Seward, meanwhile, would wait at Auburn for Weed's report.[3]

Weed went west, taking his own compromise proposals with him. He had a six-hour interview with Lincoln on December 20, and found that Chase and two other Old Democrats, Gideon Welles of Connecticut and Montgomery Blair of Maryland, were being seriously considered for Cabinet posts. Lincoln showed no interest in Adams for the Treasury.

As for the compromise proposals, Lincoln was opposed to any move that would give slavery freedom to expand southward. He presented Weed with a short draft of three propositions that he felt would do much good and that he wanted Seward to introduce. They were: (1) a constitutional amendment forbidding alteration of the Constitution in such a way as to allow Congress to abolish or interfere with slavery in the states; (2) amendment of the fugitive slave law by granting a jury trial to the fugitive; and (3) a recommendation from Congress to the states that they revise their personal liberty laws and repeal all that were in conflict with the Constitution.

Weed came back from Springfield, Seward joining him on the train at Syracuse, and between there and Albany they discussed the situation. Seward was willing to accept Lincoln's three proposals and champion them in the Senate, but the Cabinet was not shaping up as he and Weed had hoped it would.

It was a difficult problem. Weed was doubtful. Vice President-elect Hamlin thought Seward should refuse. Seward consulted Adams and avowed his dissatisfaction with the Cabinet, where, he felt, he would lack support. Adams advised him to accept. Finally, on December 28, Seward wrote to Lincoln that he would serve. He told Frances of his decision, adding, "I will try to save freedom and my country." After the news became public, Chase sent a gracious note of congratulation—"The post is yours by right and you will honor the post. My best wishes go with you." [4]

On December 22, after conferring with Weed on the train, Seward had gone on to New York and the Astor House, arriving there late in the evening. The New England Society was holding its annual meeting at the hotel. He had been invited to this gathering and had declined, but on hearing of his arrival the diners literally forced him to come to the banquet hall. South Carolina had formally seceded two days before, and they wanted to hear what he had to say.

Seward couched his remarks in a light, humorous vein, and his audience loved it. He had just told Weed, he said, that he repudiated all compromises that New York, Pennsylvania, and New England couldn't stand upon. The New England Yankees had invented confederation, and now South Carolina invented secession. This put the Union in some peril, but when one state went out they would see Canada and the Mexican states rush in (applause). Secession was unwise and unnatural. It was not surprising that attempts should be made to alter such a complex government as ours, or that one or two states should think they could do better by seceding, but he believed that no state could long exist out of the Union. Neither did he believe southerners when they said all love was lost between North and South. This was a family quarrel. He suspected that South Carolina liked the North tolerably well, and he was sure that if Louis Napoleon or the Prince of Wales or his mother made a descent upon New York City tomorrow, all the hills of South Carolina would come to its rescue (loud and prolonged applause), "just as they would go to the rescue of Charleston and South Carolina." Everybody knew that. South Carolinians didn't humbug him with their secession and they wouldn't humbug themselves much longer. Sixty days from then things would look a lot brighter.[5]

This speech was meant as reassurance, not as a sober analysis of the situation. As an indication of Seward's frame of mind, its significance lay in its assertion that a threat of danger from outside would produce a tempest of patriotic ardor that would end all thought of disunion. This represented a belief that Seward found singularly attractive during the months that lay ahead.

Seward said nothing specifically to the New England Society about compromise, but the subject was on his mind, and others wondered about his attitude toward it. He was in Albany when Weed wrote his second editorial supporting compromise, and the rumor spread that Weed was indeed speaking for him, and even that he was frightened and had taken his family and gone home. There is no real evidence, however, that Seward agreed with Weed's stand, and he was at home because he was waiting for the results of Weed's visit to Springfield. He had spent his time in Auburn trying to evolve a policy for dealing with the fast-developing crisis.

Seward's efforts to save the Union developed along three lines. First, he sought means and methods that would conciliate the South without abandoning his principles (that is, his determination to keep slavery within the limits where it already existed), thus putting it in the way of ultimate extinction. Second, he undertook to bring into the scope of this effort Lincoln's three propositions transmitted to him by Weed. Third, since he felt sure that the rebellion taking shape was the work of a relatively few hotheads, rather than the desire of a majority of southerners, he tried to discover ways of gaining time during which he might arouse southern loyalty to the Union. This was all very well, but in his overweening confidence that he was to be the real head of the incoming administration, he did not consult Lincoln before publicly outlining his own policy.[6]

Seward went back to Washington a member of the Senate Committee of Thirteen appointed to consider means of dealing with the crisis. In the committee he voted against the Crittenden Compromise extending the old Missouri Compromise line of 36° 30′ to the Pacific Ocean, and offered the Lincoln resolutions prohibiting interference with slavery in the states where it already existed, guaranteeing a jury trial for fugitive slaves, and requesting the repeal or modification of personal liberty laws. The committee adopted the first of these by a vote of eleven to two, but rejected the others. Seward voted steadily against all proposals fostering the expansion of slavery into newly acquired territories, and one proposed by Douglas that would have prohibited voting or holding office by Negroes.

The New Yorker worked closely with Adams, who was an influential member of the House Committee of Thirty-three, the counterpart of the Senate Committee of Thirteen. Adams's policy, like Seward's, was delay, so that passions might have a chance to cool and the new administration have time to take over the government. On December 21 Henry Winter Davis proposed in the House Committee of Thirty-three that New Mexico be allowed to come in, if it so wished, as a slave state. When extremists, North and South, opposed this, Seward urged postponement of its consideration. On December 28, however, he seems to have suggested a plan that almost brought harmony into the Senate Committee of Thirteen. This would have divided the territories into two parts, New Mexico coming in as a slave state, the rest of the territory north of the compromise parallel being free. When, on that same day, the committee agreed that it could find no general plan of adjustment, and adjourned, Seward prevailed upon it not to ask to be discharged, and to adjourn not *sine die* but subject to the call of the chairman. The next day Adams, in the House committee, offered a resolution that was adopted 13 to 11, admitting New Mexico as a state. These were basically time-gaining moves, just as was Seward's policy of keeping in as close touch as possible with southern statesmen, for which purpose he used southern-born Senator Gwin of California and a fast-talking New York *bon vivant* and adventurer named Sam Ward. It is more than likely that the Seward-Adams policy during those hectic days, much as it horrified men like Charles Sumner, was important in preventing a close coalition between the border slave states and the cotton states and so giving momentum to the rebellion.

While preaching coolness and moderation, Seward also tried in various ways to stiffen Buchanan's administration and to prepare the North for any possible contingency. When southerners and southern sympathizers left the Cabinet, he supported staunch Unionist John A. Dix for Secretary of the Treasury, and when Edwin M. Stanton became Attorney General the New Yorker, who was still *persona non grata* at the White House, quickly established confidential relations with him. Seward received information from Stanton as to Cabinet proceedings, and provided for the latter a contact with Congress. Seward also urged the governors of New York and Massachusetts to begin military preparations so that, in the event of a crisis, they would be able to furnish troops; and by February 1861, New York was gathering between 5000 and 10,000 militia. Concerned over the falling price of government bonds, Seward proposed that Treasury notes be sold in small denominations so that the ordinary citizen could lend money to the government, and urged the New York legislature to put the credit of the state behind the federal 6 per cents. A delegation of twenty-five New York merchants and bankers who had come to Washington looking for salvation was taken aback when Seward urged them to help the Union by lending it money at 7 per cent, rather than increasing the panic and its difficulties by extorting 12 per cent.[7]

While Seward urged others to make ready for a coming storm, he was preparing a major speech on the crisis. For this speech he was receiving a welter of conflicting advice; some, like Salmon P. Chase, begged him to avoid compromise, while others, like Gilbert C. Davidson, an Albany businessman and close to Weed, telegraphed him to propose measures that would hold the border states and so save the Union.[8]

When Seward rose to speak on January 12, Mississippi, Florida, and Alabama had followed South Carolina out of the Union, and the increasing gravity of the situation brought over 2000 men and women to the galleries of the Senate to hear him. He began by avowing his "adherence to the Union in its integrity and with all its parts. . . ." Congress, he said, ought, if possible, to redress any real grievances, and then it should furnish the President with all the means necessary to maintain an undivided nation. How was the Union to be saved, he asked, and answered that it was not by eulogiums or recriminations or by endless debates. Neither could he agree with those who advocated separation with a view to eventual reconstruction. Congressional compromises were not likely to save it. Yet it could not be dissolved by the action of individual states, but only by the people of the nation and in the manner prescribed by the Constitution. Then he pictured the chaos that would follow secession and evoked the specter of slave uprisings. Organization of a distinct confederacy was "obviously impossible of execution."

Since the Union was all-important, some basis for preserving it must be found. To save it, he was willing to see all personal liberty laws repealed; to see a Constitutional amendment forbidding forever to Congress the power to abolish or interfere with slavery in any state; with Kansas admitted as a free state, he could accept the admission of the remaining territory of the Union as two states. (His statement here was qualified and not clear, but he apparently meant with slavery, if the inhabitants so desired. He was sure they would not so desire.) He would vote for laws safeguarding states against invasions such as that of John Brown; and finally he urged the building of two railroads to the Pacific, one north, one south, as a powerful means of strengthening the Union. He closed with a plea for calmness, moderation, and conciliation.

It was a moving speech, and at times during its delivery more than one Senator bowed his head and wept. But it was susceptible to a wide range of interpretation. Some thought that it offered real concessions to the South, and Frances wrote in sorrow that its "compromises," as she called them, put Henry "in danger of taking the path which led Daniel Webster to an unhonored grave ten years ago." New York merchants praised its concessions, and border state Congressmen were pleased, though not ecstatic. Nevertheless, Israel Washburn wrote from Maine that people there interpreted the speech as offering no practicable compromises or concessions, and so they liked it. The French Minister at Washington, Henri Mercier, thought that it was hazy on the all-important point of concessions to the South, but that Seward had so managed as to enlist the support of moderates North and South. Others thought it "cautious" or "foggy," and Edward Everett declared that it disappointed almost everyone and amounted to nothing. Whittier, who had pilloried Daniel Webster for his Seventh of March speech, wrote a poem praising Seward's effort as a noble and courageous attempt to preserve peace and the Union, though he, himself, was

> constrained to hold even Union less
> Than Liberty, and Truth and Righteousness.

Edouard de Stoeckl, the Russian Minister at Washington, felt the speech made only a few slight concessions, but no compromise. Stoeckl, after talking with Seward and his friends, believed that the New Yorker wanted to rally behind him conservative Democratic-Republican support for leading the South back into the Union by giving it satisfactory guarantees, but that he hesitated through lack of courage to make the necessary moves.[9]

Seward professed to be amused by this diversity of opinion; he was in high spirits after his speech. Frances would see, he assured her, that what looked like compromises were only explanations meant to disarm the enemies of Freedom and Union. "Once for all, I must gain time for the new administration to organize and for the frenzy of passion to subside. I am doing this without making any compromise whatever, by forbearance, conciliation, magnanimity." He believed that he had moderated the crisis, and that now a re-action favorable to the Union would surely come. Frederick, on a brief visit at the capital toward the end of January, found his father overwhelmed with letters and visitors pleading with him to save the Union, but "patient with each, unconverted by any and confident, cheerful & hopeful about the result."

Seward felt himself to be on a pinnacle of power. He could not come home now, he told Frances. "It seems to me that if I am absent only three days, this Administration, the Congress, and the District would fall into consternation and despair. I am the only hopeful, calm, conciliatory person here." And he told Weed that now every-thing depended on Lincoln's inaugural: "I shall write to him about that." [10]

There was conceit here, but there was some justification for it. Henry Adams believed that Seward's speech inspired hope and con-fidence; that Seward had become "virtually the ruler of the country," and George William Curtis thought Seward greater at that moment than ever before.

All during late January and February, Seward continued his policy of playing for time, while he strove to damp the desires and stifle the impulses of ultras, both North and South. He told Frances in February that "the Republicans must give up their ultra sentiments as belonging to an issue on which they have already won the administration of the government," an observation that disturbed his wife. Various possible courses of action shaped in his restless mind, and he aired them to his friends and associates. There were times when he felt that it would be best to give the seceding states full opportunity to see that the new administration meant to deal with them fairly, and that secession meant for them only evils and hardships. Then, perhaps in three months or, at the latest, by the end of the year, Union sentiment in the seceded states would swell into an irresistible tide. Seward told Stoeckl that, if Lincoln could not carry the Republican radicals with him, he should cut loose from them and save the country by rallying conservatives of all parties to his standard. This made the Russian sure that Seward was bent on compromise.[11]

With an eye on the situation in Virginia, where he was working hard to bolster Union sentiment, Seward twice intimated to a Virginia friend that, in substance, he favored the Crittenden Compromise. Again, his thought would veer in another direction. Why wouldn't it be a good thing if the administration cashiered Major Anderson for moving from Moultrie to Sumter, he flung out one evening at an Adams dinner. It might be still better if Winfield Scott, too, were forced to resign as commanding general. Then the North would get mad, and this would loosen the ties that bound northern Democrats and the great cities to the South. Screw up the North to a war pitch, and the South would learn manners. He was attracted by the idea of using foreign policy as a means of ending the internal crisis. Twice he told Rudolf Schleiden, Minister Resident from Bremen, that he would welcome war with England, France, or Spain, for it would unite the country in a burst of patriotic fervor; and he informed Lord Lyons that he could unite America by a foreign war, if foreign governments interfered to protect their commercial interests. The British Minister, who saw him a number of times that winter, thought that as Secretary of State he would be apt to adopt a violent anti-British policy so as "to divert the public excitement to a foreign quarrel."

When the secessionist tide appeared to ebb, Seward's spirits were high. Then a spate of bad news would make him despondent. At the end of January, smarting under criticism from radical anti-slavery sources, he told Weed that he thought he would resign his seat in the Senate. He needed rest, and the animosities aroused by the radicals would render difficult his position in the State Department. Weed put an end to this idea by replying that the New York legislature was an uncertain quantity and might well elect Greeley to fill out Seward's unexpired term.

Moderation, but not submission, remained Seward's watchword. On January 27 he told Lincoln that he felt the proper policy was to continue collecting the revenues at southern ports and to regain the forts taken over by the Confederates, at the same time preparing to defend Washington against any attack. Four days later he made a speech in the Senate that was a mixture of conciliation and threat of war. Kansas had been admitted as a free state the day before. Seward noted that a considerable portion of the remaining one million miles of territory had a slave code, but that there were just twenty-four slaves in all that area. Slavery extension in the United States had ceased to be a practical question. He wished to consider every possible solution of the present crisis, including a constitutional convention, but if all efforts proved fruitless and the Union had to be upheld by force of arms, he had advised others and was himself ready to "stand in the breach, and stand with it or perish with it."

When Seward finished, Senator Mason charged him with supporting a war policy in order to maintain a Union that was no longer in existence. The Union was still in being, Seward replied. Some had departed from the Senate chamber, but others would take their places. If there was treason, he would fight to put it down.[12]

Seward was one of the promoters of the Peace Convention, summoned at the initiative of Virginia, which met in Washington during February and in which the border states were powerfully represented. It had peace-keeping value, he felt, even though it made no real progress toward settling the crisis. Henry Adams declared that Seward kept it going all through February because the Union men in Virginia and the other border states were of the opinion that no further steps toward disunion would be taken before its deliberations were completed. At the same time, through James Barbour and other prominent Virginians, Seward kept inspiriting the Unionists in the Old Dominion who were fighting a bitter battle with the secessionists. When the Peace Conference proposals, protecting slavery where it existed in almost every possible way, were brought in by a Senate committee as a thirteenth amendment to the Constitution, he and Lyman Trumbull, being on the committee, submitted a minority report in favor of a convention. This, said the Virginia *Sentinel*, was "nothingness whittled down to a point," and something of a betrayal of Seward's Virginia friends.[13]

What was the significance of Seward's role during that critical winter? More than any other man, for Lincoln's public attitude from November to March was, as James G. Randall puts it, one of "studied reticence," Seward acted as the leader of his party. His cool, moderate, pragmatic policy was designed in essence as a time-saving device. He would probably have been willing to leave the Southwest open to slavery, if that would placate the South, but there is no evidence that he was ready at any time to abandon the fundamental principle of the Republican party and leave the way clear for the expansion of slavery into Cuba, or Mexico, or Central America. Even so, his attitude aggravated extremists like Joshua Giddings and Charles Sumner. "God damn you, Seward," said a Senator to him one day, "you've betrayed your principles and your party; we've followed your lead long enough." [14]

Seward talked too much, especially when exhilarated by wine or brandy, and sometimes the ideas he threw out bred suspicion as to his designs. It is also true that he greatly underestimated the force and stamina of the secession movement. But it is equally certain that his "bridge-building," as he called it, played a significant part in keeping Virginia and the other border slave states in the Union during those critical months.

While Seward took the lead in formulating Washington policy toward the secessionists he was also revolving in his mind plans for the Cabinet. He forwarded to Lincoln a number of suggestions— Adams for the Treasury, Frémont for the War Department, and no less than five southerners for whom he did not venture to designate places. Lincoln, who had his own ideas about his official family, evinced interest in only one of these, John A. Gilmer of North Carolina, but this Unionist and close friend of the New Yorker bowed out of the picture. Seward urged an early choice of the Secretaries of War and Navy, but Lincoln did not want to make his final selections for those posts until he had exhausted his efforts to find suitable men from the South for Cabinet positions. Seward wanted a post for Cameron but, beyond expressing high regard for the Pennsylvanian and dread of the hostility of Cameron's friends if he were rebuffed, let Weed do the maneuvering for him.

The Seward-Weed and Greeley-Bryant factions in New York State engaged in furious contentions over the Cabinet, but Seward as was his wont left such operations mainly to Weed. He wrote to the latter on January 21, "Mr. L. has undertaken his Cabinet without consulting me. For the present I shall be content to leave the responsibility on his own broad shoulders."

Seward had suggestions for Lincoln on other than Cabinet appointments. He urged the President-elect to come to Washington early in February, saying that this would have a reassuring effect on the country, but Lincoln thought it unwise to appear before February 13, when the electoral vote was officially counted. When he did come, ten days after the count had been made, advices from Seward and General Scott concerning an assassination plot in Baltimore led him to take a night train through that city, a change of schedule that elicited a considerable amount of adverse comment.

Lincoln arrived in Washington at six o'clock on the morning of February 23, and during the next few days Seward played the part of both friend and social secretary, taking the President-elect to the Capitol and introducing him to members of both houses, going with him to church, receiving and transmitting invitations and requests addressed to Lincoln, and arranging details for the inauguration.

Lincoln gave Seward a draft of his inaugural, asking for suggestions. Seward went over it carefully and made numerous comments, the general tendency of which was to soften its language toward the South. Lincoln adopted some of these, rejected others. The final paragraph, beginning "I am loath to close. We are not enemies but friends," was Seward's in thought and in the figures of speech, but Lincoln gave it a simplicity and a poetic quality lacking in Seward's draft. This may have been what prompted the New Yorker to remark to Adams that the President had "a curious vein of sentiment running through his thought which is his most valuable mental attribute." [15]

About ten o'clock on the morning of inauguration day, two or three hundred New Yorkers who had come to Washington for the inauguration gathered in front of Seward's home on F Street in tribute to their Senator. He spoke to them briefly, thanking them for their demonstration of affection, telling them that he had tried to be faithful to their trust, and finishing with a tribute to Lincoln, under whose conciliatory administration the nation would be restored to unity. Then he went to the inauguration, and later attended the inaugural ball, which at his suggestion was called the "Union Ball, in honor of the Inauguration of Abraham Lincoln." He had helped to organize this festivity. His daughter-in-law, Anna Seward, was on his arm, a lady presented him with an elegant bouquet, and memory must have taken him back to the early days when as a rising young lawyer he had helped to manage dances in Auburn. On the surface all seemed harmony, but two days before he had asked to be relieved from serving in the State Department.

During February the struggle over the Cabinet had reached a feverish pitch. The anti-Seward forces were determined to put Chase in the Cabinet and, if possible, get Seward out of it, while Weed and other pro-Seward elements fought for the inclusion of Adams and Henry Winter Davis of Maryland, and the exclusion of Chase and Welles and Blair. As the month drew to its close, it became apparent that the Seward forces would have a number of disappointments. Weed, after conferring with Lincoln in New York, warned Seward that the conference had been unsatisfactory. A week later, at a dinner for Lincoln at Willard's, Seward told Adams that all was not well. Despite pressure, the President-elect was determined to have both Chase and Seward in his official family. He had also decided to include Welles and Blair, thus eliminating Adams and Henry Winter Davis. It was to be a "compound Cabinet," as Seward called it, one containing both Old Whigs and Old Democrats, some favoring and some opposing concessions to the South. Seward doubted that it would be viable.

A letter to the New York *Evening Post,* which was obviously in-

This cartoon was published in *Vanity Fair*, March 2, 1861. Weed tells Lincoln that he can rely upon Seward. *University of Rochester Library*

spired by Seward and which was published just after Lincoln reached Washington, showed Seward's deep sense of frustration because of abolitionist opposition and because he had not had Lincoln's support. The writer of this letter declared that Seward's enemies were trying to drive him out of the Cabinet. They were also seeking to defeat any form of compromise with the South, and in so doing claimed Lincoln as an ally. When the President-elect reached Washington, and learned the facts now known to only one or two, he would assent to some of the propositions pending before the Peace Convention and before Congress.

A New York *Times* editorial applauded this letter, denounced Greeley and the abolitionists in general, and expressed confidence in Lincoln. When on March 2 Seward asked "leave to withdraw," he was attempting to win the battle over the Cabinet and at the same time force Lincoln's acceptance of his leadership in devising policy.

Seward and his friends promptly spread the news of his withdrawal, doubtless as a means of bringing additional pressure on the President-elect. Had the New Yorker carried through, it would have been a heavy blow to the new administration, but Lincoln was not going to let Seward "take the first trick." On the morning of March 4 he asked Seward to "countermand the withdrawal." After the inauguration ceremonies the two men had a long and confidential talk. No record of that conversation remains, but there is some evidence that they discussed the possibility of Seward's being Minister to England, and that Lincoln mentioned the name of William L. Dayton of New Jersey as his second choice for the State Department. On the following day Seward withdrew his resignation. He told his wife that he had done so because he "did not dare to go home or to England and leave the country to chance."

Many of Seward's friends regretted his decision, but Weed thought he had chosen wisely, though he might be driven out by the voracity of his colleagues for the spoils. The Albany boss declared that Lincoln had begged Seward to remain and gave him to understand that whatever others might say or do, they two would not disagree. Lincoln doubtless put his request tactfully, but the significant thing was that Seward accepted the concept of a balanced Cabinet.[16]

Lincoln had, indeed, taken the first trick, but there remained one consoling thought for the still ambitious New Yorker. As Senator, he had brought one President under his spell. It seemed more than likely that he could repeat that performance with this railsplitter who, by a stroke of chance, had become President of the United States.

~§ 18 §~

The Head of the Family

Seward was not quite sixty years old when he became Secretary of State. His wiry hair, now silvery white, was more apt than not to be dishevelled; his clothes were scarcely ever in style; and he had a slight stoop from years of desk-sitting. His voice was husky, his face sallow, his ears protruded, and his large beaked nose and keen eyes peering out from under gray, grizzly eyebrows gave him an alert and rather bird-like appearance. Young Henry Adams, who thought him simply "great," had a yearning to dye his hair a bright crimson, paint his face a brilliant green and his nose yellow, and then exhibit him as a parrot. Prince Napoleon thought he looked like a schoolteacher.

The new Secretary was a great storyteller and was fond of banter, sometimes chuckling himself hoarse over his wit. He could recite with effect an Irishman's anathema—now unfortunately lost to posterity—and witty comments appeared repeatedly in his letters. "I send you some sympathetic verses," he wrote to Charles Sumner while the latter was recuperating from his caning at the hands of Preston Brooks. "You have endured much from Brooks. If you can stand up under this poetry you may deem yourself convalescent. You will have had the *worst from friends* as well as enemies." In the depths of the war years, he closed a letter to Weed "with love to Harriet, I am ever your unfortunate friend, who has faith in everybody and enjoys the confidence of nobody." And to an anxious female who asked him, "Governor Seward, which way *is* the army going?" he replied, "Madam, if I did not know, I would tell you."

Seward's humor sometimes had an acid touch. He was at the Adams's one evening with a number of others, among them the dignified and very conservative Senator from Rhode Island, Henry B. Anthony. Henry Adams described the scene in a letter to his brother Charles. Mrs. Adams had recently given Anthony a "tremendous hiding," apparently for some remark he had made about southern valor, and all present knew of the incident. Seward set out to make the Rhode Islander's life miserable, first by contradicting everything he said, and then dragging Abigail into the conversation. She could take care of those South Carolinians; she should be put into a dark room with some of them and let them fight it out. Everyone grinned broadly. Anthony squirmed and left at the first opportunity. Abigail did not care for being so used, but "the Governor only smiled grimly and neither apologized nor confessed his intentions."

As Seward became better acquainted with Lincoln, the two men found it easy to drop into nonsensical and preposterous dialogue, with humor that was often broad. Emerson, visiting Washington in the winter of 1862 and being taken by Sumner to the State Department, came away with what he termed an "extraordinary exordium" from Seward ringing in his ears. He wrote down his recollection of Seward's words:

> The President said yesterday, when I was going to tell him a story, "Well, Seward, don't let it be smutty." And I remember when a witness was asked in court, "Do you know this man?"
> "Yes, I know him."
> "How do you know him?"
> "Why I know him. I can't say I have carnal knowledge of him."

After this recital, Seward took a large half-smoked cigar from a shelf and lighted and pulled on it.[1]

Seward used snuff to some extent and was an inveterate smoker. He consumed a dozen or more cigars every day, and it was nothing for him to order two thousand choice Havanas from Cuba. He found Charles Francis Adams's brand to his liking and when dining at the Adams home would invariably smoke two cigars after dinner and put a third in his pocket to puff on the way home.

Cigars went with sociability, and Seward was a pre-eminently sociable individual. Friendly by nature, he attracted people of all ages and conditions. The barkeeper at Cayuga grinned with pleasure when he could furnish his neighbor some pike fresh from the lake. An old and timid secretary at the Capitol, snubbed by many, found Seward invariably kind and thoughtful. In 1845, when he had hurt his leg in a coach accident and could not walk, Seward found himself in the little village of Stockport, some twenty-four miles south of Albany. Despite pain and discomfort, he made fast friends of the inhabitants who, before he left, came to look upon him as an oracle. Nor was it only the lowly who felt the force of his personality. Carl Schurz felt drawn to him, almost as though by some sort of occult power; the actress Charlotte Cushman had faith in him and was proud of his friendship. Lord Napier, the English Minister to the United States in the 1850s, was his devoted friend, so much so that he was described back in London as "Yankee bitten."

Seward took a great interest in young people, whether they were aspiring painters, lawyers, teachers, or journalists, and the testimonials to their gratitude were numerous. One of the finest tributes he ever received came from Charles Francis Adams, Jr., after they parted company at the close of the 1860 campaign.

> I beg you not to suppose [wrote young Adams] that the continual attention & kindness you showed to me, & the thoughtfulness, which so often led to my being brought forward when there was a chance for me to show that I had anything in me, & at moments too when all your thoughts might well have been taken up by your own position:—do not suppose, that this was unnoticed by me, or that for it I did not feel deeply grateful. I had no claim on you, but you could not have taken greater interest in me had I been your son.

It is natural for sociable people to like to entertain, and Seward was no exception to this rule. He exchanged visits and dinners with Congressmen and Senators from both North and South, and with Cabinet members and foreign diplomats. On New Year's Day, two to three hundred callers would leave their cards at his Washington home, while he roamed the streets on the same errand. An eighteen-year-old relative, Mary Grier, staying at the Seward's in the winter of 1857, wrote home about the New Year festivities. There was scarcely a five-minute period when callers were not at the house. Douglas and Cass appeared, the latter at seventy-four acting like a young man but in Mary's eyes looking "as if he had been boiled down for about ten years and keeps his mouth going all the time." The guests helped themselves at a long table laden with turkey, cold ham, bread-and-butter sandwiches, coffee, New Year's cakes and fruit cake, and five kinds of wine.

Henry came in about five o'clock that day, announcing that he had invited seven men for dinner, including the Mexican Minister. They came. The ladies left the dinner table at half past eight, the gentlemen lingering over their port an hour longer. Then Henry sent word to have tables set up for whist. The party broke up about midnight, "and then I can assure you we were all very tired."

In addition to the impromptu New Year's dinner, there were at least four other social events at Seward's home that January, including two large dinner parties at which the table was brilliant with silver, crystal goblets, and imported china decorated in blue and gold with *esse quam videri* in the center of each dish.

A typical dinner lasted from six to ten o'clock, and had eleven courses. Soup, fish, and roast beef came in order. Then the plates were all changed, and roast turkey and vegetables appeared. Next asparagus was brought on by itself, then sweetbreads, followed by a sequence of quails and green peas, terrapins, ducks, a tenth course of ice cream, wine jelly, and pies, and finally apples, nuts, and prunes. The ladies then departed, leaving the gentlemen to their wine and cigars. Coffee in the drawing room marked the end of this Lucullan feast.

Such entertainment was costly. No complete record remains, but during the 1850s Frances kept a ledger of household expenses, "so far as they come to my knowledge." This indicated that, from September 1859 to September 1860, the bills for the households in Washington and Auburn amounted to $10,665.90.[2]

The master of these ceremonies was a good host, and usually gave his guests an opportunity to talk about their own interests. He himself loved to talk, was not above monopolizing the conversation, and had many moods, being by turns challenging, pontifical, a cynic, a raconteur, a mimic—altogether something of a show-off, and one whose words could not always be trusted. Dr. Henry W. Bellows, in January 1863, just back from Washington where he had been a guest at a dinner given by Samuel B. Ruggles, told how Seward talked from half past five until eleven—a regular Niagara flood— about his views and policies, past and present. Among other things he said was that in the winter of 1861 he had kept a hundred hired toughs in the Senate gallery for the protection of northern Senators. Bellows came away much impressed, but George Templeton Strong, to whom he told the story, thought the hundred toughs stationed in the gallery made Seward a rival of Baron Munchausen.

Seward never minimized his own importance. The story of the New York rowdies, for instance, undoubtedly occurred to him as a means of showing what a dramatic role he had played. Nor did he hold back in expressing his opinions on subjects far removed from the field of politics. Fanny Seward recorded in her diary an incident when Edwin Booth came to dinner. "Father said if he would allow him he would tell him where he thought his acting might be improved. He accepted Father's criticism gracefully—often saying he had felt those defects himself." Dullness seldom presided at a Seward dinner table, nor was it likely to be expected by those who had seen him posture in the Senate, calling upon the rocks and mountains to crush him on Judgment Day, if he were false to his trust, or needling Stuart of Michigan by describing with gestures how he and Benjamin had gone scraping and bowing before Franklin Pierce's footstool, saying "May it please Your Excellency." But the recipients of his hospitality usually fell victims to his charm. Such was the case with Charlotte Cushman, who thought him a wonderful man, indeed; and Sir Henry Holland, who was his guest in 1863, declared that "it is impossible to live with him without contracting sentiments of affection as well as esteem." [3]

Seward's critics charged him with making statements in private that belied his public utterances, and declared that this stamped him a hypocrite. This charge is not borne out by the evidence. Sometimes the seeming discrepancies were simply the result of his efforts to give a humorous twist to a serious conversation. The famous Duke of Newcastle incident affords a good illustration.

In November 1860, Seward attended a dinner given by Governor Morgan for the Prince of Wales, and in the Prince's entourage was the Duke of Newcastle. As Seward remembered the conversation some two years afterward, he had attempted to enlighten the Prince and his party on the intricacies of American politics by explaining that the pro-slavery Democrats were always eager to pin a British label on the Republican anti-slavery position, and that the Republicans had to take pains to avoid being so ticketed. This explanation of American political maneuvering was evidently confusing to British ears, all the more so when Seward apparently added some flippant remark about having to insult Great Britain when he became President or Secretary of State. It was this last comment that the Duke solemnly reported at home as a serious threat, and that went the rounds of the press. Seward flatly denied having made such a statement, but Weed was probably nearer the truth when he referred to what had been said as "an attempted pleasantry."

At other times, Seward tried either to shock his listeners or simply to avoid a useless argument. He stunned journalist Donn Piatt by telling him that the Constitution was a paper kite held up by a string that would one day break; that it was "a superstitution that presupposes certain impossibilities." When Mrs. Jefferson Davis asked him how he could believe the piteous appeals he made for the Negro when he had lived in the South, he looked at her quizzically, smiled, and said that he did not believe them but that they went down very well with the northern masses. Did he never speak from conviction, asked her husband? "Nev-er," responded Seward. Davis, blindfolded on account of his eye trouble, raised his head from the pillow and declared that, as God was his judge, he never spoke from any other motive, whereupon Seward, putting his arm around him, laid his head down gently and said "I know you do not—I am always sure of it." [4]

Such statements perplexed his listeners, and some of his other social traits were still harder to understand. Indeed, if the spirit moved him, he could be lawless in his social behavior. Sedate associates at male gatherings looked askance at his lolling about in undignified poses, cursing, swearing or belching before the assembled company. He had a most irritating habit, so far as his household was concerned, of setting up impromptu dinner parties. Nor did he hesitate, if his feet were damp, to take off his shoes before distinguished company and dry his feet at the fireplace. Dignified ladies found themselves patted on the head, or on their bare shoulders, while onlookers raised their eyebrows at such breaches of conventional behavior. On one occasion Seward shepherded the four Adams children to his house for dinner, but before starting went up to Mrs. Adams, a formidable lady who dressed and looked like Queen Victoria, patted her on the head, and told her that if she were lonesome without her offspring she could come down and join them after dinner. "From any other man this would make our dear mother furious," wrote her son Henry, "but he is so hopelessly lawless that she submits and feels rather flattered, I think." [5]

Seward was by nature generous. Frances once wrote to her sister that Henry could never refuse an application that appealed to his humanity, and this was scarcely an exaggeration. His Auburn real estate development, while profitable, was attractively priced from the point of view of people with little or no capital. He treated his servants well and provided decent funerals for those who died in the service of the household. He was generous with fledgling lawyers and lenient with those who owed him money. His open-handedness brought beggars down upon him. In one instance, a woman who had never met him wrote asking for one hundred dollars so that she and her father could buy some new clothes and visit their relatives back East. In another case, generous treatment of a townsman produced political embarrassment.

In October 1856, Seward and William B. Rhoades of Auburn formed a partnership for the purchase and sale of paints, oils, "and such other articles of trade as the said Rhoades shall see fit to deal in," the business to be conducted in Rhoades's name. Seward put in $2000 capital; Rhoades agreed to pay interest on that amount and to rent a store owned by Seward for $250 a year. The partnership was to run for three years, and all profits from the business were to go to Rhoades.

A few weeks after this arrangement had been made, the New York *Herald* reported that Seward and Rhoades were in the liquor business together. Could this be true, asked the *Herald* sanctimoniously; it was hard to believe. Other papers spread the news that Seward had entered "the infamous ranks of the rum sellers" for "paltry gain," and his friends became alarmed. In December an explanation, obviously inspired, appeared in the Buffalo *Express* and from there found its way into the New York *Times*. Seward had, indeed, gone into the paint and oil business with Rhoades, so this story ran, but in drawing up the contract Rhoades had asked that "etc." be added, supposedly to cover brushes, glue, and other such articles. Seward had agreed and then, to his vexation, had found that wines and liquors were sold in the store. Since he was a silent partner, he had to allow the business to go on until the partnership expired.

It is doubtful that being associated with a liquor dealer troubled Seward until it became apparent that there might be repercussions among the temperance folk. His effort to help a fellow townsman get started in business, however, was a failure. Even though liquor was the most profitable item that Rhoades sold, he fell behind in his payments. A July 1865 item in Seward's financial papers, under "Suspended Accounts," listed Rhoades as owing his erstwhile partner $1247.70.[6]

Seward's private life was never touched by the breath of scandal, and no charge of corruption was ever brought against him as a public man. He took pains to see that his reputation in this latter respect should remain unspotted. In 1856 Webb and Reverdy Johnson wanted him to use his influence with Congressman Edwin B. Morgan, his long-time friend and brother of his former law partner, Christopher Morgan, in favor of a patent extension for Cyrus McCormick's reaper. Seward, who was a leading counsel for McCormick, thought the extension was right in itself, but felt that he could not interfere. "My hold on Morgan," he wrote to Weed, "rests chiefly on his conviction that I would not suffer personal interests to induce me to ask him to modify his own rule of action in public affairs." The report that Christopher Morgan, associated with Seward as counsel for the reaper manufacturer, had asked McCormick $20,000 for his aid in getting the patent extension through Congress added to Seward's embarrassment. However, he saw nothing wrong in Weed's asking Morgan to oblige Webb and Johnson, and he looked the other way when Weed used money to buy votes for a Whig or Republican cause. It was very convenient to have the Dictator take care of the seamier side of politics.

Obliging a friend by swaying another man's vote on a bill might be unwise, but Seward did not think that it was necessarily wrong. Later that same year Weed wrote that he had $10,000 invested in Georgia railroads, and that it might be jeopardized if a bill for a naval depot on the Georgia coast failed to pass. Seward replied that he would do what he could. He undoubtedly asked friends to support the measure, and he himself spoke for the bill and voted against amendments. The measure became law.

Seward could the more easily come to Weed's assistance on the naval depot bill because he was just then making efforts to conciliate the South. In another instance his solicitation of a fellow Senator's vote was purely a matter of practical politics. As a vigorous supporter of the Collins line of steamships, he asked Sumner to vote for subsidization of that line. Sumner thought the bill economically unsound, and there was a lengthy argument. Finally Seward asked him to vote for it as a personal favor, since it would help in his own re-election. Sumner replied that he had not been sent to the Senate to re-elect Seward, and the latter, losing his temper, exclaimed, "Sumner, you're a damned fool." They did not speak, so Henry Adams averred, for six months, but Sumner finally voted for the bill.[7]

Seward had enormous vitality. He suffered from intermittent attacks of erysipelas, lumbago, swollen joints, migraine, and chills and fever, but his capacity for work showed no sign of diminution with his advancing years. He customarily rose during the summer at five or six in the morning, a little later in the wintertime. In Auburn he would vary his work routine by walks, carriage rides, and fishing expeditions to the nearby lakes of Owasco and Cayuga. In Washington, walking was his principal form of diversion, going often to the market in the early morning. Then would come a round of political and social activity. January 15, 1857, may serve as an example. He spent the day at the Capitol, where he reported a bill and participated actively in debate. After the Senate adjourned in late afternoon, he went directly to dine with Senator Philip Allen of Rhode Island, came home at ten o'clock, went with members of his family to a reception at the home of Secretary of State Marcy, left them there while he went to a supper at journalist William Seaton's, came back to the Marcy affair, and reached home with his exhausted family at two o'clock in the morning.[8]

Seward's life as a public man left him little time to devote to his children. He was, in truth, a family man only by fits and starts. His eldest son, Augustus, was away most of the time, either on the Coast Survey or serving with the army in New Mexico in the wearisome business of keeping order among the Navahoes. Henry helped in getting him promoted to an army captaincy in 1859, a promotion for which Frances had no relish because she feared that it would mean more active and therefore more dangerous service.

The busy head of the family took little interest in William Henry, Jr. Willie had little formal schooling, spelled abominably, and lacked inclination for the law or for any other intellectual pursuit, but he had ideas and was full of bounce. When he was fifteen he wanted to go to West Point—"which he will not," Frances wrote to Gus. Then he thought of going out West to make his fortune. When he was eighteen he took a job as clerk in an Albany store. This paid little, and his father doled out money to him only in small driblets. The following year he had an opportunity to buy an Auburn hardware business, but his father was cool to the idea. During the winter of 1858–59, he acted as Seward's secretary in Washington. The following summer he handled the family's business affairs while Henry toured Europe, and continued to do so for a time thereafter.

Willie married an Auburn girl, Janet McNeil Watson, in June 1860. Handling the family's business affairs gave him something to live on, and he developed an interest in finance. He wanted to set up with a partner as a banker in Auburn, but his father delayed giving assistance until Frances wrote to Frederick that she would mortgage the Seward homestead, which was in her name, in order to furnish the necessary funds. Then, early in 1861, Seward obtained a $5000 loan from Richard M. Blatchford, and Willie was launched upon what proved to be a profitable financial career.

Frances had moved through Frederick in this instance because she felt that he had more influence than she had with his father. Her appeal had a pathetic note—"if ever I possessed sufficient [influence] I do not know. I doubt whether I ever could have changed a settled purpose."

The Sewards' one living daughter, named for her mother, was fifteen years old in 1860. Fanny, as they called her, was a shy, introspective girl, observant, sensitive, and with a good sense of humor.

Conservative by temperament, an omnivorous reader, she was devoted to her father. She wanted to be a writer. She had weak lungs, and her parents were always concerned about her health. Fanny was under her mother's watchful care well into the State Department period, but she also stayed much in Seward's thoughts, and when they were separated he wrote to her often. She was his favorite child. His favorite among the boys was his second-born, Frederick William.

Frederick was trained for the law, but did not practise. After passing his bar examination, he went into the newspaper business at Albany with Weed. When Frederick was twenty-three he married Anna Wharton of Albany. Anna's father was a wholesale druggist, comfortably situated, but Frances felt that Frederick had married beneath him. This prejudice, not uncommon among doting mothers, soon gave way to a sincere liking. Anna was small, plain, and socially ambitious. She was also modest and gentle, as Frances wrote to Henry, adding a touch acidly, "I believe these are esteemed desirable qualities for wives in general."

Shortly after their marriage, Frederick became associate editor of the Albany *Evening Journal*. He and his wife came to Washington on a number of occasions while Congress was in session, and Henry quickly found that Anna, who was in her early twenties, had gifts as a hostess. She loved the capital's social whirl, and presided at dinner parties with grace and dignity. When fat Senator Preston King fell asleep at the dinner table, or on a sofa with the ladies all around him, it was tactful Anna who gently awakened him and tried to keep the other guests from laughing at his predicament. When, at the Seward dinner table, John J. Crittenden spat on the floor, Anna could take command of the awkward silence that descended upon the company. By 1861 Seward found her presence indispensable in his home.[9]

For Frances was the problem in the Seward household. Generous, idealistic, intelligent, interested in politics where a moral cause was involved, she had at first found Washington society stimulating, but by the end of a decade it had become intolerable to her. She still could discover an occasional worthwhile acquaintance among the politicians—Charles Sumner was one—but the social obligations of a Senator's wife bored her beyond words. Henry insisted upon so much entertaining, and by and large "*his guests*" were for her a burden. Then, too, she had become an ardent prohibitionist, and wine and brandy flowed freely at the Seward Washington menage. Henry was unhappy if she put her foot down on this practice, as she did on New Year's Day 1859, when no punch was served and the callers departed quickly for more hospitable havens. Indeed, when husband and wife differed on any course of procedure, the head of the family either pursued his own stubborn way, or was apt to make it appear that he thought Frances unreasonable when he gave in to her wishes. She was a passionate abolitionist, and she feared that her husband lacked her sense of commitment to the crusade against slavery; that his devotion to the Union was greater than his hatred of human bondage. There were sometimes bitter tears for these things.[10]

Trials and worries and a growing sense of frustration fostered a developing hypochondria and melancholia. Frances became morbid, convinced that her nerves were diseased, and that her vascular system was deranged. There would be brighter periods, as in 1856, when she felt a sense of "partial recovery" and could look back with a feeling of relief on "four years of almost indescribable suffering from diseased nerves." In these relatively happy times she would act as hostess, or at least come in after dinner, moving among the guests, graceful and dignified. "She did look so handsome," wrote Mary Grier to her brother, "dressed in a black satin skirt & a black velvet basque. . . . I do wish she was able to see her guests always." Then the shadows would come down again, and she would keep to her room, often to her bed as well, for months on end. For even longer periods she would not appear if guests were in the house. But even in such a welter of affliction she strove to keep up with happenings in the political world, and to keep in touch with the way Henry thought and acted about the widening chasm between North and South.

Henry was distressed by the state of his wife's health, and her periods of deep depression gave him much concern. "She is too noble a woman to think of parting from and too frail to hope to keep long," he told Sumner in 1853. He would take her out in the carriage, only to find that driving over rough pavements made her sick the rest of the day. Like Henry, she was fond of the Napiers, and the two families saw much of each other, but even a small dinner with these friends could turn out to be a trying experience. The gaslight streaming down on the Napier dining room table made her feel as though she was in a fiery furnace, and "a very powerful piano" played by a young southerner for her amusement jangled her nerves still further. She came away as soon as she decently could, but Henry stayed on and did not get home until late. She had not recovered by noon the next day. "I think I will not be persuaded to go again to so unsuitable a place," she told Lazette. "I think Lady Napier has very little nervous sensibility. Consequently she does not comprehend the condition of a person whose nerves are unnaturally acute from disease—very few do." It was all very baffling to a man of Henry's temperament, especially when she would be prostrated by suffering one day and on the next appear to be perfectly normal.[11]

The health problem inevitably created a hostess problem. In the early 1850s Frances was able to function in that capacity, but after April 1853, when Henry had to take her back to Auburn because of her extreme depression, she rarely presided at any social function. Henry did the best he could with a series of substitutes—Lazette Worden, Mrs. James Bowen from New York, Mary Grier, Anna Seward—and a faithful staff of servants.

The thought of the White House was like a nightmare to Frances, and after Lincoln's nomination in 1860 her spirits rose. It looked as though Henry's political career was coming to a close, and then would come the retirement to Auburn for which she longed. How good it was, she told him, to be free from the wranglings, envy, hatred, and malice of politics. Thirty-five years of the best part of a man's life were all that his country could reasonably claim. "Let those who are disposed to cavil go and do as well as you have done. You have earned the right to a peaceful old age."

It looked for a little while as though Henry agreed with her, and afterward Fanny remembered that, in those days following the Chicago convention, "we were the happiest family imaginable." Then Henry plunged into the campaign, and Frances could see the handwriting on the wall. "He is monopolized by the public and I am at last—resigned.— Is that the word—" she wrote to Sumner.

During the crucial secession winter, Frances stayed in Auburn, pleading the necessity of supervising repairs upon the house, and the inadvisability of interrupting Fanny's lessons. At the end of February, a week before Henry took over the State Department, she offered to come and help, if she were needed. Her health was better, she wrote, and some of the work on the house could be put off until April 1. By this time, however, Frederick had been summoned from Albany to become Assistant Secretary of State, and Anna was to be hostess in the new house on Lafayette Square. When Frances came to Washington thereafter, she came as a visitor in her own home.[12]

Times past furnish poignant memories, and ties of years standing are not easily destroyed. Henry and Frances corresponded faithfully during the 1850s. They continued to do so during the war years, her letters to "My dearest Henry" giving details about the relatives and life in Auburn, his briefer, usually accounts of the progress of the war, but always ending "your own Henry." There are from time to time expressions of affection in the letters that still exist, but such tributes are few and far between. Immersed in the cares of office, Henry seldom came to Auburn, taking elsewhere such brief relaxation as came his way. More and more, Frances lived her own life. There was not much use in waiting for him any more.

❧ 19 ❧

Crisis and Responsibility

It was only natural that the new Secretary of State should find a new Washington home, one comfortably close to the State Department. It was a spacious, red brick, three-stories-plus-a-dormer-floor mansion, facing on Lafayette Square just east and north from the White House. Built some forty years before by Commodore John Rodgers on land that had belonged to Henry Clay, it had housed various Cabinet members and had served for a time as a club house or "mess" for Congressmen. Seward rented it, unfurnished, for $1800 a year, the owner offering to do some painting and papering, put in city water and gas fixtures, and make other alterations which eventually included a furnace. Renting arrangements were concluded in February and the place was ready for occupancy some two months later. There were so many trees about it that its occupants could not see other houses, or even into the park.

Anna Seward saw to settling the new establishment, with Seward furniture, old and new, with portraits of Washington, Jackson, Webster, a clock, candlesticks, and other items all borrowed from the State Department, and with two mirrors, two small gilt tables, and a round extension dining table purchased from Mrs. Gwin. There was china enough for twenty-four settings, a necessary item for one who entertained as lavishly and as often as did the head of the household.[1]

The two months that elapsed before Seward could take possession

269

of his new establishment were among the most crucial of his career, a time of trial for which he was psychologically unprepared. By nature intensely ambitious, he still felt a smarting sense of rejection, but at the same time was convinced that the nation's salvation rested upon his shoulders; that he and not the man in the White House must guide the nation's destinies. The flattery of friends, a sense of the prominent role he had played during the winter months just passed, and memories of his dominance over another President a dozen years before, all nurtured this conviction of his own over-weening importance. He had yet to learn that he could not interfere with impunity in all the functions of the government, and that Lincoln rather than he was to be its head.

In still other ways, Seward was unprepared for the tasks that lay before him. Friendly by disposition, pacific by temperament, accustomed to having Weed fight the rough and tumble political battles, he was to find himself engaged at close quarters in a struggle for power with some of his colleagues in the Cabinet. Out of this came a sense of frustration. He felt, so he wrote to Frances, like "a chief reduced to a subordinate position, and surrounded with a guard to see that I do not do too much for my country, lest some advantage may revert to my own fame." Finally, though he liked the glitter of military pomp, war had no charms for him. Old friends such as Trumbull Cary, George W. Patterson, and George H. Boughton thought he lacked the bellicosity of temperament, the iron soul necessary for a Cabinet member in wartime. Yet there he was in the State Department, with war coming ever closer and finally bursting upon the land.

Nor were Seward's problems only those of temperament, or of how to deal with his immediate colleagues. In shaping his policies and carrying them to fruition he would have to seek the co-operation of powerful figures on Capitol Hill—the headstrong, cynical Thaddeus Stevens, chairman of the Ways and Means Committee of the House; the spotlight-loving Charles Sumner, chairman of the Senate Foreign Relations Committee, a man who felt free to go to Lincoln in matters of foreign policy. It would also be essential to establish good relations with the diplomatic corps. Baron Gerolt, Prussian Minister to the United States, was an understanding student of American affairs, a wise counselor and a friend of the Union.

Rudolph Schleiden, Minister from the Hanseatic towns since 1853, was an expert on European matters, a shrewd judge of men and political events. Friendship with such diplomats could be valuable, all the more for a man just assuming the burdens of the State Department. Still more important were the Ministers of Russia, France, and England, with whom he was to have relations of the first magnitude.

The Russian Minister, Edouard de Stoeckl, dubbed "Baron" by Americans, had come to the United States in 1841 as secretary of legation. In 1856, after he had been made *chargé d'affaires*, he married Elizabeth Howard of Springfield, Massachusetts—"American, Protestant and without property," as he informed the Emperor. Promotion to head of the legation came three years later. Now he was fifty-three years old, a very able diplomat with a large circle of friends in Washington, an admirer of the American people, and sympathetic with the Union.

Not such a friend of the United States was Henri Mercier, the French Minister. Experienced in the arts of diplomacy, energetic, devoted to the interests of his Emperor and his country, Mercier professed great friendship for the land to which he was accredited, but he was far more interested in cotton than he was in preserving the Union. In March 1861 he told the British Minister that the two of them should have discretionary power to recognize the South, and two weeks before the bombardment of Sumter he wrote to Thouvenel at the Quai d'Orsay urging recognition as a means of preventing the conflict.

More significant than Mercier, as events were to prove, was Richard Bickerton Pemell, Lord Lyons. Entering the British diplomatic service in 1839, he held only minor European posts until sent to Washington as Minister twenty years later. There he at once undertook a study of the country and its people, and became convinced that the best way to deal with Americans was with a mixture of caution and firmness. A prodigious worker with a passion for detail, he was blessed with a calm temperament and a profound conviction of the superiority of Britain and the British. Like Mercier, he was skeptical (once war came) as to the triumph of the Union but, unlike his French colleague, he had no wish to see it overthrown.[2]

Confronted by all the tasks and perplexities of his office, it was of the utmost importance that the Secretary of State should have a working rapport with his chief. This developed and, though there were times when Seward felt that the President was not equal to his task, he achieved a measure of respect for the man he had been inclined to despise. "The P. is all right," he wrote to Weed, and he told Frances of Lincoln's magnanimity and of their confidential and sympathetic relationship. "The President is the best of us," he confessed, though adding, "he needs constant and assiduous cooperation." [3]

Distributing the spoils provided one area of co-operation, for time had to be devoted to the making of major diplomatic appointments, as well as to the horde of importunate seekers for lesser office who besieged the new administration. Lincoln and Seward worked closely in the choice of ministers to foreign countries. Seward did not like the President's paying off debts incurred in his nomination at Chicago, particularly the selection of Norman Buel Judd as Minister to Berlin and William L. Dayton as Minister to England. The Judd appointment stood, but Seward insisted that Adams go to England, and Lincoln finally agreed to send Dayton to France. With Weed urging him on, Seward succeeded in placing Henry S. Sanford, a career diplomat and old acquaintance, at Brussels. Carl Schurz clamored for the Sardinian appointment, but Seward felt that it would be unwise to make this erstwhile German revolutionist the head of any European legation. The German-American vote was mighty, however, and Lincoln eventually gave Schurz the Spanish post, shifting the newly appointed Cassius M. Clay from Madrid to St. Petersburg in order to do so. James Watson Webb, an inveterate beggar for office, wanted a diplomatic appointment that would be lucrative. William M. Evarts wrote to Lincoln on Webb's behalf, urging that he be made Minister to Great Britain and intimating that, if Frémont or Seward had become President in 1856, Webb would have received that post. In 1861 the editor of the *Courier and Enquirer* was willing to settle for something less. He badgered Seward, appealed from him to Lincoln, and was finally made Minister to Brazil.

It was also a matter for consultation between Seward and the President when Sumner and Henry Wilson requested that John

Lothrop Motley be appointed Minister to The Hague. The author of *The Rise of the Dutch Republic* was a logical candidate, but James S. Pike, who had lost out to Sanford at Brussels, had been placated by being made Minister to Holland. Motley was given the Austrian mission, a major appointment at a $12,000 salary. This disappointed Seward's old friend and benefactor Richard M. Blatchford, who had applied with some urgency for Vienna, presumably because his young wife wanted the glittering society of a major European capital. All came right, however, for Seward soon found an opportunity to make "Blatch" Minister to the Court of Pius IX, and Mrs. Blatchford had a winter season in Rome.[4]

There were hundreds of lesser appointments, ministerial and otherwise, the responsibility for which was shared or individually assumed by the President and the Secretary of State. One that must have brought some pain to Seward was that of David K. Carrter of Ohio, who was made Minister to Bolivia. It had been Carrter who announced the shifting to Old Abe of the four Ohio votes that clinched the 1860 nomination at Chicago.

The State Department of 1861 was not the huge organization that it is today. Its home since 1820 had been an old, two-story brick building, drab in color but with a front portico of six white columns. This edifice stood on the corner of Fifteenth Street and Pennsylvania Avenue, where the northern wing of the Treasury Department stands today. Its thirty-odd rooms housed the diplomatic bureau proper, a consular bureau, a home bureau, a keeper of the archives, a disbursing agent, and a commissioner of patents, all save the last being supervised by the chief clerk of the Department. The two rooms occupied by the Secretary of State were on the northeast corner of the second floor, just across the hall from those of the chief clerk and the Assistant Secretary.

The chief clerk was William Hunter, an authority on every phase of the Department's work, for he had served since the days of John Quincy Adams. There were twenty-three lesser clerks, two messengers, and four watchmen. This aggregation made the building hum with activity. The accumulation of archives and books provided a space problem, but no change of location was made until the fall of 1866. Then the Treasury Department needed the site, and State moved into temporary quarters—a building belonging to the

Washington Orphan Asylum on Fourteenth near S Street—where it remained until 1875.[5]

The new Secretary of State retained Hunter as chief clerk, but a loyalty check eliminated several of the lesser fry. Two of the vacancies were filled by Seward's friends—his biographer and editor of his *Works*, George E. Baker, and his friend, the erstwhile publisher James C. Derby. He also found a place for the tempestuous Pole, Adam Gurowski, who professed his gratitude by declaring that "Savage animals, & I am one by nature, when tamed become the most devoted." This mood was transient, for Gurowski, an antislavery radical, was soon boasting that he was in the Department to spy on his chief. Even so, his tenure lasted some fifteen months.

Seward had not been long in the State Department when it became apparent that he had a wide conception of his duties and obligations. He seemed willing, even eager, to take on every task that lay within the province of government—patronage distribution in his own and other departments, military planning and policymaking, censorship of the mails and the telegraph, and a huge correspondence North and South. He even engaged the services of a charming adventurer and world traveler, one Henry Wikoff, in an attempt to get Greeley, Raymond, and James Gordon Bennett into agreement on a common policy of supporting the government, a task not unlike the labor of Sisyphus. And his attentions and advice to Lincoln were assiduous.

These multifarious activities, this inclination as Gurowski put it "to meddle in everything," scarcely endeared the Secretary of State to his colleagues in the Cabinet. That body, in addition to Seward, consisted of Chase (Treasury), Welles (Navy), Cameron (War), Bates (Attorney General), Caleb B. Smith (Interior), and Montgomery Blair (Postmaster General), a group that Charles Francis Adams characterized as "a motley mixture, consisting of one statesman, one politician, two jobbers, one intriguer, and two respectable old gentlemen." No one of them could be regarded as Seward's friend, and Chase, Welles, and Blair were Old Democrats who were hostile to him. He was, they felt, not only an Old Whig and soft on slavery, but also avid for power. One of their first grievances was what they regarded as his attempt to dominate Lincoln and cast them in distinctly subordinate roles.

Apparently at Seward's suggestion, at any rate with his full consent, Lincoln fell into the habit of having only impromptu Cabinet meetings, with Seward informing the other members as to time and place. "An artful scheme," thought Welles; a part of Seward's plan for taking over control of the government. Chase, too, was upset by this procedure, both men protested to Lincoln, and after that there were stated Cabinet meetings on Tuesdays and Thursdays. When there were special sessions, however, it was Seward who sent out the announcements.

From the beginning a sense of strain hovered over the meetings of the Cabinet, for all the members early developed real or fancied grievances. Each man was eager to obtain his full share of the patronage, and more if possible; all resented poaching by the others on what they regarded as their own preserves. Seward was peculiarly vulnerable to this accusation because the jurisdictional limits of the departments were poorly defined and State had developed a habit of assuming the duties not specifically assigned to others. The new administration was not three weeks old before Chase was complaining bitterly about the paucity of diplomatic appointments from Ohio and threatening to go to Lincoln. Seward rejected the complaint as unjust and accused Chase of persecuting him. Soon Welles and Chase were at loggerheads with Seward over appointments in New York; Chase found fault with Seward's method of stimulating enlistments in the Empire State; and Weed did not help matters by conducting a vendetta against the Blairs in the columns of the Albany *Evening Journal*. For the most part the disputes were petty and the grievances transitory, but the friction between Seward and Chase, the two strongest men in the Cabinet, was ominous for the future.[6]

During the first six weeks of the administration, the overshadowing question, in or out of the Cabinet, was whether or not the nation would be plunged into a civil war. A new government had been set up by seven states. The Confederate States of America, in Montgomery, Alabama, with Jefferson Davis as President and a written Constitution, closely resembled in form the government of the United States. One federal fort and custom house after another had been seized by the Confederates, though two principal fortresses, Pickens at Pensacola and Sumter at Charleston, were still in federal hands. No resistance to these proceedings had been offered by Buchanan's administration, which had remained supine even when, early in January, the unarmed steamer *Star of the West* with reinforcements for Sumter had been driven away by the fire of South Carolinian batteries. The Union had been split in two, and there was a real and present danger that all or most of the eight border slave states would soon join the Confederacy.

Nevertheless, the outlook was not all gloomy. The South had only two pressing grievances that were specific—difficulties in the rendition of fugitive slaves, and the ominously protective Morrill tariff which had become law two days before Lincoln's inauguration—and the former of these was disappearing as one northern state after another repealed its personal liberty laws. There were also powerful Unionist forces in the border states, and very considerable pro-Union elements in the Confederacy itself. It was logical to hope that the states just south of the Mason and Dixon line, if rightly handled, could be kept in the Union, and that the rebellion, if patiently and wisely dealt with, might in two or three months wither away.[7]

Seward's thinking, which ran along these lines, was strengthened by still other considerations. He shrank from the idea of fratricidal strife. Colonel John B. Baldwin, a Virginia Unionist who talked with him early in April, thought that he was "earnestly engaged in the effort to secure peace and safety as a means of averting the military era which he thought he saw dawning upon the country." War and disunion were alike dreadful to him. He told William H. Russell of the London *Times* that, if a majority of the southern people wanted secession, he would let them have it, but he could not believe so monstrous a thing. He also had scores of letters encouraging him to pursue a conciliatory course. These came from influential people —Leslie Combs of Kentucky, northern and southern lawyers and merchants, Virginia Unionists, and a man in whose judgment Seward had great confidence, John A. Gilmer, member of Congress from North Carolina.

Let the crisis wear itself out, Gilmer advised in repeated letters. The secessionists want a collision of arms over the collection of the revenue, a collision that will sweep Unionist southerners into the secession movement. Give up the forts, gain time so that Unionists can get control of the governments in the border states. This will give an opportunity for a resurgence of Union sympathy in the Deep South. Above all, yield the forts.

Under these circumstances, with the mails to the South still open, and with daily protestations from highly placed southerners of their devotion to peace, Seward was hopeful that war could be avoided and the Union restored. He consulted Gilmer and other southerners about federal appointments in the border slave states, kept in close touch with the Unionists in the still-existent Virginia convention, and generally exhibited a spirit of confidence and optimism. Fred Seward wrote to his mother that Unionist feeling in the South grew stronger every day, and his father urged Weed to have the New York legislature resolve that Congress call a national convention for the redress of grievances. Such a step, he declared, "would be agreeable to the Administration in all its parts." A short time later he told William H. Russell that secession would be over in three months.[8]

It was in this optimistic frame of mind that Seward faced the problem of what to do about three commissioners from the Confederate government who, early in March, arrived in Washington. These men, John Forsyth, Martin J. Crawford, and A. B. Roman, sought recognition for the Confederacy. They asked Seward to arrange an appointment with Lincoln so that they could open negotiations for a peaceful solution of questions arising between the two countries.

This request posed a problem for the Secretary of State. To open official negotiations was obviously impossible, since it would be, in effect, a recognition of the Confederacy. He considered, and then abandoned, meeting Roman "by accident" at the home of the Russian Minister. There was, of course, the danger that blunt rejection of the commissioners' request might precipitate hostilities. Sam Ward reported to him that Senators Gwin and Hunter believed that an outright rebuff would mean a Confederate attack on the forts, and Ward gave further information, apparently direct from Judah P. Benjamin, Attorney General of the Confederacy, that the government at Montgomery was getting impatient and did not intend "to await events." Under such circumstances, the obvious course of action was to make the commissioners believe that Washington was on the point of evacuating Sumter, and would perhaps make other concessions as well.

Seward now drew up a memorandum, which was approved by Lincoln, stating that the so-called Confederate government was altogether unjustifiable and unconstitutional, and that the President would have no communication with the commissioners. This Seward kept at the State Department with the consent of the Confederate emissaries, for they knew it contained a rebuff which they were anxious to avoid. Time, they felt, was useful to the Confederacy, they were especially eager to avoid a showdown over Sumter, and they had assurance that through intermediaries they could keep in touch with the Secretary of State. In fact Seward, at first through Senators Gwin and Hunter and later through Supreme Court Justices Campbell and Nelson, kept assuring them that the fort would soon be relinquished to the Confederacy.[9]

The Secretary and the commissioners alike sought delay, though for exactly opposite reasons. For the commissioners every day of peace meant a more firmly established government at Montgomery; for Seward it meant avoidance of hostilities that might push the border states into the Confederate camp and make more difficult the reconstitution of the Union.

On March 15, shortly after the curious understanding between Seward and the commissioners had been established, Lincoln asked his Cabinet if it would be wise to attempt the provisioning of Fort Sumter. The President had not yet made up his mind on this crucial question, and Weed later insisted that he had "conclusive evidence" that Lincoln had told three different men he would surrender Sumter if by so doing he could keep Virginia in the Union. To the question now posed, Blair and Chase said "yes," Smith wavered, but Seward and the rest said "no." Seward's reply stressed the importance of a non-aggressive policy as giving time for the development of that devotion to the Union that, even in South Carolina, was "a profound and permanent national sentiment." Coercion would have a disastrous effect on the border states, he said, and would give political ammunition to the Democracy. He urged continuance of a peaceful policy "a short time longer." He would collect the customs, but only by means of naval vessels outside harbors that were in dispute.

Even before Seward wrote out this reply to Lincoln's question, the press was spreading the story that it was administration policy to abandon Sumter, and Seward's mail became heavy. It showed opinion in the North and in the border states divided. Some, like Alonzo Potter, Protestant Episcopal bishop of Pennsylvania, wrote praising this wise decision and commending Seward's efforts for peace; but Weed sent a strong note of protest about surrendering the fort, declaring that "such sharp disgrace will overwhelm us." In the days that followed northern resentment at the prospect of this appeasement became more and more apparent.

On March 29 Lincoln again polled the Cabinet on relief for Sumter, and this time Seward was the only member in outright opposition. News of such action, he said, would undoubtedly get out; this would precipitate open conflict and probably defeat the effort at relief. "I do not think it wise," he declared, "to provoke a civil war beginning at Charleston and in rescue of an untenable position." Despite this advice, Lincoln told the War and Navy Departments to draw up plans for the relief of Sumter, and Seward began modifying his assurances to Judge Campbell that Sumter would be evacuated. He was satisfied, he said, that the government would not undertake to supply the fort without giving notice to Governor Pickens of South Carolina.

Seward did, however, join with the rest of the Cabinet in favor of holding Fort Pickens. In his memorandum urging the abandonment of Sumter, he declared that he would "at once and at every cost prepare for a war at Pensacola and Texas, to be taken however only as a consequence of maintaining the possession and authority of the United States." That same day he took his friend Captain M. C. Meigs, an army engineer, to see Lincoln. Meigs was confident that Pickens could be defended, Lincoln told him to draw up plans for securing the fort, and Seward provided him with $10,000 for financing the expedition.[10]

Seward's attitude toward the Confederacy hardened during the last two weeks in March, as he became less certain that war could be avoided. He told Russell on March 28 that newspaper statements about orders having been given to abandon Sumter were "a plain lie," and ten days later repeated that no federal property would be abandoned. On March 29, after he and Meigs had talked with Lincoln, he told Meigs that all men of sense saw war was coming, and that for his part he would give up Sumter but hold Pickens and make the fight there and in Texas, where Sam Houston was standing stoutly for the Union. Gilmer had advised sending the whole Union army to the Texas frontier, and Seward evidently thought there was a possibility of detaching the Lone Star State from the Confederacy and thus perhaps turning the tide of the rebellion. He still hoped that war could be avoided and the Union reunited, but these hopes were growing dimmer by the hour.

The situation was dark, and Seward's mind moved restlessly from one possibility to another. How did Europe view the American crisis, he asked Stoeckl, and, on being assured that the European states would not interfere unless their commerce was injured, he seemed reassured. The government, he said, intended to leave the seceded states in peace until they returned to the Union. A few days later, at Lord Lyons's, Stoeckl found him a different man. He spoke so belligerently of blockades and coercive measures that Lyons, startled out of his habitual reserve, declared that England had to have cotton and that she would have it, one way or another. The next time Stoeckl saw the Secretary of State, he was again talking of peace and conciliation. The Russian thought that Seward vacillated between bellicosity and fear of war.[11]

As Seward's hopes of peace and reconciliation faded, he became impatient with Lincoln, and in this he was not alone. There was much grumbling in the North over the apparent lack of a constructive presidential policy toward the rebellion. Lincoln was slowly and cautiously feeling his way toward positive action, especially in regard to the forts. This, however, was not apparent to the country at large, and other Cabinet members than the Secretary of State became restive over what seemed the President's lack of decision. During March the best that the New York *Times* and *Tribune* could do was to sum up his policy as one of "masterly inactivity." On April 3 the *Times* came out with a blistering attack upon a do-nothing government that had no policy other than a kind of Micawberish propensity for waiting for something to "turn up."

Charles Francis Adams, after conferences with Seward and other prominent men at the capital, recorded in his diary—"The impression which I have received is that the course of the President is drifting the country into war, by its want of decision. Everywhere at this place is discouragement, not loud in words but in hopelessness of a favorable issue. For my part I see nothing but incompetency in the head. The man is not equal to the hour."

Seward shared this feeling of discontent, felt it all the more keenly because Lincoln did not take his advice about Sumter. He told Adams that the President was gradually coming right, but that there was "no system, no relative ideas, no conception of his situation— much absorption in the details of office dispensation, but little application to great ideas." [12]

The reasons for the course now taken by the Secretary of State must remain, at least in part, a matter of conjecture, but certain factors in his thinking are clearly apparent. He felt that it might be necessary to warn some European countries, France especially, against recognition of the Confederacy. An avid newspaper reader, he knew of the gloomy views that were rampant about the government's lack of policy. He was still clinging desperately to his hope that the border states could be saved and the Union restored, but even his plan for a national convention was recoiling upon his head. Not only was it fruitless, as Weed told him, to try to get the New York legislature's approval of such a move, but the *Herald* declared that the convention plan was designed to pave the way for the peaceful dissolution of the Union. This assertion by Bennett's newspaper produced furious criticism of Seward. His hopes and even his position of influence in the Cabinet seemed trembling in the balance.

It was with such thoughts in mind that he decided to take action. Probably in consultation with Weed (who was in Washington toward the end of March), he outlined a proposal to put before the President. Raymond, summoned to Washington for a midnight conference at Seward's home, pledged his support if Lincoln accepted the plan. Then, on March 30, in what must have seemed a providential manner, the news broke that Spain had annexed San Domingo and by arrangement with France was about to take over Haiti as well. The next day was Sunday, and that afternoon Seward wrote out the draft of a paper entitled "Thoughts for the President's Consideration." Frederick copied it, giving it the date of April 1, and on the morning of that day delivered it to Lincoln.[13]

The "Thoughts" began with the observation that the administration, though a month old, was still "without a policy either domestic or foreign." This had been unavoidable, because of the presence of the Senate and the attendant problems of patronage distribution, but further delay would be both scandalous and dangerous. They must rid themselves of the applicants for office by making local appointments right away, leaving foreign and general ones for later action.

As to policy at home, the question before the public mind should be changed from one upon or about slavery to one on union or disunion—from a party question to one of patriotism. Since the occupation or evacuation of Fort Sumter was generally regarded as a slavery or party question, the thing to do was to "terminate" it and by so doing change the issue confronting the country. The next steps should be to defend and reinforce all the forts in the Gulf of Mexico; recall the navy from foreign stations and prepare it for a blockade; and put Key West under martial law. These moves would center popular attention upon union or disunion as the main issue confronting the country.

In foreign policy, Seward continued, he would demand explanations from Spain and France and, if satisfactory ones were not received, he would convene Congress and declare war upon them. He would also "seek explanations" from Great Britain and Russia (apparently as to their policies in the Western Hemisphere if civil war broke out in the United States) and would send agents into Canada, Mexico, and Central America to rouse a spirit of independence against European intervention.

Whatever policy was adopted, said the Secretary of State, should be prosecuted energetically. Either the President must do it, or "devolve it on some member of his Cabinet." Once adopted, all should agree and abide by it. "It is not my especial province," he concluded, "but I neither seek to evade or assume responsibility."

Here was certainly a program for vigorous and dramatic action. The note teemed with practical ideas, many of which were later implemented. The Gulf forts were reinforced; the navy was recalled from foreign parts and a blockade instituted; explanations were asked of France and Spain; federal agents were sent into Canada. Then, too, the obvious lack of confidence it displayed in the President's leadership had some justification. Historians are prone to forget that Lincoln's ability as Chief Executive had not yet been demonstrated. A month had gone by during which he had not made up his mind about Sumter, and impatience with this delay was daily growing more acute. Seward's proposal to abandon that fort and serve notice that this was a final effort at conciliation was at least a defensible effort to avert a crisis.

There were, however, two great weaknesses in the "Thoughts." One was in its obvious assumption that Seward should take over the direction of government policy—a suggestion to which no self-respecting President could possibly assent. The other lay in the Secretary's chief province, foreign policy. The obvious interest in war with France and Spain demonstrated his woeful underestimation of the strength and depth of the Rebellion. He was still clinging to the illusion that conflict with foreign nations could bring the South back into the national fold.

Lincoln replied to Seward's note the same day. There was a domestic policy, he mildly observed, and quoted the promise from his inaugural, "to hold, occupy and possess the property and places belonging to the government, and to collect the duties and imposts." This was the same policy that Seward now urged, save for evacuating Sumter. Neither could Lincoln see that the reinforcement of that fortress was more of a slavery or party issue than the reinforcement of Fort Pickens. As to foreign affairs, he and Seward had been preparing instructions to ministers "without even a suggestion that we had no foreign policy." Where direction of policy was concerned, Lincoln simply said, "if this must be done, I must do it."

Lincoln's reply evaded one of Seward's suggestions. While it was true that Lincoln had announced that he would hold the forts and collect the revenues, it was also true that no decision had been made about Sumter, a key point. The President was on stronger ground in regard to foreign policy, where no significant problem had arisen until the preceding Saturday. And he was on the strongest ground of all when he served notice, kindly but firmly, that he was master in his own house. Seward had virtually offered to take over the leadership of the administration. Lincoln brought him under control, and it was a credit to both men that the close relationship already established between them remained undisturbed.

Seward continued to press for the evacuation of Sumter, arguing that to do so would help to prevent the secession of Virginia. With this in mind, he persuaded Lincoln to see a Unionist member of the Virginia convention, John B. Baldwin, who came to Washington on April 4. What each man said to the other has long been a subject of controversy, but Lincoln evidently tried to indicate that he would evacuate Sumter if the Virginia Unionists would strike a blow at secession by forcing adjournment of the convention. Apparently Baldwin understood only that Lincoln wanted the convention adjourned, and this he rejected. The thoroughly unsatisfactory interview over, Lincoln made up his mind that Sumter must be reinforced.[14]

By April 5 Lincoln had authorized two expeditions southward—one to Fort Pickens sponsored by Seward and prepared by Montgomery Meigs and David D. Porter, the other to Fort Sumter under the supervision of irascible Gideon Welles. The Pickens expedition was kept secret from the Navy Department, for fear that southern sympathizers there would inform the Confederate government of the plan. Furthermore, while Lincoln had signed an authorization for Porter to have command of the armed ship *Powhatan,* he had also approved Welles's instructions for the Sumter expedition, instructions that included use of the *Powhatan* under the command of a Captain Mercer. The result was confusion, and a first-class row between Seward and Welles.

Late on the evening of April 5, Seward and his son Fred came to see Welles in the latter's room at the Willard Hotel. They had a telegram from Meigs in New York, where the expeditions were being outfitted, saying that orders from Welles were embarrassing the Pickens expedition. Welles immediately became upset and, when he understood that Seward had given the *Powhatan* to Porter, exceedingly irate. All agreed to appeal to Lincoln and in a state of considerable excitement made their way over to the White House, with Seward attempting to calm the waters by saying something to the effect that, old as he was, he had learned a lesson and would thereafter confine himself to the affairs of his own department. To this Welles, according to his recollection, "cordially assented."

Lincoln had not gone to bed. He heard the stories of both men, saw Welles's instructions to Mercer, and realized that he must support the Secretary in whose province the expeditions lay. He told Seward to order Porter to turn the *Powhatan* over to Mercer. Seward sent the required telegram, but signed it with his own name, and Porter, regarding an order with Lincoln's signature as superior, took the *Powhatan* down to Pensacola.

Welles suspected that Seward had diverted the *Powhatan* to Pensacola in order to wreck the Sumter expedition, but there is no reason to believe this was so. A more logical explanation of Seward's course is that he was earnestly committed to the Pickens expedition, and that in the excitement attendant upon that midnight interview with Lincoln he quite naturally sent the telegram to Porter under his own name.[15]

On April 6, the day after Seward's contretemps with Welles, James E. Harvey, erstwhile Washington correspondent of the Philadelphia *North American* and the New York *Tribune*, who had just been appointed Minister to Portugal, sent a number of puzzling telegrams to friends in Charleston about the intentions of the administration regarding Sumter. One said that Anderson definitely was to be reinforced; another just the opposite. They were based on information Seward had given Harvey about the policy toward Sumter, and when they came to light the metropolitan press and some Senators demanded Harvey's recall. This Seward refused. When he first heard of what Harvey had done, he told John G. Nicolay, Lincoln's secretary, his impulse was to demand Harvey's resignation but he had decided not to act, on the ground that Harvey had been nothing worse than imprudent.

That Seward had given Harvey information was interpreted in some quarters as an attempt on his part to checkmate the Sumter expedition, perhaps even to incite an immediate attack on the fort by the Confederates. This was, in all probability, not true. He had certainly been indiscreet in talking with Harvey, but the contradictory nature of the telegrams sent by the latter indicates that the information he had from Seward was subject to a variety of interpretations. Furthermore, had Seward really wished to see the Confederates informed of the Sumter expedition, he had only to tell Judge Campbell about it and the Confederate commissioners would promptly have relayed the word to Montgomery.

On April 7, the day after Harvey sent his telegrams to Charleston,

Seward made another effort to stay the course of events. John M. Botts came up from Richmond, went to see Seward, and with the latter's approval called at the White House. Botts, a strong Union man, urged Lincoln to let the forts go and call a national convention for the purpose of validating the withdrawal of the seceded states, with payment for federal property in the Confederacy left subject to negotiation. This would keep the border states in the Union and before long, Botts argued, the prodigals would return to the fold. Lincoln told him it was too late. Plans for the relief of Sumter had gone beyond the point of no return.[16]

News of the Sumter expedition was now very much in the air, and the Confederate commissioners saw that their waiting game was played out. On April 8 they picked up Seward's memorandum of March 15, which had been lying all this time at the State Department and which contained his refusal, approved by Lincoln, to receive them. The next day they sent a blistering letter to the Secretary of State, justifying secession and accusing him of blindness and perfidy, a letter that he "cheerfully" acknowledged. On April 11 they left Washington.

Events now moved swiftly. The bombardment of Fort Sumter began early on the morning of April 12, and on the following day, as the expedition from New York lay helplessly outside the harbor, Anderson surrendered. Lincoln issued a call for 75,000 militia. The Civil War had begun.

But even though the gates of the temple of Janus had opened, Seward still hoped that they would be soon closed. "It will be deeply to be regretted," he wrote to Anson Burlingame on the day that Sumter surrendered, "if the energy of this great Government is to have its first serious trial in a civil war instead of one against a foreign foe." To be sure, he rejected in the name of the President a suggestion by Governor Hicks of Maryland that Lord Lyons be asked to act as mediator between North and South, but on April 24 Fred Seward wrote to his mother that "Father is quite confident the whole storm will blow over. . . ." That morning Rudolf Schleiden had come to Seward offering his services in arranging an armistice for three months, or until Congress could assemble. Vice President Stephens of the Confederacy was in Richmond, and Schleiden proposed to go down there and consult with him. Seward took Schleiden to see Lincoln, who expressed interest in the project but would state no specific terms. Seward, who was determined that Schleiden go, procured a pass through the lines for him and that same day the German set off on his secret mission. He had several conferences with Stephens but could bring back no concrete proposals for an armistice. Lincoln decided that further negotiation was useless. Seward's last effort to avert the war had failed.[17]

Seward must have experienced a deep sense of frustration as he saw the battle lines forming, North and South. For months he had devoted himself to warding off this catastrophe, and his efforts had continued even after the guns had roared at Charleston harbor. He had believed that a policy of delay and conciliation would keep the border states in the Union, and pave the way for the return of the erring sisters in the Deep South. There had been delay, but during it the forces driving the Union apart had gathered strength and the President had been subjected to increasing pressure by those who did not wish to give another inch. Then Lincoln had decided to reinforce Sumter, it had fallen, and now Virginia was going out and North Carolina, Tennessee, and Arkansas were to follow. Seward's policy lay in ruins.

Why had Seward pursued a course that ended in such failure? It was partly because he had persistently underestimated the strength and determination of the secessionist movement. In part it was because he was deluded by the conviction that Lincoln was incapable of leadership, and that he, William Henry Seward, had the key to the country's salvation. Then, too, the desire for power, always a factor in his calculations, had urged him on. Intertwined with all these, and more fundamental than any one of them, was his devotion to the Union. Inadequate though his measures were, he had been trying his best to save his country from a bloody conflict, the outcome of which no man could foresee.

⚜ 20 ⚜

An Aggressive Diplomat

As the guns began to roar, Seward threw himself wholeheartedly into the conflict. He urged the calling of 100,000 rather than 75,000 militia, and the prompt purchase of arms at home and abroad. He encouraged a Union Defense Committee in New York City to enlist troops and obtain weapons, even though this private effort raised the hackles of both Secretary Cameron and Governor Morgan. Like the rest of the loyal men in Washington, he was anxious about the non-arrival of troops until one of the messengers he sent out, a young Jewish lad named Herman whom Seward promptly rechristened Flibbertygibbet, came in with a report that Ellsworth was at Annapolis and Rhode Island artillery on its way by sea. The regiments were soon pouring into Washington, and by the end of June, Seward began to feel easy about the army. He hoped that it might not be necessary to raise more troops than those already in service.

Bull Run awakened him from the dream of a war easily won. He telegraphed Governor Morgan for arms, equipment, and men—not three months' men but enlistments for three years, or the duration. "Nothing remains but to reorganize and begin again," he wrote to his wife. He still thought that the pressure of federal troops might cause the Union party in the South to declare itself, but this hope was fading fast.[1]

One important function which Seward undertook with Lincoln's approval and carried on until February 1862 was that of supervising the arrest and detention of disloyal persons. There were many people in the North whose affections and interests ranged them on the side of the Confederacy. Washington, Baltimore, and New York were full of southern sympathizers; border state families with divided loyalties were common; pro-slavery and therefore pro-southern sentiment was strong in the Middle West, especially in Indiana, Illinois, and southern Ohio. It was a situation ripe for treasonable activities, and so much information accumulated that Seward organized a special bureau in the State Department, with three clerks to take care of the paper work.

The task of uncovering active supporters of the southern cause was not an easy one. Much of the evidence placed in the hands of government officers was hearsay or inconclusive, and yet failure to apprehend any one individual might leave at large a formidable Confederate agent. In cases that involved recruiting for the Confederate army or selling Confederate bonds the testimony was usually clear enough. In others, where accusations rested mainly on alleged treasonable utterances or membership in an organization that was critical of some phase of the war effort, guilt was harder to establish.

The high military command, the Secretary of War, the Secretary of the Navy, and the Secretary of State shared the responsibility for crowding the prisons. Seward played the major role. Of 111 prisoners in Fort Lafayette, New York, on October 14, 1861, sixty-four were there by his order. To obtain evidence for the detention of supposedly disloyal persons, he relied on paid government agents, United States marshals, city police, and, to some extent, private informers. He sought, however, to keep unjust imprisonment at a minimum, and to that end he commissioned his old friend Seth Hawley to examine the propriety of releasing suspects confined in two of the principal prisons, Fort Lafayette and Fort Warren in Boston. As a result, between July 17, 1861, and February 17, 1862, sixty-nine prisoners were discharged from Fort Lafayette.

But the Secretary of State did deal severely with those whose guilt seemed clear. He jailed the "dangerous, skillful spy" Rose Greenhow, at whose dinner table he had been more than once entertained, and interposed no objection to the imprisonment of his old friend and go-between with the South, Senator Gwin. In

January 1862 the wives of two men who had been arrested three months earlier came to him with a plea for clemency. They had gone to Governor Morgan, who had written on their behalf to Lincoln, and who in turn had sent them over to the State Department. Seward told them in no uncertain terms that their husbands were traitors; and that if all the governors in the world wrote letters to Lincoln, the men would neither be released nor granted a trial.[2]

Zeal for apprehending the disloyal brought Seward at least one embarrassment. On flimsy evidence, principally an anonymous letter connecting Franklin Pierce with efforts to recruit for the Knights of the Golden Circle (a secret society of Peace Democrats in the Old Northwest), the Secretary asked for explanations from his old political foe. Pierce loathed the abolitionists, had no heart for the war, and on a recent western trip had criticized the national administration. But there was no proof that he did anything approaching treason. He bitterly resented Seward's demand. Seward apologized, saying that the note of inquiry had been written by the chief clerk of the Department and, in any case, had been designed to give Pierce an opportunity to clear his name. The former President remained irate. When the anonymous letter got into the Republican newspapers, Pierce obtained submission of the evidence to a congressional committee, and Seward's apology was then made public.[3]

Where national security was concerned, Seward lent himself readily to invasion of the freedoms supposedly protected by the bill of rights. Public danger, he declared, justified interference with the freedom of the press; if evidence of disloyalty existed, he would suppress a newspaper and jail the editor. The State Department censored mails and the telegraph, and Seward was in full agreement with Lincoln's suspension of the writ of habeas corpus. At the beginning of September he made a secret trip into Maryland, surveying the disaffection there. Two weeks later, under arrangements made on this week-end excursion to the headquarters of General Banks, came the arrest of the secessionist members of the Maryland legislature, thus destroying a plot to take that state into the Confederate camp. He was willing to go even further, when he felt the safety of the state warranted such action.

In Seward's view, when danger to the country was real and present, arrests were a weapon to be wielded by the military power of the nation and not by its courts and constables. He told Welles on one occasion that he never gave up departmental records or testified in judicial trials; that in one instance a court sent an officer to arrest him and he obtained a guard from the War Department.

During the summer of 1861, Edward A. Stevens, a soldier recently enlisted in the First Minnesota regiment, sought release from the army on the ground that Lincoln had acted unconstitutionally in calling for volunteers without prior authorization by Congress. Seward had Stevens arrested. Supreme Court Justice Wayne then issued a writ of habeas corpus, directing that Stevens appear at the Court chambers for a hearing that would determine his status. Seward, according to his own story, sent a messenger to Wayne saying that, if the Justice would find for the government, he could have the soldier; if not, the writ would be disobeyed. Wayne said the decision would be satisfactory, the soldier appeared before him, and the Justice remanded Stevens to military duty. The procedure had been against all law, Seward told Ralph Waldo Emerson, but it was necessary, for had there been an unfavorable ruling the regiments would have dissolved and the capital would have been left without protection.[4]

Seward's willingness to disregard the law gave him an opportunity to utilize his dry sense of humor at the expense of the Secretary of the Navy toward the close of the war. He told Welles he had not looked in any book on international law or admiralty law since he became Secretary of State. There had been no point in his doing so, he said, for his own thoughts came to the same conclusions as did the authorities. "He has queer fancies for a statesman . . . acts as if the ruler were omnipotent," noted the horrified Welles.[5]

To his manifold activities, legal or extra-legal, in defense of the Union, Seward added a search for military talent. He helped General Banks find officers for the force under his command; sent Lincoln (after consultation with General Scott) the names of men "fit to be generals," with McClellan and Halleck heading the list; welcomed German counts and titled Frenchmen who tendered their swords to the Union army; and as an "old, sincere, personal friend" offered Garibaldi a major-general's commission in a vain effort to enlist the services of the dashing Italian hero.[6]

But all these manifestations of patriotic energy were peripheral to the main work of the State Department. The conduct of diplomacy (the shaping of relationships with foreign countries) in a nation in the throes of civil strife, was, as Seward speedily discovered, an absorbing and delicate business. He addressed himself to this task with his customary energy and enthusiasm.

Early in March, Seward prepared a general communication for all ministers of the United States abroad. They were adjured to inform the governments to which they were accredited that an early reestablishment of national unity was anticipated, and that such a happy outcome of the internal troubles of the United States would be to the distinct advantage of every foreign country. On April 2, the day after he suggested to Lincoln the desirability of war with Spain, he sent a menacing note to Tassara, the Spanish Minister at Washington. This declared that continuation of Spain's New World enterprises, either in or out of Santo Domingo, would be met "with a prompt, persistent and, if possible, effective resistance."

Tassara replied in placatory fashion, but Seward sent blustering instructions to Horatio J. Perry, the *chargé d'affaires* at Madrid. The United States, he said, expected "to make its protest effective."

Perry delivered this communication to the Spanish authorities. They demanded to know what such language meant, and declared that reannexation of the island was a *fait accompli*. Confronted by this firm stand, the Secretary of State backed down. He explained lamely to Tassara that it was not the practice of the American government to utter threats. Any action taken would have to be by Congress, and that body was not likely to pay much attention to Santo Domingo. There the matter rested, and with good reason. Relations with other European Powers, especially England, now commanded Seward's full attention.[7]

There was some reason to believe that Seward's attitude toward England would be brusque, if not hostile. As a defender of Irish freedom, he had on occasion made critical reference to English tyranny. It was known that he looked forward to the time when Canada would fall like a ripe fruit into the American lap, and there were rumors that he was eager to hasten the separation of Canada from Great Britain. Newcastle was spreading the story that he intended to insult Great Britain. Early in January, Lyons informed Lord John Russell that Seward was a man who was wont to make political capital out of Anglo-American relations, and that he would be "a dangerous Foreign Minister, one who would play the old game of seeking popularity at home by displaying violence toward us."

But if there was evidence that Seward might be ill disposed toward Britain, there were also indicators that pointed in an opposite direction. In 1853, speaking in the Senate, he had pledged himself "to seek no factitious cause of controversy" with any European nation, and his formal pronouncements on Anglo-American affairs as a member of the Senate Committee on Foreign Relations had been generally restrained, courteous, and fair. During that same period he had become a close friend of Lord Napier, British Minister to the United States. They and their wives dined together frequently, Seward and Napier made an excursion to Niagara Falls, and when Napier left Washington in 1859, Seward was a moving spirit in arranging the farewell ball given in his honor. "I have received from him many marks of kindness, a kindness he extends to every Englishman," wrote the ex-Minister to another member of the British diplomatic corps. Furthermore, Seward had suggested that the Prince of Wales visit the United States as a means of increasing good feeling between the two countries, and he had had much to do with arranging the Prince's itinerary in the United States. He had also insisted that Adams, a known friend of Great Britain, be sent to the Court of St. James.[8] These were not the acts of an Anglophobe.

Seward's instructions to Adams and Dayton made clear three aspects of his policy. First, the American conflict was emphatically not a struggle between two states, but rather a disturbance *within* the nation which it was the duty of the government at Washington to put down. Second, no moral issue was involved in this internecine dispute; the extirpation of slavery was not an objective of the national government. Third, the United States would regard any movement toward recognition of the Confederacy by the maritime powers as an unfriendly act.[9]

Great Britain viewed with mixed feelings the developments taking place on the other side of the Atlantic. There was a widespread disposition on the part of the English to regard the division of the United States into two nations as an accomplished fact. There was also deep resentment of the Morrill tariff and real concern, especially on the part of the textile manufacturing interest, over a possible interruption of cotton supplies. The government, with Palmerston as Prime Minister and Lord John Russell in the Foreign Office, was aware of and, to a considerable extent, shared these points of view. Seven years later, Adams still remembered vividly "the crust of ice" that he encountered when he first called on Russell at Pembroke Lodge. Nevertheless Britain moved cautiously, seeking a neutral course that would at once avoid collision with the United States and protect its own interests.

Nervousness about Seward was one of the difficulties the British government encountered in formulating its policy. Palmerston declared that Lyons's fears about Seward only corroborated "what we saw of that worthy when he was here." The British Prime Minister felt that the American Secretary of State was a "vapouring, blustering, ignorant man" who might provoke a quarrel without intending to do so, or turn on Canada if he found it impossible to subdue the Confederacy. Russell shared this opinion. "If it can possibly be helped," he wrote to Lord Lyons, "Mr. Seward must not be allowed to get us into a quarrel." [10]

Immediately after the fall of Sumter came a succession of events directly affecting Anglo-American relations. On April 17 President Jefferson Davis issued a proclamation offering letters of marque and reprisal to Confederate privateers. Two days later Lincoln declared that privateers acting under such authorization would be treated as pirates and, in accordance with a recommendation from Seward, announced an intended blockade of southern ports.

With the national government's course clearly indicated, the State Department swung into action. Seward urged United States representatives abroad to exert themselves in preventing the outfitting of Confederate privateers in foreign ports, and he sent Captain William S. Walker of the United States Navy to Europe for the same purpose. He instructed Adams to make representations to Russell on blockade-running. Then, on April 24, American representatives abroad were told to enter into conventions providing American acceptance of the Declaration of Paris of 1856.

This Declaration was an agreement between Britain, France, and other maritime powers that privateering was abolished; that a neutral flag covered enemy goods, except for contraband of war;

that neutral goods, save contraband of war, were not liable for capture under the enemy's flag; and that blockades to be binding must be effective. Seward's stated purpose in offering adherence to the Declaration was "to remove every cause that any foreign power could have for the recognition of the insurgents as a belligerent power." [11] Another purpose, and an obvious one, was to obtain an international consensus outlawing southern privateering.

But while Seward moved to stifle southern privateering at its birth, a series of disturbing developments took place in London. On April 16, before news of the outbreak of hostilities had reached the British capital, a friend of the South, William Gregory, introduced a motion in Parliament for recognition of the Confederacy. At Russell's request, Commons postponed action on this motion, but only for two weeks. This was scarcely cheering to friends of the North. Worse was to follow.

As Adams told Seward somewhat later, Russell professed neutrality but regarded the Civil War as a struggle between empire and independence, one in which his sympathies inclined to the latter side. Now on May 3, shortly after commissioners seeking recognition of the Confederacy reached London, the British Foreign Minister gave them an unofficial interview. That same day he informed the House of Commons that a naval force for the protection of British shipping would be sent to the American coast. On May 6 he told the House that Britain could not regard the southern privateers as pirates, for to do so would be obviously un-neutral. Just a week later came the Queen's Proclamation of Neutrality, definitely recognizing the South as a belligerent. According to international law the Confederate government could now solicit loans and arms, bring captured vessels into prize courts, and in general be regarded as a quasi-political entity. Moreover, the Proclamation was issued without waiting for Adams to appear in London as the duly accredited Minister from the United States.

This series of steps made it appear that Britain was moving rapidly toward recognition of the Confederacy. To make the situation even more ominous, the British and French governments agreed to act jointly in regard to American affairs.[12]

While problems multiplied in England, they also appeared across the Canadian border. With the approval of the Cabinet, Seward sent a secret agent, one George Ashmun, into Canada "to keep political feelings right," as Bates recorded in his diary, and also to discover if privateers were being outfitted in the St. Lawrence. The Governor-General resented the presence of this unofficial emissary; and when Lyons asked why Ashmun had been sent, Seward "betrayed a good deal of confusion." He recalled Ashmun, but then trouble developed over the *Peerless*, an iron steamer under British registry that, Seward believed, had been taken over by Confederate agents. He asked that the ship be detained, but Lyons said that positive evidence of Confederate possession was necessary before any such action could be taken. Seward threatened to seize the steamer, even though it still flew the British flag, to which Lyons made energetic protest. The Secretary of State then softened his position somewhat, but still instructed American naval commanders to seize the *Peerless* if they had "reliable information" that the ship had been sold to the Confederates. An ironic touch was added to this controversy when it was discovered, months later, that the *Peerless* had actually been purchased by agents of the government at Washington.[13]

By the beginning of the third week in May, news of the course of events in London, including the Proclamation of Neutrality, had reached the United States and produced in the North a mood of intense irritation. Mercier reported to Paris that popular feeling was almost without restraint; that customarily calm and collected businessmen were talking openly about the advisability of war with Great Britain; that this feeling was rampant in influential New York quarters; and that Lyons, surveying the situation, thought that Washington and London were hovering on the brink of catastrophe.[14]

While popular opinion moved toward the boiling point, Seward's alarm and anger over the news from London became intense. He had earlier warned both Britain and France against any form of interference in the American conflict, but it now seemed evident that his admonitions were being flouted and that England in particular wanted to see the United States dismembered. He wrote to his wife that his latest dispatches from the two maritime powers showed them almost ready "to try and save cotton at the cost of the Union," and that Britain was "in great danger of sympathizing so much with the South, for the sake of peace and cotton, as to drive us to make war against her, as the ally of the traitors." To the historian and former Minister to Great Britain, George Bancroft, who had written optimistically about British policy, Seward replied that the dispatches he had received looked "fearfully in the opposite direction. England is demented, at least the government is." And in a dispatch to Sanford that was drafted on May 20 he remarked that England and France "seem to have been in danger of getting committed. I trust, however, they waited for Mr. Adams. He will be prepared, and I shall send him instructions bold and decisive tomorrow." [15]

The instructions to Adams, as Seward drew them up, were indeed "bold and decisive." They lodged a vigorous protest over the unofficial reception of the Confederate commissioners. So long as interviews with the commissioners continued, official or unofficial, Adams was to break off all intercourse with the British government, and a copy of the dispatch was to be shown to Russell. After doing this, Adams was to communicate with Seward, and then await further instructions. As to joint action of Great Britain and France in American affairs, Seward would not complain, though the United States had a right to expect "a more independent, if not a more friendly course." This government would maintain its blockade of southern ports, and would expect Great Britain to respect it. Any concession of belligerent rights was liable to be construed as recognition of such rights, and would not be borne unquestioned by the United States government, and recognition of the Confederacy would convert the United States from a friend into an enemy of Great Britain. The United States would continue to treat Confederate privateers as pirates, and if Britain sheltered them the laws of nations would afford "an adequate and proper remedy," to which the United States would have recourse. Britain could avoid all these difficulties by accepting the accession of the United States to the Declaration of Paris. Seward ended by deprecating war with England, while recognizing its possibility. If it came, he said, it would be a war provoked by Great Britain.

Seward went to Lincoln with this communication, and the President toned it down. He struck out the reference to the United States becoming an enemy of Great Britain, made several other modifications and, most important of all, changed it into a confidential communication to Adams, which he was not to show Russell but was to use merely for his own guidance. Seward accepted these changes, adding in the final draft that relations with Europe had reached a crisis, and that this instruction represented a basis for a permanent policy.[16]

The day on which this dispatch was signed, a report reached New York that the government was heading toward a war with European nations, and the day following the New York *Herald* published a Washington news item that Seward had read and corrected before it went to New York. It praised him for his boldness and decision in standing up to Great Britain. While he was Secretary of State, said the *Herald*'s correspondent, there would be "no blunders to regret, and certainly no timidity to deplore." [17]

The dispatch of May 21 to Adams certainly left the American Minister to Great Britain under no illusions, if he had ever had any, about Seward's "timidity." Adams thought, as he read it over, that the government in Washington was almost ready to declare war on all the European Powers, and young Henry Adams, writing to his brother in something like panic, declared that he was "shocked and horrified" that Seward, whom he had so admired and respected, should be guilty of "so wicked and criminal a course as this." Weed also, deeply disturbed, wrote to Seward that he was trying to keep out of the papers the report that there was danger of war with foreign Powers.

Seward reacted strongly to Weed's letter. Would Weed consent, he asked, "that Adams and Davis [sic] have audiences and compliments in the Minister's audience chamber and Toombs' [Confederate Secretary of State] emissaries have access to his bedroom. Shall there be no compromises at home and shall we compromise everything in Europe. Private recognition [of the Confederacy] gives currency to southern bonds." Later, Sumner remembered vividly how Seward, talking with him late in May about England, had kicked out with his foot, exclaiming as he did so, "God damn 'em, I'll give 'em hell." [18]

Seward's blistering comments on British policy were not slow in reaching the ears of Lord Lyons, who was both puzzled and distressed. At times he felt that the Secretary of State meant to have war with England; that he actually thought the North could fight and win two wars at once. Then again, Lyons told Russell, "incredible as it may appear, I believe that Mr. Seward himself is not without hope that he may really overawe England and France by threatening language." The best thing to do, he concluded, was not to give Seward any opportunity for using strong language to him.[19]

For some two weeks after the dispatch of May 21, Seward remained suspicious of England's intentions. Negotiations over the Declaration of 1856 lagged, and eventually came to naught; the idea of treating Confederate privateers as pirates met stubborn English resistance. He continued to be deeply perturbed by foreign recognition of the South's belligerent status, and by foreign animosity toward the Morrill Tariff. On June 15 he refused, albeit courteously, to receive Lyons and Mercier together, when they called to present the British Proclamation of Neutrality and instructions from Paris to support it. Letters to his wife and daughter showed his deep suspicion that England and France were promoting the disintegration of the Union, and his conviction that a strong stand against them was necessary in order to bring them to their senses.

By the middle of June, however, Seward began to believe that his hard line had effected a change in the English government's attitude. There was some reason for this point of view. News came that Canada had prevented the *Peerless* from sailing, and that Great Britain would respect the blockade, if it were in accordance with international law. An Adams dispatch stated that Russell did not expect to see the Confederate commissioners any more, and Sanford reported that they had met a decided rebuff in France. Furthermore, a spate of letters from various sources brought encouraging information as to England's attitude. Edward Everett, August Belmont, and Charles Sumner, all of whom had important English connections, wrote that influences favorable to the North were at work in London, and James Harvey on his way to Portugal gave the same account of popular feeling in England. More important still, John Lothrop Motley, fresh from conversations with Palmerston and Russell, brought reassuring evidence of the English government's desire for good relations with the United States. Finally the news came of a British order on June 1, forbidding privateers or other armed ships of either belligerent to bring their prizes into British ports. This step, followed by other nations, virtually destroyed Confederate privateering.[20]

As the news from Britain became more and more favorable,

Seward's belligerency notably abated. He could still at times take a stiff tone with Lord Lyons and in his dispatches to Adams, but the bellicosity of May and early June gave way to an obvious desire for a good understanding with Great Britain. British reinforcements sent to Canada were accepted with equanimity. Seward suspected British Consul Bunch at Charleston of pro-southern activities and asked for his recall. Russell refused. In answer to this the Secretary of State withdrew recognition of Bunch's authority, but at the same time made it clear to Lyons that he was not seeking a quarrel. He took pains to assure William Russell of the London *Times* that the United States was anxious to avoid giving any excuse for foreign interference on this side of the water.

A good illustration of Seward's more moderate stand, and also of his ingenuity in dealing with ticklish diplomatic problems, was his attitude in regard to foreign trade with the Confederacy. The problem that confronted him was how to cut off that trade without provoking recognition of the Confederacy by England and France.

There were two possible steps for the government at Washington to take in destroying the trade of foreign nations with the South. Acting on the assumption that the rebellion was merely an internal squabble, it could arbitrarily "close" the southern ports by municipal law. The alternative was the blockade. It was clear that England and France would not recognize closure by municipal law, for such action was not a right recognized in international law under the conditions of civil war that they regarded as existing in the United States. But a blockade was generally regarded as a belligerent right, one which implied that the country using this weapon was fighting an outside enemy.

Seward insisted upon regarding the struggle with the South as an internal problem but he chose blockade, which England and France were willing to recognize. In doing so, he took the position that the blockade was not at all an admission of a state of belligerency, but was simply a more lenient way of doing what he had a right to do—close the ports in question by municipal law. When Congress, on July 13, passed a bill authorizing the President to close the southern ports by proclamation, Seward used his influence to keep Lincoln from issuing any such statement. The attitude of the State Department met heated opposition in Congress and aroused the bitter hostility of Gideon Welles, but yielding to the arguments of his opponents would have greatly increased the chances of a foreign war.[21]

Seward's attitude toward England from mid-April to June has been ascribed to the persistence of his wish to involve the United States in a foreign war as a means of reuniting the country.[22] The fears of English statesmen that this was his intent, and the character of his original instructions to Adams on May 21, lend color to this theory. But that such was his purpose after hostilities between North and South had actually begun is not borne out by the evidence. Another possibility is that, as a result of the enormous responsibilities that the war had heaped upon him, his bitter resentment at the attitude of England, his impulsive nature, and the psychological difficulty of reconciling himself to Lincoln's leadership, he simply lost his head and acted in hasty fashion. This is possible, but Seward was no tyro in the field of foreign affairs, and the high stakes involved make it seem likely that something more than blind passion lay behind his actions.

The most likely supposition is that the hard line he adopted toward England, while strengthened perhaps by resentment and a desire to keep in touch with American public opinion, was undertaken in the belief that it would check a menacing trend by Britain and France toward outright recognition of the Confederacy. While he threatened, or seemed to threaten, war with England, there is no proof that he *wanted* such a war as a means of ending the conflict between North and South. Indeed, in a dispatch to Dayton on May 4, he explicitly stated that the time for conciliation of the rebellious states had passed; that the insurgents had now resorted to "open, flagrant, deadly war"; and that "the United States have accepted this civil war as an inevitable necessity." He likewise informed the new Minister to Russia, Cassius M. Clay, that the South's revolt would be "promptly and effectually suppressed." Two months later he told Adams that, "However otherwise I may at times have been understood, it has been an earnest and profound solicitude to avert foreign war that alone has prompted the emphatic and sometimes, perhaps, impassioned remonstrances I have hitherto made against any form or measure of recognition of the insurgents by the government of Great Britain." In 1863, recurring to the same point, he called the impression that he had desired war with Great Britain an "injurious error" which no one had done more than Adams to correct.[23]

Seward remarked to Emerson in 1862 that the possession of force made its demonstration quite unnecessary. Since in May 1861 the United States was only in the process of obtaining possession of such force, it is at least likely that he regarded a demonstration of firmness as essential. That Lincoln, while not wishing to go as far as Seward proposed, agreed with him as to the necessity of a strong stand is evidenced by the character of the amended dispatch of May 21, and the reaction to it by the American legation in London. Sumner later told the British statesman, John Bright, that Lincoln had never been bitter against anybody but Lord John Russell.[24]

While Seward and Russell matched wits over Anglo-American policies, the Secretary of State kept a cautious eye on France and the concert on American affairs that had been agreed upon by Russell and Thouvenel, the French Foreign Minister. Like Great Britain, France would accept American accession to the Declaration of 1856 only on condition that it would in no way involve France in the American conflict. In other words, neither country would consent to treat the privateers of the South as pirates. Seward argued that France ought to accept American accession without condition, since this was what she had solicited before the outbreak of the Civil War. This bland assumption that conditions were now what they had been in 1856 was ingenious, but ineffective.[25] He had greater success in dealing with a growing tendency on the part of France to interfere with the blockade of southern ports.

During the autumn of 1861, reports from Paris indicated that the French government inclined more and more to an early intervention that would be favorable to the Confederacy. The secessionist argument that slavery was not an issue in the war—that the Negro had no better prospects under Lincoln than under Davis—prevented the development of French sympathy for the North. Moreover, French industrialists and the government itself became alarmed over the prospect of a cotton shortage, and in the fall of 1861 Thouvenel began pressing England to join in taking steps that would give Europeans access to the southern staple.[26]

Mercier at Washington presented to Thouvenel a program for bold action. He proposed that England and France recognize the

Confederacy, and that they refuse to recognize the blockade that was being slowly tightened around the southern ports. Neither Russell nor Thouvenel looked upon this with favor. But Thouvenel, in a dispatch presented to Seward by Mercier, took the position that the disruption of the Union was permanent, and he gave a vivid portrayal of the serious effects upon the French economy of a protracted struggle in America, especially if it interfered with the French supply of cotton. He then argued cogently for a relaxation of the blockade.

Seward warned Mercier that interference in the American conflict meant war. The United States might be defeated, but France would know that she had been in a fight. The only way that France could get cotton was through a northern victory. And on October 30, in a dispatch to Dayton, Seward gave his response to Thouvenel.

Beginning with a lucid outline of Thouvenel's argument, Seward then minimized the seriousness of the French economic situation. Of course, he said, the interruption of trade had produced difficulties, for the simple reason that England, France, and the United States constituted a great economic society in which the United States supplied the raw materials and the others the manufactured goods. Indubitably, France and Great Britain had a vital interest in the speedy termination of the troubles in the United States. Their error was in looking for a settlement at the cost of the Union. Such an outcome would disrupt and destroy the economic unity that had been so profitable to all three countries and was so essential to their continued prosperity.

Relaxation of the blockade might benefit others, including the southern insurgents, but Seward pointed out that its costs would fall exclusively on the United States. Furthermore, the proposal itself was vague. Thouvenel did not suggest how far such relaxation should go, for what period of time it should be effective, or in what form the insurgent owners of the cotton should be paid. Neither did he show how such relaxation could take place without injuring "the paramount sovereignty of the United States," nor what its advantages, if any, would be to the North.

Respect for France, Seward declared, forbade belief that that country would adopt a hostile policy if concession was refused by the United States. He was convinced that the great principles of liberty and union were as dear to Frenchmen as to Americans. Neither could he believe that France would take any action prolonging African slavery in the United States, or disrupting the nation that France had helped to bring into existence.

Would relaxation of the blockade affect for the better the attitude of France toward the effort to maintain the Union? Would she open her ports to pirates preying upon American commerce? On these and the other questions raised previously in this communication, Seward asked Dayton to seek confidential explanations from the French Foreign Minister.

Seward concluded by promising that the French request for relaxation of the blockade would be given careful and serious consideration. But he also declared that he could not accept Thouvenel's belief that the conflict between North and South would be a protracted one. Long before France or any other nation was brought to the state of distress pictured in Thouvenel's communication, some or all of the southern ports would be in the hands of the Union. It would then be a pleasant duty to promote the re-establishment of normal commercial relations with the rest of the world.[27]

Seward's attitude toward France at this juncture was both firm and adroit. He told Mercier in no uncertain terms that the United States would go to war with any nation that threatened its interests. He gave Dayton a forceful exposition of the reasons for maintaining the Union. He presented Thouvenel with a series of questions as to the consequences of relaxing the blockade that put the French Minister on the defensive. This was statesmanship of a high order.

It would be absurd to claim that Seward's arguments converted Thouvenel to the American's way of thinking. But it is not too much to say that the Secretary of State's firm attitude, coupled with British reluctance to abandon a neutral position, scotched the development of a French policy orientated toward recognition of the Confederacy. This was a substantial, even a crucial achievement.

At the beginning of November 1861, Seward could look back upon his first eight months in office with a reasonable degree of satisfaction. He had demonstrated too ready a willingness to sidestep law, whether national or international, and to resort to bluster in dealing with Great Britain. Despite this aggressiveness, he had avoided a foreign war, parried the threat of outright recognition of the Confederacy, and maintained against French protests the increasingly effective blockade of southern ports. But the time for any self-congratulation was short, for suddenly a new crisis developed and the United States found itself on the brink of war with Great Britain.

◆§ 21 ◆◆

The *Trent* Affair

While the relations of the United States with England and France were not in any critical stage as the summer of 1861 drew to its close, Seward knew that Confederate agents were busily spreading their propaganda in Europe, and that the increasingly effective blockade of southern ports might very well produce difficulties with the maritime nations. He was, therefore, very eager to do everything possible to improve the image of the United States abroad. One of his favorite ways of achieving this objective was to employ the services of unofficial goodwill ambassadors in promoting sympathy for the Union cause. These special agents were usually Americans, although the list of names sent to the Senate for the period from 1861 through 1867 included such individuals as Giuseppi Garibaldi and Seward's friend of Levantine days, Ayoub bey Trabulsi, who had besought him ever since for financial assistance. Some $41,000 went to these agents during those years.

The supposed employment of Garibaldi had some peculiar angles. Seward provided £1000 to pay the expenses of the general and his entourage to the United States. This money was sent to Henry S. Sanford in Brussels and, when the Italian liberator refused a commission in the American army, Seward supposed and often stated that Garibaldi kept it as a special agent. A later examination of the State Department accounts, however, revealed no trace of payments to the hero. Some way or other, the money had been diverted to another use.[1]

The heyday of the special agents was at the beginning of the war. During 1861 alone they cost the government nearly $23,000. Adams and Dayton chafed over their presence, but on occasion the efforts of these agents yielded good results. The most important mission was that in 1861–62 of the triumvirate Thurlow Weed, Episcopal Bishop Charles P. McIlvaine of Ohio, and Archbishop Hughes of New York. Hughes was to present the case of the North to Napoleon III and the French public; McIlvaine's special field was England; Weed was to exercise his persuasive arts in both countries, but particularly at London.

As he told the story in later years, Weed gave the distinct impression that Seward was reluctant to employ him; that it was done only at the insistence of Archbishop Hughes, who refused to go without him, and that he served without financial support from the government. There can be no doubt that Seward sent his old partner abroad with considerable reluctance, knowing the storm that would be raised by their enemies if he gave Weed such a mission, but his belief in Weed's powers of diplomacy outweighed his fears. It may have been his original intention to have Weed pay his own way, but if so, he changed his mind.[2]

All three had their expenses paid, Weed's amounting to $4000, and Hughes's approximately $5200. None of the three was backward in indicating that he could spend more than he received from the government. Hughes, indeed, proposed that he make a grand tour that would take him south to Algeria and east to St. Petersburg at an extra cost of $10,000, a proposal that was politely but firmly vetoed by Lincoln and Seward.[3]

The mission performed a real service. Weed's abilities in the field of political adjustment were brought into full play, both in England and France, and Adams, normally censorious about such interlopers, bore witness to his skill. McIlvaine did good work with the English clergy and laity, and it is possible, though not very probable, that Hughes exercised a moderating influence upon Napoleon III.

It was a new and unexpected crisis in Anglo-American relations that gave these emissaries an opportunity to play a role of greater magnitude than they or Seward had anticipated. The Confederacy put great stress on sending representatives abroad to plead its cause and obtain support and recognition, and the government at Washington was extremely eager to interrupt these agents. In October a report reached the Secretary of State that two former United States Senators, James M. Mason of Virginia and John Slidell of Louisiana, were bound for Europe on the Confederate steamer *Nashville* which had run the blockade at Charleston. Seward got in touch with Welles, asking him if he did not have a steamer at Boston or New York that might waylay and capture the *Nashville.*

The information that Seward relayed to Welles, though inaccurate in detail, was substantially correct. The two men, as thoroughly hated in the North as any of the Confederates, had left Charleston on October 12 on a little Confederate steamer, the *Theodora,* which was bound for the West Indies. On the lookout for a vessel that would carry them to England, they reached Havana on October 22. There, on November 7, they embarked on the *Trent,* a British mail packet headed for St. Thomas in the Danish West Indies where they could make connections with British steamers bound for Southampton.

Around noon on November 8, as the *Trent* steamed through the Bahama Channel, she was approached by the fifteen-gun United States sloop *San Jacinto,* Captain Charles Wilkes commanding, which fired first a round shot and than a shell across her bows. The *Trent* stopped, was boarded, the two envoys and their secretaries were forcibly removed from the deck, and it was then allowed to proceed without search or other molestation to its destination. The affair was dramatic enough in itself, but there was an added touch of drama in the fact that Lieutenant Fairfax, who headed the boarding party, was a member of a Virginia family that had long been at odds with the Mason clan. On November 15 the *San Jacinto* and its prisoners arrived at Fortress Monroe.

That the seizure of Mason and Slidell would provoke a crisis in Anglo-American relations was the more likely because each nation was still suspicious of the other. Palmerston told Russell in September that Lincoln and Seward had shown themselves to be so "wild" that almost any act of intemperance could be expected of them. Sumner thought that if slavery survived, England and France would be responsible. Seward asked Sumner to tell Bright that the rebellion owed all the success it had attained "to the timidity, hesitation and indirect favor of British Statesmen and the British Press." In conversation with Mercier, the Secretary of State once more threatened war against any Power that recognized the Confederacy. Mercier retailed this to Lyons, and the information reached Russell just as Wilkes seized the Confederate commissioners.

At approximately twelve o'clock on Saturday, November 16, dispatches from General Dix announcing the seizure of the two men reached the State Department. The word spread over Washington, and knots of people on the street corners and at Willard's were soon pronouncing more or less learned opinions on points of international law and the effect on Anglo-American relations. The foreign ministers who were appealed to shrugged their shoulders and took refuge in ambiguity, making such remarks as *"C'est beau, c'est joli—mais très sérieux."* Two reports reached the Department as to how Lord Lyons received the news. One was that he looked serious, and the other was that he laughed. The gossips held both to be very ominous.[4]

The telegraph carried the news of Wilkes's exploit across the North and there was great rejoicing. Secretary Welles applauded Wilkes's action, the northern press and public followed suit; and when Congress met on December 2 the House of Representatives passed a resolution of thanks to the doughty captain "for his brave, adroit and patriotic conduct." Neverthless, the news caused something like a panic in New York City, the stock market showing distinct signs of nervousness, and in Baltimore jubilant secessionists began predicting Britain's entry into the war on the side of the Confederacy.[5]

The *Trent*'s official report of what had happened became public in England on November 27, together with news of the way in which the capture of the Confederate agents had been received in the United States. Meanwhile the British Cabinet had examined the evidence and, two days after the report appeared in the papers, decided that Wilkes had acted in clear violation of the law of nations. On November 30 it drew up a dispatch to Lord Lyons demanding the surrender of Mason and Slidell to the British Minister in Washington and an apology for the aggression committed by the American commander.

News of the Cabinet's decision produced a marked change in the attitude of the London press. At first cautious, it now turned to bluster and belligerency. It declared that the United States sought war with Great Britain. The Tory papers were particularly violent, hurling threats of massive naval action and the speedy destruction of the North's blockade of southern ports. The British public was told that soon the mills of the Midlands would be humming again with cotton from the South. There was also much talk of the great insult that had been offered to Britain's colors. Even Lord Lyons, whose even temperament was not easily disturbed, told Stoeckl that he regarded Wilkes's action as the gravest insult ever offered to the British flag.

The London *Times* did admit that there were precedents for the American action in British search and seizures during the Napoleonic Wars, but it declared, in the grand manner, that then the circumstances were very different, for Britain had been fighting for her life. "The splenetic mind of Mr. Seward," the "Thunderer" asserted, had been continually fostering a feeling of enmity toward Great Britain, and it suggested that he wanted war in order to obtain Canada as a recompense for losing the South.[6]

John Bigelow, United States consul at Paris and a shrewd observer of the contemporary scene, declared that the London *Times* made Europe suspect, if not believe, that Seward desired war with England. It was also his opinion that Great Britain was bent on pushing the Mason and Slidell issue as a means of dividing the Union. Weed wrote home that the storm of indignation in England, and in France for that matter, grew stronger every day. Everywhere he heard the Duke of Newcastle story, and again and again people friendly to the North besought him to write to Lincoln urging Seward's dismissal. The English government itself manifested the same desire. Lord Russell wrote to Lyons on December 1, "The best thing would be if Seward could be turned out, and a rational man put in his place." Adams had little doubt of being called home and Benjamin Moran, secretary to the American legation in London, heard that Mrs. Adams and Lady Palmerston had a crying match because war appeared to be so imminent.[7]

At this critical juncture, Queen Victoria and Prince Albert exercised a restraining influence. At the Queen's behest, the Prince Consort, though mortally ill, undertook the task of softening the tone of the British note. He did so mainly by including a hope that Wilkes had no authority for seizing Mason and Slidell. But despite this placatory gesture, a second dispatch from the Ministry, also sent on November 30, instructed Lord Lyons to allow Seward just seven days for compliance with the demands. If, at the end of that time, the American government had not complied, Lyons was to ask for his passports and he and his staff were to leave Washington.

It took about twelve days for these instructions to reach Washington. During that time the British government began rushing preparations for war, sending troops to Canada, putting the fleet in readiness, and canceling a large order that the North had placed in England for saltpeter, a gunpowder ingredient. An armed conflict appeared inevitable. Old, infirm General Scott, who was in Paris seeking relief from dropsy and vertigo, departed hastily for the United States lest delay result in his being captured on the high seas.

The wrath of the British lion did not go unnoticed in the United States, once the wave of jubilation over Wilkes's exploit had receded; and the American press was not slow in taking up its own cudgels. The New York *Tribune* rehearsed the wrongs suffered by neutral America at the beginning of the century from the impressment of her seamen. It declared that the complaints of the British press and the arguments of the Crown lawyers were "like the tricks of Quirk, Gammon and Snap employed for the defense of a desperate felon at the Old Bailey." The New York *Times* deplored "the bluster and menace" of the English papers, labeled as preposterous their charge that the United States sought war with Great Britain, and declared that Tory demagogues were trying to whip the Palmerston Ministry into a conflict with the United States. The New York *Herald*, though somewhat more restrained, suggested that cotton was England's conscience, and that she might wish to use the "imaginary outrage" of Captain Wilkes as an excuse for destroying a commercial rival.

James Russell Lowell caught the feeling of popular resentment at the British attitude—

> It don't seem hardly right, John,
> When both my hands was full,
> To stump me to a fight, John—
> Your cousin, tu, John Bull.

This popular indignation was something that Seward had to take into account in framing his policy. It was something of which Lyons also was well aware.

While threats and menaces emanated from the British capital, Lyons pursued a very circumspect course in Washington. He informed Russell of the congressional resolution praising Wilkes, gave his own estimate of the state of American public opinion, and supplied the British Foreign Minister with copious clippings from American newspapers, commenting that their tone was "on the whole moderate." At the same time he carefully avoided opening the subject of the *Trent* with Seward, a course which he pursued until after he had received instructions from England. Seward appreciated this attitude, for he, too, wished to avoid the subject until he knew the exact position taken by the British government.[8]

On the afternoon of December 19, Lyons came to the State Department to acquaint Seward informally with the British terms. He emphasized that he had come without any written demand, and he later reported to Russell that Seward had received him seriously and in a dignified manner, without any manifestation of dissatisfaction, saying that he was sensible of Lyon's "friendly and conciliatory" attitude. Seward said that he would talk with Lincoln and give Lyons a reply within forty-eight hours, but that same day he told Mercier that there would be no war with England, and he could so inform Thouvenel.

Seward, however, needed more time, and Lyons saw that he had it. It was not until Monday morning, December 23, that the latter made formal presentation of a copy of Russell's demands at the State Department. This written paper did not include the request for a reply within seven days, which was delivered orally, for Lyons thought that "in the (I fear) very improbable event of our terms being complied with within the time, it will be fair to Mr. Seward, and desirable with regard to our future relations with this government that the compliance shall have, as much as possible, the air of having been made spontaneously." [9]

Seward had not waited until the British demands were presented to decide as to what his attitude should be in this crisis. He probably did, as Welles later asserted, share that initial spirit of elation that swept over a country anxious for some notable victory, it scarcely mattered where, but his disposition was for peace. On November 30 he wrote as much to Adams, declaring that "this government has carefully avoided giving any cause of offence or irritation to Great Britain," and that, if Britain was similarly disposed, it would continue in the same spirit. Since Wilkes had acted without instructions, the seizure of Mason and Slidell was free from the embarrassment that might otherwise have resulted. "I trust," he concluded, "that the British Government will consider the subject in a friendly temper, and it may expect the best disposition on the part of this Government." This dispatch, received by Adams on December 17 and promptly communicated to Russell, cleared the air considerably in London.[10]

Seward reserved his final decision until he had information as to Russell's attitude, but during December the war situation, and advice from various quarters, only served to strengthen his desire for a peaceful solution of the problem before him. It was obvious, even to a man as optimistic as the Secretary of State, that the South by itself was a formidable opponent. If Britain entered the lists, the immense superiority of her fleet to one which had not yet been able to close effectively the southern ports meant that the North's navy would be swept from the sea, its own ports blockaded, and southern harbors opened to Europe's commerce. Boston's merchants alone had hundreds of millions of dollars in ships and merchandise scattered all over the globe. One Boston firm had sixteen ships bound mainly for Europe. Captured, they would involve a loss of over $1,000,000. The head of this firm wrote plaintively to Seward that, if war with England must come, he hoped it could be delayed six months. Seward also knew that New York's merchants were nervous, for there was great excitement on the Stock Exchange where, during the week beginning December 15, prices declined from 4 to 7 per cent. Furthermore, Adams and Bigelow, men for whose judgment he had great respect, were counseling him to give up the prisoners, and Mercier came to the State Department to tell him that France was giving Great Britain its moral support. Another important consideration was the paralysis of army and navy movements against the South while there was danger of war with Great Britain.[11]

But if a number of reasons favorable to the surrender of Mason and Slidell weighed upon Seward's thinking, there were others that prompted him to refuse the British demands. Public opinion had hailed the capture with joy, and to surrender the men might well produce a violent popular reaction, not only against Seward but also against the government. Congress, or a considerable proportion of it, might be affronted. Moreover, Seward would have to convince the President himself that the surrender of the prisoners was the proper course to pursue.

Lincoln was reluctant to part with the captives. Sumner had suggested to him that the case should be arbitrated, and the President drew up an argument for retaining Mason and Slidell until this could be arranged. If the United States had done anything wrong, so the President's thoughts ran, it would willingly make reparation, but either the government should submit the case to an arbitral board, or surrender Mason and Slidell and apologize with the understanding that this determination of the controversy should be a binding precedent for any similar cases that might arise between the two countries. According to Frederick Seward, Lincoln was not satisfied with his own argument. At any rate, he did not present it to the Cabinet for discussion.[12]

Seward's reply to Lyons was placed before the Cabinet on Wednesday, December 25. Beginning with a brief account of the seizure of the four men, he went on to state that Wilkes had acted without instructions from the United States government. Was his action justified? The prisoners were contraband of war and therefore the *Trent*, a merchant vessel even though it carried dispatches, was subject to seizure; Wilkes had conducted the search in a lawful and proper manner, and had a right to take possession of the contraband. The prisoners, however, were being released because they and the *Trent* should have been taken before an American prize court for adjudication of status.

Seward went on to say that he was not at all embarrassed by taking what seemed to be the British side of the argument, for he was really defending an old and honored American position. He then quoted instructions given in 1804 by Secretary of State Madison to James Monroe. These were to the effect that, in cases of contraband found on a neutral vessel, the right or wrong of seizure should be decided, not by the captor, but by a legal tribunal. Therefore, in surrendering Mason and Slidell, Seward declared that he was acting in accordance with cherished American principles. Neither was he forgetting that, if national safety required it, both right and duty would demand retention of the prisoners. Fortunately, their lack of importance and the waning character of the rebellion rendered such action unnecessary.

It was true, he said in conclusion, that Great Britain had acted in times past as Wilkes had acted now, but he would not "lift up buried injuries from their graves to oppose what national consistency and the national conscience compel us to regard as a claim intrinsically right." Rather, he wished to express his satisfaction that the case was being settled upon confessedly American principles, thus terminating a controversy over neutral rights that had kept the two nations at odds for more than half a century. The prisoners would be "cheerfully liberated" from Fort Warren into the custody of Lord Lyons.[13]

The Cabinet and Sumner (who was present as chairman of the Senate Committee on Foreign Relations), debated Seward's draft at length that Christmas Day. Sumner and Blair had always been in favor of giving up the prisoners. Bates argued that war with England would be ruinous—an obvious truth that some of those present, even Lincoln, were reluctant to admit. There was considerable talk about the popular displeasure that might be produced by the appearance of truckling to England. Chase wandered up and down the question, agreeing that the surrender should take place, though it was "gall and wormwood" to him, for Wilkes had "performed only his plain duty to his government." The session adjourned at two o'clock. On the following day, the Cabinet agreed to the draft with some minor changes in phraseology and it was sent to Lord Lyons.[14] Russell accepted the release without accepting Seward's arguments and the crisis was over.

Seward's note surrendering Mason and Slidell showed the influence of ideas that he had received from several quarters. That of purchasing freedom of the seas by giving up the prisoners was in a Winfield Scott-John Bigelow letter which appeared in the Paris and London papers, and in Bigelow's own letter of December 5 to Sew-

ard. The use of Madison's instruction to Monroe was proposed by
Adams in his dispatch of December 3, and the defense of Wilkes was
in part suggested by Benjamin R. Curtis in a letter to Justice Wayne
that was handed over to the Secretary of State. But even so it was
peculiarly a Seward composition in its adroit handling of a ticklish
problem. Written with a view to home as well as British consumption, it covered Wilkes with flowers while repudiating his action,
and gave in to Great Britain while upholding the great principle of
the freedom of the seas.

Opinions of the note varied widely. Adams confided to his diary
that it was "a very able paper," adding (wrongly) some days later
that it was "made almost entirely out of the substance of my des-
patch of the 3d of November." Hamilton Fish, between whom and
Seward there was never any great good feeling, thought it "verbose
and egotistical; in argument flimsy," an abandonment of principle.
Schleiden and the Prussian Minister, Baron Gerolt, were enthusiastic.
Richard Henry Dana, an authority on international law, thought
Seward "not only right, but sublime," though he regarded the note
as "a little too sublimated, dephlegmated and defecated for common
mortals. . . ." Sumner denied that Mason and Slidell were contraband of war, but approved the surrender on the ground that it was
necessary to maintain good relations with England. Save for John P.
Hale, who was violently critical, there was little adverse comment in
either House or Senate. As for Lord Lyons, he wrote to Russell on
December 27 that, "I cannot say that my general opinion of Mr.
Seward had undergone any change, but without enquiring into his
motives, I must allow him the merit of having worked very hard and
exposed his popularity to very great danger."

Frances Seward declared that Henry's stand was signal proof of
his patriotism; he had sacrificed himself for the nation's good,
"nobody else having sufficient magnanimity to do so." This probably reflected Seward's own fear of adverse popular reaction, although it soon became apparent that there was general relief on both
sides of the Atlantic that the crisis was over.

Seward had had his way. War with England had been avoided;
but the fires of suspicion and resentment that surrounded him were
smothered, rather than put out. Sumner continued to whisper that

the Secretary of State was an Anglophobe. And old Frank Blair came one night to the room of Lincoln's friend, Senator Orville H. Browning, to tell him that Seward was an ambitious, selfish, and incompetent man who ought to be removed before he involved the United States in war with Great Britain.[15]

~§ 22 §~

Calm and Storm

The year 1862 was one of the most difficult in Seward's entire public career. Ironically enough, it had an auspicious beginning. Grant captured Forts Henry and Donelson in Tennessee, and forced a Confederate retreat at Shiloh. The *Monitor* subdued the *Merrimac* in Hampton Roads, and McClellan prepared to move up the Peninsula toward Richmond. Farragut captured New Orleans as April drew to a close and, as always when the fortunes of the Union seemed bright, there was little danger of foreign intervention.

Favorable prospects on the battlefield led Seward to think that the southern leaders might be willing to propose terms upon which the struggle could be ended. In April 1862, Mercier requested a pass so that he might visit Richmond. The ostensible purpose of the French Minister was to see what could be done to alleviate the hardships of Frenchmen living in the South, but his real reason for going was to canvass the possibilities of an early peace. Lincoln approved his journey, on condition that he should in no way compromise Franco-American relations, and Seward gave him his blessing. He authorized Mercier to say that the North felt no desire for vengeance, and that he himself would be glad to be once more in the Senate with Senators from the South.

Seward's hope that this expedition would, as he phrased it, "produce fruits," was doomed to disappointment. The Frenchman found the southern government intent only upon victory, and came back convinced that restoration of the Union was impossible. He reported this to the President and the Secretary of State. Lincoln listened with interest, but made no comment. Seward remarked that the situation was like an election, where there is much contention up to the minute of voting and immediately afterward a calm—a comparison that Mercier thought had little substance. Seward told Lyons that the intelligence Mercier brought back from Richmond made it evident that the southern leaders were prepared to make one last great effort. That failing, they would accept terms. The observation of a southern Unionist to Mercier that a victorious North should temporarily govern the rebellious states as territories was proof, Seward declared to the skeptical Englishman, that devotion to the Union was still present in southern hearts.[1]

As Seward's hopes for an early peace soared, his attitude toward England became almost benign. When a Montreal firm asked permission to land some officers' baggage at Portland so that it might be transported to Canada across the state of Maine, the Secretary of State replied that Britain might so transport not only baggage, but also troops, military stores, arms, and munitions of war—a generosity that Lyons found similar to that of the Greeks bearing gifts. When Britain intimated its hope that the reciprocity treaty with Canada would be continued, Seward declared that the American administration was of the same mind. "In this and in all matters," he assured Lyons, "we desire to be good friends with you, if we can." Since the settlement of the *Trent* question, Lyons informed Russell in April, the attitude of the American government had been, on the whole, friendly and conciliating, and his intercourse with Seward and the other members of the administration had been "remarkably cordial and satisfactory."

Of course there were still difficulties. France and England grumbled over the North's high tariff and the interruption of their commerce. The government at Washington remained concerned over the activities of Confederate agents in Europe. But Seward opened New Orleans and two other captured southern ports to foreign ships, and made rosy predictions about a speedy resumption of the cotton trade. He also pointed out to both of the maritime Powers that the tariff and the blockade were products of wartime exigencies. If they would withdraw their recognition of the South as a belligerent, the struggle would end in a month. Then peace would bring cotton and prosperity to French factories and the English Midlands.[2]

Early that spring and with the President's hearty approval, Seward concluded a treaty with England providing for Anglo-American cooperation in suppressing the African slave trade. Welles grumbled that Seward sought to curry favor with the abolitionists, and that he had been duped by English flattery into an agreement which restricted the right of search—an objection that disappeared with modifications of the instrument. But Capitol Hill liked the treaty. Sumner, who had its management in the Senate, worked closely with Seward, and wept when he told Lyons that it had passed by a unanimous vote. When he carried the same tidings to the Secretary of State, Seward rose from the couch on which he had been resting and exclaimed, "Good God! the Democrats have disappeared! This is the greatest act of the Administration." He told the President much the same thing. It was a significant step, one undertaken at the initiative of the American government, and as such drew plaudits in the House of Commons.[3]

Indeed, a considerable change of opinion was apparent in England. Henry Adams thought that the whole tone there had been altered by Seward's diplomacy, and Weed and McIlvaine bore similar testimony. Seward himself believed the time had come for a master stroke, and on April 14 sent off to Adams a long and able dispatch, accompanied by a map that showed how the Union forces were beginning to strangle the Confederacy. He argued that the North's arms were everywhere victorious; that the opening of all southern ports was sure to come, and that it might come very soon indeed if England and France would make it clear that they had no intention of recognizing Confederate independence.[4]

Adams read this dispatch to Russell, who was unmoved. The British government felt that the outcome of the war was by no means determined, and that pressures engendered by the blockade were a menace to the British economy. There was logic in this point of view. The opening of the southern ports was of little help, so far as England was concerned, for the South restricted cotton exports and these were further hampered by United States customs regulations aimed at preventing payment of specie for the Confederate staple. Gladstone pushed hard for cotton, his speeches giving the distinct impression that the government of which he was a member favored intervention.

There were other issues besides cotton between the two governments. London did not take kindly to pleas and veiled threats from Seward about the use of Nassau and Bermuda by blockade runners. Despite all Seward and Adams could do, Confederate raiders—the *Florida* and the *Alabama*—were building in British shipyards. And then, as though in answer to Russell's skepticism about an early Union victory, came the collapse of McClellan's move on Richmond, the mauling of Pope's army at Second Bull Run, and Lee's move into Maryland.

This darkening of the Union's fortunes coincided with a worsening of relations with France and England, both of which were much impressed by the successes of the Confederate arms. Northern defeats, together with Ben Butler's threat to treat the ladies of New Orleans like women of the streets if they continued to insult Union soldiers, and the increased tariff duties of July 1862, roused a furor in the English press and in Parliament. Gladstone, at Newcastle on October 7, declared that the South had made an army, appeared to be making a navy, and had made "what is more important than either, a nation." Palmerston and Russell seriously considered an offer of mediation, and Mercier and Thouvenel were of the same mind. There was a possibility that refusal by Washington of such a proposal would lead to recognition of the Confederacy.

Alarmed by the report of such developments, Seward told Adams that he should rebuff all propositions for interference in the American conflict. Further, if Great Britain, either alone or in combination with any other government, recognized the insurgents, and if he had no further instructions, he should at once ask for his passports.

At the same time, however, the Secretary of State tried to find means of appeasing foreign sentiment. If he had had his way, foreigners would have been allowed to buy cotton from the rebels and ship it out from New Orleans, even if they paid gold for it. He asked Weed and Edward Everett to prepare to go abroad as

ambassadors of good will. Also, much to Welles's disgust, Seward requested that neutral mail found on captured ships should be forwarded unopened to its destination.

Antietam and Lee's retreat out of Maryland exercised a restraining influence on British opinion as, presumably, did Seward's warning against interference, which Adams retailed by indirection to the
Ministry. Palmerston, less willing than Russell to become involved in
American affairs, consulted the Earl of Derby. That venerable
leader of the opposition said that Gladstone's speech had been rash,
and that he himself was averse both to mediation and recognition.
The former would surely be rejected, and the latter would irritate
the North without helping the South or procuring one bale of
cotton. The result was refusal by the British Cabinet to take any
direct action, and for the moment Seward could breathe easier about
relations with Great Britain.[5]

France was a different matter. Seward had confidence in Thouvenel's judgment, but that minister was replaced in October by
Drouyn de Lhuys, an unknown quantity. It was becoming apparent
that Napoleon III had plans for interfering in the internal affairs of
Mexico, and word reached the State Department that he was seriously considering recognition of the Confederacy as a sovereign
state.

Reports of the Emperor's intent regarding the Confederacy
stirred Seward to action. He told Dayton to inform the French
government of his surprise that it contemplated recognition. Had
the French considered that such a step would be of no avail without
armed intervention; that, if they intervened, it would be to strike
down the arm raised to free the slave; that they would be committing themselves to maintain slavery? A century ago, said the aroused
American, two great revolutions had begun—the emancipation of
the American continent from European domination and the abolition of the European system of African slavery. The United States
had carried these revolutions forward, but Europe appeared to be
retrogressing in both respects.

Seward's information as to Napoleon III's intent was at least
partially correct, for late that fall the French Emperor invited both
England and Russia to join with him in proposing an armistice in
America. When they declined to do so, Seward asked no explana-

tions of the government at Paris. Finding that Dayton had brought up the subject on his own initiative, Seward instructed him to inform Drouyn de Lhuys that the United States was gratified with the *present* policy of France. But he also gave the French Foreign Minister to understand that there was no prospect of the United States surrendering any part of the Gulf of Mexico to the Confederacy, and that there was no political party in America which desired either French intervention or mediation.[6]

While Seward's main interest was, of necessity, concentrated on the diplomatic side of the war, he constantly sought information about the military and naval aspects of the struggle. He followed with close interest the increasing success of the northern blockade, Lincoln's search for a general in the eastern theater, and Grant's operations in the West as the Union forces moved down the Mississippi. Repeatedly, he forwarded to the American Ministers abroad detailed accounts of the military situation.

At times he viewed the conflict from a somewhat more philosophical perspective. Despite his diplomatic pretense that it was merely an insurgent uprising, he recognized it as being a "civil war," one with vast implications. They were participants, he told Sanford, in a revolutionary drama. "The scenes are unwritten, the parts unstudied, the actors come on without notice, and often pass off in ways unexpected. Nevertheless the dénouement is subject to calculation if the people who sit out the whole have virtue, which I religiously believe."

Cast as a leading actor in this drama, Seward maintained a determinedly optimistic attitude toward the war. His views of military affairs were almost invariably cheerful, whether in his official or unofficial correspondence. When misfortune struck, he could be calm while others were nervous and excited. He fully appreciated the importance of this quality. Writing to Frances in the spring of 1862, he explained why he had to remain closely on duty. If disaster should occur, "my imperturbability will be in requisition." [7]

Seward's ardent temperament, his extraordinary vitality, and his desire to play a vital part in the war effort, continued to lead him into a whole host of activities that lay outside the field of diplomacy. Despite repeated assertions that he had given up meddling in military affairs, he found himself involved in them. This was all the more natural when, early in 1862, New York State organized the "Seward Infantry, 103d. Regiment, New York State Volunteers." Greatly pleased, he presented the regiment with a stand of colors that cost him $270 at Tiffany's. He wanted "Presented by W. H. Seward" embroidered on the flag, but had to settle for a similar inscription on the staff. The regiment's colonel, Baron Eggloffstein, sent him reports of its prowess in the field. Other military men kept him informed as to how operations were going at various fronts; on occasion he would go out with Congressmen and military leaders to see at first hand how conditions were in the Shenandoah Valley or on the Peninsula.

Seward was also much concerned over appointments and promotions in the War Department and in the field. Early in 1862 he helped ship Simon Cameron off to Russia, and bring Stanton into the War Department. When ex-Senator Gwin heard of Stanton's appointment, he remarked, "He will tomahawk them all," but Seward had already found ways of getting along with the able but irascible Ohioan. McClellan tried his patience, but apparently he stood by the general until Stanton's vehement opposition and other pressures in and out of the Cabinet forced his dismissal. He defended and shielded Butler for his conduct at New Orleans, even though the general roused a flood of complaints by his treatment of foreign consuls and by his famous "Woman Order." The Secretary of State told Stuart, the British *chargé d'affaires*, that such were the sensibilities of the American nation in regard to the female sex, that no one in this country had looked upon Butler's order as conveying what Europeans thought it did—a remark that Stuart found simply incomprehensible. Seward finally agreed to the general's removal, but was prompt to entertain Butler at dinner when the latter came back to Washington after having been replaced by a Seward favorite, General Nathaniel P. Banks.[8]

The greatest service that Seward gave the country in 1862, outside his diplomatic role, was in supplying manpower for the army. Hope for a speedy end of the war pervaded the administration that spring, and Stanton suspended recruiting for two months while he undertook reforms in the procedures of enlistment. Then in rapid succession came heavy losses of men at Shiloh and before Richmond, and Lee began moving North. Gloom replaced optimism, volunteering lagged, and there was a crisis in manpower. Weed called for a draft and wondered if it would not be justifiable to offer a small reward for the apprehension of shirking soldiers. Seward told Orville Browning that there was danger of intervention by England and France unless enlistments speeded up and the army was greatly increased. It was obvious that something drastic must be done.[9]

Lincoln gave Seward a letter asking for 100,000 more troops. Armed with this, Seward went up to New York where, in consultation with Governor Morgan, Governor Curtin of Pennsylvania, and Weed, he developed a plan whereby the state governors should suggest a call for troops, with Lincoln responding to this appeal. Seward then drafted the governors' memorial to the President, obtained from Stanton the promise of a $25 advance on the $100 bounty given to each volunteer, and went himself to Boston, where he prevailed on Governor Andrew (who wanted emancipation linked to the call for men) to sign the memorial. He also arranged with General Buckingham of Ohio to meet the governors of the midwestern states in Cleveland and develop plans for recruitment.[10]

Seward went back to Washington fearful that volunteering would still be too slow and that a draft might be necessary. On August 8 he warned all diplomatic officials not to issue passports to men between eighteen and forty-five and liable for military duty who might be supposed to have left the United States subsequent to the date of his dispatch. He had eight District of Columbia recruits sent to him and presented each one with $50; he encouraged the State Department employees to enlist, promising their old jobs when they left the service. Toward the end of August he went north on a recruiting campaign. At Auburn he found William Henry, Jr., helping to raise three regiments, and heading one of them as lieutenant colonel. Then news came that Lee was in Maryland, and Seward hurried back to the capital.

The North responded to the gravity of the situation in a manner that restored Seward's optimism. On September 26, nine days after McClellan turned Lee back at Antietam, he wrote to a friend that some 200,000 had volunteered; that there would be 100,000 more within a month; and that a draft would not be necessary. The Confederacy had already resorted to a draft. That the North had not as yet been forced to follow the same path, was due in considerable part to the exertions of the Secretary of State.[11]

Seward felt that the North, with its immense resources, would
never go down to defeat and would never consent to a partition of
the Union. He kept looking ahead to the time when the battle flags
would be furled and America would resume her march toward
greatness. He encouraged Illinois experiments in growing cotton. He
sent abroad copies of the Homestead Act of 1862, and a circular
which painted in glowing colors the wages of labor, and the
bounties and pay received by enlisted men. Cotton-growing in the
North would hurt the South's morale, and might lead to the expanded production of that staple in the future. Immigration would
help fill the need for more men, both now and in the happy days
after the war. In preparation for those days he encouraged the
Collins plan for a telegraph line girdling the globe, and gave thought
to promoting trade and commerce with Russia, China, and Japan.
Even in the dark times after Burnside's defeat at Fredericksburg, his
thoughts turned to the future, and he inquired of Sumner if the
Senate would approve a treaty providing for an international copyright.[12]

There was, however, little time for such planning. Outside of the
grim exigencies of the struggle, a host of demands and requests bore
down on the Secretary of State. He could ignore the jibes of the
imprisoned rebel spy, Rose Greenhow, and the peace ravings of
those on the lunatic fringe of the war, such as Colorado Jewett; but
when others sought favors Seward tried to oblige them. He furnished George Bancroft information about the James Madison
Papers. He sought refuge in silence when General Scott asked $3000
for his "services" in France. He took a little contraband boy off the
hands of John J. Crittenden and had Anna give the lad a bed and
some work around the house. There was also the case of Second
Lieutenant Courtland Van Rensselaer, grandson of Seward's old
friend, Gary Van Sackett. Van Rensselaer had been in command of
a foraging detail which stole fourteen geese and a chicken. This sort
of shameful pillaging of civilians was common. Most officers winked
at it, but General Dix determined on stern measures. The unlucky
lieutenant was court-martialed, suspended for six months without
pay, and reprimanded in the presence of the regiment. It took

Seward's intervention with Dix and the President to get Van Rensselaer a pardon and restoration to his place in the army.[13]

During the war Seward pushed into the background his hopes of political preferment. He discouraged efforts to use his name in connection with the 1864 canvass, and at his request sixteen Seward clubs that sprouted in Pennsylvania changed their name to "Republican." He told New York lawyer Edwards Pierrepont that he "had abandoned party for the sake of his country," and he refused to be a candidate for the Senate in 1863, a stand for which he received glowing commendation in the New York *Times*.[14]

Turning his back on such suggestions did indeed create the image of a man who had forsaken ambition; whose one thought was for the country's good. But underneath this noble exterior the old political fires smoldered. On occasion, he still broke out resentfully against those who had prevented his nomination in 1860, nor was he indifferent to what was going on in New York State politics.

The Republican party during the war years called itself the Union party as a means of attracting War Democrats into its ranks. Seward and Weed wanted a Democratic-Republican Union party in New York State, conservative in tone on emancipation and with General John A. Dix the nominee for governor, but Greeley and other radical advocates of emancipation controlled the state convention in 1862 and nominated General James S. Wadsworth, a fervent abolitionist. Both Weed and Seward were cool to Wadsworth because of his stand on the slavery question, and suspicion was rife that they opposed him in the ensuing campaign. He went down to defeat before Democrat Horatio Seymour, and the contest ended with a legislature so evenly balanced as to leave the choice of a United States Senator in doubt.

A few days after Seymour's victory, Weed wrote to Seward in a state of great alarm. He said that the New York *Herald* and Fernando Wood, the former Mayor of New York, threatened treason, but that he would go to Seymour, Dean Richmond, and other leading Democrats and urge them to take a patriotic stand. Seward forwarded this letter to the White House, with a postscript to the effect that he had told Weed to delay his proposed mission to Europe so that he could use his influence on behalf of the administration. Both men had the Senatorial contest in mind.[15]

Seward now joined Weed in abandoning their ally, Senator Preston King, whom the radical Republicans wanted re-elected. The candidate of the Weed-Seward machine was Edwin D. Morgan, wealthy New York banker and erstwhile governor. There was apparently a deal with members of the opposite party, for a combination of moderate Republicans and War Democrats elected Morgan, and reports persisted that Seward and Weed were seeking to form a new political organization.[16]

The prospects for a new political party dominated by the Weed-Seward leadership were not bright, however, and there is no real evidence that either man had such an objective. Seward had little time to devote to politics and, so long as the Dictator could pull the strings, was content to work within the existing political framework.

Emancipation was a stormy issue in 1862, both in New York and in the nation at large. Should the war be fought for the Union, or for the freedom of the slave? How should slavery be brought to an end, by the national government as a military necessity, or by the civil authority of the states? Should it be immediate or gradual, with compensation or without? If with compensation, who should pay for it, and how much? Again, should the emancipated slaves stay in their native homes, or be removed and colonized? Should removal be forcible or optional? Where should they go, if they left the United States? As emigrants, should they establish colonies belonging to the nation? These questions were being earnestly and confusedly discussed.

Lincoln wanted to colonize the freedmen and thought he had found a place for them, the province of Chiriqui in Panama. Also, to appease the border slave states and to hasten the end of the war, he wished to offer gradual, compensated emancipation. This proposal was gall and wormwood to radical emancipationists like Chase and Sumner, men who were suspicious that Seward encouraged the President to think of the Union first and freedom afterward.

Long before the war began, Seward had shaped his approach to the problem of slavery. He believed that it must be rooted out, first because it was bad for the nation, second because it was bad for the white population, and last of all because it was bad for the Negro. By 1858 he was convinced that, with the growing northern predominance in Congress, the battle was substantially won; that popular pressures north and south, together with the power of the free states in Washington, would slowly but inexorably doom the peculiar institution.

This natural course of events, Seward felt, had been shattered by the pro-slavery fanatics. They had plunged the country into a war which threatened the existence of the Union. It was, he felt, an unnatural struggle, rending apart what should be an harmonious national household.

> My heart takes no delight in war, especially domestic, civil war [he wrote to Fanny in 1862]. Even the insurgents seem still to be my brethren and while I will not surrender, but will manfully contend with them, I pray that they may be turned from their dangerous ways and relinquish their wrongful purposes. Truth and freedom can move fast enough in peace to satisfy me. I do not like to proselyte with the sword.[17]

It was clear to Seward that the purpose of the war was the preservation of the Union, but he did not think that immediate emancipation and colonization were the proper means for ending the slavery problem. He opposed colonization because the Union needed all its manpower, and would need it in the times of peace that lay ahead. Slavery, he felt, should be dealt with pragmatically, rather than on the basis of idealistic concepts of freedom. He urged Adams, just before hostilities broke out, to avoid debating moral principles. Three weeks later he informed Dayton that the condition of slavery in the states would remain the same, whether the southern revolt succeeded or failed, and that the rights of the states over their own institutions would remain unimpaired. His position was virtually identical with that of the Crittenden resolution on the objects of the war which passed the Senate in July 1861 by a vote of 30 to 5, with men like Fessenden, Grimes and Wade voting yea.[18] But by 1862 it was anathema to the radicals.

As the war continued and sentiment for emancipation developed in and out of Congress, Seward remained cold to the idea. It is altogether likely that he shared Lincoln's distaste for Frémont's order freeing the slaves of Missouri Confederates, all the more because he had a most unflattering report on Frémont. His nephew Samuel S.

Seward wrote from San Francisco that the "best men" there regarded the general as wholly imcompetent and untrustworthy.[19] Seward informed Carl Schurz that national patriotism was far more important than was the evocation of foreign sympathy by making the war a crusade against slavery, a comment that mightily offended the idealistic Minister to Madrid.

Early in 1862, Amos Kendall, relic of Jacksonian Democracy, wrote to Seward opposing emancipation as an avowed war objective, because it would set a legal and constitutional war "adrift on the billows of revolution." It would be much better, said Kendall, to go along as now, setting free the slaves who escaped from or were without masters. As the northern armies advanced, "a portion of the South will be abandoned to the Negro and slavery will become extinct." He would be glad to help publicize this plan of action. Seward replied that he had shown this missive to Lincoln, who called it "a good letter." Seward then added, "I beg you to execute your purpose of enlightening the public mind in the manner you have proposed." A couple of months later Mercier reported to Thouvenel a conversation with the Secretary of State about the slavery problem. Seward had stated his conviction that the peculiar institution must be uprooted, but felt that it must be done with all prudence.[20]

Like Kendall, Seward saw slavery disappearing with the advance of the Union armies. He sought, in agreement with Lincoln, to facilitate this extinction by instructing the marshal of the District of Columbia to stop jailing enemy-employed fugitives and then delivering them to their masters, and by telling General McClellan to give them military protection. But he feared that an edict of emancipation would produce all kinds of evil consequences. It would rouse conflict in the North and might well provoke a servile war in the South. Issued without the ability to enforce it, it might bring foreign nations to the support of the South through their fear of anarchy in that region and a sixty-year loss of cotton supplies. It would make difficult, if not impossible, an harmonious restoration of the Union. He much preferred, as did Lincoln, a program that would gradually relieve the nation of the evils of slavery.[21]

The emancipation fever rose ever higher in the North. The Peninsular campaign of 1862 ended in failure; the radicals pressed the argument that the national war spirit must be given a moral tonic. Seward wrote to Adams that the emancipationists seemed to be acting in concert with the advocates of slavery to precipitate a slave rebellion. On July 17, 1862, Congress passed the Second Confiscation Act, declaring free the slaves of rebels and of all those committing treason. Lincoln and Seward both disliked this measure, but both saw in it the signs of the times.

Lincoln, like Seward, had grave doubts about the wisdom of freeing the slaves by presidential edict. On July 4, 1862, he told Sumner that it would make half the officers in the army fling down their swords, and would send three more states out of the Union. But a little over a week later, as the President and the Secretary of State were driving with Gideon Welles to the funeral of little James Stanton, Lincoln said that he had about come to the conclusion "that we must free the slaves or be ourselves subdued." He asked the advice of the two Cabinet members, and Seward replied that such a step involved vast consequences. He wanted time to reflect upon it, before making a decisive answer, but at present he inclined to regard it as justifiable, and even expedient and necessary. Welles agreed.[22]

No one realized better than the Secretary of State that putting the weight of the Executive Department behind emancipation was a significant step, and when, on July 22, Lincoln proposed it to the Cabinet, Seward counseled delay. Military reverses had depressed the popular mind, and to issue it now would appear like the "last shriek of the retreat." Impressed by this argument, Lincoln decided to wait.

As Lincoln waited, Seward continued to wonder about the President's plan. Emancipation, he felt, could be regarded as right in principle, but might not this proposed action be disastrous. The possibility of foreign interference, if the proclamation produced chaos in the South, haunted him, and he asked John Lothrop Motley in Vienna about this danger. Proclamations without the support of armies, he told Frances, were paper. In August he sent Lincoln letters from two correspondents, one strongly urging, the other deploring emancipation. He added this whimsical note—"Theology has no article more dogmatically disputed than the political one which the parties of the country seem determined that you should die upon. I send you an argument *pro*, and an argument *con*." He clung to the hope that Congress might even yet adopt Lincoln's idea of gradual and compensated emancipation, and that the war might still end in a truce and then a reconciliation in which every domestic difference would be buried.[23]

Counsels and passions arrayed themselves on opposite sides where emancipation was concerned. Archbishop Hughes, Weed, and Charles A. Dana opposed emancipation, while Adams, Bigelow, Motley, and Bancroft were for it. Sumner complained bitterly that from the start Lincoln had been slow and Seward wrong about slavery and the war, and declared that Seward was only a politician. Governor John A. Andrew of Massachusetts, fervent abolitionist, told Weed that Seward was a coward.[24] The Secretary of State listened to the arguments of both sides with a troubled mind. In the last analysis, only military necessity reconciled him to the Emancipation Proclamation, and then the reconciliation was partial.

Frances Seward did not consider her husband a coward, but she could not understand his attitude toward emancipation. From the beginning of the war she longed for it, and was critical of Lincoln for placing the salvation of the Union before the freedom of the black man. Again and again, she wrote to Henry on the subject, and at one time, probably in the summer of 1862, she put thoughts on paper, thoughts hastily scribbled down in words that perhaps her husband never saw. Henry had advocated liberty for forty years, she wrote, but now he told her that republican institutions were more important than the abolition of slavery. From her point of view, republican institutions and slavery were incompatible. Did he realize that, for a whole year, he had not written a line in defense of human liberty? To those who knew how he prized it, this silence might not appear strange, but she was not willing that his silence should give his enemies occasion to say that he was in favor of this great wrong. If the critics of the administration were correct, he had far better resign tomorrow "than by continuing there seem to give countenance to a great moral evil." [25]

Antietam came on September 17 and Lee retreated from Maryland. Five days later Lincoln opened the Cabinet meeting by reading Artemus Ward's "High-handed Outrage at Utica." He said that he considered the battle an indication of Divine will, and that he proposed to issue the Proclamation, which he then read to the Cabinet.

There was general, though on Blair's part doubtful, agreement. Seward suggested that the document would be more decisive if it stated that the government both recognized and would maintain freedom. He also thought that the reference to colonization should declare that it would be undertaken only with the consent of the Negroes and of the states colonized. These suggestions were agreed to. This preliminary proclamation announced that all the slaves of those in rebellion on January 1, 1863, would be "thenceforward and forever free." The states or parts of states still in revolt would be designated on that date.[26]

The Emancipation Proclamation was admittedly a military measure, designed to foster disaffection among the Negroes in the South, and to promote their use in the armed forces of the Union. Seward accepted it as a means to those ends. He sensed its importance in producing a favorable reaction abroad and utilized it for that purpose. It would also, he said, "reach a weakness in every nook and cranny of the insurrectionary region."

Nevertheless, his doubts as to its advisability continued. "It is a *coup d'état*," he told Stoeckl, who also doubted its wisdom. They must wait and see what the effect would be and, fruitlessly, he urged the Russian to give Lincoln his views on the subject. Washington buzzed with the rumor that Seward's influence over the President was waning, and Stoeckl thought Seward might well become a victim to the act which he had signed.[27]

When Lincoln read the draft of the final Proclamation to the Cabinet, Seward showed his fear of a servile insurrection. He urged that the freedmen be enjoined "to abstain from all violence unless in necessary self-defense"—a change that Lincoln adopted. On the day after its issuance, Senator Orville H. Browning asked Seward the reason for pronouncements that only exasperated and united the South while dividing and distracting the North. Seward replied that it was like the story of the man who, after the Revolution, could not rest until a liberty pole was raised in his village. When his neighbors asked if he did not feel as free without it as with it, he always answered, what is liberty without a pole? What, Seward added, is war without a proclamation? A few days later, Ewing reported to Browning that the Secretary of State agreed with them as to the pernicious influence of the document. Toward the end of January,

Seward again spoke to Browning about the proclamations. He regretted both of them, he said. The war, and slavery, too, would be nearer an end if they had not been issued. The President had been induced to take this step by abolitionist clamor and that of foreign nations, who did not understand that the war, if successful, would end slavery anyway. This was strong language, even though uttered in the privacy of his own home. It was also of more than doubtful propriety, coming from a man whose signature was affixed to both the preliminary and final documents.

Months later Seward felt that the New York City draft riots justified his attitude toward the Emancipation Proclamation. The rioters directed their vengeance primarily against Negroes and abolitionists. Seward wrote to his wife that he hoped what had occurred would show her the wisdom of his attempt to avoid giving the South an opportunity to enlist the support of "the faction that hates men for the marks which God set upon them to commend them to our pity and our care." [28]

◄§ 23 §►

Seward and Lincoln

Seward and Lincoln often differed, even on questions of major importance, but from the beginning they developed a close and friendly relationship. This intimacy, which caused heartburnings among various members of the Cabinet, was in some ways remarkable.

The backgrounds of the two men were strikingly different. Lincoln was a son of poverty who grew up amid frontier surroundings, a self-educated and self-made man. Seward came of wealthy parents, and received a formal education as good as that of most well-to-do youths of his time. One of Lincoln's great qualities was humility; one of Seward's outstanding characteristics was his vanity. The Secretary of State was ebullient, inclined to be impulsive, and was naturally cheerful, while Lincoln was of a more cautious temperament and subject to deeply pensive moods. The President avoided rather than sought attention; Seward thought of himself as a marked man and would raise his hat in salutation to apparent strangers who looked as though they might recognize him. Lincoln swore only rarely, mildly, and then when under great stress. Seward swore frequently and with vigor. Noah Brooks, newspaper correspondent and close friend of the President, was riding with Lincoln one day behind a team of mules out toward General Hooker's headquarters. The driver cursed, as mule drivers generally did. After one volley of oaths Lincoln touched him on the shoulder and said:

"Excuse me, my friend, are you an Episcopalian?"

"No, Mr. President," replied the man. "I am a Methodist."

"Well," said Lincoln, "I thought you must be an Episcopalian, because you swear just like Governor Seward, who is a church warden."

Behind such differences in temperament lay a much more likely source of discord between the two men, at least from the Sewardian point of view. The President, who once said that he had never willingly planted a thorn in any man's bosom, had nevertheless planted one in that of his first adjutant. He had kept Seward from achieving his lifelong goal, the White House. Much as the New Yorker might respect his chief, there still remained the bitterness of defeat and a sense of being supplanted by one who did not measure up to his own capacities. When Congressman John F. Potter of Wisconsin told him in 1861 that failure to give Carl Schurz a post would disappoint many people, Seward exploded. "Disappointment! You speak to me of disappointment. To me, who was justly entitled to the Republican nomination for the presidency, and who had to stand aside and see it given to a little Illinois lawyer! You speak to me of disappointment!"

Close association, together with the haunting specter of the might have been, produced in Seward an ambivalent attitude toward the man in the White House. At times he was full of criticism and complaint. Such had been the case in March of 1861, and so it was from time to time in the succeeding years. Richard M. Blatchford, in Washington for briefing on his Roman mission, undoubtedly saw his old friend the Secretary of State. "Blatch" stopped off in London en route to Italy and poured into the receptive ear of Charles Francis Adams tales of "the honest incompetency of the President." Then came the Cabinet crisis of December 1862, with Lincoln's defense of Seward, and shortly thereafter at a Washington dinner party where the latter held the center of the stage he eulogized his chief as the best and wisest man he had ever known.[1]

But though Seward was critical of the President's administrative capacity he had, as Welles once acidly remarked, a wonderful facility for adapting himself to situations over which he had no control. He simply ignored the obvious dislike of Mary Lincoln, who used such terms as "that hypocrite Seward," and "dirty abolition sneak." He even overlooked the snub that she administered to his wife in 1861 by refusing to put in an appearance when Frances called at the White House. Always fond of children, he quickly made friends with the Lincoln brood, especially bright, ten-year-old Willie.[2] Whether from a desire for security in office, or ambition for power, or a belief that his services were essential, or something of all three, he promptly set out to make himself useful. Opportunities speedily presented themselves.

The President knew nothing about White House procedures, and little about the social niceties that eastern society regarded as marks of good breeding. He met Charles Francis Adams on two occasions and then, at the first White House reception, failed to recognize him. Invited to an Adams party, the President and his wife did not come, nor did they send regrets. Receptions, balls, and even smaller social events, with crowds of new faces pressing about him, were confusing experiences, and Lincoln turned gratefully to anyone who could be of assistance. Seward was there to lend a helping hand.

Over from the State Department came memoranda on the use of visiting cards, and the order of procedure at balls and receptions. Gentlemen, it appeared, did not wear frock coats at evening affairs; titled foreigners were not addressed as "Sir"; state dinners customarily began at seven in the evening.

Seward made appointments for the President. He informed Lincoln that he would present Dr. Francis Lieber at 11:30 and Lord Lyons at 12:00 the next morning, and that "on neither occasion is any formal speech expected." He suggested that it might be helpful if the President would drop in at a reception the Secretary was giving that evening for some military figures and the diplomats of foreign nations. When Stephen A. Douglas died, Seward ordered the State Department draped in black. He had not felt at liberty to issue a general order, he told the President, lest the Senate object to it as a precedent, but "perhaps you may think it well to notice the matter in some way." Just before New Year's Day 1862 he sent word to Lincoln that it was customary for the President to receive the diplomatic corps on that day an hour before the general reception. He had "taken the liberty" to inform them that Lincoln would be at home next Wednesday. "You may expect them to be in full costume." [3]

The President soon found that he could rely upon Seward in ways other than those relating to social decorum. He consulted the Secretary of State about such matters as Cameron's suspension of Baltimore newspapers, and Frémont's emancipation of slaves in Missouri. When criticism of McClellan flooded the White House in the summer of 1862, Lincoln sent the letters over to the State Department for the Secretary to read. It was Seward who discovered, when Caleb Smith resigned, that the President had no authority to appoint an acting head of the Department of the Interior, and who drew up the necessary bill and message to Congress. He also composed papers for the President that ranged from a letter of commiseration to Queen Victoria on the death of Prince Albert to the presidential proclamation of thanksgiving for the victories of Gettysburg and Vicksburg. In his second annual message to Congress Lincoln used Seward's draft for the foreign affairs section almost verbatim.[4]

The President and his Secretary of State were together on all manner of occasions, formal and informal. Seward was assiduous in attendance at Cabinet meetings. When he could not attend he sent Frederick as a substitute, an innovation that irked the other members. He was a familiar figure at the White House and in the summer, when the President sought refuge from the city's heat and humidity, frequently visited Lincoln's cottage near the Soldiers' Home, three miles beyond the city on the Seventh Street road.

Charlotte Cushman was usually Seward's guest when she came to Washington. On one occasion, she had a favor to ask and Seward took her to see the President when he judged that Lincoln would be in "a pliant mood." There she was so much taken with the President's humor that she forgot to mention a young friend's desire for a West Point appointment. Seward sent the letter in which she wrote of this to the White House.

By the fall of 1861 Lincoln had formed the habit of dropping in at Seward's home in the evening, often taking John Hay along with him. Once they brought with them a Portuguese guide to English conversation that they found amusing and wished to share with the Secretary of State. It was the sort of break that Lincoln relished and that Seward, too, enjoyed. One evening Lincoln told the story of how "Long John" Wentworth had warned him against the trickery of "them Trumbull fellers" out in Illinois. Lincoln had replied that he did not see what he could do about it, whereupon "Long John" had looked exceedingly wise, and said, "I tell you what. You might do like Seward does. Get a feller to run you"—at which Seward, like the President, appeared to be vastly amused.[5]

Sometimes they would arrange a Sunday outing. Frederick Seward wrote to his mother about one such affair:

> Sunday, (yesterday) Father proposed to get our day of rest, which is an impossibility *in* town, by going out of it. On telling the President, he said he would go also. Gen. McClellan, & Scott (Asst. Secretary of War) and two of General Cameron's daughters were added so that our party filled three carriages. We went up through Tenallytown and Rockville to the camp of the Cayuga Regiment about 18 miles from Washington, where the President had telegraphed General Banks to meet him. Found the General, had a lunch under the trees. . . . We did not reach the City till long after dark.[6]

One winter evening Lincoln dropped in at the Seward establishment to get its proprietor to go out with him on a search for "news." Lazette Worden was a house guest, and Seward introduced his sister-in-law to the President as a "radical." Lazette demurred at being classed as an ultra, which prompted Lincoln to tell a story.

At the time of the War of 1812, said Lincoln, it was the fashion for young ladies to make belts with mottoes wrought on them for their soldier lovers. One girl asked her young man if she should put on his belt "Liberty or Death!" "Well," he replied, "I guess that's rather strong. Suppose you make it 'Liberty or *be crippled!*'" [7]

Such contacts bred intimacy, and by the fall of 1862 Welles could note that the two men were together every day, swapping stories and discussing policies; that Seward treated the President with a familiarity that was (Welles thought) akin to disrespect; and that Lincoln appeared reluctant to discuss and decide any important question in the Cabinet meetings without Seward's advice. Gurowski, always violent in his opinions, thought Seward had the President completely under his control.[8]

Both men could see that they had many things in common, even in such relatively minor matters as carelessness about grooming and fondness for animals. One of the first things Seward did after the new administration took office was to present Lincoln with a pair of kittens that played about the White House and climbed all over the chief executive of the nation. The keen sense of humor that they shared was a common bond, and Lincoln needed the laughter that Seward furnished with his stories and reminiscences. Both had an extraordinary facility for getting along with difficult people, and a marked disposition to achieve their ends by conciliating rather than overwhelming those who differed with them. Lincoln, himself always slow to anger and reluctant to hate (Montgomery Blair later told Samuel Tilden that he believed Chase was the only man Lincoln actually hated), admired Seward's lack of vindictiveness. "He is," said the President, "a man without gall"—a remark that was largely though not entirely true.

There were still deeper resemblances between the two men. They were shrewd judges of human nature, though here Lincoln carried off the palm. They shared a capacity for analyzing motives and the significance of political events. Both were conservative by nature. Though Lincoln had a sense of timing that contrasted with the impulsiveness apparent at various stages of Seward's public life, the latter's conduct in the winter of 1860–61 and his finesse in handling the dangers of foreign intervention and the Mexican problem showed that he, too, had proficiency in that great virtue of a public man.

Finally there were striking similarities in their attitudes toward the Negro. Both were sure that the black man was the social inferior of the white and probably would always be so, though at the same time they recognized that he had a right to life, liberty, and the pursuit of happiness. As for political rights, both were willing to see the southern Negro acquire the suffrage—at some future time. Seward had no enthusiasm for forcing Negro ballots down the throats of southern whites. Lincoln slowly came to the conclusion that the ballot should be given to very intelligent Negroes and those who had fought with gallantry in the Union army—this probably with a view of eventual full Negro suffrage. He was not militant on the subject, however, and a suggestion along this line to Governor Hahn of Louisiana had no constructive result. The President and his Secretary of State were as one in regarding the problem of the black

Abraham Lincoln (1809-65).
Photograph by Gardner, April 9, 1865. Library of Congress.

Ulysses S. Grant (1822-85).
U.S. Signal Corps photo (Brady Collection) in the National Archives.

Thurlow Weed (1797-1882).
Photograph by Brady. University of Rochester Library.

John L. Schoolcraft (1804-60).
Painted by Wagner *c.* 1855.
Seward House, Auburn, New York.

Abraham Lincoln (1809-65).
Painting by Carpenter, 1864.
Seward House, Auburn, New York.

Eliphalet Nott (1773-1866).
President of Union College 1804-66.
Seward House, Auburn, New York.

Archbishop John Hughes
(1797-1864). Seward House,
Auburn, New York.

Edwin M. Stanton (1814-69).
Secretary of War 1862-68.
U.S. Signal Corps photo (Brady
Collection) in the National Archives.

Salmon P. Chase (1808-73).
Secretary of the Treasury 1861-64.
U.S. Signal Corps photo (Brady
Collection) in the National Archives.

Charles Sumner (1811-74).
Library of Congress.

Montgomery Blair (1813-83).
Postmaster General 1861-64.
U.S. Signal Corps photo (Brady
Collection) in the National Archives.

Gideon Welles (1802-78). Secretary of the Navy 1861-69.
U.S. Signal Corps photo (Brady Collection) in the National Archives.

man's place in America as distinctly secondary to the harmonious restoration of the white man's Union.[9]

Seward had need of Lincoln's confidence and support, never more so than in the year 1862. During that trying period of the war, the attacks upon the Secretary of State were incessant. The successful settlement of the *Trent* affair made little difference to his detractors, and within three weeks Seward told one of his friends in the diplomatic corps that his control over Congress had well nigh vanished. Democrats, former Democrats now in the Republican ranks, most of all the radical Republicans who considered him to be soft on slavery and therefore unfit for his post—all these joined in the onslaught. It rose to its greatest heights when there were reverses in the field, which were promptly laid at his door, but the stream of obloquy also came at other times and from other quarters, east and west. His critics accused him of being a pusillanimous compromiser at home and a war monger abroad. They charged him with drunkenness. They kept alive the old stories about his complicity with John Brown and his threats to the Duke of Newcastle. Adams, who found his post in London trying enough, and who was wont to growl in his diary at Seward's lack of tact in sending ministers and unofficial agents to "range over this manor" and make mistakes for which he, Adams, would be held responsible, still considered his position a paradise compared with that of the Secretary of State.[10]

Whenever Seward's opponents thought they had discovered a chink in his armor, they swarmed to the attack. In the House of Representatives, the judiciary committee criticized his handling of the telegraph censorship. In the Senate, Sumner would rise and introduce resolutions calling for files of State Department correspondence in foreign affairs. The Senate committee in charge of printing demanded information about the publication of the Department's official correspondence as an advertisement in newspapers. At various times the Senate rejected Seward's preferences for posts at home or abroad. Democratic Senator Lazarus W. Powell of Kentucky called him a usurper and a tyrant who had without warrant imprisoned respectable citizens, and who had told a deputation from Kentucky seeking their release that "I do not care a damn for the opinion of Kentucky. . . . Why the hell are you not at home fighting traitors instead of seeking their release here?"[11]

The story was much the same outside of Congress. Thomas Ewing denounced him as "a low, vulgar, vain demagogue who had insulted every foreign power since coming into office"; Blair called him a liar; Sumner, both at home and abroad, criticized the conduct of the State Department; Chase consorted with and furnished ammunition for Seward's enemies in the Senate. The Secretary's Wisconsin foes accused him of intriguing for the defeat of Congressman John F. Potter for re-election.[12]

Nowhere did the fires of tribulation burn hotter than in New York State. There rabid Democrats had already written him off as the great failure of the administration—"egotistical, false, flippant, grotesque as usual," according to one of Tilden's friends. Now there was a formidable movement cheered on by Greeley and Henry Ward Beecher, for his dismissal from the Cabinet. If we are to have Cabinet changes, growled the *Tribune*, give us a Democrat rather "than a timid, lukewarm, compromising Republican." Hamilton Fish thought him a failure, and in the darkest days of 1862 even his old friend James Bowen felt that he was not competent to handle the crisis. The *Times* stood loyally by him, and the *Herald* paid tribute to him as the one good man in Lincoln's entourage, but James Gordon Bennett was at best a dubious ally. Repeatedly, enemies set rumors afloat that Seward would either go into retirement or replace Adams in London. Early in the year, Adams recorded in his diary that "In all my experience of public abuse and private slander of a statesman I have never known a parallel instance."[13] The situation was worse at the close of the year than it had been at its beginning.

This barrage of criticism was hard for Seward to bear, encased though he was in the armor of self-righteousness. Like Lincoln, he found Congress trying, both because of its attitude toward emancipation and its attacks upon himself. The story spread that, at a dinner at the Spanish minister Tassara's in July 1862, he incautiously remarked that he had lately begun to appreciate the value of a *coup d'état;* that, or a Cromwell, might be a good thing for Congress.[14] In July he gave an interview for the *National Intelligencer*, protesting that he worked in full co-operation with Lincoln, the Cabinet, and the army, and made no moves in Congress against any man. The President seldom overruled his advice. He would remain in the State

Department for the duration, unless the President thought it wise to relieve him.

The statements Seward made in the *Intelligencer* were largely true. Shortly after the *Trent* affair was over, Seward had repelled a suggestion from his political ally, William M. Evarts, that he use his newly won prestige to remodel the Cabinet. Charles A. Davis, prominent New York merchant and litterateur, congratulated him, justly enough, on his name never appearing in the accounts of political and military cliques and coteries at Washington. He and Lincoln worked together in harmony. Nevertheless, the appearance of this apologia showed that he felt the need of self-defense, especially when the chorus of condemnation grew so loud as to imperil his usefulness in the State Department.

Occasionally Seward would flash out in anger at some outrageous story, but his general mood was one of philosophic resignation. History was a solace, he told his daughter, for it showed that selfishness was a characteristic of mankind. Of course the complaints coming to him about the conduct of the war were hard to bear, especially since he could put them to no practical use, but her letters abounded in the cheerfulness of the young and he wanted her to keep on writing "of boys and girls and dogs and horses, and birds that sing, and stars that shine and never weep. . . ." [15]

The first really formidable demand for Seward's resignation came from his home state in the summer of 1862. A New York committee on the conduct of the war, packed with his enemies, sent four of its number to Washington to lay their grievances before Lincoln, and prominent in this delegation was James A. Hamilton, son of the first Secretary of the Treasury. No sooner had Hamilton arrived in the capital than he hurried over to see Chase and tell him what they planned to do. He later came back to the Secretary of the Treasury and reported the result of their efforts.

The committee had an audience at the White House on September 10, and proceeded to criticize the conduct of military affairs, and particularly Seward for not having his heart in the struggle. As the denunciation of the Secretary of State continued, Lincoln became excited. "You, gentlemen," he said, "to hang Mr. Seward, would destroy the government." Hamilton renewed the attack on Seward the following morning, but with as little effect, and the baffled committee made its way back to New York.[16]

The next, and more formidable onslaught against the Secretary of State came in December. It resulted partly from a practise that Seward had initiated in 1861, that of publishing each year selected parts of the State Department's diplomatic correspondence. He had delegated the choice of dispatches for the first volume and, by his own account, had had little time for supervision of the work. Both Adams and Dayton had criticized the selections, and congressional radicals had denounced and were still denouncing a dispatch to Dayton in late April 1861, which declared that the rights of the states and the condition of all persons in them would remain the same, whether the rebellion succeeded or failed. Seward himself edited the publication of the dispatches for 1862, with a view to avoid giving offense to foreign countries, but he included in the volume a confidential communication to Adams on July 5. There he declared that it seemed as though the most violent supporters of slavery and its most ardent opponents were acting together to precipitate a servile war.

The volume for 1862 reached Congress just as the session opened in December, and the radicals became furious at what they took to be a fleering comment on their efforts. The defeat of the Union army at Fredericksburg on December 13 whetted their anger, prone as they were to identify the Secretary of State with everything bad that happened in the course of the conflict.

Three days after Fredericksburg the Republican Senators met in secret caucus at the summons of the radicals among them. There Grimes, Wade and others criticized Lincoln for his conduct of the war, and bitterly denounced Seward. Grimes offered a resolution of want of confidence in the Secretary of State, but some spoke against such drastic procedure, and it was dropped. The caucus then adjourned until the next day.

On the 17th, when the caucus met again, there was renewed denunciation of the President and the Cabinet, although Browning noticed that most of those who spoke were admirers of Chase and exempted him from censure. Harris of New York offered a resolution that was adopted, asking a reconstruction of the Cabinet. On a motion by Charles Sumner, the Senators chose a committee of nine, seven of them radicals, to call on Lincoln and urge upon him a change in men and in policies.[17]

On the evening of December 18, at seven o'clock, the committee met with the President for a session of some three hours. They criticized irregular Cabinet meetings and the conduct of the war, but the burden of their complaint was Seward. They said that he was not in earnest in prosecuting the conflict and that he had too much influence in the administration; they made it clear that they wanted him dismissed.

Meanwhile, Preston King had gone to Seward with a report of the action taken by the Republican Senators, and the Secretary of State did the only thing possible under the circumstances. He and Frederick wrote out their resignations, and King and Frederick took them over to the White House.[18]

That evening Lincoln walked across Lafayette Square for a talk with Seward. He found the Secretary of State in an unhappy frame of mind, although the latter, putting the best possible face on the matter, remarked that it would be a relief to be freed from his official duties. To this the President responded, "Ah, yes, Governor, that will do very well for you, but I am like the starling in Sterne's story, 'I can't get out.' " [19]

Lincoln carefully felt his way toward a solution of the crisis. As a first step, he summoned a special meeting of the Cabinet for December 19 at half past ten in the morning. There he laid the situation before the members, Seward not being present, telling them of the latter's resignation and of his own interview with the Senate committee, and that he had assured those gentlemen that the Cabinet functioned in an harmonious fashion. The committee, Lincoln said, all blamed Seward for what had gone wrong in the war and, while they appeared to believe in his own honesty, they seemed to think that, when he had in him any good purposes, Seward "contrived to suck them out of him unperceived." The President went on to express concern over any possible disruption of his official family, and said that the assault upon it was uncalled for. He hoped that its members would, with him, meet the committee that evening. Chase demurred at this and there was considerable discussion, but at length all agreed to come.

That evening the President, all the Cabinet save Seward, and eight of the nine committee members (Wade was absent) had a long session. Grimes, Sumner, and Trumbull attacked Seward bitterly. Lincoln defended him, and said that, if there was disunity among his advisers, he was not aware of it. He asked each member of the committee if they thought it advisable to dismiss Seward, but only four of the eight present answered in the affirmative.

Chase now found himself in an impossible situation. He had fed the suspicions and irritations of the radical Senators but, when face to face with Lincoln and the committee, he at first could find nothing to say save that he had not expected to be arraigned in this meeting. He then proceeded to support the President by declaring that the Cabinet was harmonious. Later, when Browning asked one of the committee members, Jacob Collamer, how Chase could make that statement in view of what he had told others about Seward, Collamer replied succinctly, "He lied." [20]

The session with the President ended at one o'clock in the morning of December 20. The news of Seward's resignation had already broken, and a wave of apprehension swept over the capital as to what was on foot. That morning, various members of the Cabinet began rallying around the Secretary of State, if for no other reason than that the idea of the Senators dictating to Lincoln about his official family was distasteful to them. Even Blair dropped in at Seward's house, where he found him packing up, and said, "I thought I would just stop in to say, I object." Stanton, though suspicious that Seward was trying to turn the Senators' hostility against himself, came to see him. Welles decided to support him, and advised Lincoln not to accept his resignation. He later put in his diary, "Seward's foibles are not serious failings." [21]

Welles told Lincoln that he would go over to Seward's home and urge him not to press his resignation. This delighted the President. Welles found Seward deeply mortified by what had occurred, although prone to talk about his experience, sagacity and services. He was also pleased by the support of this man with whom he had so frequently differed. He would, he said, stay at his post if Lincoln so desired.

The Secretary of the Navy hastened back to the White House, where he found Stanton and Chase. Lincoln came in and said that he had sent for Chase because he was in great trouble. Chase said that he was painfully affected by the meeting of the previous evening. It had been a total surprise to him, and that morning he had written out his resignation.

On hearing this bit of news, Lincoln's eye lighted up. "Where is it," he said quickly.

"I brought it with me," said Chase. "I wrote it this morning."

"Let me have it," said Lincoln, reaching out his long arm toward the Secretary of the Treasury, who held onto the missive as though reluctant to part with it. Lincoln took it, and hastily opened it. "This," said he to Welles, "cuts the Gordian knot. I can dispose of this subject now. I see my way clear." The President was delighted and Chase looked perplexed.

"Mr. President," said Stanton, "I wish you, sir, to consider my resignation at this time in your possession."

"You may go to your Department," said Lincoln. "I don't want yours. This," holding out Chase's letter, "is all I want; this relieves me; my way is clear; the trouble is ended. I will detain neither of you longer."

Welles and Chase walked down the stairs together. Welles noticed that Chase was moody and reluctant to speak.[22]

Chase saw what Lincoln had in mind and wrote him another letter endeavoring to dissuade him, but the President sent identical communications to both Chase and Seward, requesting them to remain at their posts. Seward promptly replied, saying that he cheerfully resumed his duties. He also sent a copy of this note to Chase, and on the following day Chase, with protestations of reluctance, also indicated that he would remain at the head of his department. By December 22 the storm was over.

Lincoln had foiled his Senate critics, kept Seward, and retained a balanced Cabinet which, in turn, meant that he could command support in the country at large from both radicals and conservatives. "Now I can ride," he told Senator Harris. "I have got a pumpkin in each end of my bag." Welles, viewing the crisis with an appreciative eye, wrote in his diary, "Seward comforts him; Chase he deems a necessity."

On December 23 there was a Cabinet meeting, with Seward looking very happy, and Chase pale and complaining that he had been ill for weeks. Seward invited him to dinner on the 24th, but on that day the Secretary of the Treasury begged to be excused. He was, so he wrote to Frederick Seward, indisposed, he might almost say too really sick to trespass upon Seward's hospitality.

Shortly after the Cabinet question had been solved, David Dudley Field and Mayor Opdyke came down from New York to renew the attack on the Secretary of State. There was a stormy interview, and Seward's accusers went back home discomfited. "For once in my life," the President told John Hay, "I rather gave my temper the rein and I talked to those men pretty damned plainly." [23]

More secure than ever in the President's confidence, Seward was jaunty. He wrote to Dayton, on the day he withdrew his resignation, that the political situation had been "somewhat disturbed," but the result would probably be "not merely harmless but reinvigorating." Report had him openly defiant of those who had sought to remove him, declaring that, despite the Emancipation Proclamation, he would yet reconstitute the Union on the old basis.

Evarts urged Seward to force Chase out of the Cabinet, but he made no such move. Despite his bravado, he still had to watch his step with care, for his enemies were, if possible, more vindictive than ever. When it became known that he still intended to send Weed on another mission abroad there was such an explosion of wrath that he gave up the project.[24] He had indeed triumphed over his foes, but enmity would pursue him until his public career was closed.

❧ 24 ❧

The Difficult British

The turning point of the Civil War came in 1863. During the first six months of that year the eastern battle front provided little cheer for the Union. Neither Ambrose E. Burnside nor Joseph Hooker could make headway against the genius of Robert E. Lee. That summer the great southern general invaded the North a second time. Then the tide turned. The Union army hurled Lee's gallant troops back at Gettysburg. At the same time, Grant captured Vicksburg and as Lincoln said, "The Father of Waters once more flows unvexed to the sea." Grant then drove the Confederates out of Tennessee, and the road to Georgia lay open before the soldiers in blue.

Seward's labors in the wartime diplomatic field reached their peak in 1863, when problems rising from the blockade, the possibility of foreign intervention, and the building of Confederate rams and cruisers in the ports of the maritime powers crowded thick and fast upon him. During that eventful year, he formulated policies that required hundreds of dispatches to American representatives abroad and constant communication with foreign legations in Washington. Close to 1000 notes passed from the State Department to the British legation alone,[1] and in addition to such missives Seward had numerous conferences with Lyons, Mercier, Stoeckl, and other representatives of foreign governments.

Once again the nation that received the major part of Seward's

349

attention was Great Britain, with whom numberless controversies arose out of the blockade, the detention of mails, trade with the Mexican port of Matamoras, the seizure in neutral waters of ships carrying contraband of war, and Confederate activities in Canada. These vexing and sometimes ominous problems put a high premium on sagacity and skill.

Among Seward's lesser troubles was a chronic anxiety lest some contumacious Union naval officer insult the British flag in such flagrant fashion as to plunge the two countries into war. There were numerous cases of friction between the commanders of American and British ships in the Gulf of Mexico and the Caribbean, and the chief offender on the side of the North was Wilkes, the captor of Mason and Slidell. This irascible martinet had been for some months an acting rear admiral in command of a squadron operating in the Caribbean waters surrounding the British islands, and he was perpetually falling foul of British naval regulations. Welles defended him; the British became exceedingly irate; Seward finally asked that he be transferred. On June 1 Welles tardily recalled the obstreperous officer.[2]

A more fundamental source of dissension than bickering between naval officers was trade with the South. British merchants would ship to the Bahamas or to the Mexican town of Matamoras contraband goods, destined for the Confederacy. If these were seized while en route to a neutral port, the merchants loudly complained. Russell declared that such goods were not subject to seizure until they were cleared for a Confederate harbor. This Seward stoutly denied, pointing to the contraband character of the goods and other suspicious circumstances. Often tied into these contentions were disputes about the sanctity of private mails and the seizure of ships in neutral waters.

A typical case was that of the *Peterhoff*, which was first stopped in Danish waters and then, en route to Matamoras, was seized just off St. Thomas in the West Indies on February 25, 1863. Wilkes had a hand in the seizure, a circumstance which tended to embitter the controversy. Her captors took the *Peterhoff* to Key West and then to New York, where government officials refused to allow British mails on board to be forwarded to their destination, since these were to be searched for evidence. The neutral waters aspect was smoothed over with the Danish authorities, but the retention of the mails was another matter altogether.

In his desire for good relations with Great Britain, Seward had formally agreed to release mails found on prizes, an agreement to which Welles was not a party. The Secretary of State now ordered the federal district attorney in New York to keep the mails unopened, and informed Adams that they would be forwarded in that condition. This enraged Welles, who regarded Seward's action as officious interference in a matter belonging to the Navy Department. Lincoln was brought into the dispute and, perhaps reluctantly, supported the Secretary of State on the ground that not to do so might lead to war with Great Britain. The mails were forwarded, but the prize court upheld the seizure of both vessel and cargo.[3]

The seizure of the *Peterhoff* touched off a furor of resentment in England which was all the more keen because Adams had written a letter granting immunity to an American ship carrying a cargo of arms to Matamoras, arms destined for the Juarez government. In this missive Adams had commented dourly on the "frauds" being practised in Great Britain to furnish supplies to the confederates by pretending that they were destined for a Mexican port. British commercial interests declared that the United States wanted a monopoly on the Matamoras trade. The French were now in Mexico and Drouyn de Lhuys protested bitterly to Dayton over Adams's violation of American neutrality in Mexican affairs. Responding to this tumult from overseas, Lyons told Seward that the British government strongly upheld the legitimacy of its nationals' Matamoras trade, and could not allow hostilities to be carried on against this British commerce.

Faced by criticism both at home and abroad, Seward was nothing if not versatile. He strove to dull the edge of Welles's resentment by proposing a modification of his promise to Britain regarding the mails, a proposal that Lyons politely rejected. He assured the French that Adams had no intention of offense, and that the President regretted the unfortunate letter. He told Lyons that neither Adams nor the government he represented wished to interfere in any way with lawful British trade. He could understand, Seward declared, how an impression of unjustifiable interference had been created by Englishmen and, even more, by Americans more interested in profit than in preserving peace between the two countries. But the point was that Britain's Matamoras trade had blossomed as rapidly "as palaces, cities, states or Empires rise in the tales of the Arabian nights under the waving of a wand or the utterance of a spell." Roads in the interior of Texas "were covered with caravans of cotton of disloyal citizens," cotton used to hypothecate a foreign loan which would in turn furnish vessels constructed in British ports to prey upon the commerce of the United States. The proceedings against the *Peterhoff* and the other ships in this trade were, he declared, totally justifiable.[4]

Seward's efforts only partially soothed Welles's ruffled feelings, and Adams felt that the Secretary of State had been altogether too apologetic toward the French. Mollified though he was by a letter from Lincoln and Seward expressing their "confidence and esteem," Adams confided to his diary that Seward lacked delicacy of feeling, and that the President was no judge of men. As for Britain, the controversy over neutral trade continued but the British government was careful not to take an extreme position. "I only want to be clear of any entanglement with either North or South," Lord Russell told the venerable Henry Peter Brougham. He could see that precedents established now in regard to the rights of British merchants as neutrals might become most embarrassing when his nation next became involved in war. Such foresight, together with Seward's obvious wish to avoid a rupture and his gestures of propitiation, helped to keep these irritating disputes from endangering peaceful relations between the two countries.[5]

More serious than disputes about neutral trade was the controversy over Confederate cruisers built in English yards. Of these, the *Florida* and then the *Alabama* began their careers of destruction in 1862. Both were outfitted with armaments, officers, and crews at ports distant from their place of origin, and reports were prevalent that at least one more such vessel was being prepared. There was evidence also, by January 1863 that the Laird Brothers of Birkenhead were building for the Confederate government armored rams more powerful than any ships in the Union navy. The British government took the position that it could do nothing to prevent these ships leaving English ports unless there was satisfactory evidence that they were designed for the Confederacy. Seward's answer to this was a combination of accumulation of evidence, protest, and threat.

Adams and others had presented enough evidence in regard to the *Alabama* so that Russell ordered the ship held, but she slipped out of the Mersey River on pretense of a trial trip. Russell's reaction to American protests then hardened, and he asserted that the British Neutrality Act gave the government no power to stop such ships being built in England and equipped in foreign ports unless there was complete and absolute proof that they were destined for the Confederacy. At the same time, reports of the damage being wrought by the *Alabama* on American shipping raised a tempest of indignation in the United States.

In the summer of 1862, Seward had threatened to issue letters of marque to American privateers. Now, with his active and open support, a bill authorizing such action passed Congress. He asked Lyons to inform Russell that the departure of more ships like the *Alabama* was "a thing to be deprecated above all things"; that the situation was like that preceding the War of 1812; and that, if Britain did not take adequate steps, he feared for the preservation of peace. He also indicated that the prospects for cotton exports were growing dim. This was because the European firm of Erlanger and Company undertook in 1863 to float a $15,000,000 bond issue, these securities being exchangeable for Confederate cotton. The Confederacy profited little by this "cotton loan," but it was heavily subscribed in England. Seward declared that it would be used to finance the building of more "pirates," and meant the end of all concessions to neutrals.[6]

Anglo-American relations were becoming strained. Welles in the Cabinet and John Bigelow, then consul-general in Paris, thought the United States was headed for war with England. Sumner was of the same opinion, and a decided coolness developed between him and the Secretary of State. The issuance of letters of marque would have meant a long step in that direction. The Confederates had no merchant marine, and privateers would have been forced to prey upon neutral commerce. Seward knew this, but he was using every means at his command to push the British government into compliance with his will. Nor was he simply bluffing, for he inquired of Gov-

ernor Morgan as to the possibility of New York merchants' fitting
out privateers. Lyons told Russell that Seward was trying to intimi-
date Great Britain. Although England must be firm, he said, it was
also "desirable to avoid irritating unnecessarily their [the American
people's] ever sensitive vanity." [7]

There was no easing of the tense situation as the spring of 1863
changed into summer. Seward sent Evarts abroad to help collect
evidence that more raiders were building in English yards. He also
informed Adams, for Russell's benefit, that if the government in
London did not take effective steps, the United States would feel
free to prepare a formidable public and private naval force and that
hot pursuit of raiders into English waters might be expected. Adams,
however, had already made such strong representations to Russell
that he refrained from making this threat.[8]

Strain and amity between the two nations went hand in hand that
summer. One long standing problem was settled when, on July 1,
Seward and Lyons signed a treaty by which the United States paid
$650,000 in gold as settlement of Canadian claims south of the 49th
parallel in the Pacific Northwest. But Indian troubles on the Minnesota border were not so easy to solve. A Sioux uprising in
Minnesota late in 1862 had been crushed and the warriors were
being pushed back to the frontier. The British governor in the Red
River region feared that, if they moved into Canada, they would
fight with the Indians and halfbreeds there. The Sioux, brandishing
English flags and George III medals given them for their services in
the War of 1812, claimed asylum. They won out, and Britain refused permission for United States troops to cross the frontier in
pursuit of the hostiles.[9]

The pursuit of a few desperate, half-starved Indians was a minor
matter, but just at this time a British grievance of a serious character
came to a head. The government in London felt much distressed
over the way in which American cruisers lay in wait in British West
Indian ports until neutral vessels suspected of being blockade runners moved out beyond the three-mile limit, and then swooped
down upon them. This, Britain claimed, was an infraction of neutral
rights, all the more flagrant because the crews of the captured ships
were treated practically as prisoners of war. Secretary Welles was
reluctant to do anything about the situation, and now Russell in-

structed Lyons to tell Seward that one of two conclusions must be drawn from the attitude of the American government. Either the President was not sincere and wished to hoodwink the British Minister, or else he had no control over his Secretary of the Navy.

Here Lyons's tact and Seward's sagacity came into play. On July 16, Lyons spoke to Seward about the British grievance but, as he expressed it, "without putting the alternatives in so pointed a manner." Seward thought for some moments and then suggested that Lyons make an evening journey with him to the Soldiers' Home. The British Minister reluctantly agreed, and on the evening of July 19 they went to see Lincoln at his cottage on the grounds of the Home.

The three men canvassed the problem in its various aspects, Lyons making plain the British complaint. Lincoln said that both he and Seward wished to be fair in their treatment of Great Britain. His own disposition, where the right was not clearly on his side, was "to give up all the splits." Seward observed that it would be a very good thing to go along with the British government in this case. To do so would strengthen Palmerston and Russell in their stand supporting the validity of the American blockade. The session concluded with the President observing that Welles was a good man whom he wanted to keep, but he saw that "he must put in the strength of his hand." [10]

The aggressive tactics of American cruisers might be softened, but this did little to resolve the Laird rams issue. Slowly the British government made up its mind to prevent the sailing of the ironclads. This decision, however, was not communicated at once to the administration at Washington nor, indeed, to Adams in London. On September 5, the latter told Russell that, if the rams were permitted to depart, "It would be superfluous in me to point out to your lordship that this is war." That same day, Seward sent to Adams a stern warning for Palmerston and Russell. Did they suppose for a minute, he asked, that an assault could be made by these British-built, armed, and manned vessels "without at once arousing the whole nation, and making a retaliatory war inevitable?" The insurgent cause was waning, he declared, and there were no limits to the nation's "ultimate ability for self-defense." For the sake of both countries and of civilization, he hoped that Great Britain would not "let a blow fall from under their hands that will render peace impossible."

Before Adams received this somber warning, he had had cheering news from Russell, and by September 18 Seward could tell Welles confidentially that he had absolute assurance that the rams would not be allowed to leave England. The New York *Times* and the *Evening Post* were much alarmed about the ironclads and Welles thought, perhaps with some reason, that Seward was keeping the news secret until he could present written evidence that he and Adams had brought England to book.

As late as October 5 Seward was still keeping the British government advised about the rapid increase in the naval power of the United States, and the country's readiness to take all necessary measures in self-defense. At the same time he was anxious lest the *amour propre* of the English be unnecessarily ruffled. On September 10, 1863, Sumner made a speech at Cooper Institute in New York on "Our Foreign Relations" that occupied twenty and two-thirds columns of the New York *Tribune*. Its review of Britain's wartime conduct toward the United States was distinctly critical. Seward wrote to the orator that he had read it "without once stopping," and that it performed "a very important public service" in rousing the nationality of the American people. Shortly thereafter, however, he told the New York Young Men's Republican Union that it would be just as well not to circulate the speech abroad. Acting on his advice, the Union decided not to distribute the speech among members of the British Parliament.[11]

Indeed, there was still trouble enough between the two countries, for on the subject of depredations by the Confederate cruisers Russell was both obdurate and fretful. Claims for such damages were piling up, and when he received one based on the destruction of the ship *Nora* by the *Alabama*, he told Adams that Great Britain had no responsibility for such losses. He argued that his own position was sustained by international law and by decisions in the American courts; and added that he hoped Adams would not again be instructed to present such a claim.

Seward responded that Great Britain was obliged by international law and by treaties as well to restrain her subjects from making war upon a country with which it was at peace. The

Alabama was purposefully built for war on the United States by British subjects in a British port, and the same was true of her armament and equipment. These, and the ship itself, were clandestinely sent to a common port outside British waters. There her outfit was completed and she went out to begin her work of destruction "with a crew chiefly of British subjects, enlisted in and proceeding from a British port, in fraud of the laws of Great Britain, and in violation of the peace and sovereignty of the United States." This was a crime committed within British jurisdiction, and for the ensuing damages Britain would be held responsible. The United States recognized that the present hour was not "a time for a candid and calm examination of the question. After the civil war is over, and the passions roused by it have subsided, will be such a time." Then the United States would be willing to submit its case to any fair and just arbitrament. Adams should continue to present the claims to Russell. If he refused to receive them, they were to be registered and preserved "for some suitable future occasion." Great Britain's ultimate interest in reprobating such practises as those of the *Alabama*, Seward declared, was as great as the immediate interest in the United States.[12]

This able statement outlined the grounds on which the *Alabama* claims were to be based in later years, but as yet there was little outward indication that Britain would agree to any such settlement. "There's a curious kind of sneaking conscience about these English, and they know when they've done wrong," wrote Henry Adams in 1863. "The gingerly way in which they dodge this question of claims; ignore it or outface it, shows that they feel how hard it is to deal with. And the honest ones deplore it and pray to God we may soon catch the pirate." [13]

The Laird rams crisis was ended and the *Alabama* claims were postponed, but other causes of dispute remained. The files of the State Department filled to overflowing with vigorous protests about blockade running under the British flag, the enlistment of British subjects on Confederate cruisers, the depredations of these cruisers, and the use of Canada and the West Indies as bases for forays against the United States.

Repeatedly, in the discussion of these grievances, Seward dwelt on the evil effect of Great Britain's recognition of the Confederacy's belligerent status. This, he insisted, had prolonged the struggle, and had been a source of bad relations between the two countries. He also found British sympathy for the Confederacy hard to bear. How could the English take this attitude, he asked, especially in view of the slavery question. Where was British humanitarianism? "You can hardly omit to inform Earl Russell," he burst out in July 1864, "that the whole of the British West Indies are practically used by our insurgent enemies as a base for hostile operations against the United States." The profits from these activities, he said, were received throughout Great Britain "with as much satisfaction as if the operations were in conformity with international law and with treaties." [14] His last dispatch to Adams before the carriage accident that laid him low in April 1865, concerned British infractions of American rights on the high seas.

Canada, as well as the West Indies, furnished shelter for the enemies of the Union, and Seward kept a watchful eye to the north, where border troubles multiplied during the latter part of the war. There Confederate agents and their sympathizers sought munitions, hatched plots, and tried to stir up public opinion. In November 1863, as the result of an abortive attempt to seize Johnson's Island in Lake Erie, where there were many confederate prisoners, Seward sent General Dix to the frontier and Preston King to Quebec for the purpose of co-ordinating American and Canadian efforts in foiling such activities. This move did not prevent another unsuccessful attempt a year later to seize Johnson's Island and to attack Detroit, Buffalo, and other cities. Then came the famous St. Albans, Vermont, raid of October 1864, when a little band of Confederates set fires, wounded two inhabitants of the town, one mortally, robbed banks of $200,000, and fled back across the border.

These affairs aroused great indignation in the United States, and Seward moved with vigor. He told Adams to make the first expedition against Johnson's Island an occasion for new communications to Russell about enforcing neutrality obligations. He observed that the course adopted by Great Britain and the United States would very probably serve as a rule for other countries in the future. These Canadian difficulties might well lead to the abandonment of the reciprocity treaty that had been in existence since 1854. Adams should inquire of Russell by what steps a better neutrality situation might be obtained and, indeed, if the time had not come for Great Britain to withdraw its concession of belligerent rights to the Confederates.[15]

The St. Albans affair produced an even stronger reaction on the part of the Secretary of State. He asked extradition of thirteen raiders imprisoned by the Canadian government, urged the British to pass a stronger neutrality act, threatened abrogation of the Rush-Bagot Agreement of 1817 demilitarizing the Great Lakes, and obtained an executive order requiring passports of all travelers crossing the Canadian border into the United States.

General Dix, Commander of the Military District of the East, issued orders to pursue future raiders into Canada, and either destroy them or bring them back to be tried by martial law. Northern public opinion approved this hot-headed zeal but Seward was cautious, for he knew that action of this sort might well mean war with England. He refused to support Dix, and eventually obtained from Lincoln a revocation of the general's orders. This paved the way to better relations with English and Canadian authorities.

The British government urged and in February 1865, the Canadian Parliament passed an Alien Act expelling from Canada all foreigners suspected of hostile acts against a friendly government, and providing for the seizure of arms or vessels intended for the use of such foreigners. Seward thereupon informed Adams that the 1817 convention would remain in force and that the passport regulation was rescinded, but he could not prevent an indignant Congress from passing a joint resolution ending the reciprocity treaty with Canada.[16]

The co-operative attitude of both the English and Canadian authorities aided Seward in handling these troublesome Canadian problems. Even so, he prided himself on his patience. We had had many just causes for war with Great Britain, he told Adams, yet all we had done was end reciprocity and establish a passport system. How could we have been more patient and meek? Let Great Britain seek peace with us as earnestly as we had with her, and peace there would be. Despite this bluster, however, the accommodating spirit shown by the British and Canadians in the border troubles pleased him. Moreover, he looked to the future. There would be, he told Adams, no preposterous or exorbitant demands against Great Britain

as a result of wartime grievances. It was important that the two
nations go on harmoniously together, fostering the development of
free, responsible government and the progress of civilization, especially in Central and South America and in the Eastern world now
being reopened to Western commerce.

Some months later, on news of Palmerston's death, Seward passed
a measured judgment on British policy during the war years.

> The Palmerston administration [he wrote Adams] showed no
> sympathy with the United States at any time during our
> greatest national trial. Nevertheless, I think it due from us to
> the memory of Lord Palmerston, to admit that there were
> periods during the progress of our civil war, when a Prime
> Minister of England could have been sustained by his country-
> men in placing his Government in an attitude more unfriendly
> and more directly hostile to the United States. We can never
> forget that, in occasionally resisting at critical times the temp-
> tations which led the British people towards such an attitude,
> he prevented our deplorable civil strife from becoming a uni-
> versal war.[17]

As the war drew toward a close and American military and naval
power became formidable, reports were rife that, once the South
was vanquished, the United States would engage in retaliatory
foreign wars. One story had it that General Sherman declared he
would not be satisfied until he had pitched his tent in Hyde Park
with his army camped around him. Seward took pains to deflate
such rumors. The President, he averred, had no thought of con-
quests. Europeans who anticipated such moves reasoned from Old
World rather than New World principles. We would insist upon
the freedom of the seas for our commerce, and the safety of our
borders against extensive violence. "Beyond that there are no questions which may not be safely and surely left to the powers of
diplomacy." [18]

⚜ 25 ⚜

Other Aspects of
Wartime Diplomacy

While Seward wrestled with the manifold problems of Anglo-American relations he kept a wary eye on Napoleon III. Aways a conspirator and a dreamer, the French Emperor in his restless quest for glory showed an inveterate propensity for involving himself in the affairs of other nations. So far as America was concerned, he appeared bent on bringing about a negotiated peace between North and South. Like England, he allowed Confederate raiders to shelter in French ports and Confederate emissaries to negotiate for the construction of rams in French shipyards. And always in the background were his grandiose plans for Mexico.

Primarily because of cotton, perhaps also with some vague idea of fostering good relations with the United States, Napoleon III still seemed intent on bringing the Civil War to an end. Mercier's belief that some sort of intervention was essential to the restoration of peace probably strengthened the Emperor's determination to interfere in the American conflict. The failure of his efforts along this line in the fall of 1862 had in no wise discouraged him, and the following February, Mercier, on instructions from Paris, suggested to Seward that the United States appoint commissioners to treat with the South.

Seward replied to this suggestion in a long and able paper, asserting that it was utterly impractical. In a political sense, he declared, there was no North or South, but a nation and a group of insurgents operating in some of the southern states. The war must continue until this insurgent movement was put down. Any conference that was held should take place in Congress. There representatives of the whole United States could discuss national problems.

Seward could be the more unequivocal in his rejection of the French proposal because of the general European situation. A Polish insurrection against Russia had broken out in January 1863; along with the Schleswig-Holstein question, it was beginning to absorb Europe's attention. Also, his advices from the Continent convinced him that the Anglo-French entente was falling apart, and that, at least for the time being, there was no prospect of European interference in the Civil War.[1]

Greeley now entered the picture. The unpredictable editor was in one of his defeatist moods and suggested in the *Tribune* mediation by the Swiss Republic. Then he came down to Washington, told Mercier that this was a feeler to prepare the public for the idea of foreign intervention, and declared that he really looked to France and the good offices of Louis Napoleon. Mercier promptly became keen for joint Anglo-French action, but Lyons dampened his ardor and Seward said that any mediatory scheme was simply impossible. Privately, the Secretary of State heaped scorn on Greeley, asserting that his actions made him liable to legal penalties. Greeley heard that his former partner was threatening him with incarceration at Fort Lafayette.[2]

Mercier's pertinacity, and disquieting reports from Sanford, who spent much time in Paris, reawakened Seward's doubts as to the Emperor's intentions. There was, he told Sanford, "a hazard of an early and endless alienation between the newest empire in Europe and the oldest republic of America," but before it came there would be sufficient frank and decided warning by the United States. Meanwhile, by way of propitiating Napoleon III, he urged lifting the blockade so the France could get out of Richmond 10,000 hogsheads of tobacco purchased before the war.

Welles declared that the blockade should be lifted for all or none. He was not in favor of such "loose and inconsiderate practises." Seward, however, was not to be balked. He stopped Lyons on the street one day and asked him to come to the State Department. There he explained the situation, emphasizing that France was paying heavy storage duties to the Confederate government, and said that he was disposed to let the tobacco through in neutral vessels, if Lyons would agree that Britain would not make this a precedent for breaking the blockade.

Lyons of course said he could do nothing without authorization from London, whereupon Seward suggested that he talk to Mercier. The latter thought he might propose to his government that it reach an understanding with Great Britain on the subject, but he suspected that Seward was trying to drive a wedge between France and England by putting himself in the position of being willing to grant favors to the former but being prevented by the latter. Lyons thought this was not fair to Seward. The upshot of it was that before the end of the war France obtained some but not all of the tobacco.[3]

After Gettysburg and Vicksburg, Seward suggested to Mercier that now was an excellent time for France to withdraw its recognition of the belligerent rights of the Confederacy. French actions heretofore, said the Secretary of State, had strained the bonds of affection between herself and the United States almost to the breaking point. Now France could recover all her old popularity and more by the step which he proposed, and could do it without injuring her own commerce in the smallest degree.

Mercier countered by saying that this proposal would be beneath the dignity of France and her reputation for generosity. If Seward wished, however, he would suggest to his government that it inform the insurgents their cause was hopeless, and that they should make the best terms possible with the authorities at Washington. Seward in his turn declined this proposal, lest it be construed as willingness to permit foreign intervention. And there the matter rested.

Napoleon was still intent on splitting the Union permanently into two parts. That same month, the *Moniteur* published a statement by him to the effect that, if the British government thought recognition of the Confederacy would put an end to the war, he would be glad to follow Britain in such action. Promptly, in a tart dispatch that Dayton was instructed to read to Drouyn de Lhuys, Seward said that Lincoln had read this statement with surprise and regret. The Emperor was aware that the United States would consider such recognition as "an unfriendly proceeding" that could only bring more complications and irritations to Franco-American relations.[4]

France, Seward told Sanford, was like a huge, surcharged cloud, from which lightning would have to descend upon somebody. But that she wanted war with the United States was inconceivable, and how she could wage a victorious campaign in Europe while occupied as she was in other parts of the world was not very clear.

The better to curb the Emperor's anti-American tendencies, Seward sent to Dayton and to other American legations, in August 1863, a long circular letter. When the United States complained about the premature recognition of belligerency accorded by England and France, he declared, they always replied that the effort to maintain the Union would be unsuccessful. This misconception continued, and was the basis of all that was "designedly or undesignedly injurious to this country in the policy of foreign nations." He therefore sought to remove this prejudice by a broad review of the military situation. He emphasized the importance of Gettysburg and Vicksburg, the support given by the border states and parts of the rebellious area to the Union, the effectiveness of the blockade, and the North's superiority in resources.

In this circular the Secretary of State stressed the increasing Negro co-operation in the northern war effort. The United States now had in the field, he declared, 22,000 Negro soldiers; fifty Negro regiments of 1000 men each were in process of formation; and 62,800 Negroes were employed in other capacities by the Union army. In this way, the servile population was being transferred to the support of the Union, and any question of its "moral capacity for service" was ended by the bravery of the Negro soldiers in combat.

Seward felt that this review of the situation was conclusive. It showed, he declared, that the quickest road to peace and commercial prosperity for the nations abroad was "to withdraw support and favor from the insurgents, and to leave the adjustment of our domestic controversies exclusively with the people of the United States."[5]

It is possible that Seward's argument had some effect. A few weeks later, Bigelow wrote to Weed that Confederate influence in France and England was on the wane. Despite Slidell's effort to propagate the impression that he and the Empress slept alternate nights with the Emperor, he had had no audience with Napoleon since the spring of the year. Still Seward remained apprehensive. Confederate cruisers were refueling in French ports and Confederate ironclads were building in French shipyards. Through Dayton he launched vigorous protests. How would France like it, he inquired, if our shipbuilders furnished ships for use against France in her Mexican venture? Dayton was to tell Drouyn de Lhuys that France must abide the consequences of such unneutral acts. If the cruiser *Rappahannock*, which was being finished at Calais, left that port for the Confederate service, the United States might depart from its neutrality in the Franco-Mexican War to the extent of permitting traffic in arms to the Mexican government. France continued to allow Confederate cruisers to obtain supplies and fuel in French ports down to the close of the war, but the cruisers and rams building for the Confederacy were either countermanded by the French government, or were sold to neutral nations.[6]

While Seward dealt with the problems raised by a neutral but would-be interventionist France, he also kept watch on Napoleon's Mexican adventure. The Mexican republic had been in a state of chronic unrest ever since its liberation from Spain, and Napoleon III believed that he saw there an opportunity to accomplish great things. He would liberate the Mexican people from what he thought of as a state of social dissolution. In doing so he would re-establish the monarchical principle in the New World, check the advance of republicanism and democracy, and oppose a barrier to the commercial and territorial expansion of the United States in the Western Hemisphere.

These Napoleonic plans became full blown after it became apparent that Mexico was strife-torn by the feuds of conservative monarchists and republican liberals, and that republican President Juarez was unable either to maintain order or to fulfill his treaty obligations. Toward the close of 1861, France joined Spain and Great Britain in an armed intervention, with the avowed object of protecting the lives and property of their nationals in the unhappy country. The allies soon differed, however, over the extent of their intervention, and Great Britain and Spain withdrew as it became apparent that Napoleon had ambitious designs for setting up a Mexican monarchy under a European prince.

Southern interest in Mexican territory had not disappeared after the acquisition of California and the Southwest. It was manifest at various times during the 1850s, and in 1859 the pro-South Buchanan administration negotiated two treaties with Mexico. One granted commercial privileges and guaranteed the United States perpetual transit across that country by no less than three main highways. The other gave the American government the right of intervention to maintain order, Mexico paying the costs. The Juarez administration, hard pressed for the $4,000,000 provided by the first treaty, signed both of these extraordinary documents. They seemed tailored to the desires of southern expansionists, and in 1860 Republican votes defeated them in the Senate.

Seward had always been opposed to acquiring potential slave territory. He had no such scruples, however, about the acquisition of free land to the southward, if it were obtained in peaceful fashion. Rumors in 1861 that the Confederacy wanted Lower California and planned the conquest of all Mexico led him to act. He first instructed the American Minister to Mexico, Thomas Corwin, to investigate the possibility of purchasing Lower California. Then, alarmed by the prospect of European intervention, he tried to checkmate it by a treaty with Mexico, the fulfillment of which would be subject to the willingness of the European powers to keep hands off that troubled state. By the terms of the treaty, the United States would agree to pay 3 per cent interest for five years on the Mexican funded debt. To guarantee repayment, Mexico would give the United States a lien on the public lands and mineral rights of Lower California and three other provinces in northern and western Mexico. If at the end of six years Mexico was obviously in default, the aforesaid lands and rights would become the property of the United States.

Seward asserted that neither Lincoln nor he had designs of aggrandizement in the Mexican direction. When Mercier asked him how the proposed loan to Mexico would be guaranteed, he replied with some embarrassment that it would not be by land. This was not true. As Adams wrote from London, the proposed treaty looked like "the preliminary to an entry for inevitable foreclosure." It was, however, stillborn, for the maritime powers were cool to it, and the Senate decisively rejected the idea of a loan.[7]

Treaty or no treaty, Seward's interest in the Mexican situation remained keen. As France became involved in war with the Juarez regime, Seward made it clear that he adhered to the traditional American policy of non-intervention in foreign conflicts. But he also emphasized that, while neutral, the United States was much interested in the maintenance of republican institutions in Mexico. As early as March 1862, he informed Dayton that Lincoln wished the European governments to know that no monarchy established by foreign force in Mexico would have any prospect of security or permanence, particularly if the Mexican throne were assigned to a foreign prince. The United States "could not view with indifference" the interference of European powers in the internal affairs of a country so near the United States and so important to Mexico.[8]

Napoleon's plan for a Mexican monarchy took definite shape in 1863, and the Archduke Maximilian of Austria accepted the Mexican throne in April 1864. During those years Seward was mainly content to watch and wait.

In 1863 Sumner, who could at times work closely with the Secretary of State, smothered an effort by Democratic Senator Mac-Dougall of California to push the government into positive action against French intervention. This was in thorough accord with Seward's policy. They could not afford, he told Bigelow, to give France an opportunity to appeal to French and English jealousy of the United States in the midst of the Civil War, nor would the American people forgive an administration that suffered the country to fall into a foreign war "on a contingent and merely speculative issue like that of the future of Mexico." This country knew, he declared, that Mexico wished to have a republican government of its own choosing, not one imposed on it from abroad and monarchical in form. All foreign attempts to control American civilization must fail before the material, moral, and political forces that were peculiar to the American continent. Nor did the United States deny that "their own safety and the cheerful destiny to which they aspire are intimately dependent on the continuance of free republican institutions throughout America, and that their policy will always be directed to that end." Nevertheless, he informed Motley, this nation would not declare itself "in anticipation of contingent events." It was fully occupied in repressing rebellion at home. "Those always decide most wisely who have retained to the last the greatest freedom for consideration." He was playing a very careful role in which he sought to avoid offending both France and, at home, an increasingly apprehensive public opinion.[9]

The development of French intervention in Mexico, together with the skillful propaganda efforts of Matias Romero, Mexican Minister to the United States, produced growing irritation with France both in the country at large and in Congress, and in the spring of 1864 presented a challenge to Seward's policy of inaction. On April 4 the House of Representatives, without a dissenting vote, passed a joint resolution declaring that to acknowledge any monarchical government erected by a European power on the ruins of republicanism in America did not accord with the policy of the United States. The French *chargé d'affaires* at Washington, M. Geoffroy, asked for an explanation and, when word of the House's action reached Paris, an aroused Drouyn de Lhuys saluted Dayton with, "Do you bring us peace or bring us war?"

Three days after the passage of this resolution, Seward took it up in a dispatch to Dayton. It truly interpreted the unanimous feeling of the people of the United States about Mexico, he declared, but it was another question as to whether the government would consider it necessary or proper so to express itself at this time. That was a purely executive question, and the decision constitutionally belonged to the President. The resolution was a joint one, not deriving from any suggestion by the executive branch. Lincoln had received it with the profound respect to which it was entitled, but "he directs that you inform the Government of France that he does not at present contemplate any departure from the policy which this government has hitherto pursued in regard to the war which exists between France and Mexico."

Dayton read this dispatch to Drouyn de Lhuys. The *Moniteur* subsequently stated that the American government had made a satisfactory explanation of the House resolution. When news of this reached Washington the House called for the documents. Lincoln sent them over and, on June 27, Henry Winter Davis, chairman of the House Foreign Affairs Committee, submitted an acid report, together with a new resolution.

The Davis resolution declared that Congress had " a constitutional right to an authoritative voice in declaring and prescribing the foreign policy of the United States"; that the President had a "constitutional duty" to respect that policy; that the subjects which Congress had under discussion were not fit topics for diplomatic explanations to any foreign Power. The House did not vote on this proposal before adjournment, but the subject was to come up again later in the year. Seward had acted without stopping to think that his words might be made public, and he had stirred up a hornets' nest.[10]

During the remainder of the year the American press made intermittently strident demands for invoking the Monroe Doctrine in Mexican affairs. When the tumult swelled in volume, Seward would use strong language about France for publication, and then would soften it in official conversations. We could no more recognize an Emperor in Mexico than we could one in the United States he told Geoffroy, the French *chargé d'affaires,* and only by taking this attitude could the executive afford to stop expeditions organized by émigré Mexicans, and check the flow of arms across the border to Juarez. Again he would tell the Frenchman that American hostility to France and Maximilian was not formidable; that there was more likelihood of war with Great Britain over Canada than with France over Mexico. He himself thought Napoleon wanted to get out of that country and the United States had no desire to go there. Hence they had identical interests. On Geoffroy's once more bringing up recognition of Maximilian, Seward replied that it was an American custom to deal with one thing at a time. Just now the important thing was the conflict with the South.

On another occasion the Frenchman took over to the State Department a New York *Times* editorial indicating the probability that the United States would uphold the Monroe Doctrine as to Mexico, especially if disbanded Union and Confederate soldiers moved into that country. What did Seward think of it, he asked. The Secretary replied by writing on a piece of paper, "My impression is that fighting regiments never take idle vows." Small wonder that after one such interview Geoffroy declared that Seward's policy toward Mexico could only be found in what he did not say.

Seward's careful balancing act in regard to Mexico did not prevent his making an effort to use the situation there in an attempt to weaken the Anglo-French concert. On August 1, 1863, he had a long conversation with Lyons about Mexican affairs. The Secretary of State wanted to know how Britain viewed Napoleon III's effort to set up this empire under French patronage, and remarked in an inquiring tone that the British government could hardly favor such a move. He feared, Lyons thought, that French designs in Mexico would harden Napoleon's anxiety to ensure the independence of the Confederacy. It seemed obvious that Seward wished to enlist England's help, or even make that country bear the brunt of thwarting the French designs. This was a move to which the British Minister, a stout protagonist of the Anglo-French rapprochement, would give no countenance.[11]

It has often been remarked that Seward never mentioned the Monroe Doctrine in developing his policy toward the French in Mexico. There was reason for this omission. He knew that the Doctrine was unpopular in Europe. To cite it as justification for the American attitude would irritate rather than impress the European Powers. Also, he wished to preserve the greatest possible freedom of action to the last possible moment, and it would not have been easy to do so had he taken a hard stand on Monroe's *pronunciamento*. In 1853 Seward had declared that the Doctrine would prevail, whether affirmed or no, because of the power of the United States. He did not affirm it by name a decade later, but his policy regarding Mexico was in harmony with its principles. Later on he boasted that he had transformed the Doctrine from a myth into a reality.

During the Civil War, the Department over which Seward presided was a busy place. Dispatches from the legations and consular reports came from many quarters of the globe. These were read by a specially qualified clerk, or passed on for examination by William Hunter or by Frederick Seward. The Secretary of State read, or at least glanced through the dispatches from those countries with which the United States had significant relations, and such others as were called to his attention. In some cases he would order copies sent to the Secretary of War or the Secretary of the Navy. On others he would write instructions as to how they should be

answered. He himself drafted the replies to documents of importance.

Seward did not act as an independent agent in shaping foreign
policy. He had to think in terms of congressional reaction, and it
was important that he maintain as good relations as possible with the
chairmen of the committees on foreign relations in both House and
Senate. He was also careful to keep Lincoln *au courant* on developments in foreign affairs. When negotiations with England or France
reached a critical juncture, Seward's communications to Adams and
Dayton included such phrases as "I am instructed by the President to
say," or "The President desires you to inform the government of
Great Britain that this government looks with deep concern. . . ."

Was Seward the leader and Lincoln the follower in shaping for-
eign policy? Adams said in 1873 that this was the case. Gideon
Welles promptly denied it.[12] The truth lies somewhere in between.
The President listened to Sumner, who was fertile with suggestions,
and on occasion his views undoubtedly influenced those of Lincoln.
There were times, as when he modified the dispatch to Adams of
May 21, 1861, that the Chief Executive exercised control over State
Department policy. It is clear that he kept an eye on the conduct of
foreign relations. But Seward had had experience in dealing with
foreign affairs when he served on the Senate's Committee on Foreign Relations, experience that Lincoln wholly lacked when he came
into the White House. Of this the President must have been
conscious. The high value that he placed on retaining Seward in the
Cabinet, and the lack of evidence that he ever became dissatisfied
with the way in which Seward ran the State Department, indicate
his heavy reliance upon his Secretary of State.

Beset by jealousy and criticism, oppressed by multifarious duties,
often overworked, there were occasions on which Seward acted
hastily, without due regard for the forms and requirements of law.
At other times he could move with maddening deliberation. In
November 1864, Adams asked that he be relieved from his post as
soon as possible. Seward promised to bring this request to the attention of the President. Months went by. Nothing happened, and
Adams became more and more impatient. At last, toward the end of
March 1865, he demanded an answer. What it would have been no

one knows, for the tragic events of that spring made his resignation impossible. It was not until three years later that Adams finally laid down the burden that he carried with distinction at London.[13]

Certain aspects of Seward's wartime diplomacy were contradictory in nature. He maintained that the Civil War was only a local insurrection, but appealed to court decisions ruling the blockade legal because the rebellion was a war. He, himself, frequently used the term "civil war" in reference to the struggle between North and South. He accepted the South's status as a belligerent when he demanded that Great Britain and France observe their obligations as neutrals, but at the same time he urged both countries to withdraw their recognition of the Confederacy's state of belligerency. Nor was he in a particularly strong position when he upheld as genuine the inadequate blockade of 1861–62 in the face of traditional American opposition to paper blockades.

It may also be argued that his choices for diplomatic posts were not always above criticism. There is not much to justify sending Simon Cameron or Cassius M. Clay to represent the United States at St. Petersburg, or James Watson Webb to Brazil. Blatchford's sojourn in Rome was manifestly a return for favors received. He served only a year, four months of that time he was on leave with pay, and after that decided not to go back, the excuse being that Mrs. Blatchford could not leave her sister. Some of the consular appointments made at Seward's behest were equally questionable. Particularly so was his destressing tendency to send Irish refugees back as consuls to Ireland, a practice not exactly soothing to English nerves.

Seward's success as a wartime diplomat was not wholly due to his skill in controversy. As it became more and more apparent that the North would win, he had the advantage of an increasing strength of position. Neither Britain nor France was at any time ready to go to war in order to destroy the Union. In his controversies with Lord Russell over neutral rights the latter had always to keep in mind that precedents then established might later become embarrassing to the Mistress of the Seas. These factors eased the task of the Secretary of State.

But even when critically examined, Seward's conduct of the State Department during the Civil War merits high praise. This is true of his attitude toward important appointments in the foreign service. He insisted upon Adams going to London, an excellent choice. Anson Burlingame in the China post was a man of high caliber, as was Dayton at the French capital. After Dayton died in December 1864 there were many aspirants for his place. Raymond wanted it, as did Webb. Sumner pressed for Edward Everett. The minister resident in Belgium yearned for the promotion, and Weed urged that he be transferred to Paris. Sanford was an old friend, and he had given faithful service in Belgium. Seward was tempted, but he made the best possible selection in John Bigelow. In response to Sanford's open bid for the position, Seward replied, "What was done in regard to the French legation not only was the least but also the best that could be done and it is universally satisfactory here." [14]

Seward was particularly happy in his relations with foreign diplomats in Washington. He was careful to observe protocol and was prompt to refer requests and complaints to the proper individual or department. He flattered their vanity by filling one of his parlors with the portraits of diplomats and rulers of the countries with which the United States had relations, saying to visitors with mock solemnity, "Yes, these are my tormentors." He regularly entertained members of the diplomatic corps at his home, and took them on pleasure excursions that would also reveal the natural beauty and material resources of the country. Tassara went with him to a Philadelphia fair in 1862, and in 1863 he shepherded a covey of ministers on what Welles called a "rambling excursion" and Lyons described as a "very agreeable tour" through central New York to Niagara Falls and a boat trip on Lake Erie. When the office of the French embassy with all its archives and contents burned in the winter of 1862, Seward was on hand the next morning offering his house and his services.

All this made for good feeling and smoothed the paths of diplomacy. When Mercier was transferred to Madrid in 1864, he left with high regard for Seward's tact, to say nothing of his hospitality. Lyons, so doubtful of the Secretary of State at first and repelled by his personal and national vanity, found that his respect and liking for him grew stronger with the years. Long before the war was over, the relationship between the two men had become cordial. When in 1863 Seward asked modification of a dispatch that otherwise might be taken to imply unwise concessions on his part regarding belligerent rights, Lyons willingly complied. And the British Minister listened patiently and with understanding to Seward's explanations of how British subjects became caught in the draft for the Union Army.[15]

Personal relations were important, for they merged into the conduct of international relations at the highest levels. Here Seward steadily increased in stature. Brash at first, he developed both confidence and finesse in handling the problems of his office. Fertile of mind in seeking the proper course of action, flexible in the choice of procedures and versatile in their application, he conducted the nation's diplomacy with tact and ability. More and more he came to realize the truth of the dictum that he laid down to Adams in the fall of 1863—"The transactions in which we are engaged are too great, and our responsibilities concerning them are too grave, to allow us for a moment the indulgence of personal irritation, or even of national jealousy which is quick in seeing or giving occasions of offense." [16]

So he went on his way, able in riposte to the arguments of foreign powers, now promising opened ports and cotton, again threatening letters of marque and even possible war, but always dignified and courteous in representing the interests of the Union. A practical statesman, he cared little about whether or not he acted in accordance with international law. Sometimes he appealed to it or to American precedents, sometimes he disregarded both. But constantly he pursued his purpose of preventing any interference by foreign nations that would benefit the South.

A man in high public station must be inured to criticism and Seward, despite his vanity, recognized that necessity. Still, he was only human. The slings and arrows hurt, and praise was sweet. In the spring of 1864 a correspondent wrote that he had "read with admiration your letters of instruction to our agents abroad. They are conciliatory, yet firm and always hopeful, as if conscious of a good cause & ability to maintain it." The writer added that history would not pass over in silence the "herculean task" performed by the government. Seward wrote in the margin of this letter, "Acknowledge thankfully." [17]

Seward's task became easier as the war neared its end, but it was in the stress and tumult of the earlier years that he acquired the respect and admiration of the diplomatic corps at Washington and of statesmen abroad. Adams wrote to his friend John G. Palfrey in November 1863, "The absurd prejudices against our Administration with which I had first to contend, are nearly gone. Mr. Seward is no longer regarded as the bête noir, intending all sorts of shocking insults to the British lion. On the whole I suspect he is now considered as the best disposed to Britain of all our public men. . . ." Mercier, who often differed with the Secretary of State, summed up the general feeling of the diplomats at the American capital when he said toward the close of 1863, "*Il est très sage.*" [18]

⋍§ 26 §⋍

Of War and Peace, and Freedom

Although the problems of diplomacy commanded the major part of Seward's attention, his interest in other aspects of the war and his willingness to take a hand in them remained keen throughout the conflict. Lincoln repeatedly asked his judgment about the military command. There is evidence that the President consulted him when Meade took Hooker's place just before Gettysburg. He remained a supporter of Banks throughout the war, despite the criticism leveled at that general. It is probable that he had at least foreknowledge of Grant's elevation to high command in the winter of 1864. When Grant appeared at a presidential reception on the evening of March 9, Seward introduced him to Mrs. Lincoln and other prominent members of the assemblage. In Cabinet meeting the next day, Lincoln presented the doughty soldier with his commission as Lieutenant-General of the United States Army. Not long after this, according to Welles, the Secretary of State defeated an effort by Montgomery Blair to put McClellan in Halleck's place as chief of staff.[1]

Interest in military leadership was only one evidence of Seward's concern for victory. He urged the formation of Union and Loyal Leagues for encouraging the war effort, and lent his presence to the opening of fairs sponsored by the United States Sanitary Commission and other wartime organizations. Horses and mules were vital to Civil War transport, and Seward took pains to see that horse and mule shoes and the machines used for making them were not shipped via Halifax to the Confederacy. He prompted Stanton to suspend two New York newspapers, the *World* and the *Journal of Commerce*, for publishing a forged presidential proclamation imposing a national fast because of military failures and calling for a draft of 300,000 men. He made it his business to be confident in times of trial and to encourage confidence in others. The invasion of the North in 1863 was a time of great strain in Washington, especially since for days the government did not know the location of Lee's army. "It would be absurd to say we have no anxiety," Seward wrote to Sanford, "but we certainly have grounds for expectation of a just result." On the first day of the battle of Gettysburg he wrote to a Boston committee preparing to celebrate the Fourth of July— "Keep the sacred fire alive in Faneuil Hall. Though it glimmer and seem to go out in Richmond and New Orleans, it will yet revive there and everywhere else throughout the land." [2]

Such efforts to promote victory were laudable, but even in these Seward had to pick his way carefully because his every act was subjected to critical scrutiny by his opponents. Bitter over Seward's attitude toward emancipation, Sumner declared that the Secretary of State's "illimitable egotism" had left him no friends, either in Congress or in the Cabinet, and that some believed (though Sumner did not) that he wanted to break down the Republican party in order to avenge his defeat at Chicago. The story spread that Mercier had gone to Richmond so that Seward could exchange intelligence with the Confederates, and in 1864 an effort on his part to hasten the end of the struggle met a storm of criticism.

Andrew Jackson Hamilton, provisional governor of Texas, concocted a scheme for shipping out of the state cotton consigned to an agent of the Treasury Department. Pay for this cotton was to go to the rebel commanders who were then supposed to leave the service of the Confederacy, thus breaking up resistance to the Union in the Lone Star State. Seward had his doubts about the plan, but the idea of obtaining cotton supplies for the hungry European nations was attractive and he obtained the necessary cotton trading permit from Lincoln.

Fraudulent cotton traffic with the rebel states had already reached shameful proportions, and Hamilton's plan at once drew fire. Farragut protested that it would lead to immense swindles. The Secretary of the Treasury refused to recognize the permit. Welles, who believed Seward and Weed were using it to line their pockets, protested to Lincoln. The President was disturbed by all the furor, but said he "reckoned it was all right; it had been arranged by Seward." [3] There is no evidence that the project was ever put into operation.

The Secretary of State strove for victory, but his concept of its consequence differed widely from that held by such men as Stevens and Sumner. He had no wish to treat the southern states as though they had committed suicide or the southern people as rebels deserving condign punishment. His great desire was to see the Union restored, with peace and harmony between the white populations of North and South. Only in this way, he felt, could the way be prepared for the glorious era of national greatness that would come after the end of the struggle.

This dominant desire for reunion influenced his approach to war problems in several ways. For one thing, it helped to soften his attitude toward the South. He told Lyons early in 1862 that he wanted the United States to offer an example of leniency toward the enemy such as the world had never seen. After the capture of Forts Henry and Donelson in February 1862, Stoeckl asked him if this was not a good time to seek reconciliation and peace. He replied that for himself he could not ask a better time, but that the passions excited by the struggle made such a move impossible. Lyons felt that he looked forward to heading a great conservative party which would put the Union "above all other considerations" and would foster harmonious reconciliation of the warring sections "by making great concessions to Southern feeling and Southern prejudices, on the question of slavery as well as on other matters." Seward himself declared that he still regarded the southerners as his brothers. As late as Thanksgiving Day 1863, he wrote to his wife,

> No one knows how wearisome this dealing with war is to me. I have little of the passions I think that make war even when successful a pleasurable excitement. If I endure it better than many I think it is because I regard it as an evil that could not be avoided and that is appointed by a mysterious Providence for discipline and instruction.[4]

The vigor of the Confederate war effort, the growing strength of the demand for emancipation, and Lincoln's decision to issue the Emancipation Proclamation clouded this dream of reconciliation. But it still influenced Seward's thinking when he examined peace proposals, the Negro problem, and the political situation.

In the spring of 1863 the Secretary of State became interested in a project initiated by General Banks, military governor of Louisiana, who had visions of himself as a peacemaker. Banks sent to Washington Dr. Issacher Zacharie, a chiropodist who made a specialty of removing corns from the feet of Lincoln and other eminent men, and who had a wide circle of acquaintances in the South. Zacharie had a plan for peace negotiations. Exactly what it was no man knows, but it seems to have included a proposal to pay the Confederate debt.

As a result of Zacharie's conferences with Lincoln and Seward, the latter drew up two letters of authorization, both approved in writing by the President. By one, Banks was to furnish Zacharie with up to $5000; the other instructed Banks to make every effort to secure "decisive results in the present campaign," even though it required funds beyond those provided for the maintenance of his military force. When these results were procured and certified, money would be paid by the government as Banks directed up to $5,000,-000.

Seward sent his son, Colonel William H. Seward, to New Orleans with the letters, keeping duplicates signed by himself and Lincoln in his own files. Banks, however, backed away from the project. There would be, he wrote to Seward, opportunity for some useful expenditure, but there might be a better method of procedure for securing the same results. He was afraid that the medium of communication proposed to the President could not be relied upon for secrecy. Nothing, he assured the Secretary of State, would be done to bring reproach on the Department. He would also destroy the two letters in the presence of Colonel Seward, to whom he would explain his ideas more fully.

This ended the Zacharie project for the time being, but shortly thereafter, Banks sent Martin Gordon, Jr., and David Pretts of New Orleans to Richmond, and they paved the way for another Zacharie effort. In July the good doctor was again in Washington with another commendatory letter from Banks to Seward. Both the President and the Secretary of State received Zacharie in kindly fashion. Various Cabinet members, especially Chase, opposed his going to Richmond, however, and Seward became cool to the idea. Some two or three weeks later Lincoln, apparently without Seward's knowledge, sent Zacharie to the Confederate capital. He came back convinced that peace was in sight, and wrote to Banks that Lincoln and "Sewart" praised him highly for his efforts, but told him "to lay quiet until the time arrives for them to act." Lying quiet meant fading out of sight.[5]

But peace was in the air. Lee was retreating with his shattered army from Gettysburg, and Vice President Stephens offered to come to Washington for what appeared to be an opening of negotiations. On July 10, 1863, the New York *Herald*'s Washington correspondent announced "positively" that Seward had proposed a presidential proclamation of amnesty on generous terms that included withdrawal of the Emancipation Proclamation. The *Herald* also declared that the Cabinet was bitterly divided on the subject, and that radical Republicans were denouncing Seward as a traitor.

Seward opposed allowing Stephens to come to Washington, and that individual got no further than Fortress Monroe. But, curiously enough, on July 20 the prominent New York banker and Democrat August Belmont wrote to Seward proposing a peace settlement very similar to that which the *Herald* had attributed to the Secretary of State nine days before. Seward referred Belmont's letter to Chase, who replied that all wise men would approve leniency to repentant rebels, but all just men would condemn the re-enslavement of the Negro in violation of Lincoln's plighted faith.

About this same time, Seward told Mercier that, because of Gettysburg and Vicksburg, peace could be had, probably soon, but that it was not near because there was a lack of desire for it by all parties in the North. He then suggested withdrawing recognition of the South's belligerent rights as a means of speeding the end of hostilities, a proposal to which Mercier was unresponsive.

Sumner's attitude indicated in what quarters a fear of peace could be found. Writing to Bright, he declared that, if the rebellion should suddenly collapse, Democrats, Copperheads [Peace-at-any-price Democrats], and Seward would insist on amnesty and the Union, with no questions asked about slavery, and then added, "Lord save us from any such calamity." [6]

In the spring of 1864 Grant began the campaign in the Virginia Wilderness that cost so many lives on both sides, fighting men that Lee in particular could ill afford to spare. At the same time, Sherman began moving through Georgia toward Atlanta. Increasing reports of the South's war weariness and of possibilities for peace negotiations came to the State Department. These were mainly hints and suggestions, but an English friend of Charles Francis Adams, one J. Scott Russell, who claimed acquaintance with the views of the southern leaders, drew up a plan for peace and reconstruction in which Seward showed some interest. In essence it proposed reunion, with the repeal of all acts of proscription and confiscation. There would then be gradual, compensated emancipation. Cautious at first, Adams became interested and had considerable correspondence with Seward about the proposal. It was finally arranged that Thomas Yeatman, a southerner, should act as intermediary with the Confederate government.

When it became apparent that a statement from the government at Washington would be useful, Seward conferred with Lincoln and then outlined the views of the administration. They desired restoration of peace and harmony, he said, but its attainment by negotiation with the insurgents at Richmond seemed impracticable. The treaty-making department of the government had no constitutional power for such action. "The President could act only in virtue of his authority to execute the laws and suppress insurrection." If he sought to make guarantees for the future that affected the Treasury, he would have to "invoke the action of Congress, and it is not clear that Congress could efficiently act without a change in the Constitution." In any case there would be delays inconsistent with securing an immediate peace.

The President, Seward declared, felt that peace could be more easily and surely secured by following his plan for the states outlined in his Proclamation of December 8, 1863 (allowing each seceded state to come back into the Union when a number of its voters equal to 10 per cent of those on the rolls in 1860 took the oath of allegiance), rather than by a treaty with the "political organization" at Richmond. Second, the slaves must be made free, "but laws not inconsistent with their freedom may be passed to alleviate the inconvenience of a sudden and universal emancipation."

This obviously meant that the administration would look with favor on state laws designed to prevent freedom degenerating into chaos. There should be no armistice, Seward continued, no intervention or advice from any foreign state, and no part of the insurgent debt would be assumed by the federal government. Finally, if peace was promptly restored and fully guaranteed, the national government might furnish pecuniary aid for the reorganized states. But no funds so supplied should be used for the payment of debts or obligations incurred in levying war against the United States.[7]

Despite the pains taken to outline these conditions, Seward remained skeptical about the Russell proposal. Yeatman's independent attitude after he reached the United States, together with the start of the Wilderness campaign, gave the Secretary of State an opportunity to put an end to the venture and order the would-be negotiator out of the country. The project is of interest, however, for it elicited from Seward and Lincoln over a year before the war ended their concept of the proper terms of peace. They wished reconstruction to proceed by and through the co-operation of the southern whites, who must accept emancipation but might police the freedmen in their respective states. But submission was an essential prerequisite. As Seward had said some months earlier, hostilities could cease only when the insurgents had accepted Abraham Lincoln as President of the United States. Then, and only then, would be the time to speak of terms of peace.

Seward's views remained substantially those he had outlined in his communication to Adams. Conciliation of a South willing to come back into the Union was his motto. He continued to approve the Lincoln plan of 10 per cent governments that, despite the bitter opposition of such congressional leaders as Sumner, Henry Winter Davis and Ben Wade, the President tried to introduce in Louisiana, Arkansas, and Tennessee. Then, early in 1865, the Secretary of State again had opportunity to state his thoughts as to peace. This was at the famous Hampton Roads Conference.[8]

By January 1865 the situation of the Confederacy was desperate indeed. Sherman had captured Atlanta, captured Savannah, and was moving up the Atlantic coast. Lee's army at Richmond was dwindling. The disparity in strength between North and South was becoming more apparent every day, and peace sentiment was growing throughout the Confederacy. Under these circumstances a move by Francis Preston Blair, Sr., offered the beleaguered southern government at least a ray of hope.

Blair had what he thought was a statesmanlike idea. Without informing Lincoln of the nature of his plan, he went to Richmond with a proposal that the South abandon slavery; that there be an armistice preliminary to reunion; and that North and South unite in expelling the French from Mexico. Davis thought there were possibilities in this quixotic scheme for achieving peace by championing the Monroe Doctrine, and gave Blair a letter saying that he was willing to send commissioners to confer with Lincoln about ending war between "the two countries."

Blair came back to Lincoln with the outlines of his plan, together with the communication from Davis. The President handed the would-be negotiator a short note to the effect that he would receive commissioners sent informally with a view to ending hostilities between the people "of our common country." This was virtually a rejection of the Mexican scheme and a rebuff to the "two countries" idea, but Davis was desperate, willing to grasp at any straw. He decided to see what could be done by negotiation, and appointed three commissioners—Alexander H. Stephens, Vice President of the Confederacy, the Confederate ex-Secretary of State, R. M. T. Hunter, and Judge John A. Campbell, Assistant Secretary of War —telling them that their aim should be that "of securing peace to the two countries."

The Confederate commissioners expected to come to Washington, but Lincoln sent Seward to meet them at Hampton Roads. The latter was to lay down three indispensable conditions of peace; restoration of national authority throughout the states, North and South, no compromise on the slavery question, and no cessation of hostilities short of the end of the war and disbanding of all forces hostile to the national government. But he was not "to definitely consummate anything."

Seward arrived at Fortress Monroe on the night of February 1. He came armed with good cheer for the southerners, three bottles of whiskey (which according to report they drank thirstily), and two of champagne. Meanwhile, Grant, who had seen the Confederate emissaries, telegraphed Stanton that he thought they sincerely desired peace, and that he was sorry Lincoln could not talk to them. The President then decided to come to the meeting at Hampton Roads.

The five men met for four hours on the morning of February 3, on board the steamer transport *River Queen*. The conference began with reminiscences of earlier and happier days. Then Lincoln said he knew of only one way to bring about a restoration of harmony and good feeling, and that was for resistance to the national government to cease. Stephens proceeded to expatiate upon the possibility of a cessation of hostilities while the French were thrown out of Mexico. Lincoln manifested no interest in this, but Seward suggested that the Confederate develop the "philosophical basis" of his ideas about Mexico.

Stephens proceeded to explain that the Monroe Doctrine's underlying principle was "the sovereign right of local self-government." The French were violating this right in Mexico, and North and South should vindicate it. Settlement of the Mexican question would lead to settlement of their own differences. Once again he emphasized the right of local self-government as that on which all American institutions rested, and argued for "the ultimate absolute sovereignty of each state."

This argument, Seward replied, was specious, and no national government founded upon such a premise could work. Suppose Louisiana, in time of war, wanted to withdraw from the Union and form an alliance with a foreign power. It would not be permitted. Self-preservation was the first law of nations as well as of individuals. Stephens answered that if the Union was attractive enough no state would leave it; only wanton and causeless severance from the Union would justify war by the national government against a state. Seward then changed the subject, asking how an armistice could be made to work where there were two rival administrations, North and South, within one state. Stephens thought it could be done by a military convention.

Lincoln and Seward clearly opposed any armistice, and Stephens was at a loss as to why Seward had taken his line of argument. It seems evident that his purpose was to controvert the states' rights position of the Confederates. Never was Seward's nationalism more evident than in this exchange of views.

Discussion of the cessation of hostilities inevitably brought up the Negro question. Here, too, Seward and Lincoln had similar views. Both were for liberal treatment of a South that laid down its arms. Both appeared to regard the Emancipation Proclamation as a war measure that would terminate with the end of the struggle. They agreed that, if the war now ceased, the Proclamation would apply to only about 200,000 of the 4,000,000 southern Negroes. The status of the remainder would be subject to judicial construction.

Seward then referred to the Thirteenth Amendment, proclaiming the end of slavery, that had passed Congress three days before. He said that it, too, was a war measure, and if the war now came to a close it would not be adopted by a sufficient number of states to become part of the Constitution. He gave the impression that re-admitted southern states could by themselves defeat it.

Both northerners thought the southern states ought to be and would be admitted (undoubtedly they were thinking in terms of the 10 per cent government proposal). Lincoln told how reluctantly he had approached the Emancipation Proclamation. He had always favored freeing the slaves, but not in any immediate sense. The South should surrender now and so avoid, as much as possible, the evils of sudden action in this regard. Seward remarked that emancipation sentiment in the North had greatly increased.

Lincoln once more declared that he would be liberal in enforcing the confiscation acts and other penal laws, and spoke of $400,000,-000 as a possible indemnification for the slave owners if the war ceased and the states voluntarily abolished slavery. Hunter thought Seward opposed such indemnification, but Stephens and Campbell agreed that he said the North was weary of the war and, if it now ended, would pay as indemnity for the slaves what it would cost to continue the struggle. Shortly thereafter the conference came to an end.

After the formal discussion closed, Stephens asked Lincoln to do him a favor. Would he send back a nephew, a young southern lieutenant who was in a northern prison? Lincoln agreed to exchange him for a young northern lieutenant prisoner in the South. Hunter, who had spent much of his life in Washington as Congressman and Senator, turned to Seward—"Governor, how is the Capitol? Is it finished?" Seward then launched into a description of how the reconstruction begun before the war had been carried on until the stone cutters' equipment and the great blocks of marble that had cluttered nearby grounds and streets had been removed, and the dome, with the statue of Armed Freedom at the top, had completed a magnificent edifice.

Seward declared afterward that the Hampton Roads Conference was mainly an illustration of the truism that in wartime there are always citizens who impatiently demand peace negotiations. It had in truth produced no positive results, for Davis was stubbornly determined not to yield on Lincoln's terms. It showed once again, however, that for Lincoln and Seward restoration of the Union was a *sine qua non.* It also showed that both men were sympathetic toward the South, not only because of its war-ravaged condition, but also because of the terrible problem created by the freeing of four million slaves. They were determined to see slavery abolished, but they were also eager to accomplish this with the active co-operation of the southern states.[9]

Seward's attitude toward emancipation at Hampton Roads is inevitably linked to his views during the war on the Negro question. He believed, and said repeatedly, that slavery was doomed. It was dead, he told John Hay in the summer of 1863, and a few months later he wrote to Adams that the application of free labor when peace returned would make for greater prosperity than had been the case when slavery was part of the industrial economy. At Gettysburg with Lincoln in November of that year, he declared that the war would end with the abolition of slavery and that Americans would thereafter be united, "having only one hope, one ambition, and one destiny." In April 1864, approached by "a distinguished political gentleman" from the South as to the possibility of a peace that would leave the slave states with some option as to whether or not they should retain slavery, Seward conferred with Lincoln and then drew up a memorandum. They decided that he should not enter into any such negotiation; that the abolition of slavery must accompany peace. "The government can afford to be liberal on other points," wrote Seward, "but it cannot yield anything on the point that the Union must be maintained, or on the point the [sic] African slavery must now cease to exist." A month later he told Zachariah Chandler that slavery must be abolished as rapidly as possible under the Constitution, thus eliminating the distinction between North and South. This was essential, he said, for the promotion of national prosperity in the post-Civil War era.[10]

This point of view on emancipation was consistent with Seward's longtime record as an opponent of the peculiar institution. It was fortified, if it needed to be fortified, by the evidence which mounted during the latter part of the war that emancipation was increasingly popular in the North. As early as the spring of 1863 Bates confided to his diary that politicians now recognized abolition as a popular cause, adding sourly that "men who dont care a fig about it have become all of a sudden very zealous in that cause—Seward and Stanton are as hot as Chase." In December 1864, Seward wrote to Adams that the war, begun as a defensive struggle for the Union, had now become "a principal force in a popular revolution against African slavery," a point of view that he again emphasized at Hampton Roads. That winter he worked with Lincoln in pushing through the Thirteenth Amendment, using intermediaries to influence Seymour and other New York State Democratic politicians, and coming out openly for the measure in a speech at Washington just after the presidential election.[11]

It was all very well to recognize that the war had become a crusade against slavery and that slavery must be abolished, but how could the abolition be secured with a minimum of friction, a maximum of benefit to the country? Here Seward's legal training, together with his recognition of the white southerners as his brothers and his conception of the Negro as inferior to the white man, influenced his thought. He did not wish to see emancipation arbitrarily imposed on the South, either by the national executive or by Congress. The United States government was not "a forcible propagandist of emancipation," even though it did not hesitate to strike slavery down when it rose in rebellion. He had a genuine distaste for abolishing it by executive edict, and he was equally unwilling to see Congress take a hand in the matter. Late in 1863 Frances told him that she wished to sign a women's petition requesting Congress to abolish slavery. He asked her not to do so. She would not be sorry, he said, for putting emancipation in the hands of Congress would be impractical. That cause was where it should be, under the authority of the executive branch of the government, where practical steps were being taken to carry it forward.[12]

How did Seward wish the cause of emancipation carried for-

ward? The answer is, with consideration for the mood and problems
of the South, and with southerners, as far as possible, assuming the
initiative. His optimistic nature, letters received from southern
correspondents avowing enthusiasm for freeing the Negro, and
reports of emancipation movements in Kentucky, Tennessee, Missouri, and other slave states led him to believe that it was feasible
procedure to let the southern people carry the flag of freedom,
pushed forward, when that seemed necessary, from Washington.

Seward believed that the slavery problem was in the process of adjustment. Surrender by slavery, he wrote to Sanford shortly after
Gettysburg, would probably be equivalent to gradual and orderly
emancipation, while persevering resistance by slavery meant abolition. Writing to Adams in the late fall of 1863, he remarked that the
public was exercised over the principles in regard to slavery on
which federal authority should be restored in the rebellious states.
Lincoln thought the question was as yet premature. As for himself,
he felt that there would be little difficulty, for as the flag advanced
slavery disappeared. "No desire for the restoration or preservation
of slavery is manifested by citizens who adhere or reaccede to the
Union," he declared. Slavery was "now proved to be economically
useless and politically dangerous and revolutionary. We are, therefore, likely to find no slavery to contend with when the war for the
Union has come to an end." [13]

In a speech at Auburn on September 3, 1864, which was circulated as a campaign document, Seward also emphasized the way in
which the South was abandoning human bondage. As for governmental procedure on the slavery question, he said, while not authorized to speak for Lincoln, he had his own answer. The measures
affecting slavery were war measures that would end with the war
itself. Then slavery and all other questions would "by force of the
Constitution pass over to the arbitrament of courts of law and to the
councils of legislation."

Seward later modified this pronouncement, though only to a small
degree. There was not now a question of abandoning the war
measures against slavery, he declared in a speech the day before the
election, for the government struck at the rebellion through slavery.
But that institution was dying. It had provoked the war, and before
the end of the struggle it would be more hateful to the American
people than it now was to the rest of the world.[14]

Seward's attitude at the Hampton Roads Conference—his identification of the Emancipation Proclamation and the Thirteenth
Amendment as war measures only, his willingness to leave the fate
of some 3,800,000 Negroes to the courts, and to indemnify the
South for the loss of its slaves—was likewise a manifestation of his
fervent desire to smooth the road to reunion, a desire which Lincoln
shared. It was not that Seward wanted slavery to continue. Greeley
was right when, in one of his more perceptive moments during the
war, he told the publisher James Cephas Derby that he never
doubted Seward was true to the cause of human freedom, his way of
serving that cause being only by a different route from that of the
radicals.[15] It was only that his primary concern was for harmonious
reunion, a process which he thought would be important for the
emancipated slaves as well as for the whites.

⤙ 27 ⤚

A Possible Road to
the White House

Emancipation, the prosecution of the war, and how to bring the struggle to a close were all in one sense political questions, and Seward the diplomat was still a politician. He must have applauded, though he did not participate in, the New York State campaign of 1863, when the conservatives under the leadership of Edwin D. Morgan and Weed won a brief victory over the radicals at the convention and made a good showing in the state election. By the autumn of that year, however, talk of the next presidential election was in the air, and in the calculations of the Unionists, as the Republican-War Democrat combination was called, Seward's name sometimes appeared.

It would have been strange indeed if thoughts of the Unionist nomination in 1864 had not crossed Seward's mind, especially when a Middle West correspondent wrote of his popularity there and Lincoln's weakness. Dreams of the nomination may have been his when he suggested to a startled Lord Lyons in August 1863 that the United States might display its good will toward England by sending someone on a state visit—a kind of reciprocation for the visit of the Prince of Wales to the United States three years before. The only conjecture Lyons could make was that Seward thought of himself in this role. The absurdity of the notion that Seward could in any real sense return the Prince's visit, Lyons felt, "would alone prevent its being offensive." Still, it might be, said his lordship, that

Seward *was* thinking of such a visit as a step toward the highest office in the land.[1]

But if visions of the White House in 1864 appeared occasionally to the Secretary of State, he put them resolutely away. He refused the invitations that were showered upon him to speak at great public gatherings, using repeatedly the argument that it was best for harmony among the friends of the Union that he remain silent. They should all forget, he told one correspondent, what they ever had been or thought of becoming, all personal interests, and concentrate upon service to the country.[2]

Cool reason as well as patriotic devotion counseled this attitude. The attacks on him by the radicals had in no wise stopped after the Cabinet crisis of 1862. Zachariah Chandler told his wife that he was afraid Seward was a traitor, plotting dismemberment of the Union, one who would rather have France and England intervene than see the rebellion crushed by military means. The government would be lost, said Chandler, if Seward remained as Secretary of State, and they were going to make another mighty effort to unseat him. A story went the rounds that Weed's visit to England in 1862 had been nothing but a pleasure trip given him by Seward. There were repeated rumors that the Secretary of State was about to resign and either go back to obscurity in Auburn or take Adams's place in England, while Sumner went into the State Department. Parke Godwin in the New York *Evening Post* declared that Seward helped the French government get arms in the United States while denying the same privilege to the Mexicans. When James C. Derby defended Seward against this charge, Godwin admitted that the Secretary did seek the nation's welfare, but then lashed out against Weed as a corrupt and baleful influence upon Seward. "This is the general ending of all these newspaper attacks," commented Derby.[3]

Hardened to abuse by long experience, Seward usually took it philosophically. James E. Harvey commiserated with him on all the misrepresentations and injustice, to which he replied that they caused him neither surprise nor unhappiness, for he knew them to be incidental to his task and to the times. He could even joke about the stories of his resignation. "I am not out," he wrote to Weed, "but am going to be out, not of troubles, but segars. Can you tell me where and how I can renew my supplies." The attacks nevertheless stung, especially if the military or diplomatic situation was tense, and sometimes his temper was short. When Sumner suggested replacing Charles Wilson, the secretary of legation at London, an ardent Seward supporter, the Secretary of State flew into a violent rage. Sumner was informed that he knew nothing of political claims and services, and that Wilson was clever and should be sustained— an outburst that drew from the Massachusetts Senator a prim little note saying that he seemed to have offended Seward, but had spoken only in the public interest.

Shortly after this interchange with Sumner, Seward was in Auburn for a brief visit. On leaving, Frances and Fanny accompanied him to the Syracuse station, where an elderly baggage man came up to shake hands. Seward said, "You are not ashamed to shake hands with me then?"—to which the man replied, "Those that's worth kickin' generally gets kicked in this world." 4

Sometime late in 1863 (Frederick Seward tells the story), Lincoln remarked to Seward at one of their fireside chats that he hoped to see him his successor, adding that in this way Seward's friends who had been so disappointed at Chicago "would find all made right at last." Seward, according to Frederick's account, said no—that was all past and ended. Lincoln should run again. When it was evident that the people had reaffirmed their choice of him as President, the rebellion would collapse. In recounting this incident, Frederick gave the impression that the conversation alluded entirely to 1864. If this was so, there was good practical reason for Seward's response. In view of the hostility of the radicals, his chances of securing the nomination were practically nil. As Lyons had remarked somewhat earlier with more than a little truth, "If he thinks he has himself any chance of being taken as a candidate by either party, he is the only man who thinks so at this moment." 5 It is more likely, however, that Lincoln had 1868 in mind when he spoke of Seward as his successor.

At election time in 1863 Seward was in Auburn, called there by the illness of William Henry, Jr. He was asked to make his usual remarks to his fellow townsmen at the end of the canvass. His son's illness was in a critical state but he spoke, making a strong appeal for a Unionist victory that would give full support to Lincoln. What he said did not specifically commit him to championing the President's renomination, but it was generally regarded as doing so. Andrew B. Dickinson, veteran of the political wars and then Minister to Nicaragua, wrote to Weed that Seward's speech said the right thing at the right time in the right place. It would be the point of departure for the 1864 campaign, ensuring Lincoln's re-election and making Seward the man of the hour for 1868.[6]

New York State went strongly Unionist in that fall's election, and Seward returned to Washington declaring that the North was safe for 1864. Shortly thereafter it became an open secret that Lincoln wished a second term. Weed had his misgivings about this, but at first he and the other New York conservatives rallied to the President's support. The New York City and County Central Committee passed a unanimous resolution favoring Lincoln's re-election, and Federal District Attorney E. Delafield Smith, forwarding this to Seward, remarked that in showing it to Lincoln, "I might ask you to say for me that we, who are faithful to you, will be true to him." It is not strange that this letter and others of the same tenor found their way to the White House.[7]

Tales of a very different character were also making the rounds in the spring of 1864, and one in particular had considerable currency. Samuel Latham Mitchill Barlow, New York lawyer and Democrat, quoted in a letter to Montgomery Blair an excerpt from one written by "a distinguished member of Mr. Lincoln's Cabinet" urging organization of a conservative party on the basis of the Crittenden Compromise. Blair went about retailing this quote, and declaring that Seward must have been the author. There was such a letter, written in August 1863 by Caleb Blood Smith, but even after the 1864 election Blair was still telling his story to prove that Seward had been coquetting with the Democrats to run as their candidate on a Crittenden Compromise platform.[8]

Some of Seward's friends would have liked to see him replace Lincoln as the Union candidate in 1864. It was probably in the back of Weed's mind, and Thomas M. Ward, an Ohio broker, wrote in March that the people were tired of Lincoln; that Seward's friends were strong in Ohio, northern Indiana, Michigan, and a large part of the Northwest; and that when the convention met they would know how to act. There was, however, no open move in that direction by Weed or anyone else, and nothing remotely resembling a

A bitter attack on the Lincoln administration. Seward orders an arrest on personal grounds. 1864. New York Public Library

Seward boom developed. When the Union nominating convention met at Baltimore on June 7, 1864, Sewardites supporting Lincoln were in the ascendant. Edwin D. Morgan, chairman of the National Union Executive Committee, called the convention to order; Preston King was chairman of the committee on credentials; Henry J. Raymond chaired the platform committee. There was never a doubt of Lincoln's renomination, and opposition to Andrew Johnson, War Democrat from Tennessee, for the second place on the ticket, soon faded away. The platform commended, in substance, the State Department's policy toward Mexico, and endorsed two other pet projects of Seward, the fostering of foreign immigration and the Pacific railroad.

But the radicals were present at Baltimore and they were out to make trouble for Lincoln, Seward, and conservatives in general. They virtually read Montgomery Blair out of the Cabinet. Everyone knew that Seward favored bringing the seceded states back into the Union as expeditiously as possible, but there was opposition to Unionist delegations from states where the Lincoln program of reconstruction was beginning to get under way. Such delegates were finally given seats but the convention refused to give those from Virginia and Florida the right to vote.

There was also formidable evidence of defection in the New York State delegation. There the Weed-Seward group finally settled on Johnson as its candidate for Vice President, but the New York radicals wanted Daniel S. Dickinson, a War Democrat, for that post. The story was abroad that, with Dickinson as Vice President, Seward would have to leave the State Department, lest New York be over-represented in the national administration. On the one ballot taken, Dickinson mustered twenty-eight New York votes to thirty-two for Johnson. Hugh J. Hastings, a Weed-Seward stalwart, wrote from Baltimore at the convention's close that there had been a hard fight against Seward by "all the malignants and malcontents" in the convention.[9]

The radicals in his home state had not succeeded in reading Seward out of the Cabinet, but they had wounded his feelings. Pressed to speak at a great meeting in New York for ratification of the national ticket, he sent a brief letter instead. He had not failed to support Union candidates in the last four presidential elections, he declared, and he would not fail to do so, if wanted, in the present campaign, "But it is not now certain that I shall be wanted at all, and I am sure that I am not wanted yet." He added, somewhat lamely, that he had long approved of what the convention had done, and that the election of Lincoln and Johnson would prove that slavery had perished and the American Union was invincible.[10]

The campaign of 1864 got off to a bad start from the Union party point of view. The North was war weary, yet the government wanted 300,000 more men for the army and the prospect of a draft was in sight. Disaffected radicals, Germans, and War Democrats had nominated Frémont for President even before the Union convention. Morgan was deeply disgruntled because Lincoln persisted in naming Chase men for federal posts in New York. Weed was critical for the same reason, and even more so because Lincoln had permitted the war to become one for abolition rather than for the Union. He threatened openly to support any candidate who would take his stand on the Crittenden resolution of July 19, 1861, that the war was waged only to maintain the supremacy of the Constitution with the rights of the states unimpaired. The *Tribune* was gloom personified, and Greeley helped to organize a movement to force Lincoln's withdrawal from the race.

The low point of the campaign came in August, when Weed told Lincoln that he could not be re-elected and Raymond, convinced that only a bold step would save the party, wanted to make a peace offer to Jefferson Davis on the basis of acknowledging the supremacy of the Constitution, all other questions to be settled by a convention representing the people of all the states. Raymond came down to Washington with this project, but Lincoln and Seward, Stanton and Fessenden, persuaded him that such a step would be politically fatal.[11]

Depressed by the omens of political defeat, Seward left for Auburn to take part in the New York State campaign. He reached home on the evening of August 30, the day before the Democrats at Chicago nominated McClellan for President on a platform that declared the war a failure and that demanded prompt peace negotiations.

But then the tide began to turn. The harbinger of the change had appeared when Farragut entered Mobile Bay at the beginning of

August. Then, only four weeks later, came the electrifying news that Sherman's advance guard was in Atlanta. The mood of the war weary North began to change. At last the end of the war seemed near, and the star of the administration began to rise.

Nowhere was the shift in public opinion made manifest more quickly than in Auburn. On September 3 Stanton telegraphed Seward that Atlanta had fallen. Seward spread the news around the town and spoke at a celebration which his fellow citizens organized that afternoon.

He began with praise of Farragut and Sherman. Victory, he said, was now in sight. Then came an argument for the re-election of Lincoln as an assurance of victory, and the accusation that the Democratic platform was really an attempt to subvert the republic. This was the burden of his speech but, in an obvious effort to woo voters who were doubtful about emancipation, he made the statement already cited about the wartime anti-slavery measures ceasing to have effect, and slavery questions passing over "to the arbitraments of courts of law, and to the councils of legislation."

This speech was an opening gun for the campaign. It was published as "Campaign Document No. 1," and was widely praised. Samuel P. Lyman of Utica called it the most inspiring thing since the Tippecanoe song of 1840. Abolitionists, however, were not happy with its program for solving the slavery question. Did he mean, they asked, that the Emancipation Proclamation was to be thrown on the ash heap once the war ended? William Whitney, an eminent solicitor for the War Department, wrote to a friend that the speech was all wrong, for the preservation of the Union and the destruction of slavery were inextricable one from the other. Lincoln neither knew about nor did he sanction the speech, said Whitney, who was sure that Seward now regretted what he had said. Whitney ended by observing that Seward, like Blair, ought not to be believed when he made political statements.[12] There was considerable truth in this comment.

Seward's spirits rose that fall. Not only did signs of victory at the polls multiply but Lincoln, bowing to pressure from Morgan, Weed and Seward, used the appointing power to strengthen the hold of conservatives on important offices in New York State. Furthermore, the Cabinet situation was improved from Seward's point of view, for

Chase had resigned in July, when a New York appointment that he had urged met successful opposition from the Weed-Seward forces, and in September the President asked for and received Blair's resignation—a price Lincoln had to pay for Frémont's withdrawing from the race.

Aside from his speech in September, Seward refused all invitations to address mass meetings and rallies, but he took an active part in organizing strategy and tactics in the campaign. The Secretary of State also made his usual election eve address at Auburn, demanding victory as being essential to the safety of the Union. Perhaps with an eye to the future, he there modified somewhat his September statement about the fate of slavery. The measures against that institution, he declared, were part of the war effort, and therefore voting for the government was voting for them and for victory. But the preservation of the Union was still the paramount object of the struggle.[13]

Lincoln carried New York by only some 6000 votes, and Fenton defeated Seymour for governor of the state by a slightly larger majority. These were narrow margins, but Seward declared that New York was now safe ground for the Union party. The Democrats had lost their outstanding leaders when Toombs, Davis, and Breckinridge went South, and the best of the Democratic rank and file had now joined the Republicans. The Democracy, by its antiwar policy, had earned the same stigma that had doomed the Federalist party to destruction after the War of 1812. He had told the Democratic leaders, he said, "how they might have saved themselves and carried the next presidential election by being more loyal and earnest in support of the Administration than the Republican party. The Lord knows that would not have been hard."

Shortly after the election Lincoln showed the Cabinet a paper he had had them sign without reading when the campaign seemed to be going badly against him. It pledged co-operation with the President-elect [who, it seemed likely, would be McClellan] in a last great effort to win the war by March 4, 1865. Lincoln said he would have gone to McClellan, pledged complete co-operation, and urged him to raise troops for this "final trial."

Seward commented, "And the General would have answered you 'Yes, yes,' and the next day when you saw him again and pressed these views upon him he would have said 'Yes, yes,' and so on forever and would have done nothing at all."

"At least," said Lincoln, "I should have done my duty and have stood clear before my own conscience." [14]

Thanks to the favorable news from the war front and judicious use of the soldier vote, the administration had a rather narrow vote of confidence in November. As for Seward's political future, the crystal ball seemed for the moment clouded. There were rumors that he would retire to private life, replace Adams in London, return to the Senate in preparation for 1868. Actually he wished to remain at his post, though he assumed an air of indifference. As for staying in the Cabinet, he told Welles, he did not give a damn, but would stay or go as Lincoln wished. He probably had no reason for doubt on that subject.[15]

There was no question about the desire of the congressional radicals to see Seward ousted from the State Department. In July Lincoln had pocket-vetoed the Wade-Davis bill, which made Congress the ultimate authority on reconstruction, and its authors had upbraided him bitterly for doing so. Seward had undoubtedly approved this veto. The Lincoln-Seward ideas about reconstruction were gall and wormwood to the radicals and rumor had it that, once Congress reconvened, Davis would attack Seward on that ground. When the assault came, however, Davis chose to make it on the Secretary of State's Mexican policy.

On December 15, Davis again introduced his resolution of June 27. This declared that Congress had a right to a voice in foreign policy, and rebuked the President for making explanations to France on that subject. In his accompanying speech, the embattled chairman of the House Committee on Foreign Policy declared that Seward had virtually apologized to the French government for the House resolution about Mexico, and had "presumed to impeach Congress of usurpation." Thad Stevens and other radicals supported Davis. When the House laid his resolution on the table by a vote of 69 to 63, with 50 members not voting, he offered his resignation as chairman. His colleagues would not accept it.

Four days later, the Davis resolution, divided into two parts and rephrased so that it attacked the executive department rather than the President, passed the House.[16]

The bitterness manifested in this December assault, and the passage of the Davis resolution, were portents of the struggle that lay ahead. For that contest Seward and Lincoln needed one another's support. If they were victorious, the Secretary of State could reasonably expect to be in the White House on a certain March day in 1869.

~§ 28 §~

Private Lives

Interest in the great public questions of the day and the duties and demands of the State Department did not monopolize Seward's interests or consume his energies during the latter part of the war, any more than they had at its beginning. He found time to contract with a New York boat-builder for a craft he would use for excursions on Owasco Lake. He worried over the Arabian horses, eventually farming them out for their keep (Ezra Cornell had one of them) and finally writing them off as a loss. Eliphalet Nott's long career was coming to an end, and the Secretary of State wrote a biographical sketch of the president of Union College for a projected publication of his works. Together with Lincoln and the rest of the Cabinet he sat for Carpenter's "The First Reading of the Emancipation Proclamation," and the artist pronounced the picture "vastly improved" by Seward's suggestions for certain minor changes, such as removing a clock painted on the wall behind the head of Gideon Welles. He had the thanks of a boy volunteer for returning him from the army to "those parents I so rashly and unceremoniously left," and of an inventor for "getting my Torpedo discoverer and exploder at once before the proper board." [1] When the historian Richard Hildreth, consul at Trieste, became mentally incompetent in 1864, Seward took the initiative in raising $2150 for the relief of the sufferer and his wife.

Seward was also a prime mover in making Thanksgiving a national holiday. On September 28, 1863, Sarah Josepha Buell Hale, editor of *Godey's Lady's Book* and expositor of women's rights and duties, wrote to Lincoln urging that Thanksgiving be taken out of the realm of state festivals and made a national holiday. This moved Seward to action. He composed a proclamation which he read to Welles and which the latter declared was "very well done." It spoke of the blessings of fruitful fields and healthful skies, of the nation's increase in wealth and prosperity even in the midst of civil war. It set apart the last Thursday in November as a day for the people to thank God for those mercies, and to implore His aid in healing the nation's wounds and in restoring it "to the full enjoyment of peace, harmony, tranquillity and Union."

Lincoln liked this composition, and issued it on October 3 as a presidential proclamation. Shortly thereafter, Dr. Muhlenberg, founder of St. Luke's Hospital in New York, composed a metrical version, and Henry Bellows, head of the United States Sanitary Commission, obtained Lincoln's consent to call it "The President's Hymn." This was just before Lincoln and Seward went to the dedication of the national cemetery at Gettysburg. En route there, the train stopped at a station where the crowd demanded a speech from the President. Lincoln demurred and turning to his companion said, "Seward, you go out and repeat some of your 'poetry' to the people." [2]

The varied demands of public life and more purely social activities were often closely intertwined. A love of good conversation, as well as diplomatic protocol, prompted the Secretary of State's generous entertainment of foreign diplomats. The invitations he showered on them to accompany him to fairs and on excursions were as much a manifestation of his friendly propensities as they were of his desire to display the resources of the nation. Sometimes he would have a third objective, as in 1863, when the hegira through Central New York gave him opportunity for unobtrusive consultation with Supreme Court Justice Nelson at Cooperstown about some troublesome draft problems. Only on one occasion during the war did he go back to Auburn purely for rest and recreation. This was in August 1862, when he arrived there, in Fanny's opinion, "quite worn out and sick." But after five days he was hurrying back to Washington because of Lee's first invasion of the North. [3]

Entertainment at the "Old Club House" was often purely "family, " or for its master's own diversion and entertainment. Relatives came and stayed for more or less lengthy periods of time, and there were other visitors who had no connection with the affairs of the government. Charlotte Cushman was a house guest when in Washington, and visiting Englishmen like Sir Henry Holland, or noted scientists such as Jean Louis Rodolphe Agassiz and Benjamin Silliman, Jr., were likely to be found at his dinner table. At one time three of Auburn's leading citizens were his guests. He introduced them to the President, and Auburnians spoke of their visit as a compliment to New York's "loveliest village of the plain." [4]

When Seward entertained at dinner the wine flowed freely. His expenditure for this one article was considerable, though gifts from foreign diplomats and purchases through American representatives abroad reduced its cost. Through Sanford he ordered early in 1863 one barrel of Bordeaux and one of Burgundy for guests and a second barrel of Bordeaux for ordinary table use. James Harvey sent him two cases of port, 1815 vintage, one a gift from the Minister to Portugal. Blatchford, while in Rome purchased Valernian wines for Seward and (a Seward favorite) Lachrima Christi, "the best that can be bought in Naples." Count Piper, head of the Swedish legation, supplied him with enough Norwegian aqua vita to last the rest of his life. When Mercier left Washington, Seward's letter of regret reminded him of his promise to forward ten or twelve dozen bottles of good Burgundy. When the Secretary of State ended his term of public service the transportation of his wine cellar to Auburn constituted a real problem.[5]

The constant round of entertainment at Washington, the maintenance of two domiciles, medical expenses for an ailing wife and delicate daughter, and a readiness to respond to requests for charitable contributions, all made for heavy expenditures. Seward told Blatchford in February 1862 that he was in some financial difficulty, with expenses exceeding his income, and the New York banker promptly sent him a check for $2000 as a present to a man who was sacrificing his pecuniary interests to the nation's welfare. Later that same year Gurowski recorded in his diary that Seward had told one of the diplomats that he was spending $16,000 a year, twice the amount of his salary.[6]

There were undoubtedly times when Seward's expenditures exceeded his income, but on the whole the expenses consequent upon his being Secretary of State were not excessively burdensome. His Chautauqua lands still brought him in considerable revenue, the Auburn real estate operation was very profitable, and Blatchford acted as his agent in sundry stock and bond operations. These transactions, which included to some extent operations in the gold market, were in the hands of a very shrewd financier and were in all probability lucrative.[7] Furthermore, while Seward made it a rule never to hold a trusteeship or official position in any corporation, he was willing to act as legal counsel for companies in cases which involved no conflict of interest. During these years he received between $9000 and $10,000 for such services to the Hudson River Bridge Company.[8]

Seward's over-all financial position improved during the war. Inventories of his estate preserved in his papers show that on January 1, 1862, the value of property held in his own name, in that of his wife, and in the Judge Miller estate totaled $273,958.43. By September 1, 1863, this total had shrunk to $243,151.24, but it increased in value some $40,000 during the next four months. By July 1, 1866, it amounted to $315,811.12.[9] When the Secretary of State wished to spend something extra on house furnishings, or have his coat of arms engraved on silver purchased at Tiffany's, he did not need to hesitate on account of the cost.

One reason for Seward's freedom from financial worry was that his sons, now all grown to man's estate, more than took care of themselves. Frederick, aside from his salary as Assistant Secretary of State, retained his interest in the Albany *Evening Journal*, and it goes without saying that he and Anna lived without expense in the home which she managed with such competence and charm. Seward not only relied upon Frederick's help in the Department but also turned over to him his duties as trustee of the Samuel Sweezy Seward Institute at Florida.

Augustus was with the army in New Mexico at the beginning of the war. His father wanted him to come back and take an active part in the field, and for this purpose secured him an appointment as major. Augustus, however, much preferred a place in the paymaster's corps. This fitted in with his mother's ideas, and she wrote to Secretary of War Cameron asking that her son be given such a post. When Augustus reached Washington the first of October 1861, he found both positions open for him and chose to be a paymaster, a place that paid $200 more and in which he eventually achieved the rank of major. He was "good, old Gus," whom children loved, a heavy-set man, quite unlike the other children in physical aspects and in other ways as well. Conspicuous as a boy of thirteen for lack of grace and conversational powers, as time went on he became more and more silent and withdrawn from society. Henry told Charlotte Cushman, who was struck by Augustus's taciturnity, that he was like Judge Miller, who had been very diffident and had never made a speech in his life; but this was largely protective. Gus never married, and died as quietly as he had lived, just before his fiftieth birthday.[10]

If Augustus lived an introvert's life with semi-tragic overtones, William Henry, Jr., was just the opposite. Dark, handsome, and outgoing, Will exuded vitality and charm. His banking business in Auburn was no sooner started than the war began, and with it his yearning to get into the fray. His partner, Clinton McDougall, was first to join the army and thought Will should stay and take care of the business, but an elderly Auburn banker, James Seymour, finally agreed to shoulder that responsibility without remuneration. Will's mother-in-law said that going to the front would kill Janet, who was pregnant, but both his wife and his mother encouraged him to go. He raised a regiment and by the fall of 1862 was on his way to the battlefields as a lieutenant-colonel of volunteers, having waited just long enough to be at home for the birth of their first child, Cornelia Margaret. He fought in many engagements, was wounded, won high praise for ability and valor, and became a brigadier-general before peace came and he returned to the life of an Auburn banker.[11]

Will and Fanny were very close. As a child, she shared lesson time with him, and also his interest in dogs, kittens, and horses. He named his favorite pony after her. Later, he invited her to army hops. She helped his wife, pert and vivacious Janet, keep his wardrobe replenished, and bought his general's star after his promotion.

Fanny was sixteen when the war came. The vivacious, tumbling infant of the 1840s who had never been so happy as when she was chasing around after her brother, had developed into a tall, slightly round-shouldered young lady with an inconsequential figure, straight brown hair, and a heavy face whose one attractive feature was her beautiful brown eyes with heavily fringed lashes. She was prone to clumsiness and, hard as she tried, could never skate or dance well. Serious, precocious, and deeply religious, she was also reserved, subject to fits of depression, and woefully lacking in poise and assurance.

Frances took charge of Fanny's education. The growing girl had home instruction from her mother and from tutors, and a winter session at the Mapes boarding school in Philadelphia in 1862, still under her mother's watchful eye. This last effort at formal education had to be given up, however, on account of Fanny's delicate health. She was subject to colds, was repeatedly wracked with quinsy, and her lungs were lamentably weak.

Frances encouraged her daughter to read and Fanny, as she grew into her teens, hoped to become a writer. Some two years before the war she began a diary that she kept up, save for the year 1864, until a month before her death. It described the life that she saw in Washington, and abounded in vignettes of the famous people she met— General Butler, "shortish, black hair and side whiskers, black eyes and clear though red style of complexion, would be well looking were he not *very very very* cross-eyed, and his best eye half shut," or Anthony Trollope, "a great homely, red, stupid faced Englishman, with a disgusting beard of iron grey." [12]

Fanny was fond of her mother, but she adored her father, who in his turn did everything he could in the midst of his busy life to develop her mind and give her opportunities for achieving a sophisticated outlook. He took her with him when he campaigned in 1860, and three years later she joined the party of diplomats that came jaunting up through central New York. When in Washington, she would go on trips with him to the Army of the Potomac, and he took pains to introduce her to the great and near-great who came to the house. Often she sat at the dinner table, shy and silent in the midst of a distinguished company for, as Seward remarked, "it would do her no harm to hear people talk who were older and therefore wiser than herself." She made her debut at the Sewards' New Year's reception in 1863, in the house on Lafayette Square.

Seward urged Fanny to write. As for marriage, he declared that he was opposed to the idea. It was, he said, a great risk. He would hate to see her tied to some scamp who would ill-treat her, and even marriage for love might prove unhappy, for at her age she wasn't capable of understanding the character of any man. All this was said to Orville Browning with Fanny listening, wide-eyed, across the dinner table. He continued to invite eligible young men to dinner, however. There was a possibility, the family thought, that Lincoln's secretary, John George Nicolay, was interested. He did pay her some attention, but the romance never bloomed, and what little chance it had vanished when, at a reception in the winter of 1862, Nicolay addressed her as "Miss Boyd." [13]

Seward's wife and daughter maintained the homestead, and when he could he made short trips to Auburn, perhaps six or eight such journeys during the war. It was after the first of these visits, at the end of August 1861, that he brought them back to Washington for their first sight of the new home, where a special room had been prepared for Frances.

The nation's capital in wartime was like a different world to Frances. The house, she wrote to Lazette, was palatial. "I do not think Henry was ever more pleased with a home—it accommodates itself marvellously to his tastes and habits—such as they are at this day." She met the President—"I was determined to like him, and I did"—but she felt unsafe in Washington. Back in Auburn she had dreamed that they were all blown up in the Capitol, and now she was so close to the conflict that she could almost hear the rumble of the guns. Mostly she kept to her room, her health forbidding participation in the social events over which Anna presided.[14]

War was still a dreadful thing to Frances. The Most High moved in a mysterious way, she felt. But that some part of the human family would be benefited by this conflict was impossible to doubt, if one were to retain one's faith in a good and just God. She believed that it was a "Holy War" for freeing the Negro. This conviction made her consent to Will's going to the front, and set her, when health permitted, to sewing and rolling bandages for the hospitals. It also made her watch and long for the time when emancipation should become the avowed objective of the government at Washington.

Frances found it hard to bear the delay in making emancipation the war's one great aim. She criticized the President for interfering with Frémont's order in 1861 freeing the blacks in Missouri. Henry pointed out to her the problems and dangers involved in precipitate action. Where, for instance, would the 24,000 blacks in Charleston go, if they were freed, he asked her. The government could not furnish food for 4,000,000 freedmen and supply an army of half a million at the same time. Colonization was impossible without treaties and money. It would not be humane to hasten freedom at the expense of the suffering, and even the lives, of those who were supposed to benefit by it. This was in December of 1861 and she seemed half convinced, but the following summer she criticized Lincoln's answer to Greeley's "Prayer of Twenty Millions" and urged Henry to ask the President to issue a proclamation of "immediate" emancipation. The one that came that fall was too gradual for her taste. Still she felt as the war continued and abolitionist feeling grew that, despite the shortcomings of the government's policy, the war was a righteous war, quite unlike the one which had called Gus to Mexico eighteen years before.[15]

There were times of respite from the strain of the war for Frances. These came when victories seemed to promise an early end of the struggle, or when her health temporarily improved, and there was one October week in 1862 when she found peace and quiet for a few days in Henry's old home town of Florida. It brought back memories, and she wrote "it is 40 years dear Henry since I went first to Orange County. We have had many pleasant and some sad visits there in that time, but it is a comfort to think our love has outlived all changes, and to hope that it will last beyond this stage of our being." [16]

In spite of such solace, worries of mind and body taxed her strength. She had a son at the front and a husband in a city where his life might be in danger. Fanny's health and Augustus's silence weighed upon her, and then there was the tense summer of 1863 when a draft riot all but broke out in Auburn. The local Irish threatened to burn the Seward home because its owners were friends of the Negro, and Frances armed her servant William Johnson with a pistol so that he could defend himself. It was all very well for Henry to tell her, if worse came to worst, to come away and let the house burn. The house was her one haven.[17]

There were still other worries for Frances, troubles that grew more formidable as the war neared its close. Life in the old home became more and more dear to her. There the children had grown up. There was the little library back of the south parlor where she had written so many letters to Henry, and in the garden was the summer house where she and Fanny spent many quiet hours reading together. She wrote repeatedly to Henry to come home, if only for a short visit. Perhaps it would be in the spring, when the world was quiet and the garden at its height. She tried to picture it to Fred in the spring of 1861. The lilies, she wrote, were in their glory, and the peony bed was so gay—

> The phlox is just beginning to open its eyes, while the "star of Bethlehem" and ragged Robin contend for the supremacy along the borders. The seringa perfumes the air with her pretty white blossoms & the roses yellow & pink are just beginning to show their colors. June is a beautiful month. The scarlet runners which I planted in the Labyrinth are growing almost as rapidly as Jack's bean stalk. . . .[18]

But now the plans of the men threatened the destruction of her Elysium.

It was not so bad when Will, home on sick leave, talked about building a house for himself and Janet at the southern end of the garden. She did not tell him how impossible that was, because he was weak and ill. But Henry and Fred had ideas that were more threatening and just as disruptive.

Henry had been thinking for some time of an extension on the south side of the house and Fred, who was something of an architect and had planned homes for a number of friends, drew up designs that would double the front of the dwelling. Frances would have no part of it. She wanted to keep the rural character of the place—the old cherry tree that Judge Miller had planted, "home of the robins for nearly 40 years," and which, along with other fine trees would have to be destroyed if Henry and Frederick had their way. She did not want a city mansion, for she liked irregular houses, like Bleak House, where "you go up and down steps, out of one room into another, & where you come upon more rooms when you think you have seen all there are, & where there is a bountiful provision of little halls & passages, & where you find older rooms in unexpected places with lattice windows & green growth peering through them." [19]

The devotion of Frances to the old place had little weight. The plans of the men for enlargement were not abandoned. Then came another great disappointment.

Frances went to Washington in December 1864. Fanny had been there since October, as she had been throughout the war whenever an opportunity offered, and when Frances returned to Auburn not long afterward Fanny stayed with her father. It was apparent that Henry was to remain in the State Department, and it was equally evident that Fanny wished to stay in Washington with him. The family, it seemed, was breaking up. Spring was at hand, and Frances wrote the following letter:

> March, 1865. I write this for you my daughter in the event of my not being able to talk with you on this subject. After mature consideration of the matter & supposing all parties to consent I advise that your father instead of building an addition to this house should unite with Fred and build somewhere on the Hudson or any other place they should prefer a house that will be a home for you all like that in Washington—where you all seem happy—I would reserve in this house so much as Aunty & I need to be comfortable letting Wm. take the remainder when that could be done with Aunty's consent—I think Wm. intends making his home in Auburn—I doubt whether my other children would find it so agreeable here as we who have never *lived* elsewhere—Of course if Augustus or Frederick prefer this place they are entitled to it before Wm —but I do not think they would—Should I see you all again as I hope, we will talk it over together.[20]

Frederick's wife apparently exerted herself to remedy a tense situation, for a few weeks after Frances put these words on paper she wrote to Anna that she expected Fanny to come before long to Auburn, and would like them all to spend some time there that summer. She praised her daughter-in-law for her kindness and perception, hoping that she would have many years in which "to smooth the paths of others, which is really the only true happiness." [21]

This letter was written on April 2. Shortly thereafter came a series of tragic events that threw the plans of all the Sewards into turmoil.

Lee evacuated Richmond on April 2. Three days later, Seward asked Stanton to have General Godfrey Weitzel send on immediately all the correspondence in the Richmond postoffice, since it might very well contain important letters or dispatches from Europe to the Confederate government. Lincoln was at Richmond and Seward, who had been there with him, was planning to go back with a proclamation for the President to sign closing the ports in the rebel states to foreign powers.[22]

On the afternoon of April 5, Seward and Fred with Fanny and her friend Mary Titus drove out Vermont Avenue. The carriage door kept flying open and one of the men told the coachman to dismount and fasten it securely. As he set foot on the street the horses bolted. Fred jumped out to head them, but fell. The reins were trailing on the ground. Fanny begged her father not to try and get them, but he jumped. As he did so he caught his heel and fell heavily to the ground. The runaways continued until, with the coach badly damaged and on the verge of collapse, they were caught by a soldier.[23]

Meanwhile, Seward was carried to his home, unconscious. His face was terribly swollen and bruised. The surgeon and doctor who were hastily summoned thought that, aside from the facial lacerations, he had only a dislocated right shoulder, but they soon discovered that his arm was broken and that his jaw was fractured on both sides. The setting of the injured parts was an agonizing process, and a week after the accident he was still suffering much pain, his discomfort aggravated by gout in his right foot. On the night of April 12 he was delirious, but two days later he showed signs of improvement.[24]

Frances and Will, summoned by telegraph, reached Washington on the evening of the seventh. Gruff Secretary Stanton came to the house repeatedly and, Fanny noted, was gentle as a woman with the sick man, "much more efficient than I, who did not know what to do." One morning when the Secretary of War appeared, the sick man tried to express his gratitude—"God bless you, Stanton. You have made me cry for the first time in my life, I believe."

During these pain-ridden days, the war came to an end. Lee surrendered on April 9 at Appomattox Court House, and Grant quieted his cheering soldiers by reminding them that "the rebels are our countrymen again." Lincoln was at City Point. Before he had the news of Lee's surrender he heard of Seward's accident and started at once for Washington on the steamboat *River Queen*. The boat docked early in the evening and the President hurried over to see Seward. "You are back from Richmond," whispered the invalid. Yes, Lincoln replied, adding that it looked as though the end was near. He draped his huge frame over the foot of Seward's bed and talked about his visit to Richmond. He had gone through a hospital where there were 7000 sick and wounded men, shaking hands with them—had worked as hard as though sawing wood, he said—but he seemed happy at the thought of the labor. After about an hour, he took his leave. They never saw each other again.[25]

Letters of condolence flooded into the sickroom. Martin Ryerson, philanthropist and businessman, wrote on April 13 of his great respect and esteem for Seward, adding, "I have trembled with apprehension lest he & Mr. Lincoln might both be taken from us."[26]

During the five days following Lincoln's visit, the Secretary of State gained ground but slowly, in no condition to enjoy the bands and transparencies, the shouting and singing crowds that surged around the White House, the superb fireworks in Lafayette Park. He had a male nurse, Sergeant George Robinson, who helped take care of him at night. Augustus, Fanny, Frederick, and Anna took turns watching at the invalid's bedside. Fanny read to him. Frances, deeply worried and upset, put on a bright and cheerful mien.

April 14 was Good Friday, and that morning for the first time Henry took solid food. Fanny read "Enoch Arden" to him in the afternoon. In the early evening there was a torchlight procession in front of the White House and the band played "Rally Round the Flag." Fanny had the night watch until eleven, when Gus would relieve her. Sergeant Robinson was nearby. Seward dozed off. He lay on the edge of the bed furthest from the door, that position being easiest for his broken arm. It was a little after ten o'clock when Fanny heard a noise outside the sickroom.

There had been rumors of assassination attempts at various times during the war, but both Lincoln and Seward disregarded them. The latter was convinced, he told Bigelow in the summer of 1862, that assassination was not an American practice or habit, "and one so vicious and so desperate cannot be engrafted into our political system." This conviction deepened as he saw the President traveling back and forth, unguarded, to his country house near the Soldiers' Home. Seward himself went there in the same way, "by daylight and by moonlight, by starlight and without light."

The President later had to accept a cavalry escort for these trips, but it seemed to him like fixing up a gap in a fence that was down all along the line. Seward had much the same attitude, even after an anonymous letter writer in 1864 threatened him with death—"Poison—that failing, six men to fire at once, from a concealed window; telescopic rifles." It is one of the ironies of fate that he had information of the assassination plot directed against Lincoln and himself, but disregarded it as a "twice-told tale." Later, he told Secretary of the Interior Usher that, had he been able to go out, Lincoln would not have gone to the theater that night, but this was hindsight.[27]

John Wilkes Booth, brother of Edwin and a handsome, dashing stage star, was a man of pronounced southern sympathies who saw the Civil War as a struggle for freedom from the tyrannical oppression of the North. Sometime in 1864 he began organizing a plot to kidnap the President and carry him off to Richmond. This changed, after Lee's surrender, into a plan for the assassination of Lincoln, Vice President Johnson, and Seward. Lincoln had seen Booth in 1863 in a play called *The Marble Heart*, a rather tame production according to John Hay.[28] Now Booth singled the President out as his own particular victim. The task of assassinating Seward was assigned to Lewis Powell, alias Lewis Payne, a half-mad, ex-Confederate soldier who had had two brothers killed in the war.

At approximately the same time that Booth fired a pistol bullet into the back of Lincoln's head at Ford's theater, Payne rang the bell at the Seward home. He told the Negro doorman, William H. Bell, that he had come from Seward's physician, Dr. Tullio Verdi, with medicine. On pretense that he must tell Seward how to take it, Payne mounted the stairs toward the bedroom floor.

Curious about the noise that she heard, Fanny opened the door of the sickroom to find Fred, clad only in his underwear, talking to a young man in a long overcoat who was repeating the same story he had told Bell. Fred refused to let him see the invalid, and shut the door. After a minute or two, Fanny, within, heard blows being struck, but did not at once connect them with the stranger, thinking "they were chasing a rat in the hall, remembering such a chase once." She asked Robinson, who was sitting at the head of the bed, to go and see what was the matter.

Payne, pretending to go downstairs, had suddenly turned and drawn his pistol. It missed fire and he struck Frederick savagely on the head with the muzzle of the gun. They grappled, and the assassin pushed the wounded man down the hall to the invalid's door just as Robinson opened it. Payne gashed Robinson's forehead with a bowie knife and then rushed over to the bed. Seward, sensing that it was a murderous attack, raised himself up with the idea, so he said later, that he must protect Fanny. The assassin, reaching across the bed, struck repeatedly, inflicting wounds on his intended victim's face and neck, the one on the right side laying his cheek wide open. The blade seemed cold, Seward later remembered, and then he felt what seemed like rain streaming down his neck. He slipped to the floor, blood rushing from the cuts. Meanwhile, Fanny's screams had roused Augustus who, with others, wrestled Payne out of the room. He fled down the stairs and out of the house.[29]

Seward bled copiously and was very weak. Fred, too, was terribly injured, and lay for days in a critical condition. His father later told Sanford that for three months after the attack both saw everything double.

Henry could not speak for some time, due to the condition of his face and jaw, and communicated by writing on a slate. When Dorothea Dix came to see him, he wrote, "Neither the friends nor the enemies of *our* America have left *me* anything to complain of. The friends of America ought to have watched Mr. Lincoln better. His life however is the forfeit." Miss Dix sent him some cologne and a mixture of eggs and wine. Fanny gave him some of this and asked him how he liked it. "I like it because I like Miss Dix," he replied.[30]

During the days that followed Payne's assault the reception room in the Seward home was crowded with distinguished people who came to inquire after the Secretary's health. Letters poured in, some from the great and near-great, others from obscure and humble folk, who were looking to him for leadership now that the President was gone. Motley wrote from Vienna, "Never were your invaluable services more needed than now," a tribute that expressed an opinion widely held in Europe. Stanton was assiduous in his attendance upon the invalid. That summer Union College conferred an LL.D. upon the Secretary of War, proposed in part because of character and service, but chiefly, Blatchford told Seward, "on account of his devoted friendship to you." [31]

On April 19, Seward sat up in bed to catch a glimpse of the funeral procession that made its melancholy way from the White House. A week later he had recovered sufficiently to go for short rides, but he still suffered much discomfort, especially because of his broken jaw. He was also worried about Frederick, who was unconscious for days, hemorrhaged repeatedly under his fractured skull, and was not out of danger for weeks.

President Johnson and the Cabinet called on May 9, and Seward met them in the parlor. A rigid iron frame which entered his mouth held his jaw in place and he spoke only indistinctly but, as always, he wished to talk. "Once or twice," Welles noted, "allusions to the night of the great calamity affected him more deeply than I have ever seen him." [32]

Seward started going to the State Department for brief periods by May 19, and shortly thereafter began attending Cabinet meetings. He dictated his first letter to an amanuensis on June 3, but it was not until a month later that he fully resumed the duties of his office.[33]

As Henry and Frederick toiled along the road to recovery, Frances wasted away. Tormented by neuralgia and nausea, she went as often as she felt able to Henry's room. She sat for an hour, morning and evening, by Frederick's bedside. "His pale, patient face," she wrote to Lazette, "is never out of my mind." She kept repeating, "He will die."

Long years of physical and neurotic illness had taken their toll of Frances. Now tragedy had brought her close to the family again, but the causes of division remained—Henry's determination to stay in Washington, Fanny's desire to be with him rather than in Auburn, the intent of the men to change the old home into an imposing mansion. Added to all else was the terrible memory of that night—her son and her husband gashed and bleeding, the pool of blood in the bedroom, blood spatters on her dress, Fanny's screams.

Strength held out until it became apparent that the invalids were out of danger. Then Frances became listless, lost her appetite, and developed a persistent fever. She died on June 21, 1865, three months before her sixtieth birthday. Seward took her body to Auburn and saw it buried in the family plot.[34]

Frances had wanted a useful place in society. Her interest in politics was genuine, and in her better days she had been glad to criticize the speeches Henry read to her, and make abstracts of articles and news items for him to use when he returned from his legal journeys. Always she tried to impress upon him the value of high ideals, and to persuade herself that his devotion to principle equaled her own. She loved her children and did all that she could to make their lives happy and useful. She had wit and intelligence and, though she felt superior to many, had deep compassion for the weak and lowly.

Hers was a useful life, but it was also tragic. She rebelled against social protocol and this, together with recurrent illness, kept her aloof from the society that Henry loved and from her place at the head of his household. As the years went on, her path diverged from that of the other members of her family. Henry did not need her. The children were grown up. Payne's violence, a brutal denial of all her values, was the final blow to an existence that had become less and less meaningful, and she lost the will to live.

Fanny, too, suffered shock from the attempted assassination, but she was young and wanted to live. For the next year and a half she fought against ill health, harassed by headaches, fatigue, a persistent fever, and a chronic cough. In August 1866, Dr. Robinson in Auburn found her lungs badly diseased. A hurried journey in September from Auburn to Harrisburg, where her father lay desperately ill with cholera, exhausted her strength, but she rallied, and on October 11 wrote to Will, "Yes it is true that I am much better —very much stronger. I can see marked improvement in everything but my cough—and that is not any worse." She died before the end of the month, in her twenty-second year. The coroner recorded the cause of her death as a "bilious remittent fever"; the New York

Tribune called it typhoid, but the underlying cause was undoubtedly tuberculosis.[35] Fanny was not her mother's mental equal, but there was strength and sweetness in her character.

For over a year Seward had been concerned about Fanny's health. He saw to it that she had the best medical attention available and weeks at the seashore. When apart, he made it a rule to leave no one of her letters unanswered a day. Her death was a sad blow. He told John Bigelow that no one could know how precious she had been to him. He kept repeating to those who sought to console him that he knew God was just; that he believed the dead rose to eternal life. But it was months later, in answer to a letter of condolence from Charlotte Cushman, that he poured out his grief—

> I have so long delayed to answer your kind letter only because no resources which I possess have supplied me with the spirit required for writing to even the nearest of friends concerning my great my unspeakable sorrow. I had during the last ten years dreams which formed themselves into schemes of retirement, of travel, of study at the approaching end of a life which has been active from motives of duty, but as the world will probably insist motives of ambition. Those dreams and schemes were free from all impurity and all selfishness, perhaps so entirely free, because she was associated with them all. Her pleasure and improvement the objects of them, and the solace upon which I relied. They are all rudely broken and destroyed forever. . . . I ought to know that she could not be left upon the earth after me, or even longer with me, because she was not of the earth earthly. I ought to be able to rejoice that she was withdrawn from me to be reunited with the pure and blessed spirit that formed her own. But, unfortunately, I am not spiritual enough to find support in these reflections. . . .[36]

⁊ 29 ⁊

A Maelstrom and a Plan

"With malice toward none, with charity for all," said Lincoln in 1865 as he summoned the people to bind up the nation's wounds. It was noble counsel, but difficult to follow. The Civil War ended slavery as an accepted national institution; it was a stimulus to some aspects of the nation's economy; but it left behind it disruption and demoralization such as Americans had never seen.

The South was a wreck. A quarter of a million of its soldiers had fallen in battle or died of wounds and destitution. Under the pressure of blockade on the ocean and of invasion by the Union armies its economy had ground toward a halt and by 1865 lay prostrate—wealth in slaves gone, tools and equipment of all kinds destroyed, one city after another gutted by fire. In this general holocaust, individual affluence had disappeared and grinding poverty had become the rule of life.

Nor was the destruction wholly material. The old conception of the Union as an institution to which one paid reverence had been badly damaged. While most southerners were willing to acknowledge defeat and become once again loyal citizens of the nation, there were few who could escape some measure of distrust and bitterness. Mourning for those who had died on the battlefield was universal, and many who had not been touched by death in that form believed that their men had suffered barbarous treatment in northern prisons. Others feared that the North meant to make or keep them paupers, and were irked by the appearance of carpetbaggers who came down South to make their fortunes. Southern Unionists complained about lack of support from Washington in obtaining political preferment in their states. Sidney Andrews, the able special correspondent for the Chicago *Tribune* and the Boston *Advertiser*, after traveling for over two months in the Carolinas and Georgia came away with the impression that there was little genuine Unionism in those states. Dr. Thomas Cottman of New Orleans complained of the predominance of disloyal men in the reconstructed Louisiana legislature. Eight months later, Governor Elisha Marshall Pease of Texas told Gideon Welles that there was no toleration of Union men in the Lone Star State; that five-sixths of the people there were hostile to the federal government and persecuted those who did not agree with them. In June 1866 one of Seward's correspondents, writing from Columbia, Missouri, reported that the churches in that city rejected all fraternal relations with the North. Reports came to the Secretary of State from Georgia and Virginia about the lack of loyalty to the Union.[1] Indeed, loyalty to any kind of idealism was at a low ebb in both sections, and events were to prove that corruption, which follows so easily in the path of war, could find a foothold in the North as well as in the South.

One of the main reasons for the querulous attitude taken by the South in its hour of defeat was the Negro problem that, most southerners felt, had been thrust upon them by northern fanatics —men such as Charles Sumner, Thaddeus Stevens, Ben Wade, and Henry Winter Davis—who were now anxious to punish their southern brethren for having provoked the struggle between the sections. This feeling of resentment grew during the first months of peace, as the white South found itself confronted by four million freedmen, themselves confused, uncertain, and anxious lest, by hook or crook, they be again reduced to slavery.

The racial situation in the South was chaotic. Countless thousands of Negroes wandered aimlessly along the country roads, or drifted into the cities. In August 1865 the New York *Times* published an excerpt from the Richmond *Whig* telling of the constant complaints of Virginia farmers over the uncertainty and inefficiency of Negro labor—the prevalence of idleness, theft, and breaking of contracts. The Freedmen's Bureau, created in March of that year to help southern Negroes find their new place in society, had to reduce rations and use other means of coercion to get its protégés back to work.

Nor were matters improved by the attitude of the whites toward the freedmen. While intelligent southerners wanted to see the Negro given a fair chance, the masses were either apathetic or worse. Thousands of the southern whites did not realize that slavery was gone, and expected reinstatement in the Union on the old basis or, at least, with only gradual emancipation. The great majority of them cared not a whit for the Negro's welfare, while talk of his obtaining social or political equality produced only hoots of derision. There were numerous and persistent complaints about the activities of the Freedmen's Bureau, the presence of Negro troops, and the danger of Negroes resorting to violence in seizing what they felt to be their rights. Confederate General Joseph E. Johnston thought that servile war was a probability, and the New York *Times* believed that this expectation prevailed throughout the South. Faced by this general situation, several of the states enacted codes that were virtual attempts to re-enslave the Negroes, or at least to reduce them to a state of peonage.[2]

As the South licked its wounds and took stock of its situation, the government at Washington summoned it to political reorganization. Under the circumstances it is not surprising that many of the leaders in the Confederacy found seats in the new state legislatures or won election to Congress.

The North also was a maelstrom of conflicting opinions and emotions. In his last Cabinet meeting Lincoln had said: "We must extinguish our resentments if we expect harmony and union." There were many who thought as he did, but enormous casualty lists (the North had lost some 360,000 men), the sufferings of the men in Andersonville prison, Lincoln's assassination, and the attack on Seward, all promoted a feeling of bitterness and a desire for revenge upon the late foe. Those who saw the end of slavery as the war's main objective suspected the South of eagerness to restore that hated institution. News reports from below the Mason and Dixon line dwelling on the intransigent spirit of the southerners and the cruelties practised upon Negroes increased fears and suspicions already prevalent in the North.[3]

Nor were northerners distrustful only of their southern brethren. Rancor between Old Whigs and Old Democrats still persisted within Republican ranks. Conservatives and Democrats feared the intentions of radical Republicans, and were in turn accused of being false to the idealistic aims of the late conflict. These apprehensions made for an unstable political situation.

The Union party no longer had the pressures of wartime to hold it together. There existed within it a wide spectrum of views as to the treatment of the Negro and the proper attitude toward the South. The Democratic party was an uneasy amalgam of opinions on the same subjects, and it further labored under the presence in its ranks of Copperheads like Clement L. Vallandigham and Fernando Wood. The political situation was further complicated by the prospective emergence of the South as a political force almost certain to be allied with the Democracy unless the southern Negro was given the vote.

Congress reflected this political instability. Some of its members wished to smite treason hip and thigh, while others inclined to leniency. Some were willing to follow executive leadership, others felt that the reconstruction of the South was a congressional responsibility. There were Republican members who were ready to follow the President, but many were suspicious of this states'-rights Democrat from Tennessee whom they had put in the White House. Some Congressmen wished to help the southern Negro but shrank from giving him the ballot. Others, looking ahead, thought that he must have it to prevent a rejuvenated North-South Democratic party from wiping out the national banking system and the protective tariff. Congress itself was a maelstrom of conflicting views and opinions.

The question of Negro suffrage was politically explosive. Republicans generally were inclined to favor some form of Negro voting in the South, but were hesitant about it, or opposed to it in the North. There Negroes voted in only six states, and one of these (New York) had a $250 freehold qualification. The other five were in New England. Even in that section Connecticut voters in October 1865 defeated Negro suffrage by a decided majority. There was a similar result in Wisconsin and Minnesota. Color prejudice was prevalent in the North, and the Democrats made capital out of it by stigmatizing the Republicans as the "Nigger party." [4]

The political situation prompted much talk of a reorganization of parties. The New York *Times* declared that the Democratic party was doomed because its Chicago platform had declared the war a failure. It had lost its vital principle, a national spirit, said the *Times*, and would inevitably disappear. The New York *Herald* piped to the same tune, adding that the politicians of both the old parties were adrift. Bennett foresaw a radical party crystallizing around Chief Justice Chase. It would try to Tylerize Johnson, he predicted, but the President would emerge victorious, for he would have the support of the Democracy, North and South, and also that of conservative Republicans. This political reorientation would be brought about by the question of Negro suffrage in the South. Southern loyalists, Bennett concluded, could if they would "organize under Andrew Johnson the ruling party of the future." [5]

Bennett's prognostications seemed borne out by political movements that began shortly after the end of the war, as a result of Johnson's reconstruction policy. He proposed following the general lines laid down by Lincoln, and the leaders of the Democracy rallied to his support. They had visions of a rejuvenated North-South organization, and hoped that this War Democrat from Tennessee would be a new Moses to lead them out of the wilderness of political defeat. But if he did so he would have to rid himself of their old enemy, Seward, and of Stanton, who had turned his back once for all on their party, and was advocating Negro suffrage in the South.

By the summer of 1865 leaders of the Democratic party were wooing the President, and at its convention that year the New York State Democracy endorsed Johnson's policy of reconstruction. As Seward later remarked, the opposing party "seemed anxious to prove their devotion superior to ours by committing themselves to support him as a candidate for the Presidency in 1868." [6]

The Blairs hoped and worked for a party reorganization. They were close to Johnson and tried their best to influence his policy. During the summer of 1865 Montgomery Blair made three speeches viciously attacking Seward. Blair asserted that Seward had encouraged secession; that he was responsible for not relieving Sumter; that his Mexican policy was weak; that he was a coward and politically ambitious. Mingled with these assaults were fulminations against Stanton and against Judge-Advocate General Holt, who favored vigorous prosecution of the southern war "criminals." The Blair aim was lenient treatment of the South, the ousting of Seward and Stanton from the Cabinet, and a new party headed by Johnson and composed of Democrats and conservative-minded Republicans.[7]

While these plottings and plannings went on, with Johnson listening patiently to everyone but taking no moves toward reshuffling his Cabinet, various and sundry Republicans became restive. The unpredictable Greeley, whose feud with Weed and Seward was still on, championed moderate reconstruction but took delight in needling the President. Greeley printed a two-column letter from Tennesseean Emerson Etheridge in which the latter declared that Johnson was "one of the original instigators of the Rebellion," and asserted that he had proposed secession in 1856 if Frémont were elected, had repeatedly assailed the abolitionists, and had denounced Seward and the Republicans for the John Brown raid. Sumner and Henry Winter Davis joined with Greeley in clamoring for some form of Negro suffrage in the South. Ben Wade and Thad Stevens growled as they saw one southern state after another reconstructed on the Lincoln-Johnson plan. Stevens declared that, if something were not done, opposition to the President might melt away; he might even "be crowned king before Congress meets." [8]

Amid all these alarums and excursions the Weed-Seward forces were quietly at work cementing, block by block, conservative control of the Union party in New York State. Weed was the chief builder, keeping in touch with Seward, and working closely with Edwin D. Morgan, who, in 1863, had succeeded Preston King in the Senate. Another lieutenant was Henry J. Raymond, chairman of the national executive committee of the Union party. Elected to the House of Representatives in 1864, Raymond was supposed to be the administration leader in that body.

Weed did not get all the federal office appointments in the state that he wished—he pushed hard for Blatchford as Sub-Treasurer, only to be turned down by Secretary of the Treasury McCulloch. But his old henchman, James Kelly, was the New York postmaster; he kept his ally, Abram Wakeman, as surveyor of the port of New York; and he replaced Simeon Draper with Preston King as collector of the customs. This last was particularly important, or so it seemed at the time, for Weed relied upon King's loyalty and the latter was a confidant of the President.

As fall came on it was apparent that Weed had control of the

Union organization in New York State. At odds though he was with Governor Fenton, and carrying on a running battle with Greeley, he still controlled the state convention. His subsequent report to Seward that it was an "Old Fashioned convention" and that "we are all right in the State, and need only to be let alone" was borne out by a solid victory at the polls in November.

While Weed built up his power in New York State, he made clear his support of President Johnson and a lenient southern policy. He wrote to Seward and Stanton urging that the handcuffs be stricken from imprisoned Jefferson Davis, and recommending pardon for Alexander H. Stephens. The platform adopted by the state convention recommended Johnson's plan of reconstruction. On the subject of Negro suffrage it expressed only the timid hope that when the southern states were restored to their place in the Union they would give full rights of citizenship to all their people.

Seward's close collaborator did not at this time show any real interest in a political reorganization. A few extreme radicals might bolt the state ticket, he told Seward, but they could be spared. The test of friendship for Johnson and his policy would come in Congress, where it was possible that radicals and secessionists might unite in opposition to the President. He and Raymond waged war on the state Democracy in the campaign, and the Dictator also took a hand in the defeat that was administered to the New Jersey Democrats. These were neither the thoughts nor the actions of a man who contemplated a revamping of the political structure.[9] Nevertheless the enemies of himself and Seward in the Union party were many and, as events were to prove, his hold on the New York organization was uncertain.

Seward took a deep interest in Weed's activities, for he thought that the New York Dictator was on the right path. The Secretary of State was sure also that Johnson was moving along correct lines. His own ideas about rebuilding the nation were a logical development of his wartime views.

Seward had felt throughout the war that there was much latent devotion to the nation in the South; that, with the elimination of slavery, the power of the great plantation owners would be gone, and a new social and political order would come into being; that there would then be a greater unity of viewpoint between the two sections than there had ever been before. Granted that this was so, the southern people should be brought back into the Union as though they were prodigal sons returned to the family hearth.

Because of these beliefs, he had distrusted the Emancipation Proclamation, fearing that out of it might come servile war. Because of them, he had applauded Lincoln's plan for Louisiana and Arkansas. It was best, he felt, to tread delicately in approaching the Negro problem. It was best to view the rehabilitation of the rebellious states as a function of the national executive, rather than see them subjected to the tender mercies of the congressional radicals. He had been sure that love for the Union strengthened throughout the country as the insurgents weakened; that Lincoln's proposals would either be followed *in toto*, or would open the way to a satisfactory solution of the national embarrassments. When Charles J. Grady, assistant editor of the New York *Express*, wrote in August 1864 that Georgia would come over to the Union if only the people there were satisfied that the Negroes would be freed in such a way as not to injure the white masses, Seward saw this missive as confirmation of his point of view and sent the letter over to the White House.[10]

After the tragic events of April 1865, Seward had reason to feel that his views on reconstruction would have great weight with the country. The attempted assassination, together with Lincoln's known trust in him, brought a flood of testimonials to the value of his leadership. Caleb Cushing wrote that the populace regarded the Secretary of State as hallowed by his sufferings. Henry Bowen assured him that the *Independent* would now be pro-Seward. The Massachusetts Historical Society elected him an honorary member. Democrat Anson Herrick, ex-Congressman and now editor of the New York *Atlas*, said in an editorial that Seward's party affiliations and predilections were now lost sight of; that he would be judged on his great services to his country; and that he was in reality "one of the heroes of the war." [11] Such tributes alone were enough to make him feel that it was incumbent upon him to do what he could to help solve the great problem of the day.

Seward's basic aim in reconstruction remained what it had been as the war drew toward its close—the restoration of peace, harmony, and prosperity to the country at large. In that tragic winter before the war he had tried his best to prevent dismemberment. Now his object was to make the Union function smoothly again as a national entity. To do this there would have to be a reorganization in the erstwhile Confederate states that would enable them to win the confidence of the North. Conversely, there must be a northern policy that would inspire trust among southerners.[12]

Fundamental to Seward's thinking on reconstruction was his faith in the people of the South. The willingness of many former southern Whigs of good standing to co-operate with the national administration in rebuilding that section fortified him in this conviction. In July 1865 he told Browning that the southerners were anxious to return to their allegiance, and should be permitted to do so on terms that would reconcile them to the government. A year and a half later he was just as certain of "the honest and peaceful intentions of the citizens of the southern states." He clung to this conviction during the entire Johnson administration.[13]

Seward's general attitude toward the South did not at first extend to its leaders, who, he thought, should receive severe punishment. There was criticism of Johnson in England and France for putting a price on the head of Jefferson Davis, but Seward felt that the rebel chieftain should be treated with severity. Do not apologize for the attitude of the government toward Davis, he told Sanford. "Treason and Jefferson Davis are more odious, even in the eyes of the late Confederacy, than similar crimes are or would seem to be in any other part of the world." He favored a trial by military tribunal for the head of the rebellion and approved of Joseph Holt, judge-advocate general of the army, who conducted the prosecution of those connected with Lincoln's assassination in a most rigorous manner.

But Seward was naturally kind hearted and this, together with his trust in the South, soon brought him to a more forgiving frame of mind. By the middle of July 1865 he was urging delay of Davis's trial until the papers of the rebel government could be examined, and he told Browning that there should be very little hanging done. A couple of months later he was instrumental in having Alexander H. Stephens released on parole, and long before the end of the year he obtained pardons for scores of Confederate leaders. On one occasion he entertained one hundred southerners at his Washington establishment. "When you come home," he wrote to Fanny in

November 1865, "you will find our house the chief resort of the recently rebels."

This manifestation of a forgiving spirit aroused criticism among the radicals and vindictives. How, they asked, could he take these traitors to his bosom? They coupled such attacks with the charge that he was indifferent to the plight of the southern Negroes. He sought to counter these accusations in a way that was characteristically ingenious.

Thomas Corwin died that December and a memorial service was held, with Chief Justice Chase presiding, in the reception room of the Senate. Notice of this meeting came to the Cabinet only on the day it took place and in the most informal fashion, but Seward put in an appearance and spoke a few words. His tribute to the departed statesman emphasized Corwin's humanity and his love of country. Preoccupation on his part with one of those noble interests, Seward observed, had on occasion laid the Ohioan open to criticism for being indifferent to the other, an indifference that was, at the worst, unintentional. Seward hoped that "if we shall be found to have committed errors of administration, those errors will be found to have been such as were erroneously attibuted to him, and that we have erred unintentionally in deciding which of those two great causes at particular junctures were most imminently imperilled." [14]

If Seward gave pre-eminence to the re-establishment of national harmony, what had become of his humanitarian interest in the Negro? Where did that fit into his scheme of things, or had it disappeared? There is abundant evidence that it had not died out. During the war he contributed to the support of emancipated slaves in distressed circumstances. Danforth Blair Nichols, one of the founders of Howard University, and in charge of the wartime freedmen's camp near Washington, bore witness that "no Public Officer did more or showed more interest in the condition of the Freedmen than did the Secretary of State." After the war, when southerners were objecting strenuously to being garrisoned by Negro troops, Seward told Governor Perry of South Carolina that "no discrimination founded upon color, in the assignment of service, is intended or can be made by the government." His interest in stamping out the international slave trade remained keen, and he instructed John P. Hale, Minister to Spain, to suggest to the Spanish government that now would be a good time to emancipate the slaves in Cuba and Porto Rico. He told Bigelow in November 1865 that the condition of the freedmen was a subject of deep interest, and that "The establishment of the perfect equality of men of the African race with men of other races throughout the whole continent is a policy which the United States may hereafter be expected to cultivate with constancy and assiduity."

Nevertheless, despite all this, despite the success of the wartime experiment at Port Royal in demonstrating the Negro's initiative and ability to work on his own, Seward clung to his belief in the black man's inferiority. His views in this respect were probably reinforced by Louis Agassiz, whom he knew and whose opinions on the subject strikingly paralleled his own. Both men felt that finding the Negro a legitimate place in American society would be a slow and difficult undertaking; and Seward was sure that the solution of this problem must come as much as possible from within the southern states. So it is not surprising that when Henry Wilson demanded action to stop the re-enslaving of Negroes in the South, the Secretary of State remained unresponsive. Apparently he was ready to rest upon the Thirteenth Amendment as being, at least temporarily, a sufficient safeguard for the freedmen. In the speeches made during 1865 and 1866, he argued that the continued amelioration of the Negro's condition must and would go on, but just how he did not say.[15]

The gist of the matter was that Seward regarded the reconciliation of the southern whites to the Union so important that he was willing to postpone consideration of how and when the Negro should be put in the way of becoming a first-class citizen. Furthermore, he was dubious about immediate Negro suffrage where the blacks were preponderant in the population. The best thing to do, he felt, was to leave the question of suffrage to the states, where it was plainly left by the Constitution. There was not, he declared, any soundness at all in the American political system "if the personal or civil rights of each member of the State, white or black, freeborn or emancipated, native born or naturalized, are not more secure under the administration of State government than they would be under the administration of the National Government. Harmony is essential to Union, but harmony is impossible if the citizens of every

State are not left free from unconstitutional intervention in their civil rights by the Federal government." [16]

About the same time that he made this pronouncement, Seward had an interview with Charles Eliot Norton and Edwin L. Godkin, co-founders of the *Nation*. Editor Godkin, as the columns of the *Nation* bore evidence, was solicitous for the rights of the freedmen, contemptuous of Johnson's plan of reconstruction, and mildly critical of Seward. The Civil Rights Bill was in process of being passed over Johnson's veto, much to the joy of the *Nation*, and the interview was undoubtedly somewhat strained. In its course Seward declared, according to notes written out by Norton shortly afterward, that he was not at all concerned about the Negroes in the South; that he had no more concern for them than he had for the Hottentots; that they were God's poor and always would be, and "must take their level"; and that he was willing to trust their civil rights to the southern states.[17]

Seward was on the defensive in this interview, and when this was the case he could become pugnacious. It seems likely that Norton and Godkin felt his remarks were not truly representative of his point of view about the Negro. There was no immediate reaction to them in the columns of the *Nation*, but some months later that periodical became bitterly critical of Seward's wartime and post-war course.

Seward's position in regard to the southern Negro became the subject of adverse comment, both at home and abroad. He customarily refused to enter into any discussion of his political views or policies with his domestic correspondents, but he did defend himself in some detail in an exchange of letters with one of his foreign critics. This was Agénor Etienne, Comte de Gasparin, a French political writer who had published a study of the United States in 1861 and had been pro-North during the Civil War. Gasparin had sent a copy of his book to Seward in 1862, and thereafter between the two men there developed a desultory correspondence that became more animated at the close of the war.

Gasparin criticized the Johnson administration for its failure to give the Negro opportunities for social and political equality, and to these strictures Seward replied at some length. Constitutionally, he told the Count, the people of the South had to reorganize their own state governments. The national administration sought to extend amnesty in such a way as to exclude "all disloyal citizens and persistent upholders and defenders of slavery from all part in reorganization." Such were the wealthy slaveholders who had "conscripted the poor non-slaveholding loyal white men" into the rebel armies. Relieved of the power and threats of "the slaveholding capitalists," the loyalists would reorganize the civil power. When that was done the work of amnesty and restoration would be closed.

Gasparin complained that it was a strange policy to leave the fate of the freedmen to a South that had fought for four years to uphold slavery. Seward replied at length in a letter that was read by and presumably had the sanction of President Johnson.

The urgent need, he said, was to get the southern states back into their normal relationship with the Union. "This work cannot wait without danger of disorganization, anarchy, imbecility and ultimate disunion." To establish Negro suffrage would require a constitutional amendment. This would take precious time, and would involve a procedure "unknown equally to the Constitution itself, and to the habits of the American people." Furthermore, to force Negro suffrage upon the South would involve a policy of "centralization, consolidation and imperialism" that would be repugnant to the spirit of liberty, and that would require standing armies in time of peace. No administration had ever succeeded in maintaining such a standing army, and "no one has ever stood that attempted, or was even suspected of attempting to establish one. It is wiser, safer and surer to work out the problems of freedom through popular and Constitutional forms than it would be to receive them at the hands of a military despot, even if he could confer them." [18]

Seward's correspondence with Gasparin showed that he recognized the importance of the high regard for states' rights in the South, and his anxiety to have a maximum of southern co-operation in the reconstruction of the Union. Then, too, there was the need for speedy action. The South was face to face with the enormous problem of reconstructing its life, a problem complicated by the presence of a vast mass of men, women, and children who had been suddenly transformed from slaves into freedmen. Since he felt that the southern whites were eager to resume their proper relationship with the Union and willing to accept emancipation as a reality, why was it not best to work through the southern state governments, with a minimum of interference from Washington?

There was undoubtedly a degree of logic in this point of view, and there was in it some measure of consistency. As far back as 1844, when the slavery controversy was yet young, Seward had gone on record as believing that "humanity teaches and obliges us to feel sympathy for our white brethren before or at least equally with compassion for the black." Moreover the harmonious reconstitution of the Union seemed to him the paramount consideration. He was therefore willing to forget for the time being his early argument that "the basis of the American Constitution" was "the absolute equality of all men," and that there was a supreme law of creation based on the equality of nations, races, and men. This point of view was now pushed into the background, and the impassioned pleas of Henry Wilson and others that justice be done to the Negro fell on deaf ears.

The most logical interpretation of Seward's attitude toward the Negro in the Reconstruction period is that, at least for the time being, he was willing to rely on the southern white's sense of justice. There is evidence, not conclusive but impressive, of a willingness on the part of many southerners to give the Negro guarantees of life, liberty, and property that would have set him on the road to political and social equality. Immediately after the Civil War, Seward found such a disposition among the influential southern ex-Whigs of his acquaintance. After radical reconstruction ended there were similar indications, particularly in such older slave states as Virginia and South Carolina. In those states segregation was by no means uniform, many Negroes voted, and not a few held office.[19]

Had it not been for radical reconstruction, which did so much to foster hatred of compelled equality and to create a solid Democratic South, Seward's hopes might have been realized. But of this there can be no certainty. The road at best would have been long and hard.

~§ 30 §~

Seward and Johnson

As Seward wrestled with the formulation of a policy for reconstructing the Union, he had also to reconcile himself to Lincoln's death and to the presence of a new figure in the White House. The April tragedy was a great shock to the Secretary of State. Ease and harmony had characterized the relationship between him and his former chief, and four years of trial and struggle had forged between them bonds of affection. Seward drew up and presented to the Cabinet a proposal to purchase Ford's theater and convert it into a national shrine. But only Postmaster General Dennison approved the idea, and the project had to wait for a later day.

All that now remained were memories and vanished hopes. Seward had had reason to believe that he would be Lincoln's successor. Back in 1863 the President had said as much. Weed, writing about the assassination to his old friend Sanford, let fall an enigmatic comment—"Our highest prospects are suddenly and sadly disappointed"—adding that they really knew very little about Johnson.[1]

Seward being what he was, there was probably still another reason for his concern over the passing of his chief. Like Bigelow and Adams, he realized that martyrdom cast a halo over Lincoln that set him above other men. The manner of the President's demise, Bigelow told Seward, had transfigured him in the eyes of mankind. Adams confided the same opinion to his diary, adding that now Seward would never get the credit he deserved for the record of the

432

administration. The Secretary of State himself had no doubts as to Lincoln's place in history. He told Webb that it was not necessary to ask foreign governments to put on mourning for the martyred President. "His name is to grow greater, and that of all contemporaneous magistrates and sovereigns to grow smaller as time advances." He had sacrificed his life for human rights and his fame would be imperishable. If this were so, Seward's achievements would be overshadowed.[2]

Much the same thought was in the minds of many men. A story, probably apocryphal, that went the rounds a little later illustrated the point. According to this tale, Seward and Weed were standing one day before a statue of the martyred President and Seward remarked that, if Weed had played his cards correctly, he, Seward, would now be on that pedestal instead of Lincoln. Weed replied, "Well, Seward, wouldn't you rather be here with me than up there cast in bronze?"

But regrets about the past were useless, and to indulge in them for long was not Seward's nature. The important thing now was his position in the Cabinet, and this depended to some extent upon his past relations with the new Chief of State.

Seward confided to John Bigelow in 1868 that he had "dug Johnson out and had made him governor first and afterward Vice President." Bigelow put this in his diary, together with the reflection that the Secretary of State had been bitterly punished for his choice. There is no evidence that Seward was instrumental in making Johnson military governor of Tennessee, though Lincoln probably consulted him before making the appointment. There are, however, scattered indications of cordial relations during the war years, and considerable evidence that Seward had a hand in putting Johnson on the ticket with Lincoln at the Baltimore convention of 1864. Chauncey Depew remembered carrying to the convention a message from Seward which urged the delegates to give Johnson second place on the ticket, and another New York delegate, E. Delafield Smith, who knew Seward's views on the subject, headed a committee of New Yorkers that pleaded successfully with the Ohio delegation to go for Johnson.[3]

The Secretary of State also took a charitable point of view toward Johnson's performance at the inauguration of March 1864, when the incoming Vice President was under the influence of liquor. Welles and Stanton thought that the Tennesseean's rambling remarks indicated that he was either drunk or crazy, but Seward said it was emotion aroused by revisiting the Senate. A few days later he was more critical, but even then seemed unaware of any intoxication.[4]

The new President was of a very different stripe from his predecessor. Johnson still thought of himself as a states' rights Democrat of the Jeffersonian-Jacksonian tradition. Born a poor white, his sympathies lay with the yeoman farmers of the South, and he had spent his life fighting the southern planter aristocracy. He also distrusted the urban poor and told the British Minister Sir Frederick Bruce that qualifications for voting in the United States should be raised rather than lowered. At one time a slaveholder in a small way, he had come to accept the abolition of slavery as desirable, not because of any sympathy for or understanding of the Negroes who were, he felt, inferior to the whites, but because slavery benefited the aristocratic few. Hard-working, courageous, a lover of the Union which he believed must be restored by a policy of gentleness and kindness for the white masses, he was also tactless, often uncertain how to act, stubborn, and unable to compromise. This was the man with whom Seward would have to work closely during the next four years.

Johnson was no sooner in the White House than he was importuned to reorganize his Cabinet. Ben Butler tried hard to get Seward's place. The Blairs wanted Johnson to make Frank Blair Secretary of War and put Montgomery in the State Department. Seward's enemies began spreading the word that his time in the government was short. This was denied in a semi-official report. On April 24 the Washington correspondent of the New York *Times* declared that he was authorized to state that there would be no reorganization of the President's official family. Johnson, declared the *Times* reporter, "regards the preservation of the Secretary's life as second to that of no man in the nation, and impatiently awaits the time when he will have the benefit of Mr. Seward's counsel." Lewis D. Campbell, prominent Ohioan and close friend of the President, bore similar testimony in a letter to Weed. On May 9 and again on May 12 the President and members of the Cabinet called on

Seward, who was still an invalid in his house on Lafayette Square. By the end of May Weed could write to Sanford that the Secretary of State was sure he would have the "full confidence" of the President.[5]

As for the South, Johnson's initial inclination had been toward leniency. On the day after the assassination he told the Cabinet that his policy would be in essentials that of Lincoln, but in the days that followed his denunciation of traitors filled radical members of Congress with joy. Sumner, who saw him repeatedly during this period found him deprecating haste in getting the southern states back into the Union. The President declared that there should be a period of probation, during which all loyal people without distinction of color must be treated as citizens and take part in the proceedings for reorganization. His theme was justice to the colored race, and he told Sumner "there is no difference between us."

Seward, like Johnson, as has been shown in the previous chapter, was at first inclined to be severe with the leaders of the rebellion. Treason might seem a venial sin in the eyes of Europeans, he declared, but it was not so regarded by Americans. There is no indication, however, that his fundamental views regarding reconstruction had changed and, though his convalescence was slow and he spoke with great difficulty, he was in communication with the White House. He must have discussed with the President the policy to be followed toward the South. Johnson's proclamations of May 29 on amnesty and the reorganization of North Carolina (so inconsistent with what he had told Chase, Sumner, and other radicals) were in line with Seward's ideas.

The amnesty proclamation granted pardon and restoration of property (save slaves) to all who had rebelled, with the exception of certain classes such as the high officials of the Confederacy and those owning property worth over $20,000. Even these could apply for pardons that would be liberally extended. As to North Carolina, the President appointed a provisional governor under whom steps would be taken to create a state government and elect representatives to Congress. This proclamation set qualifications for voting that made it most unlikely that colored persons would participate in the state's reorganization, and the radicals greeted it with great indignation.[6]

While Johnson and Seward agreed as to the general policy of reconstruction, it is unlikely that the relationship between the two men became extremely close during the summer of 1865. Seward's health remained poor, the death of Frances and concern over Frederick and Fanny were distracting influences, and he could only slowly assume the burdens of the State Department. Johnson, feeling his way, sought advice from many men, some of whom were inimical to Seward. There is evidence that the President promised, or appeared to promise, leading Democrats that Seward's stay in the State Department would be short, and rumors of this may well have reached the ears of the Secretary of State.[7]

Seward told Welles that fall that Johnson was friendly and confiding with him, more communicative even than Lincoln, but this may be taken with a grain of salt. Perhaps more indicative of their actual relationship was an outright statement by Seward to Chauncey M. Depew and a thinly disguised hint to James Watson Webb that Johnson's use of the patronage was not to his liking. There was also the advice he gave Weed when the latter came to Washington in December. Seward told him to keep away from Johnson, writing subsequently that experience showed it was best not to call upon Presidents except when it was necessary. There was in this admonition more than a note of caution.[8]

If any of their contemporaries had doubts as to their agreement on reconstruction policy, however, these doubts must have been resolved by a speech made at Auburn during the New York State campaign that year. After a few introductory remarks, Seward gave a rosy picture of a nation at peace, its surviving combatants fraternizing in a spirit of brotherly comradeship, and the whole country standing "collected and composed, firmer, stronger, and more majestic than ever before, without one cause of dangerous discontent at home, and without an enemy in the world."

Lincoln was now with the immortal Washington, Seward declared, but Johnson was Lincoln's fit successor. His was the same plan of reconstruction, "the only possible plan which then or ever afterward could be adopted." An essential feature of it was its voluntary acceptance by the insurrectionary states, which thereby "submit themselves to and recognize the national authority." It was never "the expectation or purpose of this Government that the southern states should be subjugated," but rather that, by a judicious mixture of power and persuasion they be brought "to a condition in which they would voluntarily return to their allegiance."

Seward then extolled Johnson's firmness of purpose and his ability to rise above partisanship for the nation's good. He also spoke a good word for the members of the Cabinet, past and present, even including Montgomery Blair.

This effort at a general reconciliation produced mixed emotions in the national audience. One Democrat called it a "Uriah Heap speech." Adams felt that its calm judgment, high principle, and magnanimity placed Seward "among the highest statesmen ever known in America." The French Minister, Montholon, thought it was designed to strengthen his position in the Cabinet, but had had the opposite effect. There could be no doubt in anyone's mind that it put all of his prestige and power squarely behind the President's plan. This was the more important because the doubts of moderates and the wrath of radical Republicans were rising over the speed and manner of Johnsonian reconstruction. They were also aroused by the South's hostility to Negro suffrage, and what appeared to be its callous indifference to the welfare of the freedmen.

Rumblings of this discontent reached Seward from various parts of the North. The distinguished Philadelphia lawyer Benjamin H. Brewster wrote of rumors that power would be handed over to traitors and their abettors, and that the White House was the scene of pardon broking, corruption, drunken brawls, and "wild licentious lust." He implored Seward and Stanton to support the President "in the hour of his temptation and affliction." Henry Wilson, about to come back to Washington for his third consecutive term in the Senate, sent a stern warning. Burning with indignation over the treatment of Negroes in the South, Wilson declared that on the opening of Congress the annulment of all laws against the freedmen would be pressed. He was not satisfied, he asserted, with the supineness of the administration in the face of such legislation, and the recent elections in the southern states showed how misplaced was confidence in the good intentions of the rebels. Sumner denounced Seward, terming him responsible for Johnson's reconstruction policy, which was "the greatest and most criminal error ever committed by any government." He brought Welles a newspaper containing a memorial for the President's impeachment.[9]

There is evidence that both Seward and Johnson wanted more liberal treatment than the South was disposed to provide for the emancipated slaves. In August 1865, Johnson sent a telegram to the provisional governor of Mississippi urging extension of the franchise to all Negroes who could read and write, and to all who owned real estate worth at least $250 (the same property qualification was in the New York State constitution). Governor Sharkey laid this before the state convention, but that body adjourned without any such action. James G. Blaine later declared that Seward's disappointment over the South's failure to come to grips with the Negro problem was well known to the Secretary's intimate friends.[10]

Seward also had occasional misgivings as to the attitude of the South toward the Union. In December, A. S. Wallace, a prominent South Carolina Unionist, wrote urging that the southern states be forced to repudiate their war debts. The South Carolina legislature had adjourned without even touching the subject. Wallace described the state legislature as largely ultra, with not more than twenty Unionists out of 124 members in the house, and a like proportion in the senate. This letter impressed Seward, and he took it over to the White House. Such doubts, however, were not fundamental. More in accord with his inner convictions was a remark he made one evening to dinner guests Bruce and Burlingame. He had no fear, he said, of the South's loyalty. That section was dependent on the North for support in keeping the Negro population in order.[11]

What did Seward think was the true role of the President in reconstructing the South? Lincoln, in his last message to Congress had declared that, with the coming of peace, the power of the Executive to deal with the rebellious states "would be greatly diminished." Seward had much the same opinion. While he was ready to defend Johnson's program, he recognized that Congress also had prerogatives. In September he drew up a letter to one of the provisional governors which acknowledged that Congress would have something to say about the newly formed state constitutions. This comment aroused Johnson's displeasure, and he saw to it that Seward took out the reference to congressional participation in reconstruction.[12] The Secretary of State, where executive-legislative relations were concerned, had a Confucian-like propensity for the middle way which was alien to the dogmatic Johnson. In November there were further evidences that the two men did not see eye to eye on the role Congress should play.

Undoubtedly at Johnson's request, Seward prepared a draft for the presidential message to Congress. It was distinctly placatory in tone. Where efficient and loyal state governments had been established, this document declared, it would be necessary and just to receive their representatives into Congress, but the power to do this lay with that body. He would leave it there "with entire confidence in the wisdom, prudence and patriotism of the National Legislature." Furthermore, "with the sanction of Congress," he would continue to hold such control over the insurrectionary states as would be necessary to prevent anarchy and favor the efforts at reconstruction. Once those states abolished slavery by organic law, accepted the Thirteenth Amendment, and repudiated the debts and obligations of the pretended secession he would be content, "so far as depends on the executive department of the government," to accept them and their citizens as equal members of the Union.

This draft would not have satisfied the ultra champions of Negro rights, but it did leave the way open for adjustments between presidential and congressional views. The message Johnson sent to Congress contained no commendations of congressional wisdom and patriotism, nor did it contain any suggestions for collaboration between Congress and the President.[13]

The North was increasingly disturbed and uneasy when, on December 1, Congress began to assemble in Washington. Stevens, Wade, and other extremists came to the capital ready for a fight with the President, but realizing that a majority of their colleagues were not yet in a mood for open battle, they sought delay until sentiment against Johnson could be whipped up. At a Republican caucus on the evening of December 2, Stevens offered a resolution for a joint committee of fifteen members from both houses of Congress to inquire into the conditions in the southern states, particularly as to whether or not they were entitled to representation in either the House or the Senate. Acceptance of this proposal would postpone indefinitely the admission of the southern representatives already elected and would cast doubt upon the validity of the state governments reconstituted in the South.

Raymond was at this caucus and voted for the Stevens resolution. He probably did not fully comprehend its object, but late that evening or the next day he talked with Seward. The latter, though engulfed in the work of the State Department, was keeping close watch on congressional maneuvers, and the news of the Stevens action showed him what was in the wind. He told Raymond that North Carolina would be restored to control of her own affairs just as soon as the Executive Department received official notification of that state's ratification of the Thirteenth Amendment. This would head off the radical plan for postponing readmission and, hopefully, bring the whole scheme to the ground.[14]

The election in the Tar Heel State scarcely showed enthusiasm for the outcome of the war, or for the abolition of slavery, but by a very light vote the state did ratify the amendment. Johnson thereupon ordered Provisional Governor Holden to turn over his office to the newly elected Governor Worth.

Twenty-seven states, including eight that had gone out of the Union, had now ratified the amendment, and on December 18 Seward proclaimed it a part of the Constitution. In so doing he took pains to announce that the whole number of states in the Union was thirty-six, thus including all the reconstructed states. On the same day Johnson informed Congress that reconstruction was proceeding in a most satisfactory fashion, and that sectional animosity was "rapidly merging itself into a spirit of nationality." Three days later Raymond declared in the House that the rebel states had never left the Union, and made a stout assault on the Stevens contention that, until some future time when new states were carved out of them, they should be treated as territories.

As the administration did its best to make its program an accomplished fact Seward, characteristically enough, was in touch with one of the radicals in the House of Representatives. On December 19 James M. Ashley, prominent abolitionist Congressman from Ohio, sent over to the Secretary of State a bill that he had introduced prescribing congressional conditions for reconstruction. Ashley called Seward's attention to a provision for recognizing the reorganized government of Tennessee, adding that he hoped to have "the benefit of any suggestions you may have to make when I see you." [15]

As Seward strove to keep his hand in with both the President and Congress, the radicals were not idle. They circulated reports that Johnson was relying on the returned states to support him for election in 1868, and that he was in collusion with New York State Democratic leaders. Sumner declared that Johnson's portrayal of the situation in the South was "like the whitewashing message of Franklin Pierce with regard to the atrocities in Kansas." Seward wanted Raymond made chairman of the House Committee on Foreign Relations, but the Speaker, Schuyler Colfax, awarded that place to Banks, with Raymond second in command. The latter, disturbed by the look of things, told Weed that the House membership in the Joint Committee of Fifteen was "thoroughly radical" and that Stevens appeared to have the House Republicans under his control. The whispering campaign against Johnson continued unabated.[16]

During the first part of January the Committee of Fifteen began to wrestle with the knotty question of how representation of Negroes could be provided by Congress. It requested Johnson to take no further steps in reconstruction for the time being, and the President replied that he wished for harmony of action between Congress and the Executive and would do nothing more for the present.

Johnson could have refused the request of the Committee of Fifteen, but it was politic for him to consent. Some members of the House and the Senate—Stevens, Sumner, Wilson, and the like—had come to Washington resolved to lock horns with the administration, and Stevens could exert real influence in a caucus. Nevertheless, Raymond's nervousness about extremism had little foundation. The Committee was not loaded with radicals. They were a minority in the House, and this was even more the case in the Senate. Seward, who watched the situation closely, had few qualms. In January he took a four weeks' holiday and went off on a Caribbean cruise, saying that he wanted to show the factionist element in Congress how indifferent he was to them.[17]

The President would have done well at this juncture to cultivate the confidence of congressional moderates and conservatives in his policy. Almon M. Clapp, a Buffalo politician and friend of Seward, came down to Washington and talked with various and sundry Congressmen. He discovered that they felt the President had no use for their counsel. Clapp believed that, by a little effort, Johnson could put himself on a friendly footing with a majority in both the House and the Senate. Looking back on the situation some months later, Senator Morgan was sure that Johnson could have put together an effective organization in Congress and rendered the extremists powerless.[18] But the President made no such move.

In January, Lyman Trumbull, chairman of the Judiciary Committee in the Senate, introduced a bill extending and enlarging the powers of the Freedmen's Bureau. It passed the Senate 37 to 10, only Democrats voting in opposition, and on February 6 passed the House by a large majority and again by an almost complete division between Republicans and Democrats. Both Morgan and Raymond voted for the bill. Johnson vetoed it on February 19, on the ground that it was unnecessary, unconstitutional, and expensive class legislation that put too much power and enormous patronage in the hands of the President. He also challenged the right of Congress to legislate for the southern states in their absence. Apparently there was nothing good that he could say about the measure.

Before he drew up his veto message, Johnson asked Seward, Welles, and others for their ideas on the subject, and the Secretary of State composed a draft written in the first person which he sent over to the White House. A comparison of this draft with the message sent to Congress shows that the President and the head of the State Department approached the bill from noticeably different points of view.

Seward would veto "not without reluctance." He praised the Bureau as being "in effective operation with beneficent results," and declared that the freedmen were entitled to adequate protection. It might develop that a prolongation of the measure was necessary. If such were the case, he would be willing to accept, even to recommend, the necessary legislation. He was pleased to see that the bill now passed contemplated restoration of the southern states in all their constitutional relations to the Union, but since the legislative and executive departments had some differences of opinion as to reconstruction, he thought it "important that Congress and the

President should first agree upon what actually constitutes a restoration" before the passage of any such measure.

Seward argued with some cogency that this Freedmen's Bureau bill was unnecessary. Slavery was ended. The South was accepting this in good faith and, in all probability the courts would furnish adequate protection for the freedmen. All the states should be represented in Congress before the passage of any new bill. Nevertheless, the message that he proposed sending to Capitol Hill was in many respects an olive branch that held out the distinct possibility of co-operation on reconstruction between the two ends of Pennsylvania Avenue. Welles thought that the Secretary of State wanted compromise with Congress, and this impression was correct.[19]

Influential New Yorkers—Bryant, Bennett, Senator Morgan, Hamilton Fish, and David Dudley Field among them—sponsored a mass meeting of Democrats and Republicans in support of Johnson's veto. They scheduled the meeting on Washington's birthday, to take place in New York at the Cooper Institute, and asked Seward to speak. Apparently he hesitated, for on February 20 Weed telegraphed urging him to come; but he finally accepted.

A crowd packed the Institute and spilled over into the street outside the hall. Businessmen and politicians came to hear one who was generally regarded as the spokesman for the administration. The painfully scarred face, so reminiscent of tragic events, and the aura that clung about him as a leader in the cause of freedom and now in the cause of peace assured him a tumultuous reception.

Seward spoke in a vein at times humorous and at times deeply serious. The ship of state was not in peril, he said. It had been rescued, and only minor difficulties remained. Some thought it might now safely enter the harbor. Others said wait. Of course there was an occasional reef ahead, the vessel might roll a little, and a few politicians and statesmen, including himself, might be washed overboard, but it would not much matter if this were the case. Both pilots were honest and sincere. There was merely a difference of opinion between them.

The Union was restored and slavery abolished, "not with freedmen and refugees abandoned to suffering and persecution, but with freedmen employed in productive, self-sustaining industry, with refugees under the protection of law and order." Things had come out all right. The trouble was over the fact that some had not had a hand in bringing about "the happy termination."

The President's way of reconstruction was the only one that could be successfully used, Seward declared. Sooner or later, loyal men from the now loyal states would be admitted to Congress, and then restoration would be complete. The idea of reducing the rebel states to territorial status had been rejected by Lincoln and was now rejected by Johnson. If it was ever practicable it was now too late for "so mad a measure," one that would be impossible to execute without imperial power. Johnson was not an autocrat willing "to plunge this country into a civil war for a political chimera."

The Committee of Fifteen had so far produced only a Constitutional amendment "to compel the excluded states to equalize suffrage upon the penalty of an abridgment of representation." He did not discuss its merits. It was expected to fail in Congress, and in any case it implied a full restoration of the southern states. Therefore it was not really a plan of reconstruction. The Committee was merely acting in an obstructive manner.

The conflict over the Freedmen's Bureau bill was relatively unimportant, said the Secretary of State. Both the President and Congress agreed that the Bureau should not be kept after the states were admitted and the transition period ended. Johnson thought that period was nearly over, and Seward agreed that this was the case. Congress thought not, and believed that the power and scope of the measure should be extended; "that more patronage, more money and more power would, like Thompson's door plate, purchased at auction by Mrs. Toodles, be a good thing to have in a house." The President should not be blamed for denying this, or for "declining imperial powers." [20]

Many of Seward's friends and associates thought this a great speech. Secretary of the Treasury McCulloch called it "happy, pertinent, conclusive." Bigelow wrote that it was "so clear, so wise, so statesmanlike, so clever." Southerners applauded.

But others were not so kind. His old friend Joseph Warren declared in blistering language that it showed Seward had deserted his party and was now side by side with Copperheads, rebel sympathizers, and would-be re-enslavers of the Negro. Benjamin Brewster wrote that he would follow Seward's lead, but that he was sorely tried. Bates confided to his diary that it was an attempt to be all things to all men and he did not see how Seward could escape the contempt of both sides in the quarrel. The *Nation* declared that the speech ignored a fundamental question—was the South being restored according to democratic and republican principles, or in accordance with those of a ruling class whose attitude was basically aristocratic.[21]

The great dailies distributed Seward's speech over the land, and he had his chief clerk frank out copies from the State Department. It was a clever attempt at propitiation, well calculated to appeal to his audience and to the country at large. Its light touches, especially coupling Congress with Mrs. Toodles of *Dombey and Son*, were designed to make faintly ridiculous the moral indignation of the extremists. Nevertheless it unduly minimized the crisis now upon the nation, gave an over-optimistic picture of the situation of the freedmen, and painted in too lurid colors the consequences of delay in reconstruction.

The President was responsible for some of the criticism leveled at Seward. He, too, had spoken on Washington's birthday, addressing a crowd of well-wishers at the White House. His extemporaneous and rambling speech showed his devotion to reconciliation of the sections, and to the Union. He defended his plan of reconstruction with some skill. But, excited by the enthusiastic crowd, he launched into an attack on the Committee of Fifteen, declared that Stevens and Sumner labored to destroy the fundamental principles of government, boasted that he had been a good tailor, and asserted that he was not afraid of those in high places who wanted to get him out of the way, possibly by assassination.

The effect of this effort, coupled as it was with the veto, was lamentable. Where Seward had soothed, Johnson inflamed. Brewster wrote of the violent indignation Johnson's speech produced in Philadelphia. "The hot breath and heavy panting of excited men was felt by me even when I was busy in court." Judge Ransom Balcom in Binghamton declared that the veto caused great excitement, and made it difficult for prudent men to prevent violent denunciations of the President by prominent members of the party. Things had quieted down, and then came the speech at the White House. Now men suspected that Johnson would go over to the Copperheads, or attempt to form a new party, and this did great harm. Joseph Warren called the speech "a maudlin performance." William Schouler wrote from Boston that Seward's speech would have made everything right, if it had not been for Johnson's remarks.[22]

Both Seward and Weed, ignoring the dubious aspects of Johnson's blast, congratulated him on his effort. Seward, exhilarated by his own reception in New York, telegraphed that the President's speech was "triumphant," the Union restored and the country safe, a statement, so the *Nation* remarked, that would "always remain among the curiosities of telegraphic literature." The Secretary of State sent word in much the same vein to Senator Morgan and to Frederick, though in both instances he omitted to mention the President's effort. He evidently thought that, due chiefly to his own exertions, the crisis was over.[23]

There was a temporary lull as excitement over the veto and the White House speech abated. The President talked in conciliatory fashion with Governor Cox of Ohio, and that state's Senator Sherman defended Johnson on the floor of the Senate. But more trouble was in the offing.

Senator Trumbull reported from the Judiciary Committee a bill declaring that all persons born in the United States and not subject to any foreign power (save Indians, not taxed) were citizens of the country, and had the civil rights of citizens in every state and territory. This measure passed both the House and the Senate with heavy majorities, the votes against it being chiefly those of Democrats; by the middle of March it was on the President's desk.

Seward was now keeping in close and careful touch with the White House. A letter from Judge Ryerson, praising the New York speech but regretting expressions in Johnson's, was copied, obviously for the President to see, with the expressions of regret omitted. Seward told Gasparin that he and the President were consulting on all communications affecting the national welfare. Johnson, determined to veto the Civil Rights bill, once more asked his Secretary of State to prepare the draft of a veto message, and Seward complied.[24]

Seward thought it might be well to pass a law declaring that Negroes were citizens, though he, himself, had no doubts on that score. He was still anxious, as his draft for the veto showed, to find common ground with Congress. He began by commending the bill's objective, adding that his reservations concerned the form, rather than the substance. He would not quarrel with the intent of section one of the bill, its very heart according to Trumbull, which contained the provisions regarding citizenship and civil rights. As to this section, Seward merely observed that he would "prefer," be "better pleased," if it simply stated that all citizens, irrespective of race, color, or previous condition of servitude, were "entitled in every state and territory in the United States to equal and impartial civil rights." In regard to subsequent sections he raised some objections regarding constitutionality and phraseology, and made it clear that he felt it invaded the rights of the states.[25]

Trumbull conferred with Johnson as to the provisions of the bill while it was in process of formulation and believed that he would sign it. The President at least hesitated before he made up his mind. On March 27 he sent the measure back to Capitol Hill with his veto, a moderately worded but decisive document. He condemned section one as discriminatory and unwise, and declared that the whole proposal was contrary to the very nature of the Union. Seward had given him a letter from Weed urging that, if the bill were vetoed, there be some evidence of Johnson's philanthropic sentiments and sympathies for the Negroes. All the President did was to state that he recognized his obligation to "protect and defend that class of our people" when it was necessary and could be done in constitutional fashion.[26]

On April 6 the Senate overrode the veto, 33 to 15. Morgan voted with the majority. "It seems to me this is terrible," wrote Raymond in a hasty note to Seward, "but I don't know how his [Morgan's] purpose can be changed."

Two days later, Morgan wrote to Weed explaining his action. "Three days before we came to the vote on the Civil Rights Bill," he declared, he had made earnest efforts with Fessenden and the President to obtain a compromise measure. The effort had been a failure, due to Johnson's objections to section one. "It was then *this* bill or *nothing*. I believed something should pass both houses of Congress, and *this* will. . . . There are many ways in which it will do good. The South will become much more sensible and there is need enough for that." Morgan added that, if the President had confined his objections to the second section of the bill (which prescribed punishments for violation of the rights laid down in section one), he could have been sustained, adding that this was "a matter of *some* consideration. . . ." [27]

On April 9 the House overrode the veto by 122 to 41 and the Civil Rights bill became a finality. So did the breach between the President and Congress.

The "ifs" of history are never certainties. Nevertheless the odds are great that, if either Lincoln or Seward had been in the White House during the winter of 1866, there would have been a meeting of minds between the President and Congress that would have moved the ship of state into much calmer waters than those that lay just ahead.

⊰ 31 ⊱

Political Disaster

Seward was a prey to conflicting emotions as battle raged between the White House and Capitol Hill. He had ambitious plans in the field of foreign relations, and for these he needed the support of both President and Congress. If he lost that of the former, he would be dismissed. If he could not get along with the latter, his projects could be wrecked by attacks upon himself and upon his ministers and consuls abroad, and by the Senate's rejection of treaties. He had to keep at least a measure of favor with Congress, and yet he felt sure that the South must be given much freedom in the business of reconstruction, an attitude that was gall and wormwood to the radicals in Congress. It was a difficult situation, and he picked his way with care.

During the spring and early summer of 1866, he took advantage of two opportunities to show his loyalty to his chief. The first of these was in connection with the application of Colorado Territory for statehood. Colorado's proposed constitution made no provision for Negro suffrage, but Johnson's opponents pushed an enabling act through Congress, for the two Senators who would represent the state were supposed to be against the President's reconstruction policy. Probably for the same reason, though others such as an insufficiency of population were adduced, Johnson determined to veto.

Only three months before, Seward had told a New York audience

"You can never keep states out of this Union, never, no never!" He would not hold a state in a territorial condition "a day longer than I should be compelled." Now he apparently felt compelled to do so, for when Johnson asked him to draft a veto message he complied. The draft that came over from the State Department to the White House, save for minor changes of phraseology, was the same as that of the message Johnson sent to Congress.[1]

Another manifestation of Seward's desire to keep in line with the President came in connection with the congressional furor over James Harvey, Minister to Portugal. On March 24, 1866, Harvey wrote a private letter to Seward severely criticizing Congress for its attitude toward the administration's policy, and for its disposition to grant Negro suffrage in the South. Seward took this letter over to the White House, as he was in the habit of doing with letters that he thought would interest the President. Johnson read it, was impressed, and asked that it be published.

The Secretary of State could not have been enthusiastic about this proposal. He knew that many of the radicals were as suspicious of him as they were of Johnson, and even regarded him as the real author of the President's policy. He knew, too, that the consular and diplomatic appropriations bill would be likely to run into heavy weather when it came before Congress that spring. Nevertheless he bowed to the President's wishes, and sent the letter to the New York *Times*.

Publication of Harvey's missive produced a congressional storm. The House insisted upon cutting off Harvey's salary, the Senate concurred, and it was done. The whole appropriations bill received the severest scrutiny, and the Senate showed itself indisposed even to grant the prayer of twenty-five clerks in the State Department for an increase in their meager salaries.

The Harvey letter gave the critics of the administration an opportunity not only to punish the offending Minister but also, by their action and by oratorical fireworks, to strike at the President and the Secretary of State. When shortly thereafter Rufus King, Minister to Rome, asked permission to leave the Eternal City during the coming summer, Seward noted on this request that every indulgence taken by a public officer exposed him to assaults for which the State Department had to defend him. The situation in the United States, he added, was "revolutionary so far as the party is concerned, and such favors ought not to be asked." [2]

While the radicals fulminated over Colorado and Harvey, the Joint Committee on Reconstruction slowly matured the proposal that eventually became the Fourteenth Amendment. This declared that all persons born or naturalized in the United States were citizens of the United States and of the states where they had residence, and that no state should deprive them of their rights as citizens. It penalized any state that disfranchised any adult male citizens by reducing its representation in Congress. It prohibited from office-holding those who had taken oath to uphold the federal Constitution and had then engaged in rebellion. It declared the Confederate debt void and the debt of the United States valid. This amendment, destined to be so important a century later in the struggle over human rights, represented a triumph of northern moderate opinion over such radicals as Stevens and Sumner. Most southerners regarded it as severely punitive, but it was mild compared to what was to follow.

Johnson polled the Cabinet as to its attitude toward the amendment, and Seward's opposition to the proposal earned the President's emphatic approbation. Nevertheless the Secretary of State was still trying to maintain his influence at the other end of Pennsylvania Avenue. Stevens introduced a bill in the House that embodied features of the Fourteenth Amendment and, presumably for its author's benefit, Seward penciled suggestions for revision on the copy of the measure. In doing so he left substantially untouched what eventually became the vital first and second sections of the amendment. It is at least worthy of note that Raymond and Morgan, outstanding members of the New York team in Congress, voted for the amendment on its final passage. The New York *Times*, which reflected Seward's opinions more closely than any other newspaper, declared that if Congress would accept this proposal as its answer to the reconstruction problem, the prospects of party peace and national unity would be wonderfully enhanced.

Seward forwarded official certificates of the amendment to the governors of the states so promptly that Welles was disgusted and Johnson declared that it had been done without executive approval. Nor did the Secretary of State share Johnson's heartburnings about its ratification by Tennessee. When that state's representatives came back to Congress in the summer of 1866, Seward welcomed the returned prodigals with a dinner of fatted calf served up in a variety of ways.[3] He obviously hoped that the amendment would not be a source of further trouble between the Chief Executive and the radicals on Capitol Hill.

Seward's hopes of an adjustment between President and Congress were thwarted by Johnson's stubborn opposition to the amendment. The President advised the southern states not to accept it, none save Tennessee did so, and the struggle with Congress intensified. With it there appeared much talk about a reorganization of parties, talk which was logical enough, for the political situation was little short of chaotic. To understand the significance of this development, and Seward's reaction to it, it is necessary to examine the attitude of the Democratic party and of the President toward a political reshuffling, and also the course of New York politics in 1865 and 1866.

There can be no doubt that Johnson wished to be elected President in his own right. His public and private comments on the political situation, his gratification when James Gordon Bennett characterized him as the logical candidate for the succession, the judgment of men who knew him well, all demonstrate that he nursed the not-so-smothered flame. But that the party which had made him Vice President would nominate him in 1868 for the presidency became every day more improbable. He therefore had need of a national political organization that would support his reconstruction policy and bring it into triumphant operation. There was some reason to believe that such a party might be made to appear. He was, as Bennett termed him, "the man with two coat-tails," one who could easily command the support of many Democrats as well as that of conservative Republicans.

There were, however, difficulties in the way of creating such a national movement. One was the President's natural hesitancy to make a clean break with the Union party machine. Instead, he appeared to be waiting for Democrats and conservative Republicans to take the initiative and in a spontaneous movement coalesce around him as their leader. A second factor was his inability to use the patronage in such a way as to satisfy both conservative Republicans and Democrats. A third factor was the attitude of the Democratic party itself.[4]

The Democracy had encountered rough weather during the past six years. War Democrats had deserted it during the great conflict, and it still labored under the stigma of having declared the war a failure. Its ranks were disorganized by differences over reconstruction, and by the often contradictory aims of commercialists, industrialists, and farmers. Nevertheless, there was evidence that it could re-emerge as a great national party. It had a noble tradition to which it could point with pride. With the coming of peace many of the War Democrats who had joined the Union party were drifting back to their old allegiance. And the Democracy could count upon the voters of the returning southern states to strengthen it at the polls.

What chance was there, then, of a third party, formed as an amalgam of Democrats and conservative Republicans? There was very little chance, and the attitude of leading Democrats speedily made this apparent. Loud in their protests of devotion to the President and his reconstruction policy, when it came to the distribution of state and national patronage they showed an inveterate propensity to demand it for none but deserving members of their own political guild.

Furthermore, where Seward was concerned Democrats displayed a vigorous hostility. The Blairs hated him with an undying hatred, and Samuel L. M. Barlow, a leader of the New York Democracy, declared that Democrats could not unite with him on any question whatever. Godkin's *Nation*, surveying the political scene in the spring of 1866, thought the possibility of a new party was dim. Not only would the Democratic rank and file dislike being known as Conservatives, but also they would have to accept some distasteful leaders. Seward in particular, said the *Nation*, "is their peculiar aversion. Their leaders hate him cordially, but the rank and file abhor him with an intensity which the leaders could not control if they would. Yet what would the new party be without him?" [5]

In the midst of these trying circumstances, Thurlow Weed undertook to remould the Union party in New York State on a conservative basis. His means to this end were twofold. He sought to control the principal appointments to office, state and federal, so that through these appointees his hand would distribute the host of lesser offices. He also undertook to establish with leading Democrats working agreements that would virtually create a new party, and leave isolated and bereft of power the radical Republicans who looked to Governor Reuben E. Fenton and Congressman Roscoe Conkling as their leaders.[6] In doing this he had the co-operation of the New York *Times* and the Albany *Evening Journal*. He also kept in touch with Senator Morgan and with Seward, and was in close contact with certain Democrats, chief among whom was Dean Richmond, a wealthy railroad man and a power in the state's Democratic machine.

So far as patronage was concerned, the most important office in the state was that of collector of the port of New York. On August 15, 1865, Johnson appointed Preston King to that position. King replaced an old Whig and Weed-Seward stalwart, Simeon Draper. The new collector took the post reluctantly and only "at the solicitation of friends," according to Weed's *Autobiography*. One of these undoubtedly was Weed himself, for this appointee was to be a key figure in the restructuring of New York politics. Close to the President and a former Democrat, King played an important role during the next few months, though with tragic results to himself. His appointment, Weed told Seward after the 1865 election was over, "accomplished all I promised. Without it the state would have been demoralized and lost. Now it is fixed with the President and for his policy." [7]

Weed's assertion of triumph followed hard on a campaign in which the state's Union party approved the President's policy and swept to a decisive victory over the Democrats. But then the New York skies began to lower. King, overwhelmed by the problems of the role in which he had been cast, became a prey to morbid fears of ruin and disgrace, and on November 13 committed suicide. The key post which he occupied at once became an object of contention, with radicals, conservatives, and Democrats fighting over who should be his successor.

What followed was a comedy of political confusion that helped to frustrate Weed's plans. He recommended at least half a dozen candidates, but Johnson and Secretary of the Treasury McCulloch, to say nothing of Congress, could not agree on King's successor. There was what seemed like endless delay, and the post remained vacant for six months. Finally Johnson appointed Henry A. Smythe, a New York banker of uncertain political antecedents who owed nothing to Weed and proved to be most unreliable, so far as the latter's political plans were concerned.[8]

Despite this setback, the reorganization Weed undertook appeared to prosper until irrepressible conflict developed between President and Congress. As that struggle grew in intensity and popular sentiment swung in behind the radicals, Weed's troubles multiplied. By the end of May 1866 it began to look as though Fenton would be renominated for governor on the Union ticket and would thereafter be a formidable candidate for the United States Senate. In June, Raymond warned that any "safe reorganization" was unlikely, and Seward received the blackest kind of reports as to the increasing strength of radicalism in the state. Three months earlier George Dawson, Albany postmaster and editor of the Albany *Evening Journal*, had declared that when the time came for a fight with the radicals the *Journal* would not skulk. But by the end of July the *Journal* had deserted the President's camp, Seward's enemies were pointing gleefully to its change of heart, and Weed asked Dawson to resign as postmaster on the ground that he was embarrassing the Secretary of State. That fall the Union party's New York State organization was under radical control, and Weed was not even present at the convention. It renominated Reuben Fenton for governor and endorsed the Fourteenth Amendment. Succeeding events were to spell complete disaster for the Dictator's plans.[9]

What was Seward's attitude toward Weed's plans for party reorganization? He was certainly glad to see efforts made to reduce the effectiveness of radicalism in the Union party, and to some extent he worked with Weed to that end. He took a hand in the struggle over King's successor, so much so that at one time it looked as though he had control of the appointment. Bruce noted that he was very civil to the Democrats and thought he aspired to be the leader of a party composed of Democrats and moderate Republicans. In May 1866, Seward employed the eminent New York jurist, Benjamin Franklin Hall, paying him $2000 for a mission that Hall described as being designed "to keep our friends from backsliding," and was evidently an effort to promote the conservative viewpoint throughout the country.

But at the same time Seward did not want an open break with the radicals, one that would destroy existing party formations. He wrote to John Bigelow in April 1866 that "It looks as if some of our Union friends were preparing a bridge upon which they may expect to see the southern states and their old Democratic allies come together once more into political ascendancy. Nevertheless there is yet time for reason." Shortly thereafter Bruce reported that Seward was dubious about the outcome of Johnson's struggle with Congress, and was fearful of congressional attacks on his foreign policy. Montholon heard that the President was not at all happy about the very equivocal support given him by Seward. Any political realignment that would put Democrats of the Blair-Barlow-Tilden stripe in power was abhorrent to the Secretary of State. E. Peshine Smith, a Rochester, New York, lawyer who knew him well, felt that he had discovered that the people were not with the President, and that it was the business of himself and Stanton to stay where they were so that they might keep out a Cabinet formed by Montgomery Blair.[10]

Seward could smile upon Democrats when he wanted Democratic support in Congress. He could address a ringing letter to Mayor John T. Hoffman and the New York Tammany Society, telling them how pleased he was with their invitation to attend Tammany's Fourth of July celebration, and how he felt at one with them in the effort to get the southern states back into the Union. But there is no real evidence that he was deeply involved in efforts at party reorganization. His general attitude indicated that he felt drastic political upheaval would be unfortunate; that Democratic control of state or nation must be avoided; and that his main objective was to hasten the reconstruction process along moderate lines. He gave further evidence of this point of view in a speech delivered at Auburn on May 14, 1866. The theme that he chose was "Reconciliation."

He began with a critical account of the professed devotion to Johnson in 1865 of the northern Democracy, which he asserted was merely an attempt to bring the South back into the Democratic party. Despite this Democratic stratagem, that party had been defeated. As for himself, he was willing to accept "the Rebels and their Democratic abettors" as brethren, but only if the friends of the administration remained united and harmonious.

Seward then referred to the "supposed divergence" between the

President and the radicals, and asserted his desire to see the Union party remain in control of reconstruction. There was no need for any quarrel between Johnson and Congress, and he indicated willingness to have a constitutional amendment changing the basis of representation in the South. Differences between the two ends of Pennsylvania Avenue were really minimal, he said. An indefinite postponement of the reconciliation of the South would be tragic. That way led to disunion and anarchy, which the American people detested. Invoking Paul's Epistle to the Romans, he declared that "neither hope nor fear, nor anger, nor ambition, nor height, nor depth, nor any other creature, can separate them from this inherent, life-saving love of Union." He then defended Johnson's vetoes, emphasizing that the enforcement provisions of the Civil Rights Act would be as disruptive as had been the Fugitive Slave Law and the Dred Scott decision. The President, Seward declared, was as loyal to the nation and to the Union party as was Congress. As for himself, he was hopeful about men and parties and the nation's future.[11]

Reaction to this speech varied. The New York *Times* praised it, emphasizing Seward's insistence on admitting to Congress loyal representatives of the southern states. The *Herald* saw nothing new in it. It endorsed his own position, said Bennett, but that was of no more importance than a pauper's endorsement on the notes of William B. Astor. From many of Seward's old supporters there rose a despairing cry, even before it appeared. "I hear that you are to speak for 'My Policy,' " wrote one old admirer. "To place rebels in power. Oh God must it be so." The *Tribune* called the speech a "Manifesto" in which Seward presented his play of Hamlet with Hamlet—the Negro—left out. Where Negro rights were concerned, he put himself with the Rebels and Copperheads. "He talks softly, smoothly, plausibly, but with no such force and cogency as in the grand old days when his voice rang over the land with his heart in it." [12]

Seward might declare his loyalty to the Union party but the rumor persisted that there was a project for a new political organization, an amalgam of the Democracy and conservative Republicans. The New York *Times* suggested that there was a germ of truth in the story, declaring that time would tell whether such a movement was needed—that it would prove to be so if the radicals were to ride roughshod over conservative men. Then came what seemed to be proof positive, the news that in August conservative Republicans and Democrats were to hold a great convention in Philadelphia.

Where the idea of the Philadelphia convention originated is uncertain. Its leader was James Rood Doolittle of Wisconsin, the Republican moderate who issued the call for the gathering. But Welles was an active participant in the plan, Browning, McCulloch, Raymond, the Blairs, Dean Richmond, Weed, Seward—a motley group—had a hand in the preparations, and the Democratic members of Congress issued a card of endorsement. Others believed that Johnson contemplated a *coup d'état*, and before Congress adjourned in late July several Senators wanted to make some provision against it.[13]

The convention had no one great, overwhelming purpose. Some of its participants hoped it meant a new political structure; others saw it as a means of bringing pressure on the radicals to mend their ways. Raymond went into it only reluctantly, fearing that it would promote the Union party's destruction, but Seward assured him that this was not so. The Secretary of State declared that he, himself, was a Union party man, and both he and Johnson told Raymond that they did not wish the Democrats to get control of the movement. Rather they wanted the convention to promote the election of Congressmen who would favor prompt admission of the southern states. Washington gossip had it that the President was determined to form a new party, an opinion that Raymond shared, but Seward declared that he and his own friends were adopting a pragmatic attitude on that point. Participation in the convention involved no necessary change of political relations. Such a change "could be effected only by approving or disapproving what it should finally do." Seward's letter of endorsement for the convention took the same ground. Welles was sure that Seward had a hand in keeping any criticism of the Fourteenth Amendment out of Doolittle's call for the meeting.[14]

The Philadelphia convention met on August 14 in a wigwam built to house this gathering of delegates from North and South. Prominent among the New Yorkers were Weed and Dean Richmond, the latter having come despite his being in the last stages of a mortal illness. Raymond and Senator Doolittle led the proceedings. Alexander H. Stephens and Governor James L. Orr of South Carolina represented southern sentiment. The sessions lasted three days and were orderly but inspiring, according to those in sympathy with the movement. Before adjournment the delegates issued a statement of principles that upheld states' rights, renounced slavery, and made an impassioned call for the election of Congressmen who would admit loyal representatives from the southern states.

The sponsors of this gathering professed enthusiasm over it, but its positive accomplishments were meager. Out of it came no new party structure, and the radical press caricatured it. At the opening session the delegates came marching in, a northerner and a southerner arm in arm, led by huge Governor Orr of South Carolina and diminutive General D. N. Couch of Massachusetts. The intent of this procedure was excellent, but it lent itself to the jibe that

> The animals came in two by two,
> The elephant and the kangaroo.

It was really a hard luck convention. Far worse than the opening performance was the appearance in the hall of Copperheads like Fernando Wood and Clement Vallandigham. They were prevailed upon to withdraw, though Vallandigham in particular was reluctant to do so, but even their temporary appearance was like a lethal weapon in the hands of the radical press. Then, too, the convention came only two weeks after a bloody massacre in New Orleans, in which white police killed thirty-seven Negroes and wounded many others. This cast doubt upon the liberal protestations of the southerners at Philadelphia, and was used to blacken the President. Sumner wrote to John Bright that Johnson might be judged "by the terrible massacre at New Orleans. Stanton confessed to me that the Pres^{dt} was its author." The breakup of Johnson's Cabinet, three of whom resigned because they were not in sympathy with the movement, was a further blight upon this effort at reconciliation.[15]

Seward was in Auburn when the Philadelphia convention began. He had gone there because he needed a vacation, because he was deeply interested in the enlargement of the Auburn house, which was now proceeding apace, and probably also because he judged it diplomatic not to appear at the convention hall. He was back in Washington on the second day of the meeting, and before it closed wired to Raymond that "Pride, Passion, Prejudice must perish. Patriotism always lives and must in the end prevail." The convention, he told Blatchford, had been "morally sublime," and he helped to welcome the delegates who reported to the President after the conference adjourned.[16]

At least one of Seward's friends was hopeful that Philadelphia marked the beginning of a new departure in politics. Democrat Richard Schell wrote from New York that "the party is launched most effectually and is going to carry the country like a whirlwind" but that much work was needed to get votes, for most of the 20,000 officeholders in New York State were radicals. Dean Richmond, Schell added, "will want some capital."

Schell's hopes were high, but Seward was waiting on events and Richmond was dying. A victim of Bright's disease, he breathed his last on August 28 at the New York home of his friend, Samuel J. Tilden, and the locomotives on the New York Central were draped in black. So, too, were the hopes of Weed and his friends for party reorganization in New York State. There is some evidence that Weed and the profane old railroad man were not in complete accord on a coalition ticket, but the Dictator and his close associates believed that Richmond's death was an irreparable loss.

The political situation was indeed gloomy both for the formation of a new, nation-wide political organization, and for healing the deepening rift in the Union party itself. Sir Frederick Bruce sized up the Union party dilemma with a fair degree of accuracy. The men of moderation, the compromisers, he wrote in a dispatch to the British Foreign Office, had lost their hold on opinion. If Seward were not in office, and if the country credited him with strong convictions, he might be able to pacify the elements. "But," added Bruce, "his views seem to have little or no weight with his former supporters, and I see no leader of prominence in favor of the President's views." [17]

Hard on the Philadelphia convention came the disastrous "Swing Around the Circle." In March, Seward had been invited to speak at the laying of the cornerstone of a Chicago monument for Stephen A. Douglas. He declined on account of his health and the pressure of official business. Nevertheless the invitation was renewed, and the administration deemed the opportunity propitious. What finally developed was a campaign tour designed to promote the election of Congressmen who would support Johnson and his policies. The President headed this expedition, accompanied by Seward, Grant, Farragut, and a number of other civil and military leaders. They went by way of Philadelphia and New York through Albany, Auburn, and Niagara to Chicago, thence down to St. Louis and Louisville and back through the Middle West and Pennsylvania to Washington. Seward was the master of arrangements for the tour.

The presidential party left Washington in late August. It was well enough received at the start, but as it moved onward more and more trouble developed. The President made the same speech over and over again, and the radicals were soon publishing it in advance of his appearance. He spoke at the whistle stops as well as in the larger cities, lost his temper under heckling, and bandied insults with the crowds. His intemperate responses were played up by radical speakers, who made innuendo and vilification the order of the day. They denounced him as a demagogue, a trickster, a perjurer, a traitor, and pictured the expedition as a presidential drunken spree. Greeley wrote to John Bright that Johnson and Seward were drunk most of the time—that Johnson in particular was "at least half crazy with drink." Schurz said the President was worse than Judas Iscariot or Benedict Arnold. The story spread that Grant left the boat at Cleveland because of his disgust with Johnson's inebriety, whereas the truth of the matter was that the General himself was drunk and stupidly loquacious to Mrs. Farragut. He was put on the boat for Detroit so that the breezes of Lake Erie might restore him to sobriety.

Even without the sneers and innuendos of the radicals, the trip would have been a failure. Stoeckl, who admired Johnson's policy toward the South, deplored the President's lapses on the tour. After it was over, Johnson supporters in Washington told the Russian Minister that the expedition had done great damage to the conservative cause, and Stoeckl lamented that a man with such talent and capacity should have been carried beyond all moderation by hatred of his enemies.

Seward defended the President's conduct on the tour, declaring that he was excellent on the stump and that his speeches did good, but for the Secretary of State the trip was scarcely a pleasant experience. At Albany the senate struck his name from the list of those to be welcomed and Governor Fenton passed him over until Seward stepped forward, saying he needed no introduction in those familiar scenes, and then shook hands with several in the crowded chamber. At Auburn, where they stayed overnight, there was bickering and jealousy. Congressman Pomeroy, a relative of Seward by marriage, was a violent radical, and many Auburnians felt as he did. To make matters worse, Grant's carriage ran over a boy, injuring him so severely that his leg had to be amputated. As with Johnson, so there were persistent reports of Seward's drunkenness. To cap the climax, shortly after leaving Louisville on the return journey, the Secretary of State had an attack of cholera or dysentery, and by the time he reached Harrisburg he was desperately ill.

At Harrisburg, Welles and Johnson went into the car where Seward lay, so weak that he could not speak above a whisper. It was evident that he thought his end was near. Taking the President's hand, he said his mind was clear and that he wished to say at this time that Johnson's course was correct; that he had felt it was his duty to sustain him in it; and that if he were spared he would continue to do so.

Welles, too, thought Seward was about to die and Fanny, whose own days were numbered, came to Harrisburg to watch over her father. But his remarkable vitality carried him through and within a week he was making a rapid recovery.[18]

The weeks that followed brought a flood of bad news and personal abuse. The evil effects of the "Swing Around the Circle" multiplied, and a barrage of radical propaganda branded the followers of Johnson as traitors, renegades, and apostates who had gone over to the Copperheads. In New York State the actions of the Democratic party gave point to this charge. Weed, Richmond, and perhaps Tilden had arranged a state nominating convention composed of Democrats and conservative Republicans that was to nominate War Democrat John A. Dix for governor. Then Richmond died, the Democrats rebelled, and the convention ended by nominating John T. Hoffman, the mayor of New York. In the ensuing campaign the Democrats showed such interest in getting control of post offices and other federal appointments that conservative Republicans feared they were becoming mere appendages of the Democratic machine.

Conservative bungling was almost as bad as Democratic greed. Weed wanted Collector Smythe removed, but he remained in office, a most independent ally. Dix, after losing the gubernatorial nomination was appointed naval officer and almost immediately was made Minister to France. Seward wanted him in France, while Secretary of the Treasury McCulloch wanted him in New York. It was an embarrassing situation. Richard Schell reported to Seward that the retention of Smythe and the showering of offices on Dix made it impossible to collect a dollar in campaign funds. Johnson, besieged by Democratic as well as Republican supplicants, made enemies by almost every appointment that could be traced to his influence. Senator Henry B. Anthony wrote to Frederick Seward that the President was playing along with the Copperheads in Rhode Island and that the result was a series of terrible blunders. They were "making a precious mess of things in Washington," Anthony declared. Similar complaints came to Weed and Seward from inside and outside New York State.[19]

The opponents of the administration leveled a considerable share of their invective at Seward. He was a drunkard. Like Johnson, he was under the control of a vicious and depraved woman who had access to the White House by night and by day, while good Union men were denied admission. He was responsible for everything bad that Johnson had done. An old Michigan friend, John R. Kellogg asked if it were true that Seward had said "Well, we have gone through the farce of another election," and if Seward had asked, "Do you want Mr. Johnson as President, or do you want him as King?"

These assaults came while Seward was recovering from his illness and was stricken with grief over Fanny's death. His response was, for the most part, silent disdain, and he preserved an outward air of cheerfulness over the election in which, he told Welles, he thought the administration would hold its own. But the doubts of old friends were hard to bear. Kellogg's letter was on his desk when he returned from taking Fanny's body to Auburn. In response he wrote,

> Your letter of the 1st. instant meets me on my arrival here
> this morning from a hurried visit at Auburn. I can do almost
> anything to gratify a faithful and constant friend such as you
> have so long been, yet I cannot even for such a reason do an

unmanly thing, and therefore you must excuse me from an-
swering either of the two idle questions you put to me. You
will live long enough, I trust, to regret that you propounded
them.

He would not reproach or complain of those who promoted discord
and anarchy by their attacks on himself and the President, he declared. He could only ask that they be forgiven, since they knew
not what they did. There was a touch of the sanctimonious in this
attitude, but for it there was much justification.[20]

November brought a Waterloo defeat. In New York the radical
Republicans re-elected Governor Fenton and obtained control of
both houses of the legislature, thus ensuring the election of Roscoe
Conkling to the United States Senate. Elsewhere, too, the opponents
of Johnson and his policy were victorious. The Union party of
wartime was no more. There was now a Republican two-thirds
majority in both House and Senate, but what a majority! Supporters
of Johnson were but a scattered few; influential conservatives such
as James A. Garfield, William Pitt Fessenden, and John Sherman
would have nothing to do with the President; the party was at the
mercy of the radicals.

Seward had predicted Republican defeat in New York State by
40,000 votes, but that was during the "Swing Around the Circle."
Now he took the result with outward calm. They must, he told Sanford, suspend all speculation as to what Congress would do. There
was no necessity for wild alarm. But he wrote of his fears to Weed.
"Who is now to lead this country back to peace, tranquillity and
union? Shall we be spared to see it done? They are beginning to
presume in Europe upon our distractions. This hurts me, but I cannot help it."

The observant Stoeckl saw the Secretary of State just after the
election and was struck by his aged appearance—more disfigured,
Stoeckl thought, by grief and disappointment than he had been by
the assassin's knife. In this crisis, the Russian wrote to his chief,
America could hardly dispense with Seward's talents, energy, and
patriotism. One could only hope that the life of this statesman
would be long conserved.

Before the news of the election reached Paris, John Hay sent a message of condolence over Fanny's death. It was his fervent hope, he said, that Seward's grief over "the gentle and lovely one who has left your house desolate" might not lead him to retire from labors that had become purely patriotic. If he still had the strength to hold his even way in such perplexed times, men could admire in him a higher ideal than that in the apostrophe of Horace to the upright and determined man who holds firm to his purpose despite the rage of those commanding what is base.

The compliment touched Seward deeply and he replied, "You have by some generous form of intuition penetrated a secret of my heart. It will remain with us two. No one else has faith in Human Nature adequate to accept it." It was indeed what Seward wished to believe about himself, and in his best moments it was true.[21]

~§ 32 §~

The End of Political Dreams

The 1866 political landslide, together with Fanny's death, cast a pall over Seward's spirits. He was seeking cheerfulness, he wrote to Senator Morgan in declining an invitation to attend the New England Festival, "but the thoughts of festivity are impossible." [1] Before the old year was out a new trouble came to vex him, one that his enemies used in their attempt to blacken his reputation.

George W. McCrackin, a New York Democrat traveling in Europe during 1866, wrote to Johnson that American diplomats criticized his conduct in such a way as to astonish Americans and amaze Europeans. Motley in particular, said McCrackin, expressed disgust with the President, declared that he despised American democracy, and asserted that both Seward and Johnson had abandoned their principles and that the Secretary of State was hopelessly degraded.

This letter made Johnson furious. He called Seward into conference, and as a result the latter addressed a letter of inquiry to American ministers abroad regarding their conduct. That to Motley recounted the charges against him and asked, as did the others, for either a denial or confirmation. This was routine procedure in cases of complaints against the service.

Motley was quick-tempered. His previous relations with Seward had been cordial and in 1865 he had declared that the latter's conduct of the State Department would form "one of the most brilliant portions of our national history," but now his feelings were ruffled. In a hasty reply that admitted private criticism of the President's reconstruction policy he denied McCrackin's allegations and submitted his own resignation.

Seward replied that Motley's response was "not unsatisfactory" to the President, and that there were no considerations of public policy requiring him to leave the diplomatic service. He added that, unless Motley wanted his retirement to be absolute, the matter was closed. This letter went in the diplomatic pouch to Vienna by way of London. The President, however, was determined that Motley should leave the service, and Seward by telegram to London withdrew his letter and sent another accepting the resignation.

Sumner, a friend of Motley, roared in protest over the affair, and at his request the Senate called for the correspondence between the two men. This promptly got into the papers, and a deluge of criticism descended upon the Secretary of State. The author of *The Rise of the Dutch Republic* had a following in the United States, and men of both parties condemned Seward. Sumner declared that it was ridiculous to accept the word of an obscure individual about a distinguished historian. The New York *Tribune* accused Seward of magnifying the tales of spies disguised as gentlemen, and remarked that he was probably the only American who could find no pleasure in reading Motley's letter.

Seward remained silent out of loyalty to his chief, but his good relations with Motley were now at an end, he knew that his reputation was being damaged, and he lashed out bitterly in private. He told John Hay that the Copperheads, now almost the entire support of the President, were continually begging the State Department for offices, and accusing him of wickedness because he kept old radical Republican appointees in their places. Motley wasn't fit for his post, Seward later confided to Bigelow. He was given it only to placate Sumner, who was "grouty" over Adams going to England and had to be conciliated. McCrackin had influence, Seward told Welles, and if Sumner and his coterie wished to fight the New York "downtown bugs, damn them, let them." Adams, over in London, thought Seward's first letter was not judiciously drawn, and feared that constant attacks had begun to wear on his chief's mind and temper.

In April a Boston friend of Motley sent two notes that he had re-

ceived from the latter to the State Department, and urged his reinstatement. Presumably they depicted the historian in a calmer and
more judicious mood than he had formerly displayed. Seward turned
this material over to the President, but Johnson was adamant, the
correspondence went back to Boston, and the legation at Vienna
remained for some time in the hands of a *chargé d'affaires*. The
tumult about the incident was slow to die, and ten months later,
again at Sumner's instigation, the Senate used it to spread abroad
Motley's complaints of ill treatment by the Secretary of State.[2]

The Motley affair was only one of the difficulties that Seward had
to face during the winter of 1866–67. Abuse descended upon him
from many different quarters. William Schouler wrote of repeated
attacks in the Boston press, and of recurrent rumors that his stay in
the Cabinet was nearly over. On Capitol Hill Sumner was hostile,
writing to a friend that Seward was perverse; that he had done nothing but blunder since 1860, had never understood the war and had
no comprehension of how peace could be secured. Senator Howard
of Michigan accused the Secretary of wishing to recognize Maximilian's regime in Mexico. Congressman Glenni W. Scofield of
Pennsylvania declared that the "old man" in the State Department
wanted to incorporate with the Union "the debris of the late Confederacy," and that he encouraged lynching and murder as a southern pastime. Then another furor was raised about Minister Harvey
in Portugal, whose salary had been cut off the previous year. It was
discovered that he was still functioning at Lisbon. How could this
be? Senator Grimes declared that Seward must be paying him in
some way or other, and there was debate over the State Department's contingent fund. It ended with a provision in the act making
appropriations for consular and diplomatic expenses that no money
should be paid to Harvey out of any fund whatsoever. But despite
this order the Minister to Portugal remained at his post.[3]

It was widely believed that all the radicals hated Seward and that
he loathed them in return. One of his lady sympathizers, a Georgia
woman, urged him to form an organization to combat radicalism. It
would not be a party, as she saw it, but simply a nation-wide combination of individuals who would bind themselves to pay dues of
from twenty-five cents to one dollar a month. The resulting slush
fund would be used in buying up newspapers, letter writers, orators,

William H. Seward. The Inman Portrait. 1843.
Art Commission, City of New York.

Home of the State Department during the Civil War.
Seward House, Auburn, New York.

Lord Francis Napier (1819-98).
British Minister to the United States
1857-58. Seward House,
Auburn, New York.

Lord Lyons (1817-87). British
Minister to the United States
1859-64. Seward House,
Auburn, New York.

Don Matias Romero (1837-98).
Mexican Minister to the United States
1863-68, 1882-98.
Seward House, Auburn, New York.

Lord John Russell (1792-1878).
Seward House,
Auburn, New York.

Giuseppi Garibaldi (1807-82).
Seward offered him a commission
in the Union Army. Seward House,
Auburn, New York.

Edward de Stoeckl.
Russian Minister to the
United States 1859-68. Seward
House, Auburn, New York.

Seward in his seventy-first year.
University of Rochester Library.

Andrew Johnson, (1808-75). Seward House, Auburn, New York.

The Impeachment Committee, 1868. Left to right: (standing) James F. Wilson, George S. Boutwell, Gen. John A. Logan, (sitting) Benjamin F. Butler, Thaddeus Stevens, Thomas Williams, John A. Bingham. U.S. Signal Corps photo (Brady Collection) in the National Archives.

Lincoln and his cabinet with Grant, *c.* 1864.
A lithograph by Thomas Kelly. Library of Congress.

Grand Reception of the Notabilities of the Nation. 1865.
Library of Congress.

ministers of the gospel, and Congressmen for a war against the radicals. Only those who were in close contact with Seward—such men as Weed, Cabinet members, diplomats, and a few leading figures on Capitol Hill—realized that his policy was one of conciliation. Bigelow probably read between the lines when Seward wrote to him, "The country needs at the Capital, in the Executive Department as elsewhere, prudence and forecast now no less than heretofore. Individual interests are less than nothing in comparison with national ones." [4]

As the time approached for the President's second annual message, Johnson asked Seward for a draft and the Secretary of State sent one over to the White House. It began with an optimistic picture of the prospects of a restored Union, and then went on to acknowledge that to Congress belonged "exclusively" the right to admit its own members. The Fourteenth Amendment had been submitted to all the states, and resolutions of concurrence had been received from six of them. In all judicious and constitutional measures directed to the improvement of the nation's condition, Congress could count on "my cheerful concurrence and cooperation." Seward ended with a comprehensive survey of America's relations with the rest of the world.

The President used Seward's survey of foreign affairs, but not the effort to conciliate Congress. The message Johnson sent to Capitol Hill never mentioned the Fourteenth Amendment, and was largely devoted to demonstrating how wrong Congress had been in refusing to admit loyal representatives of the reconstructed states to the House and Senate. Johnson persisted in urging the South to have nothing to do with the amendment. Its rejection by the southern states, together with his unyielding attitude toward his congressional opponents helped to pave the way for what followed. [5]

Despite Johnson's refusal to use Seward's suggestions in regard to the southern situation, the Secretary of State followed his own moderate course. He ignored congressional attacks upon his foreign policy and upon himself. He took pains to cultivate Stevens and Sumner. Welles noted disgustedly how he would go down to the Capitol and seat himself beside them in the House and Senate, "dancing around Stevens, Sumner, Boutwell, Banks and others," with the result that they were flattered by his attentions. Seward suggested to

McCulloch that Judge Blair be sent abroad on official business, and the Judge, so McCulloch wrote, was "quite gratified." When Anson Herrick, New York publisher and influential Democrat, appealed for Seward's aid in getting a federal appointment on the ground that he had helped push the Thirteenth Amendment through Congress, the Secretary of State turned a deaf ear. There was no sense in stirring up the radical Republicans on Capitol Hill.[6]

Before his friends Seward was calm and cheerful. John Hay, just back from Paris, found him free from bitterness toward the radicals, and intent only on his work in the State Department. Seward told Bigelow that, somehow or other, the southern states would be brought into the Union within a year. Bigelow remarked that Johnson did not know how to be President, but Seward entered upon a spirited defense of his chief, declaring that he did a great deal better than Lincoln. His remarks about Lincoln prompted Bigelow to reflect that the martyred President had more faith in the love and wisdom of his Creator than had Seward, who, while not altogether lacking faith in the Most High, "at a pinch was wont to have a little more faith in himself."[7]

Seward's equanimity was the more remarkable in view of what happened during that winter. Johnson's attitude and southern refusal to accept the Fourteenth Amendment, angered the radicals. Reports of the persecution of Negroes and Unionists in the South kept their anger hot. Aided by the Democrats, who adopted the tactic of obstructing compromise between the two wings of the Republican party, the radicals pushed on toward drastic ways of handling the South.

"I think we are rushing to a violent crisis as fast as possible," Adams recorded in his diary toward the middle of February 1867. Even as he wrote, the main features of radical reconstruction had become apparent on the other side of the Atlantic. The plan was to divide the ten southern states that had not accepted the Fourteenth Amendment into five military districts, these to remain under army control until Negroes and whites (save those disfranchised for participating in the rebellion) had elected state conventions. The latter would frame constitutions providing for universal suffrage. Only when these constitutions were ratified by popular vote and approved by Congress; only when the duly elected legislatures had accepted the Fourteenth Amendment and it had become part of the federal Constitution, would military rule cease and the southern states be restored to their former place in the Union.

The radicals in Congress had taken the bit in their teeth, and before them the President, the Democrats, and the conservatively minded were impotent. Johnson, under pressure to reshuffle his Cabinet that he might yet save something from the wreckage, talked the situation over with his private secretary, Colonel William Moore. If he put Adams in the State Department, he said, with Grant in War, Farragut in the Navy, and Greeley as Postmaster General, the war between himself and the radicals would be over. Moore asked if this could not be done, and the President said he did not see that he could take such a drastic step.

The conservatives were equally helpless. Hay found those in Washington stunned and bewildered. Hollis White, a Buffalo politician, telegraphed Seward that his friends and those of the President in that part of the country hoped that Johnson would sign the congressional reconstruction bill. Weed wrote from New York that there was a dread among conservatives of impeachment, anarchy, ruin, even revolution, and a general disposition to favor any plan of reconstruction that Congress might pass.[8]

The bill which embodied the congressional plan for reconstruction passed Congress on February 20, 1867. Johnson vetoed it on March 2 and on the same day, while the chambers rang with applause, both houses passed it over his veto. And now the South entered upon a period of military rule.

Congress was in a bellicose mood where Johnson was concerned. During the "Swing Around the Circle" he had threatened a wholesale removal of officeholders who opposed his policy, threatening to "kick them out just as fast as I can." This dire threat, the removals actually made, and the Senate's desire to protect its best ally in the Cabinet, Stanton, produced the Tenure of Office Act. This measure took away the President's power to remove officeholders appointed with the advice and consent of the Senate. Cabinet members should hold their places "for and during the term of the President by whom they may have been appointed and for one month thereafter," and then could be removed only with the Senate's consent.

The Tenure of Office Act passed Congress at the same time as the

Reconstruction Act and, as in the case of the latter, by a practically solid party vote. Johnson's Cabinet condemned the bill as unconstitutional. He then asked Seward and Stanton to prepare the veto. Stanton complained of rheumatism in his arm, and as a result the composition was largely left to Seward.

Citing historical precedents, the veto message declared the bill unconstitutional, since the Constitution vested in the President the power to remove federal officials. Lincoln had found this prerogative of great value in eliminating traitors from government offices. To bring this power into question might at some future time have the gravest consequences.

Johnson vetoed the Tenure of Office Act at the same time that he rejected the Reconstruction Act, and Congress as promptly passed it over his veto by overwhelming majorities. The Democrats voted solidly with the President.[9]

Though reconstruction was now a radical triumph, Johnson was still interested in cultivating popular favor, and he was grateful for Seward's support. Early in June the two men attended the dedication of a monument to the President's father in Raleigh, North Carolina, and some three weeks later they made an excursion into New England. There was considerable speech-making on both these journeys, and the Secretary of State did his share. At Chapel Hill, North Carolina, he pointed to the stars of the old flag, once again shining in their splendor, and prophesied that before long they would be enriched by those gleaming in the Southern Cross.

The New England tour had a somewhat embarrassing aspect, for the official purpose was participation in laying the cornerstone of the new Masonic temple at Boston. Seward spent the Sunday before the ceremonies in Quincy, the newspapers duly noting that he went to church and visited the Adams home. That evening he dined with Samuel Hooper. Agassiz, Longfellow, and Dana were there, together with the Sumners (it was just before the breakup of the Sumner marriage). He declined attending the Masonic festivities, giving Fanny's death, which had occurred eight months before, as his excuse. Antimasonry might be largely past history—a Georgia woman had recently besought his help "as a Mason"—but Boston had been a hotbed of the movement and there were memories that might be stirred, accusations of inconsistency that might be leveled. It was just as well to avoid hobnobbing with the knights of the cable tow.

About the time of the "Swing Around the Circle," Stanton had warned Johnson that his Secretary of State was a candidate for the presidency, and some of Seward's acts and speeches on the New England tour gave evidence that he might still have presidential fever. His visit to the Adams ancestral home, coupled with praise of Old Man Eloquent and Massachusetts, was one such indication. So, too, was a careful explanation that his own policy had ever been to save both the nation and human rights—a sop to right and left. He told his Springfield audience that he hoped they would yet become better acquainted, and then launched into a panegyric on the nation's glorious future, with much emphasis on the expansion of American territory. In a generation or two the United States would be the dominant world power. He had just negotiated the Alaska Treaty, and Welles, reading the reports of these speeches, commented sourly, "The purchase of Russian America has demented him. . . ."

Seward was ever a politician, one who knew the seductive power of an appeal to national glory, but that he still had any real hopes of reaching the White House is more than doubtful. He must have noticed that at Boston only a handful of the state's leading men saw fit to meet the presidential party. And at Hartford he told his listeners that the tongue which would plead for him would speak in some future age when his own was "cold and silent in the dust," a comment that moved one of his listeners almost to tears. Unfortunately, from his point of view, there was no longer any party willing to support him.[10]

Shortly after the New England journey, the President determined to rid himself of government officials who were aiding and abetting congressional reconstruction. This purge eventually extended to the army commanders in the South, but it began with the Secretary of War whom Johnson had long distrusted. On August 5 he asked for Stanton's resignation, but the latter refused to give it. The President thereupon suspended him and made Grant Secretary of War *ad interim*. He then removed General Philip Sheridan, one of the North's war heroes, from his post as military governor of Louisana and Texas.

Johnson's policy of "Thorough" produced a storm of indignation in the North. Radical newspapers raged, and conservatives could see only further disasters. Weed, who felt that the President had now lost all, thought that Seward should at once retire from the Cabinet. George W. Patterson was sure that Johnson had made a fool of himself, and that Seward should leave the sinking ship before he, too, was disgraced. Senator Anthony wrote to Frederick Seward that there was no good reason for Johnson's breaking up the Cabinet and that he was rushing into impeachment.[11]

Seward was not enthusiastic about the dismissal of Stanton, nor did he like the ouster of Sheridan. Clamor for his own dismissal came from Blair and others, rumor had it that the axe had fallen on him also, and on August 23 he sent his own resignation to the White House. Johnson asked him to remain in office.

At this point Seward must have pondered the pros and cons of resignation. It was obvious that it might be well to leave what looked like a foundering administration. He was also having a rough time with the Senate, despite the fact that in April it had ratified the Alaska Treaty. It had turned down his request that his friend Sanford be promoted to the rank of Minister to Belgium. It had refused to confirm his friend Raymond as Minister to Austria. It had cut off the funds for the Roman legation, thus depriving another friend, Rufus King, of his post, and all of Seward's efforts to get the appropriation restored had been of no avail. The duty of designating newspapers in the states and territories to publish the laws of Congress had been transferred by that body from the State Department to the Clerk of the House of Representatives. The prospects for senatorial co-operation in the field of foreign policy were certainly not bright.

But Seward enjoyed power, and felt that he still had influence with the President. Then, too, he had plans for further expansion of American territory, and was just then hopeful of obtaining Samaná Bay in Santo Domingo as a coaling station. Thad Stevens penned him a hasty note—"I hope it is true. The Bay not the removal." Gold rose in New York on the rumor that he was leaving the Cabinet, and this might be taken as evidence of the concern felt by the financial world. To what extent these factors controlled his thinking it is impossible to say, but he did remain at his post.[12]

How much influence did Seward have with the President at this time? Welles thought that he was pliant and yielding, yet shaped the presidential course. This last is doubtful, save in foreign policy. Seward's flirtations with Johnson's bitter opponents in Congress, and his obvious closeness to Stanton, were anything but pleasing to the master of the White House. The latter told his confidant, Colonel Moore, that he had the kindest feelings toward his Secretary of State, that, indeed, he liked the "old man" and would gladly help him to attain the presidency, but that Weed's influence in New York State was gone and that, in fact, Seward was rather "a dead carcass." Diplomatic gossip in Washington, transmitted to Adams by Harvey, led Adams to think that Seward remained in the Cabinet on sufferance, rather than as one of its influential members.[13] Seward himself told one of his correspondents that his efforts were "now confined almost exclusively to the conduct of foreign affairs. . . ."

That the President and the Secretary of State continued to differ as to domestic policy is shown by a comparison of two state papers prepared by Seward with those that bore the Chief Executive's signature. In both cases, similarity of phraseology shows that Johnson read and used the drafts made out by his Secretary of State.

The first of these papers was a proclamation of amnesty. Seward cited as precedents similar proclamations used in 1863 and 1864 by Lincoln, and carefully avoided any reference to congressional reconstruction. His tone was irenic, that of Johnson just the reverse. The latter began by recalling that Congress in 1861 had declared that the war was fought solely for the preservation of the Union "with all the dignity, equality and rights of the several states unimpaired. . . ." He also denounced the reconstruction now taking place as retaliatory, vindictive, and dangerous to public liberty. What the President issued was probably as belligerent a proclamation of amnesty as ever saw the light of day.[14]

The second paper was the President's annual message of December 3, 1867. Seward prepared a draft distinctly conciliatory in tone. He remarked that differences of viewpoint as to the manner and method of reconstruction were bound to develop. These made necessary mutual consultations and compromise. Congress had not accepted the wise procedure instituted by Lincoln and carried on by Johnson, and in consequence misery, wretchedness, and the "unhappy alienations" of the Civil War had been prolonged. Congressional reconstruction was unconstitutional and Johnson had vetoed it, but Congress had overridden his veto, as was its constitutional right. The results of the congressional experiment could not now be foreseen. If it was a success, it would be the duty of everyone to acquiesce. If it was impracticable, in whole or in part, some revision or modification "may be found necessary to secure the great objects of restoration and reconciliation."

It was fortunate, Seward declared in his draft, that Congress was in session, for the passions engendered by the war had considerably subsided and it was high time to speed the work of uniting the sections. This was especially true because of the impending elections. He deplored the use of a standing army in time of peace, the disfranchisement of 10 of the 37 states, and the economic demoralization of the South produced by the existing situation.

This draft was critical of congressional reconstruction, but it was also an olive branch. It ignored the Tenure of Office Act, and emphasized only the need for the nation's speedy return to normal conditions.

Johnson's message took a very different attitude from that of Seward's draft. The President blamed Congress for having thwarted the efforts of the executive and the rebellious states to repair the injuries suffered in the course of the war. There was now no Union, he said, and Congress had set at naught the Constitution. He then launched into an able argument, pointing out the contradictions inherent in the congressional policy and the folly of enforced Negro suffrage. Congress was disfranchising enough whites to give Negroes a clear majority in all the southern states. Both the means and the end sought were evil. He argued that the Negro had no capacity for ruling, and emphasized the enormous expense of congressional reconstruction. He denounced the Tenure of Office Act. At one point he referred to charges that he planned to subvert the government and declared that, if Congress passed a law producing immediate and irreparable injury to the organic structure of the government, he would have to "save the life of the nation at all hazards." [15]

There was much clear and sound reasoning in the President's message. Weed thought that, if Johnson had left out the threat of using arbitrary force to save the nation from Congress, the message would have inaugurated a reaction in popular sentiment. But logical though it was, it bristled. Once again, instead of appealing to moderates, the President had thrown down the gauntlet to the national legislature.

Aside from Johnson's talent for stimulating opposition to himself, congressional Republicans had another reason for continued war with the White House. The Democrats had made a comeback in the state and congressional elections of 1867, but this did not affect the composition of the Fortieth Congress. That body was to be in almost continuous session during 1868. Its Republican leaders were determined to discredit the Chief Executive and his Democratic supporters so thoroughly that their own triumph in the presidential election would be insured.

Johnson had in truth become a party issue, and his own actions kept that issue alive. He stated publicly that the 1867 elections vindicated his policy. He even had the temerity to ask Congress to tender a vote of thanks to Sheridan's replacement, General Winfield S. Hancock, when the latter issued an order vindicating civil rather than military government in the Louisiana-Texas district. It was almost as though he were determined upon forcing his own impeachment.[16]

There had been talk of impeaching the President as early as December 1865. Rumblings of such action had always come to naught, and when they were brought to his attention Seward discounted the possibility. But such an opportunity as Congress now had for drastic action might never come again. Just before the close of the first session of the Fortieth Congress, a majority of the House Judiciary Committee recommended impeachment on grounds of treason, bribery, and "usurpation of power and repeated violations of law." A Republican minority report proposed only censure, and a Democratic report defended Johnson. The second session of the Fortieth Congress followed immediately, and the majority report became the order of the day. The House, however, could not yet be brought to vote impeachment, and for a time it looked as though the movement had collapsed.

Then came a row between Johnson and Grant, the latter determined to get out of his anomalous position as Secretary of War *ad interim* and the President equally determined to prove that Grant had broken his promise to serve as temporary head of the War Department. The news of this futile dispute became public, fanning the hostility of Congress to fever heat. There were rumors of Republican and Democratic military companies organized to defend Congress or the President. Sumner wrote to Bright that the head of the state was now "a full-blown rebel" and should have been impeached two years ago. Grant was driven into the arms of the radicals, and on February 22 the joint Committee on Reconstruction recommended impeachment. Two days later the House voted it, 128 to 47.[17]

The House put the charges on which its case rested in eleven articles. These centered on Johnson's supposed violation of the Tenure of Office Act by his dismissal of Stanton, though he was also accused of attempting to bring Congress into "disgrace, ridicule, hatred, contempt and reproach." The eleventh article was a summary of the accusations contained in the others. The Senate was to sit as a trial court, presided over by Chief Justice Chase. A two-thirds vote was necessary for conviction. If it came and Johnson was removed, the coarse and violent Benjamin F. Wade, president *pro tempore* of the Senate, would become President of the United States.

The trial proper began March 30, the President being represented by an imposing array of counsel that included Henry Stanbery (who resigned as Attorney General so that he might act as Johnson's chief counsel), Benjamin R. Curtis, and William M. Evarts. Ben Butler was chief counsel for the House of Representatives. The final arguments of the lawyers on both sides began on April 22. The defense showed conclusively that the President's purpose in dismissing Stanton was not to violate but simply to test the constitutionality of the Tenure of Office Act.

There followed a period of some two weeks before the first vote was taken, which was on the catch-all eleventh article. During this period tremendous popular pressure was brought to bear upon five of the Senators who were thought to be wavering and inclined toward acquittal. One of these in particular, Ross of Kansas, was threatened not only with repudiation at the polls but also with assassination.

The May 16 vote showed 35 for conviction and 19 for acquittal, one less than the necessary two-thirds. Four of the five Senators upon whom pressure had been brought, Ross among them, voted not guilty. Ten days later, votes taken on the first and second arti-

cles had the same result. The Senate, sitting as a court of impeachment, then adjourned. Ben Butler's boast that "the removal of the
great obstruction is certain. Wade and prosperity are sure to come
with the apple-blossoms" had gone for naught.[18]

The country had been saved from Wade, and it is distinctly possible that the form of the national government was also preserved
from destruction. Congress had been assuming a more and more
dominant role in Washington. It had overridden vetoes with mo-
notonous regularity, and passed laws designed to weaken presidential power. It had also sought to dominate the Supreme Court.

In the famous case of *ex parte Milligan* in 1866 the Court had declared that military tribunals had no jurisdiction where the civil
courts were open. This decision cast doubt upon the constitutionality of congressional reconstruction and great was the rage of the
radicals. A bill requiring a two-thirds vote for a Court decision
passed the House and another bill depriving the Court of jurisdiction over appeals from lower federal courts in *habeas corpus* cases
became law. Gideon Welles, watching this procedure, declared that
the Court "caved in." This was scarcely true, though the judges did
refrain from rendering decisions in other cases touching congressional reconstruction.

What was clear to all, then and later, was that Capitol Hill had
assumed a dominant role in the national government, and appeared
to be paving the way for further developments along that line. Had
Johnson been removed from office, a precedent would have been established for future impeachments of Presidents; and the legislature
would have gone far toward demonstrating its predominance over
both the executive and the judiciary. Congress might well have
emerged as the ruling power in the nation.

What had been Seward's course of action during all this furor?
Before the trial began he told members of his family that he was sure
the impeachment would be sustained by the Senate. At that time he
was careful not to criticize, either directly or by implication, either
Grant or Johnson, and appeared reluctant to have the Cabinet advise
the President on the manner of his defense. Playing no favorites socially, the Secretary of State invited General Grant and his wife to
dinner one Saturday and Ben Butler with his wife and daughter a
week later. He busied himself with the affairs of his department,

doubtless turning with relief to discussing the basic theories of American government with such visiting foreigners as young Dr. Georges Clemenceau, who presented himself one day with a letter of introduction from Charles Anderson Dana. Indeed, Seward appeared to be more concerned with maintaining good relations with men like Wade and Sumner and Stevens, and in guarding his department against attacks upon its budget, than he was in what happened to the President.[19]

But as the time for the impeachment trial neared, Seward made it clear that he stood by the side of his chief. He would not take the time for a journey to Pittsburgh and a mass meeting of the friends of the President, but he wrote them that the ultimate judgment of the friends of constitutional liberty throughout the world must be that Johnson had adhered "to that great national object with the singleness and fidelity of loyal and disinterested patriotism." He rejected with scorn Weed's advice that he take Adams's place in London. He wouldn't think of going abroad and leaving the State Department to be filled with men like that rascally Democrat Jerry Black. Where foreign affairs were concerned, Seward meant to keep his hand on the helm. His letter of resignation was on the President's desk, to be used whenever Johnson so desired, or if impeachment succeeded, but his support was there as long as it was wanted.

Overtures had come to Seward, he told the President. There had been a suggestion that he would be retained in office by Wade if he did not interfere with the progress of impeachment, but his reply had been "I'll see you damned first. The impeachment of the President is the impeachment of his Cabinet." When a Kentuckian sent him a facsimile of "The Death Warrant of King Charles I of England," Seward acknowledged it ironically, "with thanks for an interesting memento." [20]

Seward took charge of collecting the funds necessary to defray Johnson's legal expenses. Weed and Richard Schell were his principal agents in New York, and by the end of February he had $7500 at his disposal. Total expenses were $11,100, all of which was raised without cost to the President. Seward also tried in a discreet way to use what influence he had with the Senators. His private secretary, Erastus D. Webster, through ex-Senator Harris and others, worked hard for Johnson's acquittal.[21]

Had Seward been put on the witness stand, he could have sworn that he and the other members of the Cabinet, including Stanton, had advised Johnson that the Tenure of Office Act was unconstitutional. He was reluctant to testify, he told Welles, because he had been friendly with Stanton, and also because Lincoln had advised with him about some removals from office. He was therefore relieved when the Senate refused the request of the President's counsel that he be sworn. His testimony, had it been permitted, would have been damaging to the prosecution.

As the trial drew toward its close, Seward became confident of Johnson's acquittal, offering to bet two baskets of champagne to one on the result. Also he was not averse to claiming some credit for the conduct of the defense. After Evarts had presented a very effective closing argument, Johnson commented favorably upon his speech. "Yes," said Seward, to the President's secret amusement, "Evarts kept in pretty close touch with me." [22]

The Cabinet met on May 16, the day of the first crucial vote on impeachment. It was also Seward's sixty-seventh birthday. Early that day he had written to Mrs. Sanford that, if Johnson were found guilty, "before the sun sets I shall retire from public life now protracted too many years," but it was characteristic of him that, though the others manifested excitement, he seemed unperturbed.

When the news came that the verdict was "not guilty," he wrote a note to the President—"I congratulate you upon the day's results." Johnson, much pleased, told his secretary that Seward had shown more interest in the trial than any other member of his Cabinet. That same day one of Seward's aides, coming to his room to learn the result, found him lying on a sofa smoking a cigar and reading Rousseau. He told the inquirer that impeachment had failed by one vote, smiled, and went on with his reading just as though it were an ordinary day.[23]

After the prosecution collapsed, Stanton abandoned his pretensions to the War Department. Some weeks before, Johnson had nominated General John M. Schofield as Secretary of War, but the Senate had taken no action, nor did it do so immediately after the trial ended. The President drew up an order making Seward Secretary of War *ad interim*, but it was never issued. Seward took a draft of his appointment to Roscoe Conkling saying, "no mischief can go on without him," and asked the Senator from New York how they should proceed. Conkling, after consultation with his fellow Senators, replied that he favored such action as would place Schofield before them without embarrassment, and that evening the Senate confirmed Schofield as Secretary of War by a nearly unanimous vote. It was a happy omen of the relative peace that was to reign between Capitol Hill and the White House during the next nine months.[24]

That summer Seward had a hand in the appointment of Evarts as Attorney General. As for the quarrel over reconstruction, the Secretary of State now took a philosophical view. The two schools of thought probably led to the same goal, he wrote to a friend. The only difference was that one was longer, harder, and more exhausting than the other. He obviously did not foresee the emergence of a "Solid South " out of radical reconstruction.

Sometimes Seward's thoughts would go back to the man under whom he had served during the war, and he would speak critically of his martyred friend. Lincoln knew little of public affairs except what related to army movements, he burst out one day in Cabinet meeting. But three days later he wrote to Adams that he had recast the appendix to the diplomatic correspondence of 1865 into quarto form, calling it "Tribute of the Nations to Abraham Lincoln," put it on finer paper than usual, and so published it in a special edition.[25]

Seward still had his troubles with Capitol Hill. Again and again attempts were made to slash appropriations or to abolish posts in the State Department. At one time it looked as though the position of Second Assistant Secretary of State, which had been created for Hunter's benefit in 1866, might be abolished. Seward generally had Sumner's help in repelling these onslaughts, but he had to keep a wary eye on Congress.[26]

Such problems with politicians were significant only because of their effect upon the conduct of foreign policy. If there were lingering thoughts of political preferment, Seward had no choice but to put them away. His power base in New York was gone. There the leaders of the Democracy had no use for him, and there Weed had reached the end of his long political career.

Weed's political demise had not come without a final struggle. After the 1866 debacle, he had taken over control of the New York *Commercial Advertiser,* and had sought through federal patronage to build up centers of strength at key points throughout the state. He was trying, he told Sanford, "to work out of a false political position. . . . There is still a mountain of prejudice to overcome. But as fast as I get the ears of old friends I win them." These were idle fancies. Everyone disappointed him—Johnson, the Democrats, the Republican party—and he became bitterly critical of the President. He believed that Farragut would be a better presidential candidate than Grant, but the latter's name was on everyone's lips. Weed made overtures to Grant, but without avail, for the Fenton crowd took the Hero of Appomattox under their wing.

By the spring of 1868 the former Dictator's hopes of a great conservative movement had faded away. A victim to vertigo and despondency, he went to Europe in search of rest and health. Worried by his physical condition, fearful that he was spending too much money, he moved restlessly from place to place and did not return to the United States until after the election was over. Old friendships remained, but the political firm of Seward and Weed was broken up forever.

While Weed was in Europe the Grant boom gathered force. The General could have had either nomination, but the quarrel with Johnson had thrown him into the radical Republican camp. The Republican convention in May nominated him with fervid unanimity, and his slogan, "let us have peace," swept across the land. The Democrats, after protracted wrangling at their convention in July, nominated an unwilling candidate, Horatio Seymour of New York. The country was thus confronted with a choice between an able man who did not want to run and a military hero with no political experience. There were a number of economic issues, but the fundamental one was radical reconstruction.

There was much speculation as to where Seward stood in regard to the presidential contest. At the Democratic national convention the report spread that he would support Grant, if Johnson was not the Democracy's choice, and the story became current that he would vote for the Hero of Appomattox. This was nothing more than political gossip, for Seward refused to commit himself. He told Bigelow that he remained aloof because of his position as a Cabinet officer. He informed another correspondent that his work was done. He had helped to save the Union from domestic treason and foreign intervention, and to abolish slavery. It did not devolve upon him to choose or to concern himself officially with the next administration. He added, and then crossed out of this letter's preliminary draft, that he would hold himself in reserve in case some subsequent need for his services arose.

Probably the best statement of Seward's position came in a conversation with Bigelow during the height of the campaign. He could have supported either Johnson or Chase on the Democratic ticket, he remarked, but he could not help elect Seymour if he would. Bigelow remarked that Seward himself should have been the Democratic nominee and he replied, disclosing the smothered flame, "Yes, that is what they ought to have done." He would not vote at all, he said. He could not identify himself with Seymour, and he could not vote for Grant without condemning the reconstruction policy that he himself had advised. Furthermore, the Darien Canal, the Alabama claims, and other matters required Democratic aid, and the congressional Democrats had stood by him very faithfully during the past two years.[27]

Seward spoke in Auburn on the eve of the election. The speech was in large part an *apologia pro vita sua*. He had been an advocate of universal suffrage for the immigrant, the laborer and even the slave. His hand and seal were upon the abolition of the African slave trade, the Emancipation Proclamation and the Thirteenth Amendment. "No act of mine has consented to the prolongation of slavery a single day." The Monroe Doctrine, a mere theory eight years ago, was now "an irreversible fact," and the country was larger than it was when he became Secretary of State. He praised Lincoln, whose death was a "calamity." He defended Johnson and his policy, but would accept the present situation in the South since nothing better could be done. As for the election, the choice of a chief magistrate was important, and those who sustained the government in the war and in the abolition of slavery should be elected. The Republican party was more reliable than the Democratic party.[28]

This speech plainly admonished the electorate to vote Republican, even though it did not mention Grant by name. It was a dexterous performance, though specious in part and not likely to please the radicals or the Republican standard bearer. Coming only three days before the election, it could not have much influence on the outcome of the contest. And it was clearly designed to portray its author as one whose record entitled him to the gratitude of the country, if not to further preferment. It was hard for Seward to accept the fact that his public career was nearly at its close.

☙ 33 ❧

Maximilian

Politics was an inescapable part of Seward's life, even while Secretary of State, but the major part of his attention, both before and after the war ended centered on the diplomatic field. There a host of questions, major and minor, commanded his attention in the postwar period. Basic to all of them was whether or not the policies of the State Department should follow procedures developed under Lincoln, or strike out on a new course. In regard to this, he and Johnson soon reached an agreement. On June 3, 1865, in the first letter he was able to dictate, Seward authorized Bigelow to inform the French government that the policy of the United States toward France and Mexico "had undergone no change with the change of Administration." Subsequent events showed that this was true of Anglo-American relations as well.

The President took real interest in foreign policy. On occasion, as will appear later, he differed with his chief adjutant as to procedures. But the head of the state had had no more experience in the conduct of foreign affairs than had his predecessor. Furthermore, the quarrel with Congress over reconstruction soon became his primary concern. Seward consulted with Johnson on important diplomatic decisions, and with the Cabinet as well. There were times when the views of the Secretary of State did not prevail. Nevertheless, the initiation and conduct of foreign relations were left chiefly in his hands.[1]

Some of the minor questions with which Seward had to deal were

486

irritating enough. Such were Cassius M. Clay's antics in St. Petersburg, where his blustering behavior and capacity for quarreling with his associates involved him in difficulties. There was Minister John P. Hale in Spain, a bad appointment, who feuded with his secretary of legation. There was what seemed like the never-ending task of finding a replacement that the Senate would accept for Motley in Vienna. And there was always James Watson Webb at Rio de Janeiro.

During the war and after it, Webb stood up so boldly for American rights and privileges, including his own, that Seward had to keep watch on the rash envoy. This was particularly the case when Webb attempted to organize a steamship line between Brazil and the United States. According to his plan, the Secretary of State would steer the contract through Congress, while he, himself, would be given a leave of absence so that he could "inaugurate the enterprise." Then they would all get rich.

This project, Seward told him, was meritorious enough in itself, but the proposed manner of its execution would not only be a breach of official trust and of a federal statute, but also contravened the fundamental principle in law and morals that no man could at the same time be a trustee for another and for himself. The Secretary of State refused to have anything to do with it and the scheme died a-borning, but Webb's lack of principle and his impulsive vanity made him at best a doubtful diplomatic agent. Apparently Seward bore with him because of his long record of personal and political devotion.[2]

Webb, Hale, and "Cash" Clay were vexatious, but they could do no more than momentarily distract the attention of the Secretary of State from the major problems of the day. These were two items of unfinished business, one with France and the other with Great Britain. They constituted the major diplomatic issues of the Johnson period.

The great problem in Franco-American relations was Mexico. Here three main considerations influenced Seward's policy—his desire to maintain and promote republican institutions in the New World, his conception of the future role of the United States in the western hemisphere, and his determination to compel the abandonment of the Mexican venture while preserving good relations with the French government and people. Underlying these objectives was his belief that it was the destiny of Mexico to become part of the United States.

As early as the spring of 1864 Seward declared in a confidential letter to John Bigelow that those impatient about the French presence in Mexico should be content to await the ever-increasing expansion of the American people to the West and South. Perhaps within five years, he predicted, Mexico would be "opening herself as cheerfully to American immigration as Montana and Idaho are now." He recurred to this same argument in 1865. Bigelow might tell Drouyn de Lhuys, he declared, that when the United States expanded further, of course with the consent of adjacent peoples, it would be preferable to bring them in as constituent republican states.

But expansion or no expansion, Seward was eager to have the Mexican government remain republican in form. He would give no official countenance to Maximilian and when, in June 1865 an agent of the latter asked for an interview, the Secretary of State refused to grant it. At almost the same time, when Bigelow intimated to the French that the United States had no objection to seeing the Mexican experiment tried, and cast some doubt on the success of republican institutions in Latin America, he was told to inform the French government that such views were not warranted by his instructions. There was to be no countenance of any Mexican empire.

During the summer and fall of 1865 Seward moved with deliberation, and his policy in regard to the French Mexican venture may best be described as one of pin pricks. He was prompt to ask for explanations when reports came that France was enlisting Italians, or negotiating with erstwhile Confederate soldiers to serve in Mexico. Again, would Drouyn de Lhuys investigate reports that Negroes in Mexico were being reduced to the status of peons? Did he realize that Dr. William M. Gwin's plan for mining in Mexico under the protection of Maximilian would be regarded as a menace by the United States? Would he give serious attention to the charge that Mexicans seized while fighting for republicanism were being denied the rights of prisoners of war?

At the same time, however, Seward informed the French government through the new French Minister to the United States, the

Marquis de Montholon, and through Bigelow, that American policy had not changed. The United States was trying to prevent the enlistment of its nationals in the forces of Juarez, and was neutral in the struggle between him and Maximilian. If France asked explanations, Bigelow was to say that we cherished our traditional friendship with that country; that the Mexican situation revealed "an apparent if not a real, a future if not an immediate antagonism between the policies of the two countries"; that we felt the people of neighboring states should be free to choose their political institutions; and that, now the Civil War was over, the American people would become more and more concerned about the Mexican situation. Bigelow was to communicate this verbally and, if requested, give Drouyn de Lhuys a copy of the dispatch.[3]

There could be no question of American interest in the Mexican situation. William M. Evarts, John A. Dix, and others spoke of French policy there with open hostility. Montgomery Blair demanded that the French troops be expelled from Mexico. Army men also made their voices heard. Grant wanted vigorous action. General Lew Wallace wrote to Seward urging a move against Maximilian, and predicting a new opposition party that, if the administration did not act, would take up the Mexican question and "assume the assertion of the Monroe Doctrine as their great political principle."

Grant, together with Mexican Minister Matias Romero and General John M. Schofield, actually worked out a plan by which Schofield was to obtain a year's leave of absence and go to the Mexican border, where men and war materials would be sent across to bolster the fight against the French. Johnson was amenable, and Stanton was not unwilling to see this scheme put into effect. Seward was not at first consulted, but when he learned of the project disposed of it in typically dexterous fashion. He issued a circular requesting the diplomats of foreign countries to carry on their business through, instead of around, the State Department. Next he commissioned Schofield as a special agent to France, telling him that his mission was "to get your legs under Napoleon's mahogany and tell him he must get out of Mexico." This was in the summer of 1865 but, on pretext of waiting for the proper moment, it was not until November that the Secretary of State permitted the flattered general to set sail for France. He never had an interview with the

Emperor, though he did communicate the substance of his message to Prince Napoleon and other members of the French government. Remaining in France some six months, he was obviously in no position for activity on the Mexican border.[4]

Bigelow warned Seward that Thiers and other Frenchmen still felt resentment over Jackson's rough treatment of the French debt question in the 1830s, and that the entire nation would resent humiliation at the hands of the United States. This was probably a factor in shaping the Secretary of State's policy during 1865. But toward the close of the year the American public's irritation with France increased and President Johnson became restive. Determined to uphold the Monroe Doctrine and critical of Bigelow as having been won over by Napoleon III, Johnson evinced an inclination to conduct his own foreign policy. Moreover, Seward began hearing from both Bigelow and Sanford that the Mexican affair was putting a heavy strain on French finances; that it was unpopular with all classes; and that in view of the generally ominous European situation, Napoleon was anxious to get his troops back home.

Seward now told Prussia's Minister Gerolt that the question was no longer in the hands of the government but in that of the nation. The people, he said, were demanding a rigorous application of the Monroe Doctrine to the Mexican question. Obviously in his opinion the time had come to step up the pressure on France, and early in November he drew up a dispatch to Bigelow which stated the American position in no uncertain terms. France in Mexico, he declared, was of serious concern to the United States, for the activities of the French army there were "in direct antagonism to the policy of this government and the principle on which it was founded." On this grave question we could not be expected to compromise. We desired to retain the friendship of France, but the importance of political relations overshadowed the possibility that Bigelow had suggested of an advantageous revision in Franco-American commercial relations.

Shortly after this warning made its way across the Atlantic, Seward announced the appointment of Major General John A. Logan as Minister to the Juarez government, a step that was the more significant since Logan was a bitter critic of France and Maximilian. Another sign of a changing American attitude came when, toward the end of November, Montholon gave Seward a statement calculated to soothe the popular temper in America. This, Montholon hoped, would be in Johnson's annual message, and was, in effect, a hope that "negotiations" now pending between France and the United States would terminate in an amicable and satisfactory fashion. Seward substituted "explanations" for "negotiations" and sent this missive over to the White House. There it remained.

Seward's own draft for Johnson's message declared baldly that misapprehensions in regard to Franco-American relations would cease when France withdrew from Mexico, and the statement made by the President was scarcely less strong. Some two weeks later the French were bluntly warned that good relations with the United States were in "imminent jeopardy" unless their troops left Mexican soil. Drouyn de Lhuys had suggested that, as a *quid pro quo* for such withdrawal, the United States recognized Maximilian's government. This, said Seward, was unacceptable.[5]

Further evidence of a sterner attitude toward the Mexican situation came following reports from Bigelow and Motley that Austria might send troops to the aid of Maximilian. Seward told Motley to warn the Austrian government that if its subjects went to Mexico, either as regular troops or volunteers, the United States could not engage to remain a silent spectator. Should such participation occur, Motley was to withdraw from Vienna and await instructions.

Napoleon III was now beset from a number of quarters. Reports of Maximilian's incapacity worried him. James Watson Webb, en route from Brazil to the United States, urged him to get out of Mexico and suggested a periodic withdrawal of the French forces, an idea that favorably impressed the French Emperor. Shortly thereafter Schofield arrived with news of Seward's attitude, and the tone of Seward's dispatches became brusque. The intense hostility of the French public to the Mexican venture alarmed the government. Drouyn de Lhuys desperately suggested the initiation of direct correspondence between Johnson and Napoleon III, but to this Seward turned a deaf ear. The French Foreign Minister also requested assurances that, if France withdrew, the United States would continue its policy of neutrality in regard to Maximilian's struggle with Juarez. Seward's reply to this was a masterpiece of ambiguity that denied while it affirmed and from which no explicit assurance could be derived. As William H. Russell, the London *Times* correspondent, remarked to Bigelow, "My dear friend King Villum's oracular style, bless him, is at times obscure, is very pleasant, but there's a smack of powder in it too. . . ."

On January 31 Napoleon wrote to Marshal Bazaine, commander of the French forces in Mexico, that circumstances obliged him to withdraw from that country, but that the move would be made slowly so that Maximilian might still be able to establish his regime. Early in April Drouyn de Lhuys informed Seward that France would withdraw its forces in three stages, beginning in November 1866 and ending in November 1867. On April 5 an official statement to this effect appeared in the *Moniteur*. The long diplomatic struggle had ended with a victory that the American administration sorely needed at home.

Seward was elated. He lost no time in publishing his correspondence with Drouyn de Lhuys and Montholon, and that with Motley as well. To Seward's irritation, Welles expressed skepticism as to French promises, but most of the partisans of the administration received the news with enthusiasm. Even the New York *Tribune* admitted grudgingly that France was getting out of Mexico, and that Austria had received a stern warning. But if Motley did leave Vienna, said Greeley, the post ought to remain vacant. There was no sense in having a mission to that country.

It is a tribute to Seward's skill as a diplomat that, at this time when the triumph of his French policy was complete, he retained the trust and admiration of the French Minister to the United States. The latter reported home that Seward had full confidence in the good intentions of the Emperor. When Madame Juarez arrived in Washington, Seward gave a dinner in her honor at which report had it that he offered a toast to her husband as President of the Mexican Republic and expressed the hope that he would re-enter his capital within a year. Montholon retailed this to Drouyn de Lhuys, but added that he attached no more importance to it than to all the more or less impolitic remarks that Seward customarily made about dessert time, remarks to which "nul de nous fait la moindre attention." As for the threat to Austria, Montholon was sure that Johnson had forced Seward's hand. The situation was grave, said the Frenchman, but Seward had such confidence in himself, was so superior as a statesman to all around him, and was so capable of seeing the problems of foreign affairs in their proper perspective that no danger of war need be apprehended.[6]

Shortly after the French capitulation on withdrawal from Mexico the former Mexican ruler Santa Anna, now a man of seventy-one, occasioned a minor furor. In January 1866, while Seward was cruising in the West Indies, the wily Mexican, in exile on the island of St. Thomas, sent him a message of welcome and good wishes. Seward called on him, they discussed the Mexican situation, and the one-legged veteran, avowing his small regard for both Maximilian and Juarez, declared his willingness to lose his other leg in the cause of his country's liberty. There is no record of any further conversation, but Santa Anna and his suite shortly appeared in New York, claiming that he came with the approval of the Secretary of State.

It was common talk that Seward had summoned the Mexican, and Weed wrote asking what it was all about. Montholon thought the Secretary of State was more surprised than pleased by Santa Anna's appearance, and indeed Seward not only published a denial of any collusion with the new arrival but also refused to receive him in Washington. The old intriguer settled on Staten Island, where he tried to interest certain Fenians in the liberation of Mexico, the idea being that they would find there, rather than in Canada, a haven for Irish freedom. The New York *Herald* had it that he was in close touch with Washington, an allegation without proof. Later he tried to get into Mexico, and Seward defended the American consul at Vera Cruz for conniving at the seizure of Santa Anna by Mexican authorities on the deck of an American man-of-war. If the Secretary of State had thought at all of using the old adventurer, it was a temporary aberration.[7]

Once Napoleon gave his promise to leave Mexico, relations between the United States and France eased. Seward felt free to replace Bigelow with General John A. Dix. This, he told Montholon, was in part because Bigelow had leaned toward France in the Mexican negotiations—a remark that led the Frenchman to put the blame for this action on the President. There was a momentary flurry when word reached Washington that Napoleon had decided to take his troops out of Mexico in the spring of 1867, instead of beginning their gradual withdrawal in 1866. Seward sent to Bigelow, on November 23, 1866, a lengthy cablegram of protest. "We cannot acquiesce," he declared. Such a change would disturb American public opinion, and interfere with plans being concerted with Juarez for the pacification of his country. Bigelow made representations, but in considerably softer language, to the French court. He received assurances that the troops would depart in the spring, and these contented the Secretary of State. True to promise, the last French forces left Mexico on March 12, 1867.

After the departure of the French troops Maximilian's fortunes became desperate. Berthemy, the new French Minister at Washington, pressed Seward to join in urging a provisional government in Mexico as a means of ensuring the Emperor's safety. Seward promised to speak to Romero about it, but said he had to move carefully lest he and Johnson be accused of embroiling the country in foreign complications as a means of solving their difficulties at home. Much to the disappointment of Berthemy, the Secretary of State finally turned down the request.

On May 14 Maximilian surrendered to the troops of Juarez while his distraught wife, Carlotta, pleaded for aid in the courts of Europe. Both France and Austria made representations, and Seward sent messages to Juarez urging humane treatment for his prisoner. These had no effect. Maximilian was court-martialed, and on June 19, 1867 he faced a firing squad. Carlotta went insane. Such was the tragic end of a second Napoleon's dream of glory in the New World.[8]

It was only natural that Seward, being a politician as well as a statesman, should try to use his victory over the French for political advantage. When he and Johnson made the "Swing Around the Circle" in the fall of 1866, they invited the Mexican Minister to accompany them and Romero accepted. Seward presented him to the crowds along the route as the representative of a nation which Johnson had saved from foreign intervention, and exhorted his listeners to cheer for Mexico. Finally Romero began to suspect that he was being used and, on plea of his health, returned to Washington.

In like manner, Seward's cablegram in cipher to Bigelow about the change in French plans for withdrawal, a communication which cost the government over $13,000, had political intent. The administration had just suffered a severe defeat at the polls, and some of its enemies were eager to attack it in Congress. Bidding defiance to

France could be depended on to enlist American sympathies. The dispatch as first drafted was stronger than the one that was sent, while at the same time Seward assured the Cabinet that there would be no difficulty with the French. He released the final draft to the American press before it reached Paris. It would seem that his strategy had some effect for when, shortly thereafter, Senator Howard of Michigan attempted to mount an attack against Seward's Mexican policy, Sumner as head of the Senate's Committee on Foreign Relations sidetracked it without difficulty.[9]

There was, of course, a wide range in the contemporary judgments passed on Seward's course regarding France and Mexico. Welles confided to his diary that it had been a muddle from beginning to end. Charles XV of Sweden remarked that it showed Seward to be "the most wise and sagacious statesman of modern times." Mercier, writing from Madrid to Seward, complained that the Secretary of State had "played too strongly upon the passions of your public at our expense," though he admitted that in this he might be mistaken. Other French diplomats professed no such heartburnings. Sanford, visiting Paris in June 1867, found no trace of bitterness toward Seward or toward the United States. Moustier, the new Minister of Foreign Affairs, told Sanford, "We have the highest opinion of him here. He will have a brilliant page in history," and Drouyn de Lhuys told another American that Seward was a skillful statesman with a high reputation in Europe.

Generally speaking, liberals were disposed to commend and conservatives to blame Seward's policy. The liberal London *Daily News* praised his courteous and patient diplomacy, and especially commended his doctrine of non-intervention in the affairs of other nations. This was, said the *News,* as old as public law and, whether called the Monroe Doctrine or by some other name, was sound and necessary. On the other hand, the Tory London *Morning Herald* declared that Seward had "arrogantly" asserted the Monroe Doctrine, and had bullied France into abandoning Maximilian.[10]

While Seward's conduct of diplomacy in the Maximilian affair was at times open to the charge of being overly subtle, it still merits high praise. During the Civil War it was only wisdom to avoid a conflict with France, and Seward, while making clear the dislike of the American government for the Napoleonic venture, had assumed and maintained an attitude of neutrality toward the Mexican situation. When peace at home freed his hands he began increasing pressure on the French for withdrawal, moving in accord with mounting public opinion, but keeping the generals and congressional fire-eaters from taking steps that might well have precipitated war. His policy showed a keen appreciation of the way in which the force of circumstance was pushing Napoleon into relinquishing his disastrous venture. In consequence the French government could abandon its course without the appearance of being forced by the open threat of American intervention. The policy pursued by the Secretary of State was not only successful in achieving its objective, but did so in a manner that made possible a continuance of good relations with a traditional friend of the United States. This was diplomacy of a high order.

⤐ 34 ⤏

The *Alabama* Claims

While Seward carried on his negotiations with France over the Mexican affair, he also devoted much attention to old and new problems in Anglo-American relations. Sir Frederick Bruce, successor to Lord Lyons as Minister to the United States, arrived in Washington during the fateful month of April 1865, and Seward drafted a letter of welcome to him in a very shaky hand. Bruce had previously been the British Minister to China and Anson Burlingame, who knew him well, was confident that he would establish good relations with the Secretary of State. Before long the characteristic hospitality of the house on Lafayette Square was put in play, and the two men developed a relationship of mutual respect and friendship.

Kindness to the British Minister did not necessarily mean kind thoughts about Great Britain. That government's delay in withdrawing recognition of Confederate belligerent rights irritated the Secretary of State. On May 15, Chief Clerk Hunter, obviously under instructions from the invalid, sent word to Adams that, if such action had not been taken by the time this dispatch reached him, he was to inform Russell that the United States might deem it necessary to destroy insurgent warships sheltered in neutral ports. Three weeks later Seward was damning the English to Welles, declaring that he was ready to let them know that they would not be allowed to insult the United States.

On June 2, 1865, Britain recognized that the war was over and peace re-established, but Seward found the phraseology of Russell's communication on the subject unsatisfactory because it was not, to his mind, clear enough on the subject of belligerent rights. Bruce understood him to say that Britain's conduct was not good and therefore he would not negotiate a new reciprocity treaty. The Secretary of State was also wroth over the raider *Shenandoah*, which coaled at Melbourne and then, unaware that the war was over, proceeded to destroy the American whaling fleet in the Northwest Pacific. Much to Seward's disgust, when the *Shenandoah* surrendered in November to the British authorities at Liverpool, Captain Waddell and his men were given their freedom. The Secretary's irritation found vent in his draft for Johnson's first message to Congress. Britain's concession of belligerent rights, he wrote, "has been, at last, completely rescinded, although the proceeding was attended with manifest reluctance and vexatious delays." [1]

This fuming over belligerent rights may have been calculated to impress the British with the importance Seward attached to them as factors in the prolongation of the war. For as he fumed he took up once more what William H. Huntington of the New York *Tribune* called "that Alabamboozle business." In May 1865, Adams renewed the claim for damages suffered from the Confederate cruisers, but Russell was adamant. He delayed his answer some three months. When it came, it teemed with compliments and expressions of good will, but on the positive side merely suggested that a joint commission be established to consider such claims as the two powers agreed should be presented for its consideration. As for the *Alabama* claims, Russell would not even consider reparation, nor would he submit them to arbitration.

Adams informed Seward of the British attitude, and the latter discussed the situation with Johnson. He then told Adams that no arbitration proposal would henceforward be insisted upon or submitted by the United States. Adams was to ask Russell if it was correct that Great Britain would not agree to refer the *Alabama* claims to the proposed joint commission. Russell replied in the affirmative, and Seward thereupon declined to have anything to do with such a commission.

While this exchange of views was going on Palmerston died and Russell became Prime Minister, with Lord Clarendon as Secretary of

State for Foreign Affairs. Clarendon proposed to Adams that the two countries set up some form of joint consultation for clarifying the vaguer aspects of international law. Adams felt that the British government was uneasy about the way in which Russell had left the claims situation, and wished to extricate itself from a vulnerable position. He was not disposed to help in this, and neither was Seward. The latter declared that it was impossible for the United States to negotiate for future contingencies "without having first due regard paid for our past injuries and damages." Adams communicated this view to Clarendon.

It looked like a stalemate. Seward would not move toward a reciprocity treaty, alleging that he could take no step because of the attitude of Congress, and Sumner told Bruce that Britain's stand on the *Alabama* claims made the renewal of reciprocity impossible. Bruce informed Clarendon that, if the United States were relieved from anxiety about Mexico, public opinion would undoubtedly demand strong measures against Great Britain.[2]

Just at this time came an event that scarcely smoothed the paths of diplomacy. On February 12, 1866 George Bancroft delivered a eulogy on Lincoln before the assembled Congress, with the diplomatic corps as invited guests. According to his custom the orator portrayed the United States as the particular recipient of God's favors, but the body of his speech consisted of a review of the events of the preceding six years. Therein he referred to Maximilian as an "Austrian adventurer," said some harsh things about British policy, and particularly criticized Palmerston and Russell for their lack of sympathy with the North.

Bancroft had suggested to Seward that he might ask Bruce to stay away, and Seward told both Bruce and Montholon that perhaps they had better make themselves conspicuous by their absence. Bruce, however, appeared and was indignant, as was Count Wydenbruck, the Austrian Minister. When news of the speech reached Europe, Russell lodged a protest with Adams, who wrote in some distress to Bancroft. The latter replied, showing conclusively that the points he had made in regard to Russell's attitude were correct, and nothing more was heard from the British Prime Minister on that particular subject.

Through Blatchford, Bancroft told Seward that he had desired to strengthen him, and the Secretary of State declared that he had done so, and done it well. Bancroft's letter to Adams, said Seward, was complete and effective. European politicians who found fault with the orator ought to remember how roughly American sensibilities had been treated during the past five years. Sumner, however, thought the speech was in bad taste, and Adams felt that, rather than causing fresh quarrels, it was now "wiser and better for both nations to cultivate more friendly relations." [3]

The *Alabama* claims were left temporarily in abeyance, but Seward had no intention of dropping them. When an American firm proposed to sell to the Chilean government a ship with guns dismantled that had been used in the merchant service, the United States moved to prevent the sale lest the transaction weaken the claims contention with Great Britain. But popular feeling against England was strong, and in July 1866 the House of Representatives, by a vote of 123 to 0, passed a bill removing the prohibition against selling ships or munitions of war to foreign citizens or to governments at peace with the United States. The Austro-Prussian conflict was on, the continent of Europe teemed with unrest, and Britain had clear notice of what might be expected of neutral America if the British empire became involved in war.[4]

A factor which complicated Anglo-American relations at this time was Great Britain's chronic Irish problem. The bitter feeling stirred by Ireland's struggle for independence had been carried across the water by emigrants from the "ould sod," and in 1858 John O'Mahoney founded in America an organization pledged to work for Irish independence. He called it the Fenian Brotherhood, a transatlantic counterpart of the Irish Revolutionary Brotherhood headed by James Stephens. Both organizations harbored a conviction that the English had brought on the famine of 1846–47 in order to exterminate the Irish people, and their feeling against the English was bitter indeed.

The Fenian Brotherhood grew slowly during the Civil War, numbering some 10,000 members by January 1865. Its members took it for granted that a rupture between Great Britain and the United States was inevitable, the only question being whether the Fenians should participate in the general melee by invading Canada, or by sending money across the water in order to hasten the emancipation back home. Despite the opposition of the Catholic clergy, Fenianism grew in strength and in 1865 raised $228,000 for the cause of Irish liberation.

The British government was fully aware of the aid and comfort provided in the United States for the Irish Revolutionary Brotherhood, and it also knew of Seward's fondness for the Irish. During the Civil War Seward encouraged Irish immigration, furnishing some of the newcomers with free passage to the New World, and the Fenians thought him their friend. In September 1865, Chicago Fenians appealed to him for money. The records of the society show that one of their leaders, Bernard D. Killian, had an interview with Seward and Johnson during which he asked their opinion of a scheme for setting up a republic in Canada across the northeast boundary line. According to Killian, they replied that the government would recognize accomplished facts. Shortly thereafter, he tried unsuccessfully to get Seward to commit himself on paper. By the end of 1865 the Fenian leaders were claiming approval of the United States for their proposed invasion of Canada.[5]

By February 1866 the agitation in Ireland had gathered such force that Great Britain suspended the Habeas Corpus Act. Arrests increased, including individuals who had come from America to join in the fray. Some of these were naturalized American citizens who had held high rank in the Union army; and Adams, at least, believed that more than one Fenian sought imprisonment in order to stir up dissension between the British government and the United States.

Seward wished to avoid trouble with Great Britain. Congress was inclined to be truculent in defending the rights of New England fishermen who, in any negotiation over the Newfoundland fisheries, were averse to lowering the duties on British fish. The Secretary of State told Justin Morrill of the House Ways and Means Committee that Congress and the fishermen were much mistaken if they thought the government would go to war over the question. If an equitable arrangement could not be reached, the fishermen might "agonize and be damned." But the Irish vote was another matter, especially in view of the developing struggle over reconstruction.

Between Britain and the Irish, the Secretary of State had to pick his way with care. Cautiously he assured Bruce that he was as eager for peace on the border as were the British. He suggested that, without divulging the source of his information, Clarendon warn the Governor-General of Canada to be on the lookout for a raid on the Maine-New Brunswick frontier. He also gave Bruce private assurance that measures—he would not say what measures—were being taken to prevent such aggression.

This was smart politics for, as Bruce remarked, the radicals would have liked nothing better than a quarrel between himself and Seward over the Fenians. Nevertheless the arrests in Ireland had to be faced, and in March 1866 the Secretary of State outlined to Adams American policy toward the situation there and toward the Fenians.

The Fenian movement, Seward declared, was controlled by Irishmen who, naturalized or not, thought and acted like Irishmen. Hence it was British, not American, in character. The government would not move against it so long as it did not initiate armed action from within the United States against friendly nations. As for the naturalized Irishmen now in Ireland, they were subject to the laws of Great Britain. Adams was to investigate their complaints and ask "strict justice," nothing more. Britain's refusal to recognize the naturalization of Irishmen constituted a problem that demanded solution, perhaps in the form of a treaty. But it must be understood that the United States could not abandon naturalized citizens who had fought for the Union in the Civil War and now languished in jail accused of treason against Great Britain.[6]

Clarendon was agreeable to releasing those who claimed to be American citizens and had been arbitrarily imprisoned by local authorities, but the picture became clouded in the spring of 1866 when the Fenians launched raids into Canada from Black Rock, St. Albans, and other places on the frontier. Seward and Johnson acted promptly, ordering General Meade with troops to the border, and issuing a proclamation warning American citizens against participation in these movements. The raids themselves amounted to little— the only exploit of 1000 Irishmen at St. Albans being the capture of one British flag. By the middle of June the "invasions" were over and the Fenians were pouring out the vials of their wrath on the President and the Secretary of State.

Seward's prompt action pleased the British as much as it irritated the Fenians. He sought to assuage the latter's resentment by vigorous efforts on behalf of imprisoned Irishmen, both in Canada and the old country. Adams was kept busy requesting release or early trials, protesting convictions and asking for clemency. For his part, Seward authorized discontinuance of trials in the United States for the conspirators and the employment of counsel for citizens on trial in Canada, while he urged clemency upon the Canadian authorities. He took care that his efforts were publicized, but many of the Irish remained resentful. Sanford Church and other Democratic politicians believed that the Republican victory of 1866 in New York State resulted from the Irish vote.[7]

Further evidence of Seward's desire to propitiate the Irish came at the close of 1866. A letter from Rufus King at Rome told of the withdrawal of the French troops there and the possible flight of the Pope. Two of the confidants of Pius IX had asked King if His Holiness could find refuge in the United States. Seward read his proposed reply to the Cabinet. He would not only give the Pope asylum, but would also convey him to America in a ship of the United States Navy, and then treat him as the nation's guest. Welles and Stanton objected to these last provisions, and Seward struck them out of his reply to the Minister Resident at Rome.[8]

Shortly after the furor over Fenian attempts on Canada died down, a dispatch from Adams announced a change of ministry in Britain. Russell's government resigned, the Tories came into power, and Lord Stanley became the new Secretary of State for Foreign Affairs. It seemed a favorable moment for reopening the *Alabama* question, and Seward prepared a list of claims which covered sixty-seven pages in longhand. The accompanying letter professed willingness to consider British claims, and rehearsed the grounds for American grievances. These included not only the losses of shipowners, but also the recognition of belligerency and other forms of sympathy for and assistance to the Confederacy such as disregard of treaties and of international law, and the allowance of warlike expeditions against the United States.

Once again the British government was dilatory. Seward pressed for action, and Bruce informed Stanley that if Congress took the bit in its teeth and called for a rupture with Great Britain, Johnson might go along as a means of smoothing over his differences with that body, thus making easier a conciliatory policy toward the South. Finally, on November 30, 1866, Stanley answered Seward's contentions point by point. Having done so, he professed willingness to accept arbitration of the American claims, save for any that involved the recognition of belligerency.[9]

Seward replied on January 12, 1867. He reiterated his arguments as to the iniquity of British policy, stressing the damage caused by the Queen's Proclamation of Neutrality. It had been of great assistance to the Confederacy, he declared, for as a result of it the rebels had received massive stores of "provisions and treasures, arms, ordnance, and munitions of war," to say nothing of great moral encouragement. The loss of ninety-five ships and $10,000,000 worth of property was "only a small part of the damages . . . sustained by the United States at the hands of British abettors of the insurgents." However, he was willing to submit "the whole controversy" to arbitration.

In this dispatch Seward ignored the legitimate British argument that the proclamation of a blockade was virtually a recognition by the United States government of the South's belligerent status. Furthermore, the reference to the loss of ships and property had an ominous ring in British ears. If this was "only a small part of the damages" suffered, were the Americans going to insist on recompense for their commerce driven off the ocean, or even for the prolongation of the war? Such indirect damages would obviously open the door to enormous claims.

Stanley was still willing to negotiate a settlement, but he rejected the "extensive and unlimited" reference of the controversy to arbitration. Seward found this unsatisfactory. The United States, he asserted, could not accept any special or peculiar limitation of arbitration, especially one that omitted the question of belligerent rights. All claims should be adjusted by one and the same form of tribunal. Adams thought he put too much emphasis on the recognition of belligerency as a basis of claims for damage, and wondered about the motives of the Secretary of State.[10]

During the spring of 1867 Seward tried in various ways to spur the British government into active negotiation. Public sympathy for Ireland and delay in settling the *Alabama* claims, he declared, fostered a movement in the United States to revise our neutrality laws in ways dangerous to British interests. He spoke to Bruce of the growing unfriendliness of Congress toward Great Britain. The British Minister should not rely on Sumner to prevent unfriendly legislation, for Sumner was weakening in the face of the rising tumult. Bruce, alarmed, wrote to Stanley that, if popular emotion provoked a crisis, Seward was unscrupulous enough to go along with it for the sake of popularity, for he was "a reckless and dangerous Minister in Foreign Affairs at this time."

The claims negotiation went on through 1867 and into 1868. At one time Seward threatened to turn the whole business over to Congress. At another time he would broaden its scope to include a revision of the Clayton-Bulwer Treaty. He also suggested to Adams that Britain might make the Bahama Islands a *quid pro quo* for the American claims. In December 1867 he proposed a comprehensive consideration of all subjects of difference between the two countries, one that would include boundaries, the fisheries, the rights of naturalized American citizens in Ireland, and everything else— lumping the lot together, as he expressed it. His communications to Adams indicated that he kept in mind the injury suffered by the United States through Britain's recognition of the South as a belligerent. Adams was convinced that he wanted British territory in the Northwest, or the West Indies islands, in exchange for American claims. Others thought so, too, and one of these, Hinton R. Helper, wrote to the Secretary of State suggesting as much. Seward did not deny this, and for a good reason. A few days before he had told Orville Browning that ere long the United States would get British Columbia. His plan, he said, was to throw all claims on both sides into one heap and then balance them off, one against the other. In this way the United States would pay for British Columbia with the *Alabama* claims, the latter being assumed eventually by the government at Washington.

Bruce died suddenly, September 19, 1867, and his successor, Edward Thornton, did not reach Washington until the following January. Meanwhile, Adams became increasingly disgusted with the apparent futility of the negotiations, to say nothing of Seward's theory of Irish patriotism which, he confided to his diary, embraced "the murder of policemen and blowing up of people with mines and gunpowder to rescue prisoners." The American Minister to Great Britain felt that he was doing nothing but reclaiming Fenians from punishment that most of them richly deserved and (for Congress insisted upon simple dress) carrying on discussions about the clothes he wore at Court. Long eager to return home, Adams served notice that he meant to do so, his resignation to take effect April 1, 1868.[11]

During this same period the country was full of sound and fury over the Irish situation. Fenian petitions for redress came, Seward declared, "from Portland to San Francisco and from St. Paul to Pensacola." In the House of Representatives, Banks introduced a bill authorizing the arrest of citizens of any country that incarcerated or unreasonably detained naturalized American citizens on the ground that they were still nationals of that country. The dispute over citizenship was now a dangerous international issue. The struggle between Johnson and Congress was also approaching its climax, and the administration needed all the home support it could muster. In view of these circumstances, Seward turned his attention from the *Alabama* claims to the Fenians imprisoned in Britain, and to the question of naturalization. Here in two instances he demonstrated his versatility of approach to diplomatic problems.

Shortly before Bruce's death, Seward showed him a letter to Johnson from Fernando Wood denouncing British imprisonment of Fenians, and urging the President to take violent measures for the sake of the Irish vote. Seward intimated that the President might do so in order to curry favor with the Democrats. If Bruce would obtain the release of certain Fenian leaders, Seward would endeavor to keep Johnson within bounds. Bruce urged the British government to be lenient, and the Fenians were eventually released.

The other case involved Canada. Fenians and their sympathizers in that country raided across the American border in efforts to abduct obnoxious opponents. United States citizens responded with forays of their own. A particularly obstreperous Canadian, Allan Macdonald, was seized, carried into American territory, and thrust into prison at St. Clair. Shortly thereafter a band of armed Canadians forced his release and conveyed him back to Canada, a proceeding which brought anguished protests to Washington from the St. Clair authorities. Seward decided to ignore the whole affair. When it came up at a dinner party given by the Turkish Minister, the Secretary of State laughed and said that Macdonald had caused trouble enough as it was, and he would take no action.

Seward's decision in the Macdonald case earned the gratitude of the Governor-General of Canada. Monck wrote to Thornton that it was marked by the same fairness and consideration that had characterized the conduct of the Secretary of State "in every case with reference to which I have had occasion to appeal to him during the now rather lengthened occupation of my present situation. . . ." [12]

Seward's anxiety to conclude the negotiations with Great Britain, if nothing else, made it essential that Adams should be replaced without undue delay, and in June 1868 the Senate confirmed Reverdy Johnson as Minister to Great Britain. Good natured, courteous, and apparently popular in the Senate, which bade him farewell with expressions of high esteem, Reverdy Johnson was known to have friendly feelings toward England, and Minister Thornton thought his appointment would have a beneficial effect upon the relations between the two countries.

There is some evidence that Seward was not enthusiastic about Johnson as Adams's successor. A year earlier he had told John Bigelow that Johnson was very untruthful, and shortly after the appointment, James E. Harvey, Seward's close friend, assured Benjamin Moran, the secretary of legation in London, that Johnson was not the choice of the Secretary of State. But even if such was the case, Seward was at first hopeful that success would now crown the long drawn out negotiations. He instructed the new minister to give precedence to a naturalization treaty, because of the excited state of American public opinion over the imprisonment of Fenians in Ireland. This taken care of, he should take up the Northwest boundary question, and finally the claims problem. In regard to the latter, Seward now proposed a joint commission for the adjudication of all claims between the two countries that had arisen since February 8, 1853, that being the date of a previous settlement.

Johnson's amiable personality, and his expressions of good will in the speeches that he was only too glad to make, produced a favorable impression in England. He wrote home cheerfully about prospects but these were slow in making an appearance, and the impatient Seward thought that the British ministry had "lost all energy and spirit." Then, too, the American Minister showed a distressing propensity for consorting with erstwhile Confederates and their British sympathizers, a circumstance that aroused much indignation in the American press and in Congress. The *Tribune* called him "a

toady and a snob," and Raymond's *Times* felt that the language he
used approached servility. Benjamin Moran thought the seventy-
two-year-old diplomat was in his dotage, an old man with a penchant for scandal and smutty stories, who would sign anything that
Stanley and Clarendon put before him.

Johnson sought to make three treaties, one for naturalization, one
to determine the boundary in the Far Northwest on San Juan Island,
and one for the final settlement of the claims question. He obtained
a protocol, or preliminary agreement, on naturalization. The two
sides were not far apart on the San Juan question. But the claims
negotiation lagged. The British government suspected that Seward
did not really want a settlement of individual claims but something
more, a suspicion that was in no whit abated by his appointment of
Fenians as consuls at Leeds and other British cities.

Johnson finally negotiated a claims convention with Stanley, but
when Seward saw it he told the Cabinet that it made him sick and he
cabled instructions for revision. Among other changes, the appointed commissioners were to meet in Washington rather than in
London, there was to be specific mention of the *Alabama* claims, and
the American commissioners should be named not merely by the
President but with the advice and consent of the Senate. These
amendments, he explained to his minister plenipotentiary, were essential in order to assure Senate approval, and time was now important.

The revisions that Seward demanded were incorporated in the
convention, and on January 14, 1869, Johnson and Clarendon signed
the document in London. By its terms each side was to appoint two
commissioners, the four to agree upon an arbitrator to whom should
be referred claims upon which they could not agree. If they could
not settle on an arbitrator, each side would name one, and in referred cases one of these would be chosen by lot to officiate. The
convention clearly indicated that the claims to be examined were
those made by citizens of one country against the other since February 8, 1853.

Reverdy Johnson evidently believed the reference to the *Alabama*
claims in the convention meant that it included consideration of indirect damages as well as individual claims. He stated in a dispatch to
Seward on January 15, that the British government had given way

on this point, and that the recognition of the Confederates as belligerents would be before the commissioners or, if they failed to agree, before the arbitrator. It is scarcely possible that Seward shared this opinion. Apparently for the sake of concluding the negotiation, for time was now short, he gave up the idea of pressing for an unequivocal statement about indirect damages. They were not specifically mentioned in the treaty.

By the middle of January 1869, Reverdy Johnson had concluded the naturalization protocol, the claims treaty, and a treaty referring the San Juan boundary to arbitration by the President of the Swiss Confederation. On January 18, President Johnson sent all three agreements to the Senate.

Seward was fearful about their fate, especially that of the claims treaty. He wrote to Reverdy Johnson that the public press was bent on making an issue of the claims for the sake of the incoming administration, and that the "only pretence of a logical principle" advanced by the Republican papers was that Great Britain owed so much additional compensation for its recognition of belligerency that there must be a cession of territory. This, he noted, was the argument advanced by the very men who had opposed all acquisitions of territory attempted by the Johnson administration. The event justified his pessimism.

At a meeting of the Senate in special session, Sumner, from the Committee on Foreign Relations, made a report adverse to the claims treaty, and attacked it in an hour-long speech. He declared that it had little to commend it; that it had been manufactured in haste; that it contained no statement of regret by England; and that it took no account whatever of the principal point of contention between the two countries—the cost of the prolongation of the war which had been the result of British policy. The Senate rejected the treaty by a vote of 54 to 1.

Adams felt that the rejection of the Johnson-Clarendon claims treaty, together with Sumner's speech, raised the scale of American demands for reparation so high that there was little room left for negotiation. As later events were to prove, Sumner and other opponents of the instrument marked Canada as the price Britain should pay for the "wrongs" that country had inflicted upon the United States during the Civil War.

The other agreements concluded by Reverdy Johnson also were given short shrift. The Senate refused to act on the San Juan treaty, and postponed action on the naturalization protocol. The San Juan agreement and a naturalization convention with Great Britain both became law under the Grant administration.

The fate of the Reverdy Johnson agreements was the result of the Senate's dislike of Great Britain and, chiefly, its hostility to Seward and Johnson. Seward talked with Sumner after the Foreign Relations Committee's adverse report on the claims treaty, and came away convinced that the opposition was primarily a party question. Grant was against the treaty, and the Republican Congress was in no mood to crown the outgoing administration with a diplomatic success. Seward also blamed Great Britain for being "too slow and too obstinate." There was some justice in this complaint. But not all the delay was London's fault. He, also, had tried to play a waiting game, and his introduction of the indirect damages claim had scarcely hastened proceedings.[13]

It was not until 1871 that the Treaty of Washington expressed regret for the escape of the raiders from British ports and provided a court of arbitration that, after a renewed claim for indirect damages almost wrecked the negotiation, awarded $15,500,000 in damages to the United States. By that time Seward had been in retirement two and one-half years.

⇜§ *35* §⇝

Westward the Star of Empire

Domestic politics, the Maximilian affair, and the *Alabama* claims absorbed much of Seward's attention during the postwar years, but there was also another subject, one to which he had long devoted thought and which he kept in mind. This was the role of the United States in the world of the future.

John Quincy Adams in 1802, misquoting Bishop Berkeley, had declared that "Westward the Star of Empire takes its way." The destinies of the American "empire," in his view, were beyond the power of human calculation. Seward held much the same belief. It was a political law, a higher law, he told his audience at Madison, Wisconsin, in 1860, that empire, moving at an ever swifter pace, makes its way constantly westward. It would continue to do so until the new and old civilizations of the world met on the shores of the Pacific.

As the strength of the Confederacy waned, Seward's thoughts turned more and more to this subject. To him the United States was the evangel of a democratic "imperialism" which would first expand its economic influence and then its way of life across the globe. He could not hope for spectacular gains in building this "empire." Circumstances were against it. His hope was, rather, to lay foundations for great achievement. A year before the close of the Civil War he spoke of it to Charles Francis Adams.

They had a continent to bring forward to a higher state of civilization than the world had yet seen, Seward told the Minister to Great Britain. To achieve this the United States must have a world-wide foreign commerce, and institutions that would find favor with all mankind. Such favor could best be established by demonstrating that America would not promote violence at home or abroad, but would be "conservative of law, order and universal peace." Three years later he found a stanza of poetry that summed up his dream of the future—

> Our nation with united interests blest,
> Not now content to poise, shall sway the rest;
> Abroad our Empire shall no limits know,
> But like the sea in boundless circles flow.[1]

Expansion of American power, in Seward's view, would be internal as well as external, for the economic potential of the country, its wealth in soil and forests and minerals, was enormous. Hence immigration was essential, not only for wartime needs but also for the future store of labor and of minds that could be put to use. How much the older nations suffered from the immobility of classes and masses, he told James Harvey. We need have no fear of new ideas, nor of the discontented elements in Europe's population. This nation of ours could absorb all the conscientious teachers of Europe "without fear of danger from imputed heresies in politics or religion." The thing to do was gather to ourselves the treasures in men and ideas that Europe had to offer.

So it was no wonder that the Secretary of State circularized American ministers and consuls, urging them to spread abroad the advantages of coming to the New World. He also besought Congress to extend a helping hand to would-be immigrants, and he would have this done without favoritism being shown to such western Europeans as Englishmen, Scotsmen, and Scandinavians.

The result of these efforts, along with those of other like-minded men, was the Act To Encourage Immigration of 1864, a bill drawn up along lines proposed by the Secretary of State. As it reached the floor of the Senate in February, it provided for a Commissioner of Immigration, whose office would be in the State Department and who would be under the direction of the Secretary. The Commissioner would see to it that suitable information about America the land of opportunity was disseminated abroad, and under his auspices an immigrant office would be established in New York headed by a Superintendent of Immigration. As finally passed, the Act declared that no immigrant should be liable for military service unless he announced his intention of becoming a citizen. It also included a contract clause by which immigrants pledged their wages for not more than one year in order to pay the expenses of their journey from the Old World.

Owing to this Act and to State Department propaganda, foreigners flocked to the United States. Seward told Adams in August 1864 that during the past six months alone 115,000 immigrants had come to America. But his efforts to promote immigration, including the Contract Labor law, as men called it, had some consequences which he did not foresee. British trade unions attempted to raise their own wages by dumping their members into the American labor market, a procedure that aroused the wrath of organized labor in the United States. As a result of the contract clause, several money-making organizations were formed to bring foreign workers to the United States. One of these, the American Emigrant Company, numbered among its sponsors Charles Sumner, Gideon Welles, and Salmon P. Chase. These companies sometimes imported strike-breakers and men willing to work for starvation wages, and American labor became still more upset. In 1868 Congress repealed the Contract Labor law.

There is no evidence that Seward opposed this repeal. The probability is that he approved it. At least, in 1868, while continuing to urge free immigration of both Europeans and Orientals, he put himself on record as opposed to legislation unfair to immigrants, and particularly to Chinese and Japanese contract labor.[2]

Using the State Department to foster immigration was only one of the many ways in which Seward sought the realization of his great American dream. That his thought girdled the globe was never more apparent than in his sponsorship of the Perry McDonough Collins plan for a world-embracing telegraph. Collins planned a line that would extend from the United States through British Columbia to Russian America, then across Bering Strait to the mouth of the Amur and down that river and across Siberia to St. Petersburg, and so to western Europe. This stupendous project was taken up by the

Western Union Telegraph Company and enthusiastically sponsored by the Secretary of State. In 1864 he drafted a bill providing subsidies for the scheme, and prevailed upon Zachariah Chandler, chairman of the Senate Committee on Commerce to introduce it.

In a lengthy communication to Chandler, Seward pointed out that this line, together with the Atlantic cable, would provide worldwide communication and, with a network of wires across North and South America, would vastly stimulate industry and commerce. It would, he said, prove comparable in value to the Portuguese passage around the Cape of Good Hope and to the wealth acquired by Holland and Great Britain through trade and conquest. The Collins line and the Atlantic cable "would naturally aid and strengthen each other," for the interests of society would soon "require more than one, and more than even two trans-oceanic world-girdling telegraphs."

Alas for these roseate predictions. An unsympathetic Senate struck out the subsidy from the bill, which passed, but with an irate Chandler declaring that it was now no good and voting against his own measure. The Collins project itself collapsed when it became apparent that the success of the Atlantic cable meant ruinous competition. But before it was abandoned the directors of Western Union slipped the $3,000,000 loss it entailed over to their stockholders.[3]

Before examining the less grandiose manifestations of Seward's vision, it is necessary to note the restrictions that he placed upon it when it came to the actual conduct of foreign affairs. He consistently opposed expansion by conquest. He was not interested in the acquisition of colonies in distant parts of the world, since they would mean control over populations alien to the United States by language, custom, and ideas. He was also unwilling to participate in conferences designed to produce joint agreement with other powers, though he would so co-operate when he considered it absolutely necessary, as in the Far East. Europe's quarrels he regarded as none of his affair. During the 1860s the "Sick Man of Europe" was troubling the waters of diplomacy, but Seward showed no interest in drawing up a will for the Turkish Empire. He did feel that the United States should have diplomatic representation in Greece and Constantinople adequate for its modest trading interests in the Levant, but he emphatically disclaimed any intention of acquiring a Mediterranean base. He told the French Minister Berthemy that the time of the crusader was past, and declared that he was glad to leave to Europe "the disentangling of the Turkish knot." Such restraints, however, left open many opportunities for advancing American interests through diplomatic activity.[4]

In Seward's diplomatic arsenal, treaties were weapons. "It is characteristic of every good treaty," he told Sanford, "that it confers great advantages upon one party without any serious cost or inconvenience to the other." Consequently he devoted a considerable part of his time to the negotiation of naturalization agreements for immigrants, extradition arrangements, and especially conventions promoting trade and commerce. While most of his important treaties never became law, the result in numbers was impressive. In 1868 the executive department made an enumeration of treaties and conventions from the time of the Articles of Confederation. There were 205, it was discovered, and of these Seward had been responsible for forty-nine. Some three months later, he announced proudly that he had negotiated fifty-six treaties during his term of office. At this Welles could not help remarking "entangling alliances," a comment that vexed the Secretary of State.[5]

Almost a third of the treaties ratified were with the countries south of the United States, lands which Seward regarded with a kind of paternal benevolence. Mexico was a case in point. When the French were about to withdraw, he told the American Minister to that strife-torn and poverty-stricken country that the United States had no interest in its conquest, or in aggrandizement by purchases of land or dominion, but only wished to see the Mexicans "reassume the conduct of their own affairs under the existing republican government." To this policy he steadily adhered. He urged clemency for Maximilian, but when the fallen emperor met death by a firing squad, Seward paid no attention to Weed's advice that public opinion would approve withdrawing the American Minister to Mexico. He repeatedly warned Romero against the schemes of outside speculators, refused to bring pressure on behalf of American claimants for damages, and in 1868 negotiated a convention that resulted in a settlement of claims arising between the two countries during the past twenty years. It must not be thought, however, that all this was pure beneficence. Seward believed that Mexico would surely become part of the United States, probably within a generation, and he was preparing the way to that end.[6]

As in the case of Mexico, Seward's policy toward the other states of Latin America was generally one of sweetness and light. When he felt that American citizens were in danger there, or when a South American state failed to live up to its obligations, he was ready to use a threat of force against the offender, but he much preferred co-operation to duress. He viewed the instability of this southern region with anxiety. "We cannot willingly abandon it to either anarchy or foreign domination," he told one of his correspondents. In consequence he was always ready to employ the good offices of the American government when disputes arose between Latin American countries, or between them and European Powers. At the same time he was reluctant to interfere in the internal affairs of the southern neighbors, an attitude that is illustrated by the following incident.

A United States citizen, an iron founder in Costa Rica, appealed for aid against the competition of a foundry owned by the Costa Rican government. Seward disapproved. "If our citizens settle in foreign countries for business purposes," he wrote to the acting American consul, who had interfered on behalf of the complainant, "they must expect competition of all kinds and if they meet it they cannot look to this country to avert it, especially in the absence of any express treaty stipulation warranting such a proceeding." Such an attitude was scarcely that of nineteenth-century economic imperialism.[7]

There were many other evidences of this disposition to deal justly with the Latin American states. Where claims of the United States were concerned Seward utilized the device of joint commissions, each nation appointing a commissioner and the two selecting a third as umpire. This equitable procedure resulted in awards totaling $5,813,613.19 to the United States while the five Latin American countries involved received $232,838.21. Bruce, who acted as umpire on one of these commissions, had high praise for the way in which the Secretary of State used this mode of settling claims.

Seward also refused to counsel Central American republics as to organic changes in their constitutions, lest it give an impression of undue interference, and he would take no part in a move to establish a union of the five Central American states, though requested to do so by Honduras. American policy, he said, was "one of entire abstinence from direct intervention in the domestic concerns of friendly states." [8]

The Secretary of State hoped that good relations with Latin America would help to invigorate republicanism in the western hemisphere, as well as promote a steady increase of commerce with the states of that region. Moreover he had a project much at heart that would spread American trade and influence not only in the southern hemisphere but also throughout the world. This was a canal across the Isthmus of Panama.

Interest in such a waterway had appeared and disappeared for half a century, but Seward brought it to light with all his customary vigor. At first he thought that "the great American Route," as he called it, might lie across Nicaragua, and in 1867 he concluded a treaty of commerce and navigation that granted the United States freedom of transit across that republic. But he was also deeply interested in building across the Panama isthmus what was then called the Darien Canal. On this he sounded out General Grant, who was favorable to the project, and United States military and naval engineers began investigating the possibilities of such a route.

The Senate did not advise ratification of the Nicaragua treaty until January 1868, and it was not proclaimed until the following August. Meanwhile, Seward began prodding New York capitalists —Peter Cooper, William H. Vanderbilt, and others—to take an interest in the Panama route, which was under the control of Colombia. The Secretary rallied Robert H. Pruyn, the former Minister to Japan, to his aid, and under Pruyn's urging a bill for the incorporation of an isthmus canal company passed the New York State legislature. Governor Fenton signed this measure and, with Seward again pushing for action, New York businessmen formed a committee to raise a capital of $100,000,000 for the project.

The next step was to obtain a treaty with Colombia, and Caleb Cushing went to Bogotá for that purpose. Dealing with the Colombians was difficult. Stories were rife of the need for bribery. A Missouri lawyer told Seward that he should bribe Panama to rebel against Colombia and then ask annexation to the United States. At

length Cushing returned with an instrument that Seward pronounced satisfactory. It provided that the United States, or a private
company of its choosing, might construct a canal over a strip of
territory twenty miles wide that would be under United States
control but not United States sovereignty. Completed within fifteen
years, the canal would be open to all nations in time of peace, but
closed to belligerents in time of war. Colombia would receive 10 per
cent of the net earnings until the builders had been reimbursed for
costs, and thereafter 25 per cent.

Seward feted Colombian representatives who came to Washington, and late in February 1869 went up to New York to inspirit the
incorporators of the company. The canal, and steam navigation, he
told them, were essential to the American future. The Suez Canal
was nearing completion and, unless this western waterway was built,
commerce would turn eastward across the Atlantic. The Darien
project would be "transcendently profitable and transcendently
useful."

The Secretary of State apparently counted upon the ambiguities
in the Clayton-Bulwer Treaty of 1850 to prevent any clash with
Great Britain over this proposed agreement with Colombia, but
there proved to be no need for British objection. Fearful that closure
in time of war might be prejudicial to Colombia's interest, but
chiefly outraged because millions in gold were not immediately
forthcoming, the Colombian Senate rejected the treaty. News of this
rejection reached the United States Senate which, in April 1869 and
to Seward's bitter disappointment, dropped consideration of the
treaty without a vote.

Seward had done his best to build a vitally important waterway,
and had failed. The irony of the situation is that, had his plans been
crowned with success, the building of the canal would probably
have collapsed under the scourge of yellow fever. Half a century
later the reason for the spread of the dread disease had been
discovered and mosquitoes were cleared from the area.[9]

One function of the Darien Canal, Seward thought, would be to
increase American commerce across the wide Pacific, and on the
opposite side of that ocean his attention centered chiefly on Japan
and China. The opening of Japan had begun in the previous decade.
Seward had favored it then, and as Secretary of State he was eager

to see it continue. So was Townsend Harris, in whose appointment to Nippon in 1855 Seward had taken an interest and who was still there in 1861 as Minister Resident. Harris was able and intelligent. He enjoyed the confidence of the Japanese government and the trust of the Secretary of State.

In January 1861, Henry Hensken, secretary of the American legation in Japan, was murdered. Seward proposed a naval demonstration, but abandoned the idea on Harris's advice. Then, to Seward's regret, Harris resigned because of ill health. He was succeeded by the Secretary of State's Albany friend, Robert H. Pruyn.

Seward told Pruyn that Japan was semi-barbarous, the government being relatively enlightened but the people and the ruling classes not yet reconciled to the opening of the country. Pruyn should be dignified and firm, prudent and moderate. He was to establish good relations with the representatives of the Western Powers and seek no exclusive advantages for the United States.

For a time all went well. Seward approved Pruyn's policy of pursuing a less "energetic" course than that of the other treaty Powers, and offered his good offices with Russia in a dispute between that country and Japan over the island of Fusima. Then there was an uprising against the opening of the Japanese door, accompanied by the persecution and murder of foreigners, and Great Britain and France began using naval demonstrations to force indemnity for the wrongs suffered by their nationals.

Seward's first reaction to the news from Japan was to counsel caution. The United States had no grievances, he said, and would not unite in hostilities against the Japanese. At the same time, Pruyn was not to embarrass or hinder the British, whose reprisals would probably mean greater security for all the Western nations. Pruyn was told that he had large discretionary powers.

Distance hampered the Secretary of State in formulating policy toward Japan, especially so in times of disturbance. Dispatches took three to four months in transit, even two months when sent by telegraph from San Francisco to Washington, and Pruyn had to rely largely on his own judgment in times of crisis. At first he was all for good relations with the Japanese, but then came the 1863 uprisings against foreigners. England thereupon obtained by threats of bombardment a promise of indemnities for those hurt. Pruyn approved this course of action and wrote to Seward that he favored stiff measures in cases of violence. When Japanese burned the legation buildings at Yedo and attacked American merchant ships, Pruyn took it upon himself to order the American warship *Wyoming* to sink the offending vessels, an order that was promptly obeyed. He also began co-operating with the other Western Powers in showing a strong hand to the Japanese government. In a long dispatch to Seward, July 24, 1863, received two and one-half months after it was written, he told of these proceedings and declared that force, or the threat of force, would alone maintain the American position in Japan. He was completely disillusioned by "Japanese dissimulation" and was confident that the President would approve his action.

What Seward's course would have been had Townsend Harris remained in Japan no one knows. Before he heard from Pruyn about the violence offered to Americans, he had instructed him to exert all his powers for peace, though for wrongs against Americans he would of course demand punishment and indemnities. He was to seek both co-operation with the European ministers and the confidence of the Japanese government and people. Seward told Pruyn repeatedly that he had large discretionary powers. The Secretary of State was also willing to have the *Wyoming* use her guns and employ all necessary force for the protection of American citizens, although Pruyn had not received this instruction when he ordered the ship into action.

Seward's policy was obviously of the either/or variety, with much left to Pruyn's judgment. The consequence was that, when he received the latter's account, he "fully and cheerfully approved" what had been done. Meantime he had worked out with the British government a program for the concerted action of the Powers in Japan as a result of which the Japanese government agreed to pay $3,000,000 for damages suffered, or open an additional port for foreign trade. He also held up the departure for Japan of the *Fusiyama*, a twenty-four gun sloop constructed through Pruyn's initiative for the Japanese government.[10]

Pruyn left Japan in 1865, and for over a year the United States representative there was *chargé d'affaires* A. L. C. Portman. During this period a policy of force majeure was dominant, and Portman went along with the representatives of the other Powers, especially Sir Harry Parkes, in negotiating the tariff convention of 1866. This substituted specific for ad valorem duties at Japanese ports, and so injured Japan. All this was done without specific instructions from the State Department, but Portman explained that it was for the best in American-Japanese relations and Seward accepted the arrangement.[11]

Civil disturbances in Japan made relations difficult during the remainder of Seward's term of office and nothing very constructive was accomplished. When the Mikado prohibited "the Christian and other evil religions," Seward urged the new Minister Resident, Robert B. Van Valkenburgh, to protest earnestly, "but not without consideration and kindness." The Secretary of State also received graciously a Japanese mission that came to the United States in 1867, partly to study naval architecture and buy a warship, and partly to air a grievance about the price that Pruyn and his associates had received for the *Fusiyama*. The former Minister Resident declared that all could be satisfactorily explained, but Seward hurried back from Auburn to meet the Japanese representatives, and Weed came down to the capital to help smooth things over.

Seward took the commissioners, Ono Tonogoro and Matsumoto Indayu, about Washington, helped them to purchase the erstwhile Confederate ram *Stonewall* for $400,000, and obtained for them a refund of $500,000 in greenbacks from Pruyn, Weed, and company on the price of the *Fusiyama*. On their return to Japan the commissioners declared themselves satisfied and grateful for the assistance of the Secretary of State.[12]

Promotion of American commerce was Seward's chief concern in Japan. There is ample evidence of his realization that good relations was the best means of accomplishing that objective, but there were many reasons for his use of violence. He believed that the Japanese were half-civilized. He relied upon advisers who were either convinced that the two-sworded gentry could only be dealt with in terms of bayonets and warships, or who were under the dominance of Sir Harry Parkes. His own disposition was to react vigorously to threats by foreigners against American lives. Also, co-operation with England and France in the Far East was in harmony with his policy of keeping on good relations with those nations during the Civil War.

Seward's attitude toward Korea was similar to that toward Japan. There, too, he reacted vigorously to actions that jeopardized American lives, but there also he was anxious to develop commerce through a policy of peace and liberality.

Early in 1867 news reached Washington that French missionaries and the crew of an American ship, the *General Sherman,* had been murdered by Koreans. Seward's first thought was an expedition that would avenge the murders and force a commercial treaty, and he proposed to M. Berthemy that it be made a joint affair. The French government declined on the ground that it had already avenged the murdered missionaries. Shortly thereafter Seward learned that the *General Sherman* had been trading where it had no business to be, and had been carrying munitions to the Koreans to aid them in resisting the French. Thereupon he abandoned all thought of punishment and, in consultation with the British, French, and Russian ministers in Washington, decided to attempt an understanding through the good offices of the Chinese government. He later proposed to send his nephew, George Seward, consul at Shanghai, to Korea in a friendly search for a commercial treaty, but this did not materialize because there was little prospect of success.

The murder of Americans still rankled. George Seward was to tell the Koreans, if he found it expedient, that the United States expected redress. The American wrongs in Korea were "unendurable," Seward wrote to Van Valkenburgh in 1868, but he added that the United States was eager to proceed with such moderation there as not to bring into question American dignity and liberality in relation to rude and unorganized Eastern communities.[13]

Seward did not think of the Chinese as semi-barbarous, and moreover he had the advantage of an able and farsighted diplomat, Anson Burlingame, as Minister to Peking. The United States had had treaty relations with China since 1844, and the Secretary of State regarded that Oriental kingdom as the proper center of American attention in the Far East. George Seward encouraged this belief. He wrote to his uncle in 1862 that the ship tonnage in Shanghai exceeded that at San Francisco; that, during the following year, 1200 ships (half of them, it was true, small coasters) would enter

Shanghai port carrying the American flag; and that American merchants ought to establish a steamship line between that Chinese harbor and San Francisco. Partly because of this report, the Secretary of State believed that trading possibilities with the Celestial Kingdom were practically limitless.

Seward was willing to use strong measures in promoting Chinese trade. In 1861 he authorized Burlingame to issue letters of marque to not more than five American ships that, supposedly, would destroy piracy in the China Sea. Despite the objections of the Chinese government, he insisted on using merchants as consuls in the treaty ports, on the ground that the United States could not afford to pay these officials. After the Civil War he urged spirited protests to China about brigandage, with demonstrations where necessary by the United States Navy.

But though Seward could be firm in defending American interests, his preference in China as in other foreign areas was for co-operation and kindness. Moreover, he had the support in this of like-minded Minister Burlingame, who received his appointment in June 1861 and who found a kindred spirit in the British Minister, Sir Frederick Bruce.

Seward recognized that time and distance made it unwise to trammel Burlingame with arbitrary instructions, and the latter had virtually a free hand. He and Bruce, together with the French and Russian ministers, agreed that they would neither take territorial concessions in the treaty ports nor interfere with the Chinese government's jurisdiction over its own people, nor ever menace the territorial integrity of the Chinese Empire. Seward commended this as "able and wise." From first to last he relied upon Burlingame's discretion and supported his open-hearted and peaceful policy, a procedure that won the confidence of the Chinese government.

While supporting Burlingame, Seward also wished to make his own contribution to good relations with China. In his draft for Johnson's annual message in 1865, he brought forward a proposal (first made by a member of the Buchanan administration) that a fund of over $200,000, derived from American claims against China, be used to establish some Chinese institution where an equal number of American and Chinese pupils might receive instruction "in the science, literature and commerce" of China. Johnson did not see fit to include this suggestion. Later Seward thought it would be better to have this school or college established in the United States, where there would be more likelihood of Chinese women receiving an education. He also urged the Chinese to send a representative to the United States with the grade of Minister.

In 1868 came proof of the esteem in which China held Burlingame and American diplomacy. The Chinese government was eager to have its views explained to the Western Powers; it also wished to guard against any further concessions to foreigners being asked at an impending revision of treaties. On learning that Burlingame was determined to resign his post, it made him China's envoy to the West, with broad powers of negotiation. Accompanied by a retinue of some thirty persons, he came to Washington in the late spring of 1868, and there he and Seward in great secrecy agreed on the details of what came to be known as the Burlingame Treaty, a draft of which had been prepared beforehand by the Secretary of State.

Afterward Seward gave a grand party at Auburn for Burlingame and the Chinese delegation. Sixteen guests were domiciled in the big house, the rest throughout the town. Worn down as he was by the humid Washington heat, Seward nevertheless directed the entertainment which included a tour of the city in carriages, a rowing match on the lake and, of course, a visit to the state prison. Burlingame, Lazette Worden noted, looked less like a Chinese than he had three years before, which she felt was an improvement. The Orientals created great excitement among the town folk, young and old, and there was always a crowd in the street before the house. Seward had a police guard stationed at the gate to keep the affair from becoming a melee. He had urged Johnson to come, but the President was not among the guests.

The Burlingame Treaty recognized China's jurisdiction over its domestic affairs, and also the right of free Chinese immigration to the United States. Emigrants from both countries should have most-favored-nation privileges, but the treaty conferred no right of naturalization. China could appoint consuls at American ports. The United States also pledged itself to give China assistance in making internal improvements.

The only controversial part of this agreement was that regarding Chinese immigration, for the Pacific Coast had already become sensitive on the subject. Here the treaty reflected Seward's anxiety to secure an adequate labor supply for the United States. He and Burlingame sought, through the appointment of Chinese consuls, to protect the rights of Chinese immigrants, but this safeguard and the most-favored-nation provision were insufficient to prevent the passage of discriminatory state laws.

Seward, however, proudly hailed the mission as the first from China to any Western country. He sent Burlingame and his Chinese associates on to Europe with his blessing and gave a copy of the treaty to Thornton, expressing the hope that Great Britain would conclude similar arrangements.[14]

Seward's attempt to pave the way for world leadership by the United States was frustrated at many points. There was little popular enthusiasm for such an American role. His hopes for a world-girdling telegraph line and for immediate construction of an isthmian canal came to naught. A recalcitrant Senate limited his use of the treaty-making power. His Far Eastern policy labored under disadvantages. Civil War problems had priority over all else. Distance limited his control over Oriental relations. He was too prone to exact swift punishment for wrongs suffered by Americans.

But in spite of all these handicaps there were some gains. His efforts on behalf of immigration increased American labor power and so fostered the great economic developments of the post-Civil War era. His Latin American policy was constructive. The Burlingame Treaty promoted good relations with the Orient. These were at least steps toward the goal of his aspirations.

❧ 36 ❧

The Quest for Island Outposts

Seward's plans for American greatness involved a steady expansion of influence in areas adjacent to the United States. He foresaw an American nation buttressed on land and sea by republics whose governments would be based on the principle of equal rights for all mankind. The time would come, he felt, when European influence and European possessions in the New World would shrink and disappear. The West Indies, for example, might eventually form a black confederacy friendly to the United States. With such thoughts in mind, he asked Welles to examine and put an estimate on French holdings in the West Indies, the Spanish Main, and the Gulf of St. Lawrence. And any rumor of European acquisitions or transfers of territory in the New World aroused his concern.[1]

The same line of reasoning made island outposts under the American flag a necessity. He had seen how difficult it was during the Civil War for the American navy to obtain coal in foreign ports, and he was convinced that such stations were essential for naval observations, for police, for fleet concentrations in war, and for protecting America's commerce when the nation was at peace. This was especially true, he believed, in the Caribbean region and in the Pacific from the Panama Isthmus northward.

The attention of the Secretary of State early fastened upon the Danish West Indies, a group some forty miles east of Porto Rico and consisting principally of three main islands, St. Thomas, St. Croix, and St. John. Early in 1865, apparently with Lincoln's blessing, he began negotiations with General Raasloff, the Danish Minister to the United States. At first reluctant, Denmark soon manifested interest in exchanging its island possessions for cash.

Seward visited the islands in January 1866 and liked what he saw. On his return he persuaded Johnson that purchase was advisable and then took his project to the Cabinet, where he found Welles hostile and the rest little more than apathetic. This opposition whetted his ardor. He obtained additional information from Stanton and Quartermaster General Montgomery C. Meigs, and in July informed Raasloff that he would pay $5,000,000 in gold for the three large islands.

Raasloff now returned to his native land where he became Minister of War, but Denmark paltered and delayed about selling the islands. It feared the reaction of Britain and France, and wanted more money. It also stipulated that, before the islands were sold, there must be a plebiscite of the inhabitants.

Seward was willing to go up to $10,000,000, but it now developed that Denmark wanted $15,000,000 for the three islands, or $10,000,000 for St. Thomas and St. John. When the Secretary of State obtained the approval of a majority of the Cabinet for an offer of $7,500,000 for all three, Denmark declared that for that sum it would sell only St. Thomas and St. John. Fearful that Denmark meant to sell all the islands to some European Power, Seward was ready to close the deal at that figure, but the Danes again raised the question of a plebiscite. The harried Secretary demurred, and more delay ensued.

By the summer of 1867 reports of the negotiation were widespread, and there was considerable adverse comment. The New York *Times* declared that the nation had no need for more territory; it had better concentrate attention on domestic problems. To the New York *Tribune* the Secretary's mania for "outlandish possessions" squinted toward monarchy, and it urged Secretary McCulloch to start paying off the public debt before "the Premier, à la Mrs. Toodles" could make ducks and drakes of the Treasury's money in the real estate market. Even Adams thought the proposed purchase denoted a policy that in the end would be fatal "to the permanency of our Institutions," and confided to his diary that he had "lost all confidence in the wisdom or judgment of Mr. Seward."

Seward now felt that the country's attention had become centered on the struggle over reconstruction; that the interest shown in expansion at the close of the Civil War had "sensibly abated"; and that the best he could hope for would be the acquisition of the two islands. Warned that France was taking an interest in what the Danes might do, he agreed to a plebiscite and concluded a treaty purchasing St. Thomas and St. John for $7,500,000.

The plebiscite went in favor of annexation, and the Secretary of State undertook to prepare the way for the realization of his plans. He enlisted the aid of Vice-Admiral David D. Porter, head of the Naval Academy, who undertook the conversion of Senator Grimes, chairman of the Committee on Naval Affairs. Seward himself rallied to his side both Sumner and Stevens, and exerted his blandishments upon various other members of Congress.

The Secretary put forth his best efforts and his hopes were high. At Christmas time Senator Anthony of Rhode Island sent him a Narragansett turkey, meant for "one of those seductive dinners at which you corrupt Senators and Representatives into voting for territorial acquisitions." Seward replied that, if American turkeys grew to the size of Anthony's gift, expansion had become a necessity. So large a bird, he added, for so small a state! He was now beginning to believe that it would not be long before all of the West Indies would be under the American flag.

But Nature took a hand in the game, and in a most unkind fashion. A violent hurricane smashed into St. Thomas and a tidal wave tossed the USS *Monongahela* high and dry into the principal town of the island. There was news of an earthquake on St. Croix. Bret Harte wrote a poem which described Volcano, Sea, and Wind conspiring to thwart Seward's plans. The press began to point the finger of derision, and Mark Twain dashed off a piece about an uncle of his who wanted peace and quiet. Chased out of Alaska by bears, he had gone to St. Thomas where he had his money stolen, contracted all of the seven prevalent fevers, had one farm washed out by a storm and another by an earthquake, while a ship on which he was doing some further prospecting was hoisted by a tidal wave into one of the interior counties. He would, however, still like to try Porto Rico, if the government was going to buy it.

This ridicule came just as the quarrel between Congress and the President culminated in the impeachment proceedings. Sumner became cool to the purchase and delayed the treaty in the Senate. Raasloff finally came to the United States to assist in its passage, upon which his future career in Denmark depended, but his efforts were in vain. President-elect Grant was hostile, remarking that he wanted absolutely nothing to do with it, and the Senate refused to act. Another of Seward's pet projects for the great American future had gone down to defeat.[2]

Another West Indies island that interested Seward was Santo Domingo. He had been disturbed by Spain's reannexation of the Dominican Republic in 1861, but had not gone beyond protests to the Spanish government. Then came an insurrection that ended in 1865 with Spain's evacuation of the island. Seward took a neutral attitude toward this uprising, for he regarded the Dominican situation as a difficult choice between the Spaniard and the Negro, but by 1864 he had become interested in Samaná Bay at the eastern end of the island as a possible naval base. In 1865 he warned Great Britain that any attempt by a foreign power to obtain the Samaná peninsula might well lead to its occupancy by the United States. A visit to Santo Domingo City in January 1866, together with reports from the island, increased his enthusiasm and in December of that year he sent Frederick to conclude a treaty with the Dominican government. He was to purchase Samaná Bay for $2,000,000, half in cash and half in arms and munitions.

The Dominicans proved to be hard bargainers. Frederick returned without a treaty, and Seward thought his plans had come to naught. Then President Cabral, sadly in need of gold, reopened negotiations, only to have them interrupted by a revolution in the island. This was early in 1868, and during the following months Seward, perforce, had to watch developments. He had become skeptical that Congress would go along with the purchase.

Seward also watched the situation in Haiti, where he feared that Great Britain meant to obtain a foothold. He told Gideon Hollister, Minister to Haiti, that the United States wished to leave the Haitians absolutely free, but only so long as they maintained republican institutions, and left American citizens the full enjoyment of rights secured by treaty and guaranteed by international law. This was a striking forerunner of the 1904 Roosevelt Corollary to the Monroe Doctrine.

The Secretary of State wished to acquire from Haiti the Môle-

Saint-Nicholas, which faces the Windward Passage. It would, he thought, make a good naval base. When the disorders in Santo Domingo spread across the island, he kept hands off the situation, but the chaos gave him another idea. Why not, if the two states consented, establish protectorates? Why not, better yet, annex the whole island? In December 1868, Johnson's message to Congress proposed annexation, but this suggestion fell on deaf ears. The Môle-Saint-Nicholas was now a vanished dream.[3]

Delay and frustration did not dull Seward's appetite for something, anything in the West Indies. He sent George Bancroft to Madrid in a fruitless effort to purchase the small, uninhabited, but strategically placed islands of Culebra and Culebrita off the east coast of Porto Rico. There was talk of acquiring from Sweden the island of St. Bartholomew, but the Swedes, at first willing to sell, backed away after the failure of his negotiation with Denmark. A similar fate attended efforts to interest the French government in disposing of the islands of St. Pierre and Martinique. Toward the end of his term of office, he told Sumner that, "instructed by the debates in Congress and the tone of the public press during the past year, I have declined all recent suggestions in regard to the acquisition of naval stations anywhere in the West Indies. . . ."

Seward also had an eye on Cuba and Porto Rico, especially after a revolution in Spain spread to the Pearl of the Antilles. In 1867 Horatio J. Perry, the secretary of legation at Madrid, reported to Thurlow Weed that France was angling with the bankrupt Spanish government for Cuba, and a rumor reached Seward that the insurgent General Prim would, if victorious in Spain, undertake to pay that nation's debts by the immediate sale of its colonial possessions. A year later the Bourbons lost their throne, and Bigelow wrote that the Spanish colonies would surely go on the market and that now was the time to obtain Cuba and Porto Rico.

Seward responded that it was best to wait upon events in Madrid, especially those that bore on the republican system and on slavery in the provinces. Would the United States now want Cuba, either with or without slavery, he asked, and which of the two political parties would undertake the financial responsibility for purchase? "How sadly domestic disturbances of ours," he added, "demoralize the national ambition."

Two days after this melancholy observation, a revolt broke out in Cuba ushering in a ten years' futile struggle for independence. Planters and businessmen suffering under harsh taxation, liberals who had vainly sought economic and social reforms, and Negroes joined in this rebellion. It spread swiftly over large sections of eastern Cuba.

Cuban insurgents came to the United States to solicit aid for this uprising. One of these was Don Miguel Aldama, a wealthy business-man and reformer. Armed with introductions from Blatchford and General Sherman, Aldama called on the Secretary of State. There is no record of their conversation, but Seward told Thornton sub-sequently of an effort by one Colonel John Gibbon to organize a filibustering expedition against Cuba. Seward had assured Thornton repeatedly that he would not countenance such a move, but the Englishman suspected that, in the present case, the Secretary of State had said "no" only after discovering that public opinion was adverse to such action.

Early in 1869, Reverdy Johnson reported that Spain would sell Cuba and Porto Rico for $120,000,000. Benjamin Moran, secretary of legation in London, suspected that this was a job being engineered by George N. Sanders, General Wigfall, and other erstwhile Con-federates. Seward's New York friend, Richard Schell, swore that the report came from a friend of his who was thoroughly loyal and had had no Confederate connections. But all this came at the close of Seward's term of office. The revolt was on in Cuba, and he made no move toward opening negotiations if, indeed, there was any such opportunity.[4]

The West Indies by no means monopolized Seward's interest in islands and naval bases in the Atlantic region. He had that insatiable expansionist Robert J. Walker draw up a report in 1867 on the resources and geopolitical importance of Greenland and Iceland. Walker enlisted the support of a scientist of national reputation, Professor Benjamin Peirce, superintendent of the United States Coast Survey, and presented a report which urged the purchase of the islands on account of their mineral resources and fisheries—also because they would flank British America on the east and stimulate the desire of the Canadians for annexation to the United States. Seward authorized the printing of this tract of the times, and Ben

Butler was prompted to remark scathingly about "one insane enough to buy the earthquakes of St. Thomas and the ice fields in Greenland." Beyond this there was scarcely a ripple. Congress was apathetic, the country at large was not interested and, after the failure of the Danish West Indies negotiation, Seward decided that further efforts in the North Atlantic region would be useless.[5]

While the Secretary of State sought in vain for island acquisitions in the Atlantic he kept looking for similar footholds in the vast Pacific region. Berthemy reported to the Quai d'Orsay in 1867 that Seward had rejected the possibility of obtaining a naval base in Borneo only after an unfavorable report on the project by Admiral Bell. There was also a rumor that the King of the Fiji Islands had given three of them to the United States as compensation for American sailors eaten by the king's subjects. Australians were reported alarmed by the possibility of the United States becoming a South Pacific neighbor. But whatever interest Seward had in such faraway ventures was little more than fitful and fleeting. Tiger Island and Hawaii, much nearer at hand in the Pacific, were more interesting possibilities for expansion.[6]

Tiger Island, in the Gulf of Fonseca on the west coast of Central America, excited Seward's interest because it was an excellent site for a coaling station on the ocean route between the Isthmus and San Francisco. The Clayton-Bulwer Treaty limited the right of territorial acquisitions on or near the possible canal routes, and Seward had Adams sound out the British government as to its attitude toward the purchase of this island from Honduras. Adams found the British Foreign Office cool to the idea, and Seward abandoned his hopes in that quarter.

Hawaii seemed a more promising field for exploration. Seward had favored its acquisition as early as 1852, but President Fillmore was not interested. American missionary and whaling ventures grew apace in the Sandwich Islands (as they were then called), and in the period just after the Civil War, when expansion had an evanescent bloom, Sumner declared that they were "wards of the United States."

Seward's interest in the islands now revived. He repelled a British suggestion that there be a joint guarantee of Hawaiian independence, for this would shut the door to annexation. At the same time he would have nothing to do with a proposal that, in order to pave the way for acquisition, the United States instigate a revolution among the islanders. Their shift into the American orbit must be fostered, not forced.

In 1865 Dowager Queen Emma of the Islands went to England for a lengthy visit. She sailed from Honolulu in HMS *Clio*, and was received with great honor as the guest of the English nation. Her visit was primarily for reasons of health and religion, but King Kamehameha V judged it necessary to allay suspicions of political intent by having her visit the United States on her return journey.

Seward received reports of how the Queen had been royally entertained at Windsor, and of how her expenses in England and on the Continent had been paid by the English government. He was eager that all honor should be accorded her in the United States. He gave a dinner in her honor, saw to it that she met the President, and arranged a trip to Niagara Falls. When she left New York she traveled to San Francisco as the guest of the Pacific Mail Steamship Company, and from the Golden Gate to Honolulu on Rear Admiral Thatcher's flagship, the *Vanderbilt*. Seward was determined to counteract any growth of British or other foreign influence in Hawaii for he believed that an influx of Americans would eventually mean the acquisition of the islands by the United States.

It was in line with Seward's general policy of expansion that he should seek to bring Hawaii gradually and peacefully within the sphere of American influence. Annexation was his main objective, but he also approved a commercial reciprocity treaty as a first step and as more within the bounds of possibility. In 1867 such a treaty was drawn up with his sanction but, as it turned out, even this was doomed to failure.

The reciprocity treaty went to the Senate on July 13, 1867. It was debated and then laid on the table. Despite Seward's insistence, the Senate again rejected it the following year. Brought up once more in March, 1869, it suffered a similar fate, and in 1870 failed to obtain a two-thirds vote. Fears of competition entertained by the sugar and rice growers of the South, the loss of tariff revenues, and the suspicions of eastern sugar refiners that their business would be hurt by free raw sugar for the California refineries probably contributed to its downfall. But the major causes were the insignificance of the

Hawaiian market, and popular reluctance to assume new obligations. Seward saw the writing on the wall before he left office. He concluded regretfully that domestic issues, especially the siren song of economy and retrenchment, were the order of the day, and that the nation had lost interest in the "more remote questions of national extension and aggrandizement." [7]

As it turned out, the only island acquisition in the Pacific or anywhere else during Seward's two terms in the State Department was Midway in 1867, and that was occupied by the navy. Just before his public career ended, however, he recommended a survey of that island for the establishment of a naval base. At the time it looked like an insignificant return for even that much effort, but Americans were to appreciate its value during the Second World War.

ᴥ 37 ᶻᴥ

Toward the Aurora Borealis

The yearning of the Secretary of State for bases in the Pacific and his interest in Greenland and Iceland were linked to his vision of a time when Russian America and the vast reaches of Canada would become part of the United States. This dream was not peculiar to Seward. Robert J. Walker and Senator William Gwin of California urged the acquisition of Alaska before the Civil War. Sumner, Banks, Butler, newspaper men James Gordon Bennett and Joseph Medill, and others led in a movement for the annexation of Canada during the 1860s, and Senator Zachariah Chandler threatened the conquest of that country by Michigan veterans of the War Between the States.

Certain aspects of the Canadian situation in the early 1860s encouraged American annexationists. Canada then consisted of present-day Ontario and Quebec together with the maritime provinces of New Brunswick, Nova Scotia, and Prince Edward Island. Westward from Ontario stretched a vast territory governed loosely by the Hudson's Bay Company, save for British Columbia on the Pacific coast, a province that, since 1858, was under the direct rule of the government in London.

At mid-century, Canadians earnestly debated their future. Should Canada have an independent existence? Should it become a confederation within the British realm? Should it join the United States? There were protagonists of all three views. With his eyes ever straying northward, Seward heard reports of American traders and emigrants moving into the Red River region north of Minnesota, and of sentiment in the eastern provinces favoring annexation.

Seward was always a peaceful expansionist, and as such there can be no doubt that he looked with longing toward Canada. In 1864 he tried, unsuccessfully, to get permission for stationing eighteen additional consuls in the British provinces. The London *Times* of December 5, 1865 declared that there would be no objection to Canada's absorption by the United States, always, of course, if it were done "freely and spontaneously" on the part of the Canadians. Seward took pains to reproduce the editorial in the published diplomatic correspondence of the United States for 1866. He made James Wicks Taylor, an ardent Minnesota expansionist, an adviser to the State Department on "the progress of American interests and institutions northwest of Lake Superior." In January 1867, Seward sent to the Senate a report by E. H. Derby, special agent of the United States in Canada, which argued that it would be Britain's true policy to cede British Columbia and Vancouver Island in payment for American claims against England.

When it came to a revival of reciprocity with Canada, however, Seward took as cautious an attitude as he did toward reciprocity with Hawaii. When this question was raised, after the close of the Civil War, he took a hands-off position on the ground that there was no demand for a resumption of the agreement of 1854. Early in 1867 he outlined this view to Johnson. The treaty of 1854, he said, had been advantageous to both countries, and he had assented to its termination in the expectation that, when a unitary authority in the English provinces over trade and finance and a thorough revision of the revenue system in the United States had been established, there could be set up a better and more permanent relationship between the two countries. Financial reform in Canada had come, but the United States had not yet simplified and reduced its taxation system. As soon as this was done, perhaps before, he would recommend consultation with Canada about enlarging the free list or, better yet, adopting a Zollverein or customs union like that among the German states.

Seward went on to say that he also favored a proposal now before Congress to invite "the English Provinces on the continent, of course upon the fullest consultation with the government of Great Britain, to become coordinate members of the United States of America." He would like to see some action; but if Congress did not find the idea acceptable, he would urge rendering the frontier "as slight a barrier as possible to social and commercial intercourse between friendly and kindred communities." [1]

There was little real sentiment in Canada for annexation to its southern neighbor. Indeed at the time Seward made his policy statement plans for the British North America Act of 1867 establishing the Dominion of Canada were far advanced. Prospects for expansion northward did not seem bright, but just then came a development that he found of absorbing interest, and that led to the one great territorial acquisition of his career.

Russian America, as Alaska was called, had from time to time during the nineteenth century aroused American interest and, indeed, anxiety. The possibility of further Russian expansion south of 54°40′ had been one of the factors back of Monroe's message of 1823, and the idea persisted that the Russian Bear was an undesirable neighbor on the American continent. There is some evidence that Robert J. Walker, as ardent an expansionist as the period produced, suggested in 1845 purchase of this Russian territory. Senator William Gwin promoted the same plan during the following decade, and in the spring of 1854 Secretary of State Marcy was ready to buy, but found Stoeckl unreceptive to the idea.

A few years later, however, Russian sentiment changed. The acquisition of the lower Amur River Valley from China between 1854 and 1860 turned the attention of St. Petersburg to that region as the proper place for expansion. Moreover, Archduke Constantin, brother of Emperor Alexander II and head of the Russian admiralty, became convinced that Russian America was a losing venture, and Stoeckl agreed with this point of view. They saw more and more Americans pushing into the Far Northwest, and there was a rumor that the Mormons might emigrate from Utah to Russian America. Would they come as conquerors or peaceful colonists, Stoeckl asked Buchanan, and the latter replied that that was up to the Russians. "As for ourselves [said the President], we shall be very happy to be rid of them."

It seemed a foregone conclusion that some Americans, Mormons or not, would try to settle in Alaska, and Stoeckl especially was fearful of all kinds of ensuing difficulties. There was also the argument that Russian America was indefensible in time of war, and its sale would surely discomfit Great Britain, perhaps lead to the loss of British territory in the Far Northwest. Constantin and other highly placed Russians worked on Foreign Minister Gortchakov, who was willing to sell if the price was high enough, but who insisted that the United States must take the initiative.[2]

The Civil War put an end for a time to negotiations over Russian America, but it also smoothed the path to their resumption. At its beginning Gortchakov assured the United States that Russia would not recognize the insurgents. In August 1861 the Emperor wrote what Seward described as "a most generous and magnanimous letter, expressing himself heart and soul in favor of the cause of the Union." So impressed was the Secretary of State that he asked Stoeckl to read the Emperor's letter to Lincoln. Again, at the time of the *Trent* affair, Seward expressed his deep appreciation of the Russian attitude—"If I knew how I could say anything more grateful or more acceptable to the Prince and the Emperor," he told Minister Clay, "I should authorize you to say it."

Opportunities were not lacking for Seward to show his gratitude. At the time of the Crimean War an American citizen, Benjamin W. Perkins, made an oral agreement with Stoeckl and a Captain Lilienfeldt, so Perkins later asserted, to supply Russia with 154 tons of powder and 35,000 stand of arms. The war came to an end, Russia refused to accept shipments and Perkins brought his claim before the United States government. Seward examined the evidence late in 1861, thought it strongly favored Perkins and, on the ground that an oral contract was binding in the United States, told Clay to reopen the question with the Russian government. Clay was dubious about getting anything from the Russians. He offered without success to settle for some $130,000, and Seward did not press the claim.

During the following years Russian-American relations were decidedly cordial. In 1863, on the ground of America's traditional policy of non-intervention, Seward refused to join France, England, and Austria in a démarche on behalf of the rebellious Russian Poles. He even gave Gortchakov permission to publish his dispatch to Dayton on the subject. When the Russian fleet visited a number of

United States ports during the fall and winter of 1862–63, its officers were sumptuously entertained by the local citizenry. Seward was unable to attend the banquet in New York, but he sent a toast to Prince Gortchakov: "not more able in defending the policy of his own country than just and liberal in conducting its relations with the United States." When the Russian squadron anchored in the Potomac, the Secretary of State gave a huge party for Russian and American naval officers and the members of the Cabinet. These friendly exchanges made easy the path to negotiations over Russian America.[3]

In the winter of 1864–65 Hiram Sibley, president of the Western Union Telegraph Company, visited St. Petersburg on behalf of the Collins project. Shortly after his arrival, Clay presented him to Gortchakov and to the Emperor. Gortchakov told Sibley, accord-into a tradition in the Sibley family, that Russia was willing to sell Alaska and through Clay this news was transmitted to Seward. No such message appears in Clay's dispatches, nor was it really necessary. Seward was ready to buy. He knew very well that the Russian territory would be strategically valuable for the United States and that its purchase, just at a time when Congress was taking over control of reconstruction from a sadly buffeted administration, would be valuable both for himself and for the President.

Clay wrote to Seward in late 1864 that, in his opinion, the time would come when it would be to the interest of the United States to buy Russian America. Subsequently Seward suggested that Clay invite the Archduke Constantin to visit the United States as the nation's guest. "I think," said the Secretary of State, "that it would be beneficial to us, and by no means unprofitable to Russia. I forebear from specifying my reasons." Clay tendered the invitation informally but the Archduke said that, much as he desired to visit America, his duties kept him at home.

Stoeckl visited St. Petersburg the following winter and there, with the Archduke and other high officials went over the Alaska problem—the hard financial situation of the Russian American Company whose profits and credit had steadily declined, Russia's growing interest in the Amur region, the straitened condition of the nation's treasury, and Stoeckl's contention that Alaska in Russian hands was bound to breed trouble with the United States. Late in

December 1866 at a meeting presided over by the Emperor, with Gortchakov, Constantin, and Stoeckl among those present, the men in charge of Russia's destiny decided to cede Alaska to the United States and made Stoeckl their agent in effecting the transaction. The price for the territory should be not less than $5,000,000.

The following February Stoeckl landed in New York where he stayed for three weeks, partly because he had sprained his foot on the rough sea voyage. In order to whet the interest of the Secretary of State he had a mutual friend, apparently either Walker or Weed, call on Seward and expatiate on the value of Russian America. Then he himself went to Washington, determined to elicit an offer of purchase.

Opportunity was soon at hand. Stoeckl called on Seward and they discussed certain Alaskan fishing and fur trading rights desired by American citizens. Stoeckl said that Russia could not possibly grant these privileges, and Seward then inquired if Russia would sell its American possessions. Before they parted they agreed that both countries would profit by such a transaction.

In the days that followed they discussed procedure and price. Stoeckl thought it might be well for the proposal to come from Capitol Hill but Seward, quite rightly, said that secrecy was important and, anyway, it was his affair. As to price, he offered $5,000,-000. Stoeckl demurred. He hoped to get $6,000,000, possibly $6,-500,000, and was delighted when additional bargaining brought the offer to $7,000,000. The Russian felt that this offer was due to the influence "de quelques personnes influentes," so the negotiations turned out to be not absolutely secret. The Cabinet seems not to have known about them, however, for the first mention that Welles and Browning made in their diaries about the transaction was on March 15, when Seward presented the draft of a treaty for the purchase of Russian America at a price of $7,000,000 in gold.

Striving to kill two birds with one stone, Seward asked that the Russian government use its influence with Denmark to cede the Danish West Indies. He wrote a note to this effect for Stoeckl to forward to St. Petersburg and the Russian reluctantly agreed to do so, warning that little good would come of it. Gortchakov replied that he could not make such a move and there the matter ended.

Before the transfer of Russian territory could be completed, one or two preliminary difficulties had to be surmounted. Criticism from Cabinet members required some minor revisions of the treaty draft, but this was easily done. Stoeckl raised a question concerning the rights of Russian companies in Alaska, particularly the Russian American Fur Company, and also asked that payment be made in the near future and at London. Seward insisted that the cession be free from any reservations, privileges, franchises, grants, or possessions by any such company, nor did he agree to the other two conditions. Instead he added $200,000 to the purchase price.

Stoeckl informed his government by telegraph of the bargain that had been struck, and the Emperor wired his approval. Exactly what followed is doubtful, owing to differences in subsequent versions of the event. According to Frederick Seward, his father was playing whist when Stoeckl appeared on the evening of March 29 and told him that he had permission for the sale. He would come over to the State Department in the morning and they would draw up the treaty.

Seward smiled, pushed back from the card table, and said, "Why wait till tomorrow, Mr. Stoeckl? Let us make the treaty tonight."

"But your Department is closed," Stoeckl is supposed to have replied. "You have no clerks, and my secretaries are scattered about the town!"

"Never mind that," said Seward. "If you can muster your legation together before midnight, you will find me waiting you at the Department, which will be open and ready for business."

Some such conversation seems to have taken place, for the way was paved for the immediate completion of the treaty. Seward went over to the State Department, which was a mile away at 14th and S Streets. A message to Sumner brought him over to Seward's house, where he learned from Frederick and Stoeckl what was in the wind and was asked to support the treaty next day in the Senate. Sumner and Stoeckl then left, Sumner going to his home at 322 I Street and Stoeckl to the State Department where, in the early hours of Saturday morning, March 30, 1867, the treaty was made ready for submission to the Senate.[4]

The regular session of Congress ended that day at noon, and Johnson and his Cabinet went to Capitol Hill at ten o'clock. Seward hoped against hope that consent could be gained that day, but talks with several Senators (including Cole of California who had angled for Alaskan trading privileges on behalf of California fur interests) convinced him that it was impossible to do so. Thereupon he and Johnson presented the Senate with a proclamation to the effect that "an extraordinary occasion" required that body to convene on Monday, April 1 at twelve o'clock. The Senate then went into executive session where Sumner had the treaty sent to the Committee on Foreign Relations. Thereafter the Senate adjourned over the weekend.

On the evening of this eventful day Bigelow, just home from Paris, dined with Seward and found him in high spirits. The Secretary of State remarked that Russia and France were leaving the continent at the same time. The purchase, he said, was the most remarkable event of half a century and was part of a series of negotiations that were headed for a successful conclusion. His imagination pictured a land where there would no longer be any North and South, one where the political parties would divide along eastern and western lines.

The treaty provided for the transfer of territory more than twice the size of the state of Texas. The Russian inhabitants had their choice of returning to their homeland within three years or remaining under American jurisdiction. The United States was to take possession immediately after ratifications had been exchanged. Seward did not expect to get the necessary appropriation until the winter session began, and he thought possession would make it easier to get the money out of the House of Representatives.

News of the treaty provoked some adverse newspaper comment. The Cincinnati *Daily Gazette* called it a dodge by Seward and Johnson to hide their domestic disgrace. The New York *Evening Post*, Richard M. Blatchford thought, was mean and malicious. Worst of all was the New York *Tribune*. It, too, declared that the treaty was just part of an effort to cover up failure at home. The United States already had more territory than it wanted and, anyway, why buy Russian icebergs? Settlers going there would be like Martin Chuzzlewit in Eden. Strategically it would be a liability, and as to its being a menace to Great Britain, there was no occasion for dealing in impertinences. As for its being a bargain, that was just like Mrs. Toodle's argument that it was a good idea to buy 178 empty watch boxes so that they would be handy if they were ever wanted.

Opposition also came from important quarters in Washington. Stanton, who had approved the treaty in Cabinet, privately criticized it as a useless extravagance. Some Senators, so Stoeckl understood, said that they would vote against it because it came from Seward. Sumner, who was at first lukewarm about the purchase, told the Russian that it could not be confirmed and asked him to withdraw it, but Stoeckl refused. He informed Berthemy that Russia had sold the territory because it wanted to be agreeable to the United States. He, Stoeckl, had proposed to take up the project with influential Congressmen but Seward's vanity had prevented this; and if the project collapsed, it would be all Seward's fault.

Faced by the manifestations of discontent, Seward was not idle. He had Stevens on his side and Sumner, though on principle he disliked the acquisition of territory "unless by the free choice of the inhabitants," finally agreed to give it his support. Stevens used his influence with the Senators, and when Sumner reported the treaty he made a powerful speech in its favor, a speech which the Secretary of State distributed with funds from his Department. Seward also gave out letters supporting the treaty from the war hero, Commodore John Rodgers, Quartermaster General Meigs, and General Halleck, "Old Brains" of wartime and now Commander of the Military Division of the Pacific. Seward telegraphed to westerners for assistance, and gave dinner parties for Senators, at which he described over the wine and brandy the beauties of Russian America. New Yorker John V. L. Pruyn used his influence, and the former Assistant Secretary of the Navy, Gustavus Vasa Fox, got leading New Englanders to telegraph in favor of the treaty, and himself praised it in the press. Despite occasional dissidents, newspaper opinion was generally favorable.

The opponents of the treaty in the Senate based their objections on the expense involved, the need for concentrating attention on domestic affairs, and sheer hatred of the administration. Its friends declared that the territory would provide a naval base, and harbors for traders and for the whaling fleet. They also argued that it would help forward the acquisition of Canada, and that it would gratify Russia. At first twelve Senators voted to postpone consideration. Then all but two (Fessenden of Maine and Morrill of Vermont) withdrew their opposition. On April 9, by a vote of 37 to 2, the Senate approved the treaty.[5]

Probably one of the most unhappy men in the United States, aside from Horace Greeley, over the confirmation of the treaty was Sir Frederick Bruce. He wrote to Lord Stanley that it signified a Russian-American rapprochement at the expense of England, one aimed at neutralizing British efforts in the Near East and enabling the United States to claim British Columbia or some other territory. The humiliation of Great Britain would complete "the self-satisfaction of this people." A step had been taken toward absorption of the whole northern continent. Both Stoeckl and Johnson assured him, however, that the deal had no political significance, and Bruce consoled himself with the thought that dislike of Seward might block the necessary appropriation in the House of Representatives.

While Bruce lamented, felicitations poured in to the Secretary of State. "I congratulate you and rejoice at your safe deliverance," wrote Thad Stevens. "I hope the afterbirth is easy." Clay declared that the new territory was worth at least $50,000,000, "and hereafter the wonder will be that we got it at all." A group of Seward's admirers, headed by Peter Cooper, commissioned Emanuel Leutze to do the famous painting that symbolically depicts the signing of the treaty, and presented it to Seward with expressions of gratitude and appreciation for his services in the State Department. Even Millard Fillmore wrote to ask for a map of the new territory. James Gordon Bennett characteristically praised the purchase and published fictitious advertisements showing how beggared European sovereigns might palm off on Seward worthless territories at handsome prices. Clay described the general Russian reaction as favorable, but Stoeckl thought the opposition there was rather strong. At least one Russian newspaper was bitter, suggesting that they might next hear rumors of the sale of the Baltic Provinces and the Crimea. Sanford reported that where Europe paid any attention to the transaction at all it was regarded as a blow at Great Britain.

Obviously the territory would have to have a new name, and about this there was considerable discussion. Some of the Secretary's admirers wanted it called "Seward Land," or "Seward Territory" until it should be made into states. "Aliaska," "Yukon," and "Sitka" (its capital), were also suggested, but Seward or possibly Sumner chose "Alaska," a corruption of an Aleut word meaning "mainland," and so it was called.[6]

As soon as the Senate confirmed the treaty, Seward moved to ensure completion of the transaction. Through Stoeckl he made arrangements to have American merchants given ready access to the Alaskan market. He asked the Smithsonian Institution to make a survey of Alaskan resources so that a report could be made to Congress, and Captain W. A. Howard of the revenue cutter service was sent out for that purpose. The Secretary of State also secured the appointment of Major General Lovell H. Rousseau to receive formal delivery from the Russians, so that the territory might be held until Congress organized a government. Rousseau reached Sitka on October 18, 1867, and the transfer was made the same day.

But would the nation's representatives make the appropriation necessary to pay for the new territory? Seward and Stevens assured Stoeckl that the money would be voted as soon as Congress convened in December, but by that time the House was in an ugly mood about the Johnson administration. There was also a report that Grant thought the purchase ill-advised and the cost ruinous; his close friend, Congressman E. B. Washburne of Illinois, declared the treaty was wastefully extravagant. The Danish West Indies Treaty was before the Senate, and on November 25, 1867, immediately after the House Judiciary Committee offered its resolution for impeachment of the President, the House passed a resolution by a vote of 93 to 43 that it would vote no more money for Seward's expansionist schemes. Washburn of Wisconsin, who offered this motion, said that it did not apply to "Walrussia," but made plain his opposition to the treaty appropriation. Ben Butler again raised the Perkins claim, which now amounted to $500,000, and a coterie in the House tried to block payment for Alaska in order to force satisfaction for the Perkins heirs. The move for impeachment of the President also worked in favor of the treaty opponents, and Stoeckl became alarmed as he saw fading from sight the reward of 25,000 roubles that his government had promised him for the sale of the territory, and which he thought was an inadequate recompense for his services in the matter.

In March 1868 the House decided to postpone discussion of the Alaska treaty for some two months. This meant that Russia could not possibly receive the purchase price before May, and violated an agreement in the treaty for payment within ten months after the exchange of ratifications which had taken place on June 20, 1867. Stoeckl fumed. It was the first time in history, he informed St. Petersburg, that the United States government had violated its solemnly contracted engagements, and he would demand explanations. But if it came out all right, the delay would be of no importance.

Once more Seward, Stoeckl, and their supporters swung into action. Thad Stevens had been favorable to the Perkins claim, but he now arrayed himself against Butler. Seward urged Johnson to use his influence with the Democratic members of the House. He, himself, worked closely with Thad Stevens's former law student and close friend, Simon Stevens, who lobbied for the appropriation. Stoeckl kept in close touch with Banks and, at Seward's suggestion, appealed to Robert J. Walker for help. That fervent expansionist lobbied on the floor of the House and composed a lengthy article arguing for both the Russian and Danish treaties. This appeared in the Washington *Daily Morning Chronicle*, edited by John W. Forney, who also published other reports extolling Alaska's mineral deposits, its fisheries, commercial opportunities, and "charming" climate, and declaring that its purchase would foster the extension of Christianity to China and Japan. These reports were all the more striking because of their violent contrast with a description the *Chronicle* had given just a day or two before of troublesome Indians, frequent brutal fights among the inhabitants, and a temperature that was 110 degrees below freezing.[7]

The failure of the impeachment proceedings, which took precedence over the treaty, caused a bitterness of feeling that manifested itself in regard to Alaska. The opponents of the administration declared that Johnson had exceeded his authority in taking possession of the territory before the House had voted the appropriation. Schenck of Ohio, though admitting that he would vote for the money because of Russia's friendship during the war, declared that Johnson's act was a usurpation for which the President should be again impeached. Forty-one of the 43 members of the House who finally voted against the appropriation had approved the impeachment proceedings against the President.

Once again the arguments for and against the appropriation resounded on Capitol Hill. Butler pressed the Perkins claim. Wash-

burn of Wisconsin and Delano of Ohio denounced the purchase.
Ferriss and McCarthy of New York declared that Congress had a
perfect right to refuse payment for a lot of worthless land. Banks
later recalled that at first a majority of the members were against the
appropriation.

The treaty's supporters, fortified by documentary evidence sent
by Seward, asserted that the territory was immensely valuable.
Banks brought the appropriation bill out of the Committee on Foreign Affairs and spoke in its favor. Washburn, he said, was a doubt-
ing Thomas. If he "could lay his hand on the print in the side, he
would not believe." The treaty's advocates assured the House that
the United States was morally obligated to pay for the territory. If
it refused to do so, the states on the Pacific Coast would be offended,
Russia would be disappointed, and Great Britain would get the
prize. It was a step, they declared, toward building up our trade in
the Pacific and toward the occupation of the whole continent.
Furthermore, it could not be gainsaid that Alaska now belonged to
the United States by treaty, and that rejection of the appropriation
would give Russia an iron-clad claim against the United States for
$7,200,000 with interest.

On June 27 the House agreed by unanimous consent to take up
the bill three days later. Banks then counted 117 votes for the
appropriation. The bill passed on July 14 by 113 to 43, with 44 not
voting. Banks told Seward that, estimating the probable positions of
the 44, the bill had a three to one majority in its favor.[8] But this was
only after there was an understanding between himself and Seward
that the President would be requested to ask the consideration of the
Russian government for the Perkins claim. This was done but
Russia remained adamant and so the matter ended.

Was money employed in assuring the passage of the appropriation? Seward later told President Johnson that Stoeckl had greased
palms liberally, paying out thousands to Forney for the use of the
Washington *Chronicle*, to Walker for his efforts, and to Banks and
Stevens in order to win them from their support of the Perkins
claim. He told much the same story to Bigelow. Stoeckl himself declared that the Perkins claim alone cost him a large part of the
$200,000 in the purchase price, and he complained to Walker that,
what with cables to St. Petersburg and all the rest, the whole busi-

ness had been very expensive. The Russian legation refused to furnish any information to a House committee that undertook to investigate the reports of bribery. In a dispatch to the Quai d'Orsay Berthemy declared categorically that the $200,000 had been used to ensure passage of the appropriation through the House of Representatives. It is certain that only $7,000,000 went into the coffers of the Russian government. The remainder went for unitemized expenditures. Walker admitted that he received $21,000 in gold and $2300 in greenbacks for his services.

Seward asserted that he had his information direct from Stoeckl about the payments to Congressmen and others, but later, before an investigating committee of the House, he declared that "I know nothing whatever of the use the Russian Minister made of the fund." This statement was undoubtedly made to shield Stoeckl and Russia itself from the charge of bribery.[9]

The purchase of Alaska stimulated expansionists. Bigelow thought it would be a good idea to balance the *Alabama* claims against British Columbia. Sanford declared that this was the time to acquire the whole Pacific coastline north of California. Bancroft believed that Canada had no geographic unity and, more and more breaking into separate parts, would be irresistibly attracted into the United States's orbit. Many leading newspapers saw the Alaska purchase as the first great step in the acquisition of all North America.

What was Seward's reaction? Sir Frederick Bruce was sure that the Secretary of State's ambiguous attitude toward the *Alabama* claims and his stress on the damage caused by British recognition of southern belligerency indicated that he was angling for Canadian territory. Adams shared this opinion, and so did the New York *Herald*. There was substance to these conjectures.

Seward declared, shortly after he signed the Alaska treaty, that he had "sounded out" the British government regarding setting off the *Alabama* claims against British Columbia, but that the British ministers dared not do it. Bruce heard him urge an American capitalist to form a company for buying up the rights of the Hudson's Bay Company and thus obtaining a line of communications between the Atlantic and the Pacific. In January 1868, Seward told Browning that he thought it would not be long before the United States had British Columbia. The previous summer he had asserted, to the resounding plaudits of a Boston audience, that Nature meant this whole continent to be, sooner or later, part of the American Union.

Such were the expressed aspirations of the Secretary of State, but there was in them no threat of force as a means of obtaining his objectives. Neither is there any evidence of subterranean plotting, or instigations of revolt against British or Canadian authorities. Seward believed that the expansion of which he dreamed was inevitable, and that it would be peacefully accomplished. Both he and the United States could afford to wait.

Alaska was a triumph, but it was the only tangible result of Seward's drive for new territories. Despite temporary manifestations of expansionist fever on the part of American leaders, the general trend of the period was against such a movement. In the troubled years following the Civil War there was nothing that could be described as a great national movement toward high and distant goals of world leadership. Such arguments as those centering on the unprecedented national debt, the need to devote the national energies to rebuilding the country and constructing the transcontinental railroad, and the racial problems that would be involved in acquiring outside territories, weighed heavily on the minds of Congressmen. Furthermore there was always the hatred of Seward and Johnson, the reluctance to give the administration any cause for self-congratulation or any hold on the popular imagination.[10]

But despite the disappointments and frustrations of his expansionist drive, Seward was right in thinking that he built for the oncoming generations. He was a follower in the footsteps of John Quincy Adams and like him dreamed of those places "where the strange roads go down." Adams had a vision of American expansion to the Pacific and helped pave the way to that goal. He foresaw the dominance of the United States on this continent. Seward's vision, larger than that of Adams, was of an expansion of American power and place that meant world leadership. In seeking the realization of his dream he pointed the way for the acquisition of the Virgin Islands, the building of the Panama Canal, the Good Neighbor policy toward Latin America, the Open Door in the Orient and the open door at home. This was no mean achievement for the little statesman from Auburn, New York.

⋙ 38 ⋘

The Last Phase

Seward dreaded retirement. Writing to Sanford, he compared it to that sleep mentioned by Hamlet in his soliloquy. Moreover, he saw complications arising from living with Will and Janet, who occupied the Auburn house. He wrote to the former, making it clear that he himself must have the responsibility for all repairs and improvements and a voice in any new furnishings. These would be at his expense, he said, and he did not propose to have their "spacious, free and simple country dwelling" cluttered up with damask, rosewood, and gold like the parlors of the merchants and bankers in their mansions on Fifth Avenue or in Madison Square.

This dread of the retreat to Auburn, together with his habitual friendliness, and his reluctance for putting public life and its responsibilities behind him, led him to hold out his hand to Grant during the last months of the Johnson administration. On a trip to New York after the election of 1868, Grant and Seward found themselves on the same train, and the President-elect invited the Secretary of State into his private car. A rather formal conversation ensued. A few weeks later Seward made Grant a present of some cigar holders, and early in the new year Grant came to the house on Lafayette Square for dinner. All this was noted by an observant world. Stoeckl was credited with the remark that the Hero of Appomattox could not drive Seward out of the State Department with a company of soldiers, and the rumor began to fly about that he was to remain at his post. But this was only talk, for Grant did not forget that Seward had supported Johnson in the trouble over the War Department. He responded to Seward's overtures with an outward cordiality, but did not ask him a single question about his department.[1]

With less than two weeks left in office, Seward confided to Sanford his reasons for retiring from public life. He had entered the State Department, he said, only from a sense of duty to his country, and had stated repeatedly that he would leave office when the country was saved from the perils it faced. Now peace had come, the federal Constitution was secure, and the time appointed by himself had arrived. "Thus you see in withdrawing I am only executing the very purpose with which I entered upon my present public service. . . ." He had neither the ambition nor the patience to sustain him in merely routine administration, and rest and quiet had "come to appear inviting and attractive." Sanford solemnly and regretfully acknowledged this explanation of the return to private life.

The last weeks in Washington were hectic, a constant round of social engagements and huge receptions at the house on Lafayette Square, where Anna strove heroically to pay off obligations. On March 3, the thirty-eight members of the State Department staff presented Seward with a testimonial to his unfailing kindness and courtesy. At two o'clock that afternoon the ministers, secretaries, and attachés of the diplomatic corps, together with their wives, came to the State Department to say farewell. They then went over to the White House, where Seward presented them severally to Johnson. "The diplomatic body then renewed their parting salutations to the Secretary of State, and retired to their respective homes."

Grant would not ride in the same carriage with Johnson, and the latter refused to take any part in the ceremonies of March 4. Seward and a number of the other members of the Cabinet thought they should go in a body to the inauguration. They all met that morning in the council room at the White House. Seward came in last, the usual cigar in his mouth, and apologized for being late. Johnson kept busy at his desk and at last the Secretary of State asked if it was not time to start. Johnson replied that they had better finish their work, and kept them busy until it was too late to attend the ceremonies. It was a good illustration of the President's stubbornness, and of Seward's willingness to forget differences of opinion that were past and gone.

His official duties ended, Seward had to face the problem of where to go and what to do. Latin America attracted him and he thought seriously of going there to study its society and politics. He told one friend that he might make a journey to eastern Asia. There was also a call of duty closer at home. The suffering Weed, who was spending the winter at Aiken in South Carolina, was anxious for his company. Seward toyed with the idea of joining his old partner and their returning north by way of Greenville, Tennessee, and a visit with Andrew Johnson. But moving back to Auburn was a mountainous labor, one that had priority over all else.

Seward spent some two months settling himself at his old home. Over one hundred boxes, packed up by Frederick, arrived from Washington—books, papers, silver, furniture, clothes, and so much wine and spirits that Seward declared there was enough to supply him for the rest of his life if he kept it under lock and key. He began the task of arranging his papers, and revolved plans for enlarging the library. There were scores of letters testifying the respect and affection of the writers, and these had to be answered. There was also a constant stream of visitors. On quiet evenings Seward had the whist table set up, with neighbors brought in for partners when not enough of the family were available for a game.

But even if there was plenty to do, a man whose life had been spent in politics and government found his thoughts straying to Washington. He was determined, he wrote to Charlotte Cushman, to refrain from criticizing the Grant administration, and to praise it wherever possible. He told his family that putting Hamilton Fish in the State Department was a wise move. But Evarts went about saying that within six months Grant would be begging Seward to take over his old post, and Seward himself would have liked to believe that this was true. When Bigelow came up to Auburn for a visit toward the end of March he found his host in a distinctly critical mood.

Fish, said Seward, would refer everything to Attorney General Hoar, and himself do nothing. There were only three men fit to be

Secretary of State—Sumner, Adams, and Bigelow. It had been a mistake not to invite Sumner into the Cabinet. He would not have accepted, but he should have been asked to take the State Department. Grant's idea of foreign policy was brute force, and he thought of his Cabinet ministers as staff officers. Only in relation to his old friend Webb, who was attacking him, was Seward in a charitable mood.

Webb was declaring to all and sundry that he, rather than Seward, should have the credit for inducing Napoleon III to leave Mexico. He asserted that in 1863 he had prevailed upon the Emperor to agree to the withdrawal of his troops; it was due to him that Napoleon had arranged for their periodic withdrawal. Webb took the documents in the case to Raymond, who supported him in a leading editorial in the *Times*.

The evidence did indicate that in 1865 Webb had suggested the withdrawal in stages of the French forces. It also showed that in 1863 Napoleon had told Webb that he would retire from Mexico only when he could do so with credit and honor, and that he would not leave under compulsion. This was scarcely the same thing as an agreement to abandon the Mexican venture. Bigelow was indignant with Webb, who owed much to Seward; but Seward remarked that the General probably thought that airing his claim would be of value to himself and would not hurt his former chief.[2]

Despite Seward's continued interest in public affairs and his still remarkable energy, it was apparent that his physical powers were on the decline. He walked slowly and somewhat unsteadily, rather than with his former confident tread. The muscle tone in his right arm was very weak, care by a personal servant was essential to his comfort, and he found the chill Auburn spring hard to take. More and more his thoughts turned to travel. He decided to go to the west coast and to Alaska, perhaps to Mexico as well. Included in his plans for the journey was a family by the name of Risley.

Seward had first met Hanson A. Risley in 1835, when he was in Westfield and Risley lived in Fredonia. The latter was a faithful Whig and later Republican, and the Weed-Seward machine found offices for him, first in New York State and later in the Treasury Department in Washington. He was a hanger-on, who professed a filial regard for his mentors, and he had two daughters, Olive and

Harriet, the former approximately the same age as Fanny Seward, while Hattie, as she was called, was six years younger.

Olive was mildly pretty, by no means a ravishing beauty. Her letters at the age of twenty-four indicate no great wit or intellectual power, being rather dull and stodgy, but Seward found her sweet and generous-spirited, and under his tutelage her mentality did show some sign of development. As he heaped favors upon her, favors that delighted her father, she appeared to be deeply appreciative.[3]

During 1868 Seward's attentions to Olive became marked. There were frequent rides in his carriage, picnics along Rock Creek, presents to Olive and her sister. He kept urging her to improve her mind and she declared that she was more than willing, though she complained that such mundane matters as health and domestic cares kept interfering with her plans for intellectual development. That summer she and Hattie went to Fredonia, but came to Auburn for the Burlingame festivities. Seward's personal physician, Dr. Dimon, ministered to the invalid Hattie and attended the girls' mother that fall in her last illness. When Mrs. Risley died Seward summoned an embalmer from New York to take care of the remains.

By October the newspapers were reporting that Seward was to be married again, and Bigelow went to Blatchford for information. Blatchford said that Seward was very fond of the girl. He himself would not be surprised if the story about marriage was true, though he did not believe it. Welles, too, who watched Seward drive past his house practically every day on his way to the Risleys, was skeptical about matrimony. Nevertheless, he thought Seward's conduct strange. "Says he is an old friend of the family," Welles noted cryptically in his diary.

There could be no question of Seward's being deeply involved with the daughter of his old friend. The best clue to his infatuation, for it was scarcely less than that, is to be found in a letter he wrote early in 1868 to Gertrude Sanford, the attractive wife of the diplomat. He told her that he was conscious of a change in himself, a change of which the world was not aware but which she had discovered. The death of his wife and daughter had left him "in want of a habitual support of life. . . . How I accept with thankfulness every expression of feminine respect and affection you have seen." Olive offered him both tributes, and he was a ready recipient.

As Seward's plans for his trip matured Frederick and Anna decided to go with him, and he invited the Risleys to join the party. Hanson Risley turned down the invitation, pleading Hattie's delicate health and the state of his affairs. Olive declared she was deeply disappointed. During the trip Seward wrote repeatedly of his regret that she had not come. He hoped vainly that she would join them in San Francisco for the Mexican trip. "Why did I ever allow myself to become dependent on you so entirely," he wrote from Mexico. Olive's letters told how lonesome she was and how she regretted their separation. She was reading Guizot and was going to study the history of the art of music so as to tell him something for his book. Would he bring her some sealskins from Alaska? She had always wanted a sealskin coat and cap. She said she was sure that he loved her.[4]

Despite Seward's disappointment that Olive was not with him, the trip was a success. The party started on June 7, traveling in a "hotel car" furnished by George Mortimer Pullman, and the journey across the continent stimulated the old statesman's propensity for looking into the future. At Chatham in Canada, a prosperous colony of erstwhile slaves prompted him to remark that Negroes in the United States, like those in Canada, should have equal political rights with the whites. The backwardness of the Canadian countryside near the head of Lake Ontario confirmed his belief that Canada would inevitably be absorbed by the United States. In a short speech on the coast he predicted that within seven years not one only but three railroads would span the continent.

After hospitable receptions at San Francisco and Sacramento they took a steamer to Sitka, from which town they explored some distance along the coast. At Sitka on August 12 Seward spoke, extolling Alaska's scenery, weather and resources, and predicting that it would become a state of the Union. On his return journey, at Victoria, British Columbia, he dwelt on the intermingling of British and American interests in the Northwest, and in Salem, Oregon, on western dynamic and the inevitability of British Columbia becoming part of the United States.

From San Francisco they moved down to Mexico, where his hosts outdid themselves in hospitality. The travelers remained there over two months and Seward declared that, if he were not the guest of the nation, he would be tempted to stay all winter. He spent much of his time in and about Mexico City, making visits to Chapultepec and Popocatapetl, and being deterred from ascending the latter only when he learned that it was always twenty degrees below zero at the summit, and that he would have to remain overnight in an open hut. In a number of short speeches, he extolled good neighborliness, assuring his listeners that the United States could be counted on to support republicanism in the Western world. While his own country was always willing to accept those nations that wished to come into its fold, he declared, it was equally willing to co-operate with those desiring to maintain their republican independence.

When the little party finally left Mexico it made a leisurely trip home, staying for some weeks in Havana. It was not until March 12 that they reached Auburn, where they found an accumulation of gifts and purchases, fruits of the trip. The Californians had given Seward a pair of matched sorrel horses, small and swift, in which he took great pride. Alaskans had sent an eagle and an Esquimaux dog. The travelers had amassed a large collection of mementos and curiosities, and Seward planned a Pacific library, for which he had ordered some 7000 feet of Alaskan yellow cedar, together with Vancouver Island laurel, Oregon pine, and California redwood, all to be sent around Cape Horn. He was in good spirits as he surveyed the spoils of the journey, and for the present seemed happy to be home.[5]

During the next five months there was much to occupy the returned traveler. Public affairs still claimed his attention. Stanton's death, which had occurred some months before, left lingering and sad memories. He had loved his former colleague, he wrote, and none the less because the quarrel over the War Department in 1868 had driven them apart. Henry Wilson asked for information about Stanton's course in the winter of 1860–61. "You made a grand record," wrote Seward's former critic, "uttered noble truths that read grandly now"; and Seward replied, giving the story of how he and Stanton, through their mutual friend, Peter Watson, had daily furnished each other with information on questions of policy. Adams came to Auburn in May, and the two men relived the memories of wartime, Seward magnifying his role in the *Trent* affair and the two men exchanging critical opinions on Lincoln's leadership. Not long thereafter Congressman James Negley of Pennsylvania urged Seward to recommend subsidization of a steamship line to southern Europe. He replied with a published letter approving the development of an American merchant marine, and urging free immigration from Europe and Asia. He asked Senator Morton to foster legislation that would promote the economic development of Mexico and, with little success, tried to act the part of intermediary between that country and its British bondholders.

But politics was now peripheral. Closer at home was an active social life. Delegations of friends and admirers came from Syracuse and other nearby towns. Sunday school classes from the surrounding area called at the house, where they consumed sponge cake and lemonade. There were Saturday night receptions. Every day Seward rode out behind the swift California sorrels, but he refused all invitations to formal gatherings or crowded assemblies.

The growing paralysis that made his right arm and hand almost useless was now appearing on his left side. Adams noted that, while he was loquacious as ever, he lacked that exuberant vivacity that had always been one of his outstanding characteristics. Subdued in manner and at times depressed, he fought fiercely against physical disintegration. His remedy for his ailments, he wrote wryly to a friend, was to raise blisters on his hands by rowing on the lake and trundling a wheelbarrow about the yard.

The prospect of a winter in Auburn was most distasteful, and another trip to foreign parts became increasingly attractive. Travel was a sovereign remedy, and there were such pleasant recollections of his reception in Mexico. Goldwin Smith, who came up from Ithaca to see him that summer, noted caustically that "old Seward" was thinking of himself as an ambassador of good will to countries having some connection with the United States.

At first Seward's thoughts turned again to South America, but there was a discouraging report about the hardships of travelers in such countries as Peru and Chile. The alternative was the Orient. Then he began to think of a trip around the world, with Olive and Hattie Risley as his principal traveling companions.

When Seward, with Fred and Anna, landed at Baltimore in February 1870, there had been telegrams from Hanson Risley in Washington. Olive was slowly recovering from typhoid fever, and would he not come to see her? Instead he forwarded presents and, to Olive's disappointment, went on to New York and Auburn. Whatever the reasons, Seward's devotion had cooled.

That spring, however, his relations with the Risleys were resumed on the old, close footing. Olive and her father came to Auburn in May and stayed for several days. The following month, after a tenday visit at Montrose, Frederick's home on the Hudson, Seward brought the Risley girls back to Auburn for another visit. It was probably at this time that they completed their plans for the great expedition. Olive would write his letters for him and keep a journal, at the same time having the cultural advantages of world travel. She was eager to go, and this time Risley gave his consent, stipulating that he would accompany them as far as San Francisco. The party that started from Auburn consisted of five persons, Seward, his personal servant, the two girls and their father. In San Francisco they were joined by Governor and Mrs. Alexander W. Randall and also by George Seward and his bride, who were en route to Shanghai.[6]

The trip, which began on August 9, was a tremendous undertaking for a man in Seward's physical condition, but he entered upon it with his accustomed verve. At the Tremont House in Chicago they met President Grant, "who seemed as much travel worn and a great deal more office worn than myself." They attended service at the tabernacle in Salt Lake City, where Seward took the Mormon communion of bread and water. Brigham Young was solicitous in his attentions, and introduced them to nine of his sixteen wives. From Ogden westward Governor Stanford placed the private car of the directors of the Union Pacific at their disposal.

During their stay in Japan the Mikado gave Seward a face-to-face audience, a most important precedent as Minister De Long wrote to Secretary Fish. After this climax to the Japanese visit, the party crossed over to China, where they remained two months, traveling through the northern and central regions and exploring as far as the Great Wall.

At Shanghai the party broke up. Randall decided to go home and Mrs. Randall, despite Seward's urging, accompanied her husband. George Seward was to remain in Shanghai, where he was consul general. This left Seward with the two girls, and their continuing around the world in their present situation would have stimulated the gossip that already swirled about him and his young protégé.

During the early stages of the trip Seward had been revolving plans for the future. En route to Japan he had written to Olive's father of how grateful he was that Risley had allowed "our children" to come on this journey, and of how he anticipated seeing their father "at no distant day in some European retreat which I shall secure for them and where with your paternal advice their plans for the future may be reviewed." Subsequent to this, he thought of buying a charming bungalow in Nagasaki. He and Olive went over the situation and finally agreed that adoption was the best way of stopping the tongues of the gossip mongers. The decision to take this step was probably made at Shanghai.

On November 5, 1870 Seward made his will, leaving the home and real estate in Auburn to his three sons in equal shares, and the remaining estate, real and personal, also in equal shares, to his sons and his adopted daughter. William Henry, Jr., and Olive were named executor and executrix. A month later Seward and Olive wrote to the family back home of the step they had taken.

The news reached Auburn and Montrose in January. Fred replied that it was a judicious and sensible arrangement, one that he hoped would save them from further annoyance. Will wrote that Lazette Worden, Jenny, and himself had resolved that it was "entirely satisfactory" to them; that they, like himself, were under many obligations to Olive "for her kind care and affection for you and I see no better or delicate way than this of rewarding its continuance." Their one wish, he added, was "to see your life made happy & comfortable be the circumstances what they may." So the family put itself on record as accepting the inevitable. Seward and Olive in turn expressed their appreciation of this attitude. The adoption had the additional merit of quieting Hanson Risley, who had begun writing to Seward about his fears for his daughters' reputations.[7]

Seward told his children that he had been sure of their acceptance of the adoption when they reflected upon his need for travel and his dependence upon Olive's patient affection. He informed Risley that he was now so fond of her that "it seems almost indelicate for me to speak her just praise even to you. She has ripened into a noble, impressive, intellectual and attractive womanhood. All women we meet give her their love and seek her confidence. All the intelligent and distinguished men converse with her as their equal or superior." He felt that it was imperative she should see Europe, where he would introduce her "to the highest, most cultivated society." He hoped Risley would meet them in Constantinople. Risley's one idea was that Seward should bring his "precious children" home.[8]

During this long-range discussion of the adoption, the travelers had been wending their way from China to Europe. They spent nearly three months in India, traveling across that country as far north as the foothills of the Himalayas and from Calcutta to Bombay. Then they moved on to Cairo and up the Nile as far as Assouan, guests of the Viceroy and the Khedive of Egypt. On this expedition they saw evidences of man's antiquity that, Seward declared, made doubtful the chronology of Archbishop Usher. Next they went to Syria and the Holy Land, spending a week in Jerusalem. They visited Athens and then Constantinople, where Seward met the Sultan and was the guest of the Turkish government. From there they made their way by the Black Sea and along the Danube to Vienna, then down to Venice, Rome, and Naples, and by way of Florence, to Geneva. In August 1871 they reached Paris.

Throughout this journey Seward grew physically weaker. Before its end he had two personal servants in attendance, but his spirits and his eagerness to be part of all that he met did not flag. While in Calcutta he wrote a long letter to the Secretary of State about the fisheries in the northern Pacific. While yet in office he had drawn up a treaty providing reciprocal rights in the fishing areas for Russia and the United States. Such an agreement now, he said, would add immensely to American prestige, and would help in negotiations with Great Britain over the northeast fisheries and the free navigation of the St. Lawrence. He was meditating a visit to St. Petersburg and would be glad to talk with Minister Curtin there about the subject, if Fish thought it proper and desirable.

This letter elicited no reply. Some months later, when he saw Bancroft in Berlin, he again raised the question of the North Pacific fisheries, saying that he felt their importance rivaled that of an interoceanic canal. It was over twenty years later that Russia and the

United Sates reached a similar agreement, one in regard to sealing in the Pacific.

There were German soldiers still quartered in Paris when Seward reached that capital and the city still bore the marks of the Franco-Prussian conflict. Seward went about, observing everything. Despite his arms being almost helpless he attended a dinner given for him by the consul general, Meredith Read. There he met Antoine Paul Laboulaye, liberal politician and author of a political history of the United States. He also heard the sad news that Count de Gasparin was dead. The following day he had a ninety-minute interview with Drouyn de Lhuys which turned out to be largely a monologue, Seward describing his trip and going over the story of American policy in the Maximilian affair.[9]

The travelers reached New York at the beginning of October. As George Bancroft wrote, Seward had done what would greatly astonish the psalmist, "if he should ever get news of it. When did a man of three score years and ten ever before go round the world?" It had, indeed, been an amazing performance. Seward calculated that over a period of fourteen months and two days he had traveled some 44,000 miles, on an average over 100 miles a day.

Will and Fred met him at the boat. At his request they had canceled a reception planned by New York friends and he went at once to Montrose. There he rested a few days, sleeping on a bed in the library so that he would not have to climb the stairs. Weed spent a day with him, and then Seward went on to Auburn, a reporter accompanying him on the train for an interview which covered the front page of the New York *Sun*.[10] On arrival he made a little speech to the neighbors who came to greet him. Many had thought this trip a proof of eccentricity, he said, but he had discovered that "rest was rust; and nothing remained to prevent rust but to keep in motion. I selected the way that would do the least harm, give the least offense, enable me to acquire the most knowledge, and increase the power, if any, to do good."

Seward now resigned himself to life at home. He went for a drive behind the California sorrels some five or six miles every day. When weather permitted he spent days at Will's cottage on Owasco Lake. Reading, studying, dictation to Fred, and later to Olive, occupied much of his time. But though journeys had come to an end, the taste for them remained. His favorite novels, he declared, were *Robinson Crusoe* and *Gulliver's Travels,* and he sent to New York for a copy of Camoen's *Lusiads,* that magnificent epic of discovery built around Vasco da Gama's voyage to India.

A succession of guests appeared at the old home. Weed came for a visit, and so did Rudolf Schleiden. Charlotte Cushman came to Auburn for a recital and the Sewards gave a dinner in her honor. John Hay paid his respects. Seward went to the opera house to hear Ole Bull, and the violinist played for sixty guests at the house on South Street. Governor Oglesby of Illinois made a special visit so that he might invite Seward to speak at the dedication of a Lincoln monument, and Seward almost accepted. There were other such invitations, all refused. A large amount of work lay ahead, for he planned to write two books, an account of his journey round the world and the story of his life.

Risley told James C. Derby that Olive had notes enough for a handsome volume, and Derby, who was connected with the publishing house of D. Appleton and Company, urged Seward to see that "the fair authoress" was amply compensated for her trouble. Other publishers liked the idea of the travel book, and they deluged Seward with offers of contracts. Olive was not unwilling to act as editor, though she declared that it would mean the breaking of old ties and associations that she held dear. Pleading such difficulties, her want of ability and her ill health, she delayed coming to Auburn until after Thanksgiving.

In the meantime, Fred and Anna arrived, and with their help Seward began work on his autobiography, a book that Adams, Bancroft, and others had urged him to write. By the close of November, he had reached the gubernatorial race of 1834, and had become deeply interested in the project. Then Olive appeared, the autobiography was dropped, and everyone went to work on the "travels."

William H. Seward's Travels Around the World, edited by Olive Risley Seward, appeared in 1873. Its 720 pages, replete with illustrations, abounded in descriptions of the places visited, together with Seward's observations concerning peoples and institutions. Primarily based on Olive's journal, it also recorded memories and later philosophical comments by the principal voyager. Frederick put considerable time and labor into the project. Its historical interest is slight, but to an American generation curious about the outside world and unable or unwilling to travel, it possessed great interest. It sold over 60,000 copies.

Just as the manuscript neared completion, the dismal presidential campaign of 1872 began gathering momentum. Grant had easily won renomination, despite the revolt of liberal Republicans disgusted with his incompetence. This discontented gentry, together with powerful newspaper editors, idealists and practical politicians, gathered in a nominating convention at Cincinnati where, amid much wrangling, they finally made Greeley their candidate. It was a strange choice, for by this time the peppery editor had lost much of the reforming zeal of his younger days. He also had a long record of despising Democrats, but that party, in the desperate hope that coalition meant victory, accepted him as their candidate.

Seward was not cheered by the doings at Cincinnati. A day or two after Greeley's nomination there the Auburn invalid delivered a short political disquisition.

> Did it ever occur to you [he remarked] that the great political problem which has vexed the political theorists and philosophers is simply this—how to prevent the government from falling into the hands of knaves or fools? In all ages and in all countries that is the question they have been trying to solve—for the most part with very indifferent success. Monarchies, republics, parliaments, and despotisms, in their various forms, were all invented to avert that danger, and have all found it impossible to entirely prevent it. Look at the proceedings of any party convention under this, the best government in the world, and see how close they run to that danger every time they meet.[11]

Adherents of both candidates solicited support from Auburn. Weed urged Seward to come out for Grant. So did Roscoe Conkling and Cornell Jewett. Seward had no love for the President, but Greeley in the White House was unthinkable. Only a few months before, the *Tribune*'s editor had published a front-page spread of the famous letter dissolving the partnership with Weed and Seward, declaring it a "bold untruth" that he had written it because they would not give him office. "What can you do," Seward remarked, "with a man of sixty ideas, and every one of the sixty an impracticable crochet?" His sister-in-law replied to a query from Augustus that none of them were for Greeley.

For a long time Seward refused to make a public commitment, but the strain was too great. Finally, on September 17, he wrote a published letter, declaring that he saw "no sufficient reason" to withdraw his support from the principles and policy that had carried the country through the war, or from the party organization and candidates who represented them. In this oblique fashion he came out for Grant.[12]

Seward planned to resume work with Fred on his autobiography as soon as he completed the *Travels*, but his paralytic condition had now reached a critical state. He watched its progress with a rather detached curiosity, remarking to one of his sons that death usually struck men at the heart or by the throat. In his case he believed that breathing would be obstructed and then fail.

Until the last day of his life he took his place at the table and went for his usual drive. On that day he was dressed and did some work on the *Travels*. Lying on the lounge to rest, he had difficulty breathing. Dr. Dimon came and told him that the end was near. His last words, indistinctly uttered, were either some reference to science and religion, or an adjuration to the members of his family to love one another. He died at four o'clock on the afternoon of October 10, 1872.[13]

William Henry Seward was a complex individual, one who does not easily fit into any stereotype—radical, liberal, conservative, or reactionary. He was equally ready to have the government or private capital build roads, canals, and railroads. He favored work relief in times of depression, would welcome men and ideas of all kinds and from all quarters to the building of America, and yet never questioned the validity of a capitalistic society. He was the political leader of the anti-slavery movement in the 1850s, and a hissing and a byword to anti-slavery zealots a decade later. He spoke noble words on behalf of humanity and freedom, but even his wife sometimes doubted his fealty to those great ideals. Such a man is not easy to classify.

This complex man had certain fundamental drives. Ambitious for public recognition, he longed for high office, the presidency most of all. He loved his country, and this devotion rivaled ambition. His dislike of slavery was genuine. He did not see the black man as the equal of the white, then or in the future, but he believed that human bondage violated the basic principles of the nation and obstructed progress; and that the Negro should have a secure place in American society. Finally, he loved the game of politics and entered into it with a zest that never failed.

Seward had many faults. His habitual optimism often led him into false predictions, a trait that was especially noticeable during the Civil War. There was a Machiavellian streak in him, a love for obfuscating his adversaries by ambiguities that on occasion bewildered even his friends. His dispatches were often clear and cogent, but sometimes, as one friendly critic remarked, were "more creditable to his physical vigor of composition and his love of scholastic dialectics than to his sagacity." He could act hastily, and on the basis of inadequate information. His predilection for unofficial envoys tried the patience of such capable diplomats as Dayton and Adams.

There were still more grave limitations. He lacked the moralistic fervor with which Greeley could move the minds and hearts of men. Seward's appeal was always on the practical side. And friendly and outgoing though he was, something within him, his vanity perhaps, prevented his giving to others the affection they gave to him. Frances loved him with a devotion he could not reciprocate. Weed was the lesser man, but Weed gave Seward a depth of loyalty which was beyond Seward's power to give in return. Lincoln recognized his great qualities. Seward could never really bring himself to recognize Lincoln's greatness.

But with all his faults, Seward was a remarkable, an outstanding figure in his era. He had an endless thirst for knowledge. Like Tennyson's Ulysses, he was determined to drink life to the lees. Like Goethe, his passion for more light never failed. He enjoyed having people about him, and had the Irish facility for making himself agreeable to them, whether they were servants, clerks, politicians, or statesmen. Even his foes acknowledged his generosity. Rarely ill-tempered, he was blessed with a keen sense of humor and an exuberant, almost boyish gaiety that was one of his most appealing traits. It was well said of him that he destroyed his enemies by making them his friends. Weed, Sanford, the formidable Abigail Brooks Adams, Eliphalet Nott, Charlotte Cushman, and many others acknowledged the power of his charm. So, too, did children, for he had a rare capacity for putting himself on their level.

Was he a statesman in the best sense of the word? His gubernatorial career which, though creditable, was not exceptional, is scarcely a fair test, for he was dogged by the economic depression of the period. Nevertheless, it showed courage and capacity for administration. His twelve years in the United States Senate demonstrated his industry, and his ability to grasp and deal intelligently with the public questions of the day. Despite unfortunate slips in the use of such phrases as "higher law" and "irrepressible conflict," his approach to the greatest problem of all, the slavery question, showed prescience of a high order.

As Secretary of State, Seward demonstrated a remarkable ability to assume great burdens of administration, and an equally remarkable versatility of approach to vital issues. He watched public opinion, sometimes using and never flouting it. He appreciated the maxim that a half loaf is better than none, remarking toward the end of his career "it is always better to accept what can be secured and call in the aid of time to perfect what we have established." A significant measure of his achievement is that, while the nation was wracked by the damage and loss of civil war and reconstruction, its standing with the other nations in no wise diminished.

And Seward did more than conduct American foreign relations from year to year with skill and success. His foreign policy built for the future. He wished to prepare America for the great era which lay ahead. So he sought bases, naval stations and, peacefully, additional territory. He recognized the importance of good relations with Britain, France, and Russia, with Latin America and the Orient. He wanted the United States to compete with Europe for the world's trade and commerce, and something more. Teaching by example, it should lead all the rest in building a happier future for mankind. A practical statesman, he was also a dreamer. This, perhaps more than his accomplishments, makes him one of the significant figures in American history.

Notes

Abbreviations Used in Notes

AANY — Archives of the Archdiocese of New York
AAE — Archives des Affaires Étrangères
ABIIP— Archives of the Foreign Policy of Russia
AJ — Andrew Johnson Papers
F. O.— Foreign Office of Great Britain
LC — Library of Congress
MVHR — *Mississippi Valley Historical Review*
NA — National Archives
NA M— R— National Archives, Microcopy — Roll —.
N.Y.P.L.— New York Public Library
OR — Official Records of the Union and Confederate Armies
PAC — Public Archives of Canada
p. d.— Preliminary draft
PRFA — Papers Relating to Foreign Affairs
RTL — Robert Todd Lincoln Papers
SP — Seward Papers
WP — Weed Papers

Notes

NOTES FOR CHAPTER I

1. *Ancestors of General William Henry Seward and His Wife Janet Mc-Neil Watson.* Arranged by P. S. deLuze (New Rochelle, N.Y., 1899); F. W. Seward, Jr., *Obadiah Seward of Long Island, New York and His Descendants* (Goshen, N.Y., 1948), 13, 90–91.
2. Samuel Sweezy Seward Papers, memoranda regarding property holdings, 1848; William Henry Seward Papers (hereafter referred to as SP), D. Berdan to W. H. Seward, May 16, 27, Aug. 11, 1822, to B. J. Seward, n.d., Frances Seward to W. H. Seward, Apr. 22, 1832, Seward to Wm. W. Goodrich, Feb. 12, 1864; F. W. Seward, *William H. Seward: An Autobiography from 1801 to 1834. With a Memoir of His Life and Selections from His Letters* (3 vols., New York, 1891), I, 20–38, 43, 187, 229. The *Autobiography* will hereafter be referred to as Seward, *Autobiography*, and the remainder of this work as F. W. Seward, *Seward.*
3. Milledgeville *Journal*, March 2, 1819, reprinted in New York *Times*, Jan. 31, 1860.
4. SP, Seward to Mary J. Seward, March 11, 1819 (copy); Iddo Ellis to Seward, May 20, 1828, J. Johnsing to Seward, July 2, 1855, R. Alexander to Seward, Apr. 11, 1866; Seward, *Autobiography*, 36–44.
5. SP, Seward to D. Jessup, Jr., Jan. 24, 1820, Seward to President of Adelphic Society, Sept. 3, 1827; Seward, *Autobiography*, 30, 32.
6. SP, Berdan's letters to Seward, *passim*, Frances Seward to Seward, Feb. 15, 1831; *The Knickerbocker*, XIV (Dec. 1839), 471–82, Seward's "Memoir of David Berdan."
7. SP, Berdan to Seward, May 16, 27, July 24, Oct. 28, 1822, Sept. 15, 1826.
8. SP, Seward to S. S. Seward, Aug. 12, 15, 1823, Berdan to Seward, July 22, 1823.

9. Berdan to Seward, Aug. 29, 1824; Seward, *Autobiography*, 55–6; B. F. Hall, "Genealogical and Biographical Sketch of the Late Honorable Elijah Miller," 84–5.

10. SP, Berdan to Seward, Sept. 15, 1826, F. A. Seward to W. H. Seward, Sept. 19 (1847); Hall, op. cit. 102–10, *et passim; Collections of the Cayuga County Historical Society* (Auburn, 1888), no. 6, 112–13. The description of Frances Seward is based on the Seward family letters, especially those from Frances to her husband and to her sister Lazette Worden. See also, M. E. White, ed., *A Sketch of Chester Harding, Artist* (Boston and New York, 1890), 215.

11. Grier Papers, W. H. Seward to S. S. Seward, Dec. 20, 1823, Aug. 5, 1824; SP, Seward to D. Jessup, Jr., Jan. 24, 1820, Berdan to Seward, March 28, Sept. 29, 1826, Seward to C. Morgan, Jan. 2, 1841(p.d.), S. S. Seward to W. H. Seward, Nov. 22, 1824, W. H. Seward to N. P. Tallmadge, Dec. 1, 1840(p.d.); Weed Papers (hereafter referred to as WP), Seward to Weed (Sept. 25, 1834); Cayuga *Republican*, Nov. 13, 20, 1822, Nov. 17, 1824, Nov. 22, 1826; G. E. Baker, ed., *The Works of William H. Seward* (3 vols., New York, 1853), III, 335–7 (hereafter referred to as Seward, *Works*); L. Benson, *The Concept of Jacksonian Democracy* (Princeton, 1961), 7–10; R. V. Remini, *Martin Van Buren and the Making of the Democratic Party* (New York, 1959), 8–11, 60–62; Seward, *Autobiography*, 27, 35–6, 47–51. In his *Autobiography* (67) Seward implies that his rejection by the senate was due to his coming out against Clinton.

12. On the origins of Antimasonry and Weed's part in it, see the Tracy Papers, Weed to Tracy, June 15, 1828; WP, Tracy to Weed, June 19, 1828; C. McCarthy, "The Antimasonic Party," *Annual Report of the American Historical Association* (1902), I, 369–83; G. H. Blakeslee, "The History of the Antimasonic Party" (Harvard University, 1903), an unpublished doctoral dissertation; Benson, op. cit. 17–26; G. G. Van Deusen, *Thurlow Weed: Wizard of the Lobby* (Boston, 1947), 38–49.

13. Cayuga *Republican*, Aug. 20, Oct. 1, 8, 15, 1828; WP, Seward to Weed, Dec. 24, 1837; *Proceedings of the Antimasonic Republican Convention of the County of Cayuga—Jan. 1, 1830* (Auburn, 1830), 4–20; Seward, *Autobiography*, 70–72, 76–7. Antimasonic and National Republican hostilities gave the Democrats an easy victory in New York State in 1828.

14. *Proceedings for the Antimasonic Convention for the State of New York, Held at Utica, August 11, 1830* (Utica, 1830), 3–6, 14; Albany *Argus*, Sept. 15, 17, Oct. 12, 1830; *Antimasonic Convention Held at Philadelphia, Sept. 11, 1830* (Philadelphia, 1830), 1, 3–7, 69–72, 84; SP, Jas. H. Woods to Seward, April 27, 1830; Tracy Papers, Weed to Tracy, July 26, 1830; McCarthy, op. cit. I, 393–400; Seward, *Autobiography*, 78–80; H. A. Weed, ed., *Autobiography of Thurlow Weed* (Boston, 1883), 367 (hereafter cited as Weed, *Autobiography*); Benson, op. cit. 34; Van Deusen, *Weed*, 56–7.

NOTES FOR CHAPTER 2

1. Tracy Papers, Seward to Tracy, May 1, 12, 1831, June 17, 1832; C. F. Adams, ed., *Memoirs of John Quincy Adams* (12 vols., Philadelphia, 1874–77), VI, 458, 464, 469, *et passim;* SP, Tracy to Seward, Feb. 2, May 4, 1831; WP, Seward to Weed, June 22, 1831; H. B. Stanton, *Random Recollections* (New York, 1887), 149.

2. SP, S. G. Andrews to Seward, May 23, 1831, Weed to Seward, June 18, 1831, May 27, 1834, William Kent to Seward, June 30, 1836; WP, Seward to Weed, June 22, 1831; F. W. Seward, *Seward,* I, 166, 172, 179–80; Van Deusen, *Weed,* 81.

3. Samuel Sweezy Seward Papers, W. H. Seward to S. S. Seward, Feb. 28, 1831; Benson, op. cit. 44–6.

4. Tracy Papers, Seward to Tracy, June 23, July 19, 1831; SP, Weed to Seward, July 15, 24, 1831; WP, Seward to Weed, Aug. 2, 8, Sept. 14, 1831; F. W. Seward, *Seward,* I, 198–206.

5. SP, Tracy to Seward, Oct. 6, 1831, J. Q. Adams to Seward, Oct. 17, 1831; Seward to Judge Miller, Dec. 26, 1831; Seward, *Autobiography,* 89–91; WP, Seward to Weed, Nov. 12, 1831; Weed, *Autobiography,* 389–91; S. R. Gammon, *The Presidential Campaign of 1832* (Baltimore, 1922), 44–52.

6. *Journal of the Senate of the State of New York,* 55th Session, 1832 (Albany, 1832), 42, *et passim;* S. S. Seward Papers, W. H. Seward to S. S. Seward, March 18, 1832; SP, J. Case to Seward, Jan. 1, 1832; F. W. Seward, *Seward,* I, 211; W. H. Seward, *Speech on the Resolution Against Renewing the Charter of the United States Bank* (Albany, 1832).

7. SP, J. C. Spencer to Seward, March 5, 1832, Wm. Kent to Seward, Feb. 21, 1832, Frances Seward to Lazette Worden, Jan. 31, 1832, "Address to the People of New York State—April 1832," draft in Seward's handwriting; WP, Seward to Weed, May 10, July 16, Aug. 19, 1832; S. S. Seward Papers, W. H. Seward to S. S. Seward, May 10, 1832; F. W. Seward, *Seward,* I, 214.

8. Blakeslee, op. cit. 253–8; Tracy Papers, Seward to Tracy, June 4, 1832; WP, Seward to Weed, Aug. 19, Sept. 5, 27, Oct. 2, 26, 1832; *Journal of the Senate,* 56th sess., 1833, 157–9, 168–74; SP, Tracy to Seward, Nov. 11, 1832, John A. Collier to Seward, Feb. 5, 1833; Albany *Evening Journal,* Nov. 21, 1832; F. W. Seward, *Seward,* I, 218–20.

9. SP, Judge Miller to Seward, March 31, 1833, Tracy to Seward, May 17, 1833, Weed to Seward, June 5, 1833, "Diary Letters," e.g. 33, 58, 62, F. A. Seward to L. Worden, March 9, 1834, W. H. Seward to F. A. Seward, July 25, 1859, Hammond to Seward, Aug. 28, 1834; Tracy Papers, F. A. Seward to Tracy, May 19, 1833, Seward to Tracy, May 23, 1833; Albany *Evening Journal,* Oct. 6, 1834.

10. W. H. Seward, *Speech on the Resolutions Concerning the Removal of*

the Government Deposites (Albany, 1834), *passim;* Seward, *Works,* I,
37–50, III, 349–55.

11. SP, J. A. Collier to Seward, Feb. 5, 1833, W. H. Seward to S. S. Seward,
June 2, 1838; *Journal of the Senate* (1833), 168–74, (1834), 453, 465–6.
Other senators from the central and northern parts of the state also voted
against these bills.

12. SP, Jan.–March, 1834, *passim,* also Seward to L. Worden, Jan. 27, 1834,
B. F. Hallett to Seward, May 5, 1834, S. M. Hopkins to Seward, July 12,
1834; Patterson Papers, Weed to Patterson, Dec. 11, 1833; E. M. Carroll,
Origins of the Whig Party (Durham, 1925), 118–41, *et passim;* G. G.
Van Deusen, *The Life of Henry Clay* (Boston, 1937), 276–7, and *Horace
Greeley* (Philadelphia, 1953), 30.

13. SP, A. Worden to Seward, March 16, 1833, Seward to A. Worden, March
19, 1833, Wm. Kent to Seward, Nov. 27, 1829, Cornelia Canfield to
Seward, Feb. 28, 1831, M. Canfield to Seward, March 7, 1831, Weed to
Seward, March 8–11, 1835.

14. SP, J. D. Hammond to Seward, Aug. 28, 1834, Weed to Seward, Aug. 6,
Sept. 8–11, 1834, Cary to Seward, Sept. 11, 1834, G. W. Lay to Seward,
Sept. 11, 1834, G. F. Talman to Seward, Oct. 9, 1834, J. L. Rathbone to
Seward, Oct. 11, 1834, F. Whittlesey to Seward, Oct. 17, 1834, D. Ullman
to Seward, Oct. 18, 1834, Tracy to Seward, May 26, 1834; Tracy Papers,
Seward to Tracy, June 1, 1834, S. P. Lyman to Tracy, July 20, 1834,
Weed to Tracy, July 21, 1834; WP, Seward to Weed, July 28, Aug. 3,
Sept. 12, 1834; I. D. Spencer, *The Victor and the Spoils: A Life of Wil-
liam L. Marcy* (Providence, 1959), 74–81.

15. SP, Weed to Seward, Sept. 20, 29, Nov. 1, 6, 1834, J. D. Hammond to
Seward, Aug. 28, 1834; WP, Seward to Weed, Nov. 6, 8, 1834; Cary
Papers, Seward to Cary, Nov. 11, 14, 1834.

NOTES FOR CHAPTER 3

1. SP, S. S. Seward to W. H. Seward, Jan. 18, Nov. 22, 1824, Berdan to
Seward, Sept. 15, 1826, D. D. Hillis to Seward, Aug. 14, 1831, W. H.
Seward to S. S. Seward, April 6, 1835, June 2, 1838; WP, Seward to Weed,
Jan. 18, 30, Feb. 15, 27, March 3, May 10, Nov. 22, 1835, March 7, 1836;
S. S. Seward Papers, W. H. Seward to S. S. Seward, June 2, 1836; Tracy
Papers, Seward to Tracy, June 1, 1834; Patterson Papers, Weed to Pat-
terson, Aug. 12, 1833; Seward, *Autobiography,* 74–6.

2. SP, Seward family letters, 1825–35, Tracy to Seward, Feb. 7, 1831, May 8,
30, 1832, April 14, Dec. 29, 1834, April 14, May 7, 1835, Seward to Tracy,
Dec. 29, 1834, June 24, 1835, Weed to Seward, May 27, 1832, June 7,
1834; Tracy Papers, Seward to Tracy, Feb. 11, May 1, 1831, June 4, 1832,
June 1, Dec. 29, 1834, F. A. Seward to Harriet Tracy, July 31, 1832, to
Tracy, May 9, 1833.

3. SP, manuscript journals of the trip; WP, Seward to Weed, June 3, 12, 21, July 5, 28, 1835; Tracy Papers, Seward to Tracy, June 24, 1835.
4. "Register of the Baptisms—in the Parish of St. Peter's Church, Westfield, N.Y.," March 26, 1837; WP, Seward to Weed, March 26, 1837; F. W. Seward, *Seward*, I, 226, 239.
5. Patterson Papers, Seward to Israel Munson, Aug. 27, 1836 (copy), Statement of the Proprietors to the American Life Insurance and Trust Company; SP, W. H. Seward to S. S. Seward, June 2, 1838; P. D. Evans, *The Holland Land Company* (Buffalo, 1924), 25–35, 329–87, 390, 393; H. G. McMahon, *Chautauqua County. A History* (Buffalo, 1958), 29; E. F. Warren, *Sketches of the History of Chautauqua County* (Jamestown, N.Y., 1846), 118 21; F. W. Seward, *Seward*, I, 303–4. The exact amount of land purchased was 364,808.18 acres.
6. SP, W. H. Seward to S. S. Seward, June 2, 1838, Weed to Seward, June 15, 1836, Personal Papers, Box 67, Aug. 1, 1837; WP, Seward to Weed, June 14, 20, 1836, Sept. 5, 1838, Rathbone to Seward, Oct. 21, 1837, Seward to Rathbone, Oct. 23, 1837; Patterson Papers, Seward to Munson, Aug. 27, 1836 (copy), Rathbone to Seward, July 30, Sept. 9, Oct. 15, 25, Nov. 18, Dec. 27, 1836, Cary to Seward, Aug. 5, Oct. 1, 1836, Lay to Seward, Sept. 30, 1836; F. W. Seward, *Seward*, I, 301. Frederick says that Weed urged Seward to go to Chautauque (as the name was then spelled), but Weed's letter of June 15, 1836, clearly shows that he was at first doubtful about Seward's taking on the project.
7. Patterson Papers, VanderKemp to G. W. Lay, Dec. 26, 1836, D. E. Evans to Seward, Jan. 3, 1837, Seward to VanderKemp, Feb. 17, 1837 (p.d.), VanderKemp to Seward, March 6, 1837, Cary to Seward, March 15, 25, 1837, Seward to VanderKemp, March 20, April 18, 1837 (p.ds.), Rathbone to Seward, May 3, 6, 1837, Seward to Biddle, Sept. 20, 22, Oct. 24, 1837 (p.ds.), Biddle to Seward, Sept. 21, Oct. 28, 1837; SP, Rathbone to Seward, April 19, 21, 24, 1837, Cary to Seward, May 21, 1837; WP, Seward to Weed, Oct. 27, 1837.
8. Patterson Papers, P. J. Van Hall to Seward, June 4, 1838, J. J. VanderKemp to Seward, Oct. 9, 1838, R. M. Blatchford to B. J. Seward, Oct. 29, 1838; SP, Seward to Van Hall, June 12, 1838 (copy), Seward to Rathbone, June 28, 1838, R. M. Blatchford to Seward, Oct. 22, 1838, Personal Papers, Box 67, Agreements of July 3, 4, 1838; Gratz Collection, Seward to Biddle, April 18, 1838; F. W. Seward, *Seward*, I, 317, 367.

NOTES FOR CHAPTER 4

1. WP, Seward to Weed, Jan. 10, 18, Feb. 8, 25, March 11, 15, April 12, July 19, Oct. 4, 11, Nov. 22, 1835, Feb. 27, March 4, 1836, Feb. 24, March 7, April 3, July 17, Nov. 12, 1837, Patterson to Weed, Sept. 23, 1869; SP, Weed to Seward, March 8, 11, April 13, 22, 24, May 13, July 8, 1835,

Feb. 7, 1836, Seward to H. Hunt, June 25, 1836 (p.d.); Patterson Papers, Weed to Patterson, June 7, 1835; B. Hammond, *Banks and Politics in America* (Princeton, 1957), 580–99; Benson, op. cit. 97–104; D. G. B. Thompson, *Ruggles of New York* (New York, 1946), 38–9.

2. WP, Seward to Weed, Sept. 8, Oct. 4, Nov. 15, Dec. 7, 1835, Feb. 24, April 4, 1837.

3. WP, Seward to Weed, June 3, 1835, Nov. 17, Dec. 8, 1836, Nov. 5, 23, 1837; SP, W. H. Seward to B. J. Seward, Sept. 27, 1837; Patterson Papers, Weed to Seward, Aug. 2, 14, 1837; W. H. Seward, *Address Delivered . . . at the Commencement of the Auburn and Owasco Canal, October 14, 1835* (Auburn, 1835); *Discourse on Education Delivered at Westfield, July 26, 1837* (Albany, 1837); *Address of the New-York and Erie Railroad Convention to the People of the State of New York* (Auburn, 1837).

4. Seward, *Works*, III, 356–62; SP, Wm. Kent to Seward, June 30, 1836, Seward's "Draft of Address to Young Men's Association at Troy, June 25, 1838," Weed to Seward (on letter from Patterson to Weed, Aug. 12, 1838); WP, Seward to Weed, Aug. 13, 30, 1838; Patterson Papers, Seward to Patterson, June 27, 1838 (copy).

5. WP, Whittlesey to Weed, Aug. 27, 1838, Pellet to Weed, Aug. 29, 1838; Patterson Papers, Weed to Patterson, Aug. 15, 1838, S. Sammons to Patterson, Aug. 16, 1838; SP, Weed to Seward, Aug. 1, 7, 13, Sept. 6, 8, 1838, Spencer to Seward, Aug. 30, 1838, Wm. Inglis to Seward, Feb. 23, 1839; *The Jeffersonian*, Sept. 12, 22, 1838; Van Deusen, *Weed*, 99–101.

6. SP, Blatchford to Seward, Oct. 23, 27, 1838, Weed to Seward, Oct. 27, 1838, N. K. Hall to Seward, Nov. 2, 1838, B. D. Silliman to Seward, Nov. 10, 1838; WP, Seward to Weed, Oct. 5, Nov. 4, 1838; New York *Tribune*, Aug. 1, 1842.

7. WP, Seward to Weed, Oct. 1, 1838; SP, Blatchford to Seward, Nov. 8, 1838, Wm. Jay and Gerrit Smith to Seward, Oct. 1, 1838, Weed to Seward, Oct. 23, 28, Nov. 2, 1838; Seward, *Works*, III, 426–32; Bradish Papers, Seward to Bradish, Oct. 27, 1838; N. P. Tallmadge Letters (N. Y. State Lib.), Tallmadge to Seward, Nov. 11, 1838; Albany *Evening Journal*, Oct. 25, 1838, Albany *Argus*, Oct. 27, 1838; *The Jeffersonian*, Nov. 17, 24, Dec. 8, 1838; R. V. Harlow, *Gerrit Smith* (New York, 1939), 137–41; I. D. Spencer, *The Victor and the Spoils*, 96–7, 105–7.

8. WP, Seward to Weed, Nov. 11, 19, 20, Dec. 5, 14, 1838, June 30, 1840; SP, Personal Papers (Box 67), W. H. Seward to B. J. Seward, Nov. 12, 1838, Weed to Seward, Nov. 21, 23, Dec. 2, 9, 1838, F. A. Seward to L. Worden, Jan. 10, 1841, Seward to H. Tupper, Sept. 4, 1841; J. C. Derby, *Fifty Years Among Authors, Books and Publishers* (New York, 1884), 58; F. W. Seward, *Seward*, I, 382–3.

9. WP, Stone to Weed, Nov. 12, 1838, Seward to Weed, Nov. 13, 19, Dec. 8, 1838; SP, Webb to Seward, Nov. 20, 22, 1838, Weed to Seward, Nov. 20, 21, 29, Dec. 1, 9, 1838, Blatchford to Seward, Nov. 12, 20, 1838, Seward

to H. Ketchum, Feb. 15, 1839 (copy); Tracy Papers, L. F. Allen to Tracy, Jan. 30, 1839.

10. Based on the correspondence in the Weed, Seward and Tracy Papers, Nov.–Dec. 1838, the Weed-Hunt Correspondence in the Yale Library, and the Buffalo Historical Society *Publications*, XI, 176–9, 181–3, 188–9.

NOTES FOR CHAPTER 5

1. SP, Augustus Seward to Aunt & Cousin, Jan. 7, 1839, Frances Seward to L. Worden, Dec. 15, 1839, S. S. Seward to W. H. Seward, Feb. 6, 1839, J. Amory to W. H. Seward, Oct. 4, 11, 1839; New York *Herald*, Jan. 5, 1839.

2. SP, Seward to C. Morgan, Jan. 1, 1839; Tracy Papers, T. M. Foote to Tracy, Jan. 6, 1839; Albany *Evening Journal*, Jan. 1, 1839; Albany *Argus*, Jan. 4, 1839; *Laws of the State of New York* (Albany, 1839), *passim.*

3. SP, Weed to Seward, Dec. 6, 1838, Frances Seward to L. Worden, July 20, 1840, Seward to Brooks, March 26, 1840 (copy), Ledger Books of Nominations (1839, 1840), Seward to C. Morgan, April 8, 1840, Seward to T. C. Chittenden, Nov. 19, 1840 (p.d.).

4. SP, Seward to C. Morgan, Feb. 15, 1839, May 30, 1840, Jan. 3, 1841, R. M. Blatchford to Seward, Dec. 2, 20, 1840, Greeley to Seward, June 12, 1841; WP, Collier to Weed, Jan. 24, 1841, Seward to Weed, May 13, 1842; Gratz Collection, Seward to Tyler, Sept. 28, 1841; Seward-Tallmadge Correspondence, Seward to Tallmadge, Nov. 14, 1838; Buffalo Historical Society *Publications*, II, 188–9. The other aspirants for the Senate were Granger, John C. Spencer, Joshua A. Spencer, and John A. Collier.

5. SP, Seward to J. Randall, May 23, 1839 (p.d.), Seward to Mark Sibley, June 29, 1839 (p.d.), Clay to Seward, Sept. 26, 1839, Seward to J. Tyler, July 10, 1841 (copy), Seward to C. B. Penrose, Nov. 26, 1839 (p.d.), Weed to Seward, Dec. 4, 9, 1839, C. Morgan to Seward, Dec. 26, 1839; WP, Seward to Weed. Aug. 17, Nov. 30, 1839, L. Hubbell to Weed, Oct. 16, 1839, E. Curtis to Weed, Nov. 18, 28, 1839, Jas. Bowen to Weed, Nov. 20, 1839, P. Potter to Weed, Nov. 29, 1839, Fillmore to Weed, Dec. 2, 1839; Etting Collection, Seward to T. Childs, March 12, 1838; Van Deusen, *Clay*, 331–2.

6. Seward, *Works*, III, 211–19; SP, Frances Seward to L. Worden, Oct. 20, 1839; Hammond, op. cit. II, 516–17; Van Deusen, *Weed*, 106–8.

7. SP, Frances Seward to L. Worden, Dec. 5, 10, 1839, Seward to M. Artcher, Dec. 12, 1839 (p. d.), Seward to S. H. Gallup *et al.*, Dec. 13, 1839; F. W. Seward, *Seward*, II, 210–21; E. P. Cheyney, *The Anti-Rent Agitation in the State of New York, 1839–1846* (Philadelphia, 1887), 30–36; Seward, *Works*, III, 211–19, D. Murray, "The Antirent Episode in the State of New York", American Historical Association, *Annual Report* (Washington, D.C., 1897), I, 139–73; D. M. Ellis, *Landlords and Farm-*

ers in the Hudson-Mohawk Region, 1790–1850 (Ithaca, 1946), 225–67; H. Christman, Tin Horns and Calico (New York, 1945), 28–45; E. Muntz, "The First Whig Governor of New York," unpublished doctoral dissertation at the University of Rochester.

8. D. L. Dix, Remarks on Prisons and Prison Discipline in the United States (Boston, 1845), 7–8, 60; SP, Seward to C. Morgan, March 15, 1839, A. Lockwood to Seward, March 16, 1839, Seward to D. L. Seymour, June 30, Aug. 11, 1841 (p. ds.), L. Dwight to Seward, April 17, 1841, M. J. Lockwood to Seward, Nov. 29, 1841; Seward, Works, II, 347–51, 405–6; W. D. Lewis, From Newgate to Dannemora, the Rise of the Penitentiary in New York, 1796–1848 (Ithaca, 1965), 201–22; J. J. Gurney, A Journey in North America (Norwich, Eng., 1841), 287, 303; P. Klein, Prison Methods in New York State (New York, 1920), 312; B. McKelvey, American Prisons (Chicago, 1936), 41–2.

9. SP, Frances Seward to L. Worden, Jan. 20, 1842, Seward to M. Schuyler, May 1, 1841 (p. d.), Seward to B. J. Ferris, July 17, 1841 (p. d.), Seward to John Tyler, Dec. 18, 1841 (p. d.), J. Harvey to Seward, Feb. 2, 1842, T. E. Ludlum to Seward, March 18 [1867]; F. W. Seward, Seward, I, 224.

10. SP, Seward to T. Clarkson, July 25, 1840 (p. d.), Seward to A. Pray and T. Paul, July 13, 1841 (p. d.), Seward to L. Tappan, March 21, 1842 (p. d.), Seward to D. S. Thomas, June 1, 1842 (copy); WP, Seward to Weed, Dec. 31, 1842; W. H. Seward, Oration Delivered at Auburn (Auburn, 1825), 15–16; F. W. Seward, Seward, II, 258; Seward, Works, IV, 317, 337, 348–58, 384, 397–9.

11. SP, A. Worden to Seward, June 14, 1838, Oct. 29, 1839, W. Duvall to Seward, July 11, 1839, C. Morgan to Seward, Oct. 31, Nov. 7, 1839, M. Butterfield to Seward, Jan. 9, 1840, Seward to H. L. Hopkins, Sept. 16, 1839, Seward to J. M. Patton, April 6, 1841 (copy), Seward to C. J. McDonald, June 15, July 14, 1841, Seward to J. Rutherford, Nov. 8, 1841, A. B. Roman to Seward, June 3, 1840, C. J. McDonald to Seward, April 29, June 8, Nov. 22, 1841, Seward to J. Q. Adams, April 20, 1841 (p. d.), S. M. Gates to Seward, March 31, 1841, Hammond to Seward, April 3, 26, Nov. 11, 1841, L. Tappan to Seward, April 27, 1841, Seward to C. Morgan, March 3, 1842; WP, I. C. Bronson to Weed, Feb. 4, 1840; Gratz Collection, Seward to J. C. Spencer, Nov. 6, 1841; New York Tribune, Feb. 25, 1842; Seward, Works, II, 391.

12. SP, Seward to J. Rutherford, June 8, 1841 (p. d.), Seward to C. J. McDonald, Dec. 27, 1841 (p. d.), E. W. Goodwin to Seward, Jan. 20, 1842, Gerrit Smith to Seward, Feb. 19, March 5, 1842, Seward to Gerrit Smith, Feb. 23, March 19, 1842 (p. ds.), L. Tappan to Seward, March 18, 1842.

13. SP, W. H. Seward, Discourse on Education (Albany, 1837), 21, Seward to W. MacNeven et al., March 14, 1829, Seward to E. Gallup, June 29, 1839 (p. d.), M. Gilbride to Seward, July 11, 1839, Weed to Seward, Aug. 6, 1839; WP, Seward to Weed, Aug. 25, 1839; Seward, Works, II, 215;

H. J. Browne, "Public Support of Catholic Education in New York, 1825–1842: Some New Aspects," *The Catholic Historical Review*, XXXIX (April 1953), 8–9; J. W. Pratt, "Governor Seward and the New York City School Controversy, 1840–1842," *New York History*, XLII (Oct. 1961), 354–5; W. O. Bourne, *History of the Public School Society of the City of New York* (New York, 1870), 163, 168, 179–86.

14. SP, S. Luckey to Seward, Nov. 25, 1840, Seward to Luckey, Nov. 29, 1840 (p. d.). Luckey was Presiding Elder of the Methodist Episcopal Church in the New York District. This letter is partially at variance with the statement by both Weed and F. W. Seward that the governor had taken counsel with Luckey and Eliphalet Nott before making his recommendation, and also with Frederick's assertion that Seward had gone to New York in October 1839 and studied the school situation there (Weed, *Autobiography*, 484; F. W. Seward, *Seward*, I, 441–2, 460–61). Seward later recalled that, sometime before the message of 1840, he had talked with Dr. Nott and with Weed, and that they had both approved the part relating to education (SP, Geo. Wardner to A. G. Johnson, Sept. 5, 1856).

15. New York *American*, Jan. 10, 1840; H. J. Browne, op. cit. 17; SP, Seward to H. C. Westervelt, March 19, 25, 1840 (p. ds.), to M. M. Noah, Aug. 29, 1840 (p. d.), to D. E. Stearns, Sept. 28, 1840 (p. d.), to S. Luckey, Nov. 29, 1840 (p. d.), to Bishop Hughes, May 11, 1841 (p. d.), to H. V. R. Schermerhorn, Feb. 20, 1849, R. M. Blatchford to John Power, March 11, 1840 (copy), Blatchford to Seward, Apr. 11, 1840, J. Costigan to Weed, Aug. 22, 1840, Weed to [Seward], Sept. 13, 1840, Frances Seward to L. Worden, Nov. 29 [1841], Jan. 14 [1842]; Seward, *Works*, II, 280.

16. SP, Hughes to Seward, May 11, 1841, May 5, 1842, S. Luckey to Seward, July 8, 1841, Seward to C. Morgan, June 10, 1841, to H. V. R. Schermerhorn, Dec. 27, 1848 (p. d.), Hammond to Seward, Feb. 4, 1854; Seward-Tallmadge Corresp., Seward to Tallmadge, May 10, 1841; Gratz Collection, Hughes to Seward, Aug. 29, 1840, Nov. 6, 1841; American Catholic Historical Society of Philadelphia, *Records and Studies*, XXIII (March 1912), 36–40.

17. Hughes Papers, J. F. Loubat to "dear Archbishop," Aug. 15, 1886; Seward, *Discourse on Education*, 7; Seward, *Works*, IV, 149; J. R. G. Hassard, *Life of the Most Reverend John Hughes, D. D.* (New York, 1866), 241–51, 434–94.

1. *Laws of the State of New York* (Albany, 1840), 52–8; Albany *Evening Journal*, March 2, 23, April 2, 25, 1840; New York *Daily Express*, March 26–31, 1840; New York *American*, March 27, April 1, 1840; WP, Seward to Weed, Jan. 30, 1835, Granger to Weed, March 28, April 2, 1840; SP, R. M. Blatchford to Seward, March 29, 31, 1840, James Bowen to Seward

[March 29, 1840], P. Hone to Seward, March 29, 1840, S. Draper to Seward, March 29, 31, 1840, John Duer *et al.* to Seward [March 30, 1840], J. Hoxie to Seward, March 31, 1840, R. C. Wetmore to Seward, March 31, 1840, R. B. Minturn to Seward, March 31, 1840, J. W. Webb to Seward [April 1, 1840], C. Morgan to Seward, April 2, 1840.

2. SP, Seward to C. Morgan, April 8, June 9, 1840, Drawer D, ms. draft of the suppressed veto, Seward to S. Starkweather, Feb. 11, 1841; WP, Seward to Weed, Jan. 10, 1843; Seward, *Works*, II, 379–81; T. W. Barnes, *Memoir of Thurlow Weed* (Boston, 1884), 86–7.

3. SP, Seward to C. Morgan, June 18, 1840, Bowen to Seward, July 17, 1840, C. Morgan to Seward, Aug. 15, 1840, S. P. Grover to Seward, Nov. 16, 1840, H. R. Filley to Seward, Nov. 20, 1840; Hone, *Diary*, I, 505; New York *American*, Oct. 3, 1840; Albany *Argus*, Sept.–Nov. 1840.

4. *Documents of the Assembly of the State of New York*, 71st sess., 1848 (Albany, 1848), I, no. 4, 9. Report of Comptroller Flagg. The debt had risen from approximately $12,000,000 to over $18,000,000; *New York State Register for 1843* (Albany, 1843), 68; SP, L. Hubbell to Seward, Nov. 7, 1840, Seward to B. D. Silliman, Nov. 12, 1840 (p. d.); WP, B. D. Silliman to Weed, Nov. 8 [1840], Patterson to Weed, Nov. 24, 1840; Seward-Tallmadge Corresp., Seward to Tallmadge, Feb. 13, 1840; Auburn *Journal and Advertiser*, Nov. 11, 1840.

5. Seward-Hunt Corresp. (Yale Library), Seward to A. Hunt, Nov. 18 [1840]; SP, Seward to C. D. Barton, Nov. 19, 1840 (p. d.), R. M. Blatchford to Seward, Nov. 20, 1840, Jan. 13, 1841, Seward to B. D. Silliman, Nov. 12, 15, 1840 (p.ds.); WP, Seward to Weed, Nov. 6, 1840.

6. SP, Blatchford *et al.* to Seward, Dec. 7, 1838; Gratz Collection, G. S. Doughty and D. Selden to Seward, Jan. 21, 1840; *The Log Cabin*, Oct. 31, 1840.

7. SP, E. Ransom to G. H. Boughton, Jan. 29, 1841, Webster to Seward, March 19, 1841, Seward to Webster, March 22, 1841 (p. d.), Seward to L. G. Mickles, Aug. 23, 1841 (p. d.), Seward to Tyler, April 20, May 10, 20, 1841 (p. ds.), Tyler to Seward, May 15, 25, 1841, R. M. Blatchford to Seward, May 16, 19, Aug. 8, 1841, Seward to Crittenden, May 31, 1841 (p. d.), C. Morgan to Seward, Aug. 9, 1841, Weed to Seward, Aug. 15, 1841, W. Hall to Seward, Oct. 12, 1841; Seward Mss. (L.C.), Seward to J. MacLean, March 20, 1846; Crittenden Papers, volume entitled "Drafts and Notes of Speeches & Letters of the Hon. J. J. Crittenden," pp. 1023–33; A. D. Kirwan, *John J. Crittenden* (Lexington, Ky., 1962), 144–6; A. Watt, "The Case of Alexander McLeod," *The Canadian Historical Review*, XII (June 1931), 145–67.

8. SP, Seward to G. A. French, May 5, 1841 (p. d.), Seward to J. J. Crittenden, May 31, 1841 (p. d.), Seward to C. Morgan, July 21, 26, 1841, Seward to Webster, Sept. 3, 1841 (p. d.), J. Harvey to Seward, Aug. 1, Oct. 23, 1841, Seward to Tyler, June 4, 1842 (p. d.), Seward to Sir Charles Bagot, June 6, Aug. 30, 1842 (p. ds.), H. A. S. Dearborn to Seward,

June 25, July 1, 1841; Ewing Papers, Seward to Ewing, May 17, 1841.

9. SP, Seward to John A. King, July 20, 1841 (p. d.), Spencer to Seward, Aug. 30, 1841, Weed to Seward, Sept. 12, 1841, Seward to A. Hazeltine, Sept. 24, 1841 (p. d.), Seward to C. Morgan, Oct. 21, 1841, Feb. 20, 1842, Seward to J. C. Spencer, June 5, 1842 (p. d.); Gratz Collection, Seward to Tyler, Sept. 28, 1841, Seward to Spencer, Nov. 9, 1841; Welles, *Diary*, I, 507.

10. Seward Letters (Albany State Library), Seward to J. A. Collier, Aug. 1, 1841; SP, J. C. Spencer to Seward, Aug. 19, Nov. 8, 1841, R. M. Blatchford to Seward, Jan. 6, 1842, S. B. Ruggles to Seward, April 23, 1842; WP, J. C. Spencer to Weed, Oct. 8, 1841; Gratz Collection, Seward to J. C. Spencer, Aug. 25, Nov. 5, 1841; Seward, *Works*, II, 257, 283–5.

11. SP, Seward to C. Morgan, June 10, 1841, Seward to J. C. Spencer, Nov. 4, 1841 (p. d.), Frances Seward to L. Worden, Nov. 5 [1841], J. A. King to Seward, Nov. 12, 1841, Seward to B. F. Hall, Nov. 10, 1841 (p. d.); Seward, *Works*, II, 309–21, 337–41, III, 365; WP, Seward to Weed, April 26, 1842; *Laws of the State of New York*, 65th sess., 1842 (Albany, 1842), 79–85; *Documents of the Assembly of the State of New York*, 65th sess., 1842 (Albany, 1842), IV, no. 61, 13–14, and 71st sess., 1848 (Albany, 1848), I, no. 4, 10–11; Hammond, op. cit. III, 273–86. Seward claimed that the damages for broken contracts amounted to $800,000.

12. Gratz Collection, Seward to Spencer, June 6, 1842; SP, Spencer to Seward, June 1, 16, 1842, Seward to C. Morgan, April 15, May 11, 1842, H. Underwood to Frances Seward, Nov. 6, 1842, S. Blatchford to Seward, Nov. 25 [1842].

13. Albany *Evening Journal*, May 9, 22, 1840; Albany *Argus*, May 22, Sept. 11, 1840; SP, Weed to Seward, Nov. 20, 22, 30, 1842, J. Bowen to Seward [Nov. 30, 1842], Webb to Seward, Dec. 6, 1842, Helen Webb to Seward, Dec. 7, 1842.

14. Seward, *Works*, II, 330–31; SP, Seward to Brodhead, Sept. 9, 1841 (p. d.), April 23, 1842 (p. d.), Brodhead to Seward, Jan. 3, Dec. 3, 1842, W. Irving to Seward, July 11, 1842, Seward to C. Anthon *et al.*, June 11, 1842 (p. d.), Seward to C. Morgan, Nov. 25, 1843, Frances Seward to L. Worden, June 26, 1842, B. Hale to Seward, Dec. 27, 1842, Jas. Wadsworth to Seward, Sept. 1841; F. W. Seward, *Seward*, I, 555, 614; *Natural History of the State of New York* (6 vols. in 4, New York, 1842–43), I, 1–178.

15. SP, Seward to T. C. Reed, Nov. 9, 1841 (p. d.), Adams to Seward, Nov. 3, 1841, Seward to Adams, Nov. 6, 1841 (p. d.), Seward to T. C. Chittenden, March 19, 1842 (p. d.), Seward to C. Morgan, April 15, 1842; Seward Letters (Huntington Library), Seward to S. B. Ruggles, Nov. 4, 1841; WP, Seward to Weed, Dec. 31, 1842.

16. SP, Frances Seward to L. Worden, Jan. 8, 1843, Weed to Seward, Jan. 21, 1843; WP, Seward to Weed, Sunday afternoon [Jan. 8, 1843]; F. W. Seward, *Seward*, I, 642–5.

NOTES FOR CHAPTER 7

1. SP, R. M. Blatchford to Seward, May 28, 1840, Jan. 15, Nov. 9, 11, 12, 1841, July 18, 1843, Seward to R. M. Blatchford, July 17, 1839, Feb. 1, 1843, to John M. Sherwood, Sept. 20, 1841, to John Duer, June 28, 1842, to Talman and Macaulay, Dec. 13, 1843 (all p.ds.), J. B. Plumb to Seward, Feb. 22, 1843, M. T. Reynolds to Seward, July 13, 1843; F. W. Seward, *Seward,* I, 646, estimates his father's indebtedness in 1843 at $400,000, but this is altogether too high.

2. SP, F. A. Seward to L. Worden, Jan. 15, May 14, 1843, Seward to Henry Hall, Aug. 24, 1868 (p.d.); WP, Seward to Weed, Jan. 28, April 14, May 13, 14, 1843; Seward Letters (Clements Library), Seward to Jas. Bowen, Sept. 25, 1843; Patterson Papers, Seward to Patterson, Dec. 22, 1843; Seward-Hunt Corresp., Seward to Hunt, May 31, 1843.

3. SP, Frances Seward to L. Worden, Feb. 20, March 7, 22, Aug. 10, 1843; Seward Mss. (L.C.), Seward to Ruggles, March 21, 1843; WP, Seward to Weed, Jan. 28, March 25, Aug. 11, 1843, Harding to Weed, Feb. 13, 1843, Ruggles to Weed, March 17, 1843; Seward-Hunt Corresp., Seward to A. Hunt, May 31, 1843; Dearborn Collection, Seward to Ruggles, June 10, 1843; Wm. H. Gerht, "Heads or Tails: The Seward Portrait in City Hall," *The Art Quarterly,* XXI (Spring 1958), 68–81.

4. SP, F. A. Seward to L. Worden, Aug. 1, 1843.

5. SP, Seward to his children, n.d., W. H. Seward to Fanny Seward, Aug. 6, 1850, Frances Seward to L. Worden, May 24, June 14, 15, Nov. 1, 1846, Dec. 24, 1848, to A. Seward, Aug. 16, Dec. 24, 1848, Mrs. Sarah Mytton Maury to Seward, May 29, Oct. 5, 1848, Feb. 2, 1849, F. A. Seward to W. H. Seward, Aug. 21, 1847, Jan. 17, 24, June 6, Sept. 20, Oct. 22, Dec. 12, 1848; WP, Seward to Weed, July 8, 1845, May 28, 1846, Aug. 15, 1847; S. S. Seward Papers, W. H. Seward to S. S. Seward, Aug. 5, 1845; W. H. Seward, *In the Supreme Court of the United States—Wilson v. Rousseau and Easton. Opening Argument for the Plaintiff* (Auburn, 1845), 5; F. Bancroft, *The Life of William H. Seward* (2 vols., New York, 1900), I, 204.

6. SP, D. L. Dix to Seward, Nov. 20, 1843, Seward to Morgan and Blatchford, Jan. 22, 1846; Seward, *Works,* I, 484, 493, 514–15, III, 14, 258, 279, 301; *Cong. Globe,* 31st Cong., 1st sess., *App.,* 261; WP, Seward to A. Worden, March 22, 1846, Seward to Weed, March 28, June 10, 1846; B. F. Hall, *The Trial of William Freeman* (Auburn, 1848), 395. Frederick Seward indicates that his father came in contact with Wyatt two days before his trial. The evidence shows that Seward had enlisted in Wyatt's defense at a considerably earlier date.

7. Hall, *Freeman,* 21–3, 195, 211, 332, 437–8, 474–94, 497–8; WP, Seward to Weed, July 8, 1846; Seward, *Works,* I, 409–75; C. F. Adams, Diary, Feb. 17, 1873.

8. WP, Seward to Weed, July 13, Aug. 1, 29, Sept. 8, 1846, March 15, Aug. 15, 1847; SP, F. A. Seward to A. Seward, July 1, Sept. 22, 1846, Feb. 15, 1847.

9. Seward Letters (Clements Library), Seward to Jas. Bowen, Jan. 6, 1845; SP, Frances Seward to L. Worden, Jan. 10, 18, 28, 1845; Seward Letters (Albany State Lib.), Seward to R. King, Feb. 15, 1845; Patterson Papers, Weed to Patterson, May 30, 1845; F. W. Seward, *Seward*, I, 736–8.

10. *Wilson v. Rousseau et al.*, 4 Howard, 1141–73 (1846), and *Jacob P. Wilson v. Daniel Barnum*, 8 Howard, 257–61 (1850); W. H. Seward, *Arguments in the Case of James G. Wilson vs. Lewis Rousseau and Charles Easton in the Circuit Court of the United States for the Northern District of New York* (Auburn, 1845), and *In the Supreme Court of the United States—Wilson v. Rousseau and Easton. Opening Argument for the Plaintiff* (Auburn, 1845); WP, Seward to Weed, Dec. 6, 1845, April 11, 1847, Nov. 29, 1848; SP, Box 70, newspaper clipping dated July 28, 1849, also W. H. Seward to C. Morgan, April 5, 1846, F. A. Seward to A. Seward, April 6, 1846.

11. SP, Seward to G. Talman and D. P. Macaulay, Dec. 13, 1843, Seward to Mrs. J. L. Rathbone, Oct. 10, 1845 (p.d.), Seward to Ira Harris, Nov. 17, 1845, Aug. 10, 1846, Seward to H. V. R. Schermerhorn, Dec. 27, 1848; WP, Seward to Weed, Aug. 13, 22, Oct. 4, Dec. 6, 1845, April 4, 1846, Jan., 1847; Patterson Papers, G. F. Talman to G. W. Patterson, Dec. 18, 1844; Weed-Hunt Corresp., Weed to Hunt, May 8, 1847.

NOTES FOR CHAPTER 8

1. Seward-Hunt Corresp., Seward to Hunt, Jan. 25, 1843; WP, Hunt to Weed, Jan. 22, 1843, Seward to Weed, March 4, Sept 24, 1843, Whittlesey to Weed, Dec. 16, 1843; Tallmadge Papers, Weed to N. P. Tallmadge, Jan. 22, 1843; Weed-Hunt Corresp., Weed to Hunt, April 5, 1843.

2. Albany *Evening Journal*, Nov. 6, 1843; SP, Frances Seward to L. Worden, Nov. 7, 1843; WP, E. Curtis to Weed, Feb. 8, 1844, Seward to Weed, Feb. 18, March 17, June 22, 1844; Patterson Papers, Seward to Patterson, Dec. 22, 1843, Weed to Patterson, June 16, 1844.

3. WP, Fillmore to Weed, Nov. 6, 1844, Seward to Weed, Nov. 7, 1844; Seward, *Works*, III, 246–53, 260–74; SP, Seward to Clay, Nov. 7, 1844 (copy); Seward Letters (Cornell University), Seward to E. A. Stansbury, Nov. 16, 1844; Seward Letters (Clements Library), Seward to Jas. Bowen, Oct. 7, 1844; Albany *Evening Journal*, Nov. 9, 11, 12, 1844; New York *Tribune*, Nov. 6, 9, 11, 12, 1844; R. J. Rayback, *Millard Fillmore* (Buffalo, 1959), 156.

4. SP, Seward to E. A. Stansbury, Sept. 2, 1844; Chase Papers (Hist. Soc. of Pa.), Seward to Chase, Aug. 4, 1845. This letter is in Frederick Seward's handwriting but is signed by his father. It is addressed to Samuel P. Chase, a slip that could scarcely have pleased the ambitious Ohioan.

5. WP, Seward to Weed, Dec. 20, 22, 1845, Dec. 13, 1846, Jan. 20, 1848; New York *Courier and Enquirer*, April 15, 1846, with quote of comment by the Buffalo *Commercial* and reproduction of Seward's letter.

6. WP, Seward to Weed, May 28, June 10, 28, Aug. 29, 1846; Patterson Papers, Seward to Patterson, May 29, 1846.

7. WP, Seward to Weed, April 11, Sept. 26, 1847; SP, C. F. Adams to Seward, March 18, 1848, Seward to B. D. Ames, Jan. 2, 1857; Seward, *Works*, I, 476–515, III, 75–110, 281–2; W. H. Seward, *Life and Public Services of John Quincy Adams* (Auburn, 1849), "Advertisement"; J. C. Derby, op. cit. 60; F. W. Seward, *Seward*, II, 39–41; Horace Mann Papers, Greeley to Mann, July 19, 1848, Mann to S. G. Howe, July 20, 1848, Mann to Mrs. Mann, July 25, 1848. If Seward sensed their attitude, he gave no sign of it in writing to his wife about the case—F. W. Seward, *Seward*, II, 72–3.

8. WP, Seward to Weed, Jan. 6, 25, 1846, Dec. 26, 1847, March 29, April 24, May 4, 27, 1848, Seward to ——, 1847 (rough draft to unknown persons who had apparently solicited his views), S. Hawley to Weed, Nov. 25, 1845, March 27, 1848; Albany *Evening Journal*, March 28, 1848; Patterson Papers, D. H. Abell to Patterson, April 6, 1848, Weed to Patterson, April 9, 1848, P. C. Fuller to Weed, May 5, 1848, T. Smith to Weed, Aug. 26, 1853; SP, Seward to Ira Harris, Aug. 10, 1846. See also H. Hamilton, *Zachary Taylor, Soldier in the White House* (Indianapolis and New York, 1951), 94–7, and R. J. Rayback, *Millard Fillmore*, 185.

9. WP, Seward to Weed, March 21, June 10, 23–5, Aug. 26, 31, Sept. 23, 27, Oct. 9, 29, 1848, S. J. Peters to Weed July 2, 1848; SP, F. A. Seward to W. H. Seward, Oct. 4, 11, 1848; New York *Tribune*, June 10, Sept. 25, 1848; Albany *Evening Journal*, April 4, 1851; Seward, *Works*, III, 291–305; F. W. Seward, *Seward*, II, 193–4; *Cong. Globe*, 36th Cong., 1st sess., 916.

10. SP, F. A. Seward to L. Worden, Feb. 12, 1849. The account of the struggle over Seward's election is based on the correspondence in the Seward, Weed, and Patterson papers. The result of the balloting is given in the New York *Tribune*, Feb. 8, 1849.

11. SP, J. W. Webb to Seward, Jan. 28, 1849, Weed to Seward, Jan. 28, 1849, Seward to Webb, Feb. 1, 1849 (p.d.); WP, Seward to Webb, Feb. 1, 1849, S. Draper, Jr., to Weed, Feb. 6, 1849; Weed, *Autobiography*, 586.

NOTES FOR CHAPTER 9

1. New York *Tribune*, Feb. 7, 9, 1849; SP, E. Nott to Seward, Feb. 13, 1849, Weed to Seward, April 15, 1849, W. H. Seward to F. A. Seward, March 16, 18, 26, April 29, May 3, 1849, Webster to Seward, April 3, 1849; WP, Seward to Weed, March 4, 8, 16, 19, 1849.

2. WP, Seward to Weed, May 14, 1847, Nov. 21, 29, 1848, Feb. 27, March 1, 7, 9, 16, 19–21, 25, 28, 29, 1849, C. A. Stetson to Weed, Jan. 14, 1849;

SP, W. H. Seward to F. A. Seward, March 10, 11, 14, 1849, Weed to Seward, March 11, 17, 1849, S. Draper to Seward, Feb. 9, 1849, N. K. Hall to C. Robinson, March 11, 1849; *National Intelligencer,* March 30, 1849; Hamilton, op. cit. 168–70; Rayback, *Millard Fillmore,* 202; G. R. Poage, *Henry Clay and the Whig Party* (Chapel Hill, 1936), 184–6.

3. SP, W. H. Seward to F. A. Seward, March 23, 26, 1849, E. G. Spaulding to Z. Taylor (copy), May 18, 1849, Fillmore to Seward, April 17, 1849, Hawley to Seward, May 24, 1849, A. Hunt to Weed, June 2, 1849; WP, Seward to Weed, March 25, 28, 1849, E. G. Spaulding to Weed, May 27, 1849, Hawley to Weed, Aug. 26, 1849; Fillmore Papers, Fillmore to Granger, April 17, 1849, Dox to Fillmore, April 14, 1849. Seward's quotation from *Henry IV,* part two, was reasonably accurate "like a sow that hath overwhelmed all her litter save one."

4. SP, S. S. Seward to W. H. Seward, Sept. 3, 1847, Legal and Financial Papers, 1849–50, Box 70, Dec. 1849, Weed to Seward, Dec. 21, 1849; Grier Papers, S. S. Seward Estate, Financial Papers, 1849–64. The official copy of the will is in the Surrogate's Office, Goshen, N.Y., Liber P, 372–9.

5. *Proceedings of the National Railroad Convention,* Seward to the Convention, Oct. 2, 1849; SP, Weed to Seward, Dec. 21, 1849, Feb. 8, 1850; WP, Seward to Weed, Feb. 3, 1850.

6. SP, W. H. Seward to F. A. Seward, May 1, 1849, F. A. Seward to L. Worden, Dec. 29, 1849, Jan. 13, 1850; Fish Papers, Seward to Fish, Jan. 31, 1850; Smith Papers, Seward to Smith, Feb. 15, 1845; WP, Seward to Weed, Nov. 30, Dec. 3, 1849, Jan. 1, 1850; Fillmore Papers, D. D. Barnard to Fillmore, July 10, 1850. Seward's estimate of the secession threat was strengthened by southern correspondents—SP, W. L. Hodge to Seward, Jan. 4, 1850, J. M. Bixby to Seward, Jan. 17, 1850.

7. WP, Seward to Weed, Dec. 7, 1849; SP, W. H. Seward to F. A. Seward, June 2 [1849], Seward to E. A. Stansbury, Sept. 2, 1844, A. Conkling to Seward, Jan. 3, 1850, Colfax to Seward, March 26, 1850, F. A. Seward to L. Worden, Dec. 29, 1849; WP, Seward to Weed, Feb. 9, 14, 1850; Seward, *Works,* I, 284–96; *Cong. Globe,* 31st Cong., 1st sess., 51–2, 59, 236–7; Seward-Hunt Corresp., Seward to Hunt, Jan. 11, 1850.

8. WP, Schoolcraft to Weed, Dec. 28, 1849; SP, F. A. Seward to L. Worden, Feb. 24, 1850; Fish Papers, Seward to Fish, Dec. 4, 1849; Fillmore Papers, J. T. Bush to Fillmore, Jan. 5, 1850, J. Fuller to Fillmore, Feb. 18, 1850. The course of these resolutions through the legislature is examined in detail by Aida DiPace Donald, "Prelude to Civil War: the Decline of the Whig Party in New York, 1848–1852," unpublished doctoral dissertation at the University of Rochester, 168–82.

9. *Cong. Globe,* 31st Cong., 1st sess., 244–7, *App.,* 115–27; SP, F. A. Seward to L. Worden, Feb. 10, March 10, 1850; WP, Seward to Weed, Jan. 25, March 11, 1850, Schoolcraft to Weed, Feb. 24, 1850.

10. New York *Tribune,* March 18, 1850; WP, S. P. Lyman to Weed, March

11, 1850; C. A. Dana, *Recollections of the Civil War* (New York, 1898), 169; C. F. Adams, *An Address on—William Henry Seward* (Albany, 1873), 72; *Cong. Globe*, 31st Cong., 1st sess., *App.*, 260–69.

11. SP, F. A. Seward to L. Worden, March 21, April 4, 27, 1850, Bishop Alonzo Potter to Seward, April 3, 1850; WP, O. B. Matteson to Weed, March 22, 1850, Schoolcraft to D. H. Abell, March 21, 1850; *Cong. Globe*, 31st Cong., 1st sess., 400; New York *Tribune*, March 19, 1850. That Seward thought of the higher law as reinforcing, not contradicting, the Constitution has been generally disregarded by historians.

12. SP, Weed to Seward, March 14, 15, 26, 1850, W. H. Seward to F. A. Seward, Nov. 19, 1852; WP, J. C. Clark to Weed, March 15, 1850, Seward to Weed, March 15, 1850, S. G. Andrews to Weed, March 20, 1850; Marcy Papers (New-York Hist. Soc.), Marcy to G. W. Newell, March 24, 1850; Fillmore Papers, J. Fuller to Fillmore, March 20, 1850.

13. SP, E. Nott to Seward, Feb. 13, 1849, F. A. Seward to W. H. Seward, June 2, 1850, T. C. Reed to Seward, March 21, 1850, L. H. Morgan to Seward, March 21, 1850, Weed to Seward, March 24, 1850, C. D. Smith to Seward, May 8, 1850; The *American Whig Review*, n.s., V (June 1850), 554, 622–39; WP, Seward to Weed, March 31, 1850.

14. That Seward's "higher law" was divine law, or at least Sydney's "law of God and nature," a combination of natural and moral law, is indicated by his earlier usage of the idea, by a second reference in the March 11 speech to "the laws of God" as the standard by which all other laws must be measured, by a quote of Sydney in a later speech (*Cong. Globe*, 31st Cong., 1st sess., *App.*, 1024), and by Wm. Hosmer, *The Higher Law in Its Relations to Civil Government* (Auburn, 1852), 13–15, 18–35. Hosmer, an Auburn clergyman, dedicated this book to Seward, used his picture as a frontispiece, and Seward approved the manuscript before publication —SP, J. C. Derby to Seward, June, 1852. For the prevalence of the "higher law" concept at this time, see the New York *Courier and Enquirer* (semi-weekly), April 24, 1850, and R. H. Gabriel, *The Course of American Democratic Thought* (rev. ed., New York, 1956), 14–19.

15. WP, Schoolcraft to Weed, March 21, 1850, Seward to Weed, March 31, 1850; SP, Weed to Seward, March 26, 1850, D. W. Holly to Seward, March 21, 1850.

1. *Cong. Globe*, 31st Cong., 1st sess., *App.*, 1021–4; SP, Weed to F. A. Seward, July 4, 1850, F. A. Seward to W. H. Seward, July 8, 1850.

2. WP, Seward to Weed, July 11, 21, 27, 1850; SP, F. A. Seward to W. H. Seward, July 31, 1850; *Cong. Globe*, 31st Cong., 1st sess., *App.*, 1442–7. There is an intensive analysis of Weed's policy and procedure in A. Donald, "Prelude to Civil War," 207–77. Rayback, *Millard Fillmore*, 254–67, gives a different interpretation.

3. SP, F. A. Seward to L. Worden, Sept. 7, 1850.

4. SP, Greeley to Seward, Dec. 4, 1850. The reference to the slavery question was in supporting a petition for repeal of the fugitive slave law—*Cong. Globe*, 31st Cong., 2nd sess., 575–6. For his letter of April 5, 1851, on the fugitive slave law to a New England anti-slavery meeting, see *Cong. Globe*, 32nd Cong., 1st sess., *App.*, 710–11.

5. W. H. Seward, "The Basis of the American Constitution" in Julia Griffiths, *Autographs for Freedom* (Auburn, 1854), 201–8; Gerrit Smith Papers, Seward to Smith, Oct. 11, 1850; SP, Colfax to Seward, Dec. 20, 1850, E. B. Morgan to Seward, Jan. 21, 1851, J. C. Woodman to Seward, Jan. 24, 1851, J. Griffiths to Seward, Apr. 8, 1851, J. G. Crofts to Seward, Sept. 25, 1851, Feb. 18, 1852, F. Douglass to Seward, July 31, 1850; *The North Star*, Jan. 16, 23, 1851; WP, Seward to C. Morgan, Jan. 11, 1851, Seward to Weed, March 31, 1851.

6. *Cong. Globe*, 31st Cong., 2nd sess., 323–4, 739–42, *App.*, 260–61; SP, Personal Papers, Box 71, Jan.–Feb. 1851, Buell and Blanchard to Seward, Aug. 23, 1851, C. A. Stetson to Seward, Jan. 27, 1851, Taney to Seward, Jan. 30, 1851, Weed to Seward, Aug. 23, 1851, A. B. Dickinson to Seward, Dec. 4, 1851, J. W. Woolsey to Seward, April 10, 1855; WP, Schoolcraft to Weed, Feb. 1, 12, Aug. 20, 1851; Greeley Papers (N.Y.P.L.), Seward to Greeley, Sept. 30 [1851]; *Argument of William H. Seward in Defense of Abel F. Fitch and Others—September 12, 13, 15, 1851* (Auburn, 1851); F. W. Seward, *Seward*, II, 154.

7. SP, F. A. Seward to W. H. Seward, Oct. 16, 1851, W. G. Snethen to Seward, Nov. 10, 1851; Greeley Papers (N.Y.P.L.), Seward to Greeley, Sept. 30, 1851; R. V. Harlow, *Gerrit Smith*, 297–303; F. W. Seward, *Seward*, II, 169–70.

8. SP, Sumner to Seward, Oct. 22, 1851, F. A. Seward to L. Worden, Dec. 25, 29, 1851, Feb. 22, March 25, 1852; Sumner Mss., Seward to Sumner, Dec. 16, 1846, May 18, 1848, June 18, July 14, 1849.

9. SP, Webster to Seward, Jan. 1852; *Cong. Globe*, 32nd Cong., 1st sess., *App.*, 243–7; S. S. Seward Papers, Seward to G. M. Grier, Dec. 13, 1851; Patterson Papers, Seward to Patterson, Dec. 6, 1851.

10. *Cong. Globe*, 32nd Cong. 1st sess., *App.*, 913–17; SP, Blatchford to Seward, Aug. 25, 1852; L. B. Shippee, *Canadian-American Relations* (New Haven, 1939), 47 and note.

11. Van Deusen, *Horace Greeley*, 168. Rayback, op. cit. 333–48, thinks Fillmore was not interested in the presidency—only in the good of the country.

12. SP, T. N. Parmelee to Seward, Dec. 15, 1850, S. Hawley to Seward, Dec. 13, 1851; WP, Seward to Weed, Dec. 29 [1850]; C. F. Adams, Diary, Dec. 13, 1851; New York *Tribune*, June 19, 1852; *Cong. Globe*, 32nd Cong. 1st sess., *App.*, 708–12; F. W. Seward, *Seward*, II, 188; F. Brown, *Raymond of the Times* (New York, 1951), 113.

13. New York *Tribune*, June 29, 1852; *Cong. Globe*, 32nd Cong., 1st sess.,

App., 1102, 1125, 34th Cong., 1st sess., *App.*, 770; WP, Schoolcraft to Weed, July 14, 1852; Sumner Papers, F. A. Seward to Sumner, Sept. 18, 1852.

14. A. Nevins and M. H. Thomas, eds., *The Diary of George Templeton Strong* (4 vols., New York, 1952), II, 109 (hereafter cited as Strong, *Diary*); New York *Times*, Nov. 3, 4, 1852; New York *Tribune*, Nov. 3, 5–7, 1852; SP, Raymond to Seward, Nov. 6, 1852, Sumner to Seward, Nov. 6, 1852, Wm. Schouler to Seward, Nov. 10, 1852, A. H. Green to F. A. Seward, Nov. 11, 1852, Scott to Seward, Dec. 8, 1852; WP, Seward to Weed, Nov. 4, 1852; Schouler Papers, Seward to Schouler, Dec. 25, 1852; C. F. Adams, Diary, Nov. 10, Dec. 4, 6, 1852; A. Donald, op. cit. 337–400; A. Craven, *The Growth of Southern Nationalism, 1848–1861* (La. St. Univ. Press, 1953), 49–57, 83, 121; A. Nevins, *Hamilton Fish* (New York, 1936), 36–42, and *Ordeal of the Union*, II, 28–38; Cole, op. cit. 245–84; W. D. Overdyke, *The Know-Nothing Party in the South* (La. St. Univ. Press, 1950), 45–52.

15. SP, F. A. Seward to W. H. Seward, May 7 [1850], June 16, 1850, May 17, 1851, A. D. Bache to Seward, Dec. 11, 1851, Weed to Seward, May 1, 1851, F. A. Seward to A. Seward, Sept. 1, 20, Nov. 25, 1851, Jan. 14, 1853, S. Blatchford to Seward, Jan. 2, 1852, F. A. Seward to L. Worden, Jan. 25, Feb. 22, 1852, Accounts, vol. 4, 1843–59, Personal Papers, Box 71, Dec. 1, 1851, Box 72, April 3, Oct. 1855; WP, Seward to Weed, May 24, Dec. 26, 1851, July 31, 1852; will of Elijah Miller, Surrogate's Office, Auburn; J. Bigelow, Diary, March 27, 1859; F. W. Seward, *Seward*, II, 171.

NOTES FOR CHAPTER II

1. *Cong. Globe*, 32d Cong., 2nd sess., 147, 248–50, *App.*, 126; New York *Times*, June 7, 1853; W. H. Seward, *The Destiny of America* (Albany, 1853), *passim*; Seward, *Works*, IV, 144–59; P. N. Garber, *The Gadsden Treaty* (Philadelphia, 1923), 118, 134.

2. SP, S. J. May to Seward, Aug. 25, Sept. 7, 1853, Parker to Seward, Oct. 1, 1853, Seward to Parker, Oct. 11, 1853, F. A. Seward to L. Worden, Jan. 15, 1853, J. Crofts to Seward, Oct. 11, 1853; J. Griffiths, ed., *Autographs for Freedom* (Boston, 1853), 1–3; New York *Herald*, Oct. 6, 1853; Van Deusen, *Weed*, 193.

3. Mrs. Archibald Dixon, in her account of the repeal of the Missouri Compromise, stated that "to the best of my knowledge and belief, Mr. Dixon consulted no one in this matter." But she also declared that northern Democrats were aghast, suspecting that Dixon's motion was a Whig bombshell thrown into the Democratic camp in order to destroy the party. In seeking to make the bill objectionable, Chase moved, Feb. 6, 1854, to strike out of the repeal clause the statement that the Missouri Compromise "was superseded by the principles of the legislation of

1850," thus leaving it, as Badger promptly noted, "a repeal without a reason." Seward, Sumner, and other northern anti-slavery Senators voted for this amendment, which was defeated 30 to 13.

I think it altogether likely that Seward made some such suggestion to Dixon and Jones. On the other hand, it is entirely possible that the idea of forcing outright repeal was already in the air when Seward talked with the two men. The Senator from New York was not at all averse to magnifying the importance of his acts. C. F. Adams, Diary, Sept. 19, 1860; G. Welles, *Lincoln and Seward* (New York, 1874), 68; Mrs. Archibald Dixon, *The True History of the Missouri Compromise and Its Repeal* (Cincinnati, 1899), 437, 444; *Cong. Globe*, 33rd Cong., 1st sess., 343; Seward, *Works*, IV, 25, F. W. Seward, *Seward*, II, 216; WP, Seward to Weed, Jan. 8, 1854; J. T. Dubois and G. S. Mathews, *Galusha A. Grow* (Boston and New York, 1917), 144–5; Nicolay and Hay, *Lincoln*, I, 345–50; R. F. Nichols, "The Kansas-Nebraska Act: A Century of Historiography," *Miss. Valley Hist. Review*, XLIII (Sept. 1956), 205.

4. WP, Seward to Weed, Jan. 7, 8, 1854; New York *Times*, Jan. 31, 1854; F. W. Seward, *Seward*, II, 219; *Cong. Globe*, 33rd Cong., 1st sess., *App.*, 150–55.

5. *Cong. Globe*, 33rd Cong., 1st sess., *App.*, 237, 331, 346–51, 34th Cong., 1st sess., *App.*, 788; J. W. Schuckers, *Salmon Portland Chase* (New York, 1874), 156; New York *Tribune*, March 7, 1854. The *Tribune*'s Washington correspondent noted that, in speaking, Douglas invariably used the term "nigger" instead of "Negro."

6. SP, Seward to Parker, March 3, April 14, 1854; Flagg Papers, Preston King to Flagg, May 20, 1854.

7. *Cong. Globe*, 33rd Cong., 1st sess., *App.*, 768–71; SP, Raymond to Seward, May 30, 1854, Everett to Seward, June 16, 1854, Seward to Parker, June 23, 1854. Parker's letter of May 19 to Seward, from which the latter borrowed, is not in the Seward Papers.

8. New York *Tribune*, June 22, 1854; Greeley Papers, Seward to Greeley, June 22, 1854; SP, F. A. Seward to W. H. Seward, June 27, 30, 1854, Seward to Parker, June 23, 1854; F. W. Seward, *Seward*, II, 234.

9. Bouck Papers, John Staats to Bouck, Feb. 2, 1853; R. A. Billington, *The Protestant Crusade, 1800–1860* (New York, 1938), chs. 11–13, 15, 16; Overdyke, op. cit. chs. 1–5; H. J. Carman and R. H. Luthin, "Some Aspects of the Know-Nothing Movement Reconsidered," *The South Atlantic Quarterly*, XXXIX (April 1940), 213–34.

10. Seward-Hunt Corresp., Seward to Hunt, May 18, 1853; Sumner Papers, Seward to Sumner, May 19, Sept. 23, Nov. 11, 1853, Sept. 12, 1854; SP, Wilson to Seward, May 28, 1854, Seward to Parker, June 23, 1854, Sumner to Seward, Oct. 26, 1854; WP, Seward to Weed, June 24, 1854; Patterson Papers, Weed to Patterson, July 11, 1854; F. W. Seward, *Seward*, II, 231; Van Deusen, *Weed*, 199–200; P. S. Foner, *Business and Slavery* (Chapel Hill, 1941), 106–8.

11. WP, Schoolcraft to Weed, March 15, 1854, C. Adams to Weed, July 14, 1854; Patterson Papers, Weed to Patterson, May 10, 1854; Van Deusen, *Weed*, 200–201, and *Greeley*, 184–7.

12. SP, Greeley to Seward, Nov. 11 (copy) and 24, 1854, G. E. Baker to Seward, Nov. 15, 1854; Van Deusen, *Greeley*, 187–92 and *Weed*, 201–4.

13. WP, R. M. Blatchford to Seward, Dec. 7, 1854, Seward to Weed, Dec. 8, 24, 1854, Seward to Schoolcraft, Dec. 29, 1854; F. W. Seward, *Seward*, II, 243; SP, Hammond to Seward, Feb. 2, 1855. My account of the election is based on material in the Seward and Weed papers, and on the files of the Albany *Evening Journal*, the Albany *Argus*, and the Albany *Evening Atlas*.

14. WP, Seward to Weed, Feb. 7, 1855; SP, D. Clarke to Seward, Feb. 6, 1855, A. B. Hodges to Seward, Feb. 7, 1855, F. A. Seward to A. Seward, Feb. 7, 1855, A. S. Hewitt to Seward, Feb. 8, 1855, T. Parker to Seward, Feb. 11, 1855, R. M. Blatchford to F. A. Seward, Feb. 15, 1855; F. W. Seward, *Seward*, II, 246.

NOTES FOR CHAPTER 12

1. *Cong. Globe*, 33rd Cong., 2nd sess., *App.*, 240–43.

2. WP, Hunt to Weed, Aug. 10, 1855, Fish to Weed, Nov. 12, 1855; SP, Weed to Seward, July 12, 23, 1855, Seward to E. A. Stansbury, Sept. 14, 1855, G. E. Baker to Seward, Oct. 19, 1855, S. J. May to Seward, Oct. 17, 1855, Sumner to Seward, Oct. 15, 1855, Clay to Seward, Nov. 16, 1855; F. W. Seward, *Seward*, II, 254.

3. Sumner Papers, Seward to Sumner, Nov. 9, 1855; F. W. Seward, *Seward*, II, 259; *Oration by William H. Seward at Plymouth* (Albany, 1856); SP, Parker to Seward, Dec. 23, 1855, Adams to Seward, Jan. 16, 1856. The Hard and Soft Democrats had run separate tickets in the election.

4. WP, Fish to Weed, Jan. 12, 1856, Seward to Weed, Jan. 26, 1856; *Cong. Globe*, 34th Cong., 1st sess., *App.*, 75–80; New York *Times*, Feb. 1, March 4, 1856; M. W. Williams, *Anglo-American Isthmian Diplomacy* (Washington, D.C., 1916), 196–223; SP, Clayton to Seward, Feb. 1, 1856, E. Conklin to Seward, Feb. 27, 1856; *The Times* (London), Feb. 15, 1856.

5. WP, Seward to Weed, Feb. 26, 1856; F. W. Seward, *Seward*, II, 267; *Cong. Globe*, 34th Cong., 1st sess., 640, and *App.*, 399–405; SP, newspaper clipping, n.d. but late 1860 or early 1861, E. H. Schuyler to Seward, April 14, 1856, W. H. Paddock to Seward, April 16, 1856, Chase to Seward, April 21, 1856.

6. *Cong. Globe*, 34th Cong., 1st sess., 1279–80, 1415–18, *App.*, 543, 664–5; SP, F. A. Seward to L. Worden, May 30, 1856; E. Everett, Diary, June 18, 1857; A. G. Riddle, *The Life of Benjamin F. Wade* (Cleveland, 1886), 208 and note.

7. *Cong. Globe*, 34th Cong., 1st sess., 1439, and *App.*, 749–805, 1107–11, 2nd

sess., 42, 4978; Nevins, *Ordeal*, II, 471–2. Governor Geary established temporary order in Kansas during the fall of 1856, but the Republicans still viewed the situation with alarm.

8. G. E. Baker, ed., *The Life of William H. Seward with Selections from His Works* (New York, 1855); SP, Greeley to Seward, April 12, 1853, Whitman to Seward, Dec. 7, 1855, Weed to Seward, Jan. 3, 1856; WP, Baker to Weed, July 20, 1853, Seward to Weed, Dec. 31, 1855, Jan. 6, 1856; Albany *Evening Journal*, Jan. 15, 1855.

9. WP, Fish to Weed, Jan. 12, 1856, Corning to Weed, Feb. 4, 1856, D. H. Abell to Weed, March 2, 1856, Seward to Weed, March 13, Sept. 18, 1856, Schoolcraft to Weed, March 15, 1856; SP, Weed to Seward, March 10, 1856.

10. Corresp. in the Seward and Weed Papers in April–June 1856, and the letters in F. W. Seward, *Seward*, II, 276–9; *Proceedings of the Republican National Convention at Philadelphia* (1856), esp. 33, 52, 60, 65–6; New York *Herald*, June 18–22, 1856; Jas. S. Pike, *First Blows of the Civil War* (New York, 1879), 344–5. Weed, writing to Blatchford in 1858, declared that Seward could not have been nominated in 1856, but this was in the midst of a bitter quarrel with Seward—SP, Weed to Blatchford, April 10, 1858.

11. SP, F. A. Seward to W. H. Seward, July 20, 1856, T. Miller to F. A. Seward, July 19, 1856; Sumner Papers, Seward to Sumner, June 19, 1856, E. Everett to Mrs. Chas. Eames, June 21, 1856; F. W. Seward, *Seward*, II, 279.

12. Sumner Papers, Seward to Sumner, Aug. 17, 1856, F. A. Seward to Sumner, Aug. 12, 1856; Gardiner Collection, E. Peshine Smith to H. C. Carey, Oct. 5, 17, 31, 1856; WP, Seward to S. Wilkeson, Jr., Sept. 10, 1856; SP, J. Henderson to Seward, Aug. 21, 1856, Jas. Bowen to Seward, Sept. 9, 1856, Sumner to Seward, Sept. 21, 1856, E. D. Morgan to Seward, Sept. 26, 1856, Weed to Seward, Oct. 5, 1856, Schoolcraft to Seward, Oct. 7, 1856; New York *Times*, Sept. 19, 1856; F. W. Seward, *Seward*, II, 287.

13. W. H. Seward, *The Slaveholding Class Dominant in the Republic* (Washington, D.C., 1857), *The Political Parties of the Day* (Washington, D.C., 1857), *Immigrant White Free Labor, or Imported Black African Slave Labor* (Washington, D.C., 1857).

14. Burnham, op. cit. 63–71; SP, C. S. Henry to Seward, Nov. 11, 1856, E. G. Spaulding to Seward, Nov. 24, 1856, Doubleday to Seward, Oct. 7, 1856, L. James to Seward, Oct. 27, 1856, Webb to Seward, Nov. 7, 1856, E. Nott to Seward, Nov. 8, 1856; Nevins, *Ordeal*, II, 487–514, and *Frémont, Pathmarker of the West* (New York, 1939), 456.

15. Gideon Welles, then very active in Republican politics, later recorded his belief that only the need of an eastern man to offset Frémont prevented Lincoln's nomination for Vice President in 1856—Welles, *Lincoln and Seward*, 205–6.

NOTES FOR CHAPTER 13

1. *Cong. Globe,* 34th Cong., 3rd sess., 10–13, 258, 395, 882; SP, Tappan to Seward, July 21, Aug. 20, 1856.

2. Seward's journal, kept during the trip, was published in the Albany *Evening Journal.* Copious extracts are given in F. W. Seward, *Seward,* II, 301–22. See also SP, A. Plamondon to Seward, Sept. 3, 1857, Seward to R. P. Toms, Sept. 3, 1857, and *Cong. Globe,* 35th Cong., 1st sess., 2054.

3. *Ibid.* 6, 406, 412–13, 518–21; Gardiner Collection (Pa. Hist. Soc.), E. P. Smith to H. C. Carey, March 3, 1858; Hay, Diary, Aug. 13, 1863; Greeley Papers (N.Y.P.L.), Seward to R. M. Blatchford, Feb. 13, 1858 (copy); SP, Weed to Seward, March 11, 1858; Patterson Papers, Seward to Patterson, March 17, 1858.

4. SP, Benedict to Seward, Jan. 18, 1858, Weed to Seward, March 15, 1858, Weed to Blatchford, April 10, 1858, Wilkeson to Seward, May 18, 1858, Blatchford to Seward, April 14, 1858; WP, Seward to Weed, March 13, 18, 24, 1858, Weed to E. B. Morgan, May 8, 1858, N. P. Banks to Weed, May 15, 1858; Van Deusen, *Weed,* 222–3.

5. *Cong. Globe,* 34th Cong., 3rd sess., 469, 682, 685–6, 1053, 35th Cong., 1st sess., 332–3; Fish Papers, Seward to Fish, Sept. 21, 1857; Chase Papers (LC), Seward to Chase, March 17, 1858; SP, S. J. May to F. A. Seward, Aug. 6, 16, 1857, J. C. Underwood to Seward, Jan. 26, 1858, Chase to Seward, March 10, 1858, J. A. Beckham to Seward, March 10, 1858, C. S. Todd to Seward, March 29, 1858; F. W. Seward, *Seward,* II, 331, 343, 346. As for Negro education in Washington, Seward may also have felt that such a project would militate against a federal appropriation for public schools in the District, a proposition that he favored but that a number of southern Senators opposed—*Cong. Globe,* 35th Cong., 1st sess., *App.,* 375.

6. SP, Seward to T. W. Higginson, Jan. 3, 1857, Cameron to Seward, July 15, 1858, F. A. Seward to A. Seward, March 3, 1858; *Cong. Globe,* 35th Cong., 1st sess., 2579; New York *Times,* Jan. 16, 1857; New York *Tribune,* Jan. 16, 1857; E. D. Morgan Papers, Seward to Morgan, Jan. 8, 1858; Bancroft, op. cit. I, 435–6.

7. *Cong. Globe,* 35th Cong., 1st sess., 698, 939–45, 959–62; SP, Smith to Seward, March 6, 1858, Chase to Seward, March 10, 1858, Bancroft to Seward, Feb. 24, 1862; Adams, Diary, March 5, 1858; Bache Papers (Huntington Library), Seward to A. D. Bache, March 14, 1859; S. Tyler, *Memoir of Roger Brooke Taney* (Baltimore, 1872), 391. On February 15, Seward had given notice of his intention to introduce a bill for reorganizing the Supreme Court and the federal circuit courts, the object being to provide for representation of the states by judges "more nearly on the basis of their federal population."

8. *Cong. Globe,* 35th Cong., 1st sess., 1894–8; Patterson Papers, Seward to

Patterson, May 17, July 1, 1858, E. Dodd *et al.* to Patterson, May 17, 1858, E. D. Morgan to Patterson, May 17, 1858, C. Vaughan and A. C. Wilder to Patterson, Sept. 26, 1859; A. Nevins, *The Emergence of Lincoln* (2 vols., New York, 1950), I, 296–301. Patterson was one of the eastern representatives sent out to Kansas. Funds were furnished the Kansans in 1859 and, presumably, in 1858.

9. F. W. Seward, *Seward*, II, 330, 332; SP, F. A. Seward to W. H. Seward, Dec. 12, 1857, Herndon to Seward, Jan. 9, June 27, 1858, T. C. Miller to Seward, March 19, 1858, J. W. Waughop to Seward, March 20, 1858; New York *Herald*, April 13, Nov. 20, 1858; Sumner Papers, Seward to Sumner, June 28, 1858; Herndon-Weik Collection (LC), Seward to Herndon, Dec. 31, 1858 (copy); Herndon Letters (New-York Hist. Soc.), Herndon to Seward, Dec. 28, 1858, Jan. 17, 1859; Trumbull Papers, E. Peck to Trumbull, Nov. 22, 1858; Bancroft, op. cit. I, 455; D. Fehrenbacher, *Prelude to Greatness* (Stanford, 1962), 117–18; D. Donald, *Lincoln's Herndon* (New York, 1948), 114–17, 125.

10. SP, Jas. Wilson to E. B. Morgan, July 21, 1858, Wilson to Seward, July 21, 1858, G. W. Curtis to Seward, Aug. 6, 9, 16, 1858, Harding to Seward, Nov. 5, 1858, Quincy to Seward, Nov. 10, 1858; Curtis Papers, Seward to Curtis, Aug. 9, 1858; Seward, *Works*, IV, 289–302; New York *Tribune*, Nov. 4, 1858; Albany *Atlas* quoted in the Albany *Evening Journal*, Oct. 28, 1858; New York *Times*, Oct. 28, 1858; Rose Greenhow, *My Imprisonment and the First Year of Abolition Rule at Washington* (London, 1863), 21.

11. Albany *Evening Journal*, Nov. 2, 1858; Webb Papers, Seward to Webb, Nov., 1858; SP, Parker to Seward, Nov. 15, 1858, Seward to Parker, Nov. 19, 1858; Herndon Letters (New-York Hist. Soc.), Herndon to Seward, Dec. 28, 1858; New York *Tribune*, Sept. 13, Nov. 3, 1858; E. D. Morgan Papers, Seward to Morgan, Nov. 8, 1858. Parker thought Seward's speeches excellent, the one at Rome "even more bold" than the one at Rochester. Gerrit Smith polled only 5470 votes. Figures on the election are given in S. C. Hutchins, *Civil List and Constitutional History of the Colony and State of New York* (Albany, 1882), 151.

12. Patterson Papers, Seward to Patterson, April 6, 1859; New York *Times*, May 9, 1859; F. W. Seward, *Seward*, II, 360.

NOTES FOR CHAPTER 14

1. This chapter is based in part on my own analysis of Seward's speeches during his public career. In addition I am glad to acknowledge my debt to two excellent, unpublished doctoral dissertations—Walter G. Sharrow, "William Henry Seward: A Study in Nineteenth Century Politics and Nationalism, 1855–1861," done under my direction, and Joseph G. Whalen, "William Henry Seward, Expansionist," done under the direction of Dexter Perkins.

W. H. Seward, *The Elements of Empire in America* (New York, 1844), 17–18; WP, Seward to Weed, April 11, 1846; New York *Tribune*, March 24, 1851; *Cong. Globe*, 32nd Cong., 1st sess., *App.*, 247, 35th Cong., 1st sess., 2495; Seward, *Works*, IV, 99, 125, 153, 397. Seward's attitude toward the Union in the pre-Civil War period is examined in P. C. Nagel, *One Nation Indivisible* (New York, 1964).

2. Seward, *Works*, I, 245, IV, 167–8, 171–2, 397–8; *Cong. Globe*, 32nd Cong., 1st sess., *App.*, 247, 34th Cong., 1st sess., 377, 35th Cong., 1st sess., 66–7, 2nd sess., 157–9; SP, Seward to E. Washburne, Jan. 27, 1856.

3. Seward Letters (Albany State Lib.), Seward to John Taylor Hall, Oct. 14, 1845; Seward, *Works*, IV, 154, 379; H. S. Commager, *Theodore Parker* (Boston, 1936), 181–5.

4. *Cong. Globe*, 35th Cong. 2nd sess., 157–9; Seward, *Works*, IV, 334–5. Sharrow, op. cit. 127–55, is excellent on Seward's land policy.

5. Seward, *Works*, III, 660–61, IV, 158–9, 162, 192; SP, Carey to Seward, March 17, 1860; *Cong. Globe*, 34th Cong., 3rd sess., *App.*, 296, 36th Cong., 2nd sess., 344.

6. Seward, *Works*, I, 108–9, 289–96, II, 198–9, III, 14; *Cong. Globe*, 34th Cong., 1–2 sess., 1505, 35th Cong., 1st sess., 215, 404, 1187; Sharrow, op. cit. 141–2.

7. Seward, *Works*, I, 88, III, 23, IV, 125, 126–8, 132, 142–3, 179, 379.

8. *Cong. Globe*, 32nd Cong., 2nd sess., *App.*, 125–6, 35th Cong., 1st sess., 1584–5; St. Louis Railroad Convention *Proceedings* (St. Louis, 1850), 57–8; Seward, *Works*, IV, 122; Townsend Harris Papers (CCNY), Seward to Harris, Oct. 21, 1861; WP, Seward to Weed, Dec. 20, 1845; J. B. G. Hutchins, *The American Maritime Industries and Public Policy, 1789–1914* (Cambridge, 1941), 349, 353, 355, 362–8.

9. New York *Times*, June 7, 1853; *Cong. Globe*, 33rd Cong., 2nd sess., 376, 35th Cong., 1st sess., 1895, 2nd sess., 159; SP, S. M. Hawley to Seward, Feb. 19, 1850, S. Wilkeson to Seward, March 4, 1853; Seward, *Works*, III, 188.

10. Seward Mss. (LC), Seward to Ruggles, Nov. 6, 1852.

11. *Cong. Globe*, 36th Cong., 1st sess., 917. Aside from the historical interpretation of the southern viewpoint to be found in such authorities as Craven, Eaton, and Sydnor, I have used William R. Taylor, *Cavalier and Yankee* (Garden City, 1963), xv–xxii, 66–71, 305–20. This study, though based primarily on literary sources, gives some interesting information about the southern psychology of the antebellum period.

NOTES FOR CHAPTER 15

1. Seward Mss. (LC), Seward to S. B. Ruggles, April 12, 1859; F. W. Seward, *Seward*, II, 379, 380, 387, 388–9; WP, Seward to Weed, July 8, 1859; SP, W. H. Seward to F. A. Seward, July 25, 1859.

2. SP, W. H. Seward to F. A. Seward, July 3, 1859; Bigelow Papers, Seward

to Bigelow, Dec. 13, 1859; New York *Tribune,* Dec. 12, 1859; Albany *Evening Journal,* Dec. 30, 1859, Jan. 3, 1860; New York *Times,* Jan. 4, 1860.

3. *Cong. Globe,* 36th Cong., 1st sess., 37–8, 238–9; SP, J. C. Jones (pseud.), to Seward, Nov. 20, 1859; Greenhow, op. cit. 190–92; F. W. Seward, *Seward,* II, 438–40; WP, E. G. Spaulding to Weed, Jan. 11, 1860.

4. SP, O. B. Matteson to Seward, Dec. 30, 1859; Seward Mss. (Univ. of Chicago), C. S. Wilson to F. W. Seward, March 11, 1860; WP, E. G. Spaulding to Weed, Jan. 24, 1860, S. J. Rea to Weed, Jan. 30, 1860, Seward to Weed, April 5, 1860, J. N. Butten to Weed, June 6, 1860.

5. SP, Blatchford to Seward, Nov. 12, 1859, Webb to Seward, April 10, 1860, Weed to Seward, July 2, 1858, Seward to C. Cole, July 1, 1858, March 19, 1859; Jos. B. Grinnell, *Men and Events of Forty Years* (Boston, 1891), 180–81; *Cong. Globe,* 36th Cong., 1st sess., 748–9; WP, Seward to Weed, June 15, 1858; H. H. Bancroft, *California* (7 vols., San Francisco, 1886–90), VI, 733.

6. WP, Seward to Weed, Feb. 15, 1860; Patterson Papers, Seward to Patterson, Feb. 27, 1860; SP, Weed to Seward, Feb. 17, 1860; Adams, Diary, Feb. 26, 29, 1860; *Cong. Globe,* 36th Cong., 1st sess., 848, 910–17.

7. SP, S. Wilkeson to Seward, Feb. 29, 1860, Jas. Bowen to Seward, March 1, 1860, Sumner to the Duchess of Argyle, March 2, 1860, Seward to E. Washburne, March 7, 1860, Bigelow to Seward, March 22, 1860, M. D. Conway to Seward, July 17, 1860; Everett Papers, Wise to Everett, March 3, 1860.

8. The preceding paragraphs are based on letters in the Seward, Weed, and Patterson Papers for the period February–May 1860, and on entries in Adams's Diary, especially those of April 19 and May 10, 13, 1860.

9. Patterson Papers, Seward to Patterson, Feb. 27, 1860; SP, Weed to Seward, May 6, 1860; WP, Jas. W. Nye to Weed, March 8, 1860, Seward to Weed, April 25, 1860, Spaulding to Weed, April 29, 1860.

10. Adams, Diary, May 13, 1860; SP, P. King to Seward, May 11, 1860, Weed to Seward, April 16, May 20, 1860, E. G. Spaulding to Seward, May 15, 16, 1860, Webb to Seward, May 16, 1860, V. W. Smith to Seward, May 29, 1860, E. B. Morgan to Seward, May 17, 1860; Montgomery Blair Papers, G. Welles to Blair, Nov. 18, 1872; New York *Tribune,* May 14, 1860; Van Deusen, *Greeley,* 242.

11. SP, King, Evarts, Blatchford, Morgan to Seward, May 18, 1860, T. Dimon to the Auburn *Advertiser,* n.d.; *Proceedings of the Republican National Convention Held at Chicago, May 16, 17 and 18, 1860* (n.l.n.d.), 99–119; Van Deusen, *Weed,* 250–53.

12. These observations on the nomination are based on both source and secondary materials. I cite, selectively, Adams, Diary, May 18, 30, 1860; SP, E. G. Spaulding to Seward, May 18, 1860, Webb to Seward, May 29, 1860, S. Wilkeson to Seward, May 18, 1860, H. P. Scholte to Seward, May 19, 1860, Weed to Seward, May 20, 1860, E. Nott to Seward, May

26, 1860; New York *Times*, May 24, 1860; Everett Papers, Everett to S. Brooks, June 11, 1860; WP, Jas. Kelly to Weed, June 9, 1860; G. G. Van Deusen, "Why the Republican Party Came to Power" in *The Crisis of the Union, 1860–1861*, G. H. Knowles, ed., (La. St. Univ. Press, 1965), 3–20; Fehrenbacher, op. cit., 154–9; R. Hofstadter, *The American Political Tradition and the Men Who Made It* (New York, 1948), 117.

NOTES FOR CHAPTER 16

1. SP, Weed to Seward, May 20, 1860, C. F. Adams, Jr., to Seward, July 16, 1860, D. Van Kleeck to "Editors Journal," May 18, 1860, Fanny Seward, Diary, May 18, 19, 1860, Seward to B. D. Silliman, July 3, 1860; WP, Seward to Weed, May 18, 1860; New York *Times*, May 25, 1860; Adams, Diary, May 30, 31, 1860; Bigelow, Diary, March 27, 1869; F. W. Seward, *Seward*, II, 454; C. F. Adams, Jr., *An Autobiography* (Boston and New York, 1916), 68–9.

2. Albany *Evening Journal*, June 14, 1860; New York *Times*, May 24, June 15, 1860; SP, Wilkeson to Seward, Feb. 20, 1860; F. W. Seward, *Seward*, II, 455–6.

3. Adams, Diary, June 21, 1860; WP, Seward to Weed, June 26, July 6, 1860, W. S. King to W. Richardson, July 3, 1860; Patterson Papers, Seward to Patterson, June 27, 1860; SP, J. Wood *et al.* to Seward, July 21, 1860; Seward to J. Wood, July 31, 1860 (Ill. State Hist. Lib.).

4. New York *Times*, Aug. 14, 15, 1860; New York *Herald*, Aug. 16, 1860; Adams, Diary, Aug. 13, 14, 1860; SP, Sumner to Seward, Aug. 15, 1860, Adams to Seward, Aug. 25, 1860. Seward's principal speeches during the campaign are given in Seward, *Works*, IV, 253–430. See also Van Deusen, "Why the Republican Party Came to Power," op. cit., 3–20.

5. Robert Todd Lincoln Papers (hereafter RTL), Seward to Lincoln, Oct. 18, 1860; Basler, *Works*, IV, 126–7.

6. Adams, *Autobiography*, 65–8; SP, J. Bigelow to Seward, March 22, 1860, E. D. Morgan to Seward, Aug. 2, Oct. 6, 1860, Weed to Seward, Oct. 25, 1860; R. W. Emerson, "Journals. War—1862," 130; New York *Times*, Nov. 3, 1860; New York *Tribune*, Nov. 3, 1860; P. S. Foner, *Business and Slavery* (Chapel Hill, 1941), 178–207, gives a valuable account of the attitude of New York merchants toward the election.

7. D. M. Potter, *Lincoln and His Party in the Secession Crisis* (New Haven, 1942), 45–74; Craven, op. cit. 352–64; Nevins, *Emergence of Lincoln*, II, 318–35.

8. *Cong. Globe*, 33rd Cong., 1st sess., *App.*, 770; Seward, *Works*, III, 293.

NOTES FOR CHAPTER 17

1. Adams, Diary, Nov. 11, 17, 1860; WP, Seward to Weed, Nov. 18, Dec. 2, 3, 1860; Fish Papers, Seward to Fish, Dec. 11, 1860; F. W. Seward, *Seward*, II, 478–81; New York *Herald*, Dec. 4, 1860.

2. SP, Adams to Seward, Nov. 11, 1860, Cameron to Seward, Nov. 13, 1860, W. G. Snethen to Seward, Nov. 26, 1860; Patterson Papers, Seward to Patterson, Nov. 14, 1860.

3. As to Lincoln's "lukewarmness," see H. K. Beale, ed., *The Diary of Edward Bates* (hereafter, Bates, *Diary*) (Washington, D.C., 1933), 164–5; H. K. Beale, ed., *Diary of Gideon Welles* (hereafter, Welles, *Diary*) (3 vols., New York, 1960), II, 388–9; Adams, Diary, Nov. 27, 1860. *Per contra*, see Bates, *Diary*, 166, note 11; Lincoln, *Works* (Basler ed.), IV, 147–9; C. E. Hamlin, *The Life and Times of Hannibal Hamlin* (Cambridge, 1899), 367–70; Weed, *Autobiography*, 605, 606; H. J. Carman and R. Luthin, *Lincoln and the Patronage* (New York, 1943), 12–15. On Seward's reaction to the invitation, see Bigelow, Diary, May 8, 1861; WP, Seward to Weed, Dec. 13, 1860; Barnes, *Memoir of Thurlow Weed*, 301–2; RTL, Seward to Lincoln, Dec. 13, 16, 1860.

4. Lincoln, *Works*, IV, 154, 156–7, 158, Bancroft, *Seward*, II, 10; New York *Times*, Dec. 21, 1860; Carman and Luthin, *Lincoln and the Patronage*, 24; SP, Weed to Seward, Dec. 25, 1860, Chase to Seward, Jan. 10, 1861; Adams, Diary, Dec. 27, 1860; RTL, Seward to Lincoln, Dec. 28, 1860; Hamlin, op. cit. 368–9. The Cabinet was shaping up along Old Whig, Old Democrat lines. Hamlin, an Old Democrat, wanted Blair in the Cabinet.

5. New York *Times*, Dec. 24, 1860; New York *Tribune*, Dec. 24, 1860; Seward, *Works*, IV, 644–50.

6. Albany *Evening Journal*, Dec. 17, 1860; WP, Seward to Weed, Dec. 2, 3, 1860; SP, I. Washburn to Seward, Dec. 19, 1860; W. C. Ford, ed., *Letters of Henry Adams, 1858–1891* (Boston and New York, 1930), 83; Lincoln, *Works*, IV, 154, 156–7, 158; Fish Papers, Seward to Fish, Dec. 11, 1860; G. S. Boutwell, *Reminiscences of Sixty Years* (2 vols., New York, 1902), I, 270–71; Jos. Schafer, *Intimate Letters of Carl Schurz* (Madison, 1928), 247.

7. RTL, Seward to Lincoln, Dec. 26, 1860; Senate *Reports*, 36th Cong., 2nd sess., No. 288; F. W. Seward, *Seward*, II, 486, 491–2; Adams, Diary, Dec. 27, 28, 29, 1860, Jan. 3, 15, 25, Feb. 4, 17, 1861; *Journal of the Committee of Thirty-three*, Dec. 21, 29, 1860; *Journal of the Committee of Thirteen*, Dec. 28, 1860; H. Adams, "The Secession Winter, 1860–1861," Massachusetts Historical Society *Proceedings*, XLIII, 675–7; B. P. Thomas and H. M. Hyman, *Stanton* (New York, 1962), 100, 106; *Cong. Globe*, 36th Cong., 2nd sess., 1019–20; Morgan Papers, Seward to Morgan, Jan. 30, 1861; SP, Morgan to Seward, Jan. 5, 1861, F. W. Seward to F. A. Seward, Jan. 30, 1861.

8. SP, Chase to Seward, Jan. 10, 1861, Davidson to Seward, Jan. 11, 1861. Davidson told him that both houses of the state legislature had passed unanimously strong conciliatory resolutions. This was not so. See the Journals of the New York State House and Senate, Jan. 10, 11, 1861.

9. *Cong. Globe*, 36th Cong., 2nd sess., 341–4; New York *Times*, Jan. 14, 1861; Central Archives, Moscow, Russia, For. Aff. 49, Stoeckl à Gortch-

akov, Jan. 21, 1861; AAE, Mercier à Thouvenel, Jan. 14, 1861; SP, F. A. Seward to W. H. Seward, Jan. 19, 1861, R. M. Blatchford to F. A. Seward, Jan. 13, 1861, A. T. Stewart to Seward, Jan. 14, 1861, I. Washburn to Seward, Jan. 22, 27, 1861, Weed to Seward, Jan. 19, 1861; Seward Corresp. (Univ. of Chicago), S. Colfax to—, Jan. 12, 1861; E. B. Washburne Papers, G. W. Southwick to Washburne, Feb. 14, 1861; Everett Papers, E. Everett to Wm. Everett, Jan. 21, 1861; Gardiner Collection, E. P. Smith to H. C. Carey, Feb. 7, 1861; F. W. Seward, *Seward*, II, 493–4, 496; Schafer, op. cit. 242–3.

10. F. W. Seward, *Seward*, II, 496–7; SP, F. W. Seward to F. A. Seward, Jan. 30, 1861; RTL, Seward to Lincoln, Jan. 15, 1861; Adams, Diary, Jan. 15, 1861.

11. H. Adams, op. cit. XLIII, 678, 680; Edw. Cary, *George William Curtis* (Boston and New York, 1894), 141; Central Archives, Moscow, Russia, For. Aff. 49, Stoeckl à Gortchakov, Feb. 1861. "Il ne néglige rien pour arriver à un compromis afin de retenir dans l'Union les Etats à esclaves des frontières et se servir plus tard de leur intermédiaire pour ramener dans la Confédération les Etats qui ont déjà sécédé."

12. R. H. Lutz, "Rudolf Schleiden and the Visit to Richmond, April 25, 1861," American Historical Association *Annual Report* (1915), 210; T. W. L. Newton, *Lord Lyons, A Record of British Diplomacy* (2 vols., London, 1913), I, 30; E. D. Adams, op. cit. I, 60; *British Sessional Papers*, 1861, LXII, Lord Lyons to Lord Russell, Feb. 4, 1861; AAE, Mercier à Thouvenel, Jan. 20, Feb. 1, 1861; Ford, ed., *Letters of Henry Adams*, 73–4, 87; *Overland Monthly*, XVIII (Nov. 1891), 465–71, "Gwin and Seward. A Secret Chapter in Antebellum History"; Bancroft, op. cit. II, 32; Lutz, op. cit. 210; WP, Seward to Weed, Jan. 30, 1861; SP, Weed to Seward, Feb. 3, 1861; RTL, Seward to Lincoln, Jan. 27, 1861; *Cong. Globe*, 36th Cong., 1st sess., 657–60. Mason and Hunter told Mercier that the gesture of the Virginia senate in offering the North a slightly modified version of the Crittenden Compromise meant nothing, and only made more evident the impossibility of an arrangement. Mercier was sure that the Virginia convention would vote in favor of secession, which Seward was striving his best to prevent.

13. R. G. Gunderson, *Old Gentlemen's Convention* (Madison, 1961), 94–5; Adams, Diary, Feb. 4, 19, 1861; SP, Jas. Barbour to Seward, Feb. 8, 1861; F. W. Seward, *Seward*, II, 503–4; H. Adams, op. cit. XLIII, 680–81; R. G. Gunderson, "Letters from the Washington Peace Conference," *Journal of Southern History*, XVII (Aug. 1951), 386–9.

14. Adams, Diary, Feb. 16, 21, 1861; Andrew Papers, C. F. Adams, Jr. to J. A. Andrew, Feb. 22, 1861; H. Adams, op. cit. XLIII, 682, 684.

15. WP, Seward to Weed, Jan. 21, 1861; Ford., ed., *Letters of Henry Adams*, 78. As to whether or not Seward met Lincoln at the station, see my "Seward and Lincoln: the Washington Depot Episode," The University of Rochester Library *Bulletin*, XX, No. 3 (Spring 1965), 33–4; F. W.

Seward, *Seward*, II, 511–12; SP, Wm. Hunter to Seward, Feb. 27, 1861, Seward to Lincoln, Feb. 24, 1861 (p.d.), Anna Seward to F. A. Seward, Feb. 28, 1861; Lincoln, *Works*, IV, 249–71; C. F. Adams, Jr., *Autobiography*, 96.

16. Seward, *Works*, IV, 692; New York *Times*, Feb. 25, 1861, which reproduces the letter to the *Evening Post;* New York *Tribune*, Feb. 26, 27, 1861; SP, Weed to Seward, Feb. 21, March 7, 1861; Adams, Diary, Feb. 28, 1861; RTL, Seward to Lincoln, March 2, 1861; Lincoln, *Works*, IV, March 4, 1861; Welles, *Diary*, II, 391–2; W. E. Baringer, *A House Dividing* (Springfield, 1945), 311–29; Carman and Luthin, op. cit. 48–51; F. W. Seward, *Seward*, II, 518; Bigelow, Diary, March 27, 1861.

NOTES FOR CHAPTER 18

1. Sumner Papers, Seward to Sumner, Jan. 9, 1858; Barnes, ed., *Memoir of Thurlow Weed*, 408; F. W. Seward, *Seward*, III, 205; Ford, ed., *Letters of Henry Adams*, 63–4; Carl Sandburg, *Abraham Lincoln: the War Years* (4 vols., New York, 1939), I, 637, 653; R. W. Emerson, "Journals. War—1862," 86.

2. B. R. Crick, *et al.*, *A Guide to Manuscripts Relating to America in Great Britain and Ireland* (London, 1961), 70; Palmerston Papers, Clarendon to Palmerston, July 25, 1857, Feb. 14, 1858; C. F. Adams, Jr., *Autobiography*, 67; WP, L. Benedict to Weed, Jan. 8, 1845; C. Schurz, *Reminiscences of Carl Schurz* (3 vols., New York, 1907–08), II, 34; SP, C. Cushman to Seward, Jan. 18, 1852, May 8, 1858, Dec. 4, 1861, C. F. Adams, Jr. to Seward, Oct. 22, 1860, S. A. Elliot to Seward, Jan. 10, 1861, Box 116, F. A. Seward, Accounts: Household, 1851–54; Grier Papers, Mary Grier to her mother, Jan. 2, 10, 1857, and to her brother, Jan. 22, 1857.

3. Fanny Seward, Diary, March 1864; WP, Holland to Weed, Sept. [?], 1863; Strong, *Diary*, III, 291–2; Ford, ed., *Letters of Henry Adams*, 73–4; F. W. Seward, *Seward*, III, 470–504; *Cong. Globe*, 33rd Cong., 1st sess., *App.*, 1164, 34th Cong., 1st sess., *App.*, 1110.

4. Emerson, "Journals. War—1862," 129–34; WP, Seward to Weed, Dec. 27, 30, 1861, Feb. 13, 19, 1862; SP, Weed to Seward, Jan. 28, Feb. 14, 1862; Barnes, ed., *Memoir of Thurlow Weed*, 355–6; D. Piatt, *Memories of the Men Who Saved the Union* (New York and Chicago, 1887), 136; V. H. Davis, *Jefferson Davis* (2 vols. New York, 1890), I, 581.

5. Ford, ed., *Letters of Henry Adams*, 74, 81; F. Bancroft Papers, C. F. Adams to Bancroft, Sept. 5, 1899; Boston *Herald*, Sept. 5, 1899; Bigelow, Diary, Feb. 21, 1868; SP, Eliza Bowen to F. A. Seward, Dec. 18, 1858; M. A. DeW. Howe, *The Life and Letters of George Bancroft* (2 vols., New York, 1908), II, 148; V. H. Davis, *Davis*, I, 582.

6. SP, Financial and Legal, 1856–58, 1861, 1863, 1865, H. A. Guild to Seward, Dec. 1, 1856, June 20, 1857; New York *Times*, Dec. 10, 1856.

7. WP, Seward to Weed, May 13, 1856; W. T. Hutchinson, *Cyrus Hall*

McCormick (2 vols., New York, 1930, 1935), II, 297–8, 427; Ford, ed., *Letters of Henry Adams*, 87; D. Donald, *Charles Sumner and the Coming of the Civil War* (New York, 1960), 271.

8. *Cong. Globe*, 34th Cong., 3rd sess., 331–41; Grier Papers, Mary Grier to her mother, Jan. 15 and later, 1857.

9. SP, Fanny Seward, Diary, Dec. 27, 1861, Jan. 30, 1862, Oct. 12, 1863; F. A. Seward to L. Worden, Jan. 1, 2, 1862, to A. Seward, March 1, 1854, to W. H. Seward, July 24, 1856, to F. W. Seward, Feb., 1861, W. H. Seward, Jr., to F. A. Seward, Sept. 16, 1857, Sept. 26, Nov. 1, 1858, Feb. 17, 1860, W. H. Seward to Lady Napier, April 8, 1859, R. M. Blatchford to F. A. Seward, Feb. 21, 1861; E. J. Doyle, "A Report on Civil War America: Sir James Fergusson's Five-Week Visit," *Civil War History*, XII, no. 4 (Dec., 1966), 348, also tells of Crittenden's spitting.

10. These observations are based upon Frances's letters to her sister and to her children, and upon the correspondence between her and Henry.

11. Sumner Papers, F. A. Seward to Sumner, May 19, 1853, Oct. 6, 1856; Grier Papers, Mary Grier to her brother, Jan. 22, 1857; SP, F. A. Seward to L. Worden, Jan., March 17, 1859.

12. SP, Fanny Seward Diary, Oct. 14, 1863, F. A. Seward to W. H. Seward, May 30, 1860, Feb. 14, 26, 1861; Sumner Papers, F. A. Seward to Sumner, June 14, Sept. 5, 1860.

NOTES FOR CHAPTER 19

1. SP, Anna Seward to F. A. Seward, Feb. 28, May 28, 1861, F. A. Seward to L. Worden, Aug., 1861; P. C. Johnson, ed., "Sensitivity and Civil War: The Selected Diaries and Papers, 1858–1866, of Frances Adeline [Fanny] Seward," Appendix C. An unpublished doctoral dissertation (1963) at the University of Rochester.

2. Pierce, *Sumner*, III, 601, IV, 120–21, 136, 145, 172; Browning, *Diary*, I, 525; Hunter Miller Ms. on "The Purchase of Alaska," 034; Newton, *Lord Lyons*, I, 1–28, 31, 34, 90, 96; E. D. Adams, *Great Britain and the American Civil War* (2 vols., N.Y., 1925), I, 192, 196 note, II, 70 note 2; Nicolay and Hay, *Lincoln*, VI, 83, 84–8; H. Blumenthal, *A Reappraisal of Franco-American Relations, 1830–1871* (Chapel Hill, 1959), 123.

3. WP, Seward to Weed, May 17, 1861; F. W. Seward, *Seward*, II, 575, 590.

4. SP, Webb to Seward, May 11, 1861, Weed to Seward, May 15, 1861, Seward to Weed, May 17, 1861, Pike to Seward, March 10, 1861, Sumner to Seward, March 16, 1861, Blatchford to Seward, Aug. 8, 1861; NA, Recommendations for Appointments, Webb folder, Evarts to Lincoln, Jan. 15, 1861; B. Donner, "Carl Schurz as Office-Seeker," *The Wisconsin Magazine of History*, XX (Dec. 1936), 127–39; Adams, Diary, March 10, 12, 19, 28, 1861; WP, Sanford to Weed, March 28, 1861; H. J. Carman and

R. H. Luthin, *Lincoln and the Patronage* (New York, 1943), 83–4, 86–8; F. W. Seward, *Seward*, II, 524–5; G. Welles, *Lincoln and Seward*, 35.

5. F. W. Seward, *Reminiscences*, 142–3, *Seward*, II, 519; G. H. Stuart, *The Department of State* (New York, 1949), 130–38; Jas. L. McCamy, *The Administration of American Foreign Affairs* (New York, 1950), 45–7; Gaillard Hunt, *The Department of State of the United States* (New Haven, 1914), 429.

6. Adams, Diary, March 5, 1861; Welles, *Diary*, I, 6–7; M. Blair Papers, Welles to Blair, Nov. 8, 1872; Dearborn Collection, Seward to Welles, March 5, 1861; SP, Chase to Seward, March 20, 27, 1861; Seward to Chase, March 1861 (Huntington Library).

7. Russell, *Diary*, 35, 60–61, 71; WP, Bigelow to Weed, March 5, 1861; Gurowski, *Diary*, I, 31.

8. Allan B. Magruder, "A Piece of Secret History," *Atlantic Monthly*, XXXV (April 1875), 444–5; WP, Seward to Weed, March 11, June 25, 1861—"The country is impatient because the army dont do up its dreadful work faster"; SP, Combs to Seward, March 8, 29, 1861, J. S. Leverett & Co. to Seward, March 14, 1861, C. Bullitt to Seward, March 25, 1861, and to S. Draper, Jr., April 1, 1861, Gilmer to Seward, March 7, 8, 12, 25, 1861, J. M. Botts to Seward, March 5, 1861, B. O. Tayloe to Seward, March 13, 16, 1861, F. W. Seward to F. A. Seward, March 12, 1861, C. K. Tuckerman to Seward, March 28, 1861; Russell, *Diary*, 35, 60–61, 71.

9. SP, Ward to Seward, March, 1861, Memorandum by Seward, March 11, 1861; Gwin Recollections, *Overland Monthly*, XVIII (Nov. 1891), 465–71; *Rebellion Record*, I, 42–4, 51; "Papers of Hon. John A. Campbell," *Southern Historical Society Papers*, n. s., no. IV (Oct. 1917), 30–42; Pickett Papers, Crawford to Toombs, March 6, 1861, Forsyth and Crawford to Toombs, March 8, 1861, Roman to Toombs, March 25, 1861, and Crawford and Roman to Toombs, March 26, 1861; Bancroft, op. cit. 109–11, 118–20. In analyzing Seward's course of action during March and April 1861 the following have been useful: D. M. Potter, *Lincoln and His Party in the Secession Crisis* (New Haven, 1942), and "Why the Republicans Rejected Both Compromise and Secession," with comment by K. M. Stampp, G. H. Knowles, ed., *op. cit.*, 90–113; J. S. Tilley, *Lincoln Takes Command* (Chapel Hill, 1941); K. M. Stampp, *And the War Came* (La. St. Univ. Press, 1950); A. Nevins, *The War for the Union*, vol. I (New York, 1959), and especially R. N. Current, *Lincoln and the First Shot* (Philadelphia, 1963).

10. SP, Meigs to Seward, May 10, 1861, Weed to Seward, Sept. 9, 1865; Seward, *Works*, V, 606–9; RTL, Seward to Lincoln, March 29, 1861; Nicolay and Hay, *Lincoln*, III, 429–34. Meigs spent $3770.45 of the $10,000.

11. Campbell Papers, loc. cit. 35; RTL, Seward to Lincoln, March 29, 1861; Russell, *Diary*, 35, 60, 70; "General M. C. Meigs on the Conduct of the Civil War," *Amer. Hist. Review*, XXVI (Jan. 1921), 300; SP, Gilmer to

Seward, April 11, 1861; Central Archives. Moscow, Russia, Stoeckl à Gortchakov, April 9, 1861.

12. Adams, Diary, March 28, 31, 1861; New York *Times,* March 21, April 3–5, 8, 1861; New York *Herald,* March 12, 19, 22, 25, 1861.

13. SP, Weed to Seward, March 13, 25, 1861, draft copy of the "Thoughts" in Seward's handwriting, F. W. Seward's unpublished account, "After Thirty Years"; New York *Tribune,* March 30, 1861; John Hay Papers (Ill. State Hist. Lib.), J. B. Swain to Hay, Feb. 21, 1888, in P. Sowle, "A Reappraisal of William H. Seward's 'Some Thoughts for the President's Consideration.'" This material was furnished me in advance of publication in *The Journal of Southern History* through the courtesy of the managing editor, S. W. Higginbotham.

14. A. B. Magruder, op cit., 438–45; J. M. Botts, *The Great Rebellion* (New York, 1866), 194–200; W. L. Hall, "Lincoln's Interview with John G. Baldwin," *South Atlantic Quarterly,* XIII (July 1914), 260–69.

15. SP, Meigs to Seward, April 1–6, May 10, 1861; S. W. Crawford Papers (LC), vol. III, Statement of Admiral Porter; Wells, *Diary,* I, 23–8; Meigs, op cit. 300–301; D. D. Porter, *Incidents and Anecdotes of the Civil War* (New York, 1885), 13–23; *War of the Rebellion—Official Records of the Union and Confederate Armies,* ser. 1, vol. I (Washington, D.C., 1880), 240–41, 368–70, 393, 394; *Official Records of the Union and Confederate Navies,* ser. 1, vol. IV, 111–12; Welles, *Lincoln and Seward,* 62–3. Nevins, *The War for the Union,* 55, 59, feels that Seward wished to give up Pickens as well as Sumter. I cannot agree, though Nevins makes a persuasive case for his opinion.

16. *War of the Rebellion—Armies,* ser. 1, vol. I, 287–8; New York *Tribune,* June 8, 10, 20, 1861; New York *Times,* June 7, 1861; *Cong. Globe,* 37th Cong., 1st sess., 432–3, letter of Harvey to Cameron, July 4, 1861; Botts, *Great Rebellion,* 195–7, 256–8, 270, 276; U. S. Dept. of State, *Papers Relating to the Foreign Affairs of the United States,* 1861, 58–9 (hereafter cited as PRFA); Current, *Lincoln and the First Shot,* 111–12.

17. *Rebellion Record,* I, 49–51; D. Rowland, ed., *Jefferson Davis, Constitutionalist, His Letters, Papers and Speeches* (10 vols., Jackson, Miss., 1923), V, 90–97; New York *Tribune,* April 24, 1861; NA M77 R13, Seward to Burlingame, April 13, 1861; SP, F. W. Seward to F. A. Seward, April 24, 1861; R. H. Lutz, op. cit. 210–14.

NOTES FOR CHAPTER 20

1. SP, Weed to Seward, May 21, 1861, R. M. Blatchford to Seward, May 1, 1861, Scott to Seward, May, 1861; Hay, Diary, April 24, May 1, 1861; Seward Letters (Alb. St. Lib.), Seward to Morgan, July 25, Aug. 7, 1861; Central Archives. Moscow, Russia, Stoeckl à Gortchakoff, May 6, 1861; F. W. Seward, *Seward,* II, 598.

2. SP, F. W. Seward to F. A. Seward, Sept. 15, Oct. 14, 1861; OR, ser. 2,

vol. II, 47, 52–4, 67, 83, 102–3, 123, 127, 154–6, 202, 271; F.O. 5, vol. 825, Lyons to Russell, Feb. 17, 1862; Morgan Papers, Mrs. F. D. Flanders and Mrs. J. R. Flanders to Morgan, Jan. 20, 1862.

3. OR, ser. 2, vol. II, 1246–66; Nichols, *Pierce*, 519–20.

4. Emerson Journals. "War. 1862," 115–17; SP, F. W. Seward to S. G. Andrews, Nov. 1, 1861, Andrews to W. H. Seward, Nov. 11, 1861; D. M. Silver, *Lincoln's Supreme Court* (Urbana, 1956), 17–18; C. A. Berdahl, *War Powers of the Executive in the United States* (Urbana, 1921), 190–91; New York *World*, Sept. 10, 1861. A different version of this incident, but also showing that Seward was ready to disregard an unfavorable court decision, is given in F. W. Seward, *Seward*, II, 604–5.

5. Welles, *Diary*, II, 232.

6. SP, Banks to Seward, Oct. 2, 1861, Seward to Sanford (p. ds.), June 27, Oct. 11, 1861, Sanford to F. W. Seward, Sept. 27, 1861; NA M77 R19, Seward to Sanford, July 27, 1861; F. W. Seward, *Seward*, II, 601.

7. NA M77 R143, Seward to Perry, May 9, 21, 28, 1861; NA M38 R86, Seward to Tassara, April 2, 1861; C. C. Tansill, *The United States and Santo Domingo, 1798–1873* (Baltimore, 1938), 214.

8. SP, Napier to Lord Bloomfield, March 30, 1859, J. Bigelow to Seward, March 22, 1860, E. D. Morgan to Seward, Aug. 2, Oct. 6, 1860; Newton, *Lyons*, I, 30; Emerson, "Journals. War—1862," 130–34; Adams, Diary, Nov. 18, 1861; E. D. Adams, op. cit. I, 62.

9. NA M77 R56, Circular of March 9, 1861; PRFA, 1861, Seward to Adams, April 10, 1861, Seward to Dayton, April 22, 1861.

10. Adams, Diary, May 3, 1868; Russell to Lyons, April 6, 1861, quoted in E. D. Adams, op. cit. I, 67; Palmerston Private Letter Books, Palmerston to Russell, May 24, 1861, Palmerston to Somerset, May 26, 1861.

11. PRFA, Seward to Dayton, July 6, 1861.

12. E. D. Adams, op. cit. I, 82–96; J. B. Moore, ed., *A Digest of International Law* (8 vols., Washington, D.C., 1906), I, 164–8, 184–6; H. Wheaton, *Elements of International Law* (Boston, 1866), 34–8 and footnote 15; Sister M. Martinice O'Rourke, "The Diplomacy of William H. Seward During the Civil War: His Policies Relating to International Law," 54–63. This is a University of California Ph. D. dissertation, 1963, and an excellent piece of work; NA M30 R73, Adams to Seward, Oct. 10, 1861.

13. Bates, *Diary*, 182; PAC, G6, IX, 50–64, May 2, 1861; NA M99 R38, Seward to Lyons, May 1, 1861; F. O. 5, vol. 775, Lyons to Russell, Dec. 6, 1861; Shippee, op. cit. 120–21.

14. PRFA (1861), 60–61, 184, Seward to Adams, April 10, 1861, Seward to Dayton, April 22, 1861; SP, Bancroft to Seward, May 16, 1861, Seward to Sanford, May 20, 1861 (p.d.); Bancroft Papers, Seward to Bancroft, May 20, 1861; NA M77 R19, Seward to Sanford, May 23, 1861; F. W. Seward, *Seward*, II, 575; AAE, Mercier à Thouvenel, May 23, 26, 31, June 4, 1861; Bright Papers, Sumner to Bright, October 15, 1861.

15. SP, Bancroft to Seward, May 16, 1861, Seward to Sanford, May 20, 1861

(p. d.); Bancroft Papers, Seward to Bancroft, May 20, 1861; NA M77 R19, Seward to Sanford, May 23, 1861; F. W. Seward, *Seward*, II, 575.

16. NA M77 R76, Seward to Adams, May 21, 1861; Nicolay and Hay, *Lincoln*, IV, 270–75. A facsimile of the original draft, with the changes suggested by Lincoln and the opening as redrafted by Seward, is given in an article by A. T. Rice in the *North American Review*, vol. 142 (April 1886), 402–10.

17. SP, Weed to Seward, May 21, 1861; F. O. 5, Lyons to Russell, May 23, 1861; New York *Herald*, May 22, 1861. See also Gurowski, *Diary*, I, 40, May, 1861; AAE, Mercier à Thouvenel, May 23, 1861.

18. Adams, Diary, June 10, 1861; SP, Weed to Seward, May 21, 1861; WP, Seward to Weed, May 23, 1861; H. Adams, *Letters*, 93; Emerson, "Journals, War—1862," 144–5. Sumner thought the date of his conversation with Seward was May 27.

19. F. O. 5, vol. 764, Lyons to Russell, May 20, 23, 1861, vol. 765, Lyons to Russell, June 8, 1861.

20. PRFA, 1861, Adams to Seward, June 14, 1861; SP, Everett to Seward, June 7, 1861, Sumner to Seward, June 7, 12, 1861, Harvey to Seward, June 11, 1861, Belmont to Seward, June 24, 1861, Motley to Seward, Oct. 18, 1861; NA M77 R19, Seward to Sanford, June 21, 1861; S. F. Bemis, ed., *The American Secretaries of State and Their Diplomacy* (15 vols. New York, 1927–66), VII, 45; F. W. Seward, *Seward*, II, 580–82, 584, 590.

21. PRFA, 1861, Seward to Adams, June 8, July 21, Sept. 7, Oct. 23, 1861; Russell, *Diary*, 380–81; E. D. Adams, op. cit. I, 246–52; O'Rourke, op. cit. 80–100. Benjamin R. Curtis believed that the Union had both belligerent and municipal rights, and could use either or both, according to its discretion—SP, Curtis to Jas. M. Wayne, Dec. 18, 1861.

22. Bancroft, op. cit. II, 173; E. D. Adams, op. cit. I, 123–32.

23. NA M77 R76, Seward to Adams, July 21, 1861, R77, Seward to Adams, June 5, 1863; PRFA, 1861, Seward to Dayton, May 4, 1861; NA M77 R136, Seward to Clay, May 6, 1861; AAE, Mercier à Thouvenel, June 10, 1861.

24. Emerson, "Journals. War—1862," 111–12; Bright Papers, Sumner to Bright, April 24, 1865.

25. PRFA, Seward to Dayton, Sept. 10, 1861.

26. SP, J. Bigelow to Seward, Sept. 23, Oct. 3, 1861, A. Belmont to Seward, Sept. 25, Oct. 21, 1861.

27. NA M77 R56, Seward to Dayton, Oct. 30, 1861.

1. F. O. 5, vols. 1129, 1130, Thornton to Clarendon, March 23, April 13, 1868; H. M. Wriston, *Executive Agents in American Foreign Relations* (Baltimore, 1929), 779–80.

2. Weed, *Autobiography*, 634–8; WP, Seward to Weed, Aug. 12, 1861; SP, Weed to Seward, Oct. 30, Nov. 6, Dec. 4, 1861, Jan. 16, 1862.

3. SP, Receipts and Vouchers, May 1862–Sept. 1867, Hughes to Seward, Dec. 18, 1861, Aug. 19, 1862; AANY, Seward to Hughes, Jan. 9, 1862.

4. SP, F. W. Seward to F. A. Seward, Nov. 17, 1861; Palmerston Private Letter Books, 860–61, Palmerston to Russell, Sept. 9, 1861; Bright Papers Seward to Sumner, Oct. 11, 1861, Sumner to Bright, Oct. 15, Dec. 30, 1861; F. O. 5, 773, Lyons to Russell, Oct. 28, 1861.

5. Cong. Globe, 37th Cong., 2nd sess., 5; New York Times, Nov. 17–21, 1861; SP, J. A. Dix to Seward, Nov. 16, 1861, Wm. C. Noyes to Seward, Nov. 18, 1861; C. F. Adams, Jr., "The Trent Affair," Mass Hist. Soc. Proceedings, XLV (Nov. 1911), 35–138.

6. Central Archives, Moscow, Russia, Stoeckl à Gortchakoff, Nov. 18, 1861; London Times, Nov. 28–Dec. 10, 1861; New York Times, Dec. 16–18, 1861; New York Tribune, Dec. 16–18, 1861.

7. SP, Weed to Seward, Dec. 2–10, 1861, Bigelow to Seward, Dec. 6, 1861; WP, Weed to Hughes, Dec. 7, 1861; Sanford Papers, Weed to Sanford, Dec. 7, 1861; Newton, Lyons I, 63; Benjamin Moran, Diary, Jan. 27, 1862.

8. F. O. 5, vol. 775, Lyons to Russell, Nov. 22, 25, 29, Dec. 2, 1861.

9. Ibid. vol. 777, Lyons to Russell, Dec. 19, 23, 1861; AAE, Mercier à Thouvenel, Dec. 19, 1861.

10. NA M77 R77, Seward to Adams, Nov. 30, 1861; SP, McIlvaine to G. T. Bedell, Jan. 13, 1862; WP, Weed to Hughes, Dec. 22, 1861.

11. SP, Bigelow to Seward, Dec. 5, 1861, S. Ward to Seward, Dec. 16, 1861, W. F. Weld to Seward, Dec. 19, 1861, C. A. Davis to Seward, Dec. 19, 21, 1861; New York Times, Dec. 23, 1861; NA M30 R74, Adams to Seward, Dec. 3, 1861, M34 R54, Dayton to Seward, Dec. 3, 1861; F. O. 5, vol. 777, Lyons to Russell, Dec. 27, 1861; AAE, Mercier à Thouvenel, Dec. 19, 1861; Bright Papers, Sumner to Bright, Dec. 30, 1866.

12. RTL, Lincoln Memorandum on the Trent affair [Dec. 1860]; Pierce, Sumner, IV, 59; Nicolay and Hay, Lincoln, V, 32–4; F. W. Seward, Seward, III, 25–6.

13. Seward, Works, V, 295–309.

14. D. Donald, ed., Inside Lincoln's Cabinet (New York, 1954), 53–5; Bates, Diary, 216.

15. Adams, Diary, Jan. 9, 24, 1862; C. F. Adams, Jr., op. cit. 63, 74–76, 130–31; Newton, Lyons, I, 72; SP, F. A. Seward to L. M. Worden, Dec. 26, 1861; Emerson, "Journals. War—1862," 144–5; New York Times, Feb. 5, 1862, citing editorial correspondence of the Albany Evening Journal; T. C. Pease and Jas. G. Randall, eds., The Diary of Orville Hickman Browning (2 vols., Springfield, 1925, 1933), I, 520.

1. RTL, Seward to Lincoln, Jan. 2, 1862[?]; F. O. 5, vols. 828, 830, Lyons to Russell, April 14, 25, 28, May 20, 1862; Central Archives. Moscow, Russia, For. Aff., Stoeckl à Gortchakoff, May 5, 1862; WP, Seward to

Weed, April 25, 1862; F. W. Seward, *Seward*, III, 82–3; AAE, Mercier à Thouvenel, April 13, 28, 1862.

2. F. O. 5, vols. 823, 827, Lyons to Russell, Jan. 17, 20, April 11, 1862; F. O. 115, vol. 298, Lyons to Russell, Feb. 14, 1862; SP, Weed to Seward, Jan. 20, 26, 28, April 15, 1862, Sanford to Seward, Jan. 24, April 10, 1862; NA M77 R77, Seward to Adams, Feb. 13, 1862, M77 R56, Seward to Dayton, Feb. 19, May 5, 1862.

3. PAC RG7 G8b, vol. 42, Lyons to A. A. Gordon, Jan. 20, March 7, 1862; Browning, *Diary*, I, 525; Malloy, *Treaties*, I, 674–88; RTL, Seward to Lincoln, April 24, 1862; Welles, *Diary*, I, 166, 167; WP, A. F. Kinnaird to Weed, July 8, 1862, with clipping; Newton, *Lyons*, I, 85; Pierce, *Sumner*, IV, 68.

4. RTL, Weed to Seward, Feb. 4, 1862, McIlvaine to Seward, Feb. 21, 1862; SP, H. Adams to F. W. Seward, April 4, 1862; Patterson Papers, Weed to Patterson, April 2, 1862; NA M77 R77, Seward to Adams, April 14, 1862; Adams, Diary, May 6, 1862.

5. NA M77 R77, Seward to Adams, Aug. 2, 1862; Chase, *Diaries*, 164–6, Sept. 30, 1862; WP, Seward to Weed, Aug. 1, 1862; SP, Everett to Seward, Sept. 9, 25, 30, 1862; Welles, *Diary*, I, 79–80, 180–81, 266–97; RTL, Lincoln to Seward and Welles, April 21, 1863; Palmerston Papers, Clarendon to Palmerston, Oct. 16, 1862; Brougham Correspondence, Parkes to Brougham, Oct. 30, 1862; E. D. Adams, op. cit. II, 26–74; C. F. Adams, Jr., *Studies Military and Diplomatic, 1775–1865* (New York, 1911), 400–410; Randall, *Lincoln*, III, 334–7.

6. NA M77 R56, Seward to Dayton, Oct. 20, Nov. 4, Dec. 11, 29, 1862; SP, Seward to T. W. Evans, Dec. 6, 1862 (p.d.).

7. NA M77 R143, Seward to Schurz, April 27, 1861, M77 R56, Seward to Dayton, July 7, 1862; Bigelow Papers, Seward to Bigelow, March 15, 1862; Sanford Papers, Seward to Sanford, Jan. 24, 1863; R. H. Lutz, op. cit. 215; Browning, *Diary*, I, 532; F. W. Seward, *Seward*, III, 83.

8. SP, W. K. Strong to Seward, April 4, 1862, Prince Felix Salm to Seward, April 11, 1862, Irwin McDowell to Seward, April 23, 1862; Welles, *Diary*, I, 93–8, 100–101, 104, 139, 209–10, 241–2; Chase, *Diaries*, 61, 129; Hay, Diary, March 11, Sept. 15, 1862; NA M77 R56, Seward to Dayton, Dec. 7, 1862; F. O. 5, vols. 831–33, 838, Lyons to Russell, May 30, June 2, Nov. 21, 1862, Stuart to Russell, July 10, 1862; SP, Fanny Seward, Diary, Jan. 3, 4, 1863. Fanny thought Butler a fascinating person.

9. NA M77 R77, Seward to Adams, April 14, 1862, R56, Seward to Dayton, June 2, 1862; SP, Weed to Seward, July 28, 29, 1862; Browning, *Diary*, I, 562.

10. SP, Seward to Stanton, June 30, July 1, 2, 1862 (p.ds.), Stanton to Seward, July 1, 1862, Seward to Lincoln [July, 1862] (p.d.); Lincoln, *Works*, V, 291–4, 296–7; OR series 3, II, 179–82, 186, 198, 200–201, 202, 205; Nicolay and Hay, *Lincoln*, VI, 115–19; F. W. Seward, *Seward*, III, 101–10; Thomas and Hyman, *Stanton*, 206–7; W. B. Hesseltine, *Lincoln and the War Governors* (New York, 1948), 198–200; H. G. Pearson, *The*

Life of John A. Andrew (2 vols., Boston, 1904), II, 29–31. I differ with Nicolay and Hay as to the letter to the governors of June 30. It was, I think, drafted by Seward rather than by Lincoln.

11. SP, Seward to Lincoln, July 30, 1862, Seward to G. G. Fogg, Sept. 26, 1862 (p. d.); NA M77 R56, Seward to Dayton, Sept. 20, 1862, M77 R38, Seward to Burlingame, Aug. 8, 1862, Circular no. 18; Browning, *Diary*, I, 618–19; F. W. Seward, *Seward*, III, 115, 121, 123, 125.

12. NA M77 R136, Seward to C. M. Clay, May 6, 1861, Seward to Cameron, June 9, 1862, R38, Seward to Burlingame, May 29, 1862; SP, Seward to R. H. Pruyn, Sept. 25, 1862 (p. d.), Seward to Sumner, Jan. 10, 1863 (p. d.); Townsend Harris Papers, Seward to Harris, Aug. 1, 1861. Pruyn's efforts to teach Japanese pupils English at the American legation were specially commended as apt to have both immediate and long-range beneficial results; AAE, Mercier à Thouvenel, Sept. 9, 1862.

13. SP, Bancroft to Seward, Aug. 11, 27, 1862, Scott to Seward, Feb. 3, 1863, Crittenden to Seward, March 17, 1863, Van Sackett to F. W. Seward, April 1, 1863, Dix to Seward, April 15, 1863, presidential pardon for Van Rensselaer, April 21, 1863.

14. SP, F. G. Troxell to Seward, Dec. 23, 1861, Pierrepont to Seward, Feb. 9, 1862, T. T. Davis to Seward, Nov. 17, Dec. 8, 1862 (p. d.), Seward to T. T. Davis, Nov. 20, Dec. 12, 1862 (p. d.).

15. SP, Weed to Seward, Nov. 5, 1862, H. J. Hastings to F. W. Seward, Nov. 8, 1862.

16. SP, A. C. Brown to Seward, June 23, 1862, Weed to Seward, Nov. 5, 1862, April 2, 1863, H. J. Hastings to F. W. Seward, Nov. 8, 1862; Welles, *Diary*, I, 154, Sept. 11, 27, 1862; New York *Herald*, Feb. 8, 1863; Stanton, *Recollections*, 216; M. Lichterman, "John Adams Dix: 1798–1879." Ph.D. dissertation at Columbia University (1952), 495, 497–8; Van Deusen, *Weed*, 301–4; Alexander, op. cit. 37, 41, 43, 50, 54, 56.

17. F. W. Seward, *Seward*, III, 74.

18. PRFA (1861), 60, Seward to Adams, April 10, 1861, and 182, Seward to Dayton, April 22, 1861; *Cong. Globe*, 37th Cong., 1st sess., 243, 257, 258, 265.

19. SP, S. S. Seward to W. H. Seward, Sept. 9, 1861; Nevins, *Frémont*, 500–501, 503.

20. NA M77 R143, Seward to Schurz, Oct. 10, 1861; Schurz, *Reminiscences*, II, 303; SP, Kendall to Seward, Jan. 26, 1862, Seward to Kendall, Jan. 31, 1862 (p. d.); AAE, Mercier à Thouvenel, March 17, 1862.

21. NA M77 R19, Seward to Sanford, May 23, 1862, M77 R56, Seward to Dayton, June 20, July 10, 1862; SP, Weed to Seward, March 9, 1862; Seward, *Works*, V, 9–10, 599–600; B. Quarles, *Lincoln and the Negro* (New York, 1962), 78; Randall, op. cit. II, 141–59; F. W. Seward, *Seward*, III, 52, 65, 143.

22. PRFA (1862), I, 124; Welles, *Diary*, I, 70; Bright Papers, Sumner to Bright, Aug. 5, 1862.

23. Chase, *Diaries*, 99; NA M77 R136, Seward to Cameron, Aug. 18, 1862,

Seward Circular, Aug. 18, 1862, M77 R77, Seward to Adams, Nov. 30, 1862, M77 R13, Seward to Motley, July 24, 1862; RTL, M. Ryerson to Seward, Aug. 11, 1862, E. Cowan to Seward, Aug. 8, 1862, Seward to Lincoln, Aug. 14, 1862; Bigelow Papers, Seward to Bigelow, Sept. 9, 1862; Richardson, *Messages and Papers*, VI, 136; F.B. Carpenter, *Six Months at the White House* (New York, 1866), 22; Nicolay and Hay, *Lincoln*, VI, 127-8.

24. Andrew Papers, John A. Andrew to Benjamin Lincoln, Sept. 16, 1862; Bright Papers, Sumner to Bright, Oct. 28, Nov. 18, 1862.

25. SP, fragment in Frances's handwriting, without date, salutation, or signature.

26. Welles, *Diary*, I, 142-4; Chase, *Diaries*, 149-50; Richardson, *Messages and Papers*, VI, 96-8.

27. Central Archives. Moscow, Russia, For. Aff. 49, Stoeckl à Gortchakoff, Sept. 25, Dec. 1, 1862; J.A. Marshall, *Private and Official Correspondence of Gen. Benjamin F. Butler During the Period of the Civil War* (5 vols., Norwood, Mass., 1917), II, 334. It is significant that H.P. Anderson, close to the British legation, made a journey through the West in the late summer of 1862, and found there much opposition to abolition, especially in the areas that had commercial outlets down the Mississippi. Not even in the pro-abolition regions did he find that emancipation was connected in men's minds with amelioration of the slaves' social condition, but there was general agreement that no immigration of Negroes into the North would be permitted.—F. O. 5, Anderson to Stuart, Oct. 1, 1862, with Stuart to Russell, Oct. 7, 1862.

28. NA M77 R19, Seward to Sanford, Oct. 10, 1862; Welles, *Diary*, I, 144, 209-11; Browning, *Diary*, I, 609, 613, 618; SP, Seward to Francis Seward, July 17, 1863; Piatt, *Memories*, 150; RTL, Seward to Lincoln, Dec. 30, 1862; Richardson, *Messages and Papers*, VI, 157-9; F. W. Seward, *Seward*, III, 151.

NOTES FOR CHAPTER 23

1. Strong, *Diary*, III, 291-2; N. Brooks, *Washington in Lincoln's Time* (New York, 1896), 27, 50-51; Schurz, *Reminiscences*, II, 221-2; Adams, Diary, Oct. 19, 1862; SP, R.M. Blatchford to Seward, Dec. 10, 1864; Sandburg, *Lincoln: The War Years*, I, 303, II, 86, 244, III, 369-70, IV, 129.

2. SP, Fanny Seward, Diary, Sept. 9, 1861; E. Keckley, *Behind the Scenes* (New York, 1868), 106-7, 131; C. Sandburg, *Mary Lincoln* (New York, 1932), 80.

3. For other illustrations of these services, see RTL, Seward to Lincoln, June 3, 25, July 1, Dec. 30, 1861.

4. RTL, Seward to Lincoln, Aug. 22, Sept. 16, 1861, Seward to [Lincoln],

Jan. 2 [1863]; SP, July, 1862; F. O. 5, Vol. 824, Lyons to Russell, Feb. 3, 1862; F. W. Seward, *Seward*, III, 176.

5. Hay, Diary, Oct. 12, 17, 22, 27, Nov. 1, 1861; RTL, Cushman to Seward, Aug. 9, 1861; Bigelow Papers, Seward to Bigelow, July 15, 1862; F. W. Seward, *Seward*, III, 208.

6. SP, F. W. Seward to F. A. Seward, [Oct.] 7 [1861].

7. SP, Fanny Seward, Diary, Jan. 17, 1863.

8. Welles, *Diary*, I, 124, 131–6; Gurowski, *Diary*, II, 242; L. H. Fischer, *Lincoln's Gadfly, Adam Gurowski* (Norman, Okla., 1964), 102.

9. Lincoln, *Works*, VI, 410–11, VII, 101–2, 499–501; J. Bigelow, ed., *Letters and Literary Memorials of Samuel J. Tilden* (2 vols., New York, 1908), I, 233; Nicolay and Hay, *Lincoln*, VI, 262; D. Donald, *Lincoln Reconsidered* (New York, 1956), 114–27; Jas. M. McPherson, *The Struggle for Equality* (Princeton, 1964), 240–46; Litwack, op. cit. 276–9.

10. WP, Seward to Weed, Jan. 2, 1862; Adams, Diary, Feb. 13, 17, Dec. 22, 1862; AAE, Mercier à Thouvenel, Jan. 14, 1862.

11. *Cong. Globe*, 37th Cong., 2nd sess., 1732, 1805, 2114.

12. Browning, *Diary*, I, 527; Bates, *Diary*, 227, 291; Welles, *Diary*, I, 127–8; SP, Seward to R. King, Jan. 3, 1863.

13. New York *Tribune*, Jan. 28, Feb. 7, 1862; J. Bigelow, ed., *Letters and Literary Memorials of Samuel J. Tilden*, I, 163; Bigelow, *Retrospections*, I, 541; New York *Herald*, Sept. 24, Nov. 9, 10, 28, 1862; SP, Weed to Seward, Nov. 5, 1862, Wm. Schouler to Seward, Nov. 13, 1862; J. C. Derby to Seward, Nov. 14, 1862, Henry Bowen to Seward, Dec. 9, 1862; Foster Papers, H. Fish to Foster, Dec. 20, 1862; Adams, Diary, Jan. 31, Nov. 20, 1862; Greenhow, *My Imprisonment*, 78–9.

14. James A. Hamilton, *Reminiscences* (New York, 1869), 536; Chase, *Diaries*, 95.

15. Emerson, "Journals. War—1862," 114; Chase, *Diaries*, 95; SP, Evarts to Seward, Dec. 22, 1862, C. A. Davis to Seward, April 15, 1862, Charles Burdett to Seward, June 11, 1862; F. W. Seward, *Seward*, III, 112–13, 117, 120, 138, 144.

16. Hamilton, *Reminiscences*, 529–36; Chase, *Diaries*, 128–30, Hamilton's account of his interviews with Lincoln was written down immediately after they occurred.

17. Browning, *Diary*, I, 596–9; F. Fessenden, *Life and Public Services of William Pitt Fessenden* (2 vols., New York, 1907), I, 231–42; Welles, *Diary*, I, 194–5; Nicolay and Hay, *Lincoln*, VI, 263–4.

18. RTL, Seward to Lincoln, Dec. 16, 1862, F. W. Seward to Lincoln, Dec. 16, 1862, Welles, *Diary*, I, 194.

19. F. W. Seward, *Seward*, III, 147.

20. Browning, *Diary*, I, 602–3; Bates, *Diary*, 269–70; Welles, *Diary*, I, 196–7, 203; Fessenden, *Fessenden*, I, 243–8.

21. Welles, *Diary*, I, 199.

22. Welles, *Diary*, I, 201–2.

23. Ibid. I, 205; RTL, F. W. Seward to [Lincoln], Dec. 16, 1862, W. H. Seward to Lincoln, Dec. 16, 21, 1862, Chase to Lincoln, Dec. 20, 22, 1862; SP, Chase to Seward [Dec. 21, 1862], Chase to F. W. Seward, Dec. 24, 1862; E. P. Oberholtzer, *Jay Cooke, Financier of the Civil War* (2 vols., Philadelphia, 1907), I, 224–6; Welles, *Diary*, I, 205; Hay, Diary, Oct. 29, 1863; Nicolay and Hay, *Lincoln*, VI, 271.

24. NA M77 R56, Seward to Dayton, Dec. 21, 1862; SP, Evarts to Seward, Dec. 22, 1862; WP, Seward to Weed, Dec. 25, 1862, Jan. 2, 1863; Seward Correspondence (Univ. of Chicago), Jas. W. White to Wm. Butler, Jan. 12, 1863; AAE, Mercier à Drouyn de Lhuys, Dec. 30, 1862.

NOTES FOR CHAPTER 24

1. Newton, *Lyons*, I, 121.

2. Welles, *Diary*, I, 298–9, 322–3, 398, 416; F. O. 5, vols. 875–6, Lyons to Russell, Jan. 30, 1863, Seward to Lyons, Feb. 7, 1863; Newton, op cit. I, 100, 105.

3. The *Peterhoff* case is examined in detail in O'Rourke "The Diplomacy of William H. Seward During the Civil War" 138–56. See also J. Monaghan, *Diplomat in Carpet Slippers* (Indianapolis, 1945), 303–4, 310–11.

4. F. O. 5, vol. 884, Seward to Lyons, May 12, 1863.

5. F. O. 5, vol. 887, Lyons to Russell, June 12, 1863; Jas. P. Baxter, 3rd, "The British Government and Neutral Rights, 1861–1865," *American Historical Review*, XXXIV (1928–29), 9–29, also "Papers Relating to Belligerent and Neutral Rights," 87; Brougham Correspondence, Russell to Brougham, Sept. 23, 1863.

6. F. O. 5, vols. 879, 881, Seward to Lyons, March 8, 1863, Lyons to Russell, March 10, 13, April 13, 1863; SP, Sanford to Seward, March 24, 1863; AAE, Mercier à Drouyn de Lhuys, March 30, 1863; Bright Papers, Sumner to Bright, April 7, 1863.

7. Welles, *Diary*, I, 250–51, 257; WP, Bigelow to Weed [Feb. 1863]; SP, J. B. Murray to Seward, April 7, 1863, E. D. Morgan to Seward, April 3, 1863, Seward to "My dear Sir," April 10, 1863 (copy); NA M77 R77, Seward to Adams, April 7, 10, 1863; F. O. 5, vol. 881, Lyons to Russell, April 13, 1863.

8. PRFA, 1863, pt. 1, 354–7, 394–5; NA M30 R79, Adams to Seward, July 16, 31, 1863, Adams to Russell, July 11, 1863.

9. F. O. 115, vol. 354, Lyons to Russell, June 22, July 3, 1863; Malloy, op. cit. I, 688–91; F. O. 5, vol. 890, Gov. Dallas to Viscount Monck, June 3, 1863, vol. 891, Lyons to Seward, July 25, 1863, Lyons to Russell, July 28, 1863.

10. F. O. 115, vols. 354 and 355, F. O. 5, vol. 891, Lyons to Russell, July 17, 20, 1863.

11. NA M77 R78, Seward to Adams, Sept. 5, Oct. 5, 1863; Sumner Papers,

Seward to Sumner, Sept. 12, 1863; SP, F. W. Ballard to Seward, Oct. 7, 1863; Welles, *Diary*, I, 435–8; New York *Tribune*, Sept. 11, 1863; Pierce, *Sumner*, IV, 160–65.

12. NA M30 R80, Adams to Seward, Sept. 18, 1863, with Russell to Adams, Sept. 14, 1863, M78 R78, Seward to Adams, Oct. 6, 23, 1863.
13. SP, Henry Adams to F. W. Seward, March 3, 1863.
14. NA M77 R78, Seward to Adams, June 20, July 2, 1864.
15. F. O. 5, vol. 897, Lyons to Russell, Nov. 17, 1863, vol. 900, Lyons to Russell, Dec. 24, 1863.
16. NA M77 R79, Seward to Adams, Dec. 14, 1864, March 8, 10, 20, 1865. Confederate activities on the Canadian border are dealt with in L. B. Shippee, *Canadian-American Relations, 1849–1874* (New Haven, 1939), 123, 136–79, and R. W. Winks, *Canada and the United States: The Civil War Years* (Baltimore, 1960), 298–336.
17. NA M77 R78, 79, Seward to Adams, Jan. 15, Dec. 27, 1864, Jan. 16, Feb. 21, Nov. 4, 1865.
18. NA M77 R79, Seward to Adams, March 1, 10, 1865; SP, Sanford to Seward, Feb. 20, March 7, 1865, A. Belmont to Seward, March 2, 1865, Seward to Sanford, April 4, 1865 (p. d.), Wm. H. Russell to Bigelow, March 8, 1865 (copy), Bigelow to Seward, March 9, 1865.

NOTES FOR CHAPTER 25

1. Bigelow Papers, Seward to Bigelow, Dec. 2, 1862, Feb. 25, 1863; NA M77 R56, Seward to Dayton, Feb. 6, 1863; Browning, *Diary*, I, 619; F. O. 5, vol. 839, Lyons to Russell, Dec. 8, 1862, Feb. 13, 1863; Central Archives, Moscow, Russia, For. Aff. 49, Stoeckl à Gortchakoff, Feb. 10, 16, 24, 1863.
2. Ibid. Stoeckl à Gortchakoff, Feb. 26, 1863; F. O. 5, vol. 879, Lyons to Russell, March 6, 1863; Van Deusen, *Greeley*, 294–96.
3. Sanford Papers, Seward to Sanford, March 6, 1863; Welles, *Diary*, I, 338–40; F. O. 5, vol. 890, Lyons to Russell, July 3, 1863.
4. NA M77 R56, Seward to Dayton, July 8, 10, 29, 1863; F. O. 5, vol. 890, Lyons to Russell, July 3, 1863.
5. NA M77 R56, Circular no. 39, Seward to Dayton, Aug. 12, 1863.
6. WP, Bigelow to Weed, Sept. 29, 1863; Adams, Diary, Feb. 10, 1865; NA M77 R56, 57, Seward to Dayton, Nov. 10, 14, 21, Dec. 17, 1863, Feb. 1, March 1, 12, 21, May 20, 21, June 27, July 2, Sept. 19, 1864, Seward to Bigelow, March 11, 15, 1865.
7. NA M77 R113, Seward to Corwin, May 7, June 3, Aug. 24, Sept. 2, 1861; AAE, Mercier à Thouvenel, Dec. 23, 1861; W. S. Holt, *Treaties Defeated by the Senate* (Baltimore, 1933), 92–6; D. Perkins, *The Monroe Doctrine, 1826–1867* (Baltimore, 1933), 421–6.
8. NA M77 R56, Seward to Dayton, March 3, 31, 1862, May 11, 1863; F. O. 5, vol. 827, Lyons to Russell, March 31, 1862.

9. Bigelow Papers, Seward to Bigelow, Jan. 27, 1864; NA M77 R13, Seward to Motley, Oct. 19, 1863, April 14, 1864; AAE, Mercier à Drouyn de Lhuys, March 30, 1863.

10. *Cong. Globe*, 38th Cong., 1st sess., 1408–9, 2427, 3309; PRFA, 1864–65, pt. 3, Dayton to Seward, April 22, 1864; R. W. Leopold, *The Growth of American Foreign Policy* (New York, 1962), 77–8.

11. F. O. 5, vol. 892, Lyons to Russell, Aug. 3, 1863; NA M77 R57, Seward to Dayton, April 7, 1864; AAE, Geoffroy à Drouyn de Lhuys, April 4, Nov. 20, 1864, Jan. 16, Feb. 27, March 30, 1865.

12. G. Welles, *Lincoln and Seward* (New York, 1874), 43, 47; C. F. Adams, *An Address on the Life, Character and Services of William Henry Seward* (Albany, 1873), 48–53.

13. Examples of hasty action are his advising Lincoln to issue a proclamation that Nevada Territory had a new constitution simply on the basis of a telegram from Governor Nye, and the secret arrest and extradiction of a Spaniard, José Augustin Arguelles, wanted in Cuba for his slave-trading activities. Both of these aroused much criticism. Welles, *Diary*, II, 36, 45–6, 163–4; Bates, *Diary*, 374, 413–14; RTL, R. Murray to Seward, May 19, 1864; SP, Jas. F. Wilson to Seward, June 20, 1864; Adams, *Diary*, Jan. 16, Feb. 24, March 18, 1865; Duberman, op. cit. 321–2.

14. SP, Sanford to Seward, Dec. 5, 6, 1864, Sanford to [Wm. Hunter], May 2, 1865, Seward to Sanford (p. d.), n.d., but obviously in answer to Sanford's letters; Bright Papers, Sumner to Bright, Jan. 1, 1865.

15. F. O. 115, vols. 355, 357, F. O. 5, vol. 892, Lyons to Russell, Aug. 11, 14, 16, 24, 1863; AAE, Mercier à Thouvenel, March 11, 1862.

16. NA M77 R78, Seward to Adams, Oct. 10, 1863.

17. SP, H. W. Bulkeley to Seward, March, 1864.

18. Adams Papers, Letterbook (Roll 170), Adams to Palfrey, Nov. 10, 1863; Hay, Diary, Dec. 12, 1863.

NOTES FOR CHAPTER 26

1. Welles, *Diary*, I, 348, 372, 538–9, II, 18, 129–130; Marshall, *Butler*, III, 77, 78; Smith, *Blair Family*, II, 274–5.

2. Sanford Papers, Seward to Sanford, June 30, 1863; SP, Seward to a Boston Committee, July 1, 1863 (p. d.).

3. Welles, *Diary*, II, 159–67; Bates, *Diary*, 414; SP, Hamilton to Seward, Aug. 8, 1864; AAE, Mercier à Drouyn de Lhuys, Jan. 24, Feb. 16, 1863; Bright Papers, Sumner to Bright, March 16, 1863.

4. F. O. 5, vols. 823, 825, 827, Lyons to Russell, Jan. 14, Feb. 17, April 11, 1862; Central Archives, Moscow, Russia, For. Aff. 49, Stoeckl à Gortchakoff, Feb. 24, 1862; SP, W. H. Seward to F. A. Seward, Thanksgiving 1863.

5. SP, Banks to Lincoln, March 6, 1863, Seward to Banks (2), March 26, 1863,

Banks to Seward, April 17, 1863, Zacharie to Seward, July 16, 18, 1863, F. A. Seward to W. H. Seward, July 12 [1863]; New York *Herald*, July 11, 1863; Banks Papers, Banks to Seward, June 20, 1863 (copy), July 2, 1863 (copy); B. W. Korn, *American Jewry and the Civil War* (Philadelphia, 1951), 194–8; F. H. Harrington, "A Peace Mission of 1863," *American Historical Review*, XLVI (Oct. 1940), 76–86, is based on the Banks Papers and consists mainly of Banks and Zacharie letters.

6. SP, Belmont to Seward, July 20, 1863, Chase to Seward, July 25, 1863; AAE, Mercier à Drouyn de Lhuys, July 15, 1863; Bright Papers, Sumner to Bright, July 21, 1863.

7. Adams Papers, Letters Received and Other Loose Papers, Dec. 1863–Feb. 1864, Seward to Adams, Feb. 1, 1864.

8. Ibid., Adams, Diary, Dec. 30, 1863, Jan. 12, March 23, 28, April 25, 1864; Adams, Letterbook (Roll 170), Adams to Seward, Dec. 31, 1863, March 3, 1864; Adams, "Letters Received and Other Loose Papers, March–April 1864," Seward to Adams, March 21, 22, 28, April 25, 1864; New York *Times*, Nov. 5, 1863; NA M77 R57, Seward to Dayton, July 26, 1864; Sanford Papers, Seward to Sanford, Sept. 17, 1865; AAE, Geoffroy à Drouyn de Lhuys, Nov. 15, 1864.

9. Nicolay and Hay, "Blair's Mexican Project," *Century Magazine*, n.s. vol. XVI (1889), 838–52; Nicolay and Hay, *Lincoln*, X, 108–12. I have used the accounts of all the participants in the Conference—Rowland, *Davis*, VIII, 128–36 (for Hunter's account); Stephens, *Constitutional View*, II, 589–622; J. A. Campbell, "Memoranda of Conversation at the Conference in Hampton Roads," *Southern Historical Society Papers*, n.s., vol. IV (Sept. 1917), 45–52; NA M77 R79, Seward to Adams, Feb. 7, 1865, and M77 R57, Seward to Bigelow, Feb. 7, 1865; Lincoln, *Works*, VIII, 284–5. The Conference is well described in Kirkland, op. cit. 206–58; Bright Papers, Sumner to Bright, Feb. 13, 20, 1865.

10. Hay, Diary, Aug. 13, 1863; NA M77 R78, Seward to Adams, Nov. 30, Dec. 7, 1863; RTL, Seward Memorandum, April 19, 1864; SP, Seward to Chandler, May 14, 1864 (p. d.); Seward, *Works*, V, 489–90.

11. Bates, *Diary*, 292; NA M77 R78, Seward to Adams, Dec. 5, 1864; Seward, *Works*, V, 512–14; SP, F. A. Seward to W. H. Seward, Feb. 3, 1865, Wm. Bilbo to Seward, Dec. 12, 20, 1864, Jan. 10, Feb. 1, 1865, R. W. Latham to Seward, Jan. 7, 9, 12, 1865, R. Schell to Seward, Jan. 23, 1865, Geo. P. Jones to Seward, Feb. 1, 1865.

12. Adams, Diary, Aug. 21, 1863; Hay, Diary, Nov. 22, 1863; NA M77 R143, Seward to H. J. Perry, Sept. 9, 1863; Carpenter, op. cit. 72–4; Welles, *Diary*, I, 549; SP, F. A. Seward to W. H. Seward [Nov. 26, 1863], W. H. Seward to F. A. Seward, Nov. 30, 1863.

13. SP, S. Duncan to M. Duncan, Aug. 25, 1863, C. A. Davis to Seward, Oct. 6, 1863, Banks to Seward, Sept. 21, 1863; NA M77 R78, Seward to Adams, Nov. 9, 1863, Feb. 4, Dec. 17, 1864, Jan. 11, 16, 1865.

14. W. H. Seward, *Issues of the Conflict* (Republican Campaign Documents, No. 1); Seward, *Works*, V, 505–12; SP, J. D. Baldwin to F. W. Seward, Sept. 10, 1864, H. T. Cheever to Seward, Sept. 10, 1864.
15. SP, Derby to G. E. Baker, Dec. 7, 1863; Richardson, op. cit. VI, 252, 254–5; Chas. H. McCarthy, *Lincoln's Plan of Reconstruction* (New York, 1901), 190–91, 398, 494–7; W. B. Hesseltine, *Lincoln's Plan of Reconstruction* (Tuscaloosa, 1960), 30, 47, 133, 135, 136–8, 140.

NOTES FOR CHAPTER 27

1. Newton, *Lyons*, I, 116–18; SP, T. M. Ward to Seward [March] 1864.
2. SP, Seward to J. Dukehart *et al.*, April 18, 1863, Seward to Dayton, July 20, 1863 (p. d.); Bigelow Papers, Seward to Bigelow, July 21, 1863; Morgan Papers, Seward to Morgan, Sept. 24, 1863.
3. Chandler Papers, Chandler to Mrs. Chandler, Feb. 10, 1863; SP, J. C. Derby to G. E. Baker, April 1, 1863, A. Goodrich to F. W. Seward, May 15, 1863, Webb to Seward, July 24, 1863.
4. SP, Seward to Harvey, March 9, 1864 (dupl.), Fanny Seward, Diary, June 1, 1863, Sumner to Seward, May 9, 1863; Welles, *Diary*, I, 300–301; WP, Seward to Weed, July 31, 1863, C. G. Halpine to Weed, Sept. 8, 1863.
5. F. W. Seward, *Seward*, III, 196; Newton, *Lyons*, I, 118; Welles, *Lincoln and Seward*, 180–85; Bright Papers, Sumner to Bright, Sept. 27, 1864.
6. RTL, Seward to Lincoln, Nov. 2, 1863 (telegram), New York *Herald*, Nov. 6, 1863; New York *Times*, Nov. 5, 1863; SP, G. W. Peck to Seward, Jan. 20, 1864; WP, A. B. Dickinson to Weed, Dec. 3, 1863.
7. Welles, *Diary*, I, 501; RTL, E. D. Smith to Seward, Jan. 25, 1864, Jas. Kelly to Seward, Feb. 18, 1864; Van Deusen, *Weed*, 306–8.
8. Welles, *Diary*, II, 28–9; Hay, Diary, Dec. 18, 1864; Barlow Papers (Huntington Library), Smith to "Dear Barnett," Aug. 17, 1863. There is no such letter from Seward in the Barlow Papers.
9. SP, Hastings to F. W. Seward, June 8, 1864; *Proceedings of the National Union Convention* (New York, 1864), 15, 33–75; Alexander, op. cit. III, 94.
10. SP, C. S. Spencer *et al.* to Seward, May 16, June 9, 11, 1864; New York *Times*, June 16, 1864.
11. RTL, Weed to Seward, Aug. 22 [1864]; Lincoln, *Works*, VII, 517, and note; Nicolay and Hay, *Lincoln*, IX, 221.
12. Wm. Whitney to T. H. Dudley, Oct. 6, 1864 (Huntington Library).
13. *Speech of William H. Seward on the Night Before the Election* (Washington, D.C., 1864).
14. Nicolay and Hay, *Lincoln*, VII, 387–8, IX, 251–2, note. Quotes are from Hay, Diary, Nov. 8, 1864.
15. Welles, *Diary*, II, 194–5, 198, 237, 244; SP, Seward to H. B. Anthony,

Jan. 13, 1865, Wm. N. Bilbo to Seward, Jan. 23, 1865, Sanford to Seward, Jan. 20, 1865.

16. *Cong. Globe*, 38th Cong., 2nd sess., 48–53, 65–7. The joint resolution of the preceding spring had died in the Senate.

NOTES FOR CHAPTER 28

1. SP, J. C. Lawrence to Seward, May 23, 1864, J. R. Benjamin to Seward, June 18, 1864, F. B. Carpenter to Seward, Sept. 20, 1864, Mrs. Richard Hildreth to Seward, April 16, 1864, S. Hooper to Seward, May 19, 1864, Jan. 20, 1865, S. E. Sewall to Seward, Jan. 1, 1865.

2. Lincoln, *Works*, VI, 496–7, and note, VIII, 56, note; Welles, *Diary*, I, 450; New York *Times*, Nov. 22, 1863, Bellows to the *Times*, Nov. 17, 1863; Carpenter, op. cit. 242.

3. SP, R. M. Blatchford to F. W. Seward, Aug. 28, 1862, Fanny Seward, Diary, Aug. 29, 1862, F. A. Seward to F. W. Seward, Sept. 3, 1862 (telegram).

4. Welles, *Diary*, I, 506; SP, C. Cushman to Seward, June 19, 1863, Chas. Hawley to Seward, Nov. 30, 1864.

5. Sanford Papers, Seward to Sanford, Feb. 28, 1863; SP, Jas. E. Harvey to Seward, April 4, 1863, J. Mitchell to Seward, July 26, 1863, R. M. Blatchford to Seward, March 7, 1863, Seward to Count Piper, June 8, 1864 (p. d.), Seward to Mercier, Oct. 19, 1864 (copy).

6. SP, Seward to Blatchford [Feb. 1862] (p. d.), Blatchford to Seward, Feb 17, 1862; Gurowski, *Diary*, I, 251.

7. SP, Blatchford to Seward, Feb. 18, Oct. 29, Nov. 1, 1864, April 1, 1865.

8. SP, Seward to Blatchford [Feb. 1862] (p. d.), July 22, 1862, (p. d.), Blatchford to Seward, Aug. 22, 1862, Nov. 21, 1863, Feb. 18, Oct. 29, Nov. 1, 10, 1864, March 19, April 1, 1865, Seward to L. L. Doty, March 29, 1865.

9. SP, Wm. H. Seward. Accounts. Personal Finances, 1861–68, 1863–67.

10. SP, F. A. Seward to W. H. Seward [June 1839], F. A. Seward to S. Cameron [March 1861], to L. M. Worden, Dec. 21, 1861, F. W. Seward to F. A. Seward, June 18, July 2, 1861, Fanny Seward, Diary, Jan. 30, 1862, Oct. 12, 13, 1863.

11. SP, F. A. Seward to F. W. Seward, April 30, 1861, W. H. Seward to W. H. Seward, Jr., Sept. 16, 1864, Fanny Seward, Diary, Oct. 12, 1862; F. W. Seward, *Seward*, III, 125; J. H. Monroe, *Historical Records of One Hundred and Twenty Years* (Geneva, 1913), 216–19.

12. SP, Fanny Seward, Diary, Sept. 10, Dec. 27, 1861.

13. SP, Fanny Seward, Diary, Sept. 10, Dec. 27, 1861, Jan. 1, 1862, Jan 22, 1863. See also the perceptive account of Fanny by Patricia Johnson Rauch in the foreward to her doctoral dissertation, "Sensitivity and Civil War: The Selected Diaries and Papers, 1858–1866, of Frances Adeline [Fanny] Seward."

14. SP, F. A. Seward to L. M. Worden, Aug. and Sept., 1861, F. A. Seward to W. H. Seward, June 7, 1861.

15. SP, F. A. Seward to W. H. Seward, April 28, Sept. 17, 1861, July 26, Aug. 24, Dec. 5, 1862, F. A. Seward to F. W. Seward, April 30, 1861, Aug. 10, 1862, F. A. Seward to L. M. Worden, Dec. 5, 11, 1861, F. A. Seward to A. Seward, May 15, 1864, F. A. Seward to W. H. Seward, Jr., May 20 [1864?], D. Dix to F. A. Seward, May 6, 1861.

16. SP, F. A. Seward to W. H. Seward, Oct. 31, 1862.

17. SP, F. A. Seward to L. M. Worden [Jan. 1862], F. A. Seward to F. W. Seward, July 23, 28, 1863; F. W. Seward, *Seward*, III, 127.

18. SP, F. A. Seward to F. W. Seward, June 15, 1861, F. A. Seward to W. H. Seward, April 21, May 16, 1862, June 6, Sept. 6, 1863, June 18, 1864.

19. SP, F. A. Seward to F. W. Seward, July 29, 1862.

20. SP, F. A. Seward to [Fanny Seward], March 1865.

21. SP, F. A. Seward to Anna Seward, April 2, 1865.

22. Welles, *Diary*, II, 274.

23. SP, Fanny Seward, Diary, April 5, 1865, C. A. Seward to W. H. Seward, June 2, 1865.

24. SP, F. W. to F. A. Seward, April 5, 6, 1865 (telegrams), F. W. Seward to A. Canfield, April 13, 1865 (p. d.), Fanny Seward, Diary, April 12–14, 1865; F. W. Seward, *Seward*, III, 270–71.

25. Welles, *Diary*, II, 269, 274; SP, Fanny Seward, Diary, April 6–9, 1865.

26. SP, Ryerson to F. W. Seward, April 13, 1865.

27. Bigelow Papers, Seward to Bigelow, July 15, 1862, "Fidies" to Seward [Oct. 1864]; Sanford Papers, Weed to Sanford, April 16, 1865; J. P. Usher, *President Lincoln's Cabinet* (Omaha, 1925), 12; Randall-Current, *Lincoln*, IV, 370.

28. Hay, Diary, Nov. 9, 1863.

29. This account is based largely on Fanny's Diary, April 14, 1865, an account by Frances Seward in F. W. Seward, *Seward*, III, 276–80, and statements of witnesses at Payne's trial—B. Pitman, comp., *The Assassination of President Lincoln and the Trial of the Conspirators* (New York, 1954), 154–68. See also H. W. Hilliard, *Politics and Pen Pictures* (New York, 1892), 349–50. There is an interesting account of the affair by John K. Lattimer, "The Stabbing of Lincoln's Secretary of State on the Night the President Was Shot," *Journal of the American Medical Association*, CXCII (April 1965), 99–106. V. Shelton, *Mask for Treason* (Harrisburg, Pa., 1965), 118–36, argues that Augustus Seward, who positively identified Payne as the would-be assassin, perjured himself at the trial. Shelton gives the Peterson transcript and the Pitman compilation of Augustus Seward's testimony. He makes an ingenious case for his thesis, but in so doing ignores the testimony of Dr. Verdi at the trial, statements in Fanny Seward's diary, and the accounts of the attack on Seward given the next day by the Washington correspondents of the New York *Times, Herald,* and *Tribune*.

30. Sanford Papers, Seward to Sanford, Dec. 22, 1865; Dix Papers, Note by Miss Dix, April 15, 1865 [?], Fanny Seward to Miss Dix, April 20 [1865].

31. SP, Fanny Seward, Diary, April 14, 1865, Motley to Seward, April 30, 1865, Schleiden to Seward, April 28, 1865, Sanford to Seward, April 28, 1865, Blatchford to Seward, July 29, 1865.

32. Welles, *Diary*, II, 304; F. W. Seward, *Seward*, III, 280.

33. G. W. Curtis Collection, Fanny Seward to Curtis, May 16, 1865; SP, F. A. Seward to L. M. Worden, June 2, 1865; NA M77 R57, Seward to Bigelow, July 3, 1865.

34. SP, Fanny Seward, Diary, June 17, 18, 1865, F. A. Seward to L. M. Worden, June 2, 1865; WP, G. E. Baker to E. W. Barnes, April 24, 1865; Derby, *Fifty Years*, 80–81; New York *Times*, June 22, 1865; F. W. Seward, *Seward*, III, 285–6.

35. SP, Fanny Seward to W. H. Seward, July 30, Aug. 1, 1866, to W. H. Seward, Jr., Oct. 11, 1866, Diary, Sept. 14, 15, 1866; Dept. of Public Health, Washington, D. C. Interments. Oct. 29, 1866; New York *Tribune*, Oct. 30, 1866.

36. Bigelow Papers, Seward to Bigelow, Nov. 11, 1866; SP, Seward to Annie L. Ash, Nov. 7, 1866, to A. D. F. Randolph, Nov. 7, 1866, to C. F. Adams, Dec. 10, 1866 (p. d.); Cushman Papers, Seward to C. Cushman, Jan. 7, 1867.

NOTES FOR CHAPTER 29

1. S. Andrews, *The South since the War, as Shown by Fourteen Weeks of Travel and Observation in Georgia and the Carolinas* (Boston, 1866), 390–92; Welles, *Diary*, II, 568, 576; SP, T. Cottman to Seward, Dec. 11, 1865, B. S. Whittin to F. H. Pierpoint, April 13, 1866, J. W. Jameson to Seward, June 7, 1866; Johnson Papers, J. Hill to Seward, Dec. 20, 1865; *Nation*, May 4, 7, 1866.

2. New York *Times*, June 6, Aug. 22, 1865; Johnson Papers, K. B. Sewall to Seward, June 2, 1865; SP, B. F. Sanford to Seward, Nov. 23, 1865, W. J. Branch to Seward, Feb. 25, 1866, A. S. Wallace to Seward, May 5, 1866; S. Andrews, op. cit., 9–10, 21–8, 101, 154–62, 178–9, 232, 321, 337, 379–80, 395–400; W. M. Caskey, *Secession and Restoration of Louisana* (University, La., 1938), 185–6; G. R. Bentley, *A History of the Freedmen's Bureau* (Philadelphia, 1955), 62, 65, 67, 79–85; L. and J. H. Cox, *Politics, Principle and Prejudice* (New York, 1963), 156–9, 166–71; Joel Williamson, *After Slavery. The Negro in South Carolina During Reconstruction, 1861–1877* (Chapel Hill, 1965), 69–102.

3. New York *Times*, May 5, 1865; SP, Henry Wilson to Seward, June 15, 1865, J. P. Hart to Seward, July 16, 1865; P. Buck, *The Road to Reunion* (Boston, 1937), 14–19; Jas. M. McPherson, *The Struggle for Equality* (Princeton, 1964), 311–16.

4. Welles, *Diary*, II, 302–3, 375; Adams, Diary, Oct. 15, 1865; McKitrick, op. cit. 55–9, an excellent survey of northern attitudes on the subject.

5. New York *Times*, May 6, June 11, 1865; New York *Herald*, May 19, July 10, 1865.

6. Welles, *Diary*, II, 595, 598; Adams, Diary, June 13, 1865; Johnson Papers, Barlow to Blair, July 19, 1865, and to Pratt, Aug. 7, 21, 1865; Seward, *The Question of Reconciliation* (Washington, D.C., 1866), 3; Thomas and Hyman, *Stanton*, 443–5; Cox, op. cit. 50–53.

7. SP, Dixon to Seward, July 17, 1865; Welles, *Diary*, II, 369–70; Smith, *Blair Family*, II, 330–32; New York *Times*, July 14, 1865; New York *Tribune*, July 19, Aug. 29, 1865; Cox, op. cit. 53–8.

8. Sanford Papers, Weed to Sanford, April 28, 1865; SP, M. Ryerson to Seward, July 24, 1865; Welles, *Diary*, II, 325–6, 330; New York *Tribune*, July 22, 1865; Rhodes, op. cit. V, 531–3; Van Deusen, *Greeley*, 318–20.

9. WP, M. Ryerson to Seward, Sept. 14, 1865, Ryerson to Weed, Sept. 27, 1865; SP, Weed to Seward, Sept. 30, 1865, Jas. Kelly to Seward, Nov. 11, 1865; New York *Times*, Oct. 3, 1865.

10. F. O. 5, vol. 834, Stuart to Russell, July 21, 1862; SP, Seward to Sanford, Nov. 9, 1863 (p. d.), Wm. C. Jewett to Seward, Feb. 16, 1864, Seward to Adams, March 21, 1864 (p. d.), Bilbo to Seward, Feb. 14, 1865, Grant to Seward, Feb. 19, 1865; SP, Seward to Sanford, Nov. 9, 1863 (p. d); NA M77 R78, Seward to Adams, Jan. 4, 1864; RTL, Grady to Seward, Aug. 12, 1864.

11. SP, T. Shankland to Seward, May 31, 1865, R. Carter to Seward, May 18, 1865, Caleb Cushing to Seward, May 5, 1865, Chandler Robbins to Seward, May 9, 1865, Bowen to Seward, June 7, 1865; New York *Atlas*, May 5, 1865.

12. SP, Seward to E. R. L. Laboulaye, Sept. 19, 1865, to L. B. Wyman, Nov. 23, 1865 (copy), to W. L. Barnes, Feb. 11, 1866 (copy), to M. Ryerson, April 30, 1866 (p. d.), to Ransom Balcom, July 14, 1866 (p. d.); New York, *Times*, Sept. 14, 1866; Hilliard, *Politics and Pen Pictures* (New York, 1892), 348.

13. Browning, *Diary*, II, 39; SP, Seward to R. M. Patton, Dec. 22, 1866 (dupl.); F. W. Seward, *Seward*, III, 284–5, B. A. Weisberger, "The Dark and Bloody Ground of Reconstruction Historiography," A. S. Eisenstadt, ed., *American History: Recent Interpretations* (2 vols., New York, 1962, 1963), I, 500, and note.

14. SP, Patterson to Seward, May 23, 1864, Jas. L. Orr to Seward, Oct. 1, 1865, Howell Cobb to Seward, Oct. 11, 1865; Johnson Papers, A. H. Stephens to Seward, Sept. 29, 1865; Welles, *Diary*, II, 335–6; Browning, *Diary*, II, 39; New York *Times*, Dec. 20, 1865; F. W. Seward, *Seward*, III, 295–6, 300.

15. Dreer Collection, Seward to M. Griffith, Jan. 29, 1864; SP, Seward to Hale, May 23, 1866 (p.d.), Nichols to Seward, Nov. 9, 1866, Wilson to

Seward, Nov. 13, 1865, L. Agassiz to Seward, Jan. 20, 1868, Mrs. Agassiz to Seward, Jan. 22, 1868; RTL, Seward to Lincoln, May 4, 1864; NA M77 R57, Seward to Bigelow, Nov. 2, 1865; F. W. Seward, *Seward*, III, 296; *Speech of the Hon. William H. Seward at Auburn, Oct. 20, 1865*, 2; W. H. Seward, *The Question of Reconciliation*, 16; E. C. Agassiz, ed., *Louis Agassiz, His Life and Correspondence* (2 vols., Boston, 1885), II, 594–612.

16. W. H. Seward, *The Question of Reconciliation*, 16; Welles, *Diary*, III, 3–4.

17. R. Ogden, *Life and Letters of Edwin Lawrence Godkin* (2 vols., New York, 1907), I, 260–66; *Nation*, March 1-April 5, 1866.

18. SP, Gasparin to Seward, July 14, 1865, March 9, 1866, Seward to Gasparin, July 10, 1865, March 5, 1866 (p.ds.), April 7, 1866 (copy).

19. C. V. Woodward, *The Strange Career of Jim Crow* (2nd rev. ed. New York, 1966), 33, 34, 47–59; G. B. Tindall, *South Carolina Negroes, 1877–1900* (La. St. Univ. Press, 1966), 19–40; C. E. Wynes, *Race Relations in Virginia*, (Charlottesville, 1961), 144–5 *et passim*; J. Williamson, *After Slavery. The Negro in South Carolina During Reconstruction, 1861–1877* (Chapel Hill, 1965), 326–62, 374–417.

NOTES FOR CHAPTER 30

1. Welles, *Diary*, II, 317; Johnson Papers, Seward statement on Ford's Theatre, April 22, 1865; F. W. Seward, *Seward*, III, 196; Sanford Papers, Weed to Sanford, April 16, 28, 1865. Weed's comment to Sanford appears to refer to the succession, but it is possible that he had in mind the future of the nation.

2. SP, Bigelow to Seward, May 5, 1865; Adams, Diary, April 26, May 1, 1865; F. W. Seward, *Seward*, III, 295; NA M77 R24, Seward to Webb, July 24, 1865.

3. Bigelow, Diary, Sept. 23, 1868; SP, Johnson to Seward, April 19, 1862, M. Ryerson to Seward, April 27, 1865, Smith to Seward, April 13, 1866; Johnson Papers, Seward to Johnson, April 28, 1862; *Proceedings of the National Union Convention . . . 1864* (New York, 1864), 73, 75; C. M. Depew, *My Memories of Eighty Years* (New York, 1922), 60–61; G. W. Curtis in *Harper's Weekly*, May 20, 1865; Welles, *Diary*, II, 47–51, 384, declared that both Seward and Lincoln were for Hamlin, but this was evidently a mistake.

4. Welles, *Diary*, II, 252, 253.

5. New York *Times*, April 25, May 13, 1865; Johnson Papers, Diary of Col. W. G. Moore, April 26, 1868; WP, Campbell to Weed, May 1, 1865; Sanford Papers, Weed to Sanford, May 28, 1865; Smith, *Blair Family*, II, 329–31.

6. Sanford Papers, Seward to Sanford, June 8, 1865; Bright Papers, Sumner to Bright, May 1, June 5, 1865; Richardson, op. cit. VI, 310–14; Welles, *Diary*, II, 289, 291.

7. AAE, Montholon à Drouyn de Lhuys, July 25, 1865; Cox, op. cit. 62, 65, 66–7.

8. SP, Seward to Webb, Aug. 9, Sept. 25, 1865 (copies), Weed to Seward, Dec. 27, 29, 1865, J. J. Peck to Seward, March 21, 1866; WP, Seward to Weed, Dec. 28 [1865]; Welles, *Diary*, II, 378; Depew, op. cit. 43.

9. Adams, Diary, Nov. 2, 1865; Welles, *Diary*, II, 363, 393–5; SP, A Goodrich to F. W. Seward, Sept. 4, 1865, to W. H. Seward, Oct. 17, 1865, Brewster to Seward, Nov. 29, 1865, Wilson to Seward, Nov. 20, 1865; AAE, Montholon à Drouyn de Lhuys, Oct. 23, 31, 1865; Cox, op. cit. 83.

10. J. W. Garner, *Reconstruction in Mississippi* (New York, 1901), 84; J. G. Blaine, *Twenty Years of Congress* (2 vols. Norwich, Conn. 1893), II, 107.

11. NA M77 R79, Seward to Adams, Dec. 16, 1865; SP, Wallace to Seward, Dec. 25, 1865, Seward to Wallace (dupl.), Feb. 18, 1866; Bright Papers, Seward to Bright, Nov. 13, 1865; Clarendon Papers, Bruce to Clarendon, Nov. 20, Dec. 12, 1865.

12. Welles, *Diary*, II, 378–9.

13. SP, Draft for Johnson's message of Dec. 4, 1865; Richardson, op. cit. VI, 353–71.

14. Gardiner Collection, E. P. Smith to H. C. Carey, Nov. 19, 1865; WP, Raymond to Weed, Dec. 3, 1865; B. B. Kendrick, *The Journal of the Joint Committee of Fifteen on Reconstruction* (New York, 1914), 140–41.

15. New York *Times*, Dec. 19, 20, 1865; *Cong. Globe*, 39th Cong., 1st sess., 75, 120–21; SP, Ashley to Seward, Dec. 19, 1865; S. A. Ashe, *History of North Carolina* (2 vols., Raleigh, 1925), II, 1031–2; H. T. Lefler and A. R. Newsome, *North Carolina* (Chapel Hill, 1954), 456–7.

16. SP, T. M. Pomeroy to Seward, Dec. 7, 1865; WP, Raymond to Weed, Dec. 15, 1865; New York *Times*, Dec. 19, 20, 1865; Bright Papers, Sumner to Bright, Nov. 5, 1865; Clarendon Papers, Bruce to Clarendon, Dec. 18, 1865.

17. Welles, *Diary*, II, 403.

18. SP, Clapp to Seward, Feb. 12, 1866; Weed to Seward, Nov. 24, 1866, Israel Washburne, Jr., to Seward, Feb. 13, 1866.

19. Johnson Papers, Reel 45, series 5A for Seward's draft; Edw. McPherson, *The Political History of the United States of America During the Period of Reconstruction* (Washington, D.C., 1880), 68–74; Rhodes, op. cit. V, 568–74; Welles, *Diary*, II, 434; Cox, op cit. 180–84.

20. New York *Times*, Feb. 23, 1866.

21. SP, McCulloch to Seward, Feb. 24, 1866, J. Warren to Seward, Feb. 24, 1866, Bigelow to Seward, March 22, 1866, J. A. Parker to Seward, April 1, 1866; Bates, *Diary*, 552; *Nation*, May 25, June 8, 1866.

22. SP, Brewster to Seward, Feb. 27, March 3, 1866, Warren to Seward, Feb. 24, 1866, Schouler to F. W. Seward, March 12, 1866; Welles, *Diary*, II, 439.

23. Johnson Papers, Weed to Johnson, Feb. 23, 1866, Seward to F. W.

Seward, Feb. 23, 1866; Morgan Papers, Seward to Morgan, Feb. 23, 1866; *Nation.* March 1, 1866; AAE, Montholon à Drouyn de Lhuys, March 6, 1866.

24. SP, Ryerson to Seward, Feb. 26, 1866, W. G. Moore to Seward, March 26, 1866, Seward to Gasparin (p. d.), March 5, 1866; Cox, op. cit. 197–8.
25. Johnson Papers, series 5A, reel 45, Seward draft, March 27, 1866; Welles, *Diary*, II, 463–4.
26. McPherson, op. cit., 74–8; Johnson Papers, Weed to Seward, March 25, 1866. For a more detailed comparison of Seward's draft with Johnson's veto see J. H. and L. W. Cox, "Andrew Johnson and His Ghost Writers," *Mississippi Valley Historical Review*, XLVIII (Dec. 1961), 473–6.
27. WP, Morgan to Weed, April 8, 1866; Rhodes, op. cit. V, 586; McKitrick, op. cit. 314–18.

1. SP, Draft, May 15, 1866, R. H. Hare to Seward, March 12, 1866, Sumner to Seward, April 25, 1866; Johnson Papers, series 5a, reel 45, a slightly different version of the draft in the Seward Papers; Richardson, op. cit. VI, 413–16; Welles, *Diary*, II, 502–3; *Cong. Globe*, 39th Cong., 1st sess., 2180; New York *Times*, Feb. 23, 1866. Sumner had voted against the bill because of the Negro suffrage provision, but it passed the Senate 19 to 13, with 17 absent.
2. *Cong. Globe*, 39th Cong., 1st sess., 2619, 2638, 3953–9; SP, King to F. W. Seward, May 21, 1866.
3. *Cong. Globe*, 39th Cong., 1st sess., 2265; SP, H. R. no. 543; Sanford Papers, E. D. Webster to Sanford, Aug. 11, 1866; Richardson, op. cit. VI, 391–2; Browning, *Diary*, II, 74–5; Welles, *Diary*, II, 495, 527, 531–3; New York *Tribune*, May 2, 1866; New York *Times*, June 4–15, 1866; J. W. Patton, *Unionism and Reconstruction in Tennessee* (Chapel Hill, 1934), 224–5.
4. See the analysis of his position in Cox, op. cit. 88–128, and H. K. Beale, *The Critical Year* (new ed., New York, 1958), 113–23.
5. Welles, *Diary*, II, 602–3; Blair Collection (Missouri Hist. Soc.), F. P. Blair to Jas. R. Doolittle, July 20, 1866; *Nation*, May 1, 1866; Cox, op. cit. 105, 114; McKitrick, op. cit. 400–403.
6. WP, A. Oakey Hall to Weed, Jan. 22, 1866, E. W. Leavenworth to Weed, Feb. 11, 1866, E. D. Morgan to Weed, Feb. 27, March 8, 1866, D. Morrison to Weed, March 31, 1866, Raymond to Weed, May 2, 1866; SP, Weed to Seward, Jan. 28, March 12, 17, 1866, G. Dawson to Seward, March 2, 1866.
7. Weed, *Autobiography*, 475; SP, Weed to Seward, Nov. 11, 1865.
8. SP, Weed to Seward, Nov. 11, 13, 1865, Jan. 29, Feb. 28, March 12, 1866, Blatchford to Seward, March 12, 1866, Raymond to Seward, Aug. 19, 1866, G. C. Davidson to F. W. Seward, Nov. 7, 1866; WP, Morgan to

Weed, April 21, 23, 1866, Raymond to Weed, June 8, 1866, H. McCulloch to Weed, Dec. 21, 1866; Patterson Papers, W. H. Wallace to Patterson, July 2, 31, 1866; Welles, *Diary*, II, 566; Cox, op. cit. 113–27.

9. WP, Morgan to Weed, May 21, 1866, Raymond to Weed, June 12, 1866, A. Hawley to Weed, July 15, 1866; SP, Dawson to F. W. Seward, July 18, 25, 1866, Weed to Dawson, July 24, 1866, A. W. Spies to Dawson, June 16, 1866, R. Balcom to Seward, July 13, 1866, S. W. Updike to F. W. Seward, July 22, 1866.

10. WP, Morgan to Weed, Dec. 15, 1865, Raymond to Weed [1866]; SP, Blatchford to Seward, March 12, 1866, B. F. Hall to Seward, May 25, 1866, March 2, 1868, H. Nicholson to M. C. C. Church [June 1866], H. Nicholson to M. C. C. Church, June 16, 1866, M. C. C. Church to Seward, June 24, 1866, Seward to J. T. Hoffman, June 26, 1866 [p. d.]; Welles, *Diary*, II, 516–17, 523, 556; Bigelow Papers, Seward to Bigelow, April 9, 1866; Gardiner Collection (Hist. Soc. of Pa.), E. P. Smith to H. C. Carey, May 4, 1866; Clarendon Papers, Bruce to Clarendon, Feb. 27, March 10, 29, April 29, July 15, 1866; AAE, Montholon à Drouyn de Lhuys, July 16, 1866.

11. SP, W. H. Seward, *Reconciliation* [n. l. n. d.].

12. New York *Times*, May 24, 1866; New York *Tribune*, May 24, 1866; New York *Herald*, May 24, 1866; SP, Isaac A. Gates to Seward, May 1866.

13. Bright Papers, Sumner to Bright, Sept. 3, 1866; New York *Times*, May 23, 1866; "Extracts from the Journal of Henry J. Raymond," IV, *Scribner's Monthly*, XX (May–Oct. 1880), 275–80; SP, Doolittle to Seward, July 10, 1866; Beale, op. cit. 125–30; McKitrick, op. cit. 404–5.

14. Raymond's Journal, *op. cit.*, 278; Browning, *Diary*, II, 81 and note; Welles, *Diary*, II, 528–32, 545, 547, 548; SP, Seward to A. W. Randall, July 11, 1866 (two p. ds.); F. O. 5, vol. 1066, Bruce to Clarendon, July 18, 1866.

15. Bright Papers, Summer to Bright, Sept. 3, 1866. Those who resigned were Attorney General Speed, Secretary of the Interior Harlan, and Postmaster General Dennison.

16. SP, Seward to Raymond, Aug. 16, 1866 (p. d.), Seward to Blatchford, Aug. 21, 1866 (p. d).

17. SP, Schell to Seward, Aug. 17, 1866; WP, D. H. Abell to Weed, Sept. 3, 1866; Sanford Papers, E. P. Webster to Sanford, Sept. 11, 1866; F. O. 5, vol. 1066, Bruce to Stanley, Aug. 31, 1866; McKitrick, op. cit. 416, and note.

18. ABПP, Stoeckl à Gortchakov, April, July 30, Sept. 17, 1866; SP, Jas. Duggan *et al.* to Seward, March 22, 1866, Seward to Duggan *et al.*, April 5, 1866 (p. d.), A. W. Randall to F. W. Seward, June 3, 1866, Seward to H. Weed, Aug. 24, 1866 (p. d.), W. H. Seward, Jr., to Seward, Aug. 30, 1866, G. B. Smith to Seward, Dec. 30, 1866; Browning, *Diary*, II, 115; Adams, Diary, Dec. 19, 1866; Welles, *Diary*, II, 588–99; Bright Papers, Greeley to Bright, Sept. 21, 1866.

19. Sanford Papers, Weed to Sanford, Sept. 25, 1866; WP, H. McCulloch to Weed, Sept. 6, 10, Oct. 11, 1866, D. H. Abell to Weed, Sept. 17, 1866, V. W. Smith to Weed, Oct. 1, 1866; SP, S. W. Crawford to F. W. Seward, Oct. 3, 1866, Schell to Seward, Oct. 1, 1866, Weed to Seward, Sept. 27, Oct. 26, 27, 1866, Anthony to F. W. Seward, Oct. 3, 1866.

20. SP, Seward to S. M. Hopkins, July 25, 1866 (p. d.), Seward to J. Segoine, Aug. 1, 1866 (p. d.), Seward to W. H. Seward, Jr., Nov. 14, 1866, S. Stebbins to Seward, Oct. 4, 1866, J. R. Kellogg to Seward, Nov. 1, 1866, Seward to Kellogg, Nov. 6, 1866 (copy); Welles, *Diary*, II, 610.

21. ABIIP, Stoeckl à Gortchakov, Nov. 13, 1866; SP, Seward to Sanford, Nov. 6, 1866 (copy), Hay to Seward, Nov. 15, 1866, Seward to Hay, Dec. 8, 1866 (p. d.); WP Seward to Weed, Nov. 7, 1866.

NOTES FOR CHAPTER 32

1. Morgan Papers, Seward to Morgan, Dec. 17, 1866.

2. NA M77 R13, Seward to Motley, Jan. 5, April 8, 1867; Welles, *Diary*, III, 24, 34-7; Hay, Diary, Feb. 2, 10, 1867; Bigelow, Diary, March 27, 1869; Adams, Diary, Feb. 14, 1867; New York *Tribune*, Jan. 29, 31, 1867; SP, Motley to Seward, July 11, 1865, Wm. Gray to Seward, April 13, 1867, Seward to Johnson, April 15, 1867; *Sen. Exec. Docs.*, 39th Cong., 2nd sess., no. 8, and 40th Cong., 2nd sess., no. 1; J. Bigelow, "Mr. Seward and Mr. Motley," *International Review* (July 1878), V, 544-56; Marjorie F. Gutheim, "John Lothrop Motley," Ph. D. dissertation at Columbia University, 1955, 258-73.

3. *Cong. Globe*, 39th Cong., 2nd sess., 458-9, 596-8, 1501-2; NA M77 R134, Seward to Harvey, July 30, 1866, March 11, April 15, 1867, Sept. 26, 1868; SP, Schouler to Seward, Feb. 21, 1867; Pierce, *Sumner*, IV, 308.

4. NA M77 R58, Seward to Bigelow, Nov. 27, 1866; SP, S. M. Chandler to Seward, Feb. [20], 1867.

5. Johnson Papers, series 5A, Seward's draft for the annual message of Dec. 3, 1866. This is in the handwriting of one of his clerks, with interlineations in his own hand; Richardson, op. cit., VI, 558-81. See also, McKitrick, op. cit. 449-55; Rhodes, op. cit., VI, 2-9.

6. Welles, *Diary*, III, 25-6, 42-4; SP, Stevens to Seward, Dec. 6, 8, 1866, John A. Bingham to Seward, Dec. 12, 1866, H. McCulloch to Seward, Dec. 15, 1866, A. Herrick to Seward, Feb. 5, 1867 (with notation by Seward).

7. Hay, Diary, Feb. 2, 1867; Bigelow, *Retrospections*, IV, 44, 48; Johnson Papers, Moore Notes, May 7, 1867.

8. Adams, Diary, Feb. 14, 1867; Andrew Papers, M. Blair to Andrew, Feb. 18, 1867; Hay, Diary, Feb. 7, 1867; Johnson Papers, Moore Notes, Feb. 14, 1867; SP, Weed to Seward, Feb. 21, 1867, White to Seward, Feb. 21, 1867, A. D. F. Randolph to Seward, Feb. 22, 1867.

9. Welles, *Diary*, II, 132, 189-90; McPherson, op. cit. 173-8; Thomas and

Hyman, op. cit. 525–7; McKitrick, op. cit., 495–7; Rhodes, op. cit. VII, 47 and note.

10. New York *Times,* June 3–9, 22–8, 1867; Welles, *Diary,* III, 119–20; Johnson Papers, Moore Notes, March 16, 1868; SP, P. Smith to Seward, Dec. 11, 1866, Wm. Schouler to Seward, July 1, 1867, F. W. Tappan to Seward, July 4, 1867; AAE, Berthemy à Moustier, July 27, 1867.

11. Sanford Papers, Weed to Sanford, Aug. 7, 1867; WP, Patterson to Weed, Aug. 8, 21, 1867; SP, Anthony to F. W. Seward, Aug. 27, 1867.

12. Sanford Papers, E. D. Webster to Sanford, March 14, 1867; SP, Stevens to Seward, Aug. 26, 1867, R. K. Cutler to Seward, Aug. 27, 1867, E. D. Webster to Seward, Sept. 9, 1867; Welles, *Diary,* III, 156, 159, 163; Bigelow, Diary, Sept. 11, 1867; Johnson Papers, Seward to Johnson, Aug. 23, 1867; St. G. L. Sioussat, "Notes of Colonel W. G. Moore," *Amer. Hist. Rev.,* XIX (Oct. 1913), 111; G. F. Milton, *The Age of Hate* (New York, 1930), 464–6; F. W. Seward, *Seward,* III, 354.

13. Welles, *Diary,* III, 67, 91, 118–19, 133–4; SP, Seward to J. P. Kennedy, Nov. 9, 1867; Johnson Papers, Moore Notes, Aug. 14, 1867; Adams, Diary, Aug. 21, 1867.

14. SP, Seward's draft for the Proclamation of Sept. 7, 1867; Richardson, op. cit. VI, 547–9.

15. SP, Seward's draft for the message of Dec. 3, 1867; Richardson, op. cit. VI, 558–81.

16. McKitrick, op. cit. 497–9; Rhodes, op. cit., VI, 93–106; D. M. Dewitt, *The Impeachment and Trial of Andrew Johnson* (New York, 1903), 289.

17. ABIIP, Stoeckl à Gortchakov, Feb. 28, 1868; Welles, *Diary,* II, 552, III, 12; SP, —— to Seward [Oct. 1866] with notation by Seward; WP, Morgan to Weed, Dec. 9, 1867, Patterson to Weed, Dec. 14, 1867; Bright Papers, Sumner to Bright, Jan. 18, March 24, 1868; McPherson, op. cit. 266.

18. Dewitt, op. cit. 515.

19. ABIIP, Stoeckl à Gortchakov, Feb. 28, 1868; SP, Dana to Seward, Nov. 25, 1867, Stevens to Seward, Nov. 25, 1867, Jan. 23, 1868, Wade to Seward, Nov. 25, 26, 1867, Seward to Sumner, Jan. 28, 1868 (p. d.), March 27, 1868 (p. d.), L. Worden to A. Seward, Jan. 12, 25, March 5, 1868.

20. SP, Seward to J. R. Butterfield, Feb. 18, 1868 (p. d.), Weed to Seward, Feb. 3 [1868], T. F. Carter to Seward, March 12, 1868, with Seward's notation; WP, Seward to Weed, Feb. 5, 1868; Bigelow, *Retrospections,* IV, 155; Johnson Papers, Moore Notes, March 8, May 15, 1868.

21. SP, Schell to Seward, March 16, April 2, 1868, Weed to Seward, April 1, 1868, H. Stanbery to Seward, May 15, 1868, R. H. Pruyn to Seward, April 8, 1868, Webster to Seward, May 6, 1868, A. Wakeman to Seward, July 11, 1868.

22. Johnson Papers, Moore Notes, May [5], 1868; Bancroft Papers, Seward to Bancroft, June 22, 1868; Welles, *Diary,* III, 335, 336, 341, 345; Dewitt, op. cit. 445–6.

23. S. J. Barrows, "Personal Reminiscences of William H. Seward," *The Atlantic Monthly*, LXIII (March 1889), 389.
24. Johnson Papers, Seward to Johnson [May 16, 1868], Johnson to Seward, May 27, 1868, Conkling to Seward, May 29, 1868, Moore Notes, May 18, 29, 30, 1868; J. M. Schofield, *Forty-six Years in the Army* (New York, 1897), 413–18.
25. SP, Seward to Adams, Sept. 7, 1868 (p. d.); Welles, *Diary*, III, 428–9.
26. SP, Seward to Sumner (p. d.), R. A. Wilson to Weed, June 2, 1868, Seward to Z. Chandler, June 22, 1868 (p. d.), Hunter to Seward, June 13, 1868, Sumner to Seward [June 1868], Seward to Sanford, Sept. 25, 1868 (p. d.); G. H. Stuart, *The Department of State* (New York, 1949), 137–8.
27. Bigelow, Diary, Sept. 23, 24, 1868, and *Retrospections*, IV, 232.
28. Seward, *Works*, V, 540–88.

NOTES FOR CHAPTER 33

1. NA M77 R57, Seward to Bigelow, June 3, 12, 17, Sept. 6, Oct. 30, Nov. 6, Dec. 16, 1865; NA M77 R79, Seward to Adams, Sept. 25, 27, 1865; Johnson Papers, 9c 64, Moore Diary, Feb. 14, 1867, and 9a 124, ibid. Oct. 24, 1866, and [1867].
2. NA M121 R31, 32, Webb to Seward, Oct. 15, 1863, June 6, 1864, R24 Seward to Webb, Dec. 7, 1863; F. O. 5, vol. 1132, Thornton to Stanley, Aug. 24, 1868; SP, Seward to Hale, Nov. 19, 1868 (dupl.); NA, Recommendations for Appointments, Webb and T. Rainey to H. J. Raymond, Nov. 3, 1865, M. A. Zabriskie to A. Johnson, April 25, 1867; D. L. Smiley, *Lion of White Hall; The Life of Cassius M. Clay* (Madison, 1962), 197–214. Another vexation was the effort of Jeremiah Black to raise a storm over the guano island of Alta Vela. The evidence indicates that Seward refused to interfere because he did not wish to prejudice his efforts to obtain Samaná Bay from Santo Domingo. See also my *Thurlow Weed*, 330–34.
3. Bigelow Papers, Seward to Bigelow, June 3, 17, Sept. 6, 1865; NA M77 R57, Seward to Bigelow, June 14, July 3, 13, 24, 31, Aug. 24, Sept. 6, 20, 1865; AAE, Montholon à Drouyn de Lhuys, Aug. 14, Sept. 5, 1865; Bigelow, *Retrospections*, II, 182–3.
4. Wriston, op. cit. 780–86; J. M. Schofield, op. cit. 380–93; P. H. Sheridan, *Personal Memoirs of P. H. Sheridan* (2 vols., New York, 1888), II, 214–19; NA M99 R70, Seward Circular, July 26, 1865; Perkins, op. cit. 470–75.
5. AAE, Montholon à Drouyn de Lhuys, Nov. 20, 1865; Clarendon Papers, Bruce to Clarendon, Dec. 18, 26, 1865, Feb. 9, 1866; NA M77 R57, Seward to Bigelow, Nov. 6, 27, Dec. 16, 1865; Johnson Papers, Montholon to Seward, Nov. 27, 1865 (copy); Seward's draft for Johnson's message of December 1865.
6. PRFA, 1865, Part 3, 818–37; NA M121 R33, Webb Memorandum (copy); M77 R57, Seward to Bigelow May 12, 1866; Welles, *Diary*, II, 479;

Bigelow, *Retrospections*, II, 215; AAE, Montholon à Drouyn de Lhuys, March 20, April 9, May 1, 7, 1866; Gardiner Collection, E. P. Smith to H. C. Carey, May 4, 1866; New York *Tribune*, April 24–28, 1866; C. A. Duniway, "Reasons for the Withdrawal of the French from Mexico," Amer. Hist. Assoc. *Annual Report* (1902), I, 321.

7. SP, Weed to Seward, May 17, 1866, P. Y. Cutler to Seward, July 23, 1866, H. Emmons to Seward, Oct. 24, 1866; New York *Times*, May 23, 1866; New York *Herald*, Sept. 29, 1866; NA M77 R58, Seward to Bigelow, Oct. 8, 1866; WP, Santa Anna to Weed, Oct. 8, 22, 1866; Welles, *Diary*, III, 131, 132; AAE, Montholon à Drouyn de Lhuys, May 29, 1866; F. W. Seward, *Reminiscences of a War-Time Statesman and Diplomat* (New York and London, 1916), 290; J. M. Callahan, *Evolution of Seward's Mexican Policy* (Morgantown, 1909), 83.

8. AAE, Berthemy à Moustier, Jan. 10, 14, 16, 20, April 22, May 2, 31, June 17, 1867.

9. Bigelow, *Retrospections*, III, 609–20; F. O. 5, vol. 1104, Bruce to Stanley, Jan. 8, 1867; SP, Bigelow to Seward, Nov. 30, 1866, J. L. O'Sullivan to O. R. Seward, Sept. 14, 1871; *Cong. Globe*, 39th Cong., 2nd sess., 267, 458–60; Welles, *Diary*, II, 622–6; Browning, *Diary*, II, 111–12; AAE, Montholon à Lavalette, Oct. 1, 1866, Montholon à Moustier, Nov. 29, Dec. 11, 1866, Berthemy à Moustier, Jan. 4, 1867; Perkins, op. cit. 534–8.

10. Welles, *Diary*, II, 648; SP, Louis De Geer to C. J. M. Stolbrand, May 5, 1866, Mercier to Seward, Jan. 6, 1867, Sanford to Seward, June 7, 1867, T. P. Smith (consul at La Rochelle) to Seward, Dec. 18, 1867; London *Morning Herald*, May 10, 1866, London *Daily News*, May 10, 1866.

NOTES FOR CHAPTER 34

1. NA M77 R79, Hunter to Adams, May 15, 1865, Seward to Adams, Sept. 7, Nov. 30, 1865; Welles, *Diary*, II, 327; SP, Hunter to Seward, June 22, 1865, Seward's draft of Johnson's message; Layard Papers, Russell to Layard, Aug. 7, 1865.

2. Bigelow, *Retrospections*, V, 36; NA M30 R86, Russell to Adams, Aug. 30, Oct. 14, 1865, M77 R79, Seward to Adams, Sept. 27, Nov. 4, 1865, Feb. 14, March 5, 1866; Adams, Diary, Sept. 4, Dec. 20, 1865, March 5, 1866; Clarendon Papers, Bruce to Clarendon, Dec. 26, 1865, Feb. 5, 1866.

3. F. O. 5, vol. 1063, Bruce to Clarendon, Feb. 14, 1866; SP, Russell to Adams, Feb. 28, 1866 (copy), Adams to Russell, March 1, 1866 (copy), Seward to Sanford, March 5, 1866 (p. d.); Bancroft Papers, Blatchford to Bancroft, May 9, 1866; M. A. DeW. Howe, *The Life and Letters of George Bancroft* (2 vols., New York, 1908), II, 158–63; R. B. Nye, *George Bancroft, Brahmin Rebel* (New York, 1944), 231–5.

4. Dudley Papers (Huntington Library), Geo. Bemis to T. H. Dudley, April 10, 1866; *Cong. Globe*, 39th Cong., 1st sess., 4194, 4197; SP, L. Bill to Seward, May 2, 1866; New York *Times*, May 2, 1866.

5. SP, Fenian Brotherhood of Chicago to Seward, Sept. 21, 1865 (copy), Bruce to Seward, Dec. 26, 1865. I have relied to a considerable extent upon Wm. D'Arcy, "The Fenian Movement in the United States," a 1947 Ph.D. dissertation at the Catholic University of America.

6. Adams, Diary, Jan. 14, 1866; NA M77 R79, Seward to Adams, March 10, 22, 31, 1866; F. O. 115, vol. 453, Bruce to Clarendon, April 17, 1866; Clarendon Papers, Bruce to Clarendon, Nov. 26, Dec. 4, 12, 31, 1865, March 5, 16, April 9, 23, May 28, 29, 1866; D'Arcy, op. cit., 95.

7. NA M77 R79, Seward to Adams, June 4, 9, 1866; SP, A. Bryson to Seward, June 5, 1866, R. Schell to Seward, June 28, 1866, M. McMahon to Seward, July 14, 1866, Weed to Seward, July 31, 1866, B. F. Mullen to Seward, Nov. 11, 1866; House Exec. Docs., 39th Cong., 1st sess., no. 154; PAC, G6, vol. 17, Bruce to Monck, July 18, 1866; F. O. 115, vol. 454, Bruce to Stanley, Oct. 30, Nov. 19, 26, 1866; D'Arcy, op. cit. 159–66, 211.

8. Welles, Diary, II, 638–9, 642; Browning, Diary, II, 117–18. There is no record of any invitation whatever to Pius IX, either in the National Archives or in the Seward Papers.

9. NA M77 R79, Seward to Adams, July 14, Aug. 27, Oct. 8, 1866; PRFA, 1867, part 1, Stanley to Bruce, Nov. 30, 1866.

10. NA M77 R80, Seward to Adams, Jan. 12, April 16, 1867; PRFA, 1867, pt. 1, 191–3, Stanley to Bruce, March 9, 1867; Adams, Diary, March 23, 1867; Bright Papers, Seward to Sumner, Dec. 6, 1867.

11. Adams, Diary, entries from May 2 to Dec. 24, 1867; NA M77 R80, Seward to Adams, May 2, 20, June 12, Aug. 12, Nov. 21, 29, Dec. 18–20, 1867, Jan. 13, 1868; F. O. 115, vols. 465–6, Bruce to Stanley, Aug. 5, 1867, Ford to Stanley, Dec. 8, 1867; SP, Adams to Seward, Nov. 21, 1867, Seward to Sumner, Dec. 6, 1867 (p. d.), Geo. Bemis to Seward, Dec. 7, 1867, Sumner to Seward, Dec. 9, 1867, Helper to Seward, Jan. 31, 1868, Seward to Helper, Feb. 5, 1868 (p. d.); Browning, Diary, II, 177.

12. F. O. 115, vol. 466, Bruce to Stanley, Aug. 26, 1867, F. O. 5, vol. 1129, Thornton to Seward, March 6, 1868, Thornton to Monck, March 5, 9, 1868, Thornton to Stanley, March 23, April 27, 1868, Monck to Thornton, March 3, 1868.

13. NA M77 R80, Seward to R. Johnson, July 20, Sept. 14, Nov. 27, Dec. 20, 1868, Jan. 11, 12, 20, 1869, M30 R94, R. Johnson to Seward, Jan. 15, 1869; F. O. 5, vol. 1131, Thornton to Stanley, July 13, 1868, 1133, Thornton to Stanley, Dec. 8, 1868; SP, R. Johnson to Seward, Dec. 26, 1868, Jan. 13, 14, 1869, Seward to R. Johnson, Jan. 13, March 3, 1869 (p. ds.), H. A. Weed to Seward [Jan. 1869]; R. Johnson Papers, Seward to R. Johnson, March 13, 1869; WP, Benj. Moran to Weed, Jan. 9, 1869; Adams, Diary, Nov. 19, 1868, April 14, 15, 19, 1869; Browning, Diary, II, 227–8; Chas. Sumner, Charles Sumner: His Complete Works, with Introduction by Hon. George Frisbie Hoar (20 vols., Boston, 1900), XVII, 53–93; Department of State, Correspondence Concerning Claims Against Great Britain (Washington, D.C., 1870), III, 742–55; Moran, Diary, Sept. 7, 19,

1868, Jan. 14, March 8, 1869; AAE, Berthemy à Lavalette, Jan. 16, 26, Feb. 2, 1869; New York *Tribune,* Nov. 9, 1868; New York *Times,* Nov. 11, 1868; Bright Papers, Henry Adams to Bright, May 30, 1869; R. Johnson Papers, Seward to Johnson, March 13, 1869; B. C. Steiner, *Life of Reverdy Johnson* (Baltimore, 1914), 233–58; Holt, op. cit. 111–20; A. Nevins, *Hamilton Fish: The Inner History of the Grant Administration* (New York, 1936), 148–52, 385–99; R. L. Morrow, "The Negotiation of the Anglo-American Treaty of 1870," *Am. Hist. Review* XXXIX (July 1934), 663–81.

NOTES FOR CHAPTER 35

1. NA M77 R78, Seward to Adams, Jan. 15, 1864; SP, Seward to P. Tomppert *et al.,* May 10, 1867 (p. d.); J. Q. Adams, *An Oration Delivered at Plymouth, December 22, 1802* (Boston, 1802), 7, 30, 31.

2. NA M77 R134, Seward to Harvey, July 9, 1862, R56, Seward to Dayton, Sept. 21, 1863, R78, Seward to Adams, Aug. 15, 1864, R104, Seward to R. B. Van Valkenburgh, July 15, 1868, R39, Seward to J. Ross Browne, Aug. 17, 1868; SP, Seward to John Sherman, Dec. 23, 1863 (copy), Blatchford to Seward, April 7, 1864, Bigelow to Sanford, May 19, 1864; *Cong. Globe,* 38th Cong., 1st sess., 865, *App.,* 259; Welles, *Diary,* I, 543; J. Grossman, *William Sylvis, Pioneer of American Labor* (New York, 1945), 145–8; T. Dennett, *Americans in Eastern Asia* (New York, 1922), 540, and note.

3. SP, Seward to Chandler, May 14, 1864 (p. d.); Morgan Papers, Seward to Morgan, May 30, 1864; *Cong. Globe,* 38th Cong., 1st sess., 3065–6, 3126; *Statement of the Origin, Organization and Progress of the Russian-American Telegraph* (Rochester, N.Y., 1866), 43–53, 134–5; R. L. Thompson, *Wiring a Continent* (Princeton, 1947), 427–39.

4. ABIIP, Stoeckl à Gortchakov, July 27, 1868; F. O. 5, vol. 1104, Bruce to Stanley, Jan. 14, 1867, vol. 1132, Thornton to Stanley, Sept. 14, 1868; F. O. 115, vol. 465, Bruce to Stanley, May 13, 1867; SP, Seward to E. J. Morris, Aug. 19, 1868, Jan. 2, 1869 (p. ds.); NA M77 R79, Seward to Adams, April 25, 1866; Johnson Papers, Seward draft for Johnson's message of Dec. 3, 1866; AAE, Berthemy à Ministre des Affaires Etrangères, Jan. 1, 1869.

5. SP, Seward to Sanford, Aug. 17, 1868 (p. d.), Wm. M. Warden to Seward, Oct. 28, 1868; Welles, *Diary,* III, 504. Malloy, op. cit. I, ix–xxii, lists 47 treaties, conventions and agreements signed from March 4, 1861 to March 4, 1869.

6. Seward, *Works,* V, 470–73; Seward Letters (N. Y. P. L.), Seward to M. O. Roberts, Dec. 26, 1866; NA M77 R58, Seward to Dix, Jan. 18, 1867; SP, Seward to Count Wydenbruck, July 1, 1867 (p. d.), Weed to Seward, July 2 [1867], E. L. Plumb to R. S. Chew, Feb. 27, 1868, Romero to Seward, Feb. 27, 1868; A. Johnson Papers, Proclamation of July 22,

1867; J. F. Rippy, *The United States and Mexico* (New York, 1931), 275–8; J. M. Callahan, *The Evolution of Seward's Mexican Policy* (Morgantown, W. Va., 1909), 87.

7. Cleveland Papers, vol. 1, series ii, Seward to J. Kilpatrick, June 2, 1866 (transcript); NA M77 R29, Seward to A. Morrell, March 9, 1868; Bright Papers, Sumner to Bright, May 21, 1866; AAE, Berthemy à Moustier, March 18, 1867, April 8, 1868.

8. NA M77 R29, Seward to R. H. Rousseau, Dec. 12, 1866; F. O. 5, vol. 1068, Bruce to Stanley, Dec. 8, 1866.

9. NA M77 R22, Seward to A.A. Hall, April 9, 1864, R28, Seward to Riotti, Sept. 8, 1863; F. O. 5, vols. 1132, 1133, Thornton to Stanley, Oct. 26, Nov. 2, 3, 1868; WP, A. B. Dickinson to E. Croswell, Jan. 4, 1865 (copy); SP, D. Ammen to Seward, June 16, 1865, Grant to Seward, Nov. 10, 1865, S. D. Fulton to Seward, June 7, 1867, Seward to Wakeman, Feb. 13, 1868 (dupl.), Pruyn to Seward, Sept. 20, 25, 1868, A. S. Hewitt to Seward, Oct. 26, 1868, Seward to Grant, Feb. 14, 1869 (copy), Cushing to Anna Seward, Feb. 16, 1869; SP, M. Samper to Cushing, March 9, 1869, T. Perez to Cushing, March 16, 1869; Caleb Cushing Papers, Seward to Cushing, April 15, 19, 1869; Seward, *Works*, V, 589–92; *Senate Docs.*, 56th Cong., 1st sess., 34–51, Doc. no. 237; AAE, Berthemy à Lavalette, Jan. 21, 1869; E. T. Parks, *Colombia and the United States* (Durham, 1935), 338–47; Holt, op. cit. 111, note.

10. AAE, Seward to Mercier, May 23, 1861; NA M77 R104, Seward to Pruyn, July 23, Aug. 1, Oct. 21, Nov. 15, 1861, Feb. 5, March 21, Sept. 25, 1862, Jan. 31, June 29, July 7, Aug. 20, Sept. 1, Oct. 3, 1863, M133 R4, Pruyn to Seward, June 16, 24, 27, 1863, M77 R78, Seward to Adams, Sept. 9, Nov. 30, 1863.

11. NA M133 R7, Portman to Seward, July 14, 1866, M77 R104, Seward to Portman, Sept. 10, 1866; Dennett, op. cit. 401–5.

12. NA M77 R104, Seward to R. H. Pruyn, Jan. 29, 1863, Dec. 14, 1864, Seward to R. B. Van Valkenburgh, July 6, 1867, July 14, 1868, M133 R8, Van Valkenburgh to Seward, Feb. 19, Oct. 7, 1867; SP, S. Williams to F. W. Seward, March 29 [1867], Weed to Seward, April 3, 1867, Pruyn to F. W. Seward, May 2, 1867, A. Wakeman to F. W. Seward, May 17, 1867, D. D. Porter to F. W. Seward, June 3, 1867, Seward to Ono Tonogoro and Matsumoto Indayu, Jan. 24, 1868 (copy).

13. SP, Moustier to Berthemy, March 29, 1867 (copy in translation); NA M77 R38, Seward to Burlingame, May 6, 1867, R104, Seward to Van Valkenburgh, Jan. 27, 1868; F. O. 5, vol. 1106, Bruce to Stanley, May 13, 1867; T. Dennett, "Seward's Far Eastern Policy," *Am. Hist. Rev.*, XXVIII (Oct. 1922–July 1923), 51–9. Seward had heard that France planned a protectorate in Korea, and Dennett believed that he proposed the Franco-American expedition because he was convinced that the partition of Asia had begun and the United States should share in the spoils. I find no evidence to support this conjecture.

14. NA M92 R25, Burlingame to Seward, Dec. 14, 1867, M77 R39, Seward to J. Ross Browne, Sept. 7, 1868; F. O. 5, vol. 1131, Thornton to Stanley, July 15, 1868, vol. 1132, Seward to Thornton, Aug. 14, 1868; SP, Lazette Worden to A. Seward, July 31, 1868, to Anna Seward, Aug. 4, 1868; Malloy, op. cit. I, 234–6; T. Dennett, *Americans in Eastern Asia*, 539–43; F. W. Williams, *Anson Burlingame and the First Chinese Mission to Foreign Powers* (New York, 1912), 144–6 and *passim;* K. Biggerstaff, "The Official Chinese Attitude Toward the Burlingame Mission," *Am. Hist. Rev.*, XLI (July 1936), 682–701. The mission had real success in England but not on the Continent.

NOTES FOR CHAPTER 36

1. Welles, *Diary*, II, 393; SP, H. E. Peck to F. W. Seward, April 3, 1866; F. O. 115, vol. 449, Clarendon to Bruce, Jan. 20, 1866; Clarendon Papers, Bruce to Clarendon, Feb. 27, 1866; F. W. Seward, *Seward*, III, 311.

2. SP, Raasloff to Seward, Dec. 6, 1864, Jan. 13, 17, 1869, Seward to Yeaman, Sept. 23, 28, 1867 (p. ds.), Porter to F. W. Seward, Nov. 11, 25, 1867, Seward to Raasloff, Nov. 15, 1867 (dupl.), draft for Johnson's December 1867 message to Congress, Seward to E. Pierrepoint, Dec. 25, 1867 (p. d.), Anthony to Seward, Dec. 26, 1867, Seward to Anthony, Dec. 31, 1867 (dupl.), Sanford to Seward, Jan. 10, 13, 1868, Schell to Seward, Feb. 9, 1868, Yeaman to Seward, March 23, 1868; Stanton Papers, Seward to Stanton, July 6, 1866; Welles, *Diary*, III, 40, 95–7, 124–5; New York *Times*, July 17, 1867; New York *Tribune*, Sept. 6, 1867; Adams, Diary, July 3, 1867; B. Harte, *The Poetical Works of Bret Harte* (Boston and New York, 1904), 43–4; M. Twain, *The Writings of Mark Twain* (37 vols., New York, 1929), VII, 134–6; C. C. Tansill, *The Purchase of the Danish West Indies* (Baltimore, 1932), 5–153; D. M. Dozer, "Anti-Imperialism in the United States," unpublished dissertation, Harvard, 1936, 13–20, 27–8; J. G. Whelan, "William Henry Seward, Expansionist," unpublished dissertation, Rochester, 1959, 186–91.

3. Welles, *Diary*, I, 519, II, 409, 630–31, 642–3, III, 7, 40; Browning, *Diary*, II, 119; NA M77 R143, Seward to Koerner, May 6, 1864; SP, H. E. Peck to F. W. Seward, April 3, 1866, J. P. O'Sullivan to F. W. Seward [Jan. 1867?], D. Hatch to D. D. Porter, Feb. 9, 20, 1867, Seward to Jos. W. Fabens, Aug. 15, 1868 (p.d.), Seward to Sumner, Nov. 9, 1868 (p.d.); F. O. 5, vol. 1066, Seward to Bruce, July 11, 1866, Bruce to Clarendon, July 16, 1866, vol. 1104, Bruce to Stanley, Jan. 8, 1867; Sumner Papers, Seward to Sumner, Nov. 9, 1868; Dozer, op. cit. 13, 32–3; Whelan, op. cit. 191–8; C. C. Tansill, *The United States and Santo Domingo* (Baltimore, 1938), 213–86; F. W. Seward, *Seward*, III, 344; R. W. Logan, *The Diplomatic Relations of the United States With Haiti, 1776–1891* (Chapel Hill, 1941), 316–22, 328–31; L. L. Montague, *Haiti and the United States, 1714–1938* (Durham, 1940), 92–3, 97–103.

4. Bancroft Papers, Seward to Bancroft, May 25, Aug. 8, 1867; NA M77 R80, Seward to Adams, Oct. 28, 1867; SP, F. W. Seward to W. H. Seward [March, 1868], Dec. 26, 1868, R. P. Noah to Seward, July 15, 1867, Bigelow to Seward, Oct. 6, 1868, Blatchford to Seward, Oct. 10, 1868, Sherman to Seward, Nov. 6, 1868, Seward to Sumner, Nov. 9, 1868 (p.d.), B. Moran to Wm. Hunter, Dec. 30, 1868, Schell to Wakeman, Feb. 3, 1869, Wakeman to Seward, Feb. 3, 1869; Bigelow Papers, Seward to Bigelow, Oct. 8, 1868; F. O. 5, vol. 1133, Thornton to Stanley, Dec. 5, 1868; Whelan, op. cit. 198–208; P. S. Foner, *A History of Cuba and Its Relations with the United States* (2 vols., N.Y., 1963), 149–78.
5. F. O. 5, vol. 1132, Thornton to Stanley, Sept. 28, 1868; B. Dyer, "Robert J. Walker on Acquiring Greenland and Iceland," *Miss. Valley Hist. Rev.*, XXVII (Sept. 1940), 263–6; Isabel C. Barrows, "Two Months with Mr. Seward," *Atlantic Monthly* (March 1889), 392.
6. AAE, Berthemy à Moustier, Oct. 16, 1867; F. O. 115, vol. 465, Bruce to Stanley, May 13, 1867; SP, W. Brooke to Seward, Dec. 30, 1867, Seward to S. Cameron, Jan. 9, 1868 (dupl.), G. R. Latham to F. W. Seward, Jan. 21, 1868.
7. NA M77 R79, Seward to Adams, April 25, 1866, R137, Seward to Clay, Aug. 31, 1868; Adams, Diary, Aug. 31, 1867; *Cong. Globe*, 32nd Cong., 1st sess., 2100, 39th Cong., 1st sess., 3858; *Senate Exec. Docs.*, 52nd Cong., 2nd sess., 139–40; SP, Thos. N. Staley to Seward, Feb. 17, 1866, A. Wakeman to Seward, Aug. 15, 1866, E. M. McCook to F. W. Seward, Nov. 18, 1867; F. O. 5, vol. 1104, Bruce to Stanley, Jan. 8, 1867, vol. 1158, Thornton to Stanley, Aug. 17, 1865, to Clarendon, Jan. 4, Feb. 6, 1869; Browning, *Diary*, II, 90; Welles, *Diary*, II, 596, 601, 604; Holt, op. cit. 102–5; Kuykendall, *The Hawaiian Kingdom, 1854–1874* (Honolulu, 1953), 198–206, 210–25; T. Morgan, *Hawaii. A Century of Economic Change, 1778–1876* (Cambridge, Mass., 1948), 210–11; Whelan, op. cit. 166–86.

1. PAC G6, vol. 17, Bruce to Monck, Feb. 21, March 2, 1866; F. O. 5, vol. 1067, Bruce to Stanley, Sept. 17, 1866, vol. 1104, Jan. 12, 19, 1867, vol. 1106, March 30, 1867; PRFA, 1866, pt. 1, 27–8; A. Johnson Papers, Seward to Johnson [Feb. 1867]; *Cong. Globe*, 39th Cong., 1st sess., 3548; *House Executive Documents*, 39th Cong., 1st sess., no. 128, 32–4; SP, Wm. Wilkeson to Seward, March 14, 19, 1865, Goldwin Smith to Seward, April 16, 1865, J. C. Maguire to Seward, May 5, 1865, Jas. W. Taylor to Seward, March 1, 1867; J. M. Callahan, *Alaska Purchase*, 19–20; A. C. Gluek, *Minnesota and the Manifest Destiny of the Canadian Northwest* (Toronto, 1965), 213; J. P. Smith, op. cit. 42–50. The bill to which Seward referred in his communication to Johnson was one drawn up by James Wickes Taylor and introduced by Banks. It proposed to admit the Canadian provinces to the United States, organized as territorial and

state governments. Seward's position on reciprocity remained the same down to the end of his term of office—SP, Seward to C. J. M. Gwinn, Nov. 30, 1868 (p.d.).

2. Russian Ministry of For. Aff., Asiatic Dept. 1857–68. I-9, no. 4, Papers relating to Alaska. Translations by Hunter Miller. Hereafter cited as Russian Archives, Alaska (in Mss. Division of the Library of Congress). Konstantin to Gortchakov, April 3, 1857, Gortchakov to Konstantin, Dec. 1, 1857, Stoeckl to Gortchakov, Dec. 23, 1859, Jan. 4, 1860; NA, U.S. Embassy, Russia. Alaska Cession. Memorandum concerning the Cession, April 29, 1857, Stoeckl à Gortchakov, Dec. 2, 1857, Dec. 23, 1859, Jan 4, 1860; Hunter Miller, "The Purchase of Alaska," 55–151; V. J. Farrar, *The Annexation of Russian America to the United States* (Washington, D.C., 1937), 1–13; A. G. Mazour, "The Prelude to Russia's Departure from America," *The Pacific Historical Review*, X (1941), 311–19; H. M. Macpherson, "The Interest of William McKendree Gwin in the Purchase of Alaska," ibid., III (1934), 28–38; T. C. Lin, "The Amur Question Between China and Russia," ibid. 1–27; R. Luthin, "The Sale of Alaska," *Slavonic Review*, XVI (July 1937), 2; F. A. Golder, "The Purchase of Alaska," *Amer. Hist. Review*, XXV (April 1920), 411–17.

3. NA M77 R136, Seward to Clay, Oct. 16, 1861, Feb. 20, 1862, Dec. 8, 1863, to B. Taylor, Dec. 7, 23, 1862, M35 R19, Clay to Seward, Nov. 13, 1861; RTL, Seward to Lincoln, Sept. 1, 1861; SP, Seward to A. Froment, Oct. 16, 1863 (copy), Stoeckl to Seward, Oct. 17, 1863; Welles, *Diary*, I, 480; AAE, Mercier à Drouyn de Lhuys, May 11, 1863; H. E. Blinn, "Seward and the Polish Rebellion of 1863," *Amer. Hist. Rev.*, XLV (1939–40), 828–33; Hunter Miller, op. cit. 151–65.

4. NA M35 R20, Clay to Seward, Nov. 14, 1864, Jan. 24, 1865; *House Exec. Docs.*, 40th Cong., 2nd sess., no. 177, Seward to Clay, Dec. 26, 1864; Sumner Papers, Seward to Sumner "Friday evening" [March 29, 1867]; Browning, *Diary*, II, 137; Welles, *Diary*, III, 66, 75; NA, U.S. Embassy. Russia. Alaska Cession, Stoeckl à Gortchakov, Feb. 26, March 18, April 19, 1867; NA M99 R82, Seward to Stoeckl, March 23, 1867; Hunter Miller, op. cit. 221–7, 230–48, 277–84; F. W. Seward, *Reminiscences*, 361–2; Farrar, op. cit. 25–53; Golder, op. cit. 418–21; H. W. Sibley, "Memoirs of Hiram Sibley," *The Rochester Historical Society, Publication Fund Series*, vol. II (Rochester, N.Y., 1923), 129–30; Hunter Miller demonstrates conclusively that Stoeckl's telegram about the details of the treaty, which cost over $9000 to send, was paid for by Stoeckl, not Seward.

5. SP, Seward to Peter Cooper *et al.*, Jan. 20, 1868 (p. d.), J. B. Weller to Seward, April 3, 1867, Blatchford to Seward, April 10, 1867, G. V. Fox to F. W. Seward, April 8, 1867, H. J. Raymond to L. L. Crounse, April 2, 1867, J. V. L. Pruyn to Seward, April 8, 1867, S. Stevens to Seward, April 10, 1867; Stanton Papers, Seward to Stanton, March 14, 1867; Johnson Papers (Moore Notes), May 2, 1867; *Cong. Globe*, 40th Cong.,

1st sess., 458; Bigelow, Diary, March 30, April 3, 1867, and *Retrospections*, IV, 58; New York *Tribune*, April 1–11, 1867; C. Cole, *Memoirs of Cornelius Cole* (New York, 1908), 281–5; V. J. Farrar, "Senator Cole and the Purchase of Alaska," *The Washington Hist. Quart.*, XIV (1923), 243–7; T. A. Bailey, "Why the United States Purchased Alaska," *The Pacific Hist. Review*, III (1934), 42–6; Dozer, op. cit. 5, 6–9; Whelan, op. cit. 107–9.

6. F. O. 115, vol. 465, Bruce to Stanley, April 2, 16, 1867; SP, T. Stevens to Seward, April 11, 1867, S. Stevens to Seward, April 10, 1867, Sanford to Seward, May 10, 1867, Peter Cooper *et al.* to Seward, Jan. 1, 1868, Fillmore to Seward, May 23, 1867, Wm. Schouler to Seward, April 9, 1867, A. B. Johnson to Seward, April 10, 1867; WP, G. F. Baker to Weed, April 30, 1868; NA M35 R21, Clay to Seward, May 10, 1867; Bailey, op. cit. 42; NA U.S. Embassy. Russia. Alaska Cession. Stoeckl à Gortchakov, April 3, 19, 1867; AAE, Berthemy à Moustier, April 4, 1867; Bright Papers, Sumner to Bright, April 16, 1867; Hunter Miller, op. cit. 322, 331, and "Russian Opinion on the Cession of Alaska," *Amer. Hist. Review*, XLVIII (April 1943), 521–31; F. W. Seward, *Reminiscences*, 364.

7. ABIIP, Stoeckl à Gortchakov, March 20, May 18, 1868; SP, Seward to Jos. Henry, April 10, 1867 (p. d.), H. B. Anthony to Seward, May 1, 1867, Seward to R. P. Spaulding, May 8, 1867 (p. d.), Seward to Banks [1867] (p. d.), Banks to Seward, Jan. 10, 1868, Walker to Seward, Feb. 9 [1868]; AAE, Berthemy à Moustier, April 8, 1867; Johnson Papers, Seward to Johnson, [July 2, 1868], Walker to Seward, July 2, 1868; Henry A. Wise Letter Books (N.-Y. Hist. Soc.), G. V. Fox to Dr. Wise, Feb. 3, 1868; Washington *Daily Morning Chronicle*, Jan. 25, 28–30, July 1, 1868; Hunter Miller, op. cit. 333–7; Farrar, op. cit. 83–8; Golder, op. cit. 422–3; Luthin, op. cit. 2–8.

8. *Cong. Globe*, 40th Cong., 2nd sess., 2528, 3663–9, 3908, *App.*, 385–92, 453–5; SP, Banks to Seward, June 27, July 15, 1868; Hunter Miller, op. cit. 467–8; Bailey, op. cit. 47–8; Dozer, op. cit. 22–5 and Appendix A.

9. Johnson Papers, Roll 51, series 9B (in Johnson's handwriting, and evidently written shortly after the conversation with Seward on Sept. 6, 1868); Bigelow, Diary, Sept. 23, 1868, and *Retrospections*, IV, 216–17; AAE, Berthemy à Moustier, Sept. 22, 1868; Hunter Miller, op. cit. 495–547, examines the bribery charge at length, but reaches no definite conclusions; House of Representatives, *Reports of Committees*, 40th Cong., 3rd sess., no. 35, Feb. 27, 1869, also *Executive Documents*, 40th Cong., 3rd sess., no. 177; New York *Herald*, Jan. 27, 1869; Golder, op. cit. 424, and "The American Civil War through the Eyes of a Russian Diplomat," *Amer. Hist. Rev.*, XXVI (April 1921), note 1, 454; Luthin, op. cit. 9–13; Wm. A. Dunning, "Paying for Alaska," *Polit. Sci. Quart.*, XXVII (Sept. 1912), 385–98; Whelan, op. cit. 115–22; AAE, Berthemy à Lavalette, March 1, 1869. There are some peculiar features of the stories regarding

the use of the $200,000. Seward's statements to Johnson and Bigelow, as recorded by them, vary as to the amounts paid to the individuals concerned. Again, while Bigelow's Diary and Johnson's memorandum agree that Seward said Stevens received $10,000, Bigelow's account in the *Retrospections* gives this amount as $1000, and adds that Seward said that, as Stevens had died, he himself still had the money. The New York *Herald* of Jan. 27, 1869, reported the testimony of one Louis Tasistro before the House committee. According to the *Herald*'s Washington correspondent, Tasistro said Stoeckl told him that only $5,000,000 went to St. Petersburg, and that he, Tasistro, "thought the balance went to Banks, Butler and Seward." This testimony does not appear in the House committee report, which is mainly remarkable for what it does not prove, and abounds in denials, charges, and countercharges.

10. SP, Sanford to Seward, May 10, 1867, Bancroft to Seward, June 15, 1867, J. W. Taylor to Seward, May 17, 1867, Feb. 26, 1868; F. O. 115, vols. 465, 466, Bruce to Stanley, April 8, 16, Aug. 30, 1867; Adams, Diary, Aug. 3, 1867; Browning, *Diary*, II, 177; Bigelow, *Retrospections*, IV, 58; Lee Kohns Memorial Collection (N.Y. P. L.), Seward to Elwood Evans. Sept. 14, 1868; Shippee, op. cit. 200; Dozer, op. cit. 1–2, 6.

NOTES FOR CHAPTER 38

1. SP, Seward to Blatchford, Dec. 12, 1867 (p. d.), L. Worden to A. Seward, Feb. 5 [1869], Seward to Sanford, Jan. 13, Feb. 20, 1869 (p. ds.), to Wm. Henry Jr., Nov. 19, 1868, A. Badeau to Seward, Dec. 13, 1868; Welles, *Diary*, III, 465, 491–2, 508; Browning, *Diary*, II, 226–7; Bigelow, Diary, Oct. 29, 1868, March 27, 1869; Johnson Papers, Moore Diary, Jan. 19, 1869.

2. SP, Seward to Sanford, Feb. 20, 1869 (p. d.), Sanford to Seward, March 16, 1869, Wm. Hunter *et al.* to Seward, March 3, 1869, L. Worden to A. Seward, March 13 [1869], Blatchford to Seward, March 18 [1869]; AAE, Berthemy à Lavalette, March 4, 1869; Welles, *Diary*, III, 540–41; Browning, *Diary*, II, 243; Cushman Papers, Seward to C. Cushman, April 24, 1869; Bigelow, Diary, March 24, 27, 1869; NA M121 R33, Dispatches from United States Ministers to Brazil, Webb Memorandum, Nov. 10, 1865; New York *Times*, March 10, 1869.

3. These judgments are based on her photograph, and on the Risley-Seward letters in the Seward Papers, also on her article "A Diplomatic Episode," *Scribner's Magazine*, II (Nov. 1887), 585–602, and the rejoinder by E. L. Pierce, which is to be found in his *Sumner*, IV, 613–24. Olive's account of the negotiation for the Danish West Indies shows considerable ability. Pierce demonstrated that she was too hard on Sumner, but his own estimate of the importance of the islands makes strange reading in the light of later events.

4. SP, letters from Olive to Seward, 1868–70, T. Dimon to Seward, Sept.

28, Oct. 1, 1868, J. D. Andrews to Seward, Sept. 29, 1868; Bigelow, Diary, Oct. 9, 1868; Welles, *Diary*, III, 449; letters from Seward to Olive are in "Journal of a Trip Across the Continent," (N.Y.P.L.).

5. "Journal of a Trip," *passim;* SP, L. Worden to A. Seward, June 10, 28, July 18, Sept. 29, 1869, Feb. 14, March 13, May 9, 1870, Romero to Seward, Oct. 8, 1868, April 4, Aug. 2, 1869, C. Sleight to Seward, Nov. 6, 1869; Seward, *Works*, V, 569–87.

6. Seward materials (N.Y. P. L.), Seward to Olive Risley, Feb. 1, 1870; SP, Wilson to Seward, May 23, 1870, Seward to Wilson, May 28, 1870 (p. d.), Seward to J. S. Negley, June 30, 1870 (p. d.), Wm. Holmes to Seward, March 20, 1870, Edw. Thornton to Seward, April 22, 1870, Seward to Romero, April 25, 1870, to T. Lewis, May 19, 1870, to W. W. Campbell, June 9, 1870 (p. ds.), L. Worden to A. Seward, April 25, May 9, June 7, 29, July 28 [1870], H. A. Risley to Seward, Feb. 21, 22, 25, March 2, 9, April 4, 1870; Adams, Diary, May 28–30, Aug. 13, 1870; Goldwin Smith Papers (Cornell University), Smith to G. Waring, Aug. 8, 1870.

7. SP, Seward to "My dear Sister & Children," Aug. 26 [1870] (copy), to H. A. Risley, Sept. 20, 1870, to L. Worden, Oct. 27, 1870 (copy), to F. W. Seward, Dec. 7, 1870 (copy), to W. H. Seward, Jr., April 10, 1871, Brigham Young to Seward, Aug. 23, 1870, C. E. De Long to Fish, Oct. 10, 1870 (copy), W. P. Mangum to Seward, Oct. 24, 1870, F. W. Seward to W. H. Seward, Jan. 31, 1871, W. H. Seward, Jr., to W. H. Seward, Feb. 12, 1871, H. A. Risley to Seward, Jan. 22, 1871; Will of W. H. Seward, Surrogate's Office, Auburn, N. Y., dated at Peking, China. I have it on the best authority that letters revealing more clearly the attitude of the Sewards toward Olive and her father were destroyed by relatives before the Seward Papers were given to the University of Rochester.

8. SP, Seward to W. H. Seward, Jr., April 10, 1871, Seward to Risley, April 24, 1871, Risley to Seward, July 7, 24, 1871.

9. Fish Papers, Seward to Fish, March 6, 1871; Bancroft Papers, Seward to Bancroft, Sept. 18, 1871; SP, Seward to F. W. Seward, Sept. 2, 1871, J. L. O'Sullivan to O. R. Seward, Sept. 14, 1871.

10. New York *Sun*, Oct. 24, 1871.

11. F. W. Seward, *Seward*, III, 492.

12. New York *Tribune*, March 15, 1872; SP, L. Worden to A. Seward, Aug. 11 [1872]; F. W. Seward, *Seward*, III, 506.

13. F. W. Seward to O. H. Browning, Oct. 22, 1872 (Ill. State Historical Library); F. W. Seward, *Seward*, III, 507–8. Olive Risley Seward's share in the estate was $63,569.35. Her father wrote to Frederick and William Henry, Jr., of how great Seward's affection for her had been, and how he hoped that she would bear herself so as to merit their approbation and approval in the delicate position in which she now found herself. At the close of the year, Anna wrote to Augustus that Fred had finished

revising the *Travels* on the Friday before Christmas. That evening, said Anna, "Olive Risley" started for New York. On leaving she told Mrs. Worden that she would return after the holidays "to pack up." But in the years that followed Will helped her with her financial affairs.

Frederick continued work on "the life." It developed into three stout volumes, the first published in 1877, the last two in 1891—SP, H. A. Risley to F. W. Seward and W. H. Seward, Jr., Nov. 4, 1872, Anna Seward to Augustus Seward, Dec. 29, 1872.

Bibliography

The best bibliography for any book with pretense to scholarship is the notes. The following lists, by no means all-inclusive, are intended for ready reference by those interested in research.

I. PRIMARY SOURCES

A. Seward Correspondence

1. The Seward Papers in Rhees Library at the University of Rochester comprise some 150,000 items. There are thousands of letters to Seward, and preliminary drafts and duplicates of letters written by him. There are also many letters written by his wife and other members of his family that throw much light on his career. The collection also includes many of Seward's public and personal papers. All in all, it is a rich mine of information on the political and social history of the period from 1820 to 1870 and beyond.

2. Other important collections in Rhees Library are the Thurlow Weed, George Washington Patterson, and Elijah Miller Papers. The Weed Papers contain some 1200 letters from Seward to Weed, and other important political correspondence. The Patterson Papers have many letters from Seward and Weed, and other materials of interest to social and economic historians. The Miller Papers have a manuscript biography of Judge Miller by B. F. Hall, legal papers, and information about real estate transactions in the central part of New York State.

3. Seward letters are scattered all over the country. The principal depositories, other than Rhees Library, are the New York State Library at Albany, the Library of Congress, the New-York Historical Society, the University of Chicago Library, the Minnesota Historical Society,

the Clements Library at the University of Michigan, the Yale University Library, the Chamber of Commerce of the State of New York in New York City, and the Pierpont Morgan Library in New York City.

4. Frederick William Seward's three-volume biography of his father contains hundreds of Seward's letters to his family and to Weed and Patterson, many of which are not otherwise available. These have to be used with care. Frederick was selective in utilizing the material at hand, omitting parts of letters that seemed to him irrelevant, or that could be construed as unfavorable to some member of the family. The dates of the letters he gives are often wrong, as is shown by comparison where originals are available. There are many inaccuracies in his biography.

B. Published Papers and Works by William H. Seward

Seward's autobiography, which carries down to the New York State election of 1834, constitutes part of the first volume of Frederick Seward's biography of his father. *The Works of William H. Seward*, G. E. Baker, editor (5 vols., New York, 1853–84, and 5 vols., Boston, 1884), contain his principal speeches and public writings. A comprehensive list of his orations and speeches that appeared in pamphlet form may be found in the catalogue of the Library of Congress.

C. Other Manuscript Collections Used

1. Jacob Abbot Collection. New York State Library at Albany.
2. The Adams Papers. Massachusetts Historical Society. Microfilm.
3. C. F. Adams, Diary. Massachusetts Historical Society. Microfilm.
4. John A. Andrew Papers. Massachusetts Historical Society.
5. Antislavery Collection. New York State Historical Society.
6. Archives du Ministère des Affaires Étrangères. Correspondance Politique. États-Unis, 1861–69.
7. ABIIP. Archives of the Foreign Policy of Russia. Moscow. Stoeckl-Gortchakov Correspondence, 1866–68.
8. Central Archives, Moscow, Russia, Foreign Affairs. Library of Congress, Manuscripts Division. Photostatic Copies.
9. Moses Kimball Armstrong Papers. Minnesota Historical Society.
10. Frederic Bancroft Papers. Columbia University.
11. George Bancroft Papers. Massachusetts Historical Society.
12. Nathaniel P. Banks Papers. Library of Congress.
13. Nicholas Biddle Papers. Library of Congress.
14. John Bigelow Papers. New York Public Library.
15. John Prescott Bigelow Papers. Houghton Library.
16. William C. Bouck Papers. Cornell University.
17. John Bright Papers. British Museum.
18. Henry Peter Brougham Correspondence. University College, London.
19. Orville H. Browning Papers. University of Illinois.

20. James Buchanan Papers. Historical Society of Pennsylvania.
21. Burlingame Family Papers. Library of Congress.
22. Robert Carter Papers. Houghton Library.
23. Trumbull Cary Papers. Buffalo Historical Society.
24. Salmon P. Chase Papers. Historical Society of Pennsylvania.
25. Salmon P. Chase Papers. Library of Congress.
26. Andrew G. Chatfield Papers. Minnesota Historical Society.
27. Chautauqua Land Office "Minutes." Westfield, New York.
28. William G. Chisholm Papers. Virginia Historical Society Library, Richmond, Va.
29. Clarendon Papers. Bodleian Library, Oxford.
30. John M. Clayton Papers. Library of Congress.
31. John J. Crittenden Papers. Duke University.
32. George William Curtis Collection. Houghton Library.
33. Richard H. Dana Papers. Massachusetts Historical Society.
34. David Davis Papers. Chicago Historical Society.
35. F. M. Dearborn Collection. Houghton Library.
36. Dorothea L. Dix Manuscripts. Houghton Library.
37. Domestic Letters. Department of State, 1861–69. National Archives (microfilm).
38. Ferdinand J. Dreer Collection. Historical Society of Pennsylvania.
39. Ralph Waldo Emerson Journals. Houghton Library.
40. Frank M. Etting Collection. Historical Society of Pennsylvania.
41. Edward Everett Papers. Massachusetts Historical Society.
42. Millard Fillmore Papers. Buffalo Historical Society.
43. Azariah Flagg Papers. Columbia University.
44. E. C. Gardiner Collection. Historical Society of Pennsylvania.
45. Joshua Giddings Papers. Ohio State Historical Society.
46. Francis Granger Papers. Library of Congress.
47. Simon Gratz Collection. Historical Society of Pennsylvania.
48. Great Britain Foreign Office Records, America, 1860–69. Photostat copies in Library of Congress Manuscripts Division.
49. George M. Grier Papers. University of Rochester.
50. Josephine Sophie White Griffing Papers. Columbia University.
51. R. W. Griswold Manuscripts. Boston Public Library.
52. Jabez D. Hammond Papers. New-York Historical Society.
53. Townsend Harris Papers. College of the City of New York.
54. Howard Harrison Papers. Cornell University.
55. John Hay, Diary. Library of Congress.
56. Timothy Otis Howe Papers. State Historical Society, Madison, Wisconsin.
57. Holland Land Company Papers. Buffalo Historical Society.
58. Hamilton Morris Hutton Autograph Collection. University of Virginia Library.
59. Andrew Johnson Papers. Library of Congress. Microfilm.
60. Reverdy Johnson Manuscripts. Library of Congress.

61. Sir Austen Henry Layard Papers. British Museum.
62. Robert Todd Lincoln Papers. Library of Congress. Microfilm.
63. Alfred Manchester Papers. Essex Institute, Salem, Mass.
64. Horace Mann Papers. Massachusetts Historical Society.
65. Mellen-Chamberlain Collection. Boston Public Library.
66. Benjamin Moran Diary. Library of Congress.
67. Edwin B. Morgan Papers. Cornell University.
68. Edwin D. Morgan Papers. New York State Library at Albany.
69. *Notes* from the Russian Legation in Washington to the Department of State, 1865–70. National Archives.
70. John Gorham Palfrey Manuscripts. Houghton Library.
71. Palmerston Private Letter Books. British Museum.
72. Palmerston Papers. Historical Manuscripts Commission. National Register of Archives, London.
73. *Papers* Relating to the Cession of Alaska. U. S. Embassy, Russia. Library of Congress. Microfilm.
74. John T. Pickett Papers. Library of Congress.
75. Edward L. Pierce Manuscripts. Houghton Library.
76. *Records* of the Department of State Diplomatic Instructions 1861–69. National Archives. Microfilm.
77. Albert Gallatin Riddle Papers. Western Reserve Historical Society.
78. Henry S. Sanford Papers. General Sanford Memorial Library, Sanford, Florida. Microfilm.
79. James Schouler Manuscripts. Massachusetts Historical Society.
80. William Schouler Papers. Massachusetts Historical Society.
81. Samuel Sweezy Seward Papers. Goshen Historical Society.
82. Letters of F. W. Seward (1861–63). New-York Historical Society.
83. Gerrit Smith Papers. Syracuse University.
84. John C. Spencer Papers. New York Public Library.
85. Edwin M. Stanton Papers. Library of Congress.
86. Charles Sumner Papers. Houghton Library.
87. Charles Sumner Autograph Collection. Houghton Library.
88. William Sidney Thayer Manuscripts. Library of Congress.
89. Albert Haller Tracy Papers, New York State Library at Albany.
90. Lyman Trumbull Papers. Library of Congress.
91. Daniel Ullmann Papers. New-York Historical Society.
92. Amasa Walker Manuscripts. Massachusetts Historical Society.
93. Washburn Autograph Collection. Massachusetts Historical Society.
94. Elkanah Watson Papers. New York State Library at Albany.
95. James Watson Webb Papers. Yale University Library.
96. Daniel Webster Manuscripts. Houghton Library.
97. Thurlow Weed. Miscellaneous Papers. New-York Historical Society.
98. Thurlow Weed, William Henry Seward, James Watson Webb Correspondence. Yale University Library.
99. Samuel Wells Williams Papers. Yale University Library.
100. Robert C. Winthrop Manuscripts. Massachusetts Historical Society.

My efforts to obtain access to the Seward letters in the papers of Archbishop Hughes were unavailing.

D. *Printed Manuscripts, Public Documents, Diaries, etc.*

C. F. Adams, *An Address on the Life, Character, and Services of William Henry Seward* (Albany, 1873).

Edward Bates, *Diary.* H. K. Beale, ed. (Washington, D. C., 1933).

Charles Sumner, His Complete Works, with Introduction by Hon. George Frisbie Hoar, 20 vols. (Boston, 1900).

L. E. Chittenden, *A Report of the Debates and Proceedings in the Secret Sessions of the Conference Convention . . . Held at Washington, D. C. in February, A. D. 1861* (New York, 1864).

Collections of the Cayuga County Historical Society, nos. 6–7 (Auburn, 1888).

"Extracts from the Journal of Henry J. Raymond," *Scribner's Monthly*, XX (June 1880), 275–80.

Adam Gurowski, *Diary* (Boston, 1862–66).

Inside Lincoln's Cabinet (S. P. Chase Diary), David Donald, ed. (New York, 1954).

"Journal of the Committee of Thirteen," *Index to the Reports of the Committees of the Senate of the United States for the Second Session of the Thirty-sixth Congress* (Washington, D. C., 1861).

Benjamin F. Hall, *The Trial of William Freeman* (Auburn, 1848).

Stephen C. Hutchins, *Civil List and Constitutional History of the Colony and State of New York* (Albany, 1880).

Intimate Letters of Carl Schurz, 1841–1869, Joseph Schafer, ed. (Madison, 1928).

Journals of the Senate of the State of New York, 54th–57th sessions (Albany, 1831–34).

B. B. Kendrick, *The Journal of the Joint Committee of Fifteen on Reconstruction* (New York, 1914).

Letters of Henry Adams, 1858–91, W. C. Ford, ed. (Boston, 1930).

Edward McPherson, *The Political History of the United States of America During the Period of Reconstruction* (Washington, D. C., 1880).

Memoirs of John Quincy Adams, C. F. Adams, ed., 12 vols. (Philadelphia, 1874–77).

Natural History of New York State, 6 vols. in 4 (New York, 1842–43).

Official Records of the Union and Confederate Armies, 70 vols. in 128 (Washington, 1880–1901).

Official Records of the Union and Confederate Navies in the War of the Rebellion, 26 vols. (Washington, D. C., 1894–1922).

Papers Relating to the Foreign Affairs of the United States, 1861–68, 19 vols. (Washington, D. C., 1862–69).

Private and Official Correspondence of Gen. Benjamin F. Butler During the Period of the Civil War, J. A. Marshall, ed., 5 vols. (Norwood, Mass., 1917).

Proceedings of a Convention of Delegates . . . Opposed to Free-Masonry, Albany 19–21 Feb., 1829 (Rochester, 1829).

Proceedings of the Anti-Masonic Republican Convention of the County of Cayuga . . . January 1, 1830 (Auburn, 1830).

Proceedings of the Anti-Masonic Convention for the State of New York: Held at Utica, August 11, 1830 (Utica, 1830).

William H. Russell, *My Diary North and South* (Boston, 1863).

George Templeton Strong, *Diary*, A. Nevins and M. H. Thomas, eds., 4 vols. (New York, 1952).

The Collected Works of Abraham Lincoln, R. P. Basler, ed., 8 vols. and index (New Brunswick, N. J., 1953–55).

The Diary of Orville Hickman Browning, T. C. Pease and Jas. G. Randall, eds. (Springfield, Ill., 1925).

The Diary of Philip Hone, 1828–1851, Allan Nevins, ed. (New York, 1936).

The Proceedings of the United States Anti-Masonic Convention Held at Philadelphia, September 11, 1830 (Philadelphia, 1830).

The Papers of Willie Person Mangum, H. T. Shanks, ed. (Raleigh, N. C., 1953).

The Rebellion Record: A Diary of American Events, F. Moore, ed., 11 vols. (New York, 1861–68).

Treaties, Conventions . . . Between the United States of America and Other Powers, Wm. M. Malloy, comp., 2 vols. (Washington, D. C., 1910).

Gideon Welles, *Diary*, H. K. Beale, ed., 3 vols. (New York, 1960).

E. *Newspapers and Periodicals*
  1. Albany *Argus*
  2. Albany *Evening Journal*
  3. Cayuga *Patriot*
  4. Cayuga *Republican*
  5. The *Independent*
  6. The *Jeffersonian*
  7. The *Log Cabin*
  8. The *Nation*
  9. New York *Evening Post*
  10. New York *Express*
  11. New York *Herald*
  12. New York *Times*
  13. New York *Tribune*
  14. *The Times of London*

II. SECONDARY MATERIALS

C. F. Adams, Jr., *An Autobiography* (Boston, 1916). "The *Trent* Affair," Massachusetts Historical Society, *Proceedings*, XLV (Nov. 1911), 35–148.

E. D. Adams, *Great Britain and the American Civil War*. 2 vols. (New York, 1925).

H. Adams, "The Secession Winter, 1860–1861," Massachusetts Historical Society *Proceedings*, XLIII (June 1910), 656–87.

D. S. Alexander, *A Political History of the State of New York*, 4 vols. (New York, 1906–23).

F. Bancroft, *The Life of William H. Seward*. 2 vols. (New York, 1900).

W. E. Baringer, *A House Dividing* (Springfield, Ill., 1945).

T. W. Barnes, *Memoir of Thurlow Weed* (Boston, 1884).

C. L. Barrows, *William M. Evarts* (Chapel Hill, N. C., 1941).

I. C. Barrows, "Two Months with Mr. Seward," *Atlantic Monthly*, LXIII (March 1889), 391–7.

S. J. Barrows, "Personal Reminiscences of William H. Seward," *Atlantic Monthly*, LXIII (March 1889), 379–91.

H. K. Beale, *The Critical Year* (new ed., New York, 1958).

H. C. F. Bell, *Lord Palmerston*, 2 vols. (London, 1936).

S. F. Bemis, ed., *The American Secretaries of State and Their Diplomacy*, 15 vols. (New York, 1927–66).

L. Benson, *The Concept of Jacksonian Democracy: New York as a Test Case* (Princeton, 1961).

J. Bigelow, *Retrospections of an Active Life*. 5 vols. (New York, 1909–13).

K. Biggerstaff, "The Official Chinese Attitude Toward the Burlingame Mission," *Am. Hist. Rev.*, XLI (July 1936), 682–701.

R. A. Billington, *The Protestant Crusade, 1800–1860* (New York, 1938).

J. G. Blaine, *Twenty Years of Congress: From Lincoln to Garfield*, 2 vols. (Norwich, Conn., 1884, 1893).

H. Blumenthal, *A Reappraisal of Franco-American Relations 1830–1871* (Chapel Hill, N.C., 1959).

W. O. Bourne, *History of the Public School Society of the City of New York* (New York, 1870).

G. S. Boutwell, *Reminiscences of Sixty Years*. 2 vols. (New York, 1902).

P. Buck, *The Road to Reunion* (Boston, 1937).

J. M. Callahan, *The Alaska Purchase and Americo-Canadian Relations* (Morgantown, 1908)

American Foreign Policy in Canadian Relations (New York, 1937).

American Foreign Policy in Mexican Relations (New York, 1932).

"Evolution of Seward's Mexican Policy," *West Va. Studies in American History*, Series 1, Diplomatic History Nos. 4, 5 and 6 (Morgantown, Apr.–June, 1909).

H. J. Carman and R. H. Luthin, *Lincoln and the Patronage* (New York, 1943).

"The Seward-Fillmore Feud and the Crisis of 1850," *New York History*, XXIV (April 1943), 163–84.

"Some Aspects of the Know Nothing Movement Reconsidered," *South Atlantic Quarterly*, XXXIX (April 1940), 213–34.

F. B. Carpenter, *Six Months in the White House with Abraham Lincoln* (New York, 1866).

E. M. Carroll, *Origins of the Whig Party* (Durham, N. C., 1925).

W. M. Caskey, *Secession and Restoration of Louisiana* (University, La., 1938).

H. Chevigny, *Russian America* (New York, 1965).

H. S. Commager, *Theodore Parker* (Boston, 1936).

L. W. and J. H. Cox, *Politics, Principles and Prejudice, 1865–1866* (New York, 1963).

S. W. Crawford, *The Genesis of the Civil War: the Story of Sumter, 1860–1861* (New York, 1887).

O. Crenshaw, *The Slave States in the Presidential Election of 1860* (Baltimore, 1945).

R. N. Current, *Lincoln and the First Shot* (New York, 1963).

C. A. Dana, *Recollections of the Civil War* (New York, 1898).

T. Dennett, *Americans in Eastern Asia* (New York, 1922).
    "Seward's Far Eastern Policy," *Am. Hist. Rev.*, XXVIII (Oct. 1922), 45–62.

C. M. Depew, *My Memories of Eighty Years* (New York, 1922).

J. C. Derby, *Fifty Years Among Authors, Books and Publishers* (New York, 1884).

D. M. DeWitt, *The Impeachment and Trial of Andrew Johnson* (New York, 1903).

D. L. Dix, *Remarks on Prisons and Prison Discipline in the United States* (Boston, 1845).

Mrs. A. Dixon, *The True History of the Missouri Compromise and Its Repeal* (Cincinnati, 1899).

D. Donald, *Charles Sumner and the Coming of the Civil War* (New York, 1960).
    Lincoln Reconsidered (New York, 1956).

C. A. Duniway, "Reasons for French Withdrawal from Mexico," *Annual Report, Amer. Hist. Assoc.*, vol. 1 (1902) 315–28.

W. A. Dunning, "Paying for Alaska," *Political Science Quarterly*, XXVII (Sept. 1912), 385–398.

H. J. Eckenrode, "The Political History of Virginia During the Reconstruction," *Johns Hopkins Univ. Studies in Historical and Political Science*, Series XXII, (Baltimore, 1904).

S. Elkins, *Slavery, a Problem in American Institutional and Intellectual Life* (Chicago, 1959).

D. M. Ellis, *Landlords and Farmers in the Hudson-Mohawk Region, 1790–1850* (Ithaca, 1946)
    A Short History of New York State (Ithaca, 1957).

P. Evans, *The Holland Land Company* (Buffalo, 1924).

V. J. Farrar, *The Annexation of Russian America to the United States* (Washington, D. C., 1937).

D. E. Fehrenbacher, *Chicago Giant: A Biography of "Long John" Wentworth* (Madison, 1957)
    Prelude to Greatness: Lincoln in the 1850's (Stanford, 1962).

F. Fessenden, *Life and Public Services of William Pitt Fessenden*, 2 vols. (Boston, 1907).

J. R. Ficklen, "History of Reconstruction in Louisiana," *John Hopkins Univ. Studies in Historical and Political Science*, Series XXVII (Baltimore, 1910).

L. H. Fischer, *Lincoln's Gadfly, Adam Gurowski* (Norman, Okla., 1964).

W. L. Fleming, *Civil War and Reconstruction in Alabama* (New York, 1905).

P. S. Foner, *Business and Slavery* (Chapel Hill, 1941).
    Frederick Douglass (New York, 1964).
    A History of Cuba and Its Relations with the United States. 2 vols. (New York, 1963).

H. S. Foote, *A Casket of Reminiscences* (Washington, D. C., 1872).

W. H. Gerht, "'Heads or Tails': The Seward Portrait in City Hall," *The Art Quarterly*, XXI (Spring 1958), 68–81.

A. C. Gluek, Jr., *Minnesota and the Manifest Destiny of the Canadian Northwest* (Toronto, 1965).

F. A. Golder, "The American Civil War Through the Eyes of a Russian Diplomat," *American Hist. Review*, XXVI (April 1921), 454–63; "The Purchase of Alaska," *American Hist. Review*, XXV (April 1920), 411–25.

Mrs. Greenhow, *My Imprisonment and the First Year of Abolition Rule at Washington* (London, 1863).

J. Griffiths, ed., *Autographs for Freedom* (Auburn, 1854).

J. B. Grinnell, *Men and Events of Forty Years* (Boston, 1891).

P. Guedalla, *Palmerston* (London, 1926).

R. G. Gunderson, *The Log Cabin Campaign* (Lexington, Ky., 1957)
    Old Gentlemen's Convention (Madison, Wis., 1961).

H. Hamilton, *Prologue to Conflict: The Crisis and Compromise of 1850* (Lexington, Ky., 1964)
    Zachary Taylor, 2 vols. (Indianapolis, 1941–1951).

J. A. Hamilton, *Reminiscences of James A. Hamilton; or, Men and Events, at Home and Abroad, During Three Quarters of a Century* (New York, 1869).

C. E. Hamlin, *The Life and Times of Hannibal Hamlin* (Cambridge, Mass., 1899).

B. Hammond, *Banks and Politics in America* (Princeton, 1957).

R. V. Harlow, *Gerrit Smith* (New York, 1939).

W. B. Hesseltine, *Civil War Prisons: A Study in War Psychology* (Columbus, Ohio, 1930)
    Lincoln's Plan of Reconstruction (Tuscaloosa, 1960).

H. W. Hilliard, *Politics and Pen Pictures at Home and Abroad* (New York, 1892).

G. F. Hoar, *Autobiography of Seventy Years*, 2 vols. (New York, 1903).

R. Hofstadter, *The American Political Tradition—and the Men Who Made It* (New York, 1948).

W. S. Holt, *Treaties Defeated by the Senate* (Baltimore, 1933).

W. Hosmer, *The Higher Law in Its Relations to Civil Government* (Auburn, 1852).

M. A. DeW. Howe, *The Life and Letters of George Bancroft*, 2 vols. (New York, 1908).

J. B. G. Hutchins, *The American Maritime Industries and Public Policy, 1789–1914* (Cambridge, Mass., 1941).

H. L. Keenleyside, "British Columbia—Annexation or Confederation?" *Canadian Historical Association Report* (1928), 34–40.

E. C. Kirkland, *The Peacemakers of 1864* (New York, 1927).

A. D. Kirwan, *John J. Crittenden* (Lexington, Ky., 1962).

G. H. Knowles, ed., *The Crisis of the Union, 1860–1861* (La. State Univ. Press, 1965).

R. S. Kuykendall, *The Hawaiian Kingdom, 1854–1874* (Honolulu, 1953).

M. Leech, *Reveille in Washington, 1860–1865* (New York, 1941).

R. W. Leopold, *The Growth of American Foreign Policy* (New York, 1962).

W. D. Lewis, *From Newgate to Danemora: The Rise of the Penitentiary in New York, 1796–1848* (Ithaca, 1965).

L. F. Litwack, *North of Slavery* (Chicago, 1961).

R. W. Logan, *The Diplomatic Relations of the United States with Haiti, 1776–1891* (Chapel Hill, N. C., 1941).

R. H. Luthin, "The Sale of Alaska," *Slavonic Review*, XVI, no. 46 (July 1937); "Salmon P. Chase's Political Career Before the Civil War," *MVHR*, XXIX (March 1943), 517–40.

C. H. McCarthy, *Lincoln's Plan of Reconstruction* (New York, 1901).

E. L. McKitrick, *Andrew Johnson and Reconstruction* (Chicago, 1960).

H. G. McMahon, *Chautauqua County: A History* (Buffalo, 1958).

J. M. Mc Pherson, *The Struggle for Equality* (Princeton, 1964).

A. B. Magruder, "A Piece of Secret History," *Atlantic Monthly*, XXXV (April 1875), 438–45.

D. H. Miller, "The Alaska Treaty," unpublished manuscript in the Department of State.

G. F. Milton, *Abraham Lincoln and the Fifth Column* (New York, 1942); *The Age of Hate* (New York, 1930).

L. L. Montague, *Haiti and the United States, 1714–1938* (Durham, N. C., 1940).

P. C. Nagel, *One Nation Indivisible* (New York, 1964).

A. Nevins, *The Emergence of Lincoln*, 2 vols. (New York, 1950);
Frémont, Pathmarker of the West (New York, 1939);
Hamilton Fish; the Inner History of the Grant Administration (New York, 1936);
Ordeal of the Union, 2 vols. (New York, 1947);
The War for the Union, 2 vols. (New York, 1959–1960).

T. W. L. Newton, *Lord Lyons, A Record of British Diplomacy*, 2 vols. (London, 1913).

R. F. Nichols, *The Disruption of American Democracy* (New York, 1948); *Franklin Pierce, Young Hickory of the Granite Hills* (Philadelphia, 1931); *The Stakes of Power, 1845-1877* (New York, 1961).

J. G. Nicolay and J. Hay, *Abraham Lincoln, A History*, 10 vols. (New York, 1886-1904).

R. B. Nye, *George Bancroft, Brahmin Rebel* (New York, 1944).

R. Ogden, ed., *Life and Letters of Edwin Lawrence Godkin*, 2 vols. (New York, 1907).

W. D. Overdyke, *The Know-Nothing Party in the South* (La. State Univ. Press, 1950).

[T. H. Parmelee], "Recollections of an Old Stager," *Harper's Monthly*, XLVII (Sept. 1873), 586-91.

J. W. Patton, *Unionism and Reconstruction in Tennessee* (Chapel Hill, N. C., 1934).

D. Perkins, *The Monroe Doctrine, 1826-1867* (Baltimore, 1933).

D. Piatt, *Memories of the Men Who Saved the Union* (New York, 1887).

E. L. Pierce, *Memoirs and Letters of Charles Sumner*, 4 vols. (Boston, 1877-93).

J. S. Pike, *First Blows of the Civil War* (New York, 1879).

G. R. Poage, *Henry Clay and the Whig Party* (Chapel Hill, 1936).

B. P. Poore, *Reminiscences of Sixty Years in the National Metropolis*, 2 vols. (Philadelphia, 1886).

D. M. Potter, *Lincoln and His Party in the Secession Crisis* (New Haven, 1942).

J. W. Pratt, "Governor Seward and the New York City School Controversy, 1840-1842," *New York History*, XLII, no. 4 (Oct. 1961), 351-64.

B. Quarles, *Frederick Douglass* (Washington, D. C., 1948); *Lincoln and the Negro* (New York, 1962).

C. W. Ramsdell, "The Natural Limits of Slavery Expansion," *MVHR*, XVI (Sept. 1929), 151-71.

J. G. Randall, *The Civil War and Reconstruction* (Boston, 1937); *Lincoln the President*. 4 vols. (New York, 1945-55). vol. 4 by J. G. Randall and R. N. Current.

J. Rawley, *Edwin D. Morgan 1811-1883, Merchant in Politics* (New York, 1955).

R. J. Rayback, *Millard Fillmore* (Buffalo, 1959).

R. V. Remini, *Martin Van Buren and the Making of the Democratic Party* (New York, 1959).

A. G. Riddle, *The Life of Benjamin F. Wade* (Cleveland, 1886).

W. L. Rose, *Rehearsal for Reconstruction; The Port Royal Experiment* (Indianapolis, Ind., 1964).

I. Ross, *Rebel Rose, Life of Rose O'Neal Greenhow, Confederate Spy* (New York, 1954).

D. Rowland, ed., *Jefferson Davis, Constitutionalist, His Letters, Papers and Speeches.* 10 vols. (Jackson, Miss., 1923).

C. Sandburg, *Abraham Lincoln. The Prairie Years.* 2 vols. (New York, 1926); *Abraham Lincoln. The War Years.* 4 vols. (New York, 1939).

J. M. Schofield, *Forty-six Years in the Army* (New York, 1897).

C. Schurz, *The Reminiscences of Carl Schurz.* 3 vols. (New York, 1907).

F. W. Seward, *Reminiscences of a War-Time Statesman and Diplomat, 1830–1915* (New York, 1916).

O. R. Seward, ed., *William H. Seward's Travels Around the World* (New York, 1873).

H. T. Shanks, *The Secession Movement in Virginia, 1847–1861* (Richmond, 1934).

R. E. Shaw, *Erie Water West. A History of the Erie Canal, 1792–1854* (Lexington, Ky., 1966).

E. M. Shepard, *Martin Van Buren* (rev. ed. Boston, 1900).

P. Sheridan, *Personal Memoirs.* 2 vols. (New York, 1888).

L. B. Shippee, *Canadian-American Relations, 1849–1874* (New Haven, 1939).

O. D. Skelton, *The Life and Times of Sir Alexander Tilloch Galt* (Toronto, 1920).

D. L. Smiley, *Lion of Whitehall* (Madison, Wis., 1962).

W. E. Smith, *The Francis Preston Blair Family in Politics,* 2 vols. (New York, 1933).

I. D. Spencer, *The Victor and the Spoils: A Life of William L. Marcy* (Providence, R. I., 1959).

K. M. Stampp, *And the War Came* (La. State Univ. Press, 1950).

A. H. Stephens, *A Constitutional View of the Late War Between the States; Its Causes, Character, Conduct and Results,* 2 vols. (Philadelphia, 1870).

C. C. Tansill, *The Purchase of the Danish West Indies* (Baltimore, 1932); *The United States and Santo Domingo, 1798–1873* (Baltimore, 1938).

W. R. Taylor, *Cavalier and Yankee* (New York, 1961).

B. P. Thomas and H. M. Hyman, *Stanton: The Life and Times of Lincoln's Secretary of War* (New York, 1962).

D. G. B. Thompson, *Ruggles of New York. A Life of Samuel B. Ruggles* (New York, 1946).

J. S. Tilley, *Lincoln Takes Command* (Chapel Hill, N. C., 1941).

H. L. Trefousse, *Benjamin Franklin Wade* (New York, 1963).

C. K. Tuckerman, "Personal Recollections of William H. Seward," *Magazine of American History,* XIX (June 1888), 499–503.

G. G. Van Deusen, *Horace Greeley: Nineteenth Century Crusader* (Philadelphia, 1953); *The Jacksonian Era, 1828–1848* (New York, 1959); *The Life of Henry Clay* (Boston, 1937); "Seward and the School Question Reconsidered," *The Journal of American History,* LII (Sept. 1965), 313–19; *Thurlow Weed: Wizard of the Lobby* (Boston, 1947).

E. F. Warren, *Sketches of the History of Chautauque County* (Jamestown, N. Y., 1846).

H. A. Weed, ed., *Autobiography of Thurlow Weed* (Boston, 1883).

G. Welles, *Lincoln and Seward* (New York, 1874).

M. E. White, ed., *A Sketch of Chester Harding, Artist Drawn by His Own Hand* (Boston, 1890).

W. M. Whitelaw, *The Maritimes and Canada Before Confederation* (Toronto, 1934).

F. W. Williams, *Anson Burlingame and the First Chinese Mission to Foreign Powers* (New York, 1912).

M. W. Williams, *Anglo-American Isthmian Diplomacy* (Washington, D. C., 1916).

J. Williamson, *After Slavery. The Negro in South Carolina During Reconstruction, 1861-1877* (Chapel Hill, N. C., 1965).

R. W. Winks, *Canada and the United States: The Civil War Years* (Baltimore, 1960).

R. C. Winthrop, Jr., *A Memoir of Robert C. Winthrop* (Boston, 1897).

C. V. Woodward, *The Strange Career of Jim Crow* (second rev. ed., New York, 1966).

A. W. Young, *History of Chautauqua County* (Buffalo, 1875).

III. UNPUBLISHED DOCTORAL DISSERTATIONS

G. H. Blakeslee, The History of the Antimasonic Party. Harvard. 1903.

J. L. Crouthamel, James Watson Webb and the New York *Courier and Enquirer, 1827-1861*. University of Rochester. 1958.

A. Di Pace (Donald), Prelude to Civil War: the Decline of the Whig Party in New York, 1848-1852. University of Rochester. 1961.

D. M. Dozer, Anti-Imperialism in the United States, 1865-1895. Harvard, 1936.

M. F. Gutheim, John Lothrop Motley. Columbia University. 1955.

P. C. Johnson (Rauch), Ed., "Sensitivity and Civil War: The Selected Diaries and Papers, 1858-1866, of Frances Adeline [Fanny] Seward." University of Rochester. 1963.

M. Lichterman, John Adams Dix: 1798-1879. Columbia University. 1952.

M. V. Miller. The Emergence of William H. Seward as a National Political Leader, 1847-1859. University of Southern California. 1957.

E. G. Muntz, The First Whig Governor of New York, William Henry Seward, 1838-1842. University of Rochester. 1960.

Sister M. M. O'Rourke, The Diplomacy of William H. Seward During the Civil War: His Policies as Related to International Law. University of California. 1963.

W. Sharrow, William Henry Seward: a Study in Nineteenth Century Politics and Nationalism. University of Rochester. 1965.

J. P. Smith, The Republican Expansionists of the Early Reconstruction Era. University of Chicago. 1930.

J. G. Whelan, William Henry Seward, Expansionist. University of Rochester. 1959.

Index